10TH EDITION

Practical Cookery

David Foskett

BEd (Hons), FHCIMA
Associate Dean
Faculty of Hospitality, Leisure and Tourism
Thames Valley University

Victor Ceserani

MBE, CPA, MBA, FHCIMA
Formerly Head of ·
The School of Hotelkeeping and Catering
Ealing College of Higher Education
(now Thames Valley University)

Ronald Kinton

BEd (Hons), FHCIMA
Formerly of
Garnett College, College of Education for Teachers
in Further and Higher Education
(now University of Greenwich)

Hodder Arnold

A MEMBER OF THE HODDER HEADLINE GROUP

Orders: please contact Bookpoint Ltd, 130 Milton Park, Abingdon, Oxon OX14 4SB. Telephone: (44) 01235 827720. Fax: (44) 01235 400454. Lines are open from 9.00 – 6.00, Monday to Saturday, with a 24 hour message answering service. You can also order through our website www.hoddereducation.co.uk.

British Library Cataloguing in Publication Data
A catalogue record for this title is available from the British Library

ISBN-10: 0 340 81147 1
ISBN-13: 978 0 340 81147 4

First Published 1962
Second edition 1967
Third edition 1972
Fourth edition 1974
Fifth edition 1981
Sixth edition 1987
Seventh edition 1990
Eighth edition 1995
Ninth edition 2000
Tenth edition 2004

Impression number   10 9 8 7 6 5 4
Year   2007 2006 2005

Cover photo by Sam Bailey
Typeset by Fakenham Photosetting Limited, Fakenham, Norfolk
Printed in Dubai for Hodder Arnold, an imprint of Hodder Education, a division of Hodder Headline, 338 Euston Road, London NW1 3BH

Foreword

This book will be seen as a bible for any young person embarking upon the career of a chef, and will also act as a text book which one can refer to time and time again. It offers a solid grounding and is written in a style that is easy to read and understand.

I have been lucky enough to know Victor personally for many years and he is to be admired for his mastery in the trade, both in the academic field as well as his culinary skills.

Practical Cookery 10th Edition will be the ultimate 'must have' guide for all young cooks and chefs alike.

Michel Roux OBE

Cookery is all about confidence and knowledge and *Practical Cookery* gives you both.

Richard A Shepherd CBE

Practical Cookery sets us all on the right culinary road, which, as it guides us, offers us intuitive thinking with creative results.

Gary Rhodes

Introduction to the Tenth Edition

The purpose of this book is to provide a sound foundation of professional cookery for all levels of students of catering.

The following points are important:

- to develop a professional attitude and appearance, acquire skills and behave in a professional manner;
- to develop knowledge and understanding of all commodities regarding cost, quality and use;
- to understand the methods of cooking and be able to produce a variety of dishes for various types of establishment;
- to understand recipe balance and be able to produce dishes of the required quality, colour, consistency, seasoning, flavour, temperature, quantity and presentation;
- with experience, to develop recipes using original ideas;
- to understand the principles of healthy eating and basic nutrition;
- to fully understand the essential necessity for healthy, hygienic and safe procedures at all times in the storage, preparation, cooking and serving of food.

These books may also assist you in your career: *Q&A for Practical Cookery*, *The Theory of Catering* and *Advanced Practical Cookery*.

As the world is getting 'smaller' due to factors such as fast transport and tourism, modern cuisine uses a wide variety of ingredients from all over the world. This has led to an intermix of cuisine cultures, for example a fusion of western and eastern styles; traditional European cuisine has blended with Oriental, and so on. This may be described as 'eclectic' cuisine, which is the deriving of ideas, tastes and styles from various sources and which originated in Australia. This development enables chefs to be creative and this has been demonstrated by the many restaurants and food service outlets taking this approach.

However, to be creative, chefs must understand and acquire the basic skills of practical professional cookery. These skills and underpinning knowledge must be formed from the subject knowledge – 'the body of knowledge' upon which every discipline relies as the source from which concepts, models and theories develop.

In practical professional cookery it is the basic principles, procedures and classical dishes that originate from the traditional French kitchen, further developed by master chefs such as Carême and Escoffier. The chefs in the traditional French kitchen were the first to practise fusion cuisine as ingredients were brought from different countries, together with different recipes and methods, which these chefs refined to suit the various types of customer. Therefore, fusion or eclectic cuisine is not new but, with globalisation, that is the bringing together of countries, peoples, cultures and cuisines, chefs have been enabled to be more creative and innovative.

Basic skills and recipes are fundamental as these provide the framework for all the essential underpinning knowledge for a successful career in professional cookery that will allow individuals to gain employment across continents.

This book provides an invaluable foundation for acquiring basic professional skill and knowledge and in this edition we have attempted to balance the traditional with the modern in the illustrations.

The decision to retain metric and imperial weights and measures was taken after consultation with catering colleges.

Nutritional Analysis

There is no such thing as unhealthy food but there are unfortunately unhealthy eating habits that in many cases lead to obesity followed by ill-health and premature death.

It is because of national concern with the alarming increase in cases of obesity, particularly with the young, that we invited Dr Jenny Poulter and Jane Cliff to develop the nutritional analysis for the recipes and healthy eating tips where appropriate.

Analysis for the nutrients has been performed using the computer software CompEat Pro Version 5.8.0 (2002). This holds the UK integrated databases of McCance & Widdowson's *The Composition of Foods 6th Summary Edition* and associated supplements, RSC.

Weights and measures were used as given in the text unless mentioned as a single item e.g. an egg, and in such cases information derived from *Food Portion Sizes, 2nd Edition*, Dept of Environment, Fisheries and Rural Affairs.

Where appropriate, the edible portion of the recipe ingredient was used; there were instances where the waste produced in the recipe would have distorted the nutritional values e.g. whole chicken as part of the recipe, but only the wing and leg quarters were used.

Vegetable oil was used as the first choice of oil unless specified otherwise, and butter was used as the first choice over margarine. Semi-skimmed milk is used as first choice milk unless otherwise specified.

Special thanks to Pat Bacon SRD who undertook the recipe analysis with efficiency and patience.

Acknowledgements

As *Practical Cookery* has been in print for over forty years it would not be possible to keep up to date and suitable for contemporary students without the help and advice from practising chefs and lecturers. We are most grateful for the comments and suggestions made by the following:

David Dorricott, Executive Chef, House of Commons.
Bill Farnsworth, Director of Catering and Bakery Studies at Birmingham College of Food.
Chris Galvin, Executive Chef at Wolseley Restaurant, Piccadilly.
Paul Heathcote, Managing Director of Heathcote's Restaurants.
Peter Richards, Chef Director at Westminster Kingsway College.
Roger Sarjent, Executive Chef at the Conrad Hotel.

We are most grateful to the following:

John Campbell (Executive Chef at the Vineyard Hotel, Stockcross) for not only supplying all the food, but also together with members of his brigade freely giving the time to prepare and cook for the majority of the illustrations.

The photographer Sam Bailey for his helpful advice and co-operation.

Glynn Johnson, Cert Ed, and Frank McDowell, Cert Ed, FHCIMA, for the interest, helpful suggestion and care taken in the preparation and presentation of the food required for some of the photographs.

Winch and Associates; The Department of Health; The British Heart Foundation; The Flour Advisory Bureau and the Dunn Nutrition Unit; the Anthony Blake Photo Library; The Robert Harding Picture Library; Marshall Cavendish Photo Library.

We are also indebted to Yolande Stanley, Anton Edelmann and Henry Brosi for their helpful contributions towards the food photography.

To all these colleagues we say thank you for your help in making a most useful exercise of co-operation between industry and education.

Our thanks go also to Reiko Hara for supplying the information on Japanese cookery.

We would also like to thank The Savoy Educational Trust for their generous contribution towards the cost of the photography.

Our appreciation also goes to Russums' and Nisbet's for the use of technical photographs and to Cobra beer and John Gray of Universal Food Service for their sponsorship.

The healthy eating input for this latest edition of *Practical Cookery* has been written by Jane Cliff and Dr Jenny Poulter. Both are public health nutritionists, who like working with chefs and caterers to translate nutritional theory into practice creatively. They have a proven track record in chef education, catering training, research and evaluation. Jenny is author of the Health Education Authority's action pack on healthy catering in the workplace. Jane has been actively involved in catering education for most of her working life.

Jane and Jenny have a life long vision to persuade all that healthy eating is primarily about fabulous food that happens to be healthy. In their view the image of healthy eating has been marred for too long by the brown rice brigade. It is books like this that will help change the hearts and minds of the next culinary generation.

David Foskett, Victor Ceserani and Ronald Kinton

Contents

Metric equivalents

	APPROXIMATE EQUIVALENT	EXACT EQUIVALENT
¼ oz	5 g	7.0 g
½ oz	10 g	14.1 g
1 oz	25 g	28.3 g
2 oz	50 g	56.6 g
3 oz	75 g	84.9 g
4 oz	100 g	113.2 g
5 oz	125 g	141.5 g
6 oz	150 g	169.8 g
7 oz	175 g	198.1 g
8 oz	200 g	227.0 g
9 oz	225 g	255.3 g
10 oz	250 g	283.0 g
11 oz	275 g	311.3 g
12 oz	300 g	340.0 g
13 oz	325 g	368.3 g
14 oz	350 g	396.6 g
15 oz	375 g	424.0 g
16 oz	400 g	454.0 g
2 lb	1 kg	908.0 g
¼ pt	125 ml	142 ml
½ pt	250 ml (¼ litre)	284 ml
¾ pt	375 ml	426 ml
1 pt	500 ml (½ litre)	568 ml
1½ pt	750 ml (¾ litre)	852 ml
2 pt (1 qt)	1000 ml (1 litre)	1.13 litres
2 qt	2000 ml (2 litres)	2.26 litres
1 gal	4½ litres	4.54 litres

Oven Temperature Chart

Approximate equivalents

½ cm = ¼ in   10 cm = 4 in
1 cm = ½ in   12 cm = 5 in
2 cm = 1 in   15 cm = 6 in
4 cm = 1½ in   16 cm = 6½ in
5 cm = 2 in   18 cm = 7 in
6 cm = 2½ in   30 cm = 12 in
8 cm = 3 in   45 cm = 18 in

1 teaspoon = 5 ml
1 dessertspoon = 10 ml
1 tablespoon = 15 ml
1 cup = 250 ml
½ cup = 125 ml
⅓ cup = 80 ml
¼ cup = 60 ml

Oven temperature chart

	°C	Gas Regulo	°F
slow (cool)	110	¼	225
	130	½	250
	140	1	275
	150	2	300
	160	3	325
moderate	180	4	350
	190	5	375
	200	6	400
hot	220	7	425
	230	8	450
very hot	250	9	475

The working environment

Maintain a safe and secure working environment

Procedures in the event of a fire

- The fire brigade must be called immediately a fire is discovered.
- Do not panic.
- Warn others in the vicinity and sound the fire alarm.
- Do not jeopardise your own safety and that of others.
- Follow the fire instructions of the establishment.
- If the fire is small use the appropriate extinguisher.
- Close doors and windows, turn off gas, electricity and fans.

It is important that passageways are kept clear at all times and that doors open outwards. Fire exits must be clearly marked and fire fighting equipment readily available and in working order. Periodic fire drills should occur and alarm bells be tested at least four times a year and staff instructed in the use of extinguishers. The extinguisher will state the kind of fire it is to be used on and that it must be refilled after use.

To extinguish a fire the three principal methods are:

- starving – removing the fuel;
- smothering – removing the air;
- cooling – removing the heat.

Fire extinguishers are predominantly red with patches of colour to show the nature of the contents.

Further information: Fire Protection Association, Bastille Court, 2 Paris Garden, London SE1 8ND www.thefpa.co.uk.

Suspicious item or package procedure

In the event of seeing a suspect item on the premises, follow the procedure of the establishment.

- Do not panic.
- Calmly warn others in the vicinity.
- Do not touch the item or allow others to do so.
- Immediately inform your employers.
- Move to a safe place.

Accidents

Accidents may be caused by:

- excessive haste;
- distraction;
- failure to apply safety rules.

Most accidents could be prevented. However, in the event of an accident, the person responsible for First Aid must be called immediately. If it is a serious accident, phone 999 and ask for the ambulance service.

- State the exact location of the incident.
- Give both the address and telephone number of the location.
- Describe the accident. If heart attack is suspected, say so immediately.
- Indicate age of casualties or casualty.

Any accident occurring to an employee on the premises must be recorded in the accident book, detailing nature of the accident, where and how it happened and names of witnesses, if any.

Accidents that are most frequent in catering establishments are cuts, burns and scalds and falls.

Cuts

Small cuts should be washed and covered with a blue waterproof dressing; more serious cuts should be treated by a First Aid person, who would decide on the need for further treatment.

Burns and scalds

Place the injured part under slowly running cold water for 10 minutes or until the pain eases. If serious, cover the burn or scald with a cloth or dressing and send the person to hospital.

Maintain a safe environment

The 1974 Health and Safety at Work Act was passed to protect employers and employees and to increase their awareness of the need for safety at work.

The employer's responsibilities are to:

- provide and maintain premises and equipment that are safe and without risk to health;
- provide supervision, information and training;
- issue written statements on general policy and procedures regarding health and safety;
- consult with employees' safety representative and to establish a safety committee.

It is the responsibility of employees to take reasonable care to avoid injury to themselves or others, to co-operate with employers so as to comply with the law and not to misuse anything provided for health and safety.

Hazards

It is desirable to develop a sense of awareness of potential hazards to prevent accidents, for example:

- power plug 'on' when cleaning electrical equipment;
- trailing electrical flexes;
- faulty electrical sockets, overloaded sockets;
- failure to replace lighting tubes or bulbs;
- not using correct steps;
- having wet hands when handling plugs etc.;
- gas not alight;
- main gas not igniting.

Prevention of accidents

- Floors in good repair and free from obstacles.
- Spillage to be cleaned up at once.
- Warning notices of slippery floors to be displayed.
- Guards on machinery to be in place.
- Extra care when guards are off during cleaning.
- One person only at a time to operate machinery.
- Never put arm or hand into bowl of electric mixer or cutter until stopped.
- Only dry, untorn gloves or cloths to be used to handle hot pans etc.
- Pan handles should not protrude over the stove.
- Lift heavy items correctly to prevent back injury.
- Use a trolley to move heavy items.
- Finger guards and safety aprons may prevent accidents.
- Never place knives in the sink.
- Use knives correctly; if they have to be carried, carry with points down, always lay knives down flat, not with the blade pointing up.
- Signs must indicate potentially hazardous machinery and chemicals.
- Protective clothing should be worn, sleeves down, apron on.
- Protective footwear should be in a good state of repair.

Further information: Health and Safety Executive (HSE) Rose Court, 2 Southwark Bridge, London SE1 9HS.

Secure environment

It is in the interests of everyone using premises that they are safe and secure. This applies to staff, customers and delivery personnel. Lockable lockers need to be provided for staff. Security systems should be installed to prevent stealing. This is particularly important with expensive food and drink. Control of keys is an important aspect of security. An effective system is dependent on the responsible attitude and practice of staff and suitable procedures of control by employers. This is essential where cash is involved – extra care is needed. In the event of anything lost or missing all staff should be aware of what action they should take.

Maintain a professional and hygienic appearance

A professional appearance is one that conveys to others the fact that the employees have pride in the job, pride in how they look and that their attitude indicates interest, willingness and keenness as well as that they care. A hygienic appearance is indicated by high standards of personal cleanliness and is shown by cleanliness of hair, hands, face, clothing and shoes.

This is important to the individual, other food handlers, consumers and employers. Hygienic standards are a legal requirement of the Food Hygiene Regulations.

Good personal hygiene helps prevent food-borne disease; therefore these points must be put into practice.

- Shower or bath daily.
- Wear clean clothes and uniform.
- Do not work if suffering from a communicable disease.

- Handle food as little as possible.
- Wash hands before and during work and after using the toilet.
- Keep hair clean and do not handle.
- Keep fingernails clean and short.
- Do not touch nose and mouth with hands.
- Do not cough or sneeze over food, use a tissue.
- Do not wear rings, earrings, jewellery or watches.
- Do not smoke in food areas.
- Taste food with a clean spoon.
- Do not sit on work surfaces.
- Footwear should be clean and safe.
- Headgear should always be worn when handling food.
- Open cuts, burns etc. must be covered with blue waterproof dressing.

Persons suffering from diarrhoea, sore throat, vomiting or head cold must not handle food. If a person becomes aware that they are suffering from or are a carrier of typhoid, paratyphoid, salmonella or staphylococcal infection, the person responsible for the premises must be informed, who then must inform the Medical Officer of Health.

Working relationships

Working in the hotel and catering industry means that you will be working with people in your own department but may also be dealing with people from other areas. In all relationships communication is a key factor to success and it is a two-way issue. It is essential that that which is communicated is understood by the person receiving it as it was intended. To create a good relationship it is necessary for junior staff to be able to communicate upwards and for senior staff to communicate downwards. Constructive, positive and clear instructions and comments should be given.

Speech

It is not only what is said but how it is said, and also when and where it is said, that may affect the way the person spoken to interprets or misinterprets what is said. Emphasis, loudness of voice, tone of voice, rapidity or slowness of speech and accent may have an effect. If spoken to alone or in front of others, in the office or by the range, there and then or at some other time, may change the intentions of the communication.

Communicating

Listening is an important skill for giving and receiving information, instructions etc. so that both parties receive the same message. The art of listening has to be learned and eye contact is desirable for all verbal communication. Body language is a form of communication; facial expression, gestures etc. convey feelings without words. The distance people are apart, the stance of the body, the position of arms and hands convey messages intended or otherwise.

Good working relationships are dependent on co-operative attitudes and clear communication so that team work is promoted to achieve the standards of work required, on time, safely, hygienically, harmoniously, with no excess of energy by the members of the team.

For new staff it is necessary to brief them on what is expected of them at work, conditions of employment, details regarding procedures for fire, first aid, health, hygiene, safety.

In addition to having a range of craft skills and knowledge and understanding, a good chef needs to develop other skills to make a successful career. To acquire the right attitude to colleagues, employers and customers and also to yourself by being honest, loyal, tidy, punctual, friendly, helpful and willing to help others and being prepared to accept constructive criticism.

Teamwork

Teamwork is essential in a busy kitchen and can be identified by:

- everyone working to the same objective;
- everyone pulling their weight;
- each member of the team ready to support the others;
- each member of the team accepts the others;
- getting help when needed;
- working together to retrieve a disaster;
- co-operating together without complaint in a crisis;
- enjoying each other's successes, commiserating with others' setbacks; sharing success and failure;
- having people to talk to who understand;
- enjoying working as a team.

Self development

A positive attitude to attainable aims is essential to achieving a worthwhile career in the catering industry. There may be setbacks, conditions not always good, changes beyond your control but consider:

- believe in yourself;
- list your strengths and weaknesses;
- act to reduce your weaknesses;
- listen to constructive feedback;
- set yourself objectives;
- practise your skills;
- concentrate on your personal hygiene and appearance;
- avoid bad habits;
- create good impressions, be polite and friendly;

- be assertive and a team player;
- be determined to reach your career goal;
- assist others – job satisfaction is enhanced if you can assist others to achieve.

Cutting equipment

Knives must be handled with respect, used correctly and taken care of so that a professional performance can be achieved.

Safety rules

- When carrying knives, the points must be held downwards.
- Knives on the table must be placed flat and not project over the edge of the table.
- When using knives, concentrate on the job in hand.
- Keep knives sharp and use the correct knife for the correct purpose.

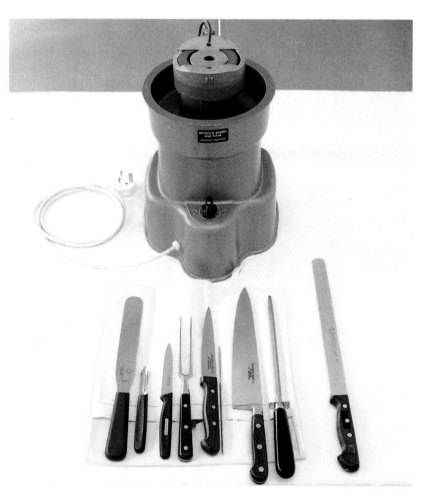

Fig 1.1 Knife sharpener and knives and small equipment

- After use, always wipe the knife, blade away from the hand.
- Keep knife handles clean and do not leave in the sink.
- Never misuse knives. After use wash, rinse, dry and safely put away.
- Colour coding of knife handles can assist in preventing cross-contamination.

Two tools are available for sharpening knives, a steel and carborundum stone. Periodically knives may need to be ground. To retain sharpness, always use a cutting board. A good craftsman or craftswoman never blames his or her tools since they always take good care of them.

Cutting machines

Persons under 18 must not use or clean any mechanical machinery. Machines used for cutting must be thoroughly cleaned after careful use. Instructions for use and safety precautions must be displayed.

Procedure for cleaning:

- Switch off the machine and remove the plug.
- Remove particles of food with a cloth, palette knife, needle or brush.
- Take extra care if guards have had to be moved to facilitate cleaning.
- Clean with hot detergent water all removable and fixed parts; take extra care with threads and plates with holes.
- Rinse, dry and reassemble.
- Guards must be replaced and any specific instructions must be followed.
- Test that it is properly assembled, plug in and switch on.

Mandolins and graters

Extra care must be taken when using these items. When cleaning the mandolin, close the blade; graters need to be thoroughly cleaned under a fast running water tap.

Mechanical equipment, power and manual driven

Manufacturers' instructions must be available and a record of maintenance sited near the machine. All machines must be used with care. They should not be overloaded and only persons instructed in the use of the machine are allowed to use it. Extra care is needed when using hot foods.

Cleanliness of food production areas, equipment and utensils

Hygiene is the science and practice of maintaining health and preventing disease. In every catering establishment providing food, it is essential that:

- persons employed are hygienic in themselves and work hygienically;
- ingredients to be used are stored and prepared in a hygienic manner;
- premises, equipment and utensils are kept clean and maintained hygienically;
- a plentiful supply of hot water and cleaning materials is available;
- suitable detergents and bactericide are available;
- the premises are properly maintained to ease cleaning;
- there is adequate lighting and ventilation;
- sinks, handbasins, gullies etc. are kept clean at all times;
- evidence of vermin must be reported;

- a sterilising solution should be used on work surfaces;
- shelves, cupboards, drawers are kept clean;
- harmful cleaning materials should be stored separately;
- food waste and refuse areas should be clean and tidy;
- bins and lids are kept clean and the lids used.

Correct cleaning and handling of waste helps prevent accidents, contamination, pest infestation, unpleasant odours, fire hazard and pollution as well as complying with the law.

Cleaning of surfaces

All surfaces should be thoroughly cleaned with hot water containing detergent, rinsed and then dried.

Cleaning of large equipment

Allow equipment to cool, turn off the fuel supply, wash with hot detergent water and dry. Re-assemble any parts that had been removed. Test that the equipment is functioning.

Cleaning small equipment

All small equipment should be washed in hot detergent water, rinsed, dried and stored ready for use. Particular care is needed with sieves, conical strainers and colanders.

Food hygiene

Unless preserved, foods deteriorate; to keep them in an edible condition it is necessary to know what causes food spoilage. Deterioration is caused by moulds, yeasts and bacteria, which cause the food to decompose, putrify and go sour; the food may then discolour, smell unpleasant and/or become sticky or slimy.

Moulds

These appear like whiskers on foods. To grow, they require warmth, moisture, air. They are killed by heat and sunlight. Moulds can grow where there is too little moisture for yeasts and bacteria to grow.

Yeasts

These are single-cell organisms, larger than bacteria, that grow on foods containing moisture and sugar. Foods containing a small percentage of sugar and a large amount of liquid, such as fruit juices and syrups, are liable to ferment because of yeasts. Yeasts are destroyed by heat.

Bacteria

There are three kinds of bacteria that concern the caterer:

- helpful bacteria, which assist in the manufacture of items such as cheese and yoghurt;
- harmful bacteria, which cause food spoilage and food poisoning;
- spoilage bacteria, which would not be seen as harmful, like pathogenic forms.

Transference of bacteria

Bacteria cannot move on their own, they must be carried by any of the following:

- hands;
- cuts, sores and burns;
- coughs and sneezing;
- different types of food;
- unclean equipment, utensils and work surfaces;
- air;
- water;
- insects or birds;

DEPARTMENT OF HEALTH

ASSURED SAFE CATERING · CRITICAL CONTROL POINTS

Step	Hazard	Action
1 Purchase	High-risk* (ready-to-eat) foods contaminated with food-poisoning bacteria or toxins (Poisons produced by bacteria).	 Buy from reputable supplier only. Specify maximum temperature at delivery.
2 Receipt of food	High-risk* (ready-to-eat) foods contaminated with food-poisoning bacteria or toxins.	 Check it looks, smells and feels right. Check the temperature is right.
3 Storage	Growth of food poisoning bacteria, toxins on high-risk* (ready-to-eat) foods. Further contamination.	 High-risk* foods stored at safe temperatures. Store them wrapped. Label high-risk foods with the correct 'use by' date. Rotate stock and use by recommended date.
4 Preparation	Contamination of High-risk* (ready-to-eat) foods. Growth of food-poisoning bacteria.	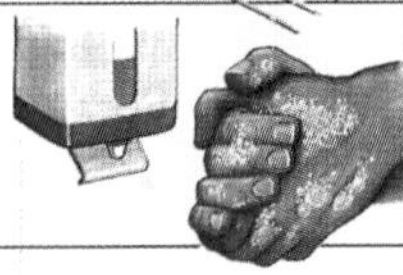 Wash your hands before handling food. Limit any exposure to room temperatures during preparation. Prepare with clean equipment, and use this for high-risk* (ready-to-eat) food only. Separate cooked foods from raw foods.
5 Cooking	Survival of food-poisoning bacteria.	 Cook rolled joints, chicken, and re-formed meats eg. burgers,so that the thickest part reaches at least 75°C. Sear the outside of other, solid meat cuts (eg. joints of beef, steaks) before cooking.
6 Cooling	Growth of any surviving spores or food poisoning bacteria. Production of poisons by bacteria. Contamination with food-poisoning bacteria.	 Cool foods as quickly as possible. Don't leave out at room temperatures to cool, unless the cooling period is short, eg place any stews or rice, etc, in shallow trays and cool to chill temperatures quickly.
7 Hot-holding	Growth of food-poisoning bacteria. Production of poisons by bacteria.	 Keep food hot, above 63°C.
8 Reheating	Survival of food-poisoning bacteria.	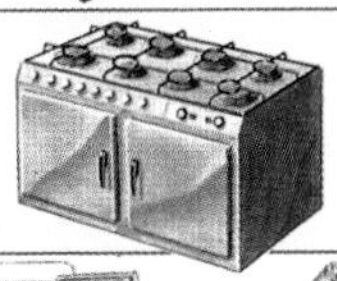 Reheat to above 75°C.
9 Chilled storage	Growth of food-poisoning bacteria.	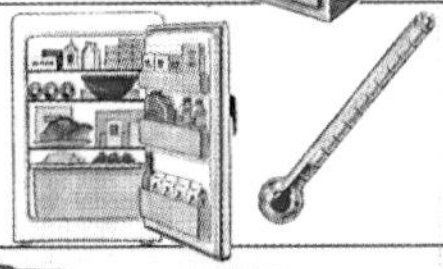 Keep temperature at right level. Label high-risk ready-to-eat foods with correct date code.
10 Serving	Growth of disease-causing bacteria. Production of poisons by bacteria. Contamination.	 COLD SERVICE FOODS - serve high-risk foods as soon as possible after removing from refrigerated storage to avoid them getting warm. HOT FOODS - serve high-risk foods quickly to avoid them cooling down.

A. *High-risk foods are those which may easily support the growth of food poisoning organisms and won't be cooked any further before you serve them, for example; cooked fish, meat patés, cooked egg dishes, pre-prepared dairy products that may only be re-heated.
B. Some food-poisoning bacteria can form spores which may survive cooking.

If cooling is delayed or takes a long time, these spores may grow or produce toxins (poisons). After cooking, food should be cooled quickly to prevent or reduce this. The list above is not exhaustive but shows some of the hazards likely to be present in any operation. In your catering operation you may be able to identify other hazards not listed above. If you do so make sure you control these as well.

Fig 1.2 🖋 Control of hygiene – assured safe catering, critical control points

- vermin;
- poor waste disposal.

Cross contamination means that unaffected food becomes contaminated by transference of bacteria from another item or medium, for example raw and cooked meat on the same board.

Some types of bacteria that could cause food poisoning:

Salmonella present in the intestine of animals and human beings. Foods affected include poultry, meat, eggs and shellfish. Prevention should include:

- good standards of personal hygiene;
- elimination of insects and rodents;
- washing hands and equipment and surfaces after handling raw poultry;
- not allowing carriers of the disease to handle food;
- use of effective food processing techniques e.g. cooking, re-heating etc.

Staphylococcus aureus: Food poisoning due to poisons produced in the food. The source includes human hands and other parts of the skin: sores, spots, boils etc. Prevention includes good hygiene habits.

Clostridium perfringens: lives in the intestines of humans and animals and in soil. Foods affected include raw meats, poultry and raw vegetables.

Escherichia Coli (E Coli) is a normal part of the intestines of humans and animals. It is found in human excreta and raw meat. E Coli causes abdominal pain, fever, diarrhoea and vomiting. High standards of hygiene and thorough cooking of foods must be applied. Raw and cooked meat must be stored at correct temperatures. Cross contamination must be avoided.

Growth of bacteria

Bacteria multiply by splitting in half under favourable conditions for growth. This means that they can double in numbers every twenty minutes so that in about six hours, 1,000,000 could be produced from one bacterium. Favourable conditions for growth are warmth, moisture, time and suitable food on which to multiply.

Foods that need extra care are:

- stocks and sauces, gravies and soup;
- meat and meat products;
- milk and milk products
- eggs and egg products
- all foods that are handled and reheated.

Bacteria grow between 7°C (45°F) and 63°C (145°F). Food poisoning bacteria multiply rapidly at body temperature. Whilst boiling kills most bacteria, it is important that a sufficient length of time is allowed at a high temperature to be sure of safe food.

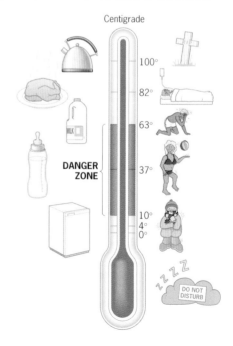

Fig 1.3 🖋 Germometer

Control of bacteria

There are three methods of controlling bacteria.

- Protect food from bacteria in the air by keeping foods covered. To prevent cross contamination, use separate boards and knives for cooked and uncooked foods. Use different coloured boards for particular foods, e.g. red for meat, blue for fish, yellow for poultry etc. Store cooked and uncooked foods separately. Wash hands frequently.

- Do not keep foods in the danger zone between 5°C and 63°C for longer than absolutely necessary.

- To kill bacteria, subject bacteria to a temperature of 77°C for 30 seconds or a higher temperature for less time. Certain bacteria develop into spores and can withstand higher temperatures for longer periods of time. Certain chemicals also kill bacteria and can be used for cleaning equipment and utensils.

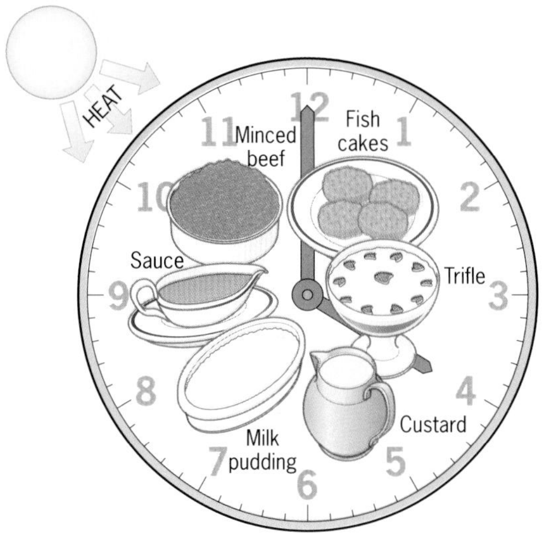

Fig 1.4 Germs multiplying in moist foods in warm temperature over time

The main food hygiene regulations of importance to the caterer are the following:

- Food Safety (General Food Hygiene) Regulations 1995.
- Food Safety (Temperature Control) Regulations 1995.

These implemented the EC Food Hygiene directive (93/43 EEC).

The 1995 Regulations are similar in many respects to earlier regulations. However, as with the Health and Safety legislation, these regulations place a strong emphasis on owners and managers to identify the safety risks, to design and implement appropriate systems to prevent contamination; these systems and procedures are covered by Hazard Analysis Critical Control Points (HACCP) and/or Assured Safe Catering.

The regulations place two general requirements on the owners of food businesses:

1. To ensure that all food handling operations are carried out hygienically and according to the 'Rules of Hygiene'.

2. To identify and control all potential food safety hazards, using a systems approach, either HACCP or Assured Safe Catering.

In addition there is an obligation on any food handler who may be suffering from or carrying a disease that could be transmitted through food to report this to the employer. The employers' responsibility is to decide appropriate action in the case of an employee reporting illness.

Catering establishments have a general obligation to supervise and instruct and provide training in food hygiene commensurate with their employees' responsibilities. Details with regard to how much training is required are not specified in the regulations, however, the HMSO Industry Guide to Catering provides guidance on training, which can be

Fig 1.5 🖋 Using a hand-held digital thermometer

taken as a general standard to comply with the legislation.

The HMSO guide suggests three categories of food handler, all three of which need training.

Category A

Support and front of house staff including: storekeeper, waiter/waitress, bar staff, counter staff, servery assistant, cellar person etc.

Category B

Those involved in the preparation of high risk (unwrapped) foods including: chefs, cooks, catering supervisors, kitchen assistants and bar staff who prepare food.

Category C

Managers or supervisors who may handle food including all such persons based on site.

Before any food handler starts work they must be given written and verbal instructions in the essentials of food hygiene.

The second stage of training is hygiene awareness instruction.

Formal training

Formal food hygiene training as suggested by the industry guide, beyond essentials and awareness, is recommended to comply with the law.

Essentials	Awareness
Personal cleanliness and dress.	The organisation's policy on food hygiene.
Hand washing.	Personal hygiene.
The need to report infections and cover cuts.	Cross contamination and food storage.
No smoking, eating or drinking in food rooms.	Waste disposal, cleaning and disinfection.
The need for temperature control i.e. keeping food either hot or cold.	Awareness of pests.
Keeping surfaces clean.	

A guide to the training of individuals in food handling:

Category of staff	Essentials of food hygiene	Hygiene awareness instruction	Formal training level 1	Formal training level 2 and or 3
A Storekeeper Waiting Staff Bar Staff Catering Assistants	Yes before starting work.	Yes within 4 weeks (8 weeks for part-time staff).	No	No
B Chefs Cooks Supervisors Food Preparation Assistants	Yes before starting work.	Yes within 4 weeks or 3 months for part-timers.	Yes	No
C Managers Supervisors	Yes before starting work.	Yes within 4 weeks.	Yes within 3 months.	Yes but only good practice, not essential.

The Food Safety (Temperature Control) Regulations 1995

These regulations came into force on 15 September 1995 and replace earlier and quite complex regulations.

Foods that may be subject to microbiological multiplication must be held at no more than 8°C or above 63°C. There are a few exceptions, which include food on display, which can be displayed for up to four hours, and also low risk and preserved foods, which can be stored at ambient (surrounding) temperatures. Manufacturers can vary upward the 8°C ceiling if there is a scientific basis to do so.

Food that is to be served hot should be held at over 63°C.

Food reheated in Scotland must retain a temperature of 82°C unless this will adversely affect the food.

This requires that any food that is likely to support the growth of pathogens, micro organisms or the formation of toxins must be kept at or below 8°C. In other words high risk foods, those that are ready for consumption without further heat treatment, must be stored under temperature control. These exceptions include food that has been cooked or re-heated or is for service on display for sale and needs to be kept hot. Also, there is an agreed time maximum of 2 hours for food to be kept hot that may be displayed below 63°C. It also applies to food where there is no health risk if it is kept at ambient temperature. Any preserved foods, including dehydrated, canned or perhaps where sugar or vinegar is added, fall into this category, providing that these containers have not been opened. If the containers of such foods are open it may be necessary to store the food using temperature control.

Foods that require ripening or maturing, such as cheese, may be kept outside of temperature control, however, once the process has been completed, they should then be refrigerated.

In a number of salmonella food poisoning cases raw eggs have been suspected of being the cause. Most infections cause only mild stomach upsets but the effects can be serious in vulnerable people such as the elderly, the infirm, pregnant women, and young children. Consumers, particularly the more vulnerable, are advised to avoid eating raw and lightly cooked eggs, uncooked foods made from raw eggs and products such as mayonnaise, mousses, ice creams. Caterers are advised to use pasteurised eggs. Dishes with an obvious risk of passing on contamination also include soft boiled eggs, scrambled eggs and omelettes. The Department of Health has issued the following guidelines that apply to raw eggs:

- Eggs should be stored in a cool dry place, preferably under refrigeration.
- Eggs should be stored away from possible contaminants such as raw meat.

- Stocks should be rotated first in first out.
- Hands should be washed before and after handling eggs.
- Cracked eggs should not be used.
- Preparation surfaces, utensils and containers should be regularly cleaned and always cleaned between the preparation of different dishes.
- Egg dishes should be consumed as soon as possible after preparation or, if not for immediate use, refrigerated.

Food poisoning

Food poisoning is an illness characterised by stomach pains, diarrhoea and sometimes vomiting, which can develop within 1 to 36 hours after eating affected food.

Prevention

Almost all food poisoning can be prevented by:

- complying with the rules of hygiene;
- taking care and thinking ahead;
- ensuring that high standards of cleanliness are applied to premises and equipment;
- preventing accidents.

More specifically, pay attention to:

- high standards of personal hygiene;
- physical fitness;
- maintaining good working conditions;
- maintaining equipment in good repair and clean condition;
- using separate equipment and knives for cooked and uncooked foods;
- ample provision of cleaning facilities and equipment;
- storing foods at the right temperature;
- safe reheating of foods;

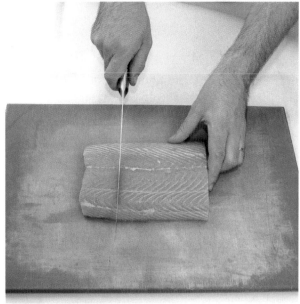

Fig 1.6 ✎ Separate chopping boards for different foods will help to prevent cross-contamination

- quick cooling of foods prior to storage;
- protection of foods from vermin and insects;
- hygienic washing-up procedures;
- knowing how food poisoning is caused;
- carrying out procedures to prevent food poisoning.

Causes

Causes include *chemicals* having entered food accidentally during the growth, preparation or cooking of the food, and *bacteria* (germs) (see page 8). Chemical food poisoning can occur from:

- arsenic, used in sprays during growth of fruit;
- lead, from using water that has been in contact with lead pipes;
- poor-quality enamelled or galvanised containers;
- copper pans, used for storing foods;
- certain plants, such as rhubarb leaves and parts of potatoes exposed above the soil;

- fungi;
- rat poison;
- poorly prepared cleaning chemicals (at incorrect strength).

Chemical food poisoning can be prevented by:

- use of properly maintained utensils;
- obtaining foods from reliable sources;
- taking care in the use of rat poison, etc.

Infestations

Infestations can be caused by:

- inadequate cleaning;
- poor building maintenance;
- suppliers' deliveries.

Rodent infestation can be caused by rats and mice contaminating food. Insect infestation includes flies, cockroaches, beetles and silver fish.

Prevention

Rats, mice, cockroaches, flies, other insects and birds must be controlled.

- Ensure buildings are sound with no holes or structural defects whereby mice and rats can enter premises.
- Use screens on windows to keep insects and birds out.
- Install ultraviolet electrical fly killers.
- Have no narrow spaces between equipment and fittings and no false bottoms.
- Store all food supplies off the floor.
- Keep all foods in lidded containers where practical.
- Do not allow waste to accumulate in the kitchen or outside.
- Keep all waste bins with lids on.
- Employ a pest control contractor.

Surplus prepared foods or left-overs

Ideally, there should be no foods remaining after the meal service. Over-production should be kept to a minimum as left-over foods can be a source of food poisoning. Therefore, to be safe and to avoid waste, such food must be stored at 5°C (41°F) or below.

Practices to prevent problems with surplus food items include:

- If items have been excessively handled or subjected to high temperature for a long time,

they may not be reusable and should be discarded.
- Hot items must be cooled as quickly as possible and when cold kept at 5°C (41°F) or below.
- If food is required to be served hot, reheat to above 70°C (158°F) and keep at above 63°C (145°F) until served; reheat only once, then discard.
- If required to be served cold, use within 48 hours. Keep at 5°C (41°F) below until required.
- Be extra careful to prevent contamination by practising high standards of food, personal and kitchen hygiene.
- Take extra care with meat, fish, poultry and egg dishes and those dishes containing milk and cream.
- Cover items to be stored and keep fresh foods away from cooked foods to avoid risk of cross-contamination.
- If in doubt, it is wiser to throw it out having checked with the person responsible.

Further information: Food Hygiene Bureau Ltd, Long Hanborough, Oxford, OX8 8LH.

Note For further information on storage, please refer to Foskett, Ceserani and Kinton (2003) *The Theory of Catering*, 10th edition, London: Hodder and Stoughton.

Healthier cooking methods

Baked jacket potato with fromage
frais and chive dressing

Selection of fresh herbs

What is healthy eating?

Food, nutrition and exercise are crucial to our health and well being. There is no doubt that making the right choices of food and drink combined with taking regular exercise can protect against many of the killer diseases like coronary heart disease and cancer. There are also lots of immediate benefits and a really positive result is keeping slim for life.

It may seem confusing in the media, but the scientists are all united on what is a healthy style of eating – unfortunately many myths still prevail. Contrary to popular opinion it is not about taking chips off the menu, or eating small portions of salad – but simply eating more bulky, filling foods, piling on the fruit and vegetables and less of the high fat sugary foods. Some of the greatest dishes and most exciting cuisines in the world are based on these principles (e.g. Paella, Biryani, Chinese vegetables stir fried with noodles, Sushi and rice, couscous, cannelloni stuffed with ricotta and spinach).

Summing Up Healthy Eating

What it is about	What it is not about	Immediate benefits
Filling up on bread, pasta, rice and potatoes Eating more fruit and vegetables Eating a little less of some food items Enjoying good food Making small, gradual changes Knowing more about food Altering food shopping patterns Feeling satisfied and good about food	Cutting down on food Going hungry Depriving yourself of treats Spending more money on food Not enjoying food 'Brown and boring food' Just salads Making major changes Going on a 'special diet'	Better weight control More self esteem Looking and feeling better Feeling fitter with more energy Enjoying a wide variety of foods Not buying expensive 'diet' products Knowing that changes made today will have long-term benefits

The balance of good health

There are no 'good' or 'bad' foods – it is the overall balance of the diet that matters. How people choose to put together meals and snacks with drinks will determine whether their style of eating is healthy or not. The balance to strive for is illustrated in the nationally recognised model (Figure 2.1). It simply says that people should consume:

- **more starchy foods** (e.g. cereals, breads, pasta, potatoes, rice)

- **more fruit and vegetables** (aiming for five portions of fruits and vegetables per day)
- **moderate** amounts of foods from the 'dairy' and 'meat' groups – as a guideline 2–3 portions from each group per day
- **very small amounts** of foods containing fats and sugars and select lower fat options where possible.

Information on the portions of different types of foods that make up a healthy diet is given in the Balance of Good Health leaflet available from the Food Standards Agency (FSA).

enjoying a healthy diet is all about

getting the balance right

fruit & vegetables

bread, other cereals & potatoes

meat, fish & alternatives

milk & dairy foods

foods containing fat, foods & drinks containing sugar

There are no healthy or unhealthy foods – only healthy or unhealthy diets

Fig 2.1

Translating this into practice means:

- bigger portions of starchy foods, vegetables and fruit within meals;

- getting more energy (kcals) from starchy carbohydrate and less from fatty and sugary foods;
- there is scope for the occasional treat;
- aiming to achieve this balance over a period of days – not necessarily at every meal;
- often making very small changes to favourite meals.

Fig 2.2 🖊 Putting healthy eating into practice

Foods into nutrients

Healthy eating is about selecting certain foods that provide nutrients that are needed by the body in different amounts. If people choose foods in the proportions shown in the Balance of Good Health leaflet (Fig 2.1) then they should obtain all the nutrients they need in the quantities that promote good health. Nutrients perform different functions in the body and you can find out more about this in any basic nutrition text book (see More information section, page 23). This table summarises some of the key nutritional terms you will encounter plus the current guidance for health.

Foods provide:	For health
Energy: is locked up in food and comes from carbohydrate, fat, protein and alcohol. It is measured in calories or joules, which are so tiny they are usually expressed in kilocalories (kcals) or kilojoules (kJ).	To balance energy intake through food with energy output through activity. This helps control body weight. Specific figures for energy intakes are given in the Government's report on Dietary Reference Values (see More information, page 23).

Fat: is a very concentrated source of energy. The same weight of pure fat has over twice as much energy as sugar or starch.
Fat is present in foods in two main types:
  saturated fat in foods from animal sources like butter, cheese, meat and milk, fatty meats;
  unsaturated fat in foods from plant (e.g. oils, nuts and seeds) and oily fish (e.g. tuna, salmon, mackerel) sources.
	To cut down on fat intake, particularly the saturated type – aiming for 30%–35% energy from fat. It is the saturated fat that pushes up blood cholesterol and this is why it is important to switch to foods containing unsaturated types of fat. For example, using oils instead of butter or lard in recipes, incorporating more oily fish like salmon and mackerel plus white meats into menu planning.

Carbohydrate: is made up of two types
  sugars (occur naturally in certain foods like fruit and honey) but added to many manufactured foods, particularly confectionery, cakes and biscuits;
  starches found naturally in filling foods like bread, breakfast cereals, rice, pasta and potatoes.
	We should aim for 50% of our energy from starch and cut back on sugars.

Fibre: is the 'roughage' in plant foods and is great for the digestive system. Good sources include all wholegrain cereals, pulses, fruits, vegetable, and nuts.	On current estimates we all eat around 20 g dietary fibre per day. The healthy goal is around 30 g/day.
Protein: is the 'body building' nutrient found in animal foods like meat, fish, cheese and eggs – but also in vegetable sources including cereals (e.g. pasta, breakfast cereals, bread) pulses and nuts.	Protein requirements are often overestimated. For example, adults only need between 35–50 g protein per day. This can be provided by a 100 g portion of chicken plus a carton of yoghurt and 200 g of baked beans.
Vitamins and Minerals: are needed in minute amounts for many bodily processes. Since the body cannot make these essential micronutrients, they have to be provided by diet.	Recommended daily amounts for nine vitamins and eleven minerals are given in the Government's report on Dietary Reference Values (see more information).
Salt: is sodium chloride, which is involved in maintaining the body's water balance. Sodium is a type of mineral and as sodium chloride is added to many manufactured foods and is particularly high in cured and snack foods.	There is now stronger evidence that the high intakes of salt in this country (estimated at about 8 g/day salt) can lead to high blood pressure. The goal is around 4g salt/day.

Fig 2.3 🏃 Mexican bean pot and salad

Fig 2.4 🏃 Navarin of lamb

The chef's role

Chefs are vital in making healthy eating an exciting reality for us all. Customer trends show that many people are looking for healthier options within menus, particularly if they eat away from home every day. Healthy eating is one of the major consumer trends to emerge over the past decade and represents an important commercial opportunity for caterers across the UK. This is not a passing fad; healthy eating is here to stay.

As well as escalating consumer demand, some sectors of catering have strict requirements relating to health and nutrition. For example, by law, school caterers have to provide meals that meet a minimum nutritional standard. Often there are health related specifications for workplace catering contracts because employers feel they have a commitment to the health of their staff.

Chefs can be highly influential in the health arena. The amount of ingredients and the proportion in which they are used, plus careful choice of cooking and service methods, can make an enormous difference to the nutritional content of a dish or meal. Research has shown that the most effective approach to healthy catering is to make small changes to popular dishes. This may involve:

- Small shifts in portion sizes (as in Figs. 2.2 and 2.4) or adding a bread roll, jacket potato to a meal. This yields more starch in proportion to fat (effectively diluting the fat).

- Subtle modifications to recipes for composite dishes. For instance making a pizza with a thicker base and adding mushrooms and roasted peppers topped with less mozzarella but adding a sprinklng of parmesan for flavour. Omitting the salt, but relying on the parmesan, black pepper and chopped oregano to add flavour.

This is where chefs are vital in developing healthier recipes that work. The skill in all this is deciding when and where dishes can be modified without losing quality. Some highly traditional dishes are best left alone, whilst subtle changes can be made to others with no loss in texture, appearance or flavour. The 'Healthy Tips' throughout the recipe sections can help in making some of these changes.

In summary the key to healthier catering is to:

- make small changes to best selling items;
- increase the amount of starchy foods;
- increase the amount of fruit and vegetables;
- increase the fibre content of dishes where it is practical and acceptable;
- reduce fat in traditional recipes;
- change the type of fat used;
- select healthier ways to prepare dishes and be adventurous;
- be moderate in the use of sugar and salt.

Note – Take care when providing nutritional information on menus: there may be danger of making misleading claims which could break the law. Take advice.

Traditional lasagne – 4 portions	'Healthier' lasagne – 4 portions
Made with 33 g oil to brown off 500 g ordinary minced beef and 125 g streaky bacon. Béchamel made from butter and whole milk, layered with 500 g lasagne and topped with 125 g cheddar cheese.	Made with lean mince and dry fried. Bacon omitted. Béchamel made up with unsaturated margarine and semi skimmed milk. More lasagne added (700 g) but slightly less cheddar cheese (100 g).

Per portion		Per portion	
Energy (kJ)	2545	Energy (kJ)	2061
(kcals)	608	(kcals)	493
Total fat (g)	33.1	Total fat (g)	15.5
Saturates (g)	16.3	Saturates (g)	5.9
Fibre (g)	3.4	Fibre (g)	4.8

Serving the lasagne with a salad and French bread or a jacket potato would further dilute the fat content and bump up the starch and fibre content. All these recipe and serving suggestions drive the balance in a healthier direction.

More information

Dietary Reference Values for Food Energy and Nutrients for the United Kingdom (1991)
Sets the current main benchmarks for nutrient intakes in the UK. Produced by the Department of Health and available from the Stationery Office.

The Manual of Nutrition (1995)
Basic text book on nutrition. Was produced by the Ministry of Agriculture, Fisheries and Food and available from the Stationery Office.

Catering For Health (2001)
Sets out the fundamentals of nutrition without the baffling science and is a fountain of practical advice to enthuse the next culinary generation. Produced in partnership by the FSA and DH, available from the Stationery Office for £5.

Catering For Health: The Recipe File (1988)
Provides healthier recipe ideas for caterers. Available from the Stationery Office.

Tipping The Balance (1999)
23 minute video on practical tips aimed at encouraging healthier catering practice in the workplace. Available from the FSA.

The Balance of Good Health (1996)
A pictorial model for food selection. Available in A4 leaflet or A3 poster format. Available from the FSA.

The transference of heat to food

(Oven temperature chart page xiii.)
All methods of cooking depend on one or more of the following principles.

Radiation

Heat passes from its source in direct rays until it falls on an object in its path such as in grilling.

Conduction

This is the transferring of heat through a solid object by contact. Some materials, for example, metal used for pans, transfer heat more quickly than, say, wood used for wooden spoons. Conduction is the principle involved in the solid electric ranges.

Convection

This is the movement of heated particles of gases or liquids. On heating, the particles expand, become less dense and rise. The colder particles sink to take their place, thus causing convection currents, which distribute heat. This principle is used in heating a gas oven and in the heating of liquids.

The effect of heat on food

Protein

Protein is coagulated by heat. The process is gradual, for example when heat is applied to egg white it thickens, becomes opaque and then firm. Over-heating will harden the protein, making it tough, unpalatable and shrunken. This characteristic coagulation of protein when heated is employed in its use as a coating for deep and shallow fried foods and in the development of crust in bread formed by the protein gluten in wheat.

Carbohydrates

Moist heat on starch causes the starch grains to soften and swell. Near boiling point the cellulose framework bursts, releasing the starch, which thickens the liquid.

Dry heat causes the starch to change colour from creamy white to brown and after prolonged heat will carbonise and burn. Water is given off during heating and the starch on the surface is changed to dextrin, a form of sugar, as in toast.

Moist heat causes sugar to dissolve in water – more rapidly in hot water than in cold. On heating it becomes syrup; on further heating it colours then caramelises and will eventually turn to carbon and ash.

Dry heat causes sugar to caramelise quickly and burn.

Fats

Fats melt to oils when heated. Water is given off with a bubbling noise as heating continues. When all the water has been driven off a faint blue haze appears; further heating will result in smoking and burning. The unpleasant smell of burning fat is caused by the presence of fatty acids.

Vitamins

Vitamin A and *carotene* are insoluble in water so they are not lost by moist methods of cooking, such as boiling and steaming, or by soaking. Therefore boiled vegetables contain the same amount of carotene as raw vegetables.

Vitamin D is not destroyed by heat or lost by solubility.

Thiamine (vitamin B_1) is very soluble in water and about 50% will dissolve in the cooking liquid. High temperatures, e.g. pressure cooking, destroy vitamin

B_1 and alkali (baking powder) will cause some destruction.

Riboflavin (vitamin B$_2$) is soluble in water and will dissolve out in the cooking liquid; some is lost in normal cooking but more losses occur in pressure cooking.

Nicotinic acid (niacin) is soluble in water and dissolves to some extent in the cooking liquid. It is stable in the presence of heat but is easily oxidised, which means that the chemical process of the products is adversely affected by taking in oxygen.

Vitamin C is lost or destroyed very easily in cooking and care must be taken to preserve it as much as possible. It is soluble in water and is easily dissolved in cleaning and cooking water; therefore vegetables containing vitamin C should not be soaked in water and cooking liquid should be made use of. It is best to cook in small quantities and as quickly as possible as vitamin C is destroyed by heat. Raw fruit and vegetables contain most vitamin C.

Vitamin C oxidises (see nicotinic acid) to form a substance that is useless to the body; to minimise oxidation cook with a lid on; also food containing vitamin C should only be stored for short periods and must be used as fresh as possible.

There is an enzyme present with vitamin C in foods which, once the cells of the plant are damaged by bruising or cutting, begins to destroy the vitamin by oxidising it. The optimum or most favourable condition for destruction of the enzyme is between 65°–88°C (149–190°F) so if the vegetable is put into boiling water the enzyme activity will be quickly destroyed.

Ways of cooking food

- boiling
- poaching
- stewing
- braising
- steaming
- baking
- roasting
- grilling (griddling)
- frying (shallow and deep)
- paper bag (en papillotte)
- microwave
- pot roasting (poêlé)

Boiling
Definition
Boiling is the cooking of prepared foods in a liquid at boiling point. This could be water, court-bouillon, milk or stock.

Purpose
The purpose of boiling is to cook food so that it is:

- pleasant to eat with an agreeable flavour;
- of a suitable texture, tender or slightly firm according to the food;
- easy to digest and safe to eat.

Methods
There are two ways of boiling:

- Place the food into boiling liquid, reboil, then reduce the heat for gentle boiling to take place, this is known as simmering.
- Cover food with cold liquid, bring to the boil, then reduce heat to allow food to simmer.

Effects of boiling
Gentle boiling helps to break down the tough fibrous structure of certain foods that would be less tender if cooked by other methods. When boiling meats for long periods the soluble meat extracts are dissolved

in the cooking liquid. Cooking must be slow in order to give time for the connective tissue in tough meat to be changed into soluble gelatine, so releasing the fibres and making the meat tender. If the connective tissue gelatinises too quickly the meat fibres fall apart and the meat will be tough and stringy. Gentle heat will ensure coagulation of the protein without hardening.

Advantages of boiling

- Older, tougher, cheaper joints of meat and poultry can be made palatable and digestible.
- It is appropriate for large-scale cookery and is economic on fuel.
- Nutritious, well-flavoured stock can be produced.
- Labour saving, as boiling needs little attention.

a) The advantages of food started slowly in cold liquid, brought to the boil and allowed to boil gently:

- helps to tenderise the fibrous structure (meat), extracts starch (vegetable soups) and flavour from certain foods (stocks);

Fig 3.1 🖌 Boiling crab

- can avoid damage to foods that would lose their shape if added to boiling liquid, e.g. whole fish.

b) adding food to boiling liquid:

- is suitable for green vegetables as maximum colour and nutritive value are retained, provided boiling is restricted to the minimum time;
- seals in the natural juices as with meat.

Time and temperature control

Temperature must be controlled so that the liquid is brought to the boil, or reboil, then adjusted in order that gentle boiling takes place until the food is cooked to the required degree. Stocks, soups and sauces must only simmer, pasta cooked slightly firm (*al dente*), meat and poultry well cooked and tender; vegetables should not be overcooked.

Although approximate cooking times are given for most foods, the age, quality and size of various foods will nevertheless affect the cooking time required.

General rules

- Select pans that are neither too small nor too large.
- When cooking in boiling liquid ensure there is sufficient liquid and that it is at boiling point before adding food.
- Frequently skim during the cooking.
- Simmer whenever possible so as to minimise evaporation, maintain volume of liquid and minimise shrinkage.

Safety

- Select containers of the right capacity – if they are too small there is danger of boiling liquid splashing over, forming steam and causing scalds.

- Always move pans of boiling liquid on the stove with care.
- Position pan handles so that they do not protrude from the stove or become hot over the heat.
- Extra care is required when adding or removing foods from containers of boiling liquid.

Poaching

Definition

Poaching is the cooking of foods in the required amount of liquid at just below boiling point.

Purpose

The purpose of poaching is to cook food so that it is:

- easy to digest;
- a suitable tender texture;
- safe and pleasant to eat because, where appropriate, an agreeable sauce is made with the cooking liquid.

Methods

There are two ways of poaching: shallow and deep.

- *Shallow poaching.* Foods to be cooked by this method, such as cuts of fish and chicken, are cooked in the minimum of liquid, that is, water, stock, milk or wine. The liquid should never be allowed to boil but kept at a temperature as near to boiling point as possible. To prevent the liquid boiling, bring to the boil on top of the stove and complete the cooking in a moderate hot oven, approximately 180°C (356°F).
- *Deep poaching.* Eggs are cooked in approximately 8 cm (3 inch) of gently simmering water. (The practice of poaching eggs in individual shallow metal pans over boiling water

is cooking by steaming.) Whole fish, e.g. salmon; slices of fish on the bone e.g. turbot, grilled cod and salmon; and whole chicken may be deep poached.

Effects of poaching

Poaching helps to tenderise the fibrous structure of the food, and the raw texture of the food becomes edible by chemical action.

Temperature and time control

- Temperature must be controlled so that the cooking liquid does not fall below, or exceed, the correct degree required:

  shallow poaching is just below simmering point (and may be carried out in an oven); *deep poaching* is just below gentle simmering.
- Time is important so that the food is neither undercooked, therefore unpalatable, nor overcooked, when it will break up and also lose nutritive value.
- The various types and qualities of food will affect both time and temperature needed to achieve successful poaching.

Safety

- Select suitably sized pans to prevent spillage and possible scalding.
- Move trays, etc. carefully on and off stove, or from the oven, as tilting or jarring may cause spillage.
- Carefully place food in the pan when adding to simmering liquid.
- When a hot container is removed from the oven, sprinkle with a little flour to warn that it is hot.

Stewing

Definition

Stewing is the slow cooking of food cut into pieces and cooked in the minimum amount of liquid (water, stock or sauce); the food and liquid are served together.

Purpose

Because stewing is both economical and nutritional, cheaper cuts of meat and poultry, which would be unsuitable for roasting and grilling, can be made tender and palatable. Stewing also produces an acceptable flavour, texture and eating quality.

Methods of stewing

All stews have a thickened consistency achieved by:

* the unpassed ingredients in the stew, such as Irish stew (page 230);
* thickening of the cooking liquor, such as white stew (*blanquette*) (page 231);
* cooking in the sauce, such as brown stew (*navarin*) (page 226).

Stewed foods can be cooked in a covered pan on the stove or in a moderate oven.

Fig 3.2 Preparation for an Irish stew

Effects of stewing

In the slow process of cooking in gentle heat, the connective tissue in meat and poultry is converted into a gelatinous substance so that the fibres fall apart easily and become digestible. The protein is coagulated without being toughened. Unlike boiling, less liquid is used and the cooking temperature is approximately 5°C lower.

See also 'effects of boiling' (page 27) as this also applies to stewing.

Advantages

* The meat juices that escape from the meat during cooking are retained in the liquid, which is part of the stew.
* Correct slow cooking results in very little evaporation.
* Nutrients are conserved.
* Tough goods are tenderised.
* It is economical in labour because foods can be cooked in bulk.

Temperature and time control

* Temperature control is essential to the slow cooking required for efficient stewing; therefore, the liquid must barely simmer.
* A tight-fitting lid is used to retain steam, which helps maintain temperature and reduce evaporation.
* Time will vary according to the quality of the food used.
* The ideal cooking temperature for stewing on top of the stove is approximately 82°C (180°F) (simmering temperature); or cooking in the oven at 170°C (gas mark 3, 340°F).

Care and cleanliness

Thoroughly wash equipment with hot detergent water, rinse with hot water and dry. Moving parts of large-scale equipment should be greased occasionally. Store pans upside-down on clean racks. Check that handles are not loose and that copper pans are completely tinned. Report any faults with large equipment.

General rules

- Stews should not be over-thickened. The sauce should be light in consistency; therefore, correct ratios of thickening agents are essential.
- Adjustment to the consistency should be made as required during cooking.
- Overcooking causes: a) evaporation of liquid; b) breaking up of the food; c) discoloration; and d) spoilage of flavour.

Safety

- Select suitably sized pans.
- Care is essential when removing hot pans from the oven.
- When removing lids be careful of escaping steam, which may cause scalds.
- Sprinkle flour on hot pans and lids after removal from the oven as a warning that they are hot.
- Ensure that pan handles are not over the heat or sticking out from the stove.

Braising

Definition

Braising is a method of cooking in the oven; unlike roasting or baking, the food is cooked in liquid in a covered pan, casserole or cocotte. It is a combination of stewing and pot roasting.

Purpose

The purpose of braising is:

- to give variety to the menu and the diet;
- to make food tender, digestible, palatable and safe to eat;
- to produce and enhance flavour, texture and eating quality.

Methods of braising

There are two methods: brown braising, used, for example, for joints and portion-sized cuts of meat; white braising, used, for example, for vegetables and sweetbreads.

Brown braising:

- Joints such as beef and venison are marinaded and may be larded, then sealed quickly by browning on all sides in a hot oven or in a pan on the stove. Sealing the joints helps retain flavour, nutritive value and gives a good brown colour. Joints are then placed on a bed of root vegetables in a braising pan, with the liquid and other flavourings, covered with a lid and cooked slowly in the oven.
- Cuts (steaks, chops, liver). The brown braising of cuts of meat is similar to that of joints.

White braising (celery, cabbage and sweetbreads). Foods are blanched, refreshed, cooked on a bed of root vegetables with white stock in a covered container in the oven.

Effects of braising

Cooking by braising causes the breakdown of the tissue fibre in the structure of certain foods, which softens the texture, thus making it tender and edible. The texture is also improved by being cooked in the braising liquid.

Advantages

- Tougher, less expensive meats and poultry can be used.
- Maximum flavour and nutritional value are retained.
- Variety of presentation and flavour is given to the menu.

Time and temperature control

- Slow cooking is essential for efficient braising; the liquid must barely simmer.
- To reduce evaporation and maintain temperature, use a tight-fitting lid.
- Time needed for braising will vary according to the quality of the food.
- Ideal oven temperature for braising is 160°C (gas mark 3, 320°F).

General rules

These are the same as for stewing. However, if the joint is to be served whole, the lid is removed three-quarters of the way through cooking. The joint is then frequently basted to give a glaze for presentation.

Safety

- Select a suitably sized pan with a tight-fitting lid and handles.
- Care is required when removing hot pans from the oven and when removing the lid.
- Sprinkle flour on hot pans and lids after removal from the oven as a warning that they are hot.

Steaming

Definition

Steaming is the cooking of prepared foods by steam (moist heat) under varying degrees of pressure.

Purpose

The purpose of steaming food is to cook it so that it is:

- easy to digest;
- of an edible texture, pleasant and safe to eat;
- as nutritious as possible (steaming minimises nutritive loss).

Methods of steaming

Atmospheric or low-pressure steaming:

- *direct:* in a steamer or in a pan of boiling water (steak and kidney pudding);
- *indirect:* between two plates over a pan of boiling water.

High-pressure steaming in purpose-built equipment, which does not allow the steam to escape, therefore enabling steam pressure to build up, thus increasing the temperature and reducing cooking time.

Vacuum cooking in a pouch: this is known as *sous-vide*, a method of cooking in which food contained in vacuum-sealed plastic pouches is cooked by steam. The advantages of *sous-vide* cooking of food are:

- minimal change of texture and weight loss;
- no drying out and very little colour loss;
- dishes can be garnished and decorated before the vacuum packing and cooking process;
- the food cooks in its own natural juices;
- labour saving;
- uniformity of standard.

In this latter method, raw food products (cuts of fish, breast of chicken or duck) are lightly seasoned and any required cut vegetables, herbs, spices, stock or wine added and placed into specially made plastic pouches.

A vacuum packing machine seals the pouch, which is then cooked in a temperature-controlled convection steam cooker. The length of cooking time must be carefully controlled. Once cooked, the pouch is quickly cooled and kept at a temperature of 3°C (37°F).

When required for service the pouches are either placed in boiling water or a steam oven.

Effects of steaming

When food is steamed the structure and texture is changed by chemical action and becomes edible. The texture will vary according to the type of food, type of steamer and degree of heat; sponges and puddings are lighter in texture if steamed rather than baked.

Advantages of steaming

These include:

- retention of goodness (nutritional value);
- makes some foods lighter and easy to digest, e.g. suitable for invalids;
- low-pressure steaming reduces risk of overcooking protein;
- high-pressure steaming enables food to be cooked or reheated quickly because steam is forced through the food, thus cooking it rapidly;
- labour-saving and suitable for large-scale cookery;
- high-speed steamers used for 'batch' cooking enable the frequent cooking of small quantities of vegetables throughout the service, keeping vegetables freshly cooked, retaining colour, flavour and nutritive value;
- with steamed fish, the natural juices can be retained by serving with the fish or in making the accompanying sauce;
- steaming is economical on fuel as a low heat is needed and a multitiered steamer can be used.

Time and temperature control

For high-pressure steaming, foods should be placed in the steamer when the pressure gauge indicates the required degree of pressure. This will ensure that the necessary cooking temperature has been reached.

Cooking times will vary according to the equipment used and the type, size and quality of food to be steamed. Manufacturers' instructions are an essential guide to successful steaming.

Cleaning

The inside of the steamer, trays and runners are washed in hot detergent water, rinsed and dried. Where applicable the water-generating chamber should be drained, cleaned and refilled. Door controls should be lightly greased occasionally and the door left open slightly to allow air to circulate when the steamer is not in use.

Before use check that the steamer is clean and safe to use. Any fault must be reported immediately.

Metal containers (sleeves and basins), may be thoroughly cleaned with kitchen paper or a clean cloth; other containers must be washed in hot detergent water, rinsed in hot water and dried. Containers are stored in closed cupboards.

Specific points

Meat and sweet pudding basins must be greased, then, after being filled, efficiently covered with greased greaseproof or silicone paper and foil to prevent moisture penetrating and resulting in a soggy pudding.

Safety factors

- Where applicable, check that the water in the water well is at the correct level and that the ball-valve arm moves freely.

- Before opening the steamer door, allow the steam pressure to drop.
- Take extra care when opening the door, use it as a shield from escaping steam as a severe scald may result.
- Follow manufacturers' instructions at all times regarding cleaning and operating procedures.

Baking

Definition

Baking is the cooking of food by dry heat in an oven in which the action of the dry convection heat is modified by steam.

Purpose

The purpose of baking is:

- to make food digestible, palatable and safe to eat;
- to create eye-appeal through colour and texture and produce an enjoyable eating quality;
- to lend variety to the menu.

Methods

Note: Ovens must be preheated prior to baking.

- *Dry baking*: when baking, steam arises from the water content of the food; this steam combines with the dry heat of the oven to cook the food (cakes, pastry, baked jacket potatoes).
- *Baking with increased humidity*: when baking certain foods, such as bread, the oven humidity is increased by placing a bowl of water or injection steam into the oven, thus increasing the water content of the food and so improving eating quality.
- *Baking with heat modification*: placing food in a container of water (*bain-marie*), such as baked

egg custard, modifies the heat so that the food cooks more slowly, does not overheat and lessens the possibility of the egg mixture overcooking.

Effects of baking

Chemical action caused by the effect of heat on certain ingredients, such as yeast and baking powder, changes the raw structure of many foods to an edible texture (pastry, cakes). However, different ingredients, methods of mixing and types of product required will cause many variations.

Advantages of baking

- A wide variety of sweet and savoury foods can be produced.
- Bakery products yield appetising goods with eye-appeal and mouth-watering aromas.
- Bulk cooking can be achieved with uniformity of colour and degree of cooking.
- Baking ovens have effective manual or automatic temperature controls.
- There is straightforward access for loading and removal of items.

Time and temperature control

- Ovens must always be heated to the required temperature before the food is added.
- In general-purpose ovens, shelves must be placed according to the food being cooked, because the hotter part of the oven is at the top. With convection ovens the heat is evenly distributed.
- Accurate timing and temperature control are essential to baking. The required oven temperature must be reached before each additional batch of goods is placed in the oven. This is known as *recovery time*.

General rules

- Always preheat ovens so that the required cooking temperature is immediately applied to the product, otherwise the product will be spoiled.
- Accuracy is essential in weighing, measuring and controlling temperature.
- Trays and moulds must be correctly prepared.
- Minimise the opening of oven doors as draughts may affect the quality of the product, and the oven temperature is reduced.
- Utilise oven space efficiently.
- Avoid jarring of products (fruit cake, sponges, soufflés) before and during baking as the quality may be affected.

Safety

- Use thick, dry, sound oven cloths for handling hot trays, etc.
- Jacket sleeves should be rolled down to prevent burns from hot trays and ovens.
- Trays and ovens should not be overloaded.
- Extra care is needed to balance and handle loaded trays in and out of the oven.

Roasting

Definition

Roasting is cooking in dry heat with the aid of fat or oil in an oven or on a spit. Radiant heat is the means of cooking when using a spit; oven roasting is a combination of convection and radiation.

Purpose

The purpose of roasting is to cook food so that it is tender, easy to digest, safe to eat and palatable. It also gives variety to the menu and the diet.

Methods

- Placing prepared foods (meat, poultry) on a rotating spit over or in front of fierce radiated heat.
- Placing prepared foods in an oven with either:
    applied dry heat;
    forced air-convected heat;
    convected heat combined with microwave energy.

Effects of roasting

The surface protein of the food is sealed by the initial heat of the oven, thus preventing the escape of too many natural juices. When the food is lightly browned, the oven temperature is reduced to cook the inside of the food without hardening the surface.

Advantages

- Good quality meat and poultry is tender and succulent when roasted.
- Meat juices issuing from the joint are used for gravy and enhance flavour.
- Both energy and oven temperature can be controlled.
- Ovens with transparent doors enable cooking to be observed.
- Access, adjustment and removal of items is straightforward.
- Minimal fire risk.

Spit roasting

- Skill and techniques can be displayed to the customer.
- Continual basting with the meat juice over the carcass or joint on the revolving spit gives a distinctive flavour, depending on the fuel used (wood, charcoal).

Time and temperature control

- Ovens must be preheated.
- Oven temperature and shelf settings in recipes must be followed.
- Shape, size, type, bone proportion and quality of food will affect the cooking time.
- Meat thermometers or probes can be inserted to determine the exact temperature in the centre of the joint.

The following table gives approximate cooking times:

	Approximate cooking times	Degree of cooking
beef	15 minutes per ½ kg (1 lb) and 15 minutes over	underdone
lamb	20 minutes per ½ kg (1 lb) and 20 minutes over	cooked through
lamb	15 minutes per ½ kg (1 lb) and 15 minutes over	cooked pink
mutton	20 minutes per ½ kg (1 lb) and 20 minutes over	cooked through
veal	20 minutes per ½ kg (1 lb) and 25 minutes over	cooked through
pork	25 minutes per ½ kg (1 lb) and 25 minutes over	thoroughly cooked

For internal temperature of meat, see page 246.

Safety

- Roasting trays should be of a suitable size: if too small, basting becomes difficult and dangerous; if too large, fat in the tray will burn, spoiling the flavour of the meat and gravy.
- Handle hot roasting trays carefully at all times, using a thick, dry cloth.
- Ensure food is securely held before removing from roasting tray.

Pot roasting

Definition

Pot roasting (poêlé) is cooking on a bed of root vegetables in a covered pan. This method retains maximum flavour of all ingredients.

Method

Place the food on a bed of roots and herbs, coat generously with butter or oil, cover with a lid and cook in an oven.

General rules

- Select pans neither too large nor too small.
- Use the vegetables and herbs with a good stock as a base for the sauce.

Tandoori cooking

Definition

Tandoori cooking is by dry heat in a clay oven called a tandoor. Although the heat source is at the base of the oven, the oven heat is evenly distributed because of the clay, which radiates heat evenly.

Method

Meat (small cuts and small joints), poultry (small cuts and whole chickens) and fish, such as prawns, are usually placed vertically in the oven. No fat or oil is used. The food is cooked quickly and the flavour is similar to that of barbecued food. Oven temperatures reach 375°C (700°F). Depending on the type, foods may be marinaded for 20 minutes to 2 hours before being cooked and in some cases they may be brushed with the marinade during cooking.

Naan, a flat leavened bread, is slapped onto the inside walls of a tandoor and cooks alongside other skewered foods.

If a traditional tandoor is not available, then an oven, grill rôtisserie or barbecue can be used provided the basic rules and principles of tandoori cooking are applied. However, as the spices for a tandoori marinade should be well cooked at a high temperature, then the spices in this case should be briefly cooked over a fierce heat before being added to the marinade.

Advantages

- The distinctive flavour of tandoori-cooked food comes from both the marinade and the cooking process.
- Marinading tenderises and also adds flavour to foods.
- Colour change may occur depending on the spices used: a red colouring agent is used in some marinades, also onions, garlic, herbs, spices and oil, wine or lemon juice.

Grilling

Definition

This is a fast method of cooking by radiant heat sometimes known as broiling.

Purpose

The purpose of grilling is:

- to make foods digestible, palatable and safe to eat;
- to utilise the speed of the cooking process to produce a distinctive flavour, colour, texture and eating quality;
- to bring variety to the menu and to introduce into the diet simple, uncomplicated dishes.

Methods of grilling

Grilled foods can be cooked:

- over heat (charcoal, barbecues, gas or electric heated grills/griddles);
- under heat (gas or electric salamanders (overfired grills));
- between heat (electrically heated grill bars or plates);

Over heat

Grill bars must be preheated and brushed with oil prior to use, otherwise food will stick. The bars

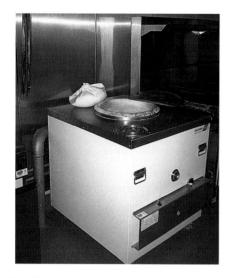

Fig 3.3 🥄 A contemporary tandoor oven

should char the food on both sides to give the distinctive appearance and flavour of grilling. Most foods are started on the hottest part of the grill and moved to a cooler part to complete the cooking. The thickness of the food and the heat of the grill determine the cooking time, which is learned by experience.

Under heat (salamander)

The salamander should be preheated and the bars greased. Steaks, chops and items that are likely to slip between the grill bars may be cooked under the salamander.

Degrees of cooking grills	Appearance of juice issuing from the meat when pressed
rare	red and bloody
underdone	reddish pink
just done	pink
well done	clear

Food items that are difficult to handle because they may easily break up may be placed in between a well-greased, centre-hinged, *double wire grid* with a handle, making it both easy and swift to cook food such as whole sole, whole plaice.

Tomatoes, mushrooms, bacon, sausages and kidneys may be grilled under a salamander on a flat tray. A rim is required on the tray to prevent spillage of fat and articles of food sliding from the tray.

The salamander can also be used for browning, gratinating and glazing certain dishes such as duchess potato border, macaroni au gratin, fillets of sole bonne femme, and for toasting bread.

Between heat

This is grilling between electrically heated grill bars or plates and is applied to small cuts of meat.

Barbecuing (see page 250)

This is grilling on preheated, greased bars over a fierce heat (gas, charcoal or wood). When using solid fuel, the flames and smoke must be allowed to die down before placing food on the bars, otherwise the food will be tainted and spoiled. Certain foods, such as brochettes or chicken, may be marinaded before cooking. Other foods (e.g. pork spare ribs) are brushed liberally with a barbecue sauce on both sides during cooking (page 284).

Effects of grilling

Because of the speed of cooking there is maximum retention of nutrients and flavour. Grilling is only suitable for certain cuts of best quality meat; inferior meat would be tough and inedible. The effect of fierce heat on the surface of the meat rapidly coagulates and seals the surface protein, thus helping to retain the meat juices. Grilled meats lose less of their juices than meat cooked by any other method provided they are not pierced with a fork while cooking.

Advantages

- Speed of grilling enables food to be quickly cooked to order.
- Charring foods gives a distinctive appearance and improves flavour.
- Control of cooking is aided because food is visible whilst being grilled.
- Variety is given to menu and diet.
- Grills may be situated in view of the customer.

General rules for efficient grilling

- Smaller, thinner items require cooking quickly.
- Seal and colour food on the hot part of the grill then move to a cooler part to complete cooking.
- Slow cooking results in the food drying out.
- Basting of food and oiling of bars prevents dryness.
- Tongs are used for turning and lifting cutlets and steaks. Palette knives and slices are used for turning and lifting tomatoes, mushrooms, whole or cut fish, from trays.

Safety

- Take extra care when moving hot salamander and grill bars.

Fig 3.4 Selection of modern pans

- Trays used for grilling must have raised edges and not be overloaded.
- Never place trays on the top surface of the heated salamander.
- Take care when removing foods from grills and salamanders.

Shallow frying

Definition

Shallow frying is the cooking of food in a small quantity of preheated fat or oil in a shallow pan or on a flat surface (griddle plate).

Purpose

The purpose of shallow frying is:

- to give variety to the menu and the diet by making food palatable, digestible and safe to eat;
- to brown food, giving it a different colour and an interesting and attractive flavour.

Methods

There are four methods of frying using a shallow amount of fat or oil: shallow fry; sauté; griddle; stir fry.

Clarified butter

Butter is melted and the fat is then carefully strained off leaving behind the liquid. Clarified butter has a higher burning point and will not burn so easily as unclarified butter. This makes it more suitable for shallow frying and therefore clarified butter should always be used if the shallow fried food is required to be cooked in butter.

Shallow fry

Food is cooked in a small amount of fat or oil in a frying pan or sauté pan. The presentation side of the food should be fried first, as this side will have the better appearance because the fat is clean, then turned so that both sides are cooked and coloured. This applies to small cuts of fish, meat and poultry, also small whole fish (up to 400 g/1 lb). Eggs, pancakes and certain vegetables are cooked by this method. The term *meunière* refers to shallow-fried fish, which is passed through seasoned flour, shallow fried and finished with lemon juice, nut-brown butter and chopped parsley.

Sauté

Tender cuts of meat and poultry are cooked in a sauté or frying pan. After the food is cooked on both sides it is removed from the pan, the fat is discarded and the pan deglazed with stock or wine. This then forms an important part of the finished sauce.

Sauté is also used when cooking, for example, potatoes, onions or kidneys, when they are cut into slices or pieces and tossed (*sauter* means to jump or toss) in hot shallow fat or oil in a frying pan until golden brown and cooked.

Griddle

Foods can be cooked on a griddle (a solid metal plate): hamburgers, sausages or sliced onions are placed on a lightly oiled preheated griddle and turned frequently during cooking. Pancakes may be cooked this way but are turned only once.

Stir fry

Vegetables, strips of fish, meat and poultry can be fast fried in a wok or frying pan in a little fat or oil.

Effects of shallow frying

The high temperature used in shallow frying produces almost instant coagulation of the surface protein of the food and prevents the escape of the natural juices. Some of the frying medium will be absorbed by the food being fried, which will change the nutritional content.

Advantages

Shallow frying is a quick method of cooking prime cuts of meat and poultry as suitable fats or oils can be raised to a high temperature without burning. As the food is in direct contact with the fat, it cooks rapidly.

Time and temperature control

This is particularly important as all shallow-fried foods should have an appetising golden brown colour on both sides. This can only be achieved by careful control of the temperature, which should be initially hot; the heat is then reduced and the food turned when required.

General rules

- When shallow frying continuously over a busy period, prepare and cook in a systematic way.
- Pans should be cleaned after every use.

Safety

- Select the correct type and size of pan: not too small, as food, such as fish, will not brown evenly and may break up; not too large, as areas not covered by food will burn and spoil the flavour of the food being cooked.
- Always keep sleeves rolled down as splashing fat may burn the forearm.
- Avoid being splashed by hot fat when placing food in the pan – add it carefully away from you.
- Use a thick, clean, dry cloth when handling pans.
- Move pans carefully in case they jar and tip fat onto the stove.

Deep frying

Definition

This is the cooking of food in preheated deep oil or clarified fat.

Purpose

The purpose of deep frying is:

- to cook appetising foods of various kinds thus giving variety to the diet and the menu;
- to produce food with an appetising golden brown colour, crisp, palatable and safe to eat.

Methods

Conventional deep-fried foods, with the exception of potatoes, are coated with either milk and flour, egg and crumbs, batter or pastry to:

- protect the surface of the food from intense heat;
- prevent the escape of moisture and nutrients;
- modify the rapid penetration of the intense heat.

The food is carefully placed into deep preheated oil or fat, fried until cooked and golden brown, well drained and served.

Partial deep-frying is known as *blanching* and may be applied to chipped potatoes. The purpose is to partly cook in advance of service and to complete the cooking to order. With certain types of potato this gives an eating quality of a floury inside and crisp exterior to the chips.

Effects of deep frying

Deep frying of items coated with milk or egg seals the surface by coagulation of the protein, with the minimum absorption of fat. However, the interior may be raw, as in apple fritters, and will require to be cooked. A cooked interior, as in croquette potatoes, needs only to be heated through. The coating (batter, etc.) does need to be cooked. With uncoated items, such as chipped potatoes, the food absorbs a large amount of fat thus affecting the texture and nutritional content.

The effect of deep frying on the structure of the item being cooked will vary according to the nature of the food.

Advantages

- Blanching, or partial cooking, enables certain foods to be held for cooking later, which helps during busy service and saves time.
- Coating foods enables a wide variety to be cooked by this method.
- Foods can be cooked quickly and easily handled for service.
- Coated foods are quickly sealed, thus preventing the enclosed food becoming greasy.

Temperature and time control

With deep fat frying it is essential for fat temperatures to be maintained at the correct degree. When quantities of food are being continuously fried, after the removal of one batch the temperature of the fat must be allowed to recover before the next batch is cooked. If this is not done the food will be pale and insipid in appearance and soggy to eat.

Timing is important: if thicker pieces of food are being cooked, the temperature must be lowered to allow for sufficient cooking time otherwise the food will be overcoloured and undercooked. The reverse is also true: the smaller the pieces of food the hotter the frying temperature and the shorter the cooking time.

General rules

- Systematic preparation and cooking are essential.
- Never overfill fryers with fat or oil or food to be cooked.
- When using free-standing fryers without a thermometer never allow smoke to rise from the fat; this will give a disagreeable taste and smell to food being fried.

OIL TEMPERATURES

Type	Approximate flash-point (°C)	Smoke point (°C)	Recommended frying temp (°C)
finest quality vegetable oils	324	220	180
finest vegetable fat	321	220	180
high-class vegetable oil	324	204	180
pure vegetable fat	318	215	180
pure vegetable oil	330	220	170–182
finest quality maize oil	224	215	180
finest fat	321	202	180
finest quality dripping	300	165	170–180
finest natural olive oil	270–273	148–165	175

- The normal frying temperature is between 175°C and 195°C (350–380°F), this is indicated by a slight heat haze rising from the fat.
- Do not attempt to fry too much food at one time.
- Allow fat to recover its heat before adding the next batch of food.
- Ensure a correct oil/fat ratio to food. If too much food is cooked in too little fat, even if the initial temperature of the fat is correct, the effect of a large amount of food will reduce the temperature drastically and spoil the food.
- Reduce frying temperatures during slack periods to conserve fuel.
- Restrict holding time to a minimum – fried foods soon lose their crispness.
- Oil and fat should be strained after use, otherwise remaining food particles will burn when the fat is next heated thus spoiling the appearance and flavour of the food.
- Always cover oil or fat when not in use to prevent oxidation.

Safety

- Always only half-fill fryers with fat or oil.
- Never overload fryers with food.
- Dry foods such as potatoes thoroughly before frying, otherwise they will splutter and cause burns.
- Always place food carefully in the fryer *away* from you. If it is added towards you, hot fat could splash and burn.
- Always have a frying basket and spider to hand in case food is required to be lifted out of the fryer quickly. A combination of the fat being too hot, fat almost ready for discarding and the food being damp can result in the fat boiling over. If it is a free-standing friture on the stove then there is a risk of fire.

- Move free-standing fryers with great care so as not to jar them and spill fat on the stove.
- Ensure that correct fire prevention equipment is to hand and that you are familiar with the fire drill procedure.
- Keep sleeves rolled down at all times when handling fryers.
- Use clean, dry, thick, sound cloths when handling fritures.
- Allow fat to cool before straining.

Paper bag cooking

Known as *en papillotte*, this is a method of cookery in which food is tightly sealed in oiled greaseproof paper or foil so that no steam escapes during cooking and maximum natural flavour and nutritive value is retained.

Thick items of food, such as veal chops or red mullet, may be partly and quickly precooked, usually by grilling or shallow frying, then finely cut vegetables, herbs and spices can be added. The bags are tightly sealed, placed on a lightly greased tray and cooked in a hot oven. When cooked, the food is served in the bag and opened by or in front of the customer.

See Vacuum Cooking in *The Theory of Catering 10th Edition*.

Microwave cooking
Definition

This is a method of cooking and reheating food using electromagnetic waves in a microwave oven powered by electricity. The microwaves are similar to those that carry television signals from the transmitter to the receiver but are at a higher frequency. The microwaves activate the water molecules or particles of food and agitate them, causing heat by friction, which cooks or reheats the food.

Purpose

- Raw, preprepared or precooked foods are cooked quickly and made palatable and digestible.
- Foods are safer to eat, particularly reheated foods, because the total food is heated at the same time.

Application

Microwave cooking can be used for cooking raw food, reheating cooked food and defrosting frozen foods.

Advantages

- A saving of between 50 and 70 per cent over conventional cooking times on certain foods.
- A quick way to cook and reheat foods.
- A fast method of defrosting foods.
- Economical on:
  electricity – less energy required;
  labour – less washing up as foods can be cooked in serving dishes.
- Hot meals can be available 24 hours a day and completely operated on a self-service basis, thereby increasing consumer satisfaction and reducing costs.
- Food is cooked in its own juices so flavour and goodness are retained.
- Minimises food shrinkage and drying-out.
- When used with conventional cooking methods, production can be more flexible.

Disadvantages

- Not suitable for all foods.
- Limited oven space restricts use to small quantities.
- Many microwave ovens do not brown food, although browning elements are available within certain models.
- Not all containers are suitable for use.
- Microwaves can only penetrate 5cm (1½ inches) into food (from all sides).

Special points for attention

- Correct selection of cooking and time controls according to the manufacturer's instructions is essential.
- Certain foods must be removed when underdone to finish cooking, so standing time is important; during this time for example fish turns from opaque to flaky, scrambled eggs turn creamy. Tender, crisp vegetables do not need to stand.
- Baked potatoes and whole unpeeled apples must have the skin pierced in order to release pressure and prevent them bursting.
- Eggs must not be cooked in their shells or they will burst.
- Cover foods when possible to reduce condensation and spluttering.

Factors that affect efficient cooking

- Only use suitable containers: glass, china, plastic. Only use metal or foil if the particular cooker has been developed to take metal without causing damage. For the best results use straight-sided, round, shallow containers.
- Even-shaped items cook uniformly; arrange uneven-shaped items with the thickest part to the outside of the dish.
- Keep food as level as possible, do not pile into mounds.
- Allow sufficient space to stir or mix.
- Turn items, such as corn on the cob, during

cooking because dense items take longer to cook than porous items.

- Foods with a high water content cook faster than those that are drier.

- Most foods should be covered when cooked in a microwave oven. Microwave clingfilm is available to cover food.

Safety

- Should the door seal be damaged, do not use the oven. This should be reported to the employer immediately.

- Do not operate the oven when it is empty.

- Remember to pierce foods and cover foods that are likely to burst.

- Regular inspection is essential and manufacturers' instructions must be followed.

Supplementary information

When preparing food for microwave heating:

1 Certain foods and container materials absorb energy at a faster rate than others and, as a result, are heated more quickly.

2 The lower the starting temperature of the food, the longer it will take to heat.

3 The denser the food, the longer it will take to heat.

4 The thicker or deeper the food, the more awkward it is to heat, i.e. there is an ideal microwave depth of penetration for each food item.

5 The shape of the food is an influence, i.e. in a ring shape, liquids in taller containers instead of low flat ones, composite meals in a compact even mass.

6 The weight or quantity of items influences the overall heating times.

7 A cover is an important aid to faster heating, more moisture retention and less cleaning up afterwards.

Frozen, dense or larger amounts of food benefit by being heated in stages with rest intervals.

Foods that are not suitable for microwave cookery

You cannot deep fry items in a microwave, boil eggs in their shells or make Yorkshire pudding, or bake items such as choux pastry goods or make meringues.

However, although deep frying is not possible because the temperature of the cooking fat can't be controlled, microwaving breadcrumbed fish in a tablespoon of oil will give a similar result. Eggs cooked in their shells would burst because of the build up of pressure inside the shell, but scrambled, poached and fried eggs (in a browning dish) are successful. Yorkshire pudding, eclairs and meringues cannot be cooked by microwave because it is impossible to achieve a crispy crust while maintaining a soft interior. Meringue toppings, for example on a lemon meringue pie, can be microwaved.

Microwaves tend to cook more round the edges of the food than in the centre, so that stirrable foods will cook more evenly. The pattern of the microwaves is sometimes uneven, with the result that some parts will not cook as quickly as others. To test whether an oven has 'hot' or 'cold' spots, quarter-fill approximately nine microwave suitable glasses or bowls with cold water. Spread them out evenly on the oven shelf and switch on the oven at full power. The hottest spot is where the water boils first. The test will enable the chef to place the dishes in the best position in the oven. Small items or dishes should be arranged in a circle and be turned individually during the cooking, even when the oven has a turntable.

Dishes that cannot be stirred should be rotated a quarter turn three times during cooking. Should the edges of the food become cooked while the centre is still raw, this can be remedied by securing small pieces of microwave cling film over the parts that are ready. Another way of ensuring even cooking for unstirrable dishes is to choose even-shaped round or square containers and arrange the food in them to a uniform thickness. It is desirable to keep to a depth of 1½ to 2 inches (4–5 cm). The shape and consistency of foods are very important when deciding on how best to cook them. Items with skin, such as jacket potatoes, tomatoes and peppers, must be pierced or scored with a knife; otherwise the steam created inside will burst the skins and food particles will spatter all over the cavity. Eggs are similarly affected and even the yolks of poached eggs should be lightly pricked. Kidney and liver, although usually cooked after slicing, have a thin covering of membrane. Any 'popping' sounds that are heard will be these membranes splitting, but if the dishes are lightly covered, all will be well. Other 'popping' foods are those containing bones, which act as tunnels storing up the pressure so that the food alongside spits, and poultry with the skin on. Boilable pouches behave the same way. The plastic must be slashed on top and it is prudent to put the bag on a plate as it will become difficult to handle when it is hot and soft.

Always cover food that is to be cooked moist, such as stews and conventionally boiled foods. Cling film is suitable to cover with but it must be applied loosely. The cling film must be removed carefully to avoid a scald from the escaping steam, pulling it towards you. When cooking food in a considerable quantity of liquid that will require stirring, only three quarters cover, so that you are able to stir through the gap – it is not possible to replace cling film covering during cooking.

Under- rather than overcook because overcooking cannot be remedied and reheating must be taken into account. For food safety reasons, a thermometer should be used for high risk foods, especially meat and poultry and when reheating foods.

Foods containing sugar and fat

Sugar heats slowly at first and then suddenly becomes very hot very quickly and will burn in the microwave oven if left for too long. Sugar attracts microwaves and, when dissolved in liquid, it will heat even more rapidly. Fat also attracts microwaves. Therefore good effects can be obtained by brushing food with fat or oil to achieve a crispy result.

Standing time

Cooking may continue after the oven is switched off and the food removed. During this period the heat spreads evenly throughout the food. Dense and large pieces of food, therefore, such as joints of meat and chicken, need to stand for 10–15 minutes after being taken out of the oven.

Stocks, soups and sauces

Green pea soup
John Campbell

French onion soup
John Campbell

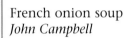

Minestrone soup
John Campbell

Prepare and cook stocks

Stock is a liquid containing some of the soluble nutrients and flavours of food that are extracted by prolonged and gentle simmering (with the exception of fish stock, which requires only 20 minutes); such liquid is the foundation of soups, sauces and gravies. Stocks are the foundation of many important kitchen preparations; therefore the greatest possible care should be taken in their production.

- Unsound meat or bones and decaying vegetables will give stock an unpleasant flavour and cause it to deteriorate quickly.
- Scum should be removed, otherwise it will boil into the stock and spoil the colour and flavour.
- Fat should be skimmed, otherwise the stock will taste greasy.
- Stock should always simmer gently, for if it is allowed to boil quickly, it will evaporate and go cloudy.
- It should not be allowed to go off the boil, otherwise, in hot weather, there is a danger of its going sour.
- Salt should not be added to stock.
- When making chicken stock, if raw bones are not available, then a boiling fowl can be used.
- If stock is to be kept, strain, reboil, cool quickly and place in the refrigerator.

Health, safety and hygiene

Read the sections in Chapter 1 on 'Maintain a safe and secure working environment' and 'Maintain a professional and hygienic appearance', and also 'Maintain clean food production areas, equipment and utensils; and food hygiene'.

- After stock, sauces, gravies and soups have been rapidly cooled they should be stored in a refrigerator at a temperature below 5°C (41°F).
- If they are to be deep-frozen they should be labelled and dated, and stored below −20°C to −18°C.
- When taken from storage they must be boiled for at least 2 minutes before being used.
- They must not be reheated more than once.
- Ideally stocks should be made fresh daily and discarded at the end of the day.
- If stocks are not given the correct care and attention, particularly with regard to the soundness of the ingredients used, they can easily become contaminated and a risk to health.
- Never store a stock, sauce, gravy or soup above eye level as this could lead to an accident by someone spilling the contents over themselves.

Types of stock

White stock made from beef, mutton or chicken can be used in white soups, sauces or stews.

Brown stocks made from beef, mutton, veal, chicken or game can be used in brown soups, gravies, sauces and stews.

1 portion (100 ml) provides:
4 kJ/1 kcal energy
0.0 g fat
(of which 0.0 g saturated)
0.2 g carbohydrate
(of which 0.2 g sugars)
0.0 g protein
0.0 g fibre

1 Stock (white)

The general proportion of ingredients and methods for all stocks (except fish stock) is to use 2 kg (4 lb) of bones for 4½ litres (1 gallon) of stock.

	4½ litres (1 gal)	10 litres (2½ gal)
raw meaty bones	1 kg (2 lb)	2½ kg (5 lb)
water	5 litres	10½ litres
onion, carrot, celery, leek	400 g (1 lb)	1½ kg (2½ lb)
bouquet garni		
peppercorns	8	16

1 Chop the bones into small pieces, remove any fat or marrow.
2 Place the bones in the stockpot, cover with cold water, bring to the boil.
3 Wash off the bones under cold water, clean the pot.
4 Return the bones to the cleaned pot, add the water and re-boil.
5 Skim as and when required, wipe round inside the pot and simmer gently.
6 After two hours, add washed, peeled whole vegetables, bouquet garni and peppercorns.
7 Simmer 6–8 hours. Skim, strain and if to be kept, cool quickly and refrigerate.

Brown stocks

1 Chop the beef bones and brown well on all sides either by:
    (a) placing in a roasting tin in the oven, or
    (b) carefully browning in a little fat in a frying-pan.
2 Drain off any fat and place the bones in stock pot.
3 Brown any sediment that may be in the bottom of the tray, deglaze (swill out) with ½ litre (1 pint) of boiling water, simmer for a few minutes and add to the bones.
4 Add the cold water, bring to the boil and skim. Simmer for 2 hours.
5 Wash, peel and roughly cut the vegetables, fry in a little fat until brown, strain and add to the beef pieces.
6 Add the bouquet garni and peppercorns.
7 Simmer for 6–8 hours. Skim and strain.

Note: For brown stocks a few squashed tomatoes and washed mushroom trimmings can also be added to improve the flavour, as can a calf's foot and/or a knuckle of bacon.

2 Fish stock

Fumet de poisson

	4½ litres	12 litres
margarine or butter or oil	50 g (2 oz)	125 g (5 oz)
onions	200 g (8 oz)	500 g (1¼ lb)
white fish bones (preferably sole, whiting, or turbot)	2 kg (4 lb)	4 kg (10 lb)
lemon, juice of	½	1½
peppercorns	8	16
1 bay leaf		
parsley stalks		
water	4½ litres (1 gal)	12 litres (2½ gal)

1 Melt the margarine or butter in a thick-bottomed pan.

2 Add the sliced onions, the well-washed fish bones and remainder of the ingredients except the water.

3 Cover with greaseproof paper and a lid and sweat (cook gently without colouring) for 5 minutes.

4 Add the water, bring to the boil, skim and simmer for 20 minutes, then strain. Longer cooking time will spoil the flavour.

1 portion (100 ml) provides:
4 kJ/1 kcal energy
0.0 g fat
(of which 0.0 g saturated)
0.2 g carbohydrate
(of which 0.2 g sugars)
0.0 g protein
0.0 g fibre

HEALTHY EATING TIP
Use an oil rich in unsaturates to lightly oil the pan. Drain off any excess after the frying is complete. Skim the fat from the finished dish.

3 White vegetable stock

	4 portions	10 portions
onion	100 g (4 oz)	250 g (10 oz)
carrots	100 g (4 oz)	250 g (10 oz)
celery	100 g (4 oz)	250 g (10 oz)
leek	100 g (4 oz)	250 g (10 oz)
water	1½ litres (3 pt)	3¾ litres (7½ pt)

1 Roughly chop all the vegetables.

2 Place all the ingredients into a saucepan, add the water, bring to the boil.

3 Allow to simmer for approximately 1 hour.

4 Skim if necessary. Strain and use.

1 portion (100 ml) provides:
4 kJ/1 kcal energy
0.0 g fat
(of which 0.0 g saturated)
0.2 g carbohydrate
(of which 0.2 g sugars)
0.0 g protein
0.0 g fibre

4 Brown vegetable stock

1 portion (100 ml) provides:
4 kJ/1 kcal energy
0.0 g fat
(of which 0.0 g saturated)
0.2 g carbohydrate
(of which 0.2 g sugars)
0.0 g protein
0.0 g fibre

	4 portions	10 portions
onions	100 g (4 oz)	250 g (10 oz)
carrots	100 g (4 oz)	250 g (10 oz)
celery	100 g (4 oz)	250 g (10 oz)
leeks	100 g (4 oz)	250 g (10 oz)
sunflower oil	60 ml (⅛ pt)	150 ml (⅓ pt)
tomatoes	50 g (2 oz)	125 g (5 oz)
mushroom trimmings	50 g (2 oz)	125 g (5 oz)
6 peppercorns		
water	1½ litres (3 pts)	3¾ litres (7 pts)
yeast extract	5 g (¼ oz)	10 g (½ oz)

HEALTHY EATING TIP

Lightly oil the pan and drain off any excess after the frying is complete. Skim the fat from the finished dish. The yeast extract contains salt, so very little or no salt should be required when this stock is used for sauces.

1 Roughly chop all the vegetables.
2 Fry the onions, carrots, celery and leeks in the sunflower oil until golden brown.
3 Drain the vegetables, place into a suitable saucepan.
4 Add all the other ingredients except the yeast extract.
5 Cover with the water, bring to the boil.
6 Add the yeast extract, simmer gently for approximately 1 hour.
7 Skim if necessary. Strain and use.

Fungi stock

White or brown fungi stock can be made using the vegetable stock recipes above adding 200–400 g, ½–1 lb white mushrooms, stalks and trimmings (all well washed) for white fungi stock.

For brown fungi stock use the brown vegetable stock recipe adding 200–400 g, ½–1 lb open or field mushrooms, stalks and trimmings (all well washed).

Glazes

Glazes are made by boiling steadily white or brown beef stock or fish stock and allowing them to reduce to a sticky or gelatinous consistency. They are then stored in jars and when cold kept in the refrigerator for up to one week. If they are to be deep frozen then place into small preserving jars that have been sterilised for 1 hour. The glaze can then be kept for several months.

Glazes are used to improve the flavour of a prepared sauce that may taste bland or be lacking in strength. They may also be used as a base for sauces, such as a fish glaze for fish white wine sauce. Butter and/or cream may be added.

Prepare and cook sauces

A sauce is a liquid that has been thickened by either:

- beurre manié (kneaded butter),
- egg yolks,

- roux,
- cornflour, arrowroot or starch,
- cream, and/or butter added to reduced stock,
- reducing cooking liquor or stock.

All sauces should be smooth, glossy in appearance, definite in taste and light in texture; the thickening medium should be used in moderation.

Roux

A roux is a combination of fat and flour, which are cooked together. There are three degrees to which a roux may be cooked, namely:

- white roux,
- blond roux,
- brown roux.

A boiling liquid should never be added to a hot roux as the result may be lumpy and the person making the sauce may be scalded by the steam produced. If allowed to stand for a time over a moderate heat a sauce made with a roux may become thin due to chemical change (dextrinisation) in the flour.

White roux is used for white (béchamel) sauce and soups. Equal quantities of margarine or butter and flour are cooked together without colouring for a few minutes to a sandy texture.

Alternatively, use polyunsaturated vegetable margarine or make a roux with vegetable oil, using equal quantities of oil to flour. This does give a slack roux but enables the liquid to be easily incorporated.

Blond roux is used for veloutés, tomato sauce and soups. Equal quantities of margarine, butter or vegetable oil and flour are cooked for a little longer than a white roux, but without colouring, to a sandy texture.

Brown roux was traditionally used for brown (espagnole) sauce and soups.

Other thickening agents for sauces
Thickening sauces with sauce flour

Sauce flour is a specially milled flour that does not require any addition of fat to prevent it going lumpy. Sauces may be thickened using this flour.

> This flour is useful when making sauces for those on a low fat diet.

Béchamel sauce (reduced fat)

> 1 portion (100 ml) provides:
> 302 kJ/73 kcal energy
> 1.8 g fat
> (of which 1.1 g saturated)
> 10.9 g carbohydrate
> (of which 4.8 g sugars)
> 4.2 g protein
> 0.3 g fibre

milk	500 ml
sauce flour	40 g
seasoning	

1 The milk may be first infused with a studded onion clouté, carrot and a bouquet garni. Allow to cool.
2 Place the milk in a suitable saucepan, gradually whisk in the sauce flour. Bring slowly to the boil until the sauce has thickened.
3 Season, simmer for approximately 5–10 minutes. Use as required.

Cornflour, arrowroot or starch, such as potato starch, is used for thickening gravy and sauces. These are diluted with water, stock or milk, then stirred into the boiling liquid and allowed to reboil for a few minutes and strained. For large-scale cooking and economy, flour may be used.

Beurre manié is used chiefly for fish sauces. Equal quantities of butter or margarine and flour are kneaded to a smooth paste and mixed into a boiling liquid.

Egg yolks are used in mayonnaise, hollandaise and custard sauces. Refer to the appropriate recipe as the yolks are used in a different manner for each sauce.

Vegetables or fruit purées are known as a cullis (*coulis*). No other thickening agent is used.

Blood is traditionally used in recipes such as jugged hare, but not normally today.

Cooking liquor from certain dishes and/or stock can be reduced to give a light sauce.

Basic sauce recipes

	4 portions	**10 portions**
margarine, oil or butter	100 g (4 oz)	400 g (1 lb)
flour	100 g (4 oz)	400 g (1 lb)
milk	1 litre (1 qt)	4½ litres (1 gal)
1 studded onion		

Try using a 'soft' margarine and semi-skimmed milk. Some cornflour milk could be used to extend the sauce and reduce the fat content.

5 White sauce

Béchamel

This is a basic white sauce made from milk and a white roux.

Using whole milk/hard margarine, this recipe provides for 1 litre:
7228 kJ/1721 kcal
120.3 g fat
(of which 59.5 g saturated)
124.8 g carbohydrate
(of which 48.6 g sugars)
42.5 g protein
3.6 g fibre

Using skimmed milk/hard margarine, this recipe provides:
5884 kJ/1401 kcal
83.3 g fat
(of which 36.1 g saturated)
127.8 g carbohydrate
(of which 51.6 g sugars)
43.5 g protein
3.6 g fibre

1 Melt the margarine or butter in a thick-bottomed pan.
2 Add the flour and mix in.
3 Cook for a few minutes over a gentle heat without colouring.
4 Remove from the heat to cool the roux.
5 Gradually add the warmed milk and stir until smooth.
6 Add the onion studded with a clove.
7 Allow to simmer for 30 minutes.
8 Remove the onion, pass the sauce through a conical strainer.
9 Cover with a film of butter or margarine to prevent a skin forming.

Other sauces made from basic white sauce

(Quantities for ½ litre (1 pint): 8–12 portions)

Sauce	Served with	Additions per ½ litre (1 pt)
6 anchovy	poached or fried or boiled fish	1 tbsp anchovy essence
7 egg	poached fish or boiled fish	2 hard-boiled eggs, diced
8 cheese or Mornay sauce	fish or vegetables	50 g (2 oz) grated cheese, 1 egg yolk. Mix well in boiling sauce, remove from heat. Strain if necessary but do not allow to reboil
9 onion	roast lamb or mutton	100 g (4 oz) chopped or diced onions cooked without colour either by boiling or sweating in butter
10 soubise	roast lamb or mutton	As for onion sauce but passed through a strainer
11 parsley	poached or boiled fish and vegetables	1 tbsp chopped parsley
12 cream	poached fish and boiled vegetables	Add cream, milk, natural yoghurt or fromage frais to give the consistency of double cream
13 mustard	grilled herrings	Add diluted English or continental mustard to make a fairly hot sauce.

HEALTHY EATING TIP: Try using yoghurt or fromage frais. Add a little cornflour prior to heating to stabilise the sauce.

14 Velouté (chicken, veal, fish, mutton)

This is a basic white sauce made from white stock and a blond roux.

	4 portions	10 portions
margarine, butter or oil	100 g (4 oz)	400 g (1 lb)
flour	100 g (4 oz)	400 g (1 lb)
stock (chicken, veal, fish, mutton) as required	1 litre (1 qt)	4½ litres (1 gal)

1 Melt the fat or oil in a thick-bottomed pan.
2 Add the flour and mix in.
3 Cook out to a sandy texture over gentle heat without colouring it.
4 Allow the roux to cool.
5 Gradually add the boiling stock.
6 Stir until smooth and boiling.

Using hard margarine, this recipe provides for 1 litre:
4594 kJ/1094 kcal
82.6 g fat
(of which 35.4 g saturated)
79.0 g carbohydrate
(of which 1.6 g sugars)
13.3 g protein
3.6 g fibre

Using sunflower oil, this recipe provides for 1 litre:
5304 kJ/1263 kcal
101.5 g fat
(of which 13.3 g saturated)
78.9 g carbohydrate
(of which 1.5 g sugars)
13.2 g protein
3.6 g fibre

continued over ▶

▶ *Velouté continued*

Make sure all the fat has been skimmed from the stock before adding it to the roux.

7   Allow to simmer for approximately 1 hour.

8   Pass it through a fine conical strainer.

Note: A velouté sauce for chicken, veal or fish dishes is usually finished with cream and, in some cases, also egg yolks. The finished sauce should be of a light consistency barely coating the back of a spoon.

Sauce suprême is a chicken velouté flavoured with 25 g (1 oz) of mushroom trimmings finished with a liaison of 1 egg yolk and 60 ml (⅛ pint) of cream and 2–3 drops of lemon juice.

Sauces made from veloutés

(Quantities for ½ litre (1 pint): 8–12 portions)

Sauce	Served with	Additions per ½ litre (1 pt)
15 caper	boiled leg of mutton	2 tbsp capers
16 aurore	poached or boiled chicken, poached eggs, chaud-froid sauce	25 g (1 oz) mushroom trimmings, 60 ml (⅛ pt) cream, 1 egg yolk, 2–3 drops lemon juice, 1 tbsp tomato purée
17 mushroom	poached or boiled chicken, sweetbreads	as (16) but substitute for tomato purée, 100 g (4 oz) well-washed, sliced, sweated white button mushrooms after straining velouté, simmer for 10 minutes and add yolk and cream
18 ivory	poached or boiled chicken	as (17) but add a little meat glaze for an ivory colour

The recipe provides:
4805 kJ/1144 kcal
90.4 g fat
(of which 39.0 g saturated)
77.8 g carbohydrate
(of which 1.6 g sugars)
9.5 g protein
3.6 g fibre

19   Fish velouté

	4 portions	10 portions
margarine or butter	100 g (4 oz)	250 g (10 oz)
flour	100 g (4 oz)	250 g (10 oz)
fish stock	1 litre (1 qt)	2½ litres (4½ pt)

1   Prepare a blond roux using the margarine or butter and flour.

2   Gradually add the stock, stirring continuously until boiling point is reached.

3   Simmer for approximately 1 hour.

4   Pass through a fine conical strainer.

Note: This will give a thick sauce that can be thinned down with the cooking liquor from the fish for which the sauce is intended.

Make sure all the fat has been skimmed from the stock before adding it to the roux.

Espagnole

This is a traditional brown sauce made from brown roux and brown stock, simmered for several hours and skimmed frequently to produce a refined sauce. Because of the lengthy time-consuming process and a move away from heavy flour-based sauces, in many kitchens a reduced veal stock (recipe 20) is used as a base for most brown sauces.

Demi-glace

Demi-glace is used as the base for a number of derivative sauces. Current practice in most kitchens is to use either stock reduced sauce (recipe 20), jus-lié or a commercially produced powder or granule base product.

20 **Reduced veal stock for sauce**

Reduced to half, 1 portion (100 ml) provides:
8 kJ/2 kcal energy
0.0 g fat
(of which 0.0 g saturated)
0.5 g carbohydrate
(of which 0.4 g sugars)

	4½ litres (1 gal)
veal bones	4 kg (8 lb)
2 calves' feet, split lengthways	
water	4 litres (1 gal)
carrots	400 g (1 lb)
onions	200 g (½ lb)
celery	100 g (¼ lb)
tomatoes	1 kg (2 lb)
mushrooms	200 g (½ lb)
1 large bouquet garni	
4 unpeeled cloves of garlic (optional)	

1 Brown the chopped bones and calves' feet (split lengthways) on a roasting tray in the oven.

2 Place the browned bones in a stock pot, cover with cold water and bring to simmering point.

3 Roughly chop the carrots, onions and celery. Using the same roasting tray and the fat from the bones, brown them off.

4 Drain off the fat, add vegetables to the stock and deglaze the tray.

5 Add the quartered tomatoes and chopped mushrooms, simmer gently for 4–5 hours. Skim frequently.

6 Strain the stock into a clean pan and reduce until a light consistency is achieved.

HEALTHY EATING TIP

Drain off all the fat before deglazing the tray. Skim all fat from the stock as it simmers and the fat from the finished product.

Sauces made from demi-glace or stock-reduced base

21 **Red wine sauce**

Sauce Bordelaise

Reduced to half, using butter 1 portion provides:
95 kJ/23 kcal energy
0.1 g fat
(of which 0.0 g saturated)
5.1 g carbohydrate
(of which 3.8 g sugars)
0.6 g protein
0.7 g fibre

	4 portions	10 portions
chopped shallots	50 g (2 oz)	125 g (5 oz)
red wine	125 ml (¼ pt)	300 ml (⅝ pt)
pinch mignonette pepper		
sprig of thyme		
bay leaf		
demi-glace jus-lié or stock-reduced base	250 ml (½ pt)	625 ml (1¼ pt)

continued over ▶

▶ *Red wine sauce continued*

1 Reduce the shallots, red wine, pepper, thyme and bay leaf.

2 Place the reduction in a small sauteuse.

3 Allow to boil until reduced to a quarter.

4 Add the demi-glace. Simmer for 20–30 minutes.

5 Correct the seasoning. Pass through a fine strainer.

Note: This sauce traditionally included poached beef marrow either:

- in dice, poached and added to the sauce;
- cut in slices, poached and placed on meat before being sauced over.

May be served with fried steaks.

22 Chasseur sauce

Sauce chasseur

> Reduced to half, using butter, 1 portion provides:
> 227 kJ/55 kcal
> 5.3 g fat
> (of which 2.5 g saturated)
> 1.4 g carbohydrate
> (of which 1.2 g sugars)
> 0.5 g protein
> 0.5 g fibre

	4 portions	10 portions
butter, margarine or oil	25 g (1 oz)	60 g (2½ oz)
chopped shallots	10 g (½ oz)	25 g (1 oz)
1 clove chopped garlic (optional)		
sliced button mushrooms	50 g (2 oz)	125 g (5 oz)
white wine (dry)	60 ml (⅛ pt)	150 ml (⅓ pt)
tomatoes, skinned, de-seeded, diced	100 g (4 oz)	250 g (10 oz)
demi-glace jus-lié or reduced stock	250 ml (½ pt)	625 ml (1¼ pt)
chopped parsley and tarragon		

HEALTHY EATING TIP

Use an unsaturated oil (sunflower or olive). Lightly oil the pan and drain off any excess after the frying is complete. Skim the fat from the finished dish. Season with minimum amounts of salt.

1 Melt the butter in a small sauteuse.

2 Add the shallots and cook gently for 2–3 minutes without colour.

3 Add the garlic and the mushrooms, cover, and gently cook for 2–3 minutes.

4 Strain off the fat.

5 Add the wine and reduce by half. Add the tomatoes.

6 Add the demi-glace; simmer for 5–10 minutes.

7 Correct the seasoning and add the tarragon and parsley.

Note: May be served with fried steaks, chops, chicken, etc.

23 Pepper sauce

Sauce poivrade

> Reduced to half, using margarine, 1 portion provides:
> 247 kJ/60 kcal energy
> 5.3 g fat
> (of which 2.5 g saturated)
> 2.6 g carbohydrate
> (of which 2.0 g sugars)
> 0.5 g protein
> 0.6 g fibre

	4 portions	10 portions
margarine, butter or oil	25 g (1 oz)	60 g (2½ oz)
onion	50 g (2 oz)	125 g (5 oz)
carrot	50 g (2 oz)	125 g (5 oz)
celery	50 g (2 oz)	125 g (5 oz)
1 bay leaf		
sprig of thyme		
2 tbsp white wine		
2 tbsp vinegar		
mignonette pepper	5 g (¼ oz)	12 g (⅝ oz)
demi-glace jus-lié or reduced stock	250 ml (½ pt)	625 ml (1¼ pt)

Use an unsaturated oil (sunflower or olive). Lightly oil the pan and drain off any excess after the frying is complete.
Skim the fat from the finished dish.
Season with minimum amounts of salt.

1 Melt the fat or oil in a small sauteuse.
2 Add the vegetables and herbs (mirepoix) and allow to brown.
3 Pour off the fat.
4 Add the wine, vinegar and pepper.
5 Reduce by half. Add the demi-glace.
6 Simmer for 20–30 minutes. Correct the seasoning.
7 Pass through a fine conical strainer.

Note: Usually served with joints or cuts of venison.

24 Italian sauce

Sauce italienne

Reduced to half, using margarine, 1 portion provides:
258 kJ/63 kcal energy
5.6 g fat
(of which 2.6 g saturated)
1.3 g carbohydrate
(of which 1.2 g sugars)
1.8 g protein
0.4 g fibre

	4 portions	10 portions
margarine, oil or butter	25 g (1 oz)	60 g (2½ oz)
shallots, chopped	10 g (½ oz)	25 g (1 oz)
mushrooms, chopped	50 g (2 oz)	125 g (5 oz)
demi-glace jus-lié or reduced stock	250 ml (½ pt)	625 ml (1¼ pt)
chopped lean ham	25 g (1 oz)	60 g (2½ oz)
tomatoes, skinned, de-seeded, diced	100 g (4 oz)	250 g (10 oz)
chopped parsley, chervil and tarragon		

Use an unsaturated oil (sunflower or olive). Lightly oil the pan and drain off any excess after the frying is complete. Trim as much fat as possible from the ham. The ham is also salty, so do not add more salt. Flavour will come from the herbs. Skim all fat from the finished sauce.

continued over ▶

▶ *Italian sauce continued*

1   Melt the fat or oil in a small sauteuse.

2   To make a duxelle, add the shallots and gently cook for 2–3 minutes, then the mushrooms and gently cook for a further 2–3 minutes.

3   Add the demi-glace, ham and tomatoes.

4   Simmer for 5–10 minutes. Correct the seasoning. Add the chopped herbs.

Note: Usually served with fried cuts of veal, lamb or chicken.

25 Brown onion sauce

Sauce lyonnaise

Reduced to half, using margarine, 1 portion provides:
240 kJ/58 kcal energy
5.2 g fat
(of which 2.5 g saturated)
2.3 g carbohydrate
(of which 1.7 g sugars)
0.3 g protein
0.4 g fibre

	4 portions	10 portions
margarine, oil or butter	25 g (1 oz)	60 g (2½ oz)
sliced onions	100 g (4 oz)	250 g (10 oz)
2 tbsp vinegar		
demi-glace jus-lié or reduced stock	250ml (½ pt)	625 ml (1¼ pt)

HEALTHY EATING TIP

Use an unsaturated oil (sunflower or olive). Lightly oil the pan and drain off any excess afer the frying is complete.
Skim the fat from the finished dish.
Season with minimum amounts of salt.

1   Melt the fat or oil in a sauteuse.

2   Add the onions, cover with a lid.

3   Cook gently until tender.

4   Remove the lid and colour lightly.

5   Add the vinegar and completely reduce.

6   Add the demi-glace, simmer for 5–10 minutes.

7   Skim and correct the seasoning.

Note: May be served with burgers, fried liver or sausages.

26 Madeira sauce

Sauce Madère

Reduced to half, 1 portion provides:
43 kJ/10 kcal energy
0.1 g fat
(of which 0.0 g saturated)
1.6 g carbohydrate
(of which 1.2 g sugars)
0.3 g protein
0.3 g fibre

	4 portions	10 portions
demi-glace jus-lié or reduced stock	250 ml (¼ pt)	625 ml (1¼ pt)
Madeira wine	2 tbsp	5 tbsp
butter	25 g (1 oz)	60 g (2½ oz)

1   Boil the demi-glace in a small sauteuse.

2   Add the Madeira; reboil. Correct the seasoning.

3   Pass through a fine conical strainer. Gradually mix in the butter.

Note: May be served with braised ox tongue or ham. Dry sherry or port wine may be substituted for Madeira and the sauce re-named accordingly.

27 Piquant sauce

Sauce piquante

Using gherkins, reduced to half, 1 portion provides:
197 kJ/48 kcal energy
5.1 g fat
(of which 3.3 g saturated)
0.3 g carbohydrate
(of which 0.3 g sugars)
0.0 g protein
0.0 g fibre

	4 portions	10 portions
vinegar	60 ml (⅛ pt)	150 ml (⅓ pt)
shallots, chopped	50 g (2 oz)	125 g (5 oz)
demi-glace jus-lié or reduced stock	250 ml (½ pt)	625 ml (1¼ pt)
gherkins, chopped	25 g (1 oz)	60 g (2½ oz)
capers, chopped	10 g (½ oz)	25 g (1 oz)
chopped chervil, tarragon and parsley	½ tbsp	1¼ tbsp

1 Place vinegar and shallots in a small sauteuse and reduce by half.

2 Add demi-glace; simmer for 15–20 minutes.

3 Add the rest of the ingredients. Skim and correct the seasoning.

Note: May be served with made-up dishes, sausages and grilled meats.

28 Robert sauce

Sauce Robert

Reduced to half, using margarine, 1 portion provides:
229 kJ/56 kcal energy
2.6 g fat
(of which 1.0 g saturated)
7.2 g carbohydrate
(of which 6.8 g sugars)
0.6 g protein
0.2 g fibre

	4 portions	10 portions
margarine, oil or butter	10 g (½ oz)	25 g (1 oz)
onions, finely chopped	50 g (2 oz)	125 g (5 oz)
vinegar	60 ml (⅛ pt)	150 ml (⅓ pt)
demi-glace jus-lié or reduced stock	250 ml (½ pt)	625 ml (1¼ pt)
1 level tbsp English or continental mustard		
level tbsp caster sugar		

HEALTHY EATING TIP

Use an unsaturated oil (sunflower or olive). Lightly oil the pan and drain off any excess after the frying is complete. Skim the fat from the finished dish. Season with minimum amounts of salt.

1 Melt the fat or oil in a small sauteuse. Add the onion.

2 Cook gently without colour. Add the vinegar and reduce completely.

3 Add the demi-glace; simmer for 5–10 minutes.

continued over ▶

▶ *Robert sauce continued*

4   Remove from the heat and add the mustard diluted with a little water and the sugar; do not boil. Skim and correct the seasoning.

Note: May be served with fried sausages and burgers or grilled pork chops.

29 Charcutière sauce

Sauce charcutière

Proceed as for Robert sauce and finally add 25 g (1 oz) sliced or julienne of gherkins.

Miscellaneous sauces

30 Curry sauce

Sauce kari

Use a small amount of an unsaturated oil (e.g. sunflower or olive) to fry the onion and garlic. Add a minimum amount of salt, taste first, lots of flavour from the spices, ginger etc.

Using sunflower oil, this recipe provides for 4 portions:
1092 kJ/260 kcal
14.1 g fat
(of which 4.1 g saturated)
30.3 g carbohydrate
(of which 19.9 g sugars)
4.9 g protein
4.1 g fibre

1   Gently cook the onion and garlic in the fat in a small sauteuse without colouring.

2   Mix in the flour and curry powder. Cook gently to a sandy mixture.

3   Mix in the tomato purée, cool.

4   Gradually add the boiling stock and mix to a smooth sauce.

5   Add the remainder of the ingredients; season with salt, and simmer for 30 minutes. Skim and correct the seasoning.

Note: This sauce has a wide range of uses with prawns, shrimps, vegetables, eggs, etc.

For poached or soft-boiled eggs it may be strained and for all purposes it may be finished with 2–3 tbsp cream or natural yoghurt.

For a traditional recipe the curry powder would be replaced by either curry paste, or a mixture of freshly ground spices such as turmeric, cumin, allspice, fresh ginger, chilli and clove.

	4 portions	10 portions
onion, chopped	50 g (2 oz)	125 g (5 oz)
clove of garlic	¼	½
oil, butter or margarine	10 g (½ oz)	25 g (1¼ oz)
flour	10 g (½ oz)	25 g (1¼ oz)
curry powder	5 g (¼ oz)	12 g (½ oz)
tomato purée	5 g (¼ oz)	12 g (½ oz)
stock	375 ml (¾ pt)	1 litre (2 pt)
apple, chopped	25 g (1 oz)	60 g (2½ oz)
chutney, chopped	1 tbsp	2 tbsp
desiccated coconut	5 g (¼ oz)	12 g (½ oz)
sultanas	10 g (½ oz)	25 g (1 oz)
ginger root, *or*	10 g (½ oz)	25 g (1 oz)
ground ginger	5 g (¼ oz)	12 g (½ oz)
salt		

31 Roast gravy

Jus rôti

	4 portions	10 portions
raw veal bones or beef and veal trimmings	200 g (8 oz)	500 g (1¼ lb)
stock or water	500 ml (1 pt)	1¼ litres (2½ pt)
onion	50 g (2 oz)	125 g (5 oz)
celery	25 g (1 oz)	60 g (2½ oz)
carrot	50 g (2 oz)	125 g (5 oz)

Using sunflower oil, this recipe provides for 4 portions:
504 kJ/120 kcal
10.0 g fat
(of which 1.3 g saturated)
1.8 g carbohydrate
(of which 0.0 g sugars)
5.6 g protein
0.0 g fibre

HEALTHY EATING TIP

Use an unsaturated oil (sunflower or olive). Lightly oil the pan and drain off any excess after the frying is complete. Season with minimum amounts of salt.

For preference use beef bones for roast beef gravy and the appropriate bones for lamb, veal, mutton and pork.

1 Chop the bones and brown in the oven or brown in a little oil on top of the stove in a frying-pan. Drain off all the fat.
2 Place the bones in saucepan with the stock or water.
3 Bring to the boil, skim and allow to simmer.
4 Add the lightly browned vegetables, which may be fried in a little fat in a frying-pan, or added to the bones when partly browned.
5 Simmer for 1½–2 hours.
6 Remove the joint from the roasting tin when cooked.
7 Return the tray to a low heat to allow the sediment to settle.
8 Carefully strain off the fat, leaving the sediment in the tin.
9 Return the joint to the stove and brown carefully; deglaze with the brown stock.
10 Allow to simmer for a few minutes.
11 Correct the colour and seasoning. Strain and skim off all fat.

32 Thickened gravy

Jus-lié

Is made

a) by simmering roast gravy with the addition of a little tomato purée, a few mushroom trimmings and a pinch of thyme for 10–15 minutes. Then lightly thicken by stirring in to the simmering gravy some arrowroot diluted in cold water. Re-boil, simmer for 5–10 minutes and pass through a strainer.

b) by using reduced veal stock (recipe 20)

Variations: add a little rosemary, thyme or lavender.

33 Bread sauce

Using semi-skimmed milk, this recipe provides for 1 portion:
318 kJ/77 kcal
3.8 g fat
(of which 2.3 g saturated)
7.6 g carbohydrate
(of which 4.6 g sugars)
3.8 g protein
0.1 g fibre

	4 portions	**10 portions**
milk	375 ml (¾ pt)	1 litre (2 pt)
small onion studded with a clove	1	2
fresh white breadcrumbs	25 g (1 oz)	60 g (2½ oz)
salt, cayenne		
butter	10 g (½ oz)	25 g (1 oz)

HEALTHY EATING TIP

Use semi-skimmed milk and a minimum amount of salt.

1 Infuse the simmering milk with the studded onion for 15 minutes.

2 Remove the onion, mix in the crumbs. Simmer for 2–3 minutes.

3 Season, correct the consistency.

4 Add the butter on top of the sauce to prevent a skin forming.

5 Mix well when serving.

Note: Served with roast chicken, turkey and roast game.

34 Tomato sauce

Sauce tomate

Using hard margarine, this recipe provides for 4 portions:
931 kJ/221 kcal
12.5 g fat
(of which 5.1 g saturated)
20.2 g carbohydrate
(of which 11.5 g sugars)
8.5 g protein
2.9 g fibre

Using butter, this recipe provides for 4 portions:
936 kJ/223 kcal
12.6 g fat
(of which 6.7 g saturated)
20.2 g carbohydrate
(of which 11.5 g sugars)
8.5 g protein
2.9 g fibre

	4 portions	**10 portions**
margarine, butter or oil	10 g (½ oz)	25 g (1 oz)
onion	50 g (2 oz)	125 g (5 oz)
carrot (mirepoix)	50 g (2 oz)	125 g (5 oz)
celery	25 g (1 oz)	60 g (2½ oz)
bay leaf	½	1½
sprig of thyme	1	3
bacon scraps (optional)	10 g (½ oz)	25 g (1 oz)
flour	10 g (½ oz)	25 g (1 oz)
tomato purée	50 g (2 oz)	125 g (5 oz)
stock	375 ml (¾ pt)	1 litre (2 pt)
clove garlic	½	1
salt, pepper		

HEALTHY EATING TIP

Use an unsaturated oil (sunflower or olive).
The fat and salt content will be reduced if the bacon is left out.

1   Melt the margarine or butter in a small sauteuse.

2   Add the vegetables and herbs (mirepoix) and bacon scraps and brown slightly.

3   Mix in the flour and cook to a sandy texture. Allow to colour slightly.

4   Mix in the tomato purée, allow to cool.

5   Gradually add the boiling stock, stir to the boil.

6   Add the garlic, season. Simmer for 1 hour.

7   Correct the seasoning and cool.

8   Pass through a fine conical strainer.

Note: This sauce has many uses, served with pasta, eggs, fish, meats, etc.

The amount of tomato purée used may need to vary according to its strength. The sauce can also be made without using flour by adding 400 g (1 lb) of fresh fully ripe tomatoes or an equivalent tin of tomatoes for 4 portions.

35 Pesto

Pesto is a green basil sauce used in some pasta dishes, salads and fish dishes.

	4 portions	**10 portions**
fresh basil leaves	4 small bunches	10 small bunches
garlic clove, chopped	1	2–3
pine nuts (lightly toasted)	1 tbsp	2½ tbsp
Parmesan cheese, grated	2 tbsp	5 tbsp
extra virgin olive oil		
salt		

1   Pound in a mortar (or use a food processor) the basil leaves, garlic, salt, and pine nuts into a smooth paste.

2   Place in a bowl, mix in the cheese and sufficient olive oil to make a sauce-like consistency.

Salsa

Salsa is a Spanish word for a sauce. A wide variety of ingredients can be used and chunky mixtures made to serve with grilled or fried fish, meat and poultry dishes.

36 Tomato and cucumber salsa

> 1 portion provides:
> 202 kJ/49 kcal energy
> 4.3 g fat
> (of which 0.7 g saturated)
> 2.0 g carbohydrate
> (of which 2.0 g sugars)
> 0.6 g protein
> 0.7 g fibre

ripe, chopped tomatoes	400 g (1 lb)
cucumber, chopped	¼
spring onions	6
chopped fresh basil	1 tbsp
chopped fresh parsley	1 tbsp
olive oil	3 tbsp
lemon or lime (juice)	1
salt and pepper	

HEALTHY EATING TIP

Rely on the herbs for flavour with a minimum amount of salt. Extra vegetables can be added and the salsa used liberally with grilled fish or chicken. Rice could be served or the salsa used to fill a tortilla.

Add all ingredients together.

Note: This recipe may be varied by using any chopped salad ingredients and fresh herbs e.g. tarragon, chervil. Do not be afraid to experiment.

37 Salsa verde

Per tablespoon provides:
281 kJ/69 kcal energy
7.5 g fat
(of which 1.1 g saturated)
0.2 g carbohydrate
(of which 0.1 g sugars)
0.1 g protein
0.0 g fibre

mint	1 tbsp	
parsley	3 tbsp	coarsely chopped
capers	3	
garlic clove (optional)	1	
Dijon mustard	1 tsp	
lemon juice	½	
extra virgin olive oil	120 ml (4 fl oz)	
salt		

Combine all ingredients. Serve with grilled fish.

38 Avocado and coriander salsa

1 portion provides:
361 kJ/87 kcal energy
8.6 g fat
(of which 1.4 g saturated)
1.8 g carbohydrate
(of which 1.4 g sugars)
0.8 g protein
1.0 g fibre

ripe avocado peeled and diced	1
ripe peeled tomatoes (de-seeded), diced	3
peeled shallot, cut in rings	1
chopped fresh coriander	1 tsp
toasted pine kernels	10 g (½ oz)
diced cucumber	25 g 1 oz
lemon or lime (juice)	1
virgin olive oil	3 tbsp
salt and pepper	

HEALTHY EATING TIP

Although avocado is rich in fat, it is unsaturated and healthier. Try using the salsa to fill a tortilla and add grilled fish or chicken to make a healthy meal.

Variations: peeled, destoned, diced mango in place of avocado
1 tsp finely chopped garlic or garlic juice
1 tsp finely chopped red chilli
2 tbsp of finely chopped lemon grass
25 g (1 oz) chopped red onion in place of shallot

39 Béarnaise sauce

Sauce béarnaise

1 portion provides:
1728 kJ/420 kcal energy
45.2 g fat
(of which 27.2 g saturated)
0.6 g carbohydrate
(of which 0.5 g sugars)
2.6 g protein
0.0 g fibre

	4–6 portions
egg yolks	3
chopped shallots	10 g (½ oz)
crushed peppercorns	6
tarragon	5 g (¼ oz)
tarragon vinegar	1 tbsp
butter or good quality oil	200 g (8 oz)
sprig chopped chervil	

1 Make a reduction with the shallots, peppercorns, tarragon stalks and vinegar.

2 Proceed as for hollandaise sauce. (recipe 42).

3 After passing add the chopped tarragon leaves and chervil.

Usually served with grilled meat and fish, e.g.
Chateaubriand grillé, sauce béarnaise. This sauce
should be twice as thick as hollandaise.

40 Smitaine sauce

Sauce smitaine

> Per tablespoon provides:
> 254 kJ/62 kcal energy
> 6.0 g fat
> (of which 3.8 g saturated)
> 1.2 g carbohydrate
> (of which 1.1 g sugars)
> 0.8 g protein
> 0.0 g fibre

butter or margarine	25 g (1 oz)
finely chopped onion	50 g (2 oz)
white wine	60 ml (⅛ pt)
sour cream	½ litre (1 pt)
seasoning	
juice of ¼ of a lemon	

1 Melt butter or margarine in a sauteuse and cook onion without colour.
2 Add the white wine and reduce by half.
3 Add sour cream and season lightly, reduce by one-third.
4 Pass through a fine strainer and finish with lemon juice.

41 Melted butter

Beurre fondu

> Per tablespoon provides:
> 388 kJ/94 kcal energy
> 10.3 g fat
> (of which 6.5 g saturated)
> 0.1 g carbohydrate
> (of which 0.1 g sugars)
> 0.1 g protein
> 0.0 g fibre

	4 portions	10 portions
butter	200 g (8 oz)	500 g (1¼ lb)
water or white wine	2 tbsp	5 tbsp

Method I
Boil the butter and water gently together until combined, then pass through a fine strainer.

Method II
Melt the butter and carefully strain off the fat leaving the water and sediment in the pan.

Note: Usually served with poached fish and certain vegetables, for example blue trout, salmon; asparagus and sea kale.

For butter sauce see page 175. For compound butter sauces see page 68.

42 Hollandaise sauce

Sauce hollandaise

> This recipe provides for 4 portions:
> 6789 kJ/1616 kcal
> 176.2 g fat
> (of which 107.9 g saturated)
> 0.1 g carbohydrate
> (of which 0.1 g sugars)
> 7.3 g protein
> 0.0 g fibre

	4 portions	10 portions
crushed peppercorn reduction (optional)	6	15
vinegar	1 tbsp	2½ tbsp
egg yolks	2	5
butter or good quality oil	200 g (8 oz)	500 g (1¼ lb)
salt, cayenne		

continued over ▶

▶ *Hollandaise sauce continued*

1 Place the peppercorns and vinegar in a small sauteuse or stainless steel pan and reduce to one-third.

2 Add 1 tbsp cold water, allow to cool.

3 Mix in the yolks with a whisk.

4 Return to a gentle heat and, whisking continuously, cook to a sabayon (this is the cooking of the yolks to a thickened consistency, like cream, sufficient to show the mark of the whisk).

5 Remove from the heat and cool slightly.

6 Whisk in gradually the melted warm butter until thoroughly combined.

7 Correct the seasoning. If reduction is not used, add a few drops of lemon juice.

8 Pass through a muslin, tammy cloth, or fine conical strainer.

9 The sauce should be kept at only a slightly warm temperature until served.

10 Serve in a slightly warm sauceboat.

Note: The cause of hollandaise sauce curdling is either because the butter has been added too quickly, or because of excess heat, which will cause the albumen in the eggs to harden, shrink and separate from the liquid.

Should the sauce curdle, place a teaspoon of boiling water in a clean sauteuse and gradually whisk in the curdled sauce. If this fails to reconstitute the sauce, then place an egg yolk in a clean sauteuse with 1 dessertspoon of water. Whisk lightly over a gentle heat until slightly thickened. Remove from the heat and gradually add the curdled sauce, whisking continuously. To stabilise the sauce during service, 60 ml (⅛ pint) thick béchamel may be added before straining (see page 54).

To reduce the risk of salmonella infection pasteurised egg yolks may be used. Do not keep the sauce for longer than 2 hours before discarding. This applies to all egg-based sauces.

Served with hot fish (salmon, trout, turbot), and vegetables (asparagus, cauliflower, broccoli).

Note: Variations, e.g. béarnaise, will be found in recipe 39.

Compound butter sauces

Compound butters are made by mixing the flavouring ingredients into softened butter, which can then be shaped into a roll 2 cm (1 inch) in diameter, placed in wet greaseproof paper or foil, hardened in a refrigerator and cut into ½ cm (¼ inch) slices when required.

- *Parsley butter*: chopped parsley and lemon juice.
- *Herb butter*: mixed herbs (chives, tarragon, fennel, dill) and lemon juice.
- *Chive butter*: chopped chives and lemon juice.
- *Garlic butter*: garlic juice and chopped parsley or herbs.
- *Anchovy butter*: few drops anchovy essence.
- *Shrimp butter*: finely chopped or pounded shrimps.
- *Garlic*: mashed to a paste.
- *Mustard*: continental type mustard.
- *Liver pâté*: mashed to a paste.

Compound butters are served with grilled and some fried fish and with grilled meats.

Flavoured oils

Flavoured oils are now used to enhance certain types of food and dishes, especially pasta, fish and salads.

43 Walnut oil

olive or walnut oil	500 ml (1 pt)
walnuts finely crushed	75 g (3 oz)
Parmesan cheese	75 g (3 oz)
salt	
mill pepper	

1 Mix all ingredients together and bottle until required.

44 Basil oil

olive oil	500 ml (1 pt)
fresh basil	25 g (1 oz)
salt	
mill pepper	

1 Blanch and refresh the basil, purée with a little oil.
2 Combine with rest of ingredients.
3 Store in bottles with a sprig of blanched basil.

Alternatively basil extract can be used in place of fresh basil.

50 g of grated Parmesan or gorgonzola cheese may also be added into the basil oil.

45 Garlic oil

vegetable, sunflower, soya and olive oil	250 ml (½ pt)
garlic, chopped and crushed	3 tbsp

1 Heat the oil in a suitable pan, add the crushed garlic, heat until the garlic is golden, allow to cool, add to the oil, store, use as required.

46 Sun dried tomato oil

olive oil	500 ml (1 pt)
sun dried tomatoes	75 g (3 oz)
salt	
mill pepper	

1 Lightly warm oil and purée in a liquidiser.
2 Reconstitute tomatoes in olive oil.
3 Add mill pepper and salt.
4 Store in bottle until required.

Soups

Soups may be served for luncheon, dinner, supper and snack meals. A portion is usually between 200–250 ml (⅓–½ pint), depending on the type of soup and the number of courses to follow.

Soup classification	Base	Passed or unpassed	Finish	Example	
clear	stock	strained	usually garnished	consommé	
broth	stock cut vegetables	unpassed	chopped parsley	Scotch broth minestrone	
purée	stock fresh vegetables pulses	passed	croûtons	lentil soup potato soup	
velouté	blond roux vegetables stock	passed	liaison of yolk and cream	velouté of chicken	
cream	stock and vegetables vegetable purée and bechámel velouté	passed	cream, milk or yoghurt	cream of vegetable cream of fresh pea cream of tomato	
bisque	shellfish fish stock	passed	cream	lobster soup	Recipes will be found in
miscellaneous (soups that are not classified under the other headings) e.g. chowders				mulligatawny mussel	*Advanced Practical Cookery*

47 Clear soup (basic recipe)

Consommé

	4 portions	10 portions
chopped or minced beef	200 g (8 oz)	500 g (1¼ lb)
salt		
egg whites	1–2	3–5
cold white or brown beef stock	1 litre (2 pt)	2½ litres (5 pt)
mixed vegetables (onion, carrot, celery, leek)	100 g (4 oz)	250 g (10 oz)
bouquet garni		
peppercorns	3–4	8–10

1 portion provides:

126 kJ/30 kcal

0.0 g fat

(of which 0.0 g saturated)

1.8 g carbohydrate

(of which 0.0 g sugars)

5.6 g protein

0.0 g fibre

HEALTHY EATING TIP

NOTE: this soup is fat free.
Keep the salt to a minimum and serve as a low calorie starter for anyone watching their weight.

1 Thoroughly mix the beef, salt, egg white and ¼ litre (½ pint) cold stock in a thick-bottomed pan.

2 Peel, wash and finely chop the vegetables.

3 Add to the beef with the remainder of the stock, the bouquet garni and the peppercorns.

4 Place over a gentle heat and bring slowly to the boil; stirring occasionally.

5 Allow to boil rapidly for 5–10 seconds. Give a final stir.

6 Lower the heat so that the consommé is simmering very gently.

7 Cook for 1½–2 hours without stirring.

8 Strain carefully through a double muslin.

9 Remove all fat, using both sides of 8 cm (3 inch) square pieces of kitchen paper.

10 Correct the seasoning and colour, which should be a delicate amber.

11 Degrease again, if necessary. Bring to the boil and serve.

Note: A consommé should be crystal clear. The clarification process is caused by the albumen of the egg white and meat coagulating, rising to the top of the liquid and carrying other solid ingredients. The remaining liquid beneath the coagulated surface should be gently simmering.

Cloudiness is due to some or all of the following:

- poor quality stock;
- greasy stock;
- unstrained stock;
- imperfect coagulation of the clearing agent;

Practical Cookery 10th Edition

Fig 4.1a-b Ingredients for and clarification of consommé

- whisking after boiling point is reached, whereby the impurities mix with the liquid;
- not allowing the soup to settle before straining;
- lack of cleanliness of the pan or cloth;
- any trace of grease or starch.

Consommés are varied in many ways by altering the flavour of the stock (chicken, chicken and beef, game, etc.), also by the addition of numerous garnishes (julienne or brunoise of vegetables – shredded savoury pancakes or pea-sized profiteroles) added at the last moment before serving, or small pasta.

Cold lightly jellied consommés, served in cups, with or without garnish (diced tomato), may be served in hot weather.

48 Mutton broth

1 portion provides:
410 kJ/100 kcal energy
4.5 g fat
(of which 2.0 g saturated)
8.5 g carbohydrate
(of which 2.8 g sugars)
6.8 g protein
1.0 g fibre

	4 portions	**10 portions**
scrag end of mutton	200 g (8 oz)	500 g (1¼ lb)
water or mutton or lamb stock	1 litre (2 pt)	2½ litre (5 pt)
barley	25 g (1 oz)	60 g (2½ oz)
vegetables (carrot, turnip, leek, celery, onion), chopped	200 g (8 oz)	500 g (1¼ lb)
bouquet garni		
salt, pepper		
chopped parsley		

72

1 Place the mutton, free from fat, in a saucepan and cover with cold water.

2 Bring to the boil, immediately wash off under running water.

3 Clean the pan, replace the meat, cover with cold water, bring to the boil and skim.

4 Add the washed barley, simmer for 1 hour.

5 Add the vegetables, bouquet garni and season.

6 Skim when necessary; simmer until tender for approximately 30 minutes.

7 Remove the meat, allow to cool and cut from the bone, remove all fat, and cut the meat into neat dice the same size as the vegetables; return to the broth.

8 Correct the seasoning, skim off all the fat, add the chopped parsley and serve.

Scotch broth

Use beef stock in place of mutton. Barley and vegetable garnish is the same as for mutton broth.

Chicken broth

Use chicken stock, garnish with rice and vegetables.

49 Pulse soup basic recipe

Any type of pulse can be made into soup, for example, split green and yellow peas, haricot beans and lentils.

	4 portions	10 portions
pulse (soaked overnight if necessary)	200 g (8 oz)	500 g (1¼ lb)
white stock or water	1½ litres (3 pt)	3¾ litres (7½ pt)
onions, chopped	50 g (2 oz)	125 g (5 oz)
carrots, chopped	50 g (2 oz)	125 g (5 oz)
bouquet garni		
knuckle of ham or bacon (optional)	50 g (2 oz)	125 g (5 oz)
salt, pepper		
Croûtons **slice stale bread**	1	2½
butter or margarine or oil	50 g (2 oz)	125 g (5 oz)

HEALTHY EATING TIP

Remove all fat from the meat and skim any fat from the finished dish. Use a small amount of salt. There are lots of healthy vegetables in this dish and the addition of a large bread roll will increase the starchy carbohydrate.

1 portion provides (no croûtons):
728 kJ/177 kcal energy
1.3 g fat
(of which 0.2 g saturated)
32.0 g carbohydrate
(of which 3.3 g sugars)
11.3 g protein
3.6 g fibre

1 portion provides (with croûtons):
1223 kJ/291 kcal energy
111.7 g fat
(of which 6.8 g saturated)
36.5 g carbohydrate
(of which 3.6 g sugars)
12.1 g protein
3.8 g fibre

continued over ▶

▶ *Pulse soup basic recipe continued*

HEALTHY EATING TIP

The fat and salt are reduced if the ham is omitted.
Try lightly brushing the stale bread with olive oil and oven baking with garlic and herbs.
Alternatively, serve with sippets.

1   Pick and wash the pulse (if presoaked, change the water).

2   Place in a thick-bottomed pan; add the stock or water, bring to the boil and skim.

3   Add remainder of ingredients, season lightly.

4   Simmer until tender; skim when necessary.

5   Remove bouquet garni and ham.

6   Liquidise and pass through a conical strainer.

7   Return to a clean pan and reboil; correct seasoning and consistency.

8   Serve accompanied by ½ cm (¼ inch) diced bread croûtons shallow fried in butter.

Note: Variations can be made with the addition of:

→   Chopped fresh herbs (parsley, chervil, tarragon, coriander, chives etc.).

→   Spice/s (e.g. garam masala).

→   Crisp lardons of bacon.

→   Toasted sippets. (illustrated on page 80)

1 portion provides:
1356 kJ/323 kcal
23.6 g fat
(of which 12.8 g saturated)
19.6 carbohydrate
(of which 8.0 g sugars)
9.3 g protein
8.3 g fibre

50   Cream of green pea soup (fresh or frozen peas)

Crème St. Germain

	4 portions	**10 portions**
onion	25 g (1 oz)	60 g (2½ oz)
leek	25 g (1 oz)	60 g (2½ oz)
celery	25 g (1 oz)	60 g (2½ oz)
butter, margarine or oil	25 g (1 oz)	60 g (2½ oz)
peas (shelled) or frozen	250 ml (½ pt)	625 ml (1½ pt)
water or white stock	500 ml (1 pt)	1¼ litres (2½ pt)
sprig of mint		
bouquet garni		
thin béchamel	500 ml (1 pt)	1¼ litres (2½ pt)
cream	60 ml (⅛ pt)	150 ml (⅓ pt)

HEALTHY EATING TIP

Use an unsaturated oil (sunflower or olive).
Lightly oil the pan and drain off any excess after the frying is complete.
Season with minimum amounts of salt.

1   Sweat onion, leak and celery in the butter.

2   Moisten with water or stock and bring to the boil.

3   Add peas, mint and bouquet garni, and allow to boil for approximately 5 minutes.

4   Remove bouquet garni, add béchamel and bring to the boil.

5   Remove from the heat and liquidise or pass through a sieve. Skim off any fat.

6   Correct seasoning, pass through medium strainer.

7   Finish with cream, natural yoghurt or fromage frais.

Note: Variations can be made with the addition of:

→ a garnish of 25 g (1 oz) cooked and washed tapioca added at the same time as the cream;

→ a garnish of 25 g (1 oz) cooked and washed vermicelli and julienne of sorrel cooked in butter;

→ natural yoghurt, skimmed milk or non-dairy cream may be used in place of cream;

→ see also variations following pulse soup, page 74.

51 Potato soup

Purée Parmentier

	4 portions	10 portions
butter, margarine or oil	25 g (1 oz)	60 g (2½ oz)
onion	50 g (2 oz)	125 g (5 oz)
white of leek	50 g (2 oz)	125 g (5 oz)
white stock or water	1 litre (2 pt)	2 ½ litres (5 pt)
peeled potatoes	400 g (1 lb)	1¼ kg (2½ lb)
bouquet garni		
salt, pepper		
chopped parsley		
Croûtons **slice stale bread**	1	3
butter, margarine or oil	50 g (2 oz)	125 g (5 oz)

Using butter, 1 portion provides:
1063 kJ/253 kcal
15.7 g fat
(of which 9.8 g saturated)
26.1 g carbohydrate
(of which 2.1 g sugars)
3.6 g protein
2.9 g fibre

HEALTHY EATING TIP

Use an unsaturated oil (sunflower or olive). Lightly oil the pan and drain off any excess after the frying is complete. Season with minimum amounts of salt. Serve with toasted croutons.

1   Melt the butter or margarine in a thick-bottomed pan.

2   Add the peeled and washed sliced onion and leek, cook for a few minutes without colour with a lid on.

3   Add the stock and the peeled, washed, sliced potatoes and the bouquet garni and season.

4   Simmer for approximately 30 minutes. Remove the bouquet garni, skim off all fat.

5   Liquidise or pass the soup firmly through a sieve then pass through a medium conical strainer.

6   Return to a clean pan, reboil, correct the seasoning and consistency and serve.

7   Sprinkle with chopped parsley. Serve fried or toasted croûtons separately.

52 Potato and watercress soup

Purée cressonnière

1 Ingredients as for potato soup plus a small bunch of watercress.
2 Pick off 12 neat leaves of watercress, plunge into a small pan of boiling water for 1–2 seconds. Refresh under cold water immediately, these leaves are to garnish the finished soup.
3 Add the remainder of the picked and washed watercress, including the stalks, to the soup at the same time as the potatoes.
4 Finish as for potato soup.

53 Leek and potato soup

Potage de poireaux et pommes

	4 portions	10 portions
leeks, trimmed and washed	400 g (1 lb)	1¼ kg (2½ lb)
butter, margarine or oil	25 g (1 oz)	60 g (2½ oz)
white stock	750 ml (1½ pt)	2 litre (4 pt)
bouquet garni		
potatoes	200 g (8 oz)	½ kg (1¼ lb)
salt, pepper		

1 Cut the white and light green of leek into ½ cm (¼ inch) paysanne.
2 Slowly cook in the butter in a pan with a lid on until soft, but without colouring.
3 Add the stock, the bouquet garni, the potatoes cut into ½ cm (¼ inch) paysanne, 2 mm (½₂ inch) thick and season with salt and pepper.
4 Simmer until the leeks and potatoes are cooked, for approximately 15 minutes.

Note: This soup can be enriched by adding 25–50 g (1–2 oz) of butter and ¹⁄₁₆ litre (⅛ pint) of cream and stirring, just before serving.

Using butter, 1 portion provides:
531 kJ/126 kcal
5.3 g fat
(of which 3.3 g saturated)
16.7 g carbohydrate
(of which 6.3 g sugars)
3.9 g protein
4.2 g fibre

HEALTHY EATING TIP

Use an unsaturated oil (sunflower or olive). Lightly oil the pan and drain off any excess after the frying is complete.
Season with minimum amounts of salt.
Try using natural yoghurt or fromage frais to finish the soup.

54 Chive and potato soup

Vichyssoise

	4 portions	10 portions
butter, margarine or oil	25 g (1 oz)	60 g (2½ oz)
onion, peeled, washed and sliced	50 g (2 oz)	125 g (5 oz)
white of leek, washed and sliced	50 g (2 oz)	125 g (5 oz)
white stock	1 litre (2 pt)	2½ litres (5 pt)
potatoes, peeled, washed and sliced	400 g (1 lb)	1¼ kg (2½ lb)
bouquet garni		
salt, pepper		
cream	125–250 ml (¼–½ pt)	500 ml (1 pt)
chopped chives		

Using 200 ml single cream, 1 portion provides:
949 kJ/228 kcal energy
15.0 g fat
(of which 9.3 g saturated)
20.3 g carbohydrate
(of which 3.2 g sugars)
4.1 g protein
1.8 g fibre

HEALTHY EATING TIP

Use an unsaturated oil (sunflower or olive). Lightly oil the pan and drain off any excess after the frying is complete.
Season with minimum amounts of salt.
Try using natural yoghurt or fromage frais to finish the soup.

1   Melt the butter or margarine or oil in a thick-bottomed pan.

2   Add the onion and leek, cook for a few minutes without colour with a lid on.

3   Add the stock and the potatoes and the bouquet garni and season.

4   Simmer for approximately 30 minutes. Remove the bouquet garni, skim.

5   Liquidise or pass the soup firmly through a sieve, then through a medium conical strainer.

6   Return to a clean pan and reboil; correct the seasoning and consistency, skim off any fat.

7   Finish with cream and garnish with chopped chives, either raw or cooked in a little butter. Usually served chilled.

HEALTHY EATING TIP

Use soft margarine or sunflower/olive oil in place of the butter. Serve with toasted croûtons and use a minimum amount of salt – there is plenty in the bacon.

55 Tomato soup

Potage de tomates

	4 portions	10 portions
butter, margarine or oil	50 g (2 oz)	125 g (5 oz)
bacon trimmings, optional	25 g (1 oz)	60 g (2½ oz)
onion, diced	100 g (4 oz)	250 g (10 oz)
carrot, diced	100 g (4 oz)	250 g (10 oz)
flour	50 g (2 oz)	125 g (5 oz)
tomato purée	100 g (4 oz)	250 g (10 oz)
stock	1¼ litres (2½ pt)	3½ litres (6 pt)
bouquet garni		
salt, pepper		
Croûtons **slice stale bread**	1	3
butter	50 g (2 oz)	125 g (5 oz)

1 Melt the butter, margarine or oil in a thick-bottomed pan.
2 Add the bacon, onion and carrot (mirepoix) and brown lightly.
3 Mix in the flour and cook to a sandy texture.
4 Remove from the heat, mix in the tomato purée.
5 Return to heat. Gradually add the hot stock.
6 Stir to the boil. Add the bouquet garni, season lightly.
7 Simmer for approximately 1 hour. Skim when required.
8 Remove the bouquet garni and mirepoix.
9 Liquidise or pass firmly through a sieve, then through a conical strainer.
10 Return to a clean pan, correct the seasoning and consistency. Bring to the boil.
11 Serve fried or toasted croûtons separately.

Note: If a slight sweet/sour flavour is required, reduce 100 ml (³⁄₁₆ pint) vinegar and 35 g (1½ oz) caster sugar to a light caramel and mix into the completed soup.

Variations can be made with the addition of:

- juice and lightly grated zest of 1–2 oranges;
- tomato concassé;

- cooked rice;

- chopped fresh coriander, basil or chives;

- 200 g (8 oz) peeled, sliced potatoes with the stock.

56 Tomato soup (using fresh tomatoes)

Crème de tomates fraîche

1 Prepare the soup as recipe 55, using 1 litre (2 pints) stock.

2 Substitute 1–1 ½ kg (2–3 lb) fresh fully ripe tomatoes for the tomato purée.

3 Remove the eyes from the tomatoes, wash them well and squeeze them into the soup after the stock has been added and has come to the boil.

4 If colour is lacking, add a little tomato purée soon after the soup comes to the boil.

57 Cream of tomato soup

Crème de tomates

1 Prepare soup as for tomato soup using only 1 litre (2 pints) stock.

2 When finally reboiling the finished soup, add ¼ litre (½ pint) of milk or ⅛ litre (¼ pint) of cream or yoghurt.

> HEALTHY EATING TIP
>
> Use semi-skimmed milk and finish with natural yoghurt or fromage frais.

58 Cream of tomato and potato soup

Crème Solférino

Mix half the cream of tomato and half the potato soup together and garnish with small balls of carrots and potatoes, cooked separately in a little salted water, refreshed and added to the soup just before serving.

59 Brown onion soup

Soupe à l'oignon

onions	600 g (1½ lb)
butter or margarine	25 g (1 oz)
1 clove of garlic, chopped (optional)	
flour, white or wholemeal	10 g (½ oz)
brown stock	1 litre (2 pt)
salt, mill pepper	
¼ of a flute	
grated cheese	50 g (2 oz)

Using butter, 1 portion provides:
197 kcals/827 kj
9.7 g fat of which 5.8 g saturated
20.4 g carbohydrate of which 8.1 g sugars
8.3 g protein
3.1 g fibre

continued over ▶

79

▶ *Brown onion soup continued*

1 Peel the onions, halve and slice finely.

2 Melt the butter in a thick-bottomed pan, add the onions and garlic and cook steadily over a good heat until cooked and well browned.

3 Mix in the flour and cook over a gentle heat, browning slightly.

4 Gradually mix in the stock, bring to the boil, skim and season.

5 Simmer approximately 10 min until the onion is soft. Correct the seasoning.

6 Pour into an earthenware tureen or casserole or individual dishes.

7 Cut the flute (French loaf, 2 cm (1 inch) diameter) into slices and toast on both sides.

8 Sprinkle the toasted slices of bread liberally over the top.

9 Sprinkle with grated cheese and brown under the salamander.

10 Place on a dish and serve.

Fig 4.2 Ingredients for brown onion soup;
Right: preparation and service of brown onion soup

Using hard margarine, 1 portion provides:
712 kJ/170 kcal
11.8 g fat
(of which 5.2 g saturated)
12.6 g carbohydrate
(of which 3.0 g sugars)
3.8 g protein
1.6 g fibre

60 Mushroom soup

Crème de champignons

	4 portions	**10 portions**
onion, leek and celery	100 g (4 oz)	250 g (10 oz)
margarine or oil	50 g (2 oz)	125 g (5 oz)
flour	50 g (2 oz)	125 g (5 oz)
white stock (preferably chicken)	1 litre (2 pt)	2½ litre (5 pt)
white mushrooms	200 g (8 oz)	500 g (1¼ lb)
bouquet garni		
salt, pepper		
milk (or cream)	125 ml (¼ pt) or 60 ml (⅛ pt) cream	300 ml (⅝ pt) or 150 ml (⅓ pt) cream

1   Gently cook the sliced onions, leek and celery in the margarine or oil in a thick-bottomed pan without colouring.

2   Mix in the flour, cook over a gentle heat to a sandy texture without colouring.

3   Remove from the heat; cool slightly.

4   Gradually mix in the hot stock. Stir to the boil.

5   Add the well-washed, chopped mushrooms, bouquet garni and season.

6   Simmer for 30–45 minutes. Skim when needed.

7   Remove the bouquet garni. Pass through a sieve or liquidise.

8   Pass through a medium strainer. Return to a clean saucepan.

9   Reboil, correct the seasoning and consistency; add the milk or cream.

Note:

- Natural yoghurt, skimmed milk or non-dairy cream may be used in place of dairy cream.

- A garnish of thinly sliced mushrooms may be added.

- Wild mushrooms may also be used.

61 Chicken soup

Crème de volaille or Crème reine

	4 portions	**10 portions**
onion, leek and celery	100 g (4oz)	250 g (10 oz)
butter, margarine or oil	50 g (2 oz)	125 g (5 oz)
flour	50 g (2 oz)	125 g (5 oz)
chicken stock	1 litre (2 pt)	2½ litres (5 pt)
bouquet garni		
salt, pepper		
milk or cream	250 ml (½ pt)	625 ml (1¼ pt)
	125 ml (¼ pt)	300 ml (⅝ pt)
cooked dice of chicken (garnish)	25 g (1 oz)	60 g (2½ oz)

Using hard margarine, 1 portion provides:
836 kJ/199 kcal
13.6 g fat
(of which 6.2 g saturated)
14.0 g carbohydrate
(of which 4.2 g sugars)
5.9 g protein
1.0 g fibre

1   Gently cook the sliced onions, leek and celery in a thick-bottomed pan, in the butter, margarine or oil without colouring.

2   Mix in the flour; cook over a gentle heat to a sandy texture without colouring.

3   Cool slightly; gradually mix in the hot stock. Stir to the boil.

4   Add the bouquet garni and season.

5   Simmer for 30–45 minutes; skim when necessary. Remove the bouquet garni.

HEALTHY EATING TIP

Use soft margarine or sunflower/olive oil in place of the butter and use a minimum amount of salt. The least fatty option is to use semi-skimmed milk and yoghurt or fromage frais in place of the cream.

HEALTHY EATING TIP

Use soft margarine or sunflower/olive oil in place of the butter and use a minimum amount of salt. The least fatty option is to use semi-skimmed milk and yoghurt or fromage frais in place of the cream.

continued over ▶

► *Chicken soup continued*

6 Liquidise or pass firmly through a fine strainer.

7 Return to a clean pan, reboil and finish with milk or cream; correct the seasoning.

8 Add the garnish and serve.

Note: Natural yoghurt, skimmed milk or non-dairy cream may be used in place of dairy cream.

Add cooked small pasta or sliced mushrooms for variations.

Using hard margarine, 1 portion provides:
1105 kJ/263 kcal
20.7 g fat
(of which 11.1 g saturated)
17.2 g carbohydrate
(of which 3.7 g sugars)
3.1 g protein
2.8 g fibre

HEALTHY EATING TIP

Use soft margarine or sunflower/olive oil in place of the butter. Serve with toasted croûtons and watch the salt.

62 Vegetable soup

Purée de légumes

	4 portions	10 portions
mixed vegetables (onion, carrot, turnip, leek, celery)	300 g (12 oz)	1 kg (2½ lb)
butter, margarine or oil	50 g (2 oz)	125 g (5 oz)
flour	25 g (1 oz)	60 g (2½ oz)
white stock	1 litre (2 pt)	2½ litres (5 pt)
potatoes	100 g (4 oz)	300 g (12 oz)
bouquet garni		
salt, pepper		
Croûtons		
slice stale bread	1	3
butter	50 g (2 oz)	125 g (5 oz)

1 Peel, wash and slice all the vegetables (except the potatoes).

2 Cook gently in the butter or margarine in a covered pan, without colouring.

3 Mix in the flour and cook slowly for a few minutes without colouring; cool slightly.

4 Mix in the hot stock. Stir and bring to the boil.

5 Add the sliced potatoes, bouquet garni and season. Simmer for 30–45 minutes; skim when necessary. Remove the bouquet garni.

6 Liquidise or pass through a sieve and then through a medium strainer.

7 Return to a clean pan and reboil; correct the seasoning and the consistency.

8 Serve with croûtons separately.

Note: For variations see pulse soup (recipe 49).

63 Cream of vegetable soup

Crème de légumes

Ingredients and method as for vegetable soup (recipe 62). Either replace ½ litre (1 pint) stock with ½ litre (1 pint) béchamel; or finish with milk or ⅛ litre (¼ pint) cream (see note recipe 61), simmer for 5 minutes and serve as for vegetable soup. For variations see below.†

64 Basic soup recipe for purées

	4 portions	**10 portions**
onions, leek and celery	100 g (4 oz)	250 g (10 oz)
suitable vegetables*, sliced	200 g (8 oz)	500 g (1¼ lb)
butter, margarine or oil	50 g (2 oz)	125 g (5 oz)
flour	50 g (2 oz)	125 g (5 oz)
white stock or water	1 litre (2 pt)	2 ½ litres (5 pt)
bouquet garni		
salt, pepper		

Using hard margarine, 1 portion provides:
601 kJ/143 kcal
10.3 g fat
(of which 4.4 g saturated)
11.4 g carbohydrate
(of which 1.8 g sugars)
1.9 g protein
1.9 g fibre

1 Gently cook all the sliced vegetables, in the fat under a lid, without colour.

2 Mix in the flour and cook slowly for a few minutes without colour. Cool slightly.

3 Gradually mix in the hot stock. Stir to the boil.

4 Add the bouquet garni and season.

5 Simmer for approximately 45 minutes; skim when necessary.

6 Remove the bouquet garni; liquidise or pass firmly through a sieve and then through a medium strainer.

7 Return to a clean pan, reboil and correct the seasoning and consistency.

Note: For cream soups see note to recipe 61.

*Suitable vegetables include Jerusalem artichokes, cauliflower, celery, leeks, onions, parsnips, turnips and fennel.

†Variations:

● add a little spice, sufficient to give a subtle background flavour, e.g. garam masala with parsnip soup;

● just before serving add a little freshly chopped herb/s, e.g. parsley, chervil, tarragon, coriander.

HEALTHY EATING TIP

Use an unsaturated oil (sunflower or olive) to lightly oil the pan. Drain off any excess after the frying is complete and skim the fat from the finished dish. Season with minimum amounts of salt. Try using more vegetables to thicken the soup in place of the flour.

Using hard margarine, 1 portion provides:
1515 kJ/361 kcal
25.3 g fat
(of which 11.9 g saturated)
27.1 g carbohydrate
(of which 8.1 g sugars)
7.7 g protein
2.5 g fibre

Using butter, 1 portion provides:
919 kJ/223 kcal energy
13.1 g fat
(of which 8.0 g saturated)
18.9 g carbohydrate
(of which 8.8 g sugars)
8.4 g protein
2.6 g fibre

HEALTHY EATING TIP

Use an unsaturated oil (sunflower or olive) to lightly oil the pan. Drain off any excess after the frying is complete and skim the fat from the finished dish. Season with minimum amounts of salt. Milk with a little cornflour can be added to reach the desired consistency.

65 Basic soup for creams

Suitable vegetables as for basic soup recipe (64).

As basic recipe but in place of ½ litre (1 pint) stock use ½ litre (1 pint) thin béchamel or use ⅛–¼ litre (¼–½ pint) less stock and finish with ¼ litre (½ pint) milk or ⅛ litre (¼ pint) of cream.

66 Asparagus soup

Crème d'asperges

	4 portions	10 portions
onion	50 g (2 oz)	125 g (5 oz)
celery	50 g (2 oz)	125 g (5 oz)
butter, oil or margarine	50 g (2 oz)	125 g (5 oz)
flour	50 g (2 oz)	125 g (5 oz)
white stock (preferably chicken)	1 litre (2 pt)	2½ litres (5 pt)
asparagus stalk trimmings or	200 g (½ lb)	500 g (1¼ lb)
tin of asparagus	150 g (6 oz)	325 g (15 oz)
bouquet garni		
salt, pepper		
milk or cream (see note recipe 61)	250 ml or 125 ml (½ pt or ¼ pt)	625 ml or 300 ml (1¼ pt or ⅝ pt)

1 Gently sweat the sliced onions and celery, without colouring, in the butter or margarine.

2 Remove from the heat, mix in the flour, return to a low heat and cook out, without colouring, for a few minutes. Cool.

3 Gradually add the hot stock. Stir to the boil.

4 Add the well-washed asparagus trimmings or the tin of asparagus, bouquet garni and season.

5 Simmer 30–40 minutes, remove bouquet garni.

6 Liquidise and pass through a strainer.

7 Return to a clean pan, re-boil, correct seasoning and consistency.

8 Add the milk or cream and serve.

67 Roasted butternut squash soup

	4 portions	10 portions
butternut squash, peeled and de-seeded	600 g (1½ lbs)	2 kg (4 lbs)
onion	100 g (4 oz)	250 g (10 oz)
olive oil	2 tbsp	5 tbsp
garlic (optional) finely chopped	1 clove	2 cloves
bacon, back rashers, in small pieces	4	10
chicken or vegetable stock	625 ml (1¼ pt)	1½ litres (3 pt)
salt and pepper		
cream or thick natural yoghurt	6 tbsp	15 tbsp

1 portion provides:
923 kJ/220 kcal energy
12.0 g fat
(of which 3.5 g saturated)
19.6 g carbohydrate
(of which 13.1 g sugars)
9.9 g protein
2.8 g fibre

HEALTHY EATING TIP

Use an unsaturated oil (sunflower or olive), lightly oil the pan to sweat the garlic and onions. Drain off any excess fat after cooking the bacon. Use low fat yoghurt to reduce the fat. Add a little cornflour to stabilise the yoghurt before adding to the soup.

1 Cut squash into thick pieces, place on a lightly oiled baking sheet and roast for 20–25 minutes in a hot oven until the flesh is soft and golden brown.

2 Sweat onions and garlic without colouring, approx 5 minutes.

3 Add bacon and lightly brown.

4 Add roasted squash, pour in stock, bring to boil, simmer 20 minutes.

5 Allow to cool, liquidise or blend until smooth.

6 Season lightly, add yoghurt or cream, reheat gently and serve.

Variation: 3–4 saffron strands soaked in 1 tbsp hot water added at point 4.

68 Minestrone

	4 portions	10 portions
mixed vegetables (onion, leek, celery, carrot, turnip, cabbage)	300 g (12 oz)	750 g (30 oz)
butter, margarine or oil	50 g (2 oz)	125 g (5 oz)
white stock or water	¾ litre (1½ pt)	2 litres (4½ pt)
bouquet garni		
salt, pepper		
peas	25 g (1 oz)	60 g (2½ oz)
French beans	25 g (1 oz)	60 g (2½ oz)
spaghetti	25 g (1 oz)	60 g (2½ oz)
potatoes	50 g (2 oz)	125 g (5 oz)
tomato purée	1 tspn	3 tspn
tomatoes, skinned, de-seeded, diced	100 g (4 oz)	250 g (10 oz)
fat bacon }		
chopped parsley } Optional	50 g (2 oz)	125 g (5 oz)
1 clove garlic }		

1 Cut the peeled and washed mixed vegetables into paysanne.

2 Cook slowly without colour in the oil or fat in the pan with a lid on.

3 Add stock, bouquet garni and seasoning; simmer for approximately 20 minutes.

4 Add the peas, beans cut in diamonds and simmer for 10 minutes.

5 Add the spaghetti in 2 cm (1 inch) lengths, the potatoes cut in paysanne, the tomato purée and the tomatoes and simmer gently until all the vegetables are cooked.

6 Meanwhile finely chop the fat bacon, parsley and garlic and form into a paste.

7 Mould the paste into pellets the size of a pea and drop into the boiling soup.

8 Remove the bouquet garni, correct the seasoning.

9 Serve grated Parmesan cheese and thin toasted flutes separately.

Chowders

Chowders are American-style fish soups usually made from shellfish. The most popular is clam chowder.

69 New England clam chowder

	8 portions
salt pork cut into ¼ cm (⅛ inch) dice	100 g (4 oz)
finely chopped onion	100 g (4 oz)
cold water	625 ml (1¼ pt)
potatoes cut in ½ cm (¼ inch) dice	1 kg (2 lb)
fresh trimmed clams or 2 × 200 g (½ lb) tins and their juices	400 g (1 lb)
cream	375 ml (¾ pt)
thyme, crushed or chopped	⅛ tsp
salt, white pepper	
butter	25 g (1 oz)
paprika	

Using bacon for salt pork, 1 portion provides:
1109 kJ/269 kcal energy
14.9 g fat
(of which 7.7 g saturated)
24.5 g carbohydrate
(of which 2.5 g sugars)
14.9 g protein
1.8 g fibre

HEALTHY EATING TIP

Dry fry using a well-seasoned pan and drain or skim off all excess fat. This will significantly reduce the overall fat content.
Use a minimum amount of salt; the customer can add more if required.

1   Dry fry the pork in a thick bottomed saucepan for about 3 minutes stirring constantly until a thin film of fat covers the bottom of the pan.

2   Stir in the chopped onion and cook gently until a light golden brown.

3   Add the water and potatoes, bring to the boil and simmer gently until the potatoes are cooked but not mushy.

4   Add the chopped clams, juice, cream, thyme and heat until almost boiling, season with salt and pepper.

5   Correct seasoning, stir in the softened butter and serve, dusting each soup bowl with a little paprika.

The traditional accompaniment is salted cracker biscuits.

Note: an obvious variation would be to use scallops in place of clams.

Mixed salad   Tomato salad

Couscous salad

John Campbell

Potato salad

Recipe No.		page no.	Recipe No.		page no.
77	Mixed salad	125	5	Green	94
55	Niçoise salad	119	8	Horseradish	95
41	Potato salad	114	3	Mayonnaise	93
52	Rice salad	118	9	Mint	95
40	Seafood salad	113		Pesto	65
58	Three bean salad	120		Red onion confit	183
50	Tomato salad	117	7	Remoulade	95
51	Tomato and cucumber salad	118		Salsa	65
42	Vegetable salad	115		Shellfish cocktail sauce	108
38	Vegetable salad with peanut dressing	363	6	Tartare	94
				Thai fish	389
56	Waldorf salad	119	2	Thousand Island	93
Cold sauces and dressings			1	Vinaigrette	92
4	Andalusian	94			

Cold food preparation (hors-d'oeuvre, salads, cooked/cured/prepared foods)

Cold food is popular in every kind of food service operation for at least three good reasons:

- *Visual appeal* When the food is attractively displayed, carefully arranged and neatly garnished, the customers can have their appetites stimulated by seeing exactly what is being offered.
- *Efficiency* Cold food can be prepared in advance allowing a large number of people to be served in a short space of time. Self service is also economic on staff.
- *Adaptability* If cold food is being served from a buffet, the range of foods can be simple or large depending on the type of operation.

Cold foods can either be preplated or served from large dishes and bowls. In both cases presentation is important; the food should appear fresh, neatly arranged and not overgarnished.

Health, safety and hygiene

Read Chapter 1 and in addition:

- Where possible use plastic gloves when handling food.
- Keep unprepared and prepared food under refrigeration at a temperature not exceeding 4–5°C (39–41°F). Refrigeration will not kill the bacteria that are present in the foods, but it does help to prevent their growth.
- Whenever possible, the food on display to the public should be kept under refrigeration and the temperature should be checked to ensure that a safe temperature is being maintained.
- Where customers are viewing the food closely, ideally it should be displayed behind a sneeze screen.
- Dishes prepared in advance should be covered with film and refrigerated at 1–3°C (34–37°F) to prevent them drying.
- Personal, food and equipment hygiene of the highest order must be observed with all cold work.

Cold preparations

Definition

The preparation of raw and/or cooked foods into a wide variety of cold items.

Purpose

The purpose of these dishes is:

- to add variety to the menu and diet by preparing food that has eye appeal, is palatable and digestible;
- to produce a variety of flavours and textures and provide food that is particularly suitable for hot weather;
- to prepare food that can be conveniently wrapped for take-aways.

Cold food characteristics

- Appearance must be clean and fresh. Presentation should be eye appealing, neither too colourful or overdecorative, therefore stimulating the appetite.
- Nutritional value is obtained because of the mixture of raw and cooked foods.

Techniques associated with cold preparation

Peeling

This is the removal of the outer skin of fruit or vegetables using a peeler or small knife, according to the thickness of the skin.

Chopping

This is cutting into very small pieces (parsley, onions).

Cutting

This is using a knife to divide food into required shapes and sizes.

Carving

This means cutting meat or poultry into slices.

Seasoning

This is the light addition of salt, pepper and possibly other flavouring agents.

Dressing

This can either mean an accompanying salad dressing such as vinaigrette, *or* the arrangement of food for presentation on plates, dishes or buffets.

Garnishing

This is the final addition to the dish, such as lettuce, quarters of tomato and sliced cucumber added to egg mayonnaise.

Marinade

A richly spiced pickling liquid used to give flavour and to assist in tenderising meats such as venison.

Simple marinades, e.g. olive oil with herbs or soy sauce with herbs and/or spices can be used for cuts of fish, chicken or meat.

Equipment

Bowls, tongs, whisks, spoons, etc., as well as food processors, mixing machines and blenders are used in cold preparations.

Preparation for cold work

Well planned organisation is essential to ensure adequate prepreparation (*mise-en-place*), so that foods are assembled with a good work flow and ready on time.

Before, during and after assembling, and before final garnishing, foods must be kept in a cool place, cold room or refrigerator so as to minimise the risk of food contamination. Garnishing and final decoration should take place as close to the serving time as possible.

General rules

- Be aware of the texture and flavour of many raw foods that can be mixed together or combined with cooked foods (coleslaw, meat salad).
- Understand what combination of foods, for example salads, is best suited to be served with other foods, such as cold meat or poultry.
- Develop simple artistic skills that require the minimum of time for preparation and assembly.
- Provide an attractive presentation of food at all times.
- Because of the requirements of food safety, cold foods are often served straight from the refrigerator. This is wrong because, at refrigerator temperature, food flavours are not at their best. Individual portions should be removed from refrigeration and allowed to stand at room temperature for 5–10 minutes before being served.

Types of hors-d'oeuvre

The choice of a wide variety of foods, combination of foods and recipes is available for preparation and services as hors-d'oeuvre and salads.

Hors-d'oeuvre can be divided into three categories:

- single cold food items (smoked salmon, pâté, melon, etc.);
- a selection of well-seasoned cold dishes;
- well-seasoned hot dishes.

Hors-d'oeuvre may be served for luncheon, dinner or supper and the wide choice, colour appeal and versatility of the dishes make many items and combinations of items suitable for snacks and salads at any time of day.

Salads may be served as an accompaniment to hot and cold foods and as dishes in their own right. They can be served for lunch, tea, high tea, dinner, supper and snack meals. Salads may be divided in two sections:

- simple, using one ingredient;
- mixed or composite, using more than one ingredient.

Some salads may form part of a composite hors-d'oeuvre.

Accompaniments include dressings and cold sauces.

Dressings, cold sauces, chutneys and relishes
Salad dressings

These dressings may be varied by the addition of other ingredients. Salads should be lightly dressed or the dressing offered separately to give the customer the choice.

1 Vinaigrette

Using 3 tbsp oil, this recipe provides for 4–6 portions:
1740 kJ/415 kcal
45.5 g fat
(of which 6.3 g saturated)
0.5 g carbohydrate
(of which 0.1 g sugars)
0.6 g protein
0.0 g fibre

Using 6 tbsp oil, this recipe provides for 4–6 portions:
3439 kJ/819 kcal
90.5 g fat
(of which 12.6 g saturated)
0.5 g carbohydrate
(of which 0.1 g sugars)
0.6 g protein
0.0 g fibre

	4–6 portions
olive oil, according to taste	3–6 tbsp
French mustard	1 tsp
vinegar	1 tbsp
salt, mill pepper	

Combine all the ingredients together.

Note: Variations to vinaigrette include:

- English mustard in place of French mustard;
- chopped herbs (chives, parsley, tarragon, etc.);
- chopped hard-boiled egg;
- other good quality oils, e.g. sesame seed or walnut;
- different flavoured vinegars or lemon juice.

2 Thousand Island dressing

This recipe provides for 4–6 portions:
15055 kJ/3584 kcal
387.0 g fat
(of which 56.5 g saturated)
10.2 g carbohydrate
(of which 9.8 g sugars)
16.1 g protein
1.8 g fibre

	4–6 portions
salt, pepper	
tabasco	3–4 drops
vinegar	125 ml (¼ pt)
oil	375 ml (¾ pt)
red pimento	50 g (2 oz)
green pimento	50 g (2 oz)
chopped parsley	
hard-boiled eggs	2
tomato ketchup (optional)	2 tbsp

1 Place the salt, pepper, tabasco and vinegar in a basin.

2 Mix well. Mix in the oil.

3 Add the chopped pimentos and parsley.

4 Mix in the sieved hard-boiled eggs.

Cold sauces

3 Mayonnaise sauce

This recipe provides for 8 portions:
10030 kJ/2388 kcal
26.2 g fat
(of which 38.9 g saturated)
0.3 g carbohydrate
(of which 0.1 g sugars)
6.8 g protein
0.0 g fibre

This is a basic cold sauce and has a wide variety of uses, particularly in hors-d'oeuvre dishes. It should always be available on any cold buffet. Because of the risk of salmonella food poisoning it is strongly recommended that pasteurised egg yolks be used.

	8 portions
egg yolks (pasteurised)	2
vinegar	2 tsp
salt, ground white pepper	
English or continental mustard	⅛ tsp
olive or other good quality oil	250 ml (½ pt)
boiling water (approximately)	1 tsp

HEALTHY EATING TIP
Try using a little less oil and thin with boiling water or lemon juice. The sauce can be extended with a little low fat yoghurt to reduce the fat content. Add a minimum amount of salt.

continued over ▶

▶ *Cold sauces continued*

1 Place the yolks, vinegar and seasoning in a bowl and whisk well.

2 Gradually pour on the oil very slowly, whisking continuously.

3 Add the boiling water, whisking well. Correct the seasoning.

Note: If, during the making of the sauce, it should become too thick, then a little vinegar or water may be added. Mayonnaise will turn or curdle for several reasons:

- if the oil is added too quickly;
- if the oil is too cold;
- if the sauce is insufficiently whisked;
- if the yolk is stale and therefore weak.

The method of rethickening a turned mayonnaise is either:

- by taking a clean basin, adding 1 teaspoon boiling water and gradually whisking in the curdled sauce; or
- by taking another yolk thinned with ½ teaspoon cold water whisked well, then gradually whisking in the curdled sauce.

Many ingredients can be used to vary mayonnaise, such as fresh herbs; garlic juice; Parmesan or blue cheese; red pepper purée; chopped sun dried tomatoes. Lemon juice may be useful in place of vinegar.

4 Andalusian sauce

Sauce andalouse

Add to ¼ litre (½ pt) of mayonnaise, 2 tbsp tomato juice or ketchup and 1 tbsp pimento cut in julienne. Makes ¼ litre (½ pint).

May be served with cold salads.

5 Green sauce

Sauce verte

	8 portions
spinach, tarragon, chervil, chives, watercress	50 g (2 oz)
mayonnaise	250 ml (½ pt)

1 Pick, wash, blanch and refresh the green leaves. Squeeze dry.

2 Pass through a very fine sieve. Mix with the mayonnaise.

Note: May be served with cold salmon or salmon trout.

6 Tartare sauce

Sauce tartare

Using gherkins, 1 portion provides:
938 kJ/228 kcal energy
24.8 g fat
(of which 3.6 g saturated)
0.3 g carbohydrate
(of which 0.3 g sugars)
0.7 g protein
0.1 g fibre

	8 portions
mayonnaise	250 ml (½ pt)
capers, chopped	25 g (1 oz)
gherkins	50 g (2 oz)
sprig of chopped parsley	

Proportionally reduce the fat by adding some low fat yoghurt.

Combine all the ingredients.

Note: This sauce is usually served with deep-fried fish.

7 Remoulade sauce

Sauce remoulade

Prepare as for tartare sauce adding 1 teaspoon of anchovy essence and mixing thoroughly. Makes ⅛ litre (¼ pint).

This sauce may be served with fried fish. It can also be mixed with a fine julienne of celeriac to make an accompaniment to cold meats, terrines etc. (see Fig 5.1).

Using gherkins, 1 portion provides:
938 kJ/228 kcal energy
24.8 g fat
(of which 3.6 g saturated)
0.3 g carbohydrate
(of which 0.3 g sugars)
0.8 g protein
0.1 g fibre

8 Horseradish sauce

Sauce raifort

	8 portions
grated horseradish	25 g (1 oz)
vinegar or lemon juice	1 tbsp
salt, pepper	
lightly whipped cream or crème fraîche	125 ml (¼ pt)

This recipe provides for 8 portions:
1807 kJ/430 kcal
43.8 g fat
(of which 27.8 g saturated)
6.0 g carbohydrate
(of which 5.0 g sugars)
3.6 g protein
2.1 g fibre

1 Wash, peel and rewash the horseradish. Grate finely.

2 Mix all the ingredients together.

Note: Serve with roast beef, smoked trout, eel or halibut.

9 Mint sauce

	8 portions
mint	2–3 tbsp
caster sugar	1 tsp
vinegar	125 ml (¼ pt)

This recipe provides for 8 portions:
204 kJ/49 kcal
0.0 g fat
(of which 0.0 g saturated)
11.3 g carbohydrate
(of which 11.3 g sugars)
1.5 g protein
1.8 g fibre

1 Chop the washed, picked mint and mix with the sugar.

2 Place in a china basin and add the vinegar.

3 If the vinegar is too sharp dilute it with a little water.

Note: Serve with roast lamb. A less acid sauce can be produced by dissolving the sugar in 125 ml (¼ pint) boiling water and, when cold, adding the chopped mint and 1–2 tablespoon vinegar to taste.

Fig 5.1 Celeriac remoulade

Chutneys and relishes

Chutneys are made from a variety of ingredients, usually fruit, preserved in sugar and acid after careful cooking. They are flavoured with a range of spices.

Chutneys are served as an accompaniment to terrines and pâtés, salads, cold meats and cheese. They may also accompany a traditional curry.

Relishes are similar to chutneys except they are generally smoother and do not always contain as much sugar.

Fruits and vegetables for relishes and chutneys must be unblemished and well washed. Good quality vinegars must be used at 4% acetic acid.

When making chutneys and relishes, never use copper or unsealed cast iron pans; the acid in the preserve will damage the metal and colour and flavour of the ingredients.

10 Tomato chutney

	Makes 1 litre
tomatoes, peeled	1.5 kg (3¾ lb)
onions, finely chopped	450 g (1 lb 2 oz)
brown sugar	300 g (12 oz)
malt vinegar	375 ml (¾ pt)
mustard powder	1½ tsp
cayenne pepper	½ tsp
coarse salt	2 tsp
mild curry powder	1 tbsp

1 Peel and coarsely chop tomatoes, combine with remaining ingredients in a large heavy duty saucepan.

2 Stir over heat without boiling until sugar dissolves. Simmer uncovered, stirring occasionally about 1¼ hours until mixture thickens.

3 Place in hot, sterilised jars. Seal while hot.

11 Rhubarb and tomato chutney

	Makes approximately 2 litres
rhubarb	1 kg (2 lb)
olive oil	1 tbsp
black mustard seeds	1½ tbsp
ground cumin	1½ tbsp
ground cloves	½ tsp
ground coriander	1½ tbsp
tomatoes, peeled, coarsely chopped	2 kg (4 lb)
onions, finely chopped	400 g (1 lb)
coarse salt	1 tsp
garlic cloves, chopped	2
raisins	400 g (1 lb)
brown sugar	200 g (½ lb)
malt vinegar	250 ml (½ pt)

1 Peel rhubarb, cut into 2 cm (1 inch) pieces.

2 Heat oil in a large heavy-duty saucepan, add seeds and spices, sweat for 2–3 minutes.

3 Add tomatoes, onion, salt, garlic, raisins, sugar and vinegar.

4 Stir over heat without boiling until sugar dissolves. Simmer uncovered, stirring occasionally, for approximately 35 minutes until mixture thickens.

5 Stir in rhubarb, simmer for 5–10 minutes until rhubarb is tender.

6 Pour hot chutney into sterilised jars. Seal while hot.

12 Beetroot relish

	Makes 1.75 litres
beetroots peeled, chopped coarsely	1 kg (2¼ lb)
onions finely chopped	800 g (2 lb)
caster sugar	225 g (9 oz)
coarse suet	1 tbsp
ground allspice	1 tsp
malt vinegar	500 ml (1 pt)
plain flour	1 tbsp

1 Mix chopped beetroot and onion together, add sugar, salt, allspice and 375 ml (¾ pint) of vinegar to a large saucepan, bring to boil, simmer for 30 minutes.

2 Mix the flour with the remaining vinegar, whisk well together. (Make sure this is smooth and does not contain any lumps.) Add to the beetroot mixture. Stir until all is well blended and thickens.

3 Place in hot sterilised jars. Seal while still hot.

13 Date and tamarind relish

	Makes 625 ml
dried tamarind	75 g (3 oz)
boiling water	500 ml (1 pt)
olive oil	2 tsp
black mustard seeds	2 tsp
cumin seeds	2 tsp
fresh dates, stoned, chopped	500 g (1¼ lb)
malt vinegar	60 mls (⅛ pt)

1 In a suitable bowl, pour boiling water over the tamarind, allow to stand for 30 minutes.

2 Strain the liquid, press to extract all moisture, discard tamarind.

3 Heat the oil in a suitable saucepan, cook mustard seeds until they pop, stir in dates, tamarind

continued over ▶

▶ *Date and tamarind relish continued*

liquid and vinegar, bring to boil. Simmer for 5 minutes until almost dry.

4   Purée in a processor until smooth.

5   Place hot relish into hot sterilised jars. Seal while hot.

Single food hors-d'oeuvre

Serve hors-d'oeuvre with bread or toast, butter separately. Add a salad garnish.

14 Oysters

Oysters should be kept in boxes or barrels covered with damp seaweed in a cold room or refrigerator to keep them moist and alive. The shells should be tightly shut to indicate freshness. The oysters should be carefully opened with a special oyster knife so as to avoid scratching the inside shell, then turned and arranged neatly in the deep shell and served on a bed of crushed ice on a plate. They should not be washed unless gritty and the natural juices should always be left in the deep shell.

Accompaniments include brown bread and butter and lemon. It is usual to serve six oysters as a portion.

15 Caviar

This is the fresh, salted roe of the sturgeon, a very expensive imported commodity usually served in its original tin or jar, in a timbale of crushed ice. One spoonful, 25 g (1 oz), represents a portion.

16 Smoked salmon

> 1 portion (25 g) provides:
> 149 kJ/36 kcal
> 1.1 g fat
> (of which 0.3 g saturated)
> 0.0 g carbohydrate
> (of which 0.0 g sugars)
> 6.4 g protein
> 0.0 g fibre

> 1 portion (35 g) provides:
> 209 kJ/50 kcal
> 1.6 g fat
> (of which 0.4 g saturated)
> 0.0 g carbohydrate
> (of which 0.0 g sugars)
> 8.9 g protein
> 0.0 g fibre

HEALTHY EATING TIP

Oily fish (e.g. salmon, trout, mackerel, rollmops, sprats) are high in omega 3 fatty acids which are beneficial for health.

Before service, a side of smoked salmon must be carefully trimmed to remove the dry outside surface. All bones must be removed; a pair of pliers is useful for this. The salmon is carved as thinly as possible on the slant and neatly dressed, overlapping, on a plate or dish, decorated with sprigs of parsley 35–50 g (1–2 oz) per portion. Accompaniments include brown bread and butter and lemon.

Other smoked fish served as hors-d'oeuvre include halibut, eel, conger eel, trout, mackerel, herring (buckling), cod's roe, sprats.

Fig 5.2   An untrimmed side of smoked salmon

17 Foie gras

This is a ready-prepared delicacy made from goose liver, and it may be served in its original dish. If tinned, it should be thoroughly chilled, removed from the tin and cut into 1 cm (½ inch) slices.

Foie gras may be cut in thick slices, lightly fried on both sides in butter or good quality oil, served on a bed of salad leaves (lightly dressed with vinaigrette) accompanied by freshly toasted brioche or bread.

18 Salami and assorted cooked or smoked sausages

These are ready-bought sausages usually prepared from pork by specialist butchers. Most countries have their own specialities, and a variety of them is exported. They are thinly sliced and either served individually or an assortment may be offered. Mortadella, garlic sausage and zungenwurst are other examples of this type of sausage.

Terrines and pâté

A slice of terrine served with a suitable garnish e.g. a small tossed salad dressed with vinaigrette and chopped fresh herbs, makes an ideal first course or a small portion can form part of an hors-d'oeuvre selection.

19 Liver pâté

Pâté de foie

1 portion provides:
213 kcals/896 kj
19.1 g fat of which 8.5 g saturated
0.7 g carbohydrate of which 0.1 g sugars
9.8 g protein
0 g fibre

This is a home-made preparation often seen on the menu as pâté maison. A typical recipe is:

	4 portions
liver (chicken, pigs, calves, lambs, etc.)	100 g (4 oz)
butter, oil or margarine	25 g (1 oz)
chopped onion	10 g (½ oz)
clove garlic	½
sprig of thyme, parsley, chervil	
fat pork	50 g (2 oz)
lean pork	50 g (2 oz)
salt, pepper	
fat bacon	25 g (1 oz)

HEALTHY EATING TIP

Use an unsaturated oil (sunflower or olive). Lightly oil the pan and drain off any excess after the frying is complete. The bacon is high in salt, so very little (or no) added salt is necessary.

1 Cut the liver in 2 cm (1 inch) pieces.

2 Toss quickly in the butter in a frying-pan over a fierce heat for a few seconds with the onion, garlic and herbs.

3 Allow to cool.

4 Pass, with the pork, twice through a mincer. Season.

5 Line an earthenware terrine with wafer-thin slices of fat bacon.

6 Place in the mixture. Cover with fat bacon.

7 Stand in a tray half full of water and bring to simmering point.

8 Cook in a moderate oven for 1 hr.

When quite cold cut in ½ cm (¼ inch) slices and serve on lettuce leaves. Usually accompanied with freshly made toast.

20 Haddock and smoked salmon terrine

	10 portions
smoked salmon	350 g (14 oz)
skinned haddock fillets	800 g (2 lb)
eggs lightly beaten	2
crème fraîche	105 ml (7 tbsp)
capers	7 tbsp
green or pink peppercorns	2 tbsp
seasoning	2 tbsp

1 portion provides:
563 kJ/133 kcal energy
3.4 g fat
(of which 0.7 g saturated)
0.1 g carbohydrate
(of which 0.1 g sugars)
25.7 g protein
0.1 g fibre

HEALTHY EATING TIP
Season with a minimum amount of salt. Offer the customer the mayonnaise separately. Serve with a warm bread or rolls (butter optional).

1   Grease a 1 litre (2 pt) loaf tin with oil, or alternatively line with clingflim.

2   Line the tin with thin slices of smoked salmon, let the ends overhang the mould. Reserve the remaining salmon until needed.

3   Cut two long slices of haddock the length of the tin and set aside.

4   Cut the rest of the haddock into small pieces. Season all the haddock with salt and pepper.

5   In a suitable basin, combine the eggs, crème fraîche, capers and green or pink peppercorns. Add the pieces of haddock.

6   Spoon the mixture into the mould until ⅓ full. Smooth with a spatula.

7   Wrap the long haddock fillets in the reserved smoked salmon. Lay them on top of the layer of the fish mixture in the terrine.

8   Fill with the remainder of the haddock and crème fraîche mixture.

9   Smooth the surface and fold over the overhanging pieces of smoked salmon.

10   Cover with tin foil, secure well.

11   Cook in a water bath (known as a bain-marie) of boiling water. Place in the oven 200°C–400°F for approximately 45 minutes until set.

12   Remove from oven and bain-marie. Allow to cool. Do not remove foil cover.

13   Place heavy weights on top, leave in refrigeration for 24 hours.

14   When ready to serve, remove weights and foil. Remove from mould.

15   Cut into thick slices, serve on suitable plates with a dill mayonnaise and garnished with salad leaves and fresh dill.

Alternative to haddock – halibut or Arctic bass.

21 Terrine of chicken and vegetables

	8–10 portions
minced chicken (white meat only)	400 g (1 lb)
each of carrots, turnips, swedes, peeled & cut to ¼ inch dice	50 g (2 oz)
broccoli (small florets)	50 g (2 oz)
baby corn, cut into ¼ inch rounds	50 g (2 oz)
french beans, cut to ¼ inch lengths	50 g (2 oz)
2 egg whites	
double cream	200 ml (6 fl oz)
salt and pepper	

1 portion provides:
930 kJ/226 kcal energy
17.3 g fat
(of which 9.4 g saturated)
2.0 g carbohydrate
(of which 1.8 g sugars)
15.5 g protein
0.9 g fibre

1   Blanch the vegetables individually in boiling salted water, ensuring that they remain firm. Refresh in cold water, and drain well.

2   Blend the chicken and egg whites in a food processor until smooth. Turn out into a large mixing bowl and gradually beat in the double cream.

3   Season with salt and mill pepper, and fold in the vegetables.

4   Line a lightly greased 2-pint terrine with clingfilm.

5   Spoon the farce into the mould and overlap the clingfilm.

6   Cover with foil, put the lid on and cook in a bain-marie in a moderate oven for about 45 minutes.

7   When cooked, remove the lid and leave to cool overnight.

HEALTHY EATING TIP

Keep the added salt to a minimum. Serve with plenty of salad vegetables and bread or toast (optional butter or spread).

Fig 5.3 Slice of terrine on salad

Terry Farr

Using common mushrooms, 1 portion provides:
1436 kJ/347 kcal energy
30.4 g fat
(of which 7.3 g saturated)
1.2 g carbohydrate
(of which 1.0 g sugars)
17.0 g protein
1.4 g fibre

HEALTHY EATING TIP

Soaking the bacon overnight will remove some of the salt.
Use only a little butter to cook the mushrooms.
Use a minimum amount of salt to season the vinaigrette.
Serve with warm bread rolls, butter optional.

22 Terrine of bacon, spinach and mushrooms served with a leek and mushroom vinaigrette

	12 portions
collar of bacon	1 kg (2 lb 8 oz)
fresh spinach	500 g (1 lb)
mushrooms (preferably morels)	200 g (8 oz)
butter	50 g (2 oz)
onion clouté	1
carrot	1
bouquet garni	1
celery	2 sticks
peppercorns	8
Vinaigrette	
leek julienne blanched	100 g (4 oz)
diced cooked mushrooms	4 oz (100 g)
shallot, freshly chopped	1
balsamic vinegar	50 ml (⅛ pt)
lemon juice	1 tbsp
olive oil	250 ml
seasoning	

1 If necessary soak the bacon overnight. Drain.

2 Place the bacon in cold water, bring to boil, add carrot, onion, bouquet garni, celery and peppercorns.

3 Poach until tender.

4 Pick some large leaves of spinach to line the terrine, blanch the leaves, refresh and drain.

5 Lightly cook the rest of the spinach gently, refresh, drain and shred.

6 Alternatively shred the spinach raw, quickly cook in butter, drain, blast chill.

7 Cook the mushrooms in a little butter, chill well, season.

8 When cool, remove the bacon from the cooking liquor, chop into small pieces.

9 Line the terrine with cling film, then the spinach leaves. Layer with bacon, mushrooms and spinach. Cover with spinach leaves and cling film. Wait for 12 hours or overnight.

10 When ready turn out, slice and serve on plates with the vinaigrette served separately.

23 Vinaigrette

1 Mix the olive oil, vinegar and lemon juice together.

2 Add the chopped shallot, mushrooms and seasoning.

3 Season.

4 Add the blanched julienne of leek.

24 Duck and chicken terrine

Reduce the fat content by removing the skin from the chicken and duck breasts.

1 of 6 portions provides:	1 of 8 portions provides:
1444 kJ/347 kcal energy	1083 kJ/260 kcal energy
22.4 g fat	16.6 g fat
(of which 9.5 g saturated)	(of which 7.1 g saturated)
0.6 g carbohydrate	0.4 g carbohydrate
(of which 0.3 g sugars)	(of which 0.2 g sugars)
35.8 g protein	26.9 g protein
0.1 g fibre	0.1 g fibre

	6–8 portions
chicken breasts	2 large approx 150 g (6 oz) each
duck breasts	1 large approx 150 g (6 oz)
chicken livers, trimmed	100 g (4 oz)
brandy	62 ml (⅛ pt)
rosemary leaves, finely chopped	¼ tsp
bay leaf	1
orange zest	2 dried strips
streaky bacon	10–12 slices
seasoning	
Mousse **chicken livers**	100 g (4 oz)
port	100 ml (³⁄₁₆ pt)
brandy	62 ml (⅛ pt)
shallot, finely chopped	25 g (1 oz)
garlic, crushed and chopped	2 cloves
egg	1
butter	50 g (2 oz)

1 Carefully prepare the chicken breasts, removing all the sinews.

2 Slice each chicken breast into two and the duck breast into four.

3 Prepare the chicken livers, remove all traces of green.

4 Marinade chicken livers, duck and chicken breasts in the brandy, rosemary, bay leaf, orange zest and season.
Allow to marinade in a refrigerator for 24 hours.

5 Prepare the mousse.
In a saucepan reduce the port and brandy with the shallot and garlic until almost dry. Place in a food processor with the chicken livers, purée until smooth.

6 Add the egg and butter, purée until smooth and light.

7 Place through a fine sieve.

8 Prepare the terrine mould 15 cm × 6 cm (6 inch × 2½ inch)

9 Place a layer of mousse in the bottom of terrine.

10 Place on top one piece of chicken and one piece of duck.

11 Cover with another layer of mousse and another piece of chicken and duck.

12 Cover with mousse again, then all the remaining chicken livers.

13 Layer up with the remaining chicken, duck and mousse, alternating the position of the dark and light meats each time to create a mosaic effect.

14 Finish with the last of the mousse, fold the streaky bacon over, then wrap the cling film over the top.

15 Cover with foil and cook in an oven in a bain-marie of water or in a combination oven with

continued over ▶

▶ *Duck and chicken terrine continued*

steam injection 150°C, 300°F for approximately 1¼ hours, until the blade of a small knife comes out warm from the centre.

16 When the terrine is cooked, transfer to a bain-marie of cold water or a blast chiller. First press down the foil, place a sheet of foil covered cardboard on top of the terrine, press down with a 500 g weight (1¼ lb) during chilling.

17 Keep refrigerated until required.

18 Serve sliced, garnished with salad leaves and a suitable chutney and warm brioche.

Fig 5.4 🪶 Duck and chicken terrine

John Campbell

25 Potted meats

1 of 4 portions provides:
1160 kJ/280 kcal energy
23.8 g fat
(of which 14.5 g saturated)
0.2 g carbohydrate
(of which 0.2 g sugars)
16.4 g protein
0.0 g fibre

cooked meat e.g. beef, salt beef, or tongue, venison, chicken	200 g (8 oz)
clarified butter	100 g (4 oz)
salt, pepper and mace	

HEALTHY EATING TIP

Keep the added salt to a minimum. Serve with plenty of salad vegetables and bread or toast (optional butter or spread)

1 Using an electric blender or chopper reduce the meat, seasoning and 3 oz butter to a paste.

2 Pack firmly into an earthenware or china pot and refrigerate until firm.

3 Cover with 1 cm (¼ inch) of clarified butter and refrigerate.

4 Serve with a small tossed green salad and hot toast.

Note: Chicken can also be combined in equal quantities with the other meats, e.g. chicken and ham.

26 Potted shrimps

Potted shrimps are freshly cooked and peeled shrimps mixed with warmed butter and a little spice, chiefly mace, served in small dishes. Ready prepared commercial potted shrimps are available. Potted shrimps have a better flavour when served warm, accompanied by thin toast or brown bread and butter.

All these fruit dishes and juices contribute to the recommended '5 portions of fruit and vegetables per day'. Include them as often as possible on the menu.

27 Grapefruit

Pamplemousse

These are halved crosswise, not through the stalk, the segments individually cut with a small knife, then chilled. Serve with a maraschino cherry in the centre. The common practice of sprinkling with caster sugar is incorrect, as some customers prefer their grapefruit without sugar. Serve half a grapefruit per portion in a coupe. Grapefruit may also be served hot sprinkled with rum and demerera sugar.

28 Grapefruit cocktail

The fruit should be peeled with a sharp knife in order to remove all the white pith and yellow skin. Cut into segments and remove all the pips. The segments and the juice should then be dressed in a cocktail glass or grapefruit coupe and chilled. A cherry may be added. Allow ½–1 grapefruit per head.

Variations include:

- *Grapefruit and orange cocktail*, allowing half an orange and half a grapefruit per head.

- *Orange cocktail*, using oranges in place of grapefruit.

- *Florida cocktail*, a mixture of grapefruit, orange and pineapple segments.

29 Avocado pear

L'avocat

The pears must be ripe (test by pressing gently, the pear should give slightly).

Serve with plenty of salad vegetables and bread or toast (optional butter or spread).

1 Cut it in half length-wise. Remove the stone.
2 Serve garnished with lettuce accompanied by vinaigrette (page 92) or variations on vinaigrette.

Note: Avocado pears are sometimes filled with shrimps or crabmeat bound with a shellfish cocktail sauce or other similar fillings, and may be served hot or cold using a variety of fillings and sauces.

Avocado pear may also be halved lengthwise, the stone removed, the skin peeled and the pear sliced and fanned onto a plate. Garnish with a simple or composed salad. Allow half a pear per portion.

Fig 5.5 ✒ Preparation of avocado pear

30 Fruit cocktail

This is a mixture of fruits such as apples, pears, pineapples, grapes, cherries, etc., washed, peeled and cut into neat segments or dice and added to a syrup (100 g (4 oz) sugar to ¼ litre (½ pint) water) and the juice of half a lemon. Neatly place in cocktail glasses and chill. Allow ½ kg (1 lb) unprepared fruit for 4 portions, 1¼ kg (2½ lb) for 10.

Variations include a tropical fruit cocktail, which uses a variety of tropical fruits, such as mango, passion fruit, lychees, pineapple, kiwi fruit.

31 Melon cocktail

The melon, which must be ripe, is peeled, then cut into neat segments or dice or scooped out with a parisienne spoon, dressed in cocktail glasses and chilled. A little liqueur, such as crème de menthe or maraschino, may also be added. Allow approximately half a melon for 4 portions, 1½ for 10.

32 Chilled melon

> 1 portion provides:
> 82 kJ/20 kcal
> 0.0 g fat
> (of which 0.0 g saturated)
> 4.7 g carbohydrate
> (of which 4.7 g sugars)
> 0.6 g protein
> 0.9 g fibre

Fig 5.6 a–c 🖎 Preparation of grapefruit, orange and Florida cocktails

Fig 5.7 🖎 Clockwise from top-left: half grapefruit; orange cocktail; Florida cocktail; orange cocktail in coupe

Cut the melon in half, remove the pips and cut it into thick slices. Cut a piece off the skin so that the slice will stand firm and serve on crushed ice. Use caster sugar and ground ginger as accompaniments. Allow approximately half a honeydew or cantaloup melon for 4 portions.

Tropical fruit plate (without accompaniments)

See page 529.

33 Fruit juices

These can be bought ready prepared, but may be made from the fresh fruit, e.g. pineapple, orange or grapefruit.

34 Tomato juice

Jus de tomate

1 portion provides:
74 kJ/18 kcal
0.0 g fat
(of which 0.0 g saturated)
3.5 g carbohydrate
(of which 3.5 g sugars)
1.1 g protein
0.0 g fibre

Fresh ripe tomatoes must be used. Wash them, remove the eyes, then liquidise and pass them through a strainer. The juice is then served in cocktail glasses and chilled. Offer Worcester sauce when serving. Use ½ kg (1 lb) tomatoes for 4 portions, 1¼ kg (2½ lb) for 10.

35 Shellfish cocktails: crab, lobster, shrimp, prawn

Cocktail de crabe, homard, crevettes, crevettes roses

	4 portions	**10 portions**
lettuce	½	1½
prepared shellfish	100–150 g (4–6 oz)	250–350 g (10–15 oz)
shellfish cocktail sauce	125 ml (¼ pt)	300 ml (⅝ pt)

1   Wash, drain well and finely shred the lettuce, avoiding long strands.
2   Place about 2 cm (1 inch) deep in cocktail glasses or dishes.
3   Add the prepared shellfish:
    - crab (shredded white meat only);
    - lobster (cut in 2 cm (¼ inch) dice);
    - shrimps (peeled and washed);
    - prawns (peeled, washed, and if large cut into two or three pieces).
4   Coat with sauce.
5   Decorate with an appropriate piece of the content, such as a prawn with the shell on the tail removed, on the edge of the glass of a prawn cocktail.

Shellfish cocktail sauce

Method I

Keep added salt to a minimum. Extend the high fat mayonnaise with low fat yoghurt to proportionally reduce the fat content.

	4 portions	**10 portions**
egg yolk (pasteurised)	1	3
vinegar	1 tsp	2½ tsp
salt, pepper, mustard		
olive oil or sunflower oil	5 tbsp	12 tbsp
tomato juice or ketchup to taste	3 tbsp	8 tbsp
Worcester sauce (optional)	2–3 drops	6–8 drops

Make the mayonnaise with the egg yolk, vinegar, seasonings and oil. Combine with the tomato juice and Worcester sauce (if using).

Method II

lightly whipped cream or unsweetened non-dairy cream	5 tbsp	12 tbsp
tomato juice or ketchup to taste	3 tbsp	8 tbsp
salt, pepper		
few drops of lemon juice		

> 1 portion provides:
> 889 kJ/216 kcal energy
> 22.7 g fat
> (of which 14.2 g saturated)
> 1.9 g carbohydrate
> (of which 1.9 g sugars)
> 1.2 g protein
> 0.1 g fibre

Mix all the ingredients together. Fresh or tinned tomato juice or diluted tomato ketchup may be used for both the above methods, but the use of tinned tomato purée gives an unpleasant flavour.

36 Soused herring or mackerel

	4 portions	10 portions
herrings or mackerel	2	5
salt, pepper		
button onions	25 g (1 oz)	60 g (2½ oz)
carrots, peeled and fluted	25 g (1 oz)	60 g (2½ oz)
bay leaf	½	1½
peppercorns	6	12
thyme	1 sprig	2 sprigs
vinegar	60 ml (⅛ pt)	150 ml (⅓ pt)

> This recipe provides for 4 portions:
> 2419 kJ/576 kcal
> 44.5 g fat
> (of which 9.4 g saturated)
> 3.0 g carbohydrate
> (of which 3.0 g sugars)
> 41.0 g protein
> 1.1 g fibre

> *HEALTHY EATING TIP*
> Serve with plenty of salad vegetables and bread or toast (optional butter or spread).
> Keep the added salt to a minimum.

1 Clean, scale and fillet the fish.
2 Wash the fillets well and season with salt and pepper.
3 Roll up with the skin outside. Place in an earthenware dish.
4 Peel and wash the onion. Cut the onion and carrot into neat thin rings.
5 Blanch for 2–3 minutes.
6 Add to the fish with the remainder of the ingredients.
7 Cover with greaseproof paper and cook in a moderate oven for 15–20 minutes.
8 Allow to cool, place in a dish with the onion and carrot.
9 Garnish with picked parsley, dill or chives.

HEALTHY EATING TIP

Serve with plenty of
salad vegetables and
bread or toast
(optional butter or
spread)
Use minimum
amounts of salt.

37 Smoked mackerel mousse

	4 portions	10 portions
smoked mackerel, free from bone and skin	200 g (8 oz)	500 g (1¼ lb)
optional seasoning: pepper, chopped parsley, fennel or chervil, 1 tbsp tomato ketchup, two ripe tomatoes free from skin and pips		
double cream (or non-dairy cream)	90 ml (3½ fl oz)	250 ml (½ pt)

1   Ensure that the mackerel is completely free from skin and bones.
2   Liquidise with required seasoning.
3   Three quarter whip the cream.
4   Remove mackerel from liquidiser and fold into the cream. Correct the seasoning.
5   Serve in individual dishes accompanied with hot toast.

Note: This recipe can be used with smoked trout or smoked salmon trimmings. It can also be used for fresh salmon, in which case 50 g (2 oz) of cucumber can be incorporated with the selected seasoning.

Assorted hors-d'oeuvre

The following recipes may be served in four ways unless otherwise indicated:

(A)   as a single hors-d'oeuvre; (1st course)

(B)   as part of a composite hors-d'oeuvre;

(C)   as a main course, when it will be suitably garnished with salad items;

(D)   as an accompaniment to a main course.

38 Tartare of smoked haddock (A)

	4 portions	10 portions
smoked haddock (free from bone and skin, and diced)	300 g (12 oz)	150 g (6 oz)
cucumber, (peeled, seeded and finely diced)	50 g (2 oz)	125 g (5 oz)
new potatoes, (cooked and diced)	50 g (2 oz)	125 g (5 oz)
chopped parsley		
mayonnaise, cream or natural yoghurt	60 ml (⅛ pt)	125 ml (¼ pt)
salt, cayenne, lemon juice		
avocado, full ripe	2	5
plum tomatoes, peeled, de-seeded, diced	50 g (2 oz)	125 g (5 oz)
mixed salad, vinaigrette dressing	50 g (2 oz)	125 g (5 oz)

1 portion provides:
1471 kJ/354 kcal energy
28.8 g fat
(of which 5.3 g saturated)
4.8 g carbohydrate
(of which 1.6 g sugars)
19.5 g protein
2.9 g fibre

HEALTHY EATING TIP

Try using half mayonnaise and half natural yogurt/fromage frais. The smoked haddock is high in salt, no added salt is necessary.
Serve with bread or toast, butter optional.

1   Mix haddock, cucumber, potatoes, parsley, mayonnaise and season lightly.

2   Place into moulds, set into centre of plates, remove moulds.

3   Peel avocado, cut in halves, remove stones, slice and lightly sprinkle with lemon juice to prevent discoloration.

4   Arrange the avocado in a fan around the base of the tartare.

5   Sprinkle the tomato around the plates.

6   Garnish the tops with lightly dressed salad and serve.

Variations: Layers of creamed horseradish and tomato chutney can be placed in the tartare. Sieved hard-boiled egg can be sprinkled on. A few chives can be used as garnish.

Fig 5.8   Tartare of smoked haddock, adapted from a recipe by Henry Brosi

1 portion provides:
763 kJ/182 kcal
15.7 g fat
(of which 3.4 g saturated)
2.4 g carbohydrate
(of which 2.4 g sugars)
8.1 g protein
1.6 g fibre

HEALTHY EATING TIP

Thin the mayonnaise to coat the eggs. Serve with plenty of bread or toast and salad garnish (offer butter separately).

39 Egg mayonnaise (A, B or C)

Oeuf mayonnaise

To cook hard-boiled eggs, place the eggs in boiling water; reboil and simmer for 8–10 minutes. Refresh until cold.

Note: When started in cold water cook for 12 minutes. If the eggs are overcooked, iron in the yolk and sulphur compounds in the white are released to form the blackish ring (ferrous sulphide) around the yolk. This will also occur if the eggs are not refreshed immediately they are cooked.

As part of a selection for hors-d'oeuvre
Cut the hard-boiled eggs in quarters or slices, dress neatly and coat with mayonnaise.

As an individual hors-d'oeuvre
Allow one hard-boiled egg per portion, cut in half and dress on a leaf of lettuce; coat with mayonnaise and garnish with quarters of tomatoes and slices of cucumber.

As a main dish
Allow two hard-boiled eggs per portion, cut in halves and dress on a plate, coat with mayonnaise sauce. Surround with a portion of lettuce, tomato, cucumber, potato salad, beetroot or coleslaw.

40 Seafood and French bean salad with roasted garlic mustard vinaigrette (A)

	4 portions	10 portions
prawns, cooked, shelled, deveined	8	20
mussels, large cooked, debearded	8	20
scallops, poached, sliced	4	10
cooked lobster	4 slices	10 slices
artichoke bottoms	2	5
french beans, blanched	100 g (4 oz)	250 g (10 oz)
mixed leaves, raddiccio, rocket, lamb's lettuce, watercress		
chopped tarragon	1 tbsp	2½ tbsp
Roasted garlic mustard vinaigrette ***seasoning***		
garlic bulb ⎫	1	2½
milk ⎬ roasted garlic purée	250 ml (½ pt)	625 ml (1¼ pt)
olive oil ⎭	125 ml (¼ pt)	312 ml (⅝ pt)
dijon mustard	1 tsp	
rice wine vinegar	2 tbsp	
olive oil	6 tbsp	

Using approx 170 g lobster meat, 1 portion provides:
3465 kJ/839 kcal energy
81.7 g fat
(of which 12.3 g saturated)
6.9 g carbohydrate
(of which 4.3 g sugars)
19.6 g protein
1.0 g fibre

HEALTHY EATING TIP
Keep the amount of added salt to a minimum.
Serve with a large portion of starchy carbohydrate – bread or new potatoes.

1   First prepare the roasted garlic purée. Peel the garlic bulb, simmer in the milk for 10 minutes. Drain, discard the milk. Place the garlic in a small roasting tray, add the olive oil.

2   Bake in a hot oven at 350°F until the garlic is soft. This will take approximately 1 hour.

3   Once soft, purée until smooth.

4   Mix in the Dijon mustard, rice vinegar and the olive oil, season. The vinaigrette is now ready to use.

5   Prepare the salad by carefully tossing together the seafood, artichoke bottoms, French beans and tarragon.

6   Sprinkle with the vinaigrette, then season.

7   Serve on a bed of mixed leaves, drizzle the plate with some additional vinaigrette.

continued over ▶

▶ *Seafood and French bean salad continued*

Alternatively

Other types of seafood may also be included and others omitted, such as shrimps, scallops, squid, oysters etc.

Asparagus, mushrooms and mange-tout may also be included in the salad.

Using mayonnaise, this recipe provides for 4 portions:
2013 kJ/479 kcal
34.9 g fat
(of which 5.1 g saturated)
40.0 g carbohydrate
(of which 1.3 g sugars)
4.0 g protein
2.6 g fibre

41 Potato salad (B or D)

Salade de pommes de terre

	4 portions	10 portions
cooked potatoes	200 g (8 oz)	500 g (1½ lb)
vinaigrette, salt, pepper	1 tbsp	2½ tbsp
chopped onion or chive (optional)	10 g (½ oz)	25g (1 oz)
mayonnaise or natural yoghurt	125 ml (¼ pt)	300 ml (⅜ pt)
chopped parsley or mixed fresh herbs		

1 Cut the potatoes in ½–1 cm (¼–½ inch) dice; sprinkle with vinaigrette.

2 Mix with the onion or chive, add the mayonnaise and correct the seasoning. (The onion may be blanched to reduce the harshness.)

3 Dress neatly and sprinkle with chopped parsley.

Note: Not usually a single hors-d'oeuvre or main course. Potato salad can also be made by dicing raw peeled or unpeeled potato, cooking them preferably by steaming (to retain shape) and mixing with vinaigrette whilst warm.

Variation includes the addition of 2 chopped hard-boiled eggs, or 100 g (4 oz) of peeled dessert apple mixed with lemon juice, or a small bunch of picked watercress leaves.

Cooked small new potatoes tossed in vinaigrette with chopped fresh herbs (mint, parsley, chive).

42 Vegetable salad (Russian salad) (B)

Salade de légumes (salade russe)

	4 portions	10 portions
carrots	100 g (4 oz)	250 g (10 oz)
turnips	50 g (2 oz)	125 g (5 oz)
French beans	50 g (2 oz)	125 g (5 oz)
peas	50 g (2 oz)	125 g (5 oz)
vinaigrette	1 tbsp	2–3 tbsp
mayonnaise or natural yoghurt	125 ml (¼ pt)	300 ml (⅝ pt)
salt, pepper		

1   Peel and wash the carrots and turnips, cut into ½ cm (¼ inch) dice or batons.

2   Cook separately in salted water, refresh and drain well.

3   Top and tail the beans, and cut in ½ cm (¼ inch) dice; cook, refresh and drain well.

4   Cook the peas, refresh and drain well.

5   Mix all the well-drained vegetables with vinaigrette and then mayonnaise.

6   Correct the seasoning. Dress neatly.

Using mayonnaise, this recipe provides for 4 portions:
1566 kJ/373 kcal
35.0 g fat
(of which 5.2 g saturated)
10.1 g carbohydrate
(of which 8.2 g sugars)
5.0 g protein
11.9 g fibre

HEALTHY EATING TIP

Try half mayonnaise and half natural yoghurt. Season with a minimum amount of salt.

43 Fish salad (A, B or C)

Salade de poisson

	4 portions	10 portions
cooked fish (free from skin and bone)	200 g (8 oz)	500 g (1¼ lb)
hard-boiled egg	1	2–3
cucumber (optional)	50 g (2 oz)	125 g (5 oz)
chopped parsley or fennel		
salt, pepper		
vinaigrette	1 tbsp	2–3 tbsp
lettuce	½	1

1   Flake the fish. Cut the egg and cucumber in ½ cm (¼ inch) dice.

2   Finely shred the lettuce. Mix ingredients together, add the parsley.

3   Correct the seasoning. Mix with the vinaigrette.

4   May be decorated with lettuce, anchovies and capers.

This recipe provides for 4 portions:
978 kJ/233 kcal
13.5 g fat
(of which 3.0 g saturated)
1.5 g carbohydrate
(of which 1.4 g sugars)
26.4 g protein
1.3 g fibre

HEALTHY EATING TIP

Use salt sparingly.

This recipe provides for 4 portions:
1616 kJ/385 kcal
15.2 g fat
(of which 4.8 g saturated)
2.7 g carbohydrate
(of which 2.5 g sugars)
59.7 g protein
2.7 g fibre

HEALTHY EATING TIP

The 'balance' of this dish is improved with less meat, more vegetables and a light dressing.

44 Meat salad (A, B or C)

Salade de viande

	4 portions	10 portions
cooked lean meat	200 g (8 oz)	500 g (1¼ lb)
gherkins	25 g (1 oz)	60 g (2½ oz)
cooked French beans	50 g (2 oz)	125 g (5 oz)
tomatoes	50 g (2 oz)	125 g (5 oz)
chopped onion or chives (optional)	5 g (¼ oz)	12 g (⅝ oz)
vinaigrette	1 tbsp	2½ tbsp
chopped parsley or mixed fresh herbs		

1 Cut the meat, gherkins and beans in ½ cm (¼ inch) dice.
2 Skin tomatoes, de-seed and cut into ½ cm (¼ inch) dice.
3 Mix with remainder of the ingredients, blanching the onions if required.
4 Correct the seasoning. Dress neatly.
5 Decorate with lettuce leaves, tomatoes and fans of gherkins.

Note: Well-cooked braised or boiled meat is ideal for this salad.

45 Beetroot

Wash and cook the beetroot in a steamer or in gently simmering water till tender (test by skinning), cool and peel. Cut into ½ cm (¼ inch) dice or ½ × 1 cm (¼ × ½ inch) batons. Beetroot may be served plain or with vinegar or sprinkled with vinaigrette, not as a main course.

1 portion provides:
134 kJ/32 kcal energy
2.0 g fat
(of which 0.3 g saturated)
3.2 g carbohydrate
(of which 3.1 g sugars)
0.7 g protein
0.9 g fibre

46 Beetroot salad (B)

Salade de betterave

	4 portions	10 portions
neatly cut or sliced beetroot	200 g (8 oz)	500 g (1¼ lb)
chopped parsley		
chopped onion or chive (optional)	10 g (½ oz)	25 g (1 oz)
vinaigrette	1 tbsp	2½ tbsp

1 Combine all the ingredients, blanching the onion if required.
2 Dress neatly. Sprinkle with chopped parsley.

Note: Variations include addition of 60–120 ml (⅛–¼ pint) mayonnaise or natural yoghurt in place of vinaigrette (150–200 ml (⅓–½ pint) for 10 portions).

47 Cucumber

Peel the cucumber if desired; cut into thin slices and dress neatly. Not as a single hors-d'oeuvre or main course.

48 Cucumber salad (B or D)

Salade de concombres

	4 portions	10 portions
cucumber	½	1¼
chopped parsley or mixed fresh herbs		
vinaigrette	1 tbsp	2½ tbsp

1   Peel and slice the cucumber. Sprinkle with vinaigrette and parsley.

To remove indigestible juices from the cucumber, slice and lightly sprinkle with salt. Allow the salt to draw out the water for approximately 1 hour, wash well under cold water and drain. This will make the cucumber limp.

Alternatively, cucumber may be diced ½ cm (¼ inch) and bound with mayonnaise or yoghurt.

49 Tomato

Tomate

If of good quality, the tomatoes need not be skinned. Wash, remove the eyes, slice thinly or cut into segments. Dress neatly.

50 Tomato salad (A or B)

Salade de tomates

	4 portions	10 portions
tomatoes	200 g (8 oz)	500 g (1¼ lb)
lettuce	¼	½
vinaigrette	1 tbsp	2½ tbsp
chopped onion or chive (optional)	10 g (½ oz)	25 g (1 oz)
chopped parsley or mixed fresh herbs		

1   Peel tomatoes if required. Slice thinly. Arrange neatly on lettuce leaves.
2   Sprinkle with vinaigrette, onion (blanched if required), and parsley.

Variation: alternate slices of tomato and mozzarella with basic dressing.

HEALTHY EATING TIP

All vegetable-based salads are a healthy way to start a meal. Lightly dress with vinaigrette or serve separately. Add a minimum amount of salt.

1 portion provides:
91 kJ/22 kcal energy
2.0 g fat
(of which 0.3 g saturated)
1.0 g carbohydrate
(of which 0.9 g sugars)
0.4 g protein
0.3 g fibre

This recipe provides for 4 portions:
394 kJ/94 kcal
6.6 g fat
(of which 1.1 g saturated)
6.7 g carbohydrate
(of which 6.6 g sugars)
2.5 g protein
3.9 g fibre

51 Tomato and cucumber salad (A, B or C)

Salade de tomates et concombres

	4 portions	10 portions
tomatoes	2	5
cucumber	¼	½
vinaigrette	1 tbsp	2½ tbsp
chopped parsley or mixed fresh herbs		

1. Alternate slices of tomato and cucumber.
2. Sprinkle with vinaigrette and parsley.

1 portion provides:
112 kJ/27 kcal energy
2.0 g fat
(of which 0.3 g saturated)
1.9 g carbohydrate
(of which 1.8 g sugars)
0.5 g protein
0.6 g fibre

52 Rice salad (B or D)

Salade de riz

	4 portions	10 portions
tomatoes	100 g (4 oz)	250 g (10 oz)
cooked rice	100 g (4 oz)	250 g (10 oz)
peas, cooked	50 g (2 oz)	125 g (5 oz)
vinaigrette	1 tbsp	2½ tbsp
salt, pepper		

1. Skin and de-seed tomatoes; cut in ½ cm (¼ inch) dice.
2. Mix with the rice and peas.
3. Add the vinaigrette and correct the seasoning.

This recipe provides for 4 portions:
906 kJ/216 kcal
6.9 g fat
(of which 1.1 g saturated)
34.6 g carbohydrate
(of which 3.3 g sugars)
5.9 g protein
8.3 g fibre

HEALTHY EATING TIP
This dish is high in starchy carbohydrate and can be varied with different/additional vegetables. Lightly dress with vinaigrette and add salt sparingly.

53 Celeriac (B)

Céleri-rave

	4 portions	10 portions
celeriac	200 g (8 oz)	500 g (1¼ oz)
lemon	½	1
English or continental mustard	1 level tsp	2½ level tsp
salt, pepper		
mayonnaise, cream or natural yoghurt	125 ml (¼ pt)	300 ml (⅝ pt)

1 portion provides:
938 kJ/228 kcal energy
24.0 g fat
(of which 3.9 g saturated)
2.0 g carbohydrate
(of which 1.6 g sugars)
1.1 g protein
1.9 g fibre

HEALTHY EATING TIP
Try using some yoghurt in place of mayonnaise/cream which will proportionally reduce the fat.
Keep the added salt to a minimum.

1   Wash and peel celeriac. Cut into fine julienne.

2   Combine with remoulade juice and remainder of the ingredients.

Other uses: as an accompaniment to pâté or terrine either as above or mixed with remoulade sauce (page 95).

54   French bean salad (B)

Salade de haricots verts

	4 portions	10 portions
cooked French beans	200 g (8 oz)	500 g (1¼ lb)
vinaigrette	1 tbsp	3 tbsp
salt, pepper		

Combine all the ingredients.

> 1 portion provides:
> 125 kJ/30 kcal energy
> 1.9 g fat
> (of which 0.3 g sugars)
> 2.5 g carbohydrate
> (of which 1.2 g sugars)
> 0.9 g protein
> 2.0 g fibre

> *HEALTHY EATING TIP*
> Lightly dress with vinaigrette and add salt sparingly.

55   Niçoise salad (A, B or C)

	4 portions	10 portions
tomatoes	100 g (4 oz)	250 g (10 oz)
cooked French beans	200 g (8 oz)	500 g (1¼ lb)
cooked diced potatoes	100 g (4 oz)	250 g (10 oz)
salt, pepper		
vinaigrette	1 tbsp	2½ tbsp
anchovy fillets	10 oz (½ oz)	25 g (1 oz)
capers	5 g (¼ oz)	12 g (⅝ oz)
stoned olives	10 g (¼ oz)	25 g (1 oz)

> This recipe provides for 4 portions:
> 867 kJ/207 kcal
> 9.6 g fat
> (of which 1.5 g saturated)
> 25.0 g carbohydrate
> (of which 4.9 g sugars)
> 6.9 g protein
> 9.9 g fibre

> *HEALTHY EATING TIP*
> Lightly dress with vinaigrette. The anchovies are high in salt, so no added salt is necessary.

1   Peel tomatoes, de-seed and cut into neat segments.

2   Dress the beans, tomatoes and potatoes neatly.

3   Season with salt and pepper. Add the vinaigrette.

4   Decorate with anchovies, capers and olives.

56   Waldorf salad (A, B or C)

Celery or celeriac and crisp russet apples diced and mixed with shelled and peeled walnuts, bound with a mayonnaise and dressed on quarters or leaves of lettuce. This may also be served in hollowed-out apples.

> *HEALTHY EATING TIP*
> Try using some yoghurt in place of mayonnaise, which will proportionally reduce the fat. Keep the added salt to a minimum.

57 Haricot bean salad (B)

Salade de haricots blancs

	4 portions	10 portions
haricot beans, cooked	200 g (8 oz)	500 g (1¼ lb)
vinaigrette	1 tbsp	2½ tbsp
chopped parsley		
chopped onion, blanched if required, or chive (optional)	10 g (½ oz)	25 g (1 oz)
salt, pepper		

Combine all the ingredients. This recipe can be used for any type of dried bean (see page 463).

58 Three-bean salad (B)

Use 200 g (½ lb) (500 g (1¼ lb) for 10 portions) of three different dried beans (red kidney, black-eyed, flageolet, etc.). Proceed as for recipe 57.

59 Lentil and goat's cheese salad (A)

	4 portions	10 portions
puy lentils	100 g (4 oz)	250 g (10 oz)
bay leaf	1	3
spring onions, finely chopped	4	10
red pepper, finely chopped	1	3
chopped parsley	1 tbsp	3 tbsp
cherry tomatoes sliced in half	400 g (1 lb)	1 kg (2½ lb)
rocket leaves	200 g (8 oz)	500 g (1 lb 4 oz)
goat's cheese	100 g (4 oz)	250 g (10 oz)
Dressing **olive oil**	1 tbsp	2½ tbsp
balsamic vinegar	1 tbsp	2½ tbsp
clear honey	2 tbsp	5 tbsp
garlic clove, crushed and chopped	1	3

HEALTHY EATING TIP

Lightly dress with vinaigrette and add salt sparingly.

HEALTHY EATING TIP

This dish provides a 'healthy balanced' starter.

1   Rinse the lentils and place in a saucepan. Add the bay leaf, cover with water, bring to boil, simmer for 20–30 minutes until tender.

2   Drain, place in a bowl. Add the spring onions, red pepper, parsley and cherry tomatoes, mix well.

3   Whisk together in a bowl, oil, vinegar, honey, garlic and stir into the lentils. Serve on a bed of rocket, with the goat's cheese sprinkled over.

60 Coleslaw (B, D)

	4 portions	10 portions
mayonnaise, natural yoghurt or fromage frais	125 ml (¼ pt)	300 ml (⅝ pt)
white or Chinese cabbage	200 g (8 oz)	500 g (1¼ lb)
carrot	50 g (2 oz)	125 g (5 oz)
onion (optional)	25 g (1 oz)	60 g (2½ oz)

Using mayonnaise, this recipe provides for 4 portions:
2514 kJ/599 kcal
59.0 g fat
(of which 8.8 g saturated)
11.7 g carbohydrate
(of which 11.4 g sugars)
5.9 g protein
7.2 g fibre

HEALTHY EATING TIP

Replace some or all of the mayonnaise with natural yoghurt and/or fromage frais. Add salt sparingly.

1   Trim off the outside leaves of the cabbage.

2   Cut into quarters. Remove the centre stalk.

3   Wash the cabbage, shred finely and drain well.

4   Mix with a fine julienne of raw carrot and shredded raw onion. To lessen the harshness of raw onion, blanch and refresh.

5   Bind with mayonnaise sauce, natural yoghurt or vinaigrette.

61 Couscous salad with roasted vegetables and mixed herbs (A, B, C or D)

	4 portions	10 portions
couscous	250 g (10 oz)	625 g (1½ lb)
balsamic vinegar	1 tbsp	2½ tbsp
olive oil	3 tbsp	8 tbsp
lemon juice	¼ lemon	1 lemon
seasoning		
fresh mint, chopped	½ tsp	1¼ tsp
fresh coriander, chopped	½ tsp	1¼ tsp
fresh thyme, chopped	½ tsp	1¼ tsp

1 portion provides:
1248 kJ/300 kcal energy
12.5 g fat
(of which 1.7 g saturated)
42.2 g carbohydrate
(of which 8.6 g sugars)
6.6 g protein
3.8 g fibre

HEALTHY EATING TIP

Use an unsaturated oil and lightly brush the vegetables when roasting.
Use the minimum amount of salt.

1   Prepare the roasted vegetables as per page 455.

2   Place the couscous in a suitable bowl, gently pour over 300 ml (⅝ pt) of boiling water.

3   Stir well, cover and leave to stand for 5 minutes.

4   Separate the grains with a fork.

5   Add the balsamic vinegar, olive oil, lemon juice and seasoning.

continued over ▶

▶ *Couscous salad with roasted vegetables and mixed herbs continued*

6   Mix well, stir in the chopped herbs.

7   Finish by adding the roasted vegetables.

8   Serve in a suitable bowl or use individual plates.

For plated service arrange the couscous neatly in the centre of the plate, arrange the roasted vegetables around, then garnish with fresh herbs.

62 Florida salad (A or D)

Salade Florida

1   Remove the orange zest with a peeler.

2   Cut into fine julienne.

3   Blanch for 2–3 minutes and refresh.

4   Peel the oranges and remove all the white skin.

5   Cut into segments between the white pith and remove all the pips.

6   Dress the lettuce in a bowl, keeping it in quarters if possible.

7   Arrange 3 or 4 orange segments in each portion.

8   Sprinkle with a little orange zest.

9   Serve an acidulated cream dressing separately (cream mixed with a few drops of lemon juice).

Note: Allow ¼ lettuce and ½ large orange per portion.

Greek-style hors-d'oeuvre

All vegetables cooked *à la grecque* are cooked in the following liquid:

	4 portions	10 portions
water	250 ml (½ pt)	625 ml (1¼ pt)
olive oil	60 ml (⅛ pt)	150 ml (⅓ pt)
lemon, juice of	1	1½
bay leaf	½	1
sprig of thyme		
peppercorns	6	18
coriander seeds	6	18
salt		

63 Artichokes (B)

Artichauts à la grecque

Not all liquid included, 1 portion provides:
585 kJ/142 kcal energy
15.1 g fat
(of which 2.1 g saturated)
1.1 g carbohydrate
(of which 0.7 g sugars)
0.9 g protein
0.0 g fibre

1 Peel and trim six artichokes for 4 portions (15 for 10).

2 Cut the leaves short. Remove the chokes.

3 Blanch the artichokes in water with a little lemon juice for 10 minutes.

4 Refresh the artichokes. Place in cooking liquid. Simmer for 15–20 minutes.

5 Serve cold in a ravier with a little of the unstrained cooking liquid.

64 Onions (button) (B)

Oignons à la grecque

1 portion provides:
634 kJ/154 kcal energy
15.1 g fat
(of which 2.2 g saturated)
4.2 g carbohydrate
(of which 3.0 g sugars)
0.7 g protein
0.7 g fibre

HEALTHY EATING TIP

Use salt sparingly in the cooking liquid. Do not serve too much liquid with the finished dish. All these vegetable dishes are a healthy way to start a meal.

1 Peel and wash 200 g (8 oz) button onions for 4 portions (500 g (1¼ lb) for 10).

2 Blanch for approximately 5 minutes and refresh.

3 Place onions in the cooking liquor. Simmer till tender.

4 Serve cold with unstrained cooking liquor.

65 Cauliflower (B)

Chou-fleur à la grecque

1 portion provides:
687 kJ/167 kcal energy
15.8 g fat
(of which 2.3 g saturated)
2.9 g carbohydrate
(of which 2.5 g sugars)
3.3 g protein
1.6 g fibre

1 Trim and wash one medium cauliflower for 4 portions (2½ for 10).

2 Break into small sprigs about the size of a cherry.

3 Blanch for approximately 5 minutes and refresh.

4 Simmer in the cooking liquor for 5–10 minutes. Keep the cauliflower slightly undercooked, and crisp.

5 Serve cold with unstrained cooking liquor.

66 Leeks (B)

Poireaux à la grecque

This recipe provides for 4 portions:
2641 kJ/639 kcal
60.0 g fat
(of which 8.4 g saturated)
19.3 g carbohydrate
(of which 19.3 g sugars)
7.6 g protein
16.4 g fibre

1 Trim and clean ½ kg (1 lb) leeks for 4 portions (1¼ kg (2½ lb) for 10).

2 Tie into a neat bundle.

3 Blanch for approximately 5 minutes and refresh.

4 Cut into 2 cm (1 inch) lengths and place in a shallow pan.

5 Cover with the cooking liquor. Simmer until tender.

6 Serve cold with unstrained cooking liquor.

67 Mushrooms (B)

Champignons à la grecque

> 1 portion provides:
> 587 kJ/142 kcal energy
> 15.2 g fat
> (of which 2.2 g saturated)
> 0.4 g carbohydrate
> (of which 0.3 g sugars)
> 1.0 g protein
> 0.6 g fibre

1 Allow 200 g (8 oz) of small, cleaned, white button mushrooms for 4 portions.

2 Cook gently in the cooking liquor for 3 to 4 minutes.

3 Serve cold with the unstrained liquor.

Portuguese-style hors-d'oeuvre

All the vegetables prepared in the Greek style may also be prepared in the Portuguese style. They are prepared and blanched in the same way then cooked in the following liquid:

	4 portions	**10 portions**
onion, chopped	1	2½
olive oil	1 tbsp	2½ tbsp
tomatoes	400 g (1 lb)	1¼ kg (2½ lb)
garlic	1 clove	1½ cloves
bay leaf	½	3
chopped parsley		
sprig of thyme		
tomato purée	25 g (1 oz)	60 g (2½ oz)
salt, pepper		

1 Sweat the onion in the oil.

2 Skin and de-seed the tomatoes. Roughly chop.

3 Add to the onion with the remainder of the ingredients.

4 Correct the seasoning.

5 Add the vegetables and simmer until tender, with the exception of cauliflower, which should be left crisp.

6 Serve hot or cold with the unstrained cooking liquor.

Salad leaves and vegetables

As these are eaten raw they may contain live food-poisoning bacteria and must be thoroughly washed to remove any soil. Watercress as the name suggests is grown in water and, as there is always the danger that the water may have been polluted, the watercress must also be thoroughly washed in clean water.

68 Celery

Céleri

Trim and thoroughly wash the celery. Remove any discoloured outer stalks. Serve stalks whole or cut into strips.

69 Chicory

Endive belge

Trim off the root end. Cut into 1 cm (½ inch) lengths, wash well and drain.

Fig 5.9 Mixed salad

70 Curled chicory

Endive frisée

Thoroughly wash and trim off the stalk. Drain well.

71 Lettuce and iceberg lettuce

Laitue

Trim off the root and remove the outside leaves. Wash thoroughly and drain well. The outer leaves can be pulled off and the hearts cut into quarters.

72 Cos lettuce

Laitue romaine

Trim off the root end and remove the outside leaves. Wash thoroughly and drain well. Cut into quarters.

73 Mustard and cress

Trim off the stalk ends of the cress. Wash well and lift out of the water so as to leave the seed cases behind. Drain well.

74 Radishes

Radis

The green stems should be trimmed to about 2 cm (1 inch) long, the root end cut off. Wash well, drain and dress neatly.

75 Rocket

A small leafed, sharp, peppery tasting salad. Trim, wash well and drain.

76 Watercress

Cresson

Trim off the stalk ends, discard any discoloured leaves, thoroughly wash and drain.

77 Mixed salad

Salade panachée

Neatly arrange in a salad bowl. A typical mixed salad would consist of lettuce, tomato, cucumber, watercress, radishes, etc. Almost any kind of salad vegetable can be used. Offer a vinaigrette separately (see page 92).

78 Green salad

Salade verte

Any of the green salads, lettuce, cos lettuce, lamb's lettuce (also known as corn salad or mâche), curled chicory, or any combination of green salads may be used, and a few leaves of radicchio. Neatly arrange in a salad bowl; serve with vinaigrette separately.

79 French salad

Salade française

The usual ingredients are lettuce, tomato and cucumber, but these may be varied with other salad vegetables, in some cases with quarters of egg. A vinaigrette made with French mustard (French dressing) should be offered.

Fig 5.10 Salmon prepared for poaching

Fig 5.11 🖋 Dressed cold salmon

Cooking and presentation of cold fish

80 Cooking of salmon

Salmon may be obtained in varying weights from 3½–15 kg (7–30 lb): ½ kg (1 lb) uncleaned salmon yields 2–3 portions. Size is an important consideration, depending on whether the salmon is to be cooked whole or cut into darnes. A salmon of any size may be cooked whole. When required for darnes, a medium-sized salmon will be more suitable.

Fish cooking liquid (court bouillon)

	4 portions	**10 portions**
water	1 litre (2 pt)	2½ litres (5 pt)
salt	10 g (½ oz)	25 g (1 oz)
carrots (sliced)	50 g (2 oz)	125 g (5 oz)
bay leaf	1	2
parsley stalks	2–3	5–8
vinegar	60 ml (⅛ pt)	150 ml (⅓ pt)
peppercorns	6	15
onions (sliced)	50 g (2 oz)	125 g (5 oz)
sprig of thyme		

1 Simmer all the ingredients for 30–40 minutes.
2 Pass through a strainer, use as required.

Cooking of a whole salmon

1 Scrape off all scales with the back of a knife.
2 Remove all gills and clean out the head.
3 Remove the intestines and clear the blood from the backbone.
4 Trim off all fins. Wash well.
5 Place in a salmon kettle, cover with cold court bouillon.
6 Bring slowly to the boil, skim, then simmer gently.
7 Allow the following approximate simmering times:

- 3½ kg   (7 lb)   15 minutes
- 7 kg   (14 lb)   20 minutes
- 10½ kg (21 lb)   25 minutes
- 14 kg   (28 lb)   30 minutes

Always allow the salmon to remain in the court bouillon until cold.

Cold salmon

1 portion provides:
1794 kJ/427 kcal
33.6 g fat
(of which 6.0 g saturated)
1.3 g carbohydrate
(of which 1.2 g sugars)
29.9 g protein
0.7 g fibre

	8–10 portions
cleaned salmon	1¼ kg (2½ lb)
court bouillon (recipe opposite)	1 litre (2 pt)
cucumber	½
large lettuce	1
tomatoes	200 g (8 oz)
mayonnaise (page 93) or green sauce (page 94)	250 ml (½ pt)

HEALTHY EATING TIP

Reduce the salt by half – approx. ½ a level teaspoon per 4 portions and a level teaspoon per 10 portions.

1   Cook the salmon in the court bouillon either whole or cut into 4 or 8 darnes.

2   Allow to cool thoroughly in the cooking liquid to keep it moist. Divide a whole salmon into eight even portions; for darnes, remove centre bone and cut each darne in half, if required.

3   Except when whole, remove the centre bone, the skin and brown surface and dress neatly on a flat dish.

4   Peel and slice the cucumber and neatly arrange a few slices on each portion.

5   Garnish with quarters of lettuce and quarters of tomatoes.

6   Serve the sauce in a sauceboat separately.

Fig 5.12   Garnished portion of cold salmon
John Campbell

Presentation of a whole salmon

If a cooked salmon is to be presented and served cold from the whole fish, the procedure is as follows:

- Carefully remove the skin and the dark layer under the skin (which is cooked blood). The now bared salmon flesh should be perfectly smooth.

- Make sure the salmon is well drained and place it on to the serving dish or board.

- The salmon is now ready for decorating and garnishing. Keep this to the minimum and avoid overcovering the fish and the dish. Neatly overlapping thin slices of cucumber (the skin may be left on or removed), quartered tomatoes (which can be peeled and neatly cut), small pieces of hearts of lettuce can, if artistically set out, give a quick, neat-looking, appetising appearance. Remember time is money and there is no justification for spending a lot of time cutting fiddly little pieces of many different items to form patterns that often look untidy.

Cold meats

The typical meats or poultry for cold presentation are: roast beef, boiled or honey roast ham or gammon, roast chicken or turkey, and boiled ox tongue. These are available as left-over joints from previous hot meals; cooked specially for cold service; or bought in ready cooked from suppliers. The various ways of presentation and service are:

- sliced from whole joints on the bone in front of the customer (in which case all bones that may hinder carving must be removed first);
- sliced from boned joints, which in some cases may be rolled and stuffed (also in front of the customer);
- pre-sliced in the kitchen, in which case the meat or poultry should be cut as close to service time as possible, otherwise it will start to dry and curl up; pre-sliced meats or poultry can be neatly cut, dressed with the slices overlapping each other, placed on to large dishes or individual plates, covered with cling film and kept under refrigeration; when large numbers of plated meals have to be prepared, plate rings can be used and the plates stacked in sensible sized numbers.

When joints of meat, hams, tongue or turkeys are cooked fresh for serving cold, this is usually done the day before. After cooking they are allowed to cool (the hams are left in the cooking liquor), and then kept under refrigeration overnight.

When roast chickens are required for serving cold, ideally they should be cooked 1–2 hours before service, left to cool (not in the refrigerator) and then carved as required. In this way, the meat remains moist and succulent. Chickens can then be cut into eight pieces and the excess bones removed before serving.

When any meats or poultry are required for a cold buffet, the joint can be presented whole with 2–3 slices cut, laid overlapping from the base of the joint, on a suitably sized dish. The two rear sides of the joint can then be garnished (if required) with two small, neatly placed bunches of watercress dressed so that only leaves show. If a little more colour is required, then a tulip-cut tomato or two may be added. It is a mistake to overgarnish any cold dishes.

If the cut surface of any joint begins to look dry, a thin slice should be removed and discarded before cutting any slices for service or presenting the joint on a cold buffet.

Ham should not be confused with gammon. A gammon is the hind leg of a baconer weight pig, and is cut from a side of bacon. A ham is the hind leg of a porker pig, and is cut round from the side of pork with the aitch bone and usually cured by dry salting. Ham is boiled and can be served hot or cold. Certain imported hams (Parma ham, Bayonne and Ardennes) are sliced thinly and eaten raw, generally as an hors-d'oeuvre. In order to carve the ham efficiently it is necessary to remove the aitch bone after cooking. Traditional English hams include York and Bradenham.

Pre-prepared pâtés or terrines are available in a wide variety of types and flavourings, which include liver (chicken, duck, etc.), poultry and game.

Pâtés are usually cooked enclosed in a thin layer of bacon fat or they may be enclosed in hot water pastry within a special mould.

Pâtés and terrines must be kept under refrigeration at all times and should never be allowed to stand in a warm kitchen or dining room because they are easily contaminated by food poisoning bacteria. For service, the pâté or terrine can be displayed whole with one or two slices cut, or cut in slices and dressed on plates. If in either case these are to be on display to the customer, then the display counter or cabinet must be refrigerated.

Fish and vegetable pâtés and terrines are also available. When serving meat, poultry or game pâtés, a simple garnish of a fan of gherkin and a little salad is sufficient.

The use of plastic gloves when cold foods are being handled will reduce the risk of contamination. See page 99 for pâté and terrine recipes.

81 Chicken salad

	4 portions	10 portions
lettuce (washed)	1	2–3
cooked chicken, free from skin and bone	400 g (1 lb)	1¼ kg (2½ lb)
tomatoes	2	5
hard-boiled egg	1	5
anchovies	10 g (½ oz)	25 g (1 oz)
olives	4–8	10–20
capers	5 g (¼ oz)	12 g (½ oz)
vinaigrette (page 92)	4 tbsp	10 tbsp

HEALTHY EATING TIP

The anchovies, capers and olives will contribute a considerable amount of salt; no added salt is necessary.
Serve with plenty of starchy carbohydrate and additional salad vegetables.

1 Remove heart from the lettuce. Shred the remainder. Place in a salad bowl.

2 Cut the chicken in neat pieces and place on the lettuce.

3 Decorate with quarters of tomato, hard-boiled egg, anchovies, olives, quartered heart of the lettuce and capers.

4 Serve accompanied with vinaigrette.

82 Raised pork pie

Hot water paste

1 portion provides:
2867 kJ/683 kcal
41.8 g fat
(of which 17.1 g saturated)
54.1 g carbohydrate
(of which 1.5 g sugars)
26.1 g protein
3.2 g fibre

	4 portions	10 portions
lard or margarine (alternatively use 100 g (4 oz) lard and 25g (1 oz) butter or margarine)	125 g (5 oz)	300 g (12½ oz)
strong plain flour	250 g (10 oz)	500 g (1½ lb)
water	125 ml (¼ pt)	300 ml (⅝ pt)
salt		

HEALTHY EATING TIP

The paste, pork and bacon result in a high fat dish.
Serve with plenty of potato, rice or pasta and a large salad to proportionally reduce the fat.
Little or no added salt is needed – plenty in the bacon.

1 Sift the flour and salt into a basin. Make a well in the centre.

2 Boil the fat with the water and pour immediately into the flour.

3 Mix with a wooden spoon until cool.

4 Mix to a smooth paste and use while still warm.

continued over ▶

▶ *Raised pork pie continued*

Main ingredients

> 1 portion provides:
> 909 kJ/218 kcal energy
> 14.2 g fat
> (of which 4.7 g saturated)
> 3.4 g carbohydrate
> (of which 0.5 g sugars)
> 19.4 g protein
> 0.1 g fibre

	4 portions	**10 portions**
shoulder of pork (without bone)	300 g (12 oz)	1 kg (2 lb)
bacon	100 g (4 oz)	250 g (10 oz)
allspice, or mixed spice, and chopped sage	½ tsp	1½ tsp
salt and pepper		
bread soaked in milk	50 g (2 oz)	125 g (5 oz)
stock or water	2 tbsp	5 tbsp

1. Cut the pork and bacon into small even pieces and combine with the rest of the ingredients.

2. Keep one-quarter of the paste warm and covered.

3. Roll out the remaining three-quarters and carefully line a well-greased raised pie mould.

4. Add the filling and press down firmly.

5. Roll out the remaining pastry for the lid, and eggwash the edges of the pie.

6. Add the lid, seal firmly, neaten the edges, cut off any surplus paste; decorate if desired.

7. Make a hole 1 cm (½ inch) in diameter in the centre of the pie; brush all over with eggwash.

8. Bake in a hot oven (230–250°C; Reg.8–9; 450–500°F) for approximately 20 minutes.

9. Reduce the heat to moderate (150–200°C; Reg.2–6; 300–400°F) and cook for 1½–2 hours in all.

10. If the pie colours too quickly, cover with greaseproof paper or foil. Remove from the oven and carefully remove tin, eggwash the pie all over and return to the oven for a few minutes.

11. Remove from the oven and fill with approximately 125 ml (¼ pint) of good hot stock in which 5 g (¼ oz) of gelatine has been dissolved.

12. Serve when cold, garnished with picked watercress and offer a suitable salad.

83 Veal and ham pie

> 1 portion provides:
> 607 kJ/144 kcal energy
> 4.5 g fat
> (of which 1.5 g saturated)
> 3.8 g carbohydrate
> (of which 0.8 g sugars)
> 22.4 g protein
> 0.1 g fibre

	4 portions	**10 portions**
ham or bacon	150 g (6oz)	375 g (15 oz)
salt, pepper		
hard-boiled egg	1	2
lean veal	250 g (10 oz)	625 g (1½ lb)
parsley and thyme	½ tsp	1 tsp
lemon, grated zest of	1	2
stock or water	2 tbsp	5 tbsp
bread soaked in milk	50 g (2 oz)	125 g (5 oz)
hot water paste		

Proceed as for raised pork pie. Place the shelled egg in the centre of the mixture. Serve when cold, garnished with picked watercress and offer a suitable salad.

HEALTHY EATING TIP

The paste and bacon result in a high fat dish. Serve with plenty of potato, rice or pasta and a large salad to proportionally reduce the fat.
Little or no added salt is needed – plenty in the bacon.

Eggs

Spanish omelette

Jam omelette

Tomato omelette

Eggs

Types

Hens' eggs are almost exclusively used for cookery but eggs from turkeys, geese, ducks, guinea fowl, quail and gulls are also edible.

Quails' eggs are used in a variety of ways. They can be used as a garnish to many hot and cold dishes or as a starter or main course, such as a salad of assorted leaves with hot wild mushrooms and poached quail eggs, or tartlet of quail eggs on chopped mushrooms coated with hollandaise sauce.

Sizes

Hens' eggs are graded in four sizes: small, medium, large and very large.

Purchasing and quality

The size of the eggs does not affect the quality but does affect the price. Eggs are tasted for quality then weighed and graded.

When buying eggs the following points should be noted.

- The eggshell should be clean, well-shaped, strong and slightly rough.

- When eggs are broken there should be a high proportion of thick white to thin white. If an egg is kept, the thick white gradually changes into thin white and water passes from the white into the yolk.

- The yolk should be firm, round (not flattened) and of a good even colour. As eggs are kept the yolk loses strength and begins to flatten, water evaporates from the egg and is replaced by air.

Food value

Eggs are useful as a main dish as they provide energy, fat, minerals and vitamins needed for growth and repair of the body. The fat in the egg yolk is high in saturated fat. The egg white is made up of protein and water. See page 140 for egg white omelette.

Salmonella

Hens can pass salmonella bacteria into their eggs and thus cause food poisoning. To reduce this risk, pasteurised eggs may be used where appropriate, e.g. omelettes, scrambled eggs.

Storage

Store in a cool but not too dry place; 0–5°C (32–41°F) is ideal. The humidity of the air and the amount of carbon dioxide in the air are controlled. Eggs will keep up to nine months under these conditions.

Because eggshells are porous the eggs will absorb any strong odours; therefore, they should not be stored near strong-smelling foods such as onions, fish, cheese, etc.

Pasteurised eggs are washed, sanitised and then broken into sterilised containers. After combining the yolks and whites they are strained, pasteurised, that is, heated to 63°C (145°F) for one minute, then rapidly cooled.

Health, safety and hygiene

- Eggs should be stored in a cool place, preferably under refrigeration.
- Eggs should be stored away from possible contaminants, such as raw meat, strong smelling foods.
- Stocks should be rotated: first in, first out.
- Hands should be washed before and after handling eggs.
- Cracked eggs should not be used.
- Preparation surfaces, utensils and containers should be regularly cleaned and always cleaned between preparation of different dishes.
- Egg dishes should be consumed as soon as possible after preparation or, if not for immediate use, refrigerated.

Versatility

Fried, scrambled, poached and boiled eggs and omelettes are mainly served at breakfast. A variety of dishes may be served for lunch, high teas, supper and snacks.

Egg dishes

1 Scrambled eggs (basic recipe)

Oeufs brouillés

> Using hard margarine, 1 portion provides:
> 1105 kJ/263 kcal
> 22.9 g fat
> (of which 8.7 g saturated)
> 0.5 g carbohydrates
> (of which 0.5 g sugars)
> 13.9 g protein
> 0.0 g fibre

	4 portions	10 portions
eggs	6–8	15–20
milk (optional)	2 tbsp	5 tbsp
salt, pepper		
butter or oil	50 g (2 oz)	125 g (5 oz)

HEALTHY EATING TIP

Try to keep the butter in cooking to a minimum and serve on unbuttered toast. Garnish with a grilled tomato.

1 Break the eggs in a basin, add milk (if using), lightly season with salt and pepper and thoroughly mix with a whisk.

2 Melt 25 g (1 oz) butter in a thick-bottomed pan, add the eggs and cook over a gentle heat stirring continuously until the eggs are lightly cooked.

3 Remove from the heat, correct the seasoning and mix in the remaining 25 g (1 oz) butter. (A tablespoon of cream may also be added.)

4 Serve in individual egg dishes.

Note: If scrambled eggs are cooked too quickly or for too long the protein will toughen, the eggs will

continued over ▶

▶ *Scrambled eggs continued*

discolour because of the iron and sulphur compounds being released and syneresis or separation of water from the eggs will occur. This means that they will be unpleasant to eat. The heat from the pan will continue to cook the eggs after it has been removed from the stove; therefore, the pan should be removed from the heat just before the eggs are cooked.

Scrambled eggs can be served on a slice of freshly-buttered toast with the crust removed.

Variations on serving scrambled eggs: see page 139.

2 Eggs in cocotte (basic recipe)

Oeufs en cocotte

1 portion provides:
534 kJ/127 kcal
11.2 g fat
(of which 5.2 g saturated)
0.0 g carbohydrate
(of which 0.0 g sugars)
6.8 g protein
0.0 g fibre

	4 portions	**10 portions**
butter	25 g (1 oz)	60 g (2½ oz)
salt, pepper		
eggs	4	10

Serve with bread or toast with optional butter. Keep the salt to a minimum.

1   Butter four egg cocottes.

2   Break an egg carefully into each.

3   Place the cocottes in a sauté pan containing 1 cm (½ inch) water.

4   Cover with a tight-fitting lid, place on a fierce heat so that the water boils rapidly.

5   Cook for 2–3 minutes until the eggs are lightly set and serve.

Note: Variations include:

- half a minute before the cooking is completed, adding 1 dessertspoon of cream to each egg and completing the cooking;

- when cooked, adding 1 dessertspoon jus-lié to each egg;

- place diced cooked chicken mixed with cream in the bottom of the cocottes. Break the eggs on top of the chicken and cook;

- as above using tomato concassé in place of chicken.

3 Boiled eggs

Oeufs à la coque

Using 1 egg per portion, 1 portion provides:
340 kJ/81 kcal
6.0 g fat
(of which 1.9 g saturated)
0.0 g carbohydrate
(of which 0.0 g sugars)
6.8 g protein
0.0 g fibre

Allow 1 or 2 eggs per portion.

Method I

Place the eggs in cold water, bring to the boil, simmer for 2–2½ minutes, remove from the water and serve at once in an egg cup.

Method II

Plunge the eggs in boiling water, reboil, simmer for 4–5 minutes.

Note: Boiled eggs are always served in the shell.

4 Soft-boiled eggs

Oeufs mollets

Plunge the eggs into boiling water, reboil, simmer for 5 minutes. Refresh immediately. Remove the shells carefully. Reheat when required for 30 seconds in hot salted water.

All the recipes given for poached eggs (page 138) can be applied to soft-boiled eggs.

> Using one egg per portion, 1 portion provides:
> 1052 kJ/251 kcal
> 18.9 g fat
> (of which 8.7 g saturated)
> 8.0 g carbohydrate
> (of which 3.3 g sugars)
> 12.5 g protein
> 1.2 g fibre

5 Hard-boiled eggs

Oeufs durs

1 Plunge the eggs into a pan of boiling water.
2 Reboil and simmer for 8–10 minutes.
3 Refresh until cold under running water.

Note: If high temperatures or a long cooking time are used to cook eggs, iron in the yolk and sulphur compounds in the white are released to form an unsightly blackish ring around the yolk. Stale eggs will also show a black ring round the yolk.

6 Hard-boiled eggs with mushroom and cheese sauce

Oeufs Chimay

> Using 2 eggs per portion, 1 portion provides:
> 679 kJ/162 kcal
> 12.0 g fat
> (of which 3.8 g saturated)
> 0.0 g carbohydrate
> (of which 0.0 g sugars)
> 13.5 g protein
> 0.0 g fibre

	4 portions	10 portions
hard-boiled eggs	4	10
chopped shallots	10 g (½ oz)	25 g (1 oz)
butter, magarine or oil (duxelle)	10 g (½ oz)	25 g (1 oz)
mushrooms	100 g (4 oz)	250 g (10 oz)
chopped parsley or other fresh herbs		
salt, pepper		
Mornay sauce, page 55	250 ml (½ pt)	625 ml (1¼ pt)
grated Parmesan cheese		

1 Cut the eggs in halves lengthwise.
2 Remove the yolks and pass them through a sieve.
3 Place the whites in an earthenware serving dish.
4 Prepare the duxelle by cooking the chopped shallot in the butter

HEALTHY EATING TIP
Serve with french bread or toast and a green salad. There is plenty of salt in the cheese, additional salt is not necessary.

135

continued over ▶

▶ *Hard-boiled eggs with mushroom and cheese sauce continued*

without colouring, add the well-washed and finely chopped mushroom or mushroom trimmings, cook for 3–4 minutes.

5 Mix the yolks with the duxelle and parsley and correct the seasoning.

6 Spoon or pipe the mixture into the egg white halves.

7 Cover the eggs with Mornay sauce, sprinkle with grated Parmesan cheese and brown slowly under a salamander or in the top of a moderate oven and serve.

HEALTHY EATING TIP

Serve with french bread or toast and a green salad. There is plenty of salt in the cheese, additional salt is not necessary.

Fried in sunflower oil, 1 portion provides:
536 kJ/128 kcal
31.0 g fat
(of which 9.8 g saturated)
0.0 g carbohydrate
(of which 0.0 g sugars)
7.6 g protein
0.0 g fibre

7 Hard-boiled eggs with cheese and tomato sauce

Oeufs aurore

1 Proceed as for recipe 6 using béchamel in place of Mornay sauce.

2 Add a little tomato sauce or tomato purée to the béchamel to give it a pinkish colour.

3 Mask the eggs, sprinkle with grated cheese.

4 Gratinate under the salamander.

8 Fried eggs

Oeufs frits

1 Allow 1 or 2 eggs per portion.

2 Melt a little fat in a frying pan. Add the eggs.

3 Cook gently until lightly set. Serve on a plate or flat dish.

Note: To prepare an excellent fried egg it is essential to use a fresh high quality egg, to maintain a controlled low heat and use a high quality fat (butter or oil, such as sunflower oil).

Fig 6.1 Preparation for fried eggs

9 Fried eggs and bacon

Oeufs au lard

1   Allow 2–3 rashers per portion. Remove the rind and bone.
2   Fry in a little fat or grill on a flat tray under the salamander on both sides. Dress neatly around the fried egg.

Note: Fried eggs may also be served with grilled or fried tomatoes, mushrooms, sauté potatoes, sausage, black pudding, fried bread etc., as ordered by the customer.

Fried in butter, 1 portion provides:
536 kJ/128 kcal
10.7 g fat
(of which 4.1 g saturated)
0.0 g carbohydrate
(of which 0.0 g sugars)
7.6 g protein
0.0 g fibre

HEALTHY EATING TIP

The fat can be reduced by serving the eggs with grilled tomatoes and mushrooms, baked beans and unbuttered toast.

10 Poached eggs

Oeufs pochés

High quality fresh eggs should be used for poaching because they have a large amount of thick white and consequently have less tendency to spread in the simmering water. Low quality eggs are difficult to manage because the large quantity of thin white spreads in the simmering water.

1 portion provides:
358 kJ/85 kcal
6.4 g fat
(of which 2.0 g saturated)
0.0 g carbohydrate
(of which 0.0 g sugars)
6.8 g protein
0.0 g fibre

A well-prepared poached egg has a firm tender white surrounding the slightly thickened unbroken yolk. The use of a little vinegar (an acid) helps to set the egg white so preventing it from spreading; it also makes the white more tender and whiter. Too much malt vinegar will discolour and give the eggs a strong vinegar flavour; white vinegar may be used.

HEALTHY EATING TIP

Serve with a thick slice of wholegrain bread or unbuttered toast.

1   Carefully break the eggs one by one into a shallow pan containing at least 8 cm (3 inches) gently boiling water to which a little vinegar has been added (1 litre (2 pints) water to 1 tablespoon vinegar).

2   Simmer until lightly set for approximately 2½–3 minutes.

3   Remove carefully with a perforated spoon into a bowl of cold water.

4   Trim the white of egg if necessary.

5   Reheat, when required, by placing into hot salted water for approximately ½–1 minute.

6   Remove carefully from the water using a perforated spoon.

7   Drain on a cloth and use as required.

Fig 6.2 ✎ Stages involved in poaching an egg

	1 portion provides:
	1177 kJ/280 kcal
	19.1 g fat
	(of which 8.7 g saturated)
	15.2 g carbohydrate
	(of which 3.4 g sugars)
	12.8 g protein
	0.8 g fibre

11 Poached eggs with cheese sauce

Oeufs pochés Mornay

	4 portions	10 portions
eggs	4	10
short paste tartlets or	4	10
half slices of buttered toast	4	10
Mornay sauce (page 55)	250 ml (½ pt)	625 ml (1¼ pt)

1 Cook eggs as for poached eggs.

2 Place tartlets or toast in an earthenware dish (the slices of toast may be halved, cut in rounds with a cutter, crust removed).

3 Add the hot well-drained eggs.

4 Completely cover with sauce, sprinkle with grated Parmesan cheese, brown under the salamander and serve.

Variations include:

- *Florentine* – poached eggs on a bed of leaf spinach and finished as for Mornay.

- *Bombay* – poached eggs on a bed of cooked rice coated with a strained curry sauce (page 62)

- *Washington* – on a bed of sweetcorn coated with supreme sauce (page 56) or cream.

HEALTHY EATING TIP

No added salt is necessary as there is plenty in the cheese. Grilled tomatoes could be served to accompany this dish.

	1 portion provides:
	2094 kJ/499 kcal
	39.9 g fat
	(of which 11.4 g saturated)
	18.4 g carbohydrate
	(of which 0.6 g sugars)
	18.0 g protein
	1.0 g fibre

12 Scotch eggs

	4 portions	10 portions
hard-boiled eggs	4	10
sausage meat	300 g (12 oz)	1 kg (2 lb)
flour	25 g (1 oz)	60 g (2½ oz)
beaten egg	1	3
breadcrumbs	50 g (2 oz)	125 g (5 oz)

1   Completely cover each egg with sausage meat.
2   Pass it through the flour, egg and breadcrumbs. Shake off the surplus crumbs.
3   Deep fry to a golden brown in a moderately hot fat.
4   Drain well, cut in halves and serve hot or cold.

Hot: garnish with fried or sprig parsley, and a sauceboat of suitable sauce, such as tomato (page 64).

Cold: garnish with salad in season and a sauceboat of salad dressing (page 92).

Make sure the fat is hot so that less fat will be absorbed into the food during cooking. Drain the cooked scotch eggs on kitchen paper.

13 Omelettes (basic recipe)

Omelette nature

eggs per portion	2–3
butter, margarine or oil	10 g (½ oz)

1   Allow 2–3 eggs per portion.
2   Break the eggs into a basin, season lightly with salt and pepper.
3   Beat well with a fork or whisk until the yolks and whites are thoroughly combined and no streaks of white can be seen.
4   Heat the omelette pan; wipe thoroughly clean with a dry cloth.
5   Add 10 g (½ oz) butter; heat until foaming but not brown.
6   Add the eggs and cook quickly, moving the mixture continuously with a fork until lightly set; remove from the heat.
7   Half fold the mixture over at right-angles to the handle.
8   Tap the bottom of the pan to bring up the edge of the omelette.
9   Tilt the pan completely over so as to allow the omelette to fall carefully into the centre of the dish or plate.
10 Neaten the shape if necessary and serve immediately.

Using 2 eggs per portion, 1 portion provides:
990 kJ/236 kcal
20.2 g fat
(of which 9.1 g saturated)
0.0 g carbohydrate
(of which 0.0 g sugars)
13.6 g protein
0.0 g fibre

Using 3 eggs per portion, 1 portion provides:
1330 kJ/317 kcal
26.2 g fat
(of which 11.0 g saturated)
0.0 g carbohydrate
(of which 0.0 g sugars)
20.3 g protein
0.0 g fibre

Use salt sparingly and serve with plenty of starchy carbohydrate and vegetables or salad.

Note: Variations of omelette include:

- *fine herbs* (chopped parsley, chervil and chives);
- *mushroom* (cooked, sliced, wild or cultivated);
- *cheese* (25g (1oz) grated cheese added before folding);
- *tomato* (incision made down centre of cooked omelette, filled with hot tomato concassé; served with tomato sauce);
- *chicken livers* (neatly cut chicken livers fried in butter added to a light brown sauce; finished as for tomato omelette);
- *kidney* (made the same as for chicken livers);
- *shrimp* (bound with béchamel sauce, finished as for fine herbs omelette).

Egg white omelette – being prepared and cooked without the egg yolks means that it is almost fat free. The whites are three-quarter whipped, lightly seasoned and then cooked as for any other omelette, folded or flat, garnished or served plain.

Other ingredients that can be used include: ham, bacon, onion, potato, etc.

Spanish omelette has tomato concassé, cooked onions, diced red pimento and parsley added and is cooked and served flat. Many other flat omelettes can be served with a variety of ingredients. A flat omelette is made as for a basic omelette up to point 7; sharply tap the pan on the stove to loosen the omelette and toss it over as for a pancake.

A **jam omelette** is made omitting salt and pepper. When the eggs are almost set a tablespoon of warmed jam is added. The omelette is then folded, placed on the serving dish or plate, liberally sprinkled with icing sugar and branded with a red hot iron to caramelise the sugar. This is illustrated on page 131.

Fig 6.3 🥄 Stages involved in making an omelette

Fig 6.4 🌶 Spanish omelette

7 Pasta and rice

Pumpkin tortellini with brown butter balsamic vinaigrette
John Campbell

Pasta and rice

Pasta is made from a strong wheat flour, known as durum flour, made into a dough by the addition of water, olive oil and egg. There are two main types of pasta, dried and fresh home-made. Dried pasta is available in at least 56 different shapes, each of which has a name, and is widely used because of the convenience and the fact that the shelf life is up to 2 years if it is correctly stored. Fresh pasta is more and more readily available in a variety of shapes, colours and flavours from suppliers and there are machines for those who wish to produce their own pasta.

Pasta can be served for lunch, dinner, supper or as a snack meal and also used as an accompaniment or garnish to other dishes. Traditionally, dried pasta is cooked *al dente,* which means 'firm to the bite'.

Food value

Durum wheat has a 15% protein content, which makes it a good alternative to rice and potatoes for vegetarians. Pasta also contains carbohydrates in the form of starch, which gives the body energy. Eating more pasta is in line with the recommendation to 'eat more starchy carbohydrates'.

Storage

If eggs are used in the making of fresh pasta, the fresher they are the longer the keeping quality of the pasta. When fresh pasta is correctly stored it will keep for up to 3 or 4 weeks. Flat types of fresh pasta, such as noodles, which are dried and transferred to a container or bowl, will keep for up to a month in a cool, dry store. Other shapes can be stored in the freezer.

Types and sauces

There are basically four types of pasta, each of which may be left plain, or flavoured with spinach or tomato.

- dried durum wheat pasta;
- egg pasta;
- semolina pasta;
- wholewheat pasta.

Examples of sauces to go with pasta include:

- tomato sauce;
- cream, butter or béchamel-based;
- rich meat sauce;
- olive oil and garlic;
- soft white or blue cheese;
- pesto (page 65).

Cheeses

Examples of cheeses used in pasta include:

- *Parmesan*, the most popular hard cheese, ideal for grating. The flavour is best when it is freshly grated. If bought ready grated, or if it is grated and stored, the flavour deteriorates.
- *Pecorino*, a strong ewe's milk cheese, sometimes studded with peppercorns. Used for strongly flavoured dishes, it can be grated or thinly sliced.
- *Ricotta*, creamy-white in colour, made from the discarded whey of other cheeses. It is widely used in fillings for pasta, such as cannelloni, ravioli, etc., and for sauces.
- *Mozzarella*, traditionally made from the milk of the water buffalo. It is pure white and creamy, with a mild but distinctive flavour, usually round or pear-shaped. It will only keep for a few days in a container half-filled with milk and water.
- *Gorgonzola* or *dolcelatte*, distinctive blue cheeses that can be used in sauces.

Ingredients for pasta dishes

The following are some examples of ingredients that can be used in pasta dishes. The list is almost endless but can include:

- smoked salmon
- shrimps
- scallops
- lobster
- tuna fish
- crab
- anchovies
- cockles
- avocado
- mushrooms
- tomatoes
- onions
- courgettes
- peas
- spinach
- chillies
- peppers
- broad beans
- broccoli
- sliced sausage
- salami
- ham
- bacon
- beef
- chicken
- duck
- prawns
- mussels
- tongue
- chicken livers
- smoked ham
- mustard and cress
- parsley
- rosemary
- basil
- tarragon
- fennel
- chives
- spring onions
- marjoram
- pine nuts
- walnuts
- stoned olives
- capers
- cooked, dried beans
- eggs
- grated lemon zest
- saffron
- grated nutmeg
- sultanas
- balsamic vinegar

Cooking pasta

- Always cook in plenty of gently boiling salted water.

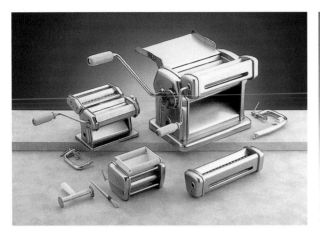

Fig 7.1 🖋 Pasta machines

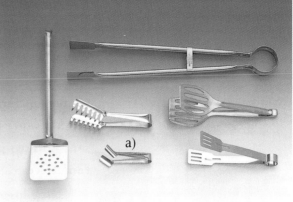

Fig 7.2 🖋 Spaghetti tongs, a)

• Stir to the boil. Do not overcook.

• If not to be used immediately, refresh and reheat carefully in hot salted water when required. Drain well in a colander.

• With most pasta, freshly grated cheese (Parmesan) should be served separately.

• Allow 50 g (2 oz) as a first course; 100 g (4 oz) as a main course.

• When cooking fresh pasta add a little oil to the water to prevent the pasta sticking together.

1 Fresh egg pasta dough

strong flour	400 g (1 lb)
eggs, beaten	4 × medium
salt	
olive oil as required	approx 1 tbsp

1 Sieve the flour and salt, shape into a well. Pour the beaten eggs into the well.

2 Gradually incorporate the flour and only add oil to adjust to required consistency. The amount of oil will vary according to the type of flour and the size of the eggs.

3 Pull and knead the dough until it is of a smooth, elastic consistency.

4 Cover the dough with a dampened cloth and allow to rest in a cool place for 30 minutes.

5 Roll out the dough on a well floured surface to a thickness of ½ mm (⅛ inch) or use a pasta rolling machine.

6 Trim the sides and cut the dough as required using a large knife.

Note: If using a pasta rolling machine, divide the dough into three or four pieces. Pass each section by hand through the machine, turning the rollers with the other hand. Repeat this five or six times adjusting the rollers each time to make the pasta thinner.

Fresh egg pasta requires less cooking time than dried pasta. When cooking fresh pasta, the addition of a few drops of olive oil in the water will help prevent the pasta from sticking together. Fresh egg pasta not for immediate use must be stored in a cool dry place. If fresh egg pasta is to be stored, it should be allowed to dry, then kept in a clean, dry container or bowl in a cool dry store.

Variations include:

• *Spinach* Add 75–100 g (3–4 oz) finely puréed, dry, cooked spinach to the dough.

• *Tomato* Add 2 tablespoons of tomato purée to the dough.

• Other flavours used include: beetroot, saffron and black ink from squid.

• *Wholewheat pasta* Use half wholewheat and half white flour.

145

2 Spaghetti with tomato sauce

Spaghetti alla pomodoro

	4 portions	10 portions
spaghetti	100 g (4 oz)	250 g (10 oz)
butter (optional) or olive oil	25 g (1 oz)	60 g (2½ oz)
tomato sauce (page 64)	250 ml (½ pt)	625 ml (1¼ pt)
salt, mill pepper		
tomato concassé (optional)	100 g (4 oz)	250 g (10 oz)

1 Plunge spaghetti into a saucepan containing boiling salted water. Allow to boil gently.

2 Stir occasionally with a wooden spoon. Cook for approximately 12–15 minutes.

3 Drain well in a colander. Return to a clean, dry pan.

4 Mix in the butter and add the tomato sauce. Correct the seasoning.

5 Add the tomato concassé and 4–5 leaves of fresh basil torn into pieces with your fingers, and serve with grated cheese.

3 Spaghetti bolognaise

Spaghetti alla bolognese

	4 portions	10 portions
butter or oil, optional	25 g (1 oz)	60 g (2½ oz)
chopped onion	50 g (2 oz)	125 g (5 oz)
clove garlic, chopped	1	2
*lean minced beef or tail end fillet, cut in ⅛ inch dice	400 g (1 lb)	1 kg (2½ lbs)
jus-lié or demi-glace	125 ml (¼ pt)	300 ml (⅝ pt)
tomato purée	1 tbsp	2½ tbsp
marjoram or oregano	⅛ tsp	¼ tsp
diced mushrooms	100 g (4 oz)	250 g (10 oz)
salt, mill pepper		
spaghetti	100 g (4 oz)	250 g (10 oz)

1 Place 10 g (½ oz) butter or oil in a sauteuse.

2 Add the chopped onion and garlic and cook for 4–5 minutes without colour.

3 Add the beef and cook, colouring lightly.

4 Add the jus-lié or demi-glace, the tomato purée and the herbs.

Using hard margarine, this recipe provides:
1672 kJ/400 kcal
17.2 g fat
(of which 9.4 g saturated)
50.0 g carbohydrate
(of which 10.2 g sugars)
11.8 g protein
4.0 g fibre

HEALTHY EATING TIP

Use very little or no salt as there is plenty from the cheese. Reduce or omit the added butter and serve with a large green salad.

Using sunflower oil, this recipe provides for 4 portions:
3188 kJ/760 kcal
32.3 g fat
(of which 5.6 g saturated)
83.4 g carbohydrate
(of which 10.4 g sugars)
39.0 g protein
9.6 g fibre

HEALTHY EATING TIP

Use an unsaturated oil (sunflower or olive). Lightly oil the pan and drain off any excess after the frying is complete. Skim the fat from the finished dish.
Season with minimum amounts of salt.
Try using more pasta and extending the sauce with tomatoes. Serve with a large green salad.

5   Simmer until tender.

6   Add the mushrooms and simmer
    for 5 minutes, then correct the
    seasoning.

7   Meanwhile cook the spaghetti in
    plenty of boiling salted water.

8   Allow to boil gently and stir
    occasionally with a wooden spoon.

9   Cook for approximately 12–15
    minutes. Drain well in a colander.

10 Return to a clean pan containing 10
    g (½ oz) butter (optional).

11 Correct the seasoning.

12 Serve with the sauce in centre of
    the spaghetti.

13 Serve grated cheese separately.

*There are many variations for
bolognaise sauce, e.g.:

•   substitute lean beef with pork
    mince or use a combination of both

•   add 50 g (2 oz) each of chopped
    carrot and celery

•   add 100 g (4 oz) chopped
    pancetta or bacon

Fig 7.3 Spaghetti bolognaise with tossed salad
John Campbell

4 Macaroni cheese (Fig 7.4)

	4 portions	10 portions
macaroni	100 g (4 oz)	250 g (10 oz)
butter or oil, optional	25 g (1 oz)	60 g (2½ oz)
grated cheese	100 g (4 oz)	250 g (10 oz)
thin béchamel	500 ml (1 pt)	1¼ litre (2½ pt)
diluted English or continental mustard	¼ tsp	1 tsp
salt, mill pepper		

This recipe provides for 4 portions:
7596 kJ/1808 kcal
116.6 g fat
(of which 64.2 g saturated)
136.6 g carbohydrate
(of which 26.6 g sugars)
60.0 g protein
6.8 g fibre

HEALTHY EATING TIP

Half the grated cheese
could be replaced with
a small amount of
Parmesan (more
flavour and less fat).
Use semi-skimmed milk
for the béchamel.
No added salt is
necessary.

1   Plunge the macaroni into a saucepan containing plenty of boiling
    salted water.

2   Allow to boil gently and stir occasionally with a wooden spoon.

3   Cook for approximately 15 minutes and drain well in a colander.

4   Return to a clean pan containing the butter.

5   Mix with half the cheese and add the béchamel and mustard.

continued over ▶

▶ *Macaroni cheese continued*

6 Place in an earthenware dish and sprinkle with the remainder of the cheese.

7 Brown lightly under the salamander and serve.

Note: Macaroni may also be prepared and served as for any of the spaghetti dishes.

Variations include addition of cooked sliced mushrooms, diced ham, sweet corn, tomato, etc.

Fig 7.4 🖊 Macaroni cheese

Using white flour and olive oil, this recipe provides for 4 portions:
2246 kJ/534 kcal
18.4 g fat
(of which 4.8 g saturated)
77.8 g carbohydrate
(of which 1.6 g sugars)
19.4 g protein
3.6 g fibre

Using wholemeal flour and olive oil, this recipe provides for 4 portions:
2116 kJ/504 kcal
19.2 g fat
(of which 4.8 g saturated)
65.8 g carbohydrate
(of which 2.2 g sugars)
22.6 g protein
8.6 g fibre

5 Noodles

	4 portions	**10 portions**
flour	100 g (4 oz)	250 g (10 oz)
salt		
olive or other vegetable oil	1 tsp	3 tsp
egg and egg yolk	1 and 1	3 and 3

Noodles are usually bought ready prepared but may be made as follows:

1 Sieve the flour and salt. Make a well.

2 Add oil and eggs. Mix to a dough.

3 Knead well until smooth. Leave to rest.

4 Roll out to a thin rectangle 45 × 15 cm (18 × 6 inches).

5 Cut into ½ cm (¼ inch) strips. Leave to dry.

Note: For wholemeal noodles use 50 g (2 oz) wholemeal flour and 50 g (2 oz) strong flour.

Semolina is a good dusting agent to use when handling this paste.

The noodles are cooked in the same way as spaghetti and may be served as for any of the spaghetti recipes. The most popular method of serving them is with butter (recipe 6).

6 | Noodles with butter

	4 portions	10 portions
noodles	100 g (4 oz)	250 g (10 oz)
salt, mill pepper		
a little grated nutmeg		
butter or margarine	50 g (2 oz)	125 g (5 oz)

Using margarine reduced to half, 1 portion provides:
796 kJ/191 kcal energy
12.3 g fat
(of which 7.1 g saturated)
18.0 g carbohydrate
(of which 0.6 g sugars)
3.1 g protein
0.7 g fibre

1   Cook noodles in plenty of gently boiling salted water.

2   Drain well in a colander and return to the pan.

3   Add the seasoning and butter and toss carefully until mixed.

4   Correct the seasoning and serve.

Note: Noodles may also be used as a garnish with meat and poultry dishes, e.g. braised beef.

HEALTHY EATING TIP

Keep the added salt to a minimum.

Noodles (oriental style)

Noodles are probably the world's oldest fast food: they are versatile and quick to cook. They may be steamed, boiled, pan-fried, stir-fried, and deep-fried. A staple food in the Far East, their popularity is spreading rapidly in the West.

Noodles are high in starch (carbohydrate). They provide some protein, especially those made from hard wheat and beans. The addition of egg also increases the protein content.

Examples of the nutritional content of some noodles:

100 g dried	Calories	Carbohydrate	Protein	Fat	Sodium salt
rice sticks	380	88%	6%	0	
rice vermicelli	363	85.5%	7.3%	0	
egg noodles	341	70%	11%	1.9%	0.8%
wheat noodles	308	60% + fibre 10%	12.5%	2%	0.8%
bean thread	320	65%	20%	0	
pasta	350	75%	11.5%	0.3%	

Source: *Noodle Book*, Pat Chapman, Hodder & Stoughton.

7 Rice noodles

rice flour	250 g (10 oz)
vegetable oil	1 tbsp
salt	1 tsp
water to form a soft sticky dough	

1 Mix the flour with the oil and salt and just enough water to form a soft, sticky dough. Knead it until it becomes elastic and cohesive.

2 Due to the lack of gluten in rice flour, substitute approx 25–50% of rice flour with strong wheat flour.

8 Rice noodles salad with duck and orange

	4 portions	10 portions
rice noodles	100 g (4 oz)	250 g (10 oz)
vegetable oil	1 tbsp	2½ tbsp
spring onions	4	10
coriander leaves, chopped	2 tbsp	5 tbsp
mint leaves, chopped	1 tbsp	2½ tbsp
cooked thinly sliced duck breast in julienne	200 g (8 oz)	500 g (1 lb 4 oz)
lime juice	½	1
orange juice	1 tbsp	2½ tbsp
orange segments (garnish)	8	20

1 Cook the noodles in boiling salted water until done, refresh and drain.

2 Add the remaining ingredients (except the orange segments), mix well and season.

3 Serve on suitable individual plates garnished with orange segments, coriander leaves. Finish with Thai coconut dressing.

9 Thai coconut dressing

coconut milk	125 ml (¼ pt)
rice vinegar	62 ml (⅛ pt)
chilli purée	1 tbsp
garlic, chopped	1 clove
lime juice	2 tbsp
palm sugar	1 tsp
Nam pla (fish sauce)	optional
seasoning	

1 Mix all ingredients together, chill.

10   Penne and mange-tout

	6 portions	10 portions
penne or macaroni	400 g (1 lb)	1 kg (2½ lb)
cream cheese	150 g (6 oz)	375 g (15 oz)
gorgonzola	75 g (3 oz)	180 g (7½ oz)
single cream	2–3 tbsp	3–7 tbsp
mange-tout	400 g (1 lb)	1 kg (2½ lb)
butter	50 g (2 oz)	125 g (5 oz)
salt and black mill pepper		

Using Stilton data instead of Gorgonzola, 2.5 tbsp single cream used, 1 portion provides:
3035 kJ/724 kcal energy
37.7 g fat
(of which 22.8 g saturated)
80.3 g carbohydrate
(of which 5.9 g sugars)
20.9 g protein
5.4 g fibre

1. Cook the pasta in plenty of boiling salted water.

2. Blend the cream cheese, gorgonzola and cream in a pan over a low heat, to a smooth sauce. If the sauce is too thick, thin with a little water from the pasta.

3. Cook the mange-tout in boiling salted water for 1–2 minutes, keeping them slightly firm.

4. Drain the pasta, add the butter, then the sauce and finally the mange-tout.

5. Finish with freshly ground black pepper. If desired, a few thin strips of red pepper may be added for decoration.

Note: Macaroni or rigatoni may be used in place of penne.

HEALTHY EATING TIP

The sauce is high in fat and salt, so additional butter and salt is not necessary. For a lower fat version, use a 'light' cream cheese. Serve with a large green salad.

11   Green fettuccine with ham and creamy cheese

Fettucine verdi in salsa cremona

	4 portions	10 portions
green fettuccine or other pasta	400 g (1 lb)	1¼ kg (2½ lb)
cream cheese, mashed	200 g (½ lb)	500 g (1¼ lb)
single cream	2 tbsp	5 tbsp
grated Parmesan cheese	50 g (2 oz)	125 g (5 oz)
melted butter	50 g (2 oz)	125 g (5 oz)
lean cooked ham, cut in thick julienne	100 g (4 oz)	250 g (10 oz)

1 portion provides:
3183 kJ/760 kcal energy
42.2 g fat
(of which 25.4 g saturated)
76.3 g carbohydrate
(of which 2.7 g sugars)
23.7 g protein
3.1 g fibre

1. Cook the fettuccine in plenty of boiling salted water.

2. Mix the cream cheese, cream, Parmesan, salt and pepper.

3. Drain the fettuccine and return to the pan.

4. Mix in butter and cheese. Add ham, toss and serve.

HEALTHY EATING TIP

The sauce is high in fat and salt, so additional butter and salt is not necessary. For a lower fat version, use a 'light' cream cheese. Serve with a large green salad.

Stuffed pasta

Examples of stuffed pasta include the following:

- *Agnolini* are small half-moon shapes usually filled with ham and cheese or minced meat.
- *Cannelloni* are squares of pasta poached, refreshed, dried, stuffed with a variety of fillings (ricotta cheese and spinach), rolled and finished with an appropriate sauce.
- *Cappelletti*, shaped like little hats, are usually filled as agnolini, and are available dried.
- *Ravioli* are usually square with serrated edges. A wide variety of fillings can be used (fish, meat, vegetarian, cheese, etc.).
- *Ravolini* or 'little ravioli' are made half the size of ravioli.
- *Tortellini*, a slightly larger version of cappelletti, are also available in dried form.
- *Tortelloni* is a double-sized version of tortellini.

Pasta that is to be stuffed must be rolled as thinly as possible. The stuffing should be pleasant in taste and plentiful in quantity. The edges of the pasta must be thoroughly sealed otherwise the stuffing will seep out during poaching.

All stuffed pasta should be served in or coated with a suitable sauce and, depending on the type of recipe, may be finished 'au gratin' by sprinkling with freshly grated Parmesan and lightly browning under the salamander.

Stuffings

The examples of stuffing for pasta that follow are for 400 g (1 lb) pasta. The list is almost endless as every district in Italy has its own variations and with thought and experimentation many more can be produced:

cooked minced chicken	200 g (8 oz)
minced ham	100 g (4 oz)
butter	25 g (1 oz)
2 yolks or 1 egg	
grated cheese	25 g (1 oz)
pinch of grated nutmeg	
salt and pepper	
fresh white breadcrumbs	25 g (1 oz)
cooked dry spinach, puréed	200 g (8 oz)
ricotta cheese	200 g (8 oz)
butter	25 g (1 oz)
nutmeg, salt and pepper	
cooked minced lean pork	200 g (8 oz)
cooked minced lean veal	200 g (8 oz)
butter	25 g (1 oz)
grated cheese	25 g (1 oz)
2 yolks or 1 egg	
fresh white breadcrumbs	25 g (1 oz)
salt and pepper	
pinch of chopped marjoram	
ricotta cheese	150 g (6 oz)
grated Parmesan	75 g (3 oz)
egg	1
nutmeg, salt and pepper	
minced cooked meat	200 g (8 oz)
spinach, cooked	100 g (4 oz)
onion, chopped and cooked	50 g (2 oz)
oregano, salt, pepper	
chopped cooked fish	200 g (8 oz)
chopped cooked mushroom	100 g (4 oz)
chopped parsley, anchovy paste	

12   Ravioli

1 portion provides:
1027 kJ/249 kcal energy
9.4 g fat
(of which 1.4 g saturated)
38.9 g carbohydrate
(of which 0.8 g sugars)
4.8 g protein
1.6 g fibre

	4 portions	10 portions
flour	200 g (8 oz)	500 g (1¼ lb)
salt		
olive oil	35 ml (1½ fl oz)	150 ml (⅓ pt)
water	105 ml (4 fl oz)	250 ml (½ pt)

1 Sieve the flour and salt. Make a well. Add the liquid.

2 Knead to a smooth dough. Rest for at least 30 minutes in a cool place.

3 Roll out to a very thin oblong 30 cm × 45 cm (12 inches × 18 inches).

4 Cut in half and eggwash.

5 Place the stuffing in a piping bag with a large plain tube.

6 Pipe out the filling in small pieces about the size of a cherry approximately 4 cm (1½ inches) apart onto one half of the paste.

7 Carefully cover with the other half of the paste, seal, taking care to avoid air pockets.

8 Mark each with the back of a plain cutter.

9 Cut in between each line of filling, down and across with a serrated pastry wheel.

10 Separate on a well-floured tray.

11 Poach in gently boiling salted water for approximately 10 minutes. Drain well.

12 Place in an earthenware serving dish.

13 Cover with 250 ml (½ pt) jus-lié, demi-glace or tomato sauce.

14 Sprinkle with 50 g (2 oz) grated cheese.

15 Brown under the salamander and serve.

13 Cannelloni

1 portion with beef provides:
1823 kJ/435 kcal energy
20.3 g fat
(of which 5.6 g saturated)
44.2 g carbohydrate
(of which 4.3 g sugars)
21.6 g protein
4.1 g fibre

Use the same ingredients as for ravioli dough (recipe 12).

1 Roll out the paste as for ravioli.

2 Cut into squares approximately 6 cm × 6 cm (2½ inches × 2½ inches).

3 Cook in gently boiling salted water for approximately 10 minutes. Refresh in cold water.

4 Drain well and lay out singly on the table. Pipe out the filling across each.

5 Roll up like a sausage roll. Place in a greased earthenware dish.

6 Add 250 ml (½ pt) demi-glace, jus-lié or tomato sauce.

7 Sprinkle with 25–50 g (1–2 oz) grated cheese.

8 Brown slowly under the salamander or in the oven and serve.

Note: a wide variety of fillings may be used such as those given for ravioli.

Fig 7.5 🖎 Leek cannelloni

John Campbell

1 portion provides:
2964 kJ/708 kcal energy
40.2 g fat
(of which 23.3 g saturated)
63.9 g carbohydrate
(of which 16.5 g sugars)
26.9 g protein
5.8 g fibre

HEALTHY EATING TIP

Sweat the leeks in a little sunflower oil and drain before adding the ricotta.
Use half Cheddar and a small amount of Parmesan to reduce the fat in the cheese sauce.

14 Leek cannelloni with lemon thyme and ricotta

	4 portions	10 portions
leeks	800 g (2 lb)	2 kilo (5 lb)
butter	50 g (2 oz)	125 g (5 oz)
garlic cloves, crushed and chopped	2	5
lemon thyme leaves	2 tsp	5 tsp
water	2 tsp	5 tsp
ricotta cheese	250 g (10 oz)	625 g (1½ lb)
fresh pasta dough (page 144)	250 g (10 oz) 12 sheets	625 g (1½ lb) 30 sheets
fresh tomato sauce (page 64)	500 ml	1 pt
cheese sauce (page 55)	500 ml	1 pt (1.25 litres)

154

1   Melt the butter in a suitable pan, add the leeks cut into julienne, garlic and chopped lemon thyme leaves and the water to prevent from browning. Sweat until tender.

2   Allow to cool, drain, add the ricotta cheese, then season.

3   Cook the pasta sheets in boiling water for approximately 3–5 minutes (size 6 cm × 6 cm (2½ inch × 2½ inch)).

4   Refresh and drain well.

5   Spoon the leek filling along one short edge of each sheet and roll up. Arrange the cannelloni seam side down on top of the tomato sauce.

6   Mask with cheese sauce, place in a hot oven to glaze and reheat the cannelloni. Serve immediately.

Note: The cheese sauce may be made with Cheddar, Parmesan, Gruyère or Beaufort.

15 Pumpkin tortellini with brown butter balsamic vinaigrette

	4 portions	10 portions
small pumpkin	1	2½
olive oil	1 tbsp	2½ tbsp
ground cinnamon	½ tsp	1¼ tsp
ground nutmeg	¼ tsp	¾ tsp
caster sugar	1 tsp	1½ tsp
seasoning		
ravioli paste (page 152)		
egg	1	2
butter	50 g (2 oz)	125 g (5 oz)
shallots, finely chopped	25 g (1 oz)	62 g (2½ oz)
balsamic vinegar	2 tbsp	5 tbsp
spinach leaves	100 g (4 oz)	250 g (10 oz)
chopped sage	1 tbsp	2½ tbsp

1 portion provides:
1744 kJ/417 kcal energy
24.6 g fat
(of which 9.0 g saturated)
43.2 g carbohydrate
(of which 4.1 g sugars)
8.2 g protein
3.0 g fibre

HEALTHY EATING TIP

Lightly brush the pumpkin with olive oil when roasting. Keep the amount of added salt to a minimum throughout.

1   First prepare the pumpkin filling. Cut in half and scoop out the seeds.

2   Place in a roasting tray. Sprinkle with olive oil, cinnamon and nutmeg. Add a little water to the pan. Roast the pumpkin at 350°C for approximately 45 minutes until tender.

3   Remove from the oven, allow to cool, scrape out the flesh. Purée the flesh with the sugar in a food processor until smooth, then season.

4   To make the tortellini, roll out the ravioli paste into ⅛ cm (¹⁄₁₆ inch) thick sheeets. Cut the pasta sheets into 8 cm (3 inch) squares.

continued over ▶

▶ *Pumpkin tortellini with brown butter balsamic vinaigrette continued*

5   Place 1 teaspoon of the pumpkin filling in the centre of the square. Lightly brush two sides of the pasta with beaten egg and fold the pasta in half, creating a triangle. Join the two ends of the long side of the triangle to form the tortellini, eggwash the seam, and firmly press the ends together to seal.

6   Cook the tortellini in boiling salted water for 3 to 4 minutes until al dente.

7   To prepare the vinaigrette, cook the butter until nut brown, remove from heat, add the shallots and balsamic vinegar, season.

8   Place the washed spinach leaves in a pan with ⅓rd of the vinaigrette and quickly wilt the spinach. Season.

9   To serve, place the wilted spinach in the centre of the plates. Arrange the well drained tortellini on the spinach. Spoon the vinaigrette around the plates. Finish with a sprinkling of fresh sage.

1 portion provides:
2416 kJ/575 kcal
28.7 g fat
(of which 11.4 g saturated)
56.1 g carbohydrate
(of which 10.0 g sugars)
26.7 g protein
5.8 g fibre

HEALTHY EATING TIP

Use an unsaturated oil (sunflower or olive). Lightly oil the pan and drain off any excess after the frying is complete. Skim the fat from the finished dish.
Season with minimum amounts of salt.
The fat content can be proportionally reduced by increasing the ratio of pasta to sauce and thinning the béchamel.

16 Lasagne

	4 portions	**10 portions**
lasagne	200 g (8 oz)	500 g (1¼ lb)
oil	1 tbsp	3 tbsp
thin strips of streaky bacon	50 g (2 oz)	125 g (5 oz)
onion, chopped	100 g (4 oz)	250 g (10 oz)
carrot, chopped	50 g (2 oz)	125 g (5 oz)
celery, chopped	50 g (2 oz)	125 g (5 oz)
minced beef	200 g (8 oz)	500 g (1¼ lb)
tomato purée	50 g (2 oz)	125 g (5 oz)
jus-lié or demi-glace	375 ml (¾ pt)	1 litre (2 pt)
clove garlic	1	1½
salt, pepper		
marjoram	½ level tsp	1½ tsp
sliced mushrooms	100 g (4 oz)	250 g (10 oz)
béchamel sauce	250 ml (½ pt)	600 ml (1¼ pt)
grated Parmesan or Cheddar cheese	25 g (2 oz)	125 g (5 oz)

1   This recipe can be made using 200 g (8 oz) of ready bought lasagne or preparing it fresh using 200 g (8 oz) flour noodle paste (recipe 5). Wholemeal lasagne can be made using noodle paste made with 100 g (4 oz) wholemeal flour and 100 g (4 oz) strong flour.

2   Prepare the noodle paste and roll out 1 mm (¹⁄₁₆ inch) thick.

3   Cut into 6 cm (2½ inches) squares.

4   Allow to rest in a cool place and dry slightly on a cloth dusted with flour.

5   Whether using fresh or ready bought lasagne, cook in gently simmering salted water for approximately 10 minutes.

6   Refresh in cold water, drain on a cloth.

7   Gently heat the oil in a thick-bottomed pan, add bacon and cook for 2–3 minutes.

8   Add the onion, carrot, celery and cover the pan with a lid and cook for 5 minutes.

9   Add the minced beef, increase the heat and stir until lightly brown.

10 Remove from the heat and mix in the tomato purée.

11 Return to the heat, mix in the jus-lié or demi-glace, stir to boil.

12 Add the garlic, salt, pepper and marjoram and simmer for 15 minutes. Remove the garlic.

13 Mix in the mushrooms, reboil for 2 minutes, remove from the heat.

14 Butter an ovenproof dish and cover the bottom with a layer of the meat sauce.

15 Add layer of lasagne and cover with meat sauce.

16 Add another layer of lasagne and cover with the remainder of the meat sauce.

17 Cover with the béchamel.

18 Sprinkle with cheese, cover with a lid and place in a moderately hot oven at 190°C (Reg. 5; 375°F), for approximately 20 minutes.

19 Remove the lid, cook for a further 15 minutes and serve in the cleaned ovenproof dish.

Note:

○ see also vegetarian lasagne, page 413.

○ fillings for lasagne can be varied in many ways.

○ tomato sauce may be used instead of jus-lié.

Traditionally, pasta dishes are substantial in quantity but because they are so popular they are also requested as lighter dishes. Obviously the portion size can be reduced but other variations can be considered.

E.g. Freshly made pasta cut into 3–4 in (8–10 cm) rounds or squares, rectangles or diamonds, lightly poached or steamed, well drained and placed on a light tasty mixture* using just the one piece of pasta on top or a piece top and bottom.

   *E.g.(1) a tablespoon of mousse of chicken, or fish or shellfish.
       (2) well cooked dried spinach flavoured with toasted pine nuts and grated nutmeg.
       (3) duxelles mixture.

A light sauce should be used.

E.g. (1) a measure of well reduced chicken stock with a little skimmed milk, blitzed to a froth just before serving
   (2) pesto sauce
   (3) a drizzle of good quality olive oil
   (4) a light tomato sauce.

The dish can be finished with a suitable garnish e.g. lightly fried wild or cultivated sliced mushrooms.

17 Gnocchi parisienne (choux paste)

Using hard margarine, 1 portion provides:
1433 kJ/341 kcal
25.0 g fat
(of which 11.8 g saturated)
19.5 g carbohydrate
(of which 3.3 g sugars)
10.7 g protein
0.8 g fibre

	4 portions	10 portions
water	125 ml (¼ pt)	300 ml (⅝ pt)
margarine or butter	50 g (2 oz)	125 g (5 oz)
salt		
flour, white or wholemeal	60 g (2½ oz)	150 g (6¼ oz)
eggs	2	5
grated cheese	50 g (2 oz)	125 g (5 oz)
béchamel (thin)	250 ml (½ pt)	625 ml (1¼ pt)

HEALTHY EATING TIP

No added salt is necessary because of the cheese.

1 Boil water, margarine or butter, and salt in a saucepan. Remove from the heat.

2 Mix in the flour with a wooden spoon. Return to a gentle heat.

3 Stir continuously until the mixture leaves the sides of the pan.

4 Cool slightly. Gradually add the eggs, beating well. Add half the cheese.

5 Place in a piping bag with ½ cm (¼ inch) plain tube.

6 Pipe out in 1 cm (½ inch) lengths into a shallow pan of gently simmering salted water. Do not allow to boil.

7 Cook for approximately 10 minutes. Drain well in a colander.

8 Combine carefully with béchamel. Correct the seasoning.

9 Pour into an earthenware dish.

10 Sprinkle with the remainder of the cheese.

11 Brown lightly under salamander and serve.

Note: gnocchi may be used to garnish goulash or navarin in place of potatoes.

18 Gnocchi romaine (semolina)

Using semi-skimmed milk, 1 portion provides:
1066 kJ/254 kcal energy
12.5 g fat
(of which 6.9 g saturated)
27.5 g carbohydrate
(of which 7.0 g sugars)
9.8 g protein
0.8 g fibre

	4 portions	10 portions
milk	500 ml (1 pt)	1¼ litre (2½ pt)
semolina	100 g (4 oz)	250 g (10 oz)
salt, pepper		
grated nutmeg		
egg yolk	1	3
grated cheese	25 g (1 oz)	60 g (2½ oz)
butter or margarine	25 g (1 oz)	60 g (2½ oz)
tomato sauce (page 64)	250 ml (½ pt)	625 ml (1¼ pt)

No added salt is necessary because of the cheese.

1 Boil the milk in a thick-bottomed pan.

2 Sprinkle in the semolina, stirring continuously. Stir to the boil.

3 Season, simmer until cooked (5–10 minutes). Remove from heat.

4 Mix in egg yolk, cheese and butter.

5 Pour into a buttered tray 1 cm (½ inch) deep.

6 When cold, cut into rounds with a 5 cm (2 inch) round cutter.

7 Place the debris in a buttered earthenware dish.

8 Neatly arrange the rounds on top.

9 Sprinkle with melted butter and cheese.

10 Lightly brown in the oven or under the salamander.

11 Serve with a thread of tomato sauce round the gnocchi.

19 Gnocchi piemontaise (potato)

Using white flour, 1 portion provides:
1045 kJ/248 kcal energy
9.7 g fat
(of which 4.7 g saturated)
35.2 g carbohydrate
(of which 2.1 g sugars)
7.2 g protein
2.1 g fibre

	4 portions	10 portions
mashed potato	300 g (12 oz)	1 kg (2 lb)
flour, white or wholemeal	100 g (4 oz)	250 g (10 oz)
egg and egg yolk	1	2
butter	25 g (1 oz)	60 g (2½ oz)
salt, pepper		
grated nutmeg		
tomato sauce (page 64)	250 ml (½ pt)	625 ml (1¼ pt)

No added salt is necessary.

1 Bake or boil the potatoes in their jackets.

2 Remove from skins and mash with a fork or pass through a sieve.

3 Mix with flour, egg, butter and seasoning while hot.

4 Mould into balls the size of a walnut.

5 Dust well with flour and flatten slightly with a fork.

6 Poach in gently boiling water until they rise to the surface. Drain carefully.

7 Dress in a buttered earthenware dish, cover with tomato or any other pasta sauce.

8 Sprinkle with grated cheese and brown lightly under the salamander and serve.

Rice

For the cultivation of rice, a hot, wet atmosphere is required and it is grown chiefly in India, the Far East, South America, Italy and in the southern states of the USA. Rice is the food crop for about half the world's population. In order to grow, rice needs more water than any other cereal crop. There are around 250 different varieties of rice. The main types are:

- *Long-grain.* A narrow, pointed grain that has had the full bran and most of the germ removed so that it is less fibrous than brown rice. Because of its firm structure, which helps to keep the grains separate when cooked, it is suitable for plain boiling and savoury dishes such as kedgeree and curry dishes, etc.

- *Brown grain.* Any rice that has had the outer covering removed, but retains its bran and as a result is more nutritious and contains more fibre. It takes longer to cook than long-grain rice. The nutty flavour of brown rice lends itself to some recipes, but does not substitute well in traditional dishes such as paella, risotto or puddings.

- Many other types of rice are now available, which can add different colours and textures to dishes.

- *Short-grain.* A short, rounded grain with a soft texture suitable for sweet dishes and risotto. *Arborio* is an Italian short-grain rice.

- *Basmati.* A narrow long-grain rice with a distinctive flavour suitable for serving with Indian dishes. Basmati rice needs to be soaked before being cooked to remove excess starch.

- *Whole-grain rice.* The whole unprocessed grain of the rice.

- *Wild rice.* The expensive seed of an aquatic plant related to the rice family.

- *Precooked instant rice.* Par-boiled, ready cooked and boil-in-the-bag rice are similar.

- *Ground rice.* Used for milk puddings (page 514). *Rice flour* can be used for thickening cream soups. *Rice paper* is used for macaroons and nougat.

Once cooked, keep hot (above 65°C for no longer than two hours) or cool quickly (90 minutes) and keep cool, below 5°C. The spores of Bacillus Cereus (a bacterium found in the soil) may revert to bacteria

and multiply in the cooked rice. Rice is a very useful and versatile carbohydrate. When added to dishes the fat content can be proportionally reduced.

20 Plain boiled rice

1 portion provides:
37 kJ/90 kcal energy
0.1 g fat
(of which 0.0 g saturated)
20.0 g carbohydrate
(of which 0.0 g sugars)
1.9 g protein
0.0 g fibre

1 Pick and wash the long-grain rice. Add to plenty of boiling salted water.
2 Stir to the boil and simmer gently until tender, for approximately 12–15 minutes.
3 Wash well under running water, drain and place on a sieve and cover with a cloth.
4 Place on a tray in a moderate oven or in the hot plate until hot.
5 Serve in a vegetable dish separately.

21 Steamed rice

1 of 4 portions provide:
1277 kJ/305 kcal energy
1.4 g fat
(of which 0.0 g saturated)
63.7 g carbohydrate
(of which 0.0 g sugars)
7.1 g protein
0.0 g fibre

Place the washed rice into a saucepan and add water until the water level is 2.5 cm (1 inch) above the rice. Bring to the boil over a fierce heat until most of the water has evaporated. Turn the heat down as low as possible, cover the pan with a lid and allow the rice to complete cooking in the steam. Once cooked, the rice should be allowed to stand in the covered steamer for 10 minutes.

22 Braised or pilaff rice

Riz pilaff

Using white rice and hard margarine, 1 portion provides:
774 kJ/184 kcal
10.4 g fat
(of which 4.5 g saturated)
22.1 g carbohydrate
(of which 0.3 g sugars)
1.9 g protein
0.6 g fibre

Using brown rice and hard margarine, 1 portion provides:
769 kJ/183 kcal
10.9 g fat
(of which 4.6 g saturated)
20.7 g carbohydrate
(of which 0.7 g sugars)
1.9 g protein
1.0 g fibre

	4 portions	10 portions
butter, margarine or oil	50 g (2 oz)	125 g (5 oz)
chopped onion	25 g (1 oz)	60 g (2½ oz)
rice, long-grain, white or brown	100 g (4 oz)	250 g (10 oz)
white stock (preferably chicken)	200 ml (approx ⅜ pt)	500 ml (1¼ pt)
salt, mill pepper		

Healthy eating tip: Use an unsaturated oil (sunflower or olive). Lightly oil the pan and drain off any excess after the frying is complete. Keep the added salt to a minimum.

1 Place 25 g (1 oz) butter in a small sauteuse. Add the onion.
2 Cook gently without colouring for 2–3 minutes. Add the rice.
3 Cook gently without colouring for 2–3 minutes.
4 Add twice the amount of stock to rice.
5 Season, cover with a buttered paper, bring to the boil.
6 Place in a hot oven 230–250°C (Reg. 8–9; 50–500°F) for approximately 15 minutes until cooked.
7 Remove immediately into a cool sauteuse.
8 Carefully mix in the remaining butter with a two-pronged fork.
9 Correct the seasoning and serve.

Note: It is usual to use long-grain rice for pilaff because the grains are firm, and there is less likelihood of them breaking up and becoming mushy. During cooking the long-grain rice absorbs more liquid, loses less starch and retains its shape as it swells; the short- or medium-grains may split at the ends and become less distinct in outline.

23 Braised rice with mushrooms

Riz pilaff aux champìgnons

Ingredients as for braised rice with the addition of 50–100 g (2–4 oz) button mushrooms.

1 Place 25 g (1 oz) butter in a small sauteuse. Add the onion.
2 Cook gently without colour for 2–3 minutes.
3 Add the rice and well-washed sliced mushrooms.
4 Complete as for braised rice from point 4 (recipe 22).

24 Braised rice with peas and pimento

Riz à l'orientale

As for braised rice (recipe 22) plus 25 g (1 oz) cooked peas and 25 g (1 oz) 1 cm (½ inch) diced pimento carefully mixed in when finishing with butter.

Note: Many other variations of pilaff may be made with the addition of such ingredients as tomato concassé, diced ham, prawns, etc.

25 Braised or pilaff rice with cheese

Riz pilaff au fromage

As recipe 22 with 50–100 g (2–4 oz) freshly grated cheese added with the butter, before serving.

26 Risotto

	4 portions	10 portions
butter or oil	50 g (2 oz)	125 g (5 oz)
chopped onion	25 g (1 oz)	60 g (2½ oz)
rice (short-grain or brown)	100 g (4 oz)	250 g (10 oz)
white stock (preferably chicken) or veal	185 ml (approx ⅜ pt)	500 ml (1 pt)
salt, mill pepper		
grated Parmesan cheese	25 g (1 oz)	60 g (2½ oz)

1   Melt the butter or oil in a small sauteuse. Add the chopped onion.

2   Cook gently without colour for 2–3 minutes. Add the rice.

3   Cook without colour for 2–3 minutes. *Gradually* add the stock, season lightly.

4   Cover with a lid. Allow to simmer on the side of the stove.

5   Stir frequently and if necessary add more stock until the rice is cooked.

6   When cooked, all the stock should have been absorbed into the rice and evaporated: a risotto should be more moist than a pilaff.

7   Finally mix in the cheese with a two pronged fork, correct the seasoning and serve.

Note: Risotto is a traditional Italian dish for which arborio or carnarolli rice is generally used.

Risotto variations include:

- *Saffron or Milanese-style* Soak ¼ teaspoon saffron in a little hot stock and mix in to the risotto near the end of cooking time.

- *Seafood* Add any one or mixture of cooked mussels, shrimp, prawns, etc., just before the rice is cooked. Use also half fish stock, half chicken stock.

- *Mushrooms.*

Using white rice, hard margarine, 1 portion provides:
881 kJ/210 kcal
12.3 g fat
(of which 5.7 g saturated)
22.1 g carbohydrate
(of which 0.3 g sugars)
4.1 g protein
0.6 g fibre

Using brown rice, hard margarine, 1 portion provides:
881 kJ/210 kcal
12.3 g fat
(of which 5.7 g saturated)
22.1 g carbohydrate
(of which 0.3 g sugars)
4.1 g protein
1.0 g fibre

HEALTHY EATING TIP

Use an unsaturated oil (sunflower or olive). Lightly oil the pan and drain off any excess after the frying is complete. Additional salt is not necessary. Serve with a large salad and tomato bread.

27 Fried rice

	4 portions	10 portions
boiled rice (cooked at least 3 hours in advance)	400 g (1 lb)	1 kg (2½ lb)
oil	2 tbsp	5 tbsp
spring onions	2	5
egg	1	2½
a pinch of salt		
thick soy sauce	2 tsp	5 tsp

Using vegetable oil, 1 portion provides:
826 kJ/196 kcal energy
7.4 g fat
(of which 1.1 g saturated)
29.9 g carbohydrate
(of which 0.3 g sugars)
4.3 g protein
0.2 g fibre

1 Separate the rice grains as much as possible.
2 Separate the white and green parts of the onions and cut into small rounds.
3 Heat a wok or thick-bottomed pan over high heat.
4 Add the oil and white spring onions; stir for 30–40 seconds.
5 Beat the egg with oil and salt, and pour into the wok, leave for 6–8 seconds until the egg sets on the bottom, but remains running on top.
6 Add the rice and turn and mix continuously for 3–4 minutes until thoroughly hot.
7 Mix in the soy sauce; if the rice is too hard add a little stock and stir for a few seconds.
8 Add the green spring onion and serve.

HEALTHY EATING TIP

Using an unsaturated oil (sunflower or olive), lightly oil the pan. Soy sauce adds sodium, so no added salt is needed.

28 Stir-fried rice

Stir-fried rice dishes consist of a combination of cold precooked rice and ingredients such as cooked meat or poultry, fish, vegetables or egg.

1 Prepare and cook meat or poultry in fine shreds; dice and lightly cook any vegetables. Add bean sprouts just before the egg.
2 Place a wok or thick-bottomed pan over fierce heat, add some oil and heat until smoking.
3 Add the cold rice and stir-fry for about 1 minute.
4 Add the other ingredients and continue to stir-fry over fierce heat for 4–5 minutes.
5 Add the beaten egg and continue cooking for a further 1–2 minutes.
6 Correct the seasoning and serve immediately.

Using 125 g chicken (average dark and light meat) and 25 g mung beans per portion, 1 portion provides:
1423 kJ/338 kcal energy
10.2 g fat
(of which 1.9 g saturated)
30.6 g carbohydrate
(of which 0.6 g sugars)
32.7 g protein
0.6 g fibre

HEALTHY EATING TIP

Using an unsaturated oil (sunflower or olive), lightly oil the pan. Soy sauce adds sodium, so no added salt is needed.

1 portion provides:
1826 kJ/439 kcal energy
18.0 g fat
(of which 4.5 g saturated)
60.1 g carbohydrate
(of which 1.5 g sugars)
8.4 g protein
1.1 g fibre

HEALTHY EATING TIP

Use an unsaturated oil
(sunflower or olive).
Lightly oil the pan and
drain off any excess
after the frying is
complete. Drain the
vermicelli on kitchen
paper. Omit the
butter/ghee.

29 Saffron and almond basmati rice

	4 portions	10 portions
basmati rice	250 g (8 oz)	625 g (1 lb 4 oz)
sunflower oil	2 tbsp	5 tbsp
vermicelli pasta	40 g (1½ oz)	100 g (4 oz)
finely chopped onion	50 g (2 oz)	125 g (5 oz)
clove of garlic (crushed)	1	2
butter or ghee	25 g (1 oz)	62 g (2½ oz)
saffron strands	½ tsp	1½ tsp
vegetable stock or water	500 ml (1 pt)	1.25 litres (2½ pt)
cardamon pods	6	15
cinnamon stick	1	2½
bay leaves	2	5
flaked almonds, lightly toasted	50 g (2 oz)	125 g (5 oz)

1 Soak the rice in cold water with cover for 30 minutes then drain in a sieve.

2 In a large saucepan, heat half the oil and break in the vermicelli. Stir-fry until brown. Carefully remove, drain off excess oil.

3 Add remaining oil, lightly fry onion and garlic until lightly coloured, add the butter or ghee.

4 Add the rice, stir well and fry for 1 minute.

5 Place saffron in 2 tablespoons of hot stock for 2 minutes.

6 Add the rest of the stock to the rice.

7 Add the vermicelli, cardamon, cinnamon, bay leaves, saffron and season.

8 Bring to the boil, cover and simmer until rice is cooked.

9 Remove from heat, allow to stand covered for approximately 3 minutes.

10 Sprinkle and stir in the almonds and serve immediately.

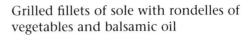

Grilled bass with red onion confit, circle of tomato concassé and parsley herb salad

Grilled fillets of sole with rondelles of vegetables and balsamic oil

Filleted red mullet on crushed potatoes with chorizo sauce, broad beans, diced tomatoes and pak choi

Grilled salmon on red pepper chutney, saffron sauce

Anton Edelmann

Fish

Because of health considerations many people choose to eat fish in preference to meat and consequently consumption of fish is and has been steadily increasing.

This popularity has resulted in a far greater selection and, due to swift and efficient transport, well over 200 types of fish are on sale throughout the year.

Fish is plentiful in the UK because we are surrounded by water, although overfishing and pollution are having a detrimental effect on the supplies of certain fish. Most catches are made off Iceland, Scotland, the North Sea, Irish Sea and the English Channel. Salmon are caught in certain English and Scottish rivers, and are also extensively farmed. Frozen fish is imported from Scandinavia, Canada and Japan and other countries worldwide; Canada and Japan both export frozen salmon to Britain.

Unfortunately the fish supply is not unlimited due to overfishing, so it is now necessary to have fish farms (such as for trout and salmon, turbot, bass, cod) to supplement the natural sources. This is not the only problem: due to contamination by humans, the seas and rivers are increasingly polluted, thus affecting both the supply and the suitability of fish, particularly shellfish, for human consumption.

Fish are valuable, not only because they are a good source of protein, but because they are suitable for all types of menus and can be cooked and presented in a wide variety of ways. The range of different types of fish of varying textures, taste and appearance is indispensable to the creative chef.

Most fish and shellfish have very little connective tissue, which unlike meat makes them naturally tender. Fish must therefore be cooked with great care and overcooking avoided, as this can both dry and toughen the product.

Types or varieties

- *Oily fish* These are round in shape (herring, mackerel, salmon, tuna, sardines).
- *White fish* Round (cod, whiting, hake) or flat (plaice, sole, turbot).
- *Shellfish* (see page 199).

Fresh fish is bought by the kilogram, by the number of fillets or whole fish of the weight that is required. For example, 30 kg (66 lb) of salmon could be ordered as 2 × 15 kg (33 lb), 3 × 10 kg (22 lb) or 6 × 5 kg (11 lb). Frozen fish can be purchased in 15 kg (33 lb) blocks.

Points to look for when buying fish

When buying whole fish the following points should be looked for to ensure freshness.

- Eyes: bright, full and not sunken; no slime or cloudiness.
- Gills: bright red in colour; no bacterial slime.
- Flesh: firm, translucent and resilient so that when pressed the impression goes quickly; the fish must not be limp.
- Scales: flat, moist and plentiful.
- Skin: should be covered with a fresh sea slime, or be smooth and moist, with a good sheen and no abrasions or bruising; there should be no discoloration.
- Smell: pleasant, with no smell of ammonia or sourness.
- Fish should be purchased daily, if possible, direct from the market or supplier.
- The fish should be well iced so that it arrives in good condition.
- Fish may be bought on the bone or filleted. (The approximate loss from boning and waste is 50% for flat fish, 60% for round fish.)

- Medium-sized fish are usually better than large fish, which may be coarse; small fish often lack flavour.

Storage

- Fresh fish are stored in a fish-box containing ice, in a separate refrigerator or part of a refrigerator used only for fish at a temperature of 1–2°C (34–36°F).
- The temperature must be maintained just above freezing point.
- Frozen fish must be stored in a deep-freeze cabinet or compartment at −18°C (0°F).
- Smoked fish should be kept in a refrigerator.

Food value

Fish is as useful a source of animal protein as meat. The oily fish (sardines, mackerel, herring, salmon, sardines) contain fat soluble vitamins (A and D) in their flesh and omega 3 fatty acids. These are unsaturated fatty acids that are essential for health. It is recommended that we eat more oily fish.

The flesh of white fish does not contain any fat. Vitamins A and D are only present in the liver (cod liver or halibut liver oil).

The small bones in sardines, whitebait and tinned salmon provide the body with calcium/phosphorus.

Owing to its fat content oily fish is not so digestible as white fish and is not suitable in cooking for invalids.

Preservation
Freezing

Fish is either frozen at sea or as soon as possible after reaching port. It should be thawed out before being cooked. Plaice, halibut, turbot, haddock, sole, cod, trout, salmon, herring, whiting, scampi, smoked haddock and kippers are available frozen.

Frozen fish should be checked for:

- no evidence of freezer burn;
- undamaged packaging;
- minimum fluid loss during thawing;
- flesh still feeling firm after thawing.

It should be stored at −18°C (0°F). *Never* refreeze frozen fish once it has thawed as this could be a major health hazard.

Canning

The oily fish are usually canned. Sardines, salmon, anchovies, pilchards, tuna, herring and herring roe are canned in their own juice (as with salmon) or in oil or tomato sauce.

Salting

In this country salting of fish is usually accompanied by a smoking process.

- Cured herrings are packed in salt.
- Caviar, the slightly salted roe of the sturgeon, is sieved, tinned and refrigerated. Imitation caviar is also obtainable.

Pickling

Herrings pickled in vinegar are filleted, rolled and skewered and known as rollmops.

Smoking

Fish to be smoked may be gutted or left whole. It is then soaked in a strong salt solution (brine), and in some cases a dye is added to improve colour. After this, it is drained and hung on racks in a kiln and exposed to smoke for 5 or 6 hours.

Fig 8.1 From top: haddock; cod; hake (left); codling; whiting

Fig 8.3 Turbot

Cold smoking takes place at a temperature of no more than 33°C (91°F) (this is to avoid cooking the flesh). Therefore all cold smoked fish is raw and is usually cooked before being eaten, the exception being smoked salmon.

Fig 8.2 From top: lemon sole; plaice; Dover sole

169

Hot smoking fish is cured at a temperature between 70–80°C (158–176°F) in order to cook the flesh, so does not require further cooking.

Choose fish with a pleasant smoky smell and a bright glossy surface. The flesh should be firm; sticky or soggy flesh means that the fish may have been of low quality or undersmoked.

Note: there is a high salt content in salted, pickled and smoked fish. Added salt is not necessary.

Safety aspects

Health and safety aspects of food hygiene are dealt with in Chapter 1. In addition:

- Store fresh fish in containers with ice (changed daily) in a refrigerator at a temperature of 1–2°C (34–36°F).
- To avoid the risk of cross-contamination fish should be stored in a separate refrigerator away from other foods; cooked and raw fish are kept separate.
- Frozen fish should be stored in a deep freezer at −18°C (0°F). When required, frozen fish should be defrosted in a refrigerator. If the frozen food is removed from the freezer and left uncovered in the kitchen, there is the danger of contamination.
- Smoked fish should be kept in a refrigerator.
- Use correct colour coded boards for preparing raw fish and different ones for cooked fish. Keep the boards clean with fresh disposable wiping cloths.
- Use equipment reserved for raw fish. If this is not possible wash and sanitise equipment before and immediately after each use.
- Unhygienic equipment, utensils and preparation areas increase the risk of cross-contamination and danger to health.
- Fish offal and bones are a high risk for contamination and must not be mixed, or stored with raw prepared fish.

- Wash equipment, knives and hands regularly using a bactericide detergent, or sanitising agent, to kill germs.
- Dispose of all wiping cloths immediately after use. Reused cloths may cause contamination.

Basic fish preparation

Unless otherwise stated, as a guide, allow 100 g (4 oz) fish off the bone and 150 g (6 oz) on the bone for a portion.

- All fish should be washed under running cold water before and after preparation.
- Whole fish are trimmed to remove the scales, fins and head using fish scissors and a knife. If the head is to be left on (as for a salmon for the cold buffet), the gills and the eyes are removed.

If the fish has to be gutted:

- Cut from the vent to two thirds along the fish.
- Draw out the intestines with the fingers or in the case of a large fish use the hook handle of a utensil such as a ladle.
- Ensure that the blood lying along the main bone is removed then wash and drain thoroughly.
- If the fish is to be stuffed then it may be gutted by removing the innards through the gill slits, thus leaving the stomach skin intact, forming a pouch in which to put the stuffing. When this method is used, care must be taken to ensure that the inside of the fish is clear from all traces of blood.

Filleting of flat fish with the exception of Dover sole

- Using a filleting knife, make an incision from the head to tail down the line of the backbone.
- Remove each fillet, holding the knife almost parallel to the work surface and keeping the knife close to the bone.

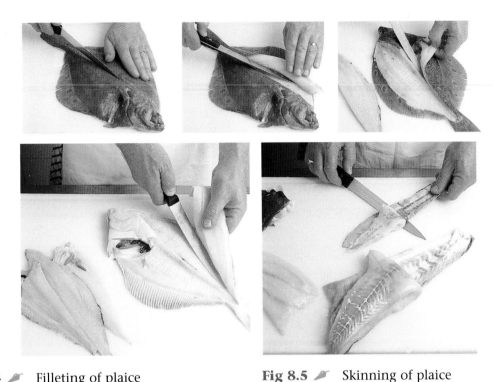

Fig 8.4 ✎ Filleting of plaice   **Fig 8.5** ✎ Skinning of plaice

Skinning of flat fish fillets with the exception of Dover sole

- Hold the fillet firmly at the tail end.
- Cut the flesh as close to the tail as possible, as far as the skin.
- Keep the knife parallel to the work surface, grip the skin firmly and move the knife from side to side to remove the skin.

Preparation of whole Dover sole

Fig 8.6 ✎ Preparation of whole Dover sole

- Hold the tail firmly, then cut and scrape the skin until sufficient is lifted to be gripped.

- Pull the skin away from the tail to the head.
- Both black and white skins may be removed in this way.
- Trim the tail and side fins with fish scissors, remove the eyes and clean and wash the fish thoroughly.

Preparation of turbot

(see fig 8.7)

- Remove the head with a large chopping knife.
- Cut off the side bones.
- Commencing at the tail end, chop down the centre of the backbone, dividing the fish into two halves.
- Divide each half into steak portions (tronçons) as required.

Note: Allow approximately 300 g (12 oz) per portion on the bone. A 3½ kg (7 lb) fish will yield approximately 10 portions.

Filleting of round fish

- Remove the head and clean thoroughly.
- Remove the first fillet by cutting along the backbone from head to tail.
- Keeping the knife close to the bone, remove the fillet.
- Reverse the fish and remove the second fillet in the same way, this time cutting from tail to head.

Methods of cooking fish

To maintain the quality and food safety of fish and shellfish dishes it is advisable to check the internal temperature by use of a probe. The following temperatures are recommended: all fish and shellfish 62°C.

Note: Environmental Health Officers may require higher temperatures.

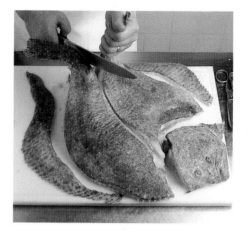

Fig 8.7 Preparation of turbot

Fig 8.8 Filleting of trout

Some examples of over 200 fish available

(O = oily, W = white)

		Baking	Boiling	Deep frying	Grilling/Griddling	Poaching	Roasting	Shallow (pan-frying)	Steaming	Stir-frying
Barracuda	O				✓			✓		
Cod	W	✓	✓	✓	✓	✓	✓	✓	✓	
Coley	W		✓	✓	✓			✓		
Dorade (red sea bream)	O	✓			✓			✓		✓
Dover Sole	W			✓	✓	✓		✓		
Emperor Bream	O	✓			✓			✓		
Grouper	W				✓		✓	✓		
Haddock	W	✓		✓	✓	✓		✓		
Hake	W	✓			✓	✓		✓		
Halibut	W	✓			✓	✓	✓	✓	✓	✓
Herring	O				✓			✓		
Huss	W			✓	✓	✓		✓		
John Dory	W	✓				✓		✓		
Lemon Sole	W	✓		✓	✓	✓		✓		
Mackerel	O	✓			✓	✓				
Marlin	O	✓			✓	✓		✓		
Monkfish	O	✓					✓	✓		✓
Plaice	W	✓		✓	✓			✓		
Red Mullet	O	✓			✓		✓	✓		
Red Snapper	O	✓			✓	✓		✓		
Salmon	O	✓	✓		✓	✓	✓	✓	✓	✓
Sardines	O				✓			✓		
Sea Bass	W	✓			✓	✓		✓	✓	
Shark	W	✓			✓	✓	✓	✓	✓	✓
Skate Wings	W		✓	✓		✓		✓		
Swordfish	W	✓			✓			✓		✓
Trout	O	✓			✓			✓		
Tuna	O				✓	✓		✓		✓
Turbot	W	✓	✓	✓	✓	✓	✓	✓		✓
Whitebait	O			✓						

Cuts of fish

Steaks

- Thick slices of fish on or off the bone.
- Steaks of round fish (salmon, cod) may be called darnes.
- Steaks of flat fish on the bone (turbot, halibut) may be called tronçons.

Fillets

- Cuts of fish free from bone: a round fish yields two fillets, a flat fish four fillets.

Suprêmes

- Prime cuts of fish without bone and skin (pieces cut from fillets of salmon, turbot, brill, etc.).

Goujons

- Filleted fish cut into strips approximately 8 × 0.5 cm (3 × ¼ inch).

Paupiettes

- Fillets of fish (sole, plaice, whiting) spread with a stuffing and rolled.

Plaited

- Also known as *en tresse*; e.g. sole fillets cut into three even pieces lengthwise to within 1 cm (½ inch) of the top, and neatly plaited.

Fish recipes
Sauces for fish

1 **Sabayon**

This is a mixture of egg yolks and a little water whisked to the ribbon stage over gentle heat. The mixture should be the consistency of thick cream. It is added to sauces to assist their glazing.

Fig 8.9 ✎ Darne of salmon

Fig 8.10 ✎ Tronçon of turbot

Fig 8.11 ✎ Suprême of salmon

Fig 8.12 ✎ Cuts of fish: (from back) fillet; suprême; délice; paupiette; goujons; goujonettes

2 Butter sauce

Beurre Blanc

	4 portions	**10 portions**
water	125 ml (¼ pt)	300 ml (⅜ pt)
wine vinegar	125 ml (¼ pt)	300 ml (⅜ pt)
finely chopped shallot	50 g (2 oz)	125 g (5 oz)
unsalted butter	200 g (8 oz)	500 g (1¼ lb)
lemon juice	1 tsp	2½ tsp
salt and pepper		

HEALTHY EATING TIP

Use minimum amounts of salt in these sauces. Do not use too much sauce with the various fish dishes.

1   Reduce the water, vinegar and shallots in a thick-bottomed pan to approximately 62 ml (⅛ pt), and allow to cool slightly.

2   Gradually whisk in the butter in small amounts, whisking continually until the mixture becomes creamy.

3   Whisk in lemon juice, season lightly and keep warm in a bain-marie.

Note: The sauce may be strained if desired. Variations include adding freshly shredded sorrel or spinach, blanched fine julienne of lemon or lime or chopped fresh herbs.

3 White wine sauce

Sauce vin blanc

This recipe provides for 4 portions:
3255 kJ/775 kcal
73.7 g fat
(of which 42.2 g saturated)
21.0 g carbohydrate
(of which 2.0 g sugars)
3.3 g protein
1.1 g fibre

	4 portions	**10 portions**
fish velouté	250 ml (½ pt)	625 ml (1¼ pt)
dry white wine	2 tbsp	5 tbsp
butter	50 g (2 oz)	125 g (5 oz)
cream	2 tbsp	5 tbsp
salt, cayenne		
few drops of lemon juice		

1   Boil the fish velouté. Whisk in the wine.

2   Remove from the heat.

3   Gradually add the butter. Stir in the cream.

4   Correct the seasoning and consistency, add the lemon juice.

5   Pass through a double muslin or fine strainer.

Note: If the sauce is to be used for a glazed fish dish then 1 egg yolk or 1 tbsp sabayon should be added as soon as the sauce is removed from the heat. (Trade practice sometimes is to whisk in 1 tbsp hollandaise sauce.)

Variations:

-   finely sliced button mushrooms and chopped parsley
-   finely sliced button mushrooms and diced, peeled, and de-seeded tomato
-   picked shrimps
-   a few strands of blanched saffron

4 Shrimp sauce

Using margarine reduced to half, 1 portion provides:
1381 kJ/332 kcal energy
22.1 g fat
(of which 10.3 g saturated)
20.0 g carbohydrate
(of which 0.9 g sugars)
14.3 g protein
0.8 g fibre

	4 portions	**10 portions**
fish velouté or béchamel	250 ml (½ pt)	625 ml (1¼ pt)
salt, cayenne		
pickled shrimps	60 ml (⅛ pt)	150 ml (⅓ pt)

1 Boil the fish velouté or béchamel.
2 Correct the seasoning and consistency using fish stock or cream.
3 Pass through double muslin or fine strainer. Mix in the shrimps.

May be served with any poached or steamed fish (for salsa see page 65).

Baking

Many fish (whole, portioned or filleted) may be oven-baked. To retain the natural moisture it is necessary to protect the fish from direct heat. There are various ways of preparing fish for baking.

* Whole fish (scaled, gutted and washed).
* Whole fish stuffed, e.g. a duxelle based mixture, breadcrumbs, herbs.
* Wrapped in pastry (puff or filo).
* Completely covered with a thick coating of dampened sea salt.
* Portions of fish can be baked, e.g.: cod, hake, haddock.

1 Place the prepared portions in a greased, oven-proof dish, brush with oil and bake slowly, basting frequently. Add herbs, e.g. parsley, rosemary, thyme etc and finely sliced vegetables, e.g. mushrooms, onions, shallots etc.

2 Depending on the size and shape of the fish, 100–150 g (4–6 oz) thick portions can be cut leaving the skin on (this helps to retain natural moisture in the fish) and baked skin side up, basting with oil. The fish can then be simply served, e.g. on a bed of creamy or flavoured mashed potato (page 468) and a suitable sauce, e.g. compound butter (page 68) or a salsa (page 65).

5 Baked cod with a herb crust

Using mustard powder (1 tsp) for herb mustard,
1 portion provides:
1882 kJ/452 kcal energy
30.8 g fat
(of which 18.7 g saturated)
12.7 g carbohydrate
(of which 0.8 g sugars)
31.7 g protein
0.4 g fibre

		4 portions	**10 portions**
cod fillet 100–150 g (4–6 oz)		4	10
herb mustard	herb crust		
fresh breadcrumbs		100 g (4 oz)	250 g (10 oz)
butter, margarine or oil		100 g (4 oz)	250 g (10 oz)
grated Cheddar cheese		100 g (4 oz)	250 g (10 oz)
chopped parsley		1 tsp	1 tbsp
salt and pepper			

Use a little sunflower oil when making the herb crust.
Cheese is salty – no added salt is needed.
Serve with a large portion of tomato or cucumber salsa and new potatoes.

1 Place prepared, washed and dried fish on a greased baking tray or oven-proof dish.

2 Combine ingredients for the herb crust and press evenly over the fish.

3 Bake in oven 180°C (350°F) mark 4 for approx 15–20 minutes until cooked and the crust is a light golden brown.

4 Serve either with lemon quarters or a suitable salsa (page 65) or sauce, e.g. tomato or egg (page 55).

Boiling

Boiling is more generally termed poaching and is suitable for (a) whole fish, e.g. salmon, trout, bass, and (b) certain cuts on the bone, e.g. salmon, turbot, brill, halibut, cod, skate. In either case, the prepared fish should be completely immersed in the cooking liquid, which can be either water, water and milk, fish stock (for white fish) or a court bouillon (water, vinegar, onion, carrot, thyme, bay leaf, parsley stalks and peppercorns) for oily fish.

Whole fish are covered with a cold liquid and brought to the boil then *gently* simmered. Cut fish are usually cooked in a *gently* simmering liquid.

Boiled turbot, brill, halibut or cod (on the bone)

1 Place the prepared fish into a shallow pan of simmering, lightly salted water containing lemon juice. The citric acid helps to make the flesh firm and white and gives a gentle flavour.

2 Allow to simmer gently. The cooking time depends on the thickness of the fish. Do **not** overcook.

3 Remove with a fish slice, remove black skin, drain and serve.

4 Garnish with picked parsley and plain boiled potato and serve with a suitable sauce, e.g. hollandaise, herb butter, shrimp or mushroom.

Deep frying

This is suitable for small whole white fish, cuts and fillets. The fish must be coated to form a surface to prevent penetration of the cooking fat or oil into the fish. Coatings can be either:

- flour, egg and breadcrumb
- milk and flour
- batter

See pages 41–3 for further information.

Any white fish are suitable for deep frying in batter, including cod, haddock, skate and rock salmon (a term used for cat-fish, coley, dog-fish etc when cleaned and skinned). Depending on size the fish may be left whole, portioned or filleted.

6 Frying batters

Pâtes à frire

Recipe 1

	6–8 portions	**10 portions**
flour	200 g (8 oz)	500 g (1¼ lb)
salt		
yeast	10 g (⅜ oz)	25 g (1 oz)
water or milk	250 ml (½ pt)	625 ml (1¼ pt)

1 Sift the flour and salt into a basin.

2 Dissolve the yeast in a little of the water.

3 Make a well in the flour. Add the yeast and the liquid.

continued over ▶

▶ *Frying batters continued*

4   Gradually incorporate the flour and beat to a smooth mixture.

5   Allow to rest for at least 1 hour before using.

Recipe 2

	6–8 portions	10 portions
flour	200 g (8 oz)	500 g (1¼ lb)
salt		
egg	1	2–3
water or milk	250 ml (½ pt)	625 ml (1¼ pt)
oil	2 tbsp	5 tbsp

1   Sift the flour and salt into a basin. Make a well. Add the egg and the liquid.

2   Gradually incorporate the flour, beat to a smooth mixture.

3   Mix in the oil. Allow to rest before using.

Recipe 3

	6–8 portions	10 portions
flour	200 g (8 oz)	500 g (1¼ lb)
salt		
water or milk	250 ml (½ pt)	625 ml (1¼ pt)
oil	2 tbsp	5 tbsp
egg whites, stiffly beaten	2	5 tbsp

As for recipe 2, but fold in the whites just before using.

Note: Other ingredients can be added to batter, e.g. chopped fresh herbs, grated ginger, garam masala, beer.

Fried fish in batter

1   Pass the prepared, washed and well dried fish through flour, shake off the surplus and pass through the batter.

2   Place carefully away from you into the hot, deep fryer 170°C until the fish turns a golden brown. Remove and drain well.

3   Serve with either lemon quarters or tartare sauce.

Fried egg and breadcrumbed fish

1   For fish fillets, pass through flour, beaten egg and fresh white breadcrumbs. (Pat the surfaces well to avoid loose crumbs falling into the fat, burning and spoiling both the fat and the fish.)

2   Deep fry at 185°C, drain well and serve with lemon quarters and a suitable sauce, e.g. tartare.

Goujons of fish

Fish fillets, e.g. sole, plaice, salmon, etc are cut into strips approx 8 × ½ cm (3 × ¼ in) then prepared, cooked and served as above.

7   Fried sole

Sole frite

For fish courses use 200–250 g (8–10 oz) sole per portion, for main course 300–400 g (12–16 oz) sole per portion.

1   Remove the black and white skin. Remove the side fins.

2   Remove the head. Clean well.

3   Wash well and drain. Pané and deep fry at 175°C (347°F).

Fig 8.13 🖋 Preparation and cooking of fried fish

4   Serve on a dish paper with picked or fried parsley and a quarter of lemon on a flat dish, and with a suitable sauce, such as tartare or anchovy.

8   Whitebait

Blanchailles

1 portion provides:
2174 kJ/525 kcal energy
47.5 g fat
(of which 0.0 g saturated)
5.3 g carbohydrate
(of which 0.1 g sugars)
19.5 g protein
0.2 g fibre

1   Pick over the whitebait, wash carefully, drain well.

2   Pass through milk and seasoned flour.

3   Shake off surplus flour in a wide mesh sieve and place fish into a frying-basket.

4   Plunge into very hot fat, just smoking (195°C/383°F).

5   Cook till brown and crisp, approximately 1 minute.

6   Drain well.

7   Season lightly with salt and cayenne pepper.

8   Serve garnished with fried or picked parsley and quarters of lemon.

Note: Allow 100 g (4 oz) per portion.

Grilling/Griddling   Read pages 37–40.

9   Grilled fish steaks, cod, swordfish, tuna, etc.

1   Wash the prepared steaks and dry them well.

2   Pass through flour, shake off surplus and brush with oil.

3   Place on hot grill bars, a griddle (page 37) or a greased baking sheet if grilling under a salamander. Brush occasionally with oil.

4   Turn the fish carefully and grill on both sides. Do not overcook.

5   Serve with lemon quarters and a suitable sauce, e.g. compound butter or a salsa.

10   Grilled round fish – herring, mackerel, bass, mullet

1   Descale fish where necessary using the back of a knife.

2   Remove heads, clean out intestines, trim off all fins and tails using fish scissors. Leave herring roes in the fish.

3   Wash and dry well.

4   Make three light incisions 2 mm (½ in) deep on either side of fish. This is known as 'scoring' and it helps the heat penetrate the fish.

5   Proceed as in previous recipe steps 2–5.

Herrings are traditionally served with a mustard sauce. Mackerel may be butterfly filleted and grilled.

11   Grilled fish fillets – sole, plaice, haddock

1   Remove the black skin from sole and plaice and proceed as for grilled fish steaks.

12   Grilled whole sole

1   Remove the black skin, descale and remove head and side bones with fish scissors.

2   Proceed as for grilled fish steaks 1–5.

Grilled salmon – proceed as for grilled fish steaks 1–4. Serve with thinly sliced cucumber and a suitable sauce, e.g. compound butter. See page 68.

Fig 8.14   Grilled salmon

13 Griddled monkfish with leeks and Parmesan

1 portion provides:
1009 kJ/239 kcal energy
8.3 g fat
(of which 5.0 g saturated)
1.0 g carbohydrate
(of which 0.8 g sugars)
40.3 g protein
0.6 g fibre

	4 portions	10 portions
prepared monkfish fillets	750 g (1½ lb)	1.8 kg (3¾ lb)
leek, finely sliced	100 g (4 oz)	250 g (10 oz)
Parmesan grated	100 g (4 oz)	250 g (10 oz)
egg white, lightly beaten	2	5
seasoning		
lemons	1	3

No added salt – plenty in the cheese. Serve with a large portion of potatoes and vegetables or salad.

1 Heat the griddled pan, lightly oil.

2 Cut the leek into fine julienne with the Parmesan, then season.

3 Cut the monkfish into 1.5 cm (¾ inch) thick slices. Dry, dip in the beaten egg white, then in the leek and Parmesan.

4 Place the monkfish on the griddle to cook approximately 3–4 minutes.

5 Garnish with lemon wedges and mixed leaves.

14 Grilled bass with red onion confit

	4 portions	10 portions
bass fillets	4 × 100 g (4 oz)	10 × 100 g (4 oz)
red onions finely chopped	4 medium	9 medium
red wine	250 ml (½ pt)	625 ml (1¼ pt)
sherry wine vinegar	4 tbsp	10 tbsp
water	4 tbsp	10 tbsp
honey	1 tsp	2½ tsp
butter or margarine	50 g (2 oz)	125 g (5 oz)
tomatoes (peeled, seeded and finely chopped)	10 medium	25 medium
olive oil	4 tbsp	10 tbsp
seasoning		
fresh basil		

Reduce the amount of olive oil used to brush the fish. Serve with new potatoes and plenty of vegetables or salad.

1 Place the finely chopped onions, red wine and sherry vinegar and water into a suitable pan and cook until the onions are tender.

2 Add the honey and 25 g (1 oz) of butter, season.

3 Place the remaining butter into a pan, add the finely chopped tomato flesh, cook to a purée, add a little water if required and a little tomato purée to improve the colour if necessary.

4 Place the fillets of bass through seasoned flour and mark criss cross with a hot poker to represent a grilling effect.

5 Brush with olive oil liberally and grill until cooked, until the fish flakes easily.

6 To serve, place the onion confit on a plate, surround with the tomato purée, place the fillets of bass on top of the confit.

7 Decorate with fresh basil leaves.

Note: John Dory, red snapper, cod, turbot may be used.

15 Grouper with crab and herb crust served on a spicy pepper sauce

1 portion provides:
1751 kJ/422 kcal energy
31.8 g fat
(of which 15.7 g sugars)
7.8 g carbohydrate
(of which 7.0 g sugars)
26.5 g protein
0.5 g fibre

	4 portions	**10 portions**
grouper fillets	4 × 100 g (4 oz)	10 × 100 g (4 oz)
butter or margarine	25 g (1 oz)	62 g (2½ oz)
freshly grated ginger	1 tsp	2½ tsp
white crab meat	100 g (4 oz)	250 g (10 oz)
chopped parsley	1 tbsp	2½ tbsp
chopped basil	1 tbsp	2½ tbsp
Parmesan cheese, freshly grated	12 g (½ oz)	30 g (1¼ oz)
seasoning		

Sauce

butter or margarine	25 g (1 oz)	62 g (2½ oz)
vegetable oil	1½ tbsp	3 tbsp
small onion, finely chopped	1	2½
red pepper, de-seeded and finely chopped	1	3
small dessert apple, finely chopped	1	3
curry powder	½ tsp	1¼ tsp
saffron	¼ tsp	1 tsp
fish stock	375 ml (¾ pt)	1 litre (2 pt)
double cream or crème fraîche	3 tbsp	8 tbsp
seasoning		

HEALTHY EATING TIP

No added salt is necessary as Parmesan cheese is added to the crust.
Use a small amount of an unsaturated oil (olive or sunflower) to fry the fish and the vegetables for the sauce. Finish the sauce with low fat fromage frais. Serve with plenty of potatoes and vegetables.

1 Heat the butter in a suitable pan and sweat gently for approximately 1 minute.

2 Remove from heat and stir in the crab meat, herbs and seasoning.

3 Season the fish and quickly fry in vegetable oil in a suitable pan on each side for approximately 1 minute.

4 Place on a suitable tray, spread each fillet with the crab mixture and sprinkle with Parmesan cheese.

continued over ▶

▶ *Grouper with crab and herb crust continued*

5 Finish cooking under the grill until the crust is lightly coloured and the fish is cooked through.

6 Serve on a bed of spicy sauce.

7 To prepare the sauce, heat the butter and oil in a suitable pan and sweat the onion without colour.

8 Add the red pepper and sweat for a further 8–10 minutes.

9 Add the apple, curry powder and saffron, stir well, cook for 5 minutes.

10 Add the fish stock, bring to the boil, simmer gently for 20 minutes.

11 Liquidise the sauce, pass through a fine strainer.

12 Return to a clean saucepan, correct the seasoning and consistency.

13 Finish with cream or crème fraîche.

16 Grilled swordfish and somen noodle salad with cilantro vinaigrette

Using vegetable oil for canola; coriander for cilantro; wheat pasta for buckwheat pasta, 1 portion provides:
2599 kJ/623 kcal energy
42.6 g fat
(of which 6.1 g saturated)
40.3 g carbohydrate
(of which 2.7 g sugars)
21.2 g protein
2.5 g fibre

	4 portions	**10 portions**
swordfish fillets	4 × 75 g (3 oz)	10 × 75 g (3 oz)
buckwheat somen noodles	200 g (8 oz)	500 g (1¼ lb)
romaine lettuce	¼	½
celery, finely diced	50 g (2 oz)	125 g (5 oz)
chopped onion (red)	50 g (2 oz)	125 g (5 oz)
Vinaigrette **olive oil**	70 ml (⅛ pt)	170 ml (¼ pt)
sesame oil	35 ml (⅙ pt)	85 ml
canola oil	35 ml (¹⁄₁₆ pt)	85 ml
rice wine	2 tbsp	4½ tbsp
lemon juice	½ lemon	1
lime juice	1 lime	2
fresh ginger, chopped	2 tbsp	5 tbsp
garlic, chopped	1 clove	3 cloves
cilantro leaves	1 tbsp	2½ tbsp
sesame seeds (black)	2 tbsp	5 tbsp
seasoning		

Fig 8.15 🖊 Grilled fillets of lemon sole
Anton Edelmann

HEALTHY EATING TIP
Keep added salt to a minimum. Adding less vinaigrette to the finished dish can reduce the fat content.

1 Prepare the vinaigrette by placing all the ingredients in a liquidiser, purée until smooth. Season to taste.

2 Season the swordfish fillets, brush with the vinaigrette. Grill for 2 to 3 minutes on each side until cooked. Allow to cool.

3   Cook the noodles in boiling water, refresh and drain. Allow to cool.

4   Shred the lettuce finely, mix with the diced celery and finely chopped red onion. Season with the vinaigrette.

5   Serve by arranging the noodles in the centre of each plate.

6   Place the swordfish fillets on the noodles, season with vinaigrette.

7   Garnish with romaine lettuce. Freshly ground black pepper may be used to finish the dish.

17   Fish kebabs

Fish kebabs or brochettes are best made using a firm fish e.g. salmon, tuna, marlin, turbot. The fish (free from skin and bone) are cut into cubes and can be (a) simply seasoned with salt and pepper or (b) lightly rolled in herbs e.g. cumin seeds and mustard or (c) placed in a simple marinade e.g. olive oil, lemon juice and chopped parsley, for 30 minutes. Other ingredients to be threaded on the skewers can be halves of small, par-boiled new potatoes, cherry tomatoes, and mushrooms.

The kebabs are lighly brushed with oil and cooked on a fierce grill or barbecue.

Note: see page 204 for scallops, which are suitable for kebabs.

Poaching

Read page 29.

Poached salmon

1   Place the prepared and washed darnes of salmon in a simmering court bouillon (page 126) for approximately 5 minutes.

2   Drain well and carefully remove centre bone and outer skin. Ensure that the fish is cleaned of any cooked blood.

3   Serve with a suitable sauce, e.g. hollandaise or melted herb butter and thinly sliced cucumber.

Note: Depending on the size of the salmon either a whole or half a darne of salmon would be served as a portion.

Poached smoked haddock

	4 portions	10 portions
smoked haddock fillets	400–600 g (1–1½ lb)	1.2 kg (2½ lb)
milk and water		

1   Cut fillets into even portions, place into a shallow pan and cover with half milk and water.

2   Simmer gently for a few minutes until cooked.

3   Drain well and serve.

Note: This is a popular breakfast dish and is also served as a lunch and a snack dish, e.g.:

(a) When cooked, garnish with slices of peeled tomato or tomato concassé, lightly coat with cream, flash under the salamander and serve.

(b) Top with a poached egg.

(c) When cooked, lightly coat with Welsh rarebit mixture (page 621), brown under the salamander and garnish with peeled slices of tomato or tomato concassé.

The following three recipes are from the classical repertoire. Although Dover sole fillets are used, any white fish fillets may be prepared and served by the same method. If shallots are used they *must* be *finely* chopped and sweated in a little butter before use.

The traditional way of making classic fish sauces is to strain off the cooking liquor (after the fish is cooked) and reduce it to a glaze (page 52). Remove the pan from the heat and gradually incorporate small pieces of butter. If the sauce is to be glazed, some lightly whipped double cream can be added.

18   Fillets of fish Duglére

Filets de poisson Duglére

> 1 portion provides:
> 699 kJ/167 kcal
> 11.6 g fat
> (of which 6.8 g saturated)
> 1.9 g carbohydrate
> (of which 1.9 g sugars)
> 11.5 g protein
> 0.9 g fibre

	4 portions	10 portions
white fish fillets sweated	400–600 g (1–1¼ lb)	1–1.5 kg (2½–3 lb)
finely chopped shallot	10 g (½ oz)	25 g (1 oz)
tomatoes concassé	200 g (8 oz)	500 g (1¼ lb)
pinch chopped parsley		
salt, pepper		
fish stock	60 ml (⅛ pt)	150 ml (⅓ pt)
dry white wine	60 ml (⅛ pt)	150 ml (⅓ pt)
lemon, juice of	¼	½
fish velouté	250 ml (½ pt)	600 ml (1¼ pt)
butter	50 g (2 oz)	125 g (5 oz)

HEALTHY EATING TIP

Keep the added salt to a minimum. Sweat the shallots in a small amount of unsaturated oil. Reduce or omit the butter when finishing the sauce.

1 Remove the black and white skins and fillet the fish.
2 Wash and drain well.
3 Butter and season an earthenware dish or sauté pan.
4 Sprinkle in the sweated chopped shallots.
5 Add the fillets, which may be folded in two, add the tomatoes and chopped parsley.
6 Season with salt and pepper.
7 Add the fish stock, wine and the lemon juice.
8 Cover with a buttered greaseproof paper.
9 Poach gently in a moderate oven at 150–200°C (Reg. 2–6; 300–400°F) for 5–10 minutes.
10 Remove the fillets and the garnish, place on a flat dish, or in a clean earthenware dish, keep warm.
11 Pass and reduce the cooking liquor in a small sauteuse, add the fish velouté, pass through a fine strainer, then incorporate the butter.
12 Correct the seasoning and consistency.
13 Coat the fillets with the sauce and serve.

Fig 8.16   Fillets of fish Duglére

19 Fillets of fish with white wine sauce

Filets de poisson vin blanc

1 portion provides:
1421 kJ/342 kcal energy
24.0 g fat
(of which 12.8 g saturated)
5.8 g carbohydrate
(of which 0.9 g sugars)
25.9 g protein
0.2 g fibre

	4 portions	10 portions
fillets of white fish	400–600 g (1–1¼ lb)	1–1.5 kg (2½–3 lb)
finely chopped sweated shallot	10 g (½ oz)	25 g (1 oz)
fish stock	60 ml (⅛ pt)	150 ml (⅓ pt)
dry white wine	60 ml (⅛ pt)	150 ml (⅓ pt)
lemon, juice of	¼	½
fish velouté	250 ml (½ pt)	625 ml (1¼ pt)
butter	50 g (2 oz)	125 g (5 oz)
cream, lightly whipped	2 tbsp	5 tbsp

HEALTHY EATING TIP

Keep the added salt to a minimum. Reduce the amount of butter and cream added to finish the sauce. Less sauce could be added, plus a large portion of potatoes and vegetables.

1 Skin and fillet the fish, trim and wash.
2 Butter and season an earthenware dish.
3 Sprinkle with the sweated chopped shallot and add the fillets of sole.
4 Season, add the fish stock, wine and lemon juice.
5 Cover with a buttered greaseproof paper.
6 Poach in a moderate oven at 150–200°C (Reg. 2–6; 300–400°F) for 5–10 minutes.
7 Drain the fish well; dress neatly on a flat dish or earthenware dish.
8 Bring the cooking liquor to the boil with the velouté.
9 Correct the seasoning and consistency and pass through double muslin or a fine strainer.
10 Mix in the butter, finally add the cream.
11 Coat the fillets with the sauce. Garnish with fleurons (puff paste crescents).

Variations: add to the fish before cooking

- Bonne-femme – 100 g (4 oz) thinly sliced white button mushrooms and chopped parsley
- Bréval – as for Bonne-femme plus 100 g (4 oz) diced, peeled and de-seeded tomatoes.

20 Fillets of fish Véronique

Filets de poisson Véronique

1 portion provides:
1077 kJ/256 kcal
19.3 g fat
(of which 10.7 g saturated)
6.9 g carbohydrate
(of which 2.1 g sugars)
11.8 g protein
0.4 g fibre

continued over ▶

▶ *Fillets of fish Véronique continued*

	4 portions	**10 portions**
fillets of white fish	400–600 g (1–1¼ lb)	1–1.5 kg (2½–3 lb)
finely chopped shallot	10 g (½ oz)	25 g (1 oz)
fish stock	60 ml (⅛ pt)	150 ml (⅓ pt)
dry white wine	60 ml (⅛ pt)	150 ml (⅓ pt)
lemon, juice of	¼	½
fish velouté	250 ml (½ pt)	625 ml (1¼ pt)
butter	50 g (2 oz)	125 g (5 oz)
cream, lightly whipped	2 tbsp	5 tbsp
white grapes (blanched, skinned and pipped)	50 g (2 oz)	125 g (5 oz)

HEALTHY EATING TIP

Keep the added salt to a minimum.
Reduce the amount of butter and cream added to finish the sauce.
Less sauce could be added plus a large portion of potatoes and vegetables.

1 Prepare and cook as for recipe 19, adding an egg yolk or spoonful of sabayon to the sauce.
2 Glaze under the salamander.
3 Arrange the grapes neatly on the dish.

21 Fillets of fish Mornay

Filets de poisson Mornay

> 1 portion provides:
> 1309 kJ/315 kcal energy
> 19.3 g fat
> (of which 9.3 g saturated)
> 5.5 g carbohydrate
> (of which 0.7 g sugars)
> 29.9 g protein
> 0.2 g fibre

	4 portions	**10 portions**
white fish fillets	500–600 g (1–1½ lb)	1.5 kg (2½ lb)
fish stock	125 ml (¼ pt)	300 ml (⅝ pt)
béchamel sauce	250 ml (½ pt)	625 ml (1¼ pt)
egg yolk or sabayon	1	3
grated cheese, preferably Gruyère or Parmesan	50 g (2 oz)	125 g (5 oz)
salt, cayenne		
butter	25 g (1 oz)	60 g (2½ oz)
cream, lightly whipped	2 tbsp	5 tbsp

HEALTHY EATING TIP

Reduce the amount of butter and cream added to finish the sauce.
Less sauce could be added plus a large portion of potatoes and vegetables.

1 Prepare the fillets; place in a buttered, seasoned earthenware dish or shallow pan, such as a sauté pan.
2 Add the fish stock, cover with a buttered paper.

3 Cook in a moderate oven at 150–200°C (Reg. 2–6; 300–400°F) for approximately 5–10 minutes.

4 Drain the fish well, place in a clean earthenware or flat dish.

5 Bring the béchamel to the boil, add the reduced cooking liquor, whisk in the yolk and remove from the heat. Add the cheese and correct the consistency. Do not reboil, otherwise the egg will curdle.

6 Correct the seasoning and pass through a fine strainer.

7 Mix in the butter and cream, check the consistency.

8 Mask the fish, sprinkle with grated cheese and gratinate under the salamander.

Note: Variations include:

- *Fillets of fish Walewska* Place a slice of cooked lobster on each fish fillet before coating with the sauce. After the dish is browned decorate each fillet with a slice of truffle.

- *Fillets of fish Florentine* Proceed as for Fillets Mornay, placing the cooked fish on a bed of well drained and heated dry leaf spinach.

22 Skate with black butter

Raie au beurre noir

1 portion provides:
725 kJ/174 kcal energy
10.8 g fat
(of which 6.5 g saturated)
0.1 g carbohydrate
(of which 0.1 g sugars)
19.0 g protein
0.0 g fibre

	4 portions	10 portions
skate wings	400–600 g (1–1½ lb)	1¼ kg (2½ lb)
court bouillon, (page 126)		
butter	50 g (2 oz)	125 g (5 oz)
vinegar	1 tsp	2½ tsp
chopped parsley		
capers	10 g (½ oz)	25 g (1¼ oz)

HEALTHY EATING TIP
Pour less black butter over the cooked fish. Serve with a large portion of potatoes and vegetables.

1 Cut the skate into 4 (or 10) even pieces.

2 Simmer in a court bouillon until cooked, approximately 10 minutes.

3 Drain well, place on a serving dish or plates.

4 Heat the butter in a frying-pan until well browned, almost black; add the vinegar, pour over the fish, sprinkle with chopped parsley and a few capers and serve.

Variation: Proceed as for 1–3, drain well and serve on a bed of plain or herb flavoured mash potato, accompanied by a compound butter sauce (page 68) or a salsa (page 65).

Roasting

Thick cuts of any fish, e.g. cod, salmon, turbot, sea-bass, monkfish etc may be roasted. Depending on size the fish may be roasted whole, e.g. sea bass.

This fish is usually portioned, skin left on, lightly seared in hot oil skin side down in a pan, and then roasted in a hot oven 230°C (450°F), gas mark 8, skin side up.

Finely sliced vegetables and sprigs of herbs can be added to the roasting tray and when the fish is cooked and removed the tray can be deglazed with a suitable wine (usually a dry white) and fish stock to form the basis of an accompanying sauce.

If the fish is skinned after it has been seared a light crust of breadcrumbs mixed with a good oil, butter or margarine, lemon juice, fresh chopped herbs, e.g. parsley, tarragon, chervil, rosemary or a duxelle based mixture or a light coating of creamed horseradish can be used.

The fish portions may be served with a sauce or a salsa or placed on a bed of creamed or flavoured mashed potato (page 468) with a compound butter sauce (page 68) and quarters of lemon.

Examples: Roast cod on garlic mash
Roast sea bass flavoured with fennel.

	4 portions	10 portions
red mullet, 200 g (8 oz)	4	10
new potatoes (medium sized)	400 g (1 lb)	1 kg (2 lb)
black olives, stoned, finely chopped	50 g (2 oz)	125 g (5 oz)
plum tomatoes, peeled, de-seeded, diced	2	5
chives	25 g (1 oz)	50 g (2 oz)
olive oil		
broad beans	200 g (8 oz)	400 g (1 lb)
diced tomatoes	100 g (4 oz)	250 g (10 oz)
salsa verde (page 66)		

HEALTHY EATING TIP

Use a minimum amount of salt. Brush the fish with a little unsaturated oil before placing on the hot grill.

23   Whole roasted red mullet on crushed potatoes, salsa verde

1 portion provides:
3120 kJ/750 kcal energy
55.5 g fat
(of which 6.9 g saturated)
21.2 g carbohydrate
(of which 3.9 g sugars)
42.6 g protein
4.9 g fibre

1   Remove scales, head and intestines, then wash and dry the fish.

2   Cut down both sides of the back bone and carefully remove the bone.

3   Trim off all fins, excess rib bones and neaten the tail.

4   Cook potatoes, drain, cool, peel and crush with a fork.

5   Mix in the olives, plum tomatoes, chives and lightly season.

6   Lighly season the fish, turn in oil and place on hot grill to mark.

7   Place on a baking sheet and bake in oven 200°C reg 6 for approx 5–6 mins.

8 Arrange potatoes in middle of plates and a ring of broad beans and tomato around it.

9 Place fish on top, coat lightly with warmed salsa and pour a little around it.

10 Garnish with a lightly steamed pak choy.

Note: This is an adapted recipe from Anton Edelmann.

Shallow or pan-frying

This method is suitable for small whole fish, cuts or fillets that are cooked in oil or fat in a frying pan. The fish are usually coated with flour but semolina, matzo meal, oatmeal or breadcrumbs may be used. If the frying medium is to be butter, it must be clarified (p. 40) otherwise there is a risk the fish may burn. Oil is the best medium to which a little butter may be added for flavour.

Method

1 Prepare, clean, wash and well dry the fish.

2 Pass through flour and shake off all surplus.*

3 Heat the frying medium in a frying pan.

4 Shallow fry on both sides (presentation side first) and serve.

* If using non-stick pans it is not necessary to flour the fish.

Note: Do not overcrowd the pan because this may cause the temperature of the fat to fall and affect the efficient cooking of the fish.

Variations

(A) *A la meunière* – when cooked, mask with nut brown butter, lemon juice and chopped parsley.

(B) As for meunière with sliced almonds lightly browned in the butter.

(C) As for meunière, with picked shrimps and finely sliced button mushrooms heated in the butter.

(D) As for meunière with a sprinkling of capers and segments of lemon or lime taken from peeled lemons (yellow and white skins removed).

(E) When cooked, sprinkle with a mixture of grated lemon zest, finely chopped garlic and chopped parsley, known as gremolata.

24 Fish meunière

1 portion (125 g white fish) provides:
1314 kJ/313 kcal
24.1 g fat
(of which 10.3 g saturated)
3.1 g carbohydrate
(of which 0.0 g sugars)
21.2 g protein
0.1 g fibre

HEALTHY EATING TIP

Use a small amount of unsaturated oil to fry the fish. Use less beurre noisette per portion. Some customers will prefer the finished dish without the additional fat.

Many fish, whole or filleted, may be cooked by this method: sole, sea bass, bream, fillets of plaice, trout, brill, cod, turbot, herring, scampi, etc.

1 Prepare and clean the fish, wash and drain.

2 Pass through seasoned flour, shake off all surplus flour.

3 Shallow fry on both sides, presentation side first, in hot clarified butter, margarine or oil.

4 Dress neatly on an oval flat dish or plate/plates.

5 Peel a lemon, removing the peel, white pith and pips.

6 Cut the lemon into slices and place one slice on each portion.

7 Squeeze some lemon juice on the fish.

8 Allow 10–25 g (½–1 oz) butter per portion and colour in a clean frying-pan to the nut-brown stage (beurre noisette).

189

continued over ▶

▶ *Fish meunière continued*

9   Pour over the fish.

10 Sprinkle with chopped parsley and serve.

Note: Variations include:

- *Fish meunière with almonds* As for fish meunière (recipe 24) adding 10 g (½ oz) of almonds cut in short julienne or coarsely chopped into the meunière butter just before it begins to turn brown. This method is usually applied to trout.

- *Fish belle meunière* As for recipe 24 with the addition of a grilled mushroom, a slice of peeled tomato and a soft herring roe (passed through flour and shallow fried), all neatly dressed on each portion of fish.

- *Fish Doria* As for fish meunière (recipe 24) with a sprinkling of small turned pieces of cucumber carefully cooked in 25 g (1 oz) of butter in a small covered pan, or blanched in boiling salted water.

- *Grenobloise* As for fish meunière (recipe 24), the peeled lemon being cut into segments, neatly dressed on the fish with a few capers sprinkled over.

- *Bretonne* As for fish meunière (recipe 24), with a few picked shrimps and cooked sliced mushroom sprinkled over the fish.

25 **Pan-fried fillets of lemon sole with rosemary mash and mushrooms**

1 portion provides:
1183 kJ/282 kcal energy
11.6 g fat
(of which 3.6 g saturated)
17.3 g carbohydrate
(of which 0.6 g sugars)
28.2 g protein
1.3 g fibre

Fig 8.17 Pan-fried fillets of lemon sole

John Campbell

	4 portions	10 portions
lemon sole fillets, skin on	4 × 150 g (6 oz)	10 × 150 g (6 oz)
mashed potato, (page 468)	400 g (1 lb)	1 kg (2½ lb)
chopped rosemary	pinch	1 tsp
sliced button mushrooms	200 g (8 oz)	600 g (1¼ lb)
vegetable oil	10 ml	25 ml
extra virgin olive oil	10 ml	25 ml
salt and pepper		

Fig 8.18 Pan-fried fillet of sea bass on rosemary mash with leeks, wild mushrooms and reduced veal stock *Henry Brosi*

Variations

(A) A sauce of light veal or chicken jus flavoured with fennel can be served around the plates.

(B) If the rosemary is in fresh sprigs it can be used to garnish the dish instead of being put into the potato.

(C) Girolle or some other wild mushrooms can be used in place of button mushrooms.

HEALTHY EATING TIP

Using an unsaturated oil (sunflower or olive), lightly oil the non-stick pan to fry the sole. Use a little olive oil to fry the mushrooms.
Keep added salt to a minimum.
Serve with plenty of seasonal vegetables and new potatoes.

1 Heat the vegetable oil in a non-stick pan and fry the lemon sole, skin side first, until it has a golden colour and is crispy.

2 Turn the fish over and gently seal without colouring.

3 Remove from the pan (skin side up) and keep warm.

4 Quickly and lightly fry the mushrooms in extra virgin olive oil.

5 Mix the rosemary into the mashed potato.

6 Arrange the potato in the centre of hot plates.

7 Place the fish on top, skin side down.

8 Garnish with the mushrooms and olive oil and serve.

26 Pan fried fillet of sea bass with spinach tagliatelle in a tomato vinaigrette

	4 portions	10 portions
sea bass	4 × 100 g (4 oz)	10 × 100 g (4 oz)
olive oil	2 tbsp	5 tbsp
seasoning		
lemon juice	1	3
seasoned flour		
spinach tagliatelle	100 g (4 oz)	250 g (10 oz)

continued over ▶

▶ *Pan fried fillet of sea bass with spinach tagliatelle in a tomato vinaigrette continued*

HEALTHY EATING TIP

Use a small amount of unsaturated oil to fry the fish and half the olive oil when reheating the tagliatelle. Increasing the amount of tagliatelle and serving the dish with extra vegetables or salad will proportionally reduce the fat content.

27 Balsamic vinegar and olive oil dressing

water	62 ml (⅛ pt)
olive oil	250 ml (½ pt)
balsamic vinegar	62 ml (⅛ pt)
sherry vinegar	2 tbsp
caster sugar	½ tsp
seasoning	

1 Whisk all ingredients together. Correct seasoning.

Note: The amount of balsamic vinegar will depend on the quality, age, etc. Add more or less as required.

28 Tomato vinaigrette

	4 portions	**10 portions**
tomatoes	200 g (8 oz)	500 g (1¼ oz)
caster sugar	½ tsp	1¼ tbsp
white wine vinegar	1 tbsp	2½ tsp
extra virgin olive oil	3 tbsp	8 tbsp
seasoning		

1 Prepare the vinaigrette: first blanch and de-seed the tomatoes, purée in a food processor.

2 Add the vinegar, olive oil and seasoning, whisk well to emulsify.

3 The vinaigrette should be smooth.

4 Cook the spinach tagliatelle, refresh and drain.

5 Cook the sea bass as for meunière.

6 Reheat the tagliatelle in hot olive oil, season, combine with the tomato vinaigrette.

7 Place the tagliatelle onto service plates, lay the sea bass fillets on top.

8 Finish the plates with a cordon of jus lié of balsamic vinegar and olive oil dressing (hot).

9 Decorate with stoned black olives and fresh basil leaves.

Other fish suitable for cooking by this method include: bream/mullet.

Steaming

Any fish that can be poached or boiled may also be cooked by steaming. This method has a number of advantages.

- It is an easy method of cooking.

- Because it is quick, it conserves flavour, colour and nutrients.

- Suitable for large scale cookery.

Fish is prepared as for poaching. The same can be prepared separately, but the liquor from the steamed fish should be strained off, reduced and incorporated into the sauce.

Preparation can also include adding finely cut ingredients e.g. ginger, spring onions, garlic, mushrooms and soft herbs, lemon juice and dry white wine to the fish on the steamer dish before cooking and being served with the fish.

Read pages 32–4.

29 Steamed fish with garlic, spring onions and ginger

	4 portions	10 portions
white fish fillets, e.g. cod, sole 4 oz	400 g (1 lb)	1.5 kg (2½ lb)
freshly chopped ginger	1 tbsp	2½ tbsp
spring onions, finely chopped	2 tbsp	5 tbsp
light soy sauce	1 tbsp	2½ tbsp
oil	1 tbsp	2½ tbsp
garlic cloves, peeled and thinly sliced		
salt		

1 Wash and well dry the fish, *lightly* rub with salt on both sides.

2 Put the fish onto plates, scatter the ginger evenly on top.

3 Put the plates into the steamer, cover tightly and gently steam until just cooked, 5–15 minutes according to the thickness of the fish.

4 Remove the plates, sprinkle on the spring onions and soy sauce.

5 Brown the garlic slices in the hot oil and pour over the dish.

Note: This is a Chinese recipe that can be adapted in many ways, e.g. replace spring onions and garlic and use thinly sliced mushrooms, diced tomato (skinned and de-seeded), *finely* chopped shallot, lemon juice, white wine, chopped parsley, dill or chervil.

Using 2 cloves of garlic, 1 portion provides:
468 kJ/112 kcal energy
3.5 g fat
(of which 0.7 g saturated)
1.2 g carbohydrate
(of which 0.4 g sugars)
18.7 g protein
0.1 g fibre

HEALTHY EATING TIP

Steaming is a healthy way of cooking. Serve with a large portion of rice or noodles and stir-fried vegetables.

Stir-frying

This is suitable for fish fillets cut into finger-sized pieces and quickly fried in hot oil in a wok or frying pan. Finely cut ginger and vegetables, e.g. garlic, shallots, broccoli sprigs, mushrooms and beanshoots may be added. Soy sauce is often used as a seasoning.

30 Hoki Stir-fry

Any firm white fish such as monkfish, hake or cod, can be used for this stir-fry. The vegetables may be varied according to what is available.

1 portion provides:
935 kJ/224 kcal energy
11.1 g fat
(of which 2.1 g saturated)
8.8 g carbohydrate
(of which 5.8 g sugars)
22.6 g protein
3.8 g fibre

HEALTHY EATING TIP

Reduce the amount of groundnut oil used for frying.
No added salt is needed – soy sauce is high in sodium.
Serve with a large portion of rice or noodles.

	4 portions	10 portions
hoki fillets	400 g (1 lb)	1 kg (2½ lb)
five spice powder	½ tsp	1¼ tsp
carrots	100 g (4 oz)	250 g (10 oz)
mange-tout	100 g (4 oz)	250 g (10 oz)
asparagus tips	100 g (4 oz)	250 g (10 oz)
spring onions	4	10
groundnut oil	3 tbsp	8 tbsp
root ginger grated	1 tsp	2½ tsp
cloves of garlic chopped	2	5
beansprouts	300 g (12 oz)	750 g (1 lb 14 oz)
baby sweetcorn	8	20
light soy sauce	2 tbsp	5 tbsp
seasoning		

1 Skin the fillets, cut into goujons (strips page 174) season with salt, pepper and five spice powder.

2 Cut the carrots in julienne and the mange-tout into large strips.

3 Trim the asparagus spears and cut in half crossways. Trim the spring onions and cut them diagonally into 2 cm (¾ inch) pieces, keeping the white and green parts separate.

4 Heat the oil in a wok. Add the ginger and garlic. Stir-fry for 1 minute, then add the white part of the spring onions and cook for 1 minute.

5 Add the hoki strips and stir-fry for 2–3 minutes. Add the beansprouts, toss together. Add carrots, mange-tout, asparagus and corn. Continue to stir-fry for 3–4 minutes.

6 Add soy sauce, toss everything together, then stir in the green parts of the spring onions. Serve immediately.

31 Seafood Stir-fry

1 portion provides:
724 kJ/172 kcal energy
4.9 g fat
(of which 0.8 g saturated)
9.1 g carbohydrate
(of which 4.9 g sugars)
23.2 g protein
2.1 g fibre

	4 portions	**10 portions**
small asparagus spears	100 g (4 oz)	250 g (10 oz)
sunflower or ground nut oil	1 tbsp	2½ tbsp
fresh ginger grated	1 tsp	2½ tsp
leek cut into julienne	100 g (4 oz)	250 g (10 oz)
carrots cut into julienne	100 g (4 oz)	250 g (10 oz)
baby sweetcorn	100 g (4 oz)	250 g (10 oz)
light soy sauce	2 tbsp	5 tbsp
oyster sauce	1 tbsp	2½ tbsp
clear honey	1 tsp	2½ tsp
cooked assorted ⎱ shellfish prawns mussels scallops	400 g (1 lb)	1 kg (2½ lb)
Garnish large cooked prawns	4	10
fresh chives	25 g (1 oz)	62 g (2½ oz)

HEALTHY EATING TIP

No added salt is needed – soy sauce is high in sodium. Increasing the ratio of vegetables to seafood to improve the 'balance' of this dish.

1   Blanch the asparagus for 2 minutes in boiling water, refresh then drain.

2   Heat the oil in a wok, add the ginger, leek, carrots and sweetcorn, stir-fry for 3 minutes without colour.

3   Add the soy and oyster sauce and honey. Stir.

4   Stir in the cooked shellfish and continue to stir-fry for 2–3 minutes until the vegetables are just tender and the shellfish is thoroughly heated through.

5   Add the blanched asparagus and stir-fry for another 1 minute.

6   Serve with fresh cooked noodles garnished with large fresh prawns and chopped chives.

Other fish recipes

32 Fish kedgeree

Cadgery de poisson

	4 portions	10 portions
fish (usually smoked haddock or fresh salmon)	400 g (1 lb)	1 kg (2½ lb)
rice pilaff (page 161)	200 g (8 oz)	500 g (1¼ lb)
hard-boiled eggs	2	5
butter	50 g (2 oz)	125 g (5 oz)
curry sauce (page 62)	250 ml (½ pt)	625 ml (1¼ pt)

The fish to be used should be named e.g. salmon kedgeree.

1 Poach the fish. Remove all skin and bone. Flake.
2 Cook the rice pilaff. Cut the eggs in dice.
3 Combine the eggs, fish, and rice and heat in the butter. Correct the seasoning.
4 Serve hot with a sauceboat of curry sauce.

Note: Traditionally served for breakfast, lunch or supper.

33 Fish cakes

	4 portions	10 portions
cooked fish (free from skin and bone)	200 g (8 oz)	500 g (1¼ lb)
mashed potatoes	200 g (8 oz)	500 g (1¼ lb)
salt, pepper		
flour	25 g (1 oz)	60 g (2½ oz)
egg	1	3
breadcrumbs	50 g (2 oz)	125 g (5 oz)

1 Combine the fish, potatoes and egg and season.
2 Divide into 4 (or 10) pieces. Mould into balls.
3 Pass through the coating of flour, egg and breadcrumbs.
4 Flatten slightly, neaten with a palette knife.
5 Deep fry in hot fat (185°C/365°F) for 2–3 minutes.

Using smoked haddock, 1 portion provides:
1974 kJ/472 kcal energy
28.2 g fat
(of which 15.3 g saturated)
29.3 g carbohydrate
(of which 4.7 g sugars)
25.7 g protein
1.2 g fibre

HEALTHY EATING TIP
Reduce the amount of butter used to heat the rice, fish and eggs. Garnish with grilled tomatoes and serve with bread or toast.

Using cod, 1 portion provides:
1130 kJ/270 kcal energy
13.6 g fat
(of which 1.9 g saturated)
23.2 g carbohydrate
(of which 1.1 g sugars)
15.1 g protein
0.8 g fibre

HEALTHY EATING TIP
The fish cakes could be shallow fried in a small amount of an unsaturated oil, then drained on kitchen paper.

Variations: use either cod, fresh haddock, salmon, crab, etc.

- Optional extra seasonings – tomato ketchup, fresh chopped herbs (e.g. chervil, dill, parsley, tarragon, chives), anchovy essence, English or Continental mustard.
- Coat lightly with flour and shallow fry.
- Serve with a sauce e.g. lemon butter, tartare, hollandaise, shrimp or tomato.
- Serve with a little dressed green salad.

34 Fish pie

	4 portions	10 portions
béchamel (thin) (page 54)	250 ml (½ pt)	625 ml (1¼ pt)
cooked fish (free from skin and bone)	200 g (8 oz)	500 g (1¼ lb)
cooked diced mushrooms	50 g (2 oz)	125 g (5 oz)
chopped hard-boiled egg	1	3
chopped parsley		
salt, pepper		
mashed or duchess potatoes	200 g (8 oz)	500 g (1¼ lb)

1 Bring the béchamel to the boil.
2 Add the fish, mushrooms, egg and parsley. Correct the seasoning.
3 Place in a buttered pie-dish.
4 Place or pipe the potato on top. Brush with eggwash or milk.
5 Brown in a hot oven or under the salamander and serve.

Note: Many variations can be made to this recipe with the addition of a) prawns or shrimps; b) herbs such as dill, tarragon or fennel; or c) raw fish, poached in white wine, the cooking liquor strained off, double cream added in place of béchamel and reduced to a light consistency.

1 portion provides:
879 kJ/209 kcal
12.0 g fat
(of which 5.3 g saturated)
11.9 g carbohydrate
(of which 3.2 g sugars)
14.1 g protein
0.9 g fibre

HEALTHY EATING TIP
Keep the added salt to a minimum. This is a healthy main course dish particularly when served with plenty of vegetables.

Using cod, 1 portion provides:
428 kJ/102 kcal energy
1.3 g fat
(of which 0.3 g sugars)
1.0 g carbohydrate
(of which 0.9 g sugars)
21.4 g protein
0.7 g fibre

35 Fish sausages

Cervelas de poisson

As with meat sausages, the variations of fish sausages that can be produced are virtually endless. Almost any type of fish or shellfish can be used, either chopped or minced. The filling can also be a combination of two or more fish, and additional ingredients can be added e.g. chopped mushrooms, brunoise of skinned red peppers etc., a suitable chopped herb e.g. dill, chervil, parsley and/or a touch of a spice.

fish and/or shellfish	400 g (1 lb)
chopped mushrooms	50 g (2 oz)
brunoise of skinned red pepper	50 g (2 oz)
fresh parsley, dill or chervil, chopped	25 g (1 oz)
salt and pepper	
sausage skins	

1 Mix all ingredients.
2 Place sausage skins in water then hang up, knot one end.
3 Using a forcing bag stuff the skins with the fish mixture then knot the other end with a piece of string. Pierce skin all over with a needle to prevent bursting.
4 Divide sausage into sections by loosely tying with string.
5 Gently poach the sausages in salted water for 15 minutes.
6 With a sharp knife, remove the sausage skins carefully so as not to spoil the shape, drain well on a clean serviette and serve with a suitable sauce e.g. white wine, and garnish e.g. shrimps, mushrooms.

Note: the filling can also be made using a mousseline mixture, page 128, *Advanced Practical Cookery*.

Shellfish

Recipe No.		page no.	Recipe No.		page no.
	Cockles	203	36	Mussels, white wine sauce	205
	Crab, dressed and uses	202		Prawns	199
	Crayfish	200		Prawn curry	345
	Crawfish	201		Scallops	204
	Dublin Bay prawns	200		Scampi	200
	Grilled scallops	205	40	Scampi, fried	207
	Lobster cocktail	108	41	Seafood in puff pastry	207
	Lobster, cooking and cleaning	200		Shellfish cocktail (crab, lobster,	
37	Lobster, grilled or barbecued	205		shrimp, prawn)	108
38	Lobster Mornay	205		Shrimps	200
39	Lobster Thermidor	206		Shrimp and vegetable fritters	358
	Lobster uses	201		Shrimps, potted	104
	Mussels	203		Tandoori prawns	346

Shellfish are divided into two main groups:

- *Crustacea* (lobster, crab, crawfish, crayfish, prawns and shrimps);
- *Mollusca* (oysters, mussels, scallops); these are also known as bivalves.

Shellfish are generally low in fat but high in dietary cholesterol. Saturated fat in the diet (not cholesterol) is linked to increased blood cholesterol. Shellfish can therefore be a 'healthy menu choice'.

Safety aspects

Health and safety aspects of food hygiene are dealt with in Chapter 1.

Quality, purchasing points and storage

- Whenever possible, all shellfish should be purchased live so as to ensure freshness.
- Shellfish should be kept in suitable containers, covered with damp seaweed or damp cloths and stored in a cold room or refrigerator.
- Shellfish should be cooked as soon as possible after purchasing.

Shrimps and prawns

These are often bought cooked either in the shells or peeled. Smell is the best guide to freshness. Shrimps and prawns can be used for garnishes, decorating fish dishes, cocktails, sauces, salads, hors-d'oeuvres, omelettes and snack and savoury dishes. They can also be used for a variety of hot dishes: stir-fry, risotto, curries, etc. Potted shrimps are also a popular dish. Freshly cooked prawns in the shells may also be served cold accompanied by a mayonnaise-based sauce, such as garlic mayonnaise.

King prawns are a larger variety, which can also be used in any of the above ways.

Raw and cooked shrimps and prawns are prepared by having the head, carapace (upper shell), legs, tail section and the dark intestinal vein running down the back removed.

(For shellfish cocktails, see page 108.)

Scampi, salt water crayfish and Dublin Bay prawns

These are also known as Norway lobster or langoustine and are sold fresh, frozen, raw or cooked. Their tails are prepared like shrimps and they are used in a variety of ways: salads, rice dishes, stir-fried, deep fried, poached and served with a number of different sauces. They are also used as garnishes to hot and cold fish dishes.

Freshwater crayfish are also known as écrevisse. These are small fresh water crustaceans with claws, found in lakes and lowland streams. They are prepared and cooked like shrimps and prawns and used in many dishes including soup. They are often used whole to garnish hot and cold fish dishes.

Lobster
Purchasing points

- Purchase alive, with both claws attached, to ensure freshness.
- Lobsters should be heavy in proportion to their size.
- The coral of the hen lobster is necessary to give the required colour for certain soups, sauces and lobster dishes.
- Hen lobsters are distinguished from cock lobsters by a broader tail.

Cooking of lobster

1   Wash, plunge them into a pan of boiling salted

Fig 8.19 🖋 From top: Scottish lobster (raw and cooked); Canadian lobster (cooked and raw); langoustine; crayfish

water containing 60 ml (⅛ pint) vinegar to 1 litre (2 pints) water.

2 Cover with a lid, reboil, then allow to simmer for 15–20 minutes according to size.

3 Overcooking can cause the tail flesh to toughen and the claw meat to become hard and fibrous.

4 Allow to cool in the cooking liquid when possible.

Cleaning of cooked lobster

* Remove the claws and remove the pincers from the claws.
* Crack the claws and joints and remove the meat.
* Cut the lobster in half by inserting the point of a large knife 2 cm (1inch) above the tail on the natural central line.
* Cut through the tail firmly.
* Turn the lobster around and cut through the upper shell (carapace).
* Remove the halves of the sac (which contains grit) from each half. This is situated at the top near the head.
* Using a small knife remove the intestinal trace from the tail and wash if necessary.

Uses

Lobsters are served cold in cocktails (page 108), lobster mayonnaise, hors-d'oeuvre, salads, sandwiches and in halves on cold buffets.

They are used hot in soups, sauces, rice dishes, stir-fry dishes and in numerous ways served in the half shell with various sauces. They are also used to garnish fish dishes.

Crawfish

These are sometimes referred to as spring lobsters but unlike lobsters they have no claws and the meat is solely in the tail. Crawfish vary considerably in size from 1–3 kg (2–6 lb); they are cooked as for lobsters and the tail meat can be used in any of the lobster recipes. Because of their impressive appearance crawfish dressed whole are sometimes used on special cold buffets. They are very expensive and are also available frozen.

Crab
Purchasing points

* Buy alive to ensure freshness.

Fig 8.20 Dressed crab

- Ensure that both claws are attached.
- Crabs should be heavy in relation to size.

Cooking

1 Place the crabs in boiling salted water with a little vinegar added.

2 Reboil, then simmer for 15–30 minutes according to size. These times apply to crabs weighing from ½–2½ kg (1–5 lb).

3 Allow the crabs to cool in the cooking liquor.

To dress

1 Remove large claws and sever at the joints.

2 Remove the flexible pincer from the claw.

3 Crack or saw carefully and remove all flesh.

4 Remove flesh from two remaining joints with handle of spoon.

5 Carefully remove the soft under-shell.

6 Discard the gills (dead man's fingers) and the sac behind the eyes.

7 Scrape out all the inside of the shell and pass through sieve.

8 Season with salt, pepper, Worcester sauce and a little mayonnaise sauce, thicken lightly with fresh white breadcrumbs.

9 Trim the shell by tapping carefully along the natural line.

10 Scrub the shell thoroughly and leave to dry.

11 Dress the brown meat down the centre of the shell.

12 Shred the white meat, taking care to remove any small pieces of shell.

13 Dress neatly on either side of the brown meat.

Fig 8.21 Dressed crab   *John Campbell*

Fig 8.22 Dressed crab, traditional

14 Decorate as desired, using any of the following: chopped parsley, hard-boiled white and yolk of egg, anchovies, capers, olives.

15 Serve the crab on a flat dish, garnish with lettuce leaves, quarters of tomato and the legs.

Serve a vinaigrette or mayonnaise sauce separately.

Allow 200–300 g (8–12 oz) unprepared crab per portion

Uses of crab meat

Crab meat can be used cold for hors-d'oeuvre, cocktails, salads, sandwiches and dressed crab. Used hot, it can be covered with a suitable sauce and served with rice, in bouchées or pancakes, or made into crab fish cakes.

Cockles

Cockles are enclosed in small, attractive, cream-coloured shells. As they live in sand it is essential to purge them by washing well under running cold water and leaving them in cold salted water (changed frequently) until no traces of sand remain.

Cockles can be cooked either by steaming; boiling in unsalted water; on a preheated griddle, or as for any mussel recipe.

Cockles should only be cooked until the shells open.

They can be used in soups, sauces, salads, stir-fry and rice dishes and as garnish for fish dishes.

Mussels

Mussels are extensively cultivated on wooden hurdles in the sea, producing tender, delicately flavoured plump fish. Mussels are produced in Britain and imported from France, Holland and Belgium. French mussels are small, Dutch and Belgian are plumper. The quality tends to vary from season to season.

Purchasing points

- The shells must be tightly closed indicating they are alive.
- Mussels should be of good size.
- There should not be an excessive number of barnacles attached.
- Mussels should smell fresh.

Storage

Mussels should be kept in containers, covered with damp

Fig 8.23 Spidercrab (top left); crab; crawfish

seaweed or cloths and stored in a cold room or refrigerator.

Use

Mussels can be used for soups, sauces, salads, and cooked in a wide variety of hot dishes.

Cooking

1 Scrape the shells to remove any barnacles, etc. Wash well and drain in a colander.

2 In a thick-bottomed pan with a tight-fitting lid, place 25 g (1 oz) chopped shallot or onion for 1 litre (1 qt) mussels.

3 Add the mussels, cover with a lid and cook on a fierce heat for 4–5 minutes until the shells open completely.

4 Remove the mussels from the shells, checking carefully for sand, weed, etc.

5 Retain the carefully strained liquid for the sauce.

Scallops

There are a number of varieties:

- Great scallops are up to 15 cm (6 inches) in size.
- Bay scallops are up to 8 cm (3 inches).
- Queen scallops, also known as Queenies, are small cockle-sized scallops.

Scallops are found on the seabed and are therefore dirty, so it is advisable to purchase them ready cleaned. If scallops are bought in the shells, the shells should be tightly shut, which indicates they are alive and fresh. The roe (orange in colour) should be bright and moist. Scallops in the shells should be covered with damp seaweed or cloths and kept in a cold room or refrigerator.

To remove from the shells, place the shells on top of the stove or in an oven for a few seconds, when they will open and the flesh can then be removed with a knife.

Fig 8.24 From top: scallops; large clams; small clams; mussels

Scallops should then be well washed; remove the trail leaving only the white scallop and orange roe.

Cooking

Scallops should be only lightly cooked.

- Poach gently for 2–3 minutes in dry white wine with a little onion, carrot, thyme, bayleaf and parsley. Serve with a suitable sauce (white wine, Mornay, etc.).

- Lightly fry on both sides for a few seconds in butter or oil in a very hot pan (if the scallops are very thick they can be cut in halves sideways) and serve with a suitable garnish (sliced wild or cultivated mushrooms or a fine brunoise of vegetables and tomato) and a liquid that need not be thickened (white wine and fish stock, or cream- or butter-mounted sauce). Fried scallops can also be served hot on a plate of salad leaves.

- Deep fry, either egg and crumbed or passed through a light batter and served with segments of lemon and a suitable sauce (tartare).

- Wrap in thin streaky bacon, place on skewers for grilling or barbecuing.

36 Mussels with white wine sauce

Moules marinière

Using mussels (750 g approx.), cooked with shells,
1 portion provides:
383 kJ/91 kcal energy
3.9 g fat
(of which 1.8 g saturated)
5.1 g carbohydrate
(of which 0.8 g sugars)
8.9 g protein
0.3 g fibre

	4 portions
fine chopped shallot	50 g (2 oz)
chopped parsley	
dry white wine	60 ml (⅛ pt)
mussels	2 litres (2 qts)
fish stock if necessary	
beurre manié (butter/flour)	25 g (1 oz)
salt, pepper	

1 Take a thick-bottomed pan.
2 Add chopped shallot, parsley, wine and the well-cleaned and washed mussels.
3 Cover with a tight-fitting lid.
4 Cook over fierce heat until shells open, approx. 4–5 minutes.
5 Drain off all cooking liquor into a basin, allow to stand in order to allow any sand to sink to the bottom.
6 Carefully check the mussels for sand, etc. If in doubt, discard.
7 Place mussels in an earthenware casserole, cover with a lid and keep warm.
8 Carefully pour the cooking liquor into a small sauteuse.
9 If necessary make up to ¼ litre (½ pt) with fish stock.
10 Bring to the boil, whisk in the beurre manié.
11 Correct the seasoning, add a little chopped parsley.
12 Pour over the mussels and serve.

37 Grilled or barbecued lobster

1 Three-quarter boil the lobsters and remove from the cooking liquid.
2 Split in halves, remove the gravel sac and intestinal tract.
3 Sprinkle with melted butter and cook for a short time under or on a hot grill.

Note: Lobsters can be split and grilled without preboiling but there is a tendency for them to become tough and chewy.

38 Lobster Mornay

Homard Mornay

Using Mornay sauce as per recipe (fillets of sole Mornay), 1 portion provides:
1490 kJ/359 kcal energy
28.3 g fat
(of which 16.0 g saturated)
5.5 g carbohydrate
(of which 0.7 g sugars)
21.1 g protein
0.2 g fibre

	4 portions	10 portions
cooked lobsters (400 g 1 lb)	2	5
butter	25 g (1 oz)	60 g (2½ oz)
salt, cayenne		
Mornay sauce	250 ml (½ pt)	625 ml (1¼ pt)
grated cheese (Parmesan)		

continued over ▶

▶ *Lobster Mornay continued*

Use a small amount of an unsaturated oil (olive or sunflower) to cook the lobster. Use little or no salt as the cheese will provide the necessary seasoning.

	4 portions	10 portions
cooked lobsters	2	5
butter	25 g (1 oz)	60 g (2½ oz)
finely chopped shallot	12 g (½ oz)	30 g (1¼ oz)
dry white wine	60 ml (⅛ pt)	150 ml (⅓ pt)
diluted English mustard	½ tsp	1 tsp
chopped parsley		
Mornay sauce	¼ litre (½ pt)	⅝ litre (1¼ pt)
grated Parmesan cheese	25 g (1 oz)	60 g (2½ oz)

1 Remove the lobsters' claws and legs.

2 Cut the lobsters carefully in half lengthwise.

3 Remove all the meat. Discard the sac and trail.

4 Wash, shell and drain on a baking sheet upside down.

5 Cut the lobster meat into escalopes.

6 Heat the butter in a thick-bottomed pan, add the lobster and season.

7 Turn two or three times; overcooking will toughen the meat.

8 Meanwhile, finish the Mornay sauce.

9 Place a little sauce in the bottom of each shell.

10 Add the lobster, press down to make a flat surface.

11 Mask completely with sauce, sprinkle with grated cheese, and brown under the salamander and serve garnished with picked parsley.

39 Lobster Thermidor

Homard Thermidor

Using Mornay sauce as per recipe 21, 1 portion provides:
1973 kJ/475 kcal energy
35.8 g fat
(of which 19.5 g saturated)
10.8 g carbohydrate
(of which 1.1 g sugars)
28.1 g protein
0.4 g fibre

Use a small amount of an unsaturated oil (olive or sunflower) to cook the lobster. Use little or no salt as the cheese will provide the necessary seasoning.

1 Remove the lobsters' claws and legs.

2 Cut the lobsters carefully in halves lengthwise. Remove the meat.

3 Discard the sac and remove the trail from the tail.

4 Wash the halves of shell and drain on a baking sheet.

5 Cut the lobster meat into thick escalopes.

6 Melt the butter in a sauteuse, add the chopped shallot and cook until tender without colour.

7 Add the white wine to the shallot and allow to reduce to a quarter of its original volume.

8 Mix in the mustard and chopped parsley.

9 Add the lobster slices, season lightly with salt, mix carefully and allow to heat slowly for 2–3 minutes. If this part of the process is overdone the lobster will become tough and chewy.

10 Meanwhile spoon a little of the warm Mornay sauce into the bottom of each lobster half shell.

11 Neatly add the warmed lobster pieces and the juice in which they were reheated. If there should be an excess of liquid it should be reduced and incorporated into the Mornay sauce.

12 Coat the half lobsters with the remaining Mornay sauce, sprinkle with Parmesan cheese and place under a salamander until a golden brown, and serve garnished with picked parsley.

40 Fried scampi

1 portion provides:
1685 kJ/403 kcal energy
23.1 g fat
(of which 2.4 g saturated)
34.9 g carbohydrate
(of which 0.0 g sugars)
16.0 g protein
0.0 g fibre

	4 portions	10 portions
shelled scampi	375–500 g (¾–1 lb)	1¼ kg (2½ lb)
flour	50 g (2 oz)	125 g (5 oz)
egg	1	3
fresh white breadcrumbs	50 g (2 oz)	125 g (5 oz)
lemon	1	2
parsley		

Make sure the fat is hot when frying the scampi – less fat will be absorbed.

1 Pass the scampi through the flour and eggwash and roll in fresh white breadcrumbs.

2 Shake off all surplus crumbs and lightly roll each piece of scampi to firm the surface.

3 Deep fry at 185°C (365°F).

4 Drain well on kitchen paper and serve.

5 Garnish with quarters of lemon and sprigs of fried or fresh parsley.

6 Accompany with a suitable sauce, such as sauce tartare.

41 Seafood in puff pastry

Bouchées de fruits de mer

Fried in peanut oil, 1 portion provides:
1327 kJ/316 kcal
17.6 g fat
(of which 3.1 g saturated)
28.9 g carbohydrate
(of which 1.1 g sugars)
12.2 g protein
1.2 g fibre

	4 portions	10 portions
button mushrooms	50 g (2 oz)	125 g (5 oz)
butter	25 g (1 oz)	60 g (2½ oz)
lemon, juice of	¼	½
cooked lobster, prawns, shrimps, mussels, scallops	200 g (8 oz)	500 g (1¼ lb)
white wine sauce (page 54)	125 ml (¼ pt)	300 ml (⅝ pt)
chopped parsley		
bouchée cases (page 583)	4	10

The white wine sauce is seasoned, so added salt is not required. Serve with a salad garnish

continued over ▶

▶ *Seafood in puff pastry continued*

1 Peel and wash the mushrooms, cut in neat dice.

2 Cook in butter with the lemon juice.

3 Add the shellfish (mussels, prawns, shrimps left whole, the scallops and lobster cut in dice).

4 Cover the pan with a lid and heat through slowly for 3–4 minutes.

5 Add the white wine sauce, chopped parsley and correct seasoning.

6 Meanwhile warm the bouchées in the oven or hot plate.

7 Fill the bouchées with the mixture and place the lids on top.

8 Serve garnished with picked parsley.

Note: Vol-au-vents can be prepared and cooked as puff pastry cases (page 583). The filling is prepared as above and dressed similarly.

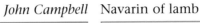

Wiener Schnitzel *John Campbell*   Navarin of lamb *John Campbell*

Chicken fricassée *John Campbell*   Seared breast of duck on its confit of root
vegetables *Anton Edelmann*

Meats

Structure of meat

To cook meat properly it is important to understand its structure.

- Meat comprises fibres bound by connective tissue.
- Connective tissue, elastin, is yellow and collagen, white.
- Yellow tissue needs to be removed.
- Small fibres are in tender cuts and young animals.
- Coarser fibres in tougher cuts and older animals.
- Fat assists in providing flavour and moistens meat in roasting and grilling.
- Tenderness, flavour and moistness are increased if meat is hung after slaughter and before being used.
- Storage times: beef up to 3 weeks, veal 1–3 weeks, lamb 10–15 days, pork 7–14 days.
- Hang and store meat between 1°C–5°C.

Full information on meat including cattle, sheep and pigs can be obtained from British Meat Service.

Offal and other edible parts of the carcass

Offal is the name given to the edible parts taken from the inside of a carcass of meat: liver, kidneys, heart and sweetbreads. Tripe, brains, tongue, head, oxtail are also sometimes included under this term.

Fresh offal (unfrozen) should be purchased as required and can be refrigerated under hygienic conditions at a temperature of −1°C (30°F), at a relative humidity of 90% for up to 7 days. Frozen offal must be kept in a deep freeze and defrosted in a refrigerator as required.

Liver

Calf's liver is considered the best in terms of tenderness and flavour. It is also the most expensive.

Lamb's liver is mild in flavour, light in colour and tender. Sheep's liver, being from an older animal, is firmer in substance, deeper in colour and has a stronger flavour.

Ox or *beef liver* is the cheapest and if taken from an older animal can be coarse in texture and strong in flavour. It is usually braised.

Pig's liver has a strong full flavour and is mainly used for pâté recipes.

Quality points

- Liver should look fresh, moist, smooth with a pleasant colour and no unpleasant smell.
- Liver should not be dry or contain an excessive number of tubes.

Food value

Liver is a good source of protein and iron and also contains vitamins A and D. It is low in fat.

Meat varies considerably in the fat content. This is found round the outside of meat, marbling and inside the meat fibres. The visible fat (saturated) should be trimmed as much as possible before cooking.

Kidneys

Lamb's kidneys are light in colour, delicate in flavour and ideal for grilling and frying.

Sheep's kidneys are darker in colour and stronger in flavour.

Calf's kidneys are light in colour, delicate in flavour and used in a variety of dishes.

Ox kidney is dark in colour, strong in flavour and is either braised, or used in pies and puddings (mixed with beef).

Pig's kidneys are smooth, long and flat and have a strong flavour.

- Suet, which is the saturated fat in which kidneys are encased, should be left on otherwise the kidneys will dry out. The suet should be removed when kidneys are being prepared for cooking.
- Both suet and kidneys should be moist and have no unpleasant smell.

Food value

This is similar to that of liver.

Hearts

Lamb's hearts are small and light and normally served whole.

Sheep's hearts are dark and solid and can be dry and tough unless carefully cooked.

Ox or *beef hearts* are dark coloured, solid and tend to be dry and tough.

Calf's hearts, coming from a younger animal, are lighter in colour and more tender.

Most hearts need slow braising to tenderise them.

Quality points

Hearts should not be too fatty and should not contain too many tubes. When cut they should be moist, not sticky and with no unpleasant smell.

Food value

Hearts are a good source of protein, which is needed for growth and repair of the body.

Sweetbreads

These are the pancreas and thymus glands known as heart breads and neck. The heart bread is round, plump and of better quality than the neck bread, which is long and uneven in shape. Calf's heart breads, considered the best, weigh up to 600 g (1½ lb), lamb's heart bread up to 100 g (4 oz).

Quality points

- Heart and neck breads should be fleshy and of good size.
- They should be creamy white in colour and have no unpleasant smell.

Food value

Sweetbreads are an easily digested source of protein, which makes them valuable for invalid diets.

Tripe

Tripe is the stomach lining or white muscle of the ox consisting of the rumen or paunch and the honeycomb tripe (considered the best); sheep tripe, darker in colour, is obtainable in some areas.

Quality points

Tripe should be fresh, with no signs of stickiness or unpleasant smell.

Food value

Tripe contains protein, is low in fat and high in calcium.

Brains

Calf's brains are those normally used. They must be fresh and have no unpleasant smell. They are a good source of protein with trace elements.

Tongues

Ox tongues and lamb and sheep tongues are those most used in cooking. Ox tongues are usually salted then soaked before being cooked. Lamb tongues are cooked fresh.

Quality points

- Tongues must be fresh and have no unpleasant smell.

- There should not be an excess of waste at the root end.

Head

Sheep's heads can be used for stock, pig's head for brawn (a cold meat preparation) and calf's head for speciality dishes (calf's head vinaigrette). Heads should be fresh, not sticky, well fleshed and free from any unpleasant smell.

Oxtail

Oxtails usually weigh 1½–2 kg (3–4 lb); they should be lean with not too much fat. There should be no sign of stickiness and no unpleasant smell.

Suet

Beef suet should be creamy white, brittle and dry. Other meat fat should be fresh, not sticky, and with no unpleasant smell.

Marrow

Marrow is obtained from the bones of the leg of beef. It should be of good size, firm, creamy white and odourless. Sliced, poached marrow may be used as a garnish for some meat dishes and savouries. Current legislation does not permit the use of marrow and beef bones.

Bones

Bones must be fresh, not sticky, with no unpleasant smell and preferably meaty as they are used for stock, the foundation for so many preparations.

Preservation of meat
Salting

Meat can be pickled in brine, and this method of preservation may be applied to silverside, brisket and ox tongues. Salting is used in the production of bacon, before the sides of pork are smoked, and for hams.

Chilling

This means that meat is kept at a temperature just above freezing-point in a controlled atmosphere. Chilled meat cannot be kept in the usual type of cold room for more than a few days, sufficient time for the meat to hang, enabling it to become tender.

Freezing

Small carcasses, such as lamb and mutton, can be frozen and the quality is not affected by freezing. They can be kept frozen until required and then thawed out before being used. Some beef is frozen, but it is inferior in quality to chilled beef.

Canning

Large quantities of meat are canned and corned beef is of importance since it has a very high protein content. Pork is used for tinned luncheon meat.

Textured vegetable protein (TVP)

This is a meat substitute manufactured from protein derived from wheat, oats, cotton-seed, soyabean and other sources. The main source of TVP is the soyabean; this is due to its high protein content.

TVP is used chiefly as a meat extender, varying from 10–60% replacement of fresh meat. Some caterers on very tight budgets make use of it, but its main use is in food manufacturing.

By partially replacing the meat in certain dishes, such as casseroles, stews, pies, pasties, sausage rolls, hamburgers, meat loaf, and pâté, it is possible to reduce costs, provide nutrition and serve food acceptable in appearance.

Soya protein can be useful in making vegetarian dishes.

Myco-protein

A meat substitute e.g. quorn, is produced from a plant that is a distant relative of the mushroom. This myco-protein contains protein and fibre and is the result of a fermentation process similar to the way yoghurt is made. It may be used as an alternative to chicken or beef or in vegetarian dishes.

Quorn

Quorn is a low fat food that can be used in a variety of dishes, e.g. oriental stir-fry. Quorn does not shrink during preparation and cooking. Quorn mince or pieces can be substituted for chicken or minced meats. Its mild savoury flavour means that it complements the herbs and spices in a recipe and it is able to absorb flavour. Frozen quorn may be cooked straight from the freezer or may be defrosted overnight in the refrigerator. Once thawed, it must be stored in the refrigerator and used within 24 hours. Quorn recipes can be found in the Vegetarian chapter. Quorn is a low fat, high protein food.

Health, safety and hygiene

Health, safety and hygiene guidelines are given in Chapter 1. In addition, to reduce the risk of cross-contamination:

- When preparing uncooked meat or poultry, and then cooked food, or changing from one type of meat or poultry to another, equipment, working areas and utensils must be thoroughly cleaned, or changed.
- If colour-coded boards are used, it is essential to always use the correct colour-coded boards for preparation of foods and different ones for cooked foods.
- Store uncooked meat and poultry on trays to prevent dripping, in separate refrigerators at a temperature of 3–5°C (37–41°F), but preferably at the lower temperature. If separate refrigerators are not available then store in separate areas within the one refrigerator.

- Wash all work surfaces with a bactericidal detergent to kill bacteria. This is particularly important when handling poultry and pork.
- When using boning knives a safety apron acts as a protection; if a great deal of boning is being done then protective gloves are also available.

To maintain the quality and safety of meat and poultry dishes it is advisable to check internal temperatures by means of a probe. The following temperatures are recommended:

Beef: rare: 52°C; medium 57°C; well done 62°C.
Lamb: pink: 57°C; well done 62°C.
Pork: 73°C.
Veal: 62°C.
Turkey and chicken: 77°C.
Duck: pink 57°C; well done 62°C.
Note: EHOs may require higher temperatures.

Cooking of meats

When cooking meats, flavour is developed. This happens when the meat proteins are heated with sugars to temperatures above 140°C, and a series of chemical reactions occur, known as the Maillard reactions. Sugars and amino acids react together. The sugars come from carbohydrates and the amino acids from the protein. In the first stage of the reactions the proteins and carbohydrates are degraded into smaller sugars and amino acids. Next the sugar rings open and the resulting aldehydes and acids react with the amino acids to produce a wide range of chemicals. These new modules then react amongst themselves to produce the main flavour compounds.

Controlling the Maillard reactions is difficult. The chef must know how much heat to apply to a piece of meat to produce the right flavour. The Maillard reactions only take place quickly at temperatures above 140°C. These high temperatures will only occur at the surface of the meat. Inside there is water, which cannot be heated above 100°C without turning to steam. Flavour will be developed more quickly if you increase the surface of the meat.

The combination of attempting not to heat those muscles that contain little connective tissue above 40°C, while heating those parts where there is lots of connective tissue to temperatures above 70°C and at the same time ensuring that some parts are heated to above 130°C makes the cooking of meats a complex process.

Always ensure the outside of the meat is cooked at a high temperature (until a dark brown colour) to seal and develop the flavour. Cook meats with little connective tissue for only a short time. Seal the outside so that it is browned and so that the inside does not become tough i.e. grilling, frying, roasting.

Meats with lots of connective tissue should be cooked for longer so that all the connective tissue denatures and the bundles of coagulated muscle proteins fall apart, rendering the meat tender i.e. stewing, braising.

(Source: Barham, P. (2000) *The Science of Cooking*, Springer)

Lamb and mutton

As a guide when ordering, allow approximately 100 g (4 oz) meat off the bone per portion, and 150 g (6 oz) on the bone per portion. It must be clearly understood that the weights given can only be approximate. They must vary according to the quality of the meat and also for the purpose for which the meat is being butchered. For example, a chef will often cut differently from a shop butcher, i.e. a chef frequently needs to consider the presentation of the particular joint whilst the butcher is more often concerned with economical cutting. We have given simple orders of dissection for each carcass. In general, bones need to be removed only when preparing joints, so as to facilitate carving. The bones are used for stock and the excess fat can be rendered down for second-class dripping.

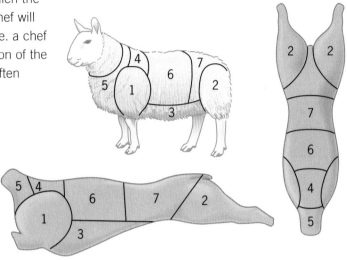

Fig 9.1 ✎ Joints of lamb

Joints, uses and weights

| Joint | Uses | Approximate weight | |
		Lamb kg (lb)	Mutton kg (lb)
whole carcass		16 (32)	25 (50)
(1) shoulder (two)	roasting, stewing	3 (6)	4½ (9)
(2) leg (two)	roasting (mutton boiled)	3½ (7)	5½ (11)
(3) breast (two)	roasting, stewing	1½ (3)	2½ (5)
(4) middle neck	stewing	2 (4)	3 (6)
(5) scrag end	stewing, broth	½ (1)	1 (2)
(6) best-end rack (two)	roasting, grilling, frying	2 (4)	3 (6)
(7) saddle	roasting, grilling, frying	3½ (7)	5½ (11)
kidneys	grilling, sauté		
heart	braising		
liver	frying		
sweetbreads	braising, frying		
tongue	braising, boiling		

Quality of lamb (sheep under 1 year old) and mutton

- A good quality animal should be compact and evenly fleshed.
- The lean flesh should be firm, of a pleasing dull red colour and of a fine texture or grain.
- There should be an even distribution of surface fat, which should be hard, brittle and flaky in structure and a clear white colour.
- In a young animal the bones should be pink and porous, so that, when cut, a degree of blood is shown in their structure. As age progresses the bones become hard, dense, white and inclined to splinter when chopped.

Order of dissection of a carcass

- Remove the shoulders.
- Remove the breasts.
- Remove the middle neck and scrag.
- Remove the legs.
- Divide the saddle from the best-end.

Preparation of joints and cuts
Shoulder

- *Roasting* Clean and trim the knucklebone so as to leave approximately 3 cm (1½ inch) of clean bone.
- *Boning* Remove the blade bone and upper arm bone (see Fig 9.2), tie with string. The shoulder may be stuffed (page 221) before tying.
- *Cutting for stews* Bone out, cut into even 25–50 g (1–2 oz) pieces.
- *Roasting* Remove the pelvic or aitchbone. Trim the knuckle cleaning 3 cm (1½ inch) of bone. Trim off excess fat and tie with string if necessary.

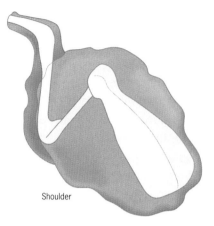

Shoulder

Fig 9.2 ✎ Shoulder of lamb showing three bones

Breasts

- Remove excess fat and skin.
- *Roasting* Bone, stuff and roll, tie with string.
- *Stewing* Cut into even 25–50 g (1–2 oz) pieces.

Middle neck

- *Stewing* Remove excess fat, excess bone and the gristle. Cut into even 50 g (2 oz) pieces. This joint, when correctly butchered, can give good uncovered second-class cutlets.

Scrag-end

- *Stewing* This can be chopped down the centre,

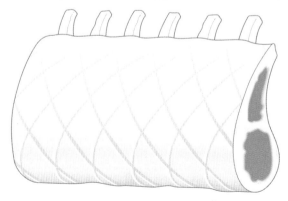

Fig 9.3 ✎ Best end (rack) of lamb

the excess bone, fat and gristle removed; cut into even 50 g (2 oz) pieces, or boned-out and cut into pieces.

Saddle

- A full saddle is illustrated in Figure 9.4a including the chumps and the tail.
- For large banquets it is sometimes found better to remove the chumps and use short saddles.
- Saddles may also be boned and stuffed.

Saddle	roasting, pot roasting (poêlé)
Loin	roasting
Fillet	grilling, frying
Loin chop	grilling, frying, stewing, braising
Chump chop	grilling, frying, stewing, braising
Kidney	grilling, sauté

The saddle may be divided as follows: remove the skin, starting from head to tail and from breast to back, split down the centre of the backbone to produce two loins; each loin can be roasted whole, boned and stuffed, or cut into loin and chump chops.

Saddle for roasting

- Skin and remove the kidney.
- Trim the excess fat and sinew.
- Cut off the flaps leaving about 15 cm (6 inches) each side so as to meet in the middle under the saddle.
- Remove the aitch or pelvic bone.
- Score neatly and tie with string.
- For presentation the tail may be left on, protected with foil and tied back.

Fig 9.4 a Clockwise from top left: pair of best-ends; chump; full saddle; loin; middle neck. b Clockwise from top left: loin chop; chump chop; Barnsley chop; fillet, loin – fillet removed. c Left to right: loin chop; cutlet; uncovered cutlets. d From left: rosettes; noisettes.

- The saddle can also be completely boned, stuffed and tied.

Loin for roasting

- Skin, remove excess fat and sinew, remove the pelvic bone, tie with string.

Loin boned and stuffed

- Remove the skin, excess fat and sinew. Bone out, replace the fillet and tie with string. When stuffed, bone out, season, stuff and tie.

Chops

Loin chops

- Skin the loin, remove the excess fat and sinew, then cut into chops approximately 100–150 g (4–6 oz) in weight.
- A first-class loin chop should have a piece of kidney skewered in the centre.

Double loin chop (also known as a Barnsley chop)

- These are cut approximately 2 cm (1 inch) across a saddle on the bone.
- When trimmed they are secured with a skewer and may include a piece of kidney in the centre of each chop.

Chump chops

- These are cut from the chump end of the loin.
- Cut into approximately 150 g (6 oz) chops, trim where necessary.

Noisette

- This is a cut from a boned-out loin.
- Cut slantwise into approximately 2 cm (1 inch) thick slices, bat out slightly, trim into a cutlet shape.

Rosette

- This is a cut from a boned-out loin approximately

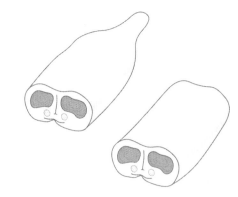

Fig 9.6 Saddle of lamb

Fig 9.5 Preparation of best-end

2 cm (1 inch) thick. It is shaped round and tied with string.

Best-end (Rack)
Best-end preparation

- Remove the skin from head to tail and from breast to back.
- Remove the sinew and the tip of the blade bone.
- Complete the preparation of the rib bones as indicated in Fig 9.3.
- Clean the sinew from between the rib bones and trim the bones.
- Score the fat neatly to approximately 2 mm (¹⁄₁₂ inch) deep.
- The overall length of the rib bones to be trimmed to two and a half times the length of the nut of meat.
- *Roasting* Prepare as above.
- *Cutlets* Prepare as for roasting, excluding the scoring, and divide evenly between the bones, or the cutlets can be cut from the best-end and prepared separately. A double cutlet consists of two bones; therefore a 6 bone best-end yields 6 single or 3 double cutlets.

Preparation of offal
Kidney

- *Grilling* Skin and split three-quarters the way through lengthwise; cut out and discard the gristle, and skewer.
- *Sauté* Skin and remove the gristle. Cut slantways into 6–8 pieces.

Hearts

- *Braising* Remove the tubes and excess fat.

Liver

- Remove skin, gristle and tubes and cut into thin slices on the slant.

Sweetbreads

- Wash well, blanch and trim.
- Soak in salted water for 2–3 hours to remove any traces of blood.

Tongue

- Remove the bone and gristle from the throat end.
- Soak in cold water for 2–4 hours. If salted, soak for 3–4 hours.

Lamb recipes

1 **Roasting of lamb and mutton**

Using leg of lamb, 1 portion (113 g/4 oz lamb) provides:
1262 kJ/301 kcal
20.2 g fat
(of which 10.5 g saturated)
0.0 g carbohydrate
(of which 0.0 g sugars)
29.5 g protein
0.0 g fibre

HEALTHY EATING TIP

Use an unsaturated vegetable oil (e.g. sunflower). Make sure the fat is hot so that less will be absorbed during the roasting. The lamb will produce additional fat as it roasts.

Where applicable name the origin and breed of the lamb e.g. Southdown, Shropshire; for further information contact British Meat.

continued over ▶

▶ *Roasting of lamb and mutton continued*

Allow approximately 150 g (6 oz) meat on the bone per portion (legs, shoulders, saddle or loin rump, best-end and breast).

1 Season the joints lightly with salt and place on a trivet, or bones, in a roasting tray.

2 Place a little vegetable oil or dripping on top and cook in a hot oven at 230–250°C (Reg. 8–9; 450–500°F).

3 Baste frequently and reduce the heat gradually when necessary, as for example in the case of large joints.

4 Roast for approximately 20 minutes per ½ kilo (1 lb) and 20 minutes over.

5 To test if cooked, place on a tray and press firmly in order to see if the juices released contain any blood.

6 In general, all joints should be cooked through. If joints are required pink, reduce the cooking time by a quarter. For internal temperatures, see page 246.

7 Allow to stand for approximately 10–15 minutes before carving; if this is not done the meat will tend to shrink and curl.

Note: Variations include: several peeled cloves of garlic inserted into the flesh of joints before roasting; a little rosemary sprinkled into boned joints before tying. Sprigs of rosemary placed on roasting joints half-way through cooking.

In small scale cookery vegetables, e.g. potatoes, parsnips, onions, carrots etc., left whole or cut into large pieces, can be roasted in with the meat.

Slow cooking – roast at 200°C (400°F) for 30 minutes then reduce temperature to 150°C (300°F), basting frequently. If required the leg can be flavoured with slices of peeled garlic cloves inserted into slashes cut into the flesh before cooking.

2 Roast gravy

This can be made at the end of roasting (see also page 63).

1 Place the roasting tray on the stove over a gentle heat to allow the sediment to settle.

2 Carefully strain off the fat, leaving the sediment in the tray.

3 Return to the stove and brown carefully, deglaze with brown stock.

4 Allow to simmer for a few minutes.

5 Correct the seasoning and colour, then strain and skim.

Note: In some establishments the gravy served with stuffed joints, lamb, pork and veal is slightly thickened with diluted cornflour, fécule or arrowroot.

Carving

Roast leg

Holding the bone, carve with a sharp knife at an angle of 45° and take off each slice as it is cut. Continue in this manner along the joint, turning it from side to side as the slices get wider.

Shoulder

To obtain reasonable sized slices of meat, carve the flesh side not the skin side of the joint. Having obtained the slices, carve round the bones. Due to the awkward shape of the bone structure, the shoulder may be boned out, rolled and tied before cooking to facilitate carving.

Roast saddle

- *Carving on the bone* There are two usual ways of carving the saddle, one is by carving lengthways either side of the backbone, the other by making a deep cut lengthwise either side of the backbone and then slicing across each loin. It is usual to carve the saddle in thick slices.

- *Carving off the bone* For economical kitchen carving it is often found best to bone the loins out whole, carve into slices, then re-form on the saddle bone.

The fillets may be left on the saddle or removed; in either case they are carved and served with the rest of the meat.

Roast loin

- *On the bone* Proceed as for the saddle.
- *Boned-out* Cut in slices across the joint; when stuffed, the slices are cut slightly thicker.

Roast best-end or racks of lamb

Divide into cutlets by cutting between bones.

Service

All roast joints are served garnished with watercress and a sauceboat of roast gravy separately.

When carved, serve a little gravy over the slices as well as a sauceboat of gravy. Mint sauce should be served with roast lamb and redcurrant jelly should be available. For roast mutton, redcurrant jelly and/or onion sauce should be served, with mint sauce available.

3 Stuffing for lamb

Using egg yolk, 1 portion provides:
824 kJ/198 kcal energy
14.1 g fat
(of which 7.7 g saturated)
15.6 g carbohydrate
(of which 1.9 g sugars)
3.1 g protein
0.8 g fibre

This is used for stuffing joints, e.g. loin, shoulder, breast. Combine all the ingredients together.

	For 1 joint
chopped suet	50 g (2 oz)
chopped onions cooked in a little butter or margarine without colour	50 g (2 oz)
egg yolk or small egg	1
white breadcrumbs	100 g (4 oz)
pinch powdered thyme	
pinch chopped parsley	
salt, pepper	
grated zest of lemon	

HEALTHY EATING TIP
Use a minimum amount of salt; the herbs, pepper and lemon provide plenty of flavour.

Note: Variations can be found on page 259. For mint sauce see page 95.

4 Best-end or rack of lamb with breadcrumbs and parsley

Roast the best-end; 10 minutes before cooking is completed cover the fat surface of the meat with a mixture of 25–50 g (1–2 oz) of fresh white breadcrumbs mixed with plenty of chopped parsley, an egg and 25–50 g (1–2 oz) melted butter or margarine. Return to the oven to complete the cooking, browning carefully.

Note: Variations include:

- mixed fresh herbs used in addition to parsley;
- finely chopped garlic added;
- chopped fresh herbs, shallots and mustard.

5 Best-end of lamb boulanger

Carré d'agneau boulanger

Any roast lamb joint may be served in this manner.

1 Prepare a dish of savoury potatoes (page 475).

2 Roast the joint.

3 Remove from the tray 15 minutes before completion of cooking.

4 Place on top of the cooked potatoes.

5 Return to the oven to complete the cooking.

6 Serve the joint whole or carved as required on the potatoes.

7 Garnish with watercress and serve with a sauceboat of gravy separately.

6 Grilled cutlets

Côtelettes d'agneau grillées

HEALTHY EATING TIP

When served with boiled new potatoes and boiled or steamed vegetables, the plate of food becomes more 'balanced'.

1 Season the cutlets lightly with salt and mill pepper.

2 Brush with oil or fat.

3 When cooked on the bars of the grill, place the prepared cutlet on the preheated bars that have been greased.

4 Cook for approximately 5 minutes, turn and complete the cooking.

5 When cooked under the salamander, place on a greased tray, cook for approximately 5 minutes, turn and complete the cooking.

6 Serve dressed garnished with a deep-fried potato and watercress. A compound butter (parsley, herb or garlic) may also be served (page 68).

7 Each cutlet bone may be capped with a cutlet frill.

7 Mixed grill

1 portion (2 cutlets) provides:
2050 kJ/488 kcal
40.8 g fat
(of which 19.3 g saturated)
0.0 g carbohydrate
(of which 0.0 g sugars)
30.4 g protein
0.0 g fibre

With straw potatoes, parsley, watercress, 1 portion provides:
3050 kJ/726 kcal
59.2 g fat
(of which 26.6 g saturated)
20.2 g carbohydrate
(of which 2.5 g sugars)
29.5 g protein
4.9 g fibre

	4 portions	10 portions
sausages	4	10
cutlets	4	10
kidneys	4	10
tomatoes	4	10
mushrooms	4	10
rashers streaky bacon	4	10
watercress		
straw potatoes		
parsley butter (page 68)		

These are the usually accepted items for a mixed grill, but it will be found that there are many variations to this list, e.g. steaks, liver, a Welsh rarebit and fried egg.

HEALTHY EATING TIP

Add a small amount of compound butter and serve with plenty of potatoes and vegetables.

1 Grill in the order given.

2 Dress neatly on an oval flat dish or plates.

3 Garnish with deep-fried potato, watercress and a slice of compound butter on each kidney or offered separately.

8 Fried cutlets

Season and carefully cook in a sauté pan. Garnish as required, e.g. page 222.

HEALTHY EATING TIP

Lightly oil the pan with an unsaturated oil to fry the cutlets. Drain off any excess fat after the frying is complete. Use a minimum amount of salt and serve with plenty of vegetables.

9 Breadcrumbed cutlets

Côtelettes d'agneau panées

HEALTHY EATING TIP

Lightly oil the pan with an unsaturated oil to fry the cutlets. Drain off any excess fat after the frying is complete. Serve with plenty of vegetables.

1 Pass the prepared and flattened cutlets through seasoned flour, eggwash and fresh white breadcrumbs. Pat firmly, then shake off surplus crumbs.

Fig 9.7 Preparation of mixed grill

2 Shallow fry in hot clarified butter, margarine or oil for the first few minutes; then allow to cook gently.

3 Turn, and continue cooking until a golden brown, for approximately 5 minutes each side.

4 To test if cooked, press firmly, no signs of blood should appear.

Note: These may be served with a garnish of pasta, such as spaghetti, noodles.

10 Lamb kebabs (shish kebab)

Kebabs, a dish of Turkish origin, are pieces of food impaled and cooked on skewers over a grill or barbecue. There are many variations and different flavours can be added by marinating the kebabs in oil, wine, vinegar or lemon juice with spices and herbs for 1–2 hours before cooking. Kebabs can be made using tender cuts, or mince of lamb and beef, pork, liver, kidney, bacon, ham, sausage and chicken, using either the meats individually, or combining two or three. Vegetables and fruit can also be added (onion, apple, pineapple, peppers, tomatoes, aubergine). Kebabs can be made using vegetables exclusively (peppers, onion, aubergine, tomatoes, etc.). Kebabs are usually served with a pilaff rice (page 161).

The ideal cuts of lamb are the nut of the lean meat of the loin, best-end or boned-out meat from a young shoulder of lamb.

1 Cut the meat into squares and place them on skewers with squares of green pepper, tomato, onion and bay leaves in between.

2 Sprinkle with powdered thyme and cook over a hot grill.

3 Serve with pilaff rice, or with chick peas and finely sliced raw onion.

Note: Variations include:

- Miniature kebabs (one mouthful) can be made, impaled on cocktail sticks, grilled and served as a hot snack at receptions.

- Fish kebabs can be made using a firm fish, such as monkfish, and marinating in olive oil, lemon or

continued over ▶

▶ *Lamb kebabs continued*

lime juice, chopped fennel or dill, garlic and a dash of tabasco or Worcester sauce.

11 **Grilled loin or chump chops or noisettes of lamb**

1 Season the chops or noisettes lightly with salt and mill pepper.

2 Brush with fat and place on hot greased grill bars or place on a greased baking tray.

3 Cook quickly for the first 2–3 minutes on each side, in order to seal the pores of the meat.

4 Continue cooking steadily, allowing approximately 12–15 minutes in all.

Note: A compound butter may also be served and deep fried potatoes. Variations include sprigs of rosemary or other herbs laid on the chops during the last few minutes of grilling to impart flavour.

12 **Braised loin or chump chops**
Chops d'agneau braisées

	4 portions	10 portions
chops	4	10
onion	100 g (4 oz)	250 g (10 oz)
carrot	100 g (4 oz)	250 g (10 oz)
flour, white or wholemeal	25 g (1 oz)	60 g (2½ oz)
tomato purée	1 level tsp	2½ level tsp
brown stock	500 ml (1 pt)	1¼ litre (2½ pt)
bouquet garni		
clove garlic, optional	1	2
seasoning		
chopped parsley		

> 1 portion provides:
> 1452 kJ/349 kcal energy
> 23.4 g fat
> (of which 10.8 g saturated)
> 9.4 g carbohydrate
> (of which 3.8 g sugars)
> 25.8 g protein
> 1.2 g fibre

1 Fry the seasoned chops in a sauté pan quickly on both sides in hot fat.

2 When turning the chops, add the mirepoix.

3 Draw aside, drain off the surplus fat.

4 Add the flour and mix in, singe in the oven or on top of the stove. (Alternatively, use flour that has been browned in the oven.)

5 Add the tomato purée and the hot stock.

6 Stir with a wooden spoon until thoroughly mixed.

7 Add the bouquet garni and garlic, season, skim and allow to simmer; cover with a lid.

8 Cook preferably in the oven, skimming off all fat and scum.

9 When cooked transfer the chops to a clean pan.

10 Correct the seasoning and consistency of the sauce.

11 Skim off any fat and pass the sauce through a fine strainer over the chops.

12 Serve sprinkled with chopped parsley.

Note: Variations include additions after the sauce has been strained:

- cooked pulse beans (haricot, butter, flageolet);
- cooked neatly cut vegetables (carrots, turnips, swede, green beans, peas).

Lamb steaks cut from the chump end of the leg can also be cooked in this way.

13 Chops Champvallon

Chops d'agneau Champvallon

	4 portions	10 portions
chops, preferably chump	4	10
flour	25 g (1 oz)	60 g (2½ oz)
onions	100 g (4 oz)	250 g (10 oz)
clove garlic (optional)	1	2
brown stock	250 ml (½ pt)	625 ml (1¼ pt)
potatoes	400 g (1 lb)	1¼ kg (2½ lb)

1 portion provides:
1727 kJ/414 kcal energy
23.5 g fat
(of which 10.8 g saturated)
24.3 g carbohydrate
(of which 2.2 g sugars)
27.6 g protein
1.9 g fibre

1   Pass the chops through seasoned flour.

2   Fry quickly on both sides in hot fat or oil.

3   Shred the onions finely and toss lightly in butter, with garlic if using, and place in a shallow earthenware dish.

4   Place the chops on top, cover with brown stock.

5   Add ¼ cm (⅛ inch) sliced potatoes neatly arranged with a knob or two of good dripping on top or brush with oil.

6   Cook in a hot oven at 230–250°C (Reg. 8–9; 450–500°F) until the potatoes are cooked and a golden brown, approximately 1½–2 hours.

7   Serve sprinkled with chopped parsley, in the cleaned earthenware dish.

HEALTHY EATING TIP

Trim fat from the chops before frying. Use a minimum amount of salt. Lightly oil the pan with an unsaturated oil to fry the cutlets. Drain off any excess fat after the frying is complete. Brush the potatoes with oil. Serve with a large portion of vegetables.

14 Noisettes of lamb or fillet of lamb sauté

Noisettes d'agneau sautées

Season and shallow fry on both sides in a sauté pan and serve with the appropriate garnish and sauce. Unless specifically stated, a jus-lié or demi-glace should be served. Fillet of lamb should be trimmed of fat and sinew before cooking.

Suitable garnishes

HEALTHY EATING TIP

Trim as much fat as possible before cooking. Grilling or braising is a healthier way of cooking. Add starchy carbohydrate and vegetables to proportionally reduce the amount of fat.

- Tomatoes filled with jardinère of vegetables and château potatoes.

- Balls of cauliflower Mornay and château potatoes.

- Artichoke bottoms filled with carrot balls and noisette potatoes.

- Artichoke bottoms filled with asparagus heads and noisette potatoes.

- Artichoke bottoms filled with peas and cocotte potatoes.

15 Valentine of lamb

1 Prepare a short saddle with all the bones, kidneys and internal fat removed.

2 Split into two loins.

3 Trim off excess fat and sinew.

4 Cut across the muscle grain into thick boneless chops.

5 Slice three parts through the lean meat and open to give a double-sized cut surface (butterfly cut).

6 Valentines are cooked in the same way as noisettes and rosettes. They may also be grilled or braised.

Note: Best-end may be used in place of the loin.

16 Brown lamb or mutton stew

Navarin d'agneau

	4 portions	**10 portions**
stewing lamb	500 g (1¼ lb)	1½ kg (3 lb)
oil	2 tbsp	5 tbsp
salt, pepper		
onion	100 g (4 oz)	250 g (10 oz)
carrot	100 g (4 oz)	250 g (10 oz)
clove garlic (if desired)	1	3
flour, white or wholemeal	25 g (1 oz)	60 g (2½ oz)
tomato purée	1 level tbsp	2½ level tbsp
brown stock (mutton stock or water)	500 g (1 pt)	1¼ litre (2½ pt)
bouquet garni		

1 Trim the meat and cut into even pieces.

2 Partly fry off the seasoned meat, then add the carrot, onion and garlic and continue frying.

3 Drain off the surplus fat, add the flour and mix.

4 Singe in the oven or brown on top of the stove for a few minutes or add previously browned flour.

5 Add the tomato purée and stir with a wooden spoon.

6 Add the stock and season.

7 Add the bouquet garni, bring to the boil, skim and cover with a lid.

8 Simmer gently until cooked, preferably in the oven, for approximately 1–2 hours.

continued over ▶

◄ Lamb noisettes on dauphinoise potatoes with minestrone vegetables

▼ Lamb valentines on gratinated fennel with white and green julienne of asparagus

▼ Lamb rosettes with mint pesto, spring onion mash, courgette boats and cherry tomatoes

Fig 9.8 ✐ Lamb rosettes, noisettes and valentine

Anton Edelmann

▶ *Brown lamb or mutton stew continued*

9 When cooked, place the meat in a clean pan.

10 Correct the sauce and pass the sauce on to the meat.

11 Serve sprinkled with chopped parsley.

Note: A variation includes a garnish of vegetables (glazed carrots and turnips, glazed button onions, potatoes, peas and diamonds of French beans) which may be cooked separately or in the stew (glazed vegetables, see page 249).

Fig 9.9 Traditional navarin of lamb *John Campbell*

Using sunflower oil, 1 portion provides:
1699 kJ/405 kcal
26.6 g fat
(of which 10.0 g saturated)
14.8 g carbohydrate
(of which 11.6 g sugars)
27.7 g protein
3.2 g fibre

HEALTHY EATING TIP

Trim as much fat as possible before frying and drain all surplus fat after frying. Use a minimum amount of salt to season the meat. Skim all fat from the finished dish and add low fat yoghurt. Serve with plenty of rice, chapatis and dhal.

17 Curried lamb

Kari d'agneau

	4 portions	10 portions
stewing lamb	500 g (1¼ lb)	1½ kg (3 lb)
oil	3 tbsp	8 tbsp
onions	200 g (8 oz)	500 g (1¼ lb)
clove garlic	1	2½
curry powder	10 g (½ oz)	25 g (1 oz)
flour, white or wholemeal	10 g (½ oz)	25 g (1 oz)
tomato purée	10 g (½ oz)	25 g (1 oz)
stock of water	½ litre (1 pt)	1¼ litre (2½ pt)
chopped chutney	25 g (1 oz)	60 g (2½ oz)
desiccated coconut	25 g (1 oz)	60 g (2½ oz)
sultanas	25 g (1 oz)	60 g (2½ oz)
chopped apple	50 g (2 oz)	125 g (5 oz)
grated root ginger		

1   Trim the meat and cut into even pieces.

2   Season and quickly colour in hot oil.

3   Add the chopped onion and chopped garlic, cover with a lid and sweat for a few minutes. Drain off the surplus fat.

4   Add the curry powder and flour, mix in and cook out.

5   Mix in the tomato purée and gradually add the hot stock; stir thoroughly; bring to the boil and season with salt and skim.

6   Allow to simmer and add the rest of the ingredients.

7   Cover with a lid and simmer in the oven or on top of the stove until cooked.

8   Correct the seasoning and consistency; skim off all fat. At this stage a little cream or yoghurt may be added.

9   Serve accompanied with rice, which may be plain boiled, pilaff or pilaff with saffron. See pages 160–1.

Note: This recipe is a European version. Authentic Asian recipes can be found in Chapter 10 on International cookery.

Other accompaniments to curry

There are many other accompaniments to curry, for example, grilled Bombay duck (dried fish fillets) and poppadums (thin vegetable wafers) which are grilled or deep fried. Also:

chopped chutney	chow-chow
sultanas	quarters of orange
desiccated coconut	sliced banana
slices of lemon	chopped onions
chopped apple	diced cucumber in natural yoghurt
segments of lime	mint in natural yoghurt

18 Braised lamb shanks with ratatouille

Using edible portion of meat – 90 g, broad beans used
to replace flageolet beans for analysis, 1 portion
provides:
2020 kJ/483 kcal energy
27.3 g fat
(of which 9.6 g saturated)
23.7 g carbohydrate
(of which 10.5 g sugars)
37.1 g protein
8.6 g fibre

HEALTHY EATING TIP

Fry the shanks in a little
olive oil and drain off any
excess fat. Skim any fat from
the cooked sauce before
adding the beans. Serve
with a large portion of
potatoes or couscous and
colourful seasonal
vegetables.
Add a minimum amount
of salt.

	4 portions	10 portions
lamb shanks	4	10
olive oil	3 tbsp	7 tbsp
red onions, finely chopped	50 g (2 oz)	125 g (5 oz)
garlic cloves, crushed, finely chopped	2	5
aubergine large, diced 1 cm (½ inch) dice	1	2
courgettes diced 1 cm (½ in) dice	3	7
plum tomatoes (canned)	400 g (1 lb)	1 kg (2½ lb)
lamb stock	250 ml (½ pt)	625 ml (1¼ pts)
flageolet beans (canned), rinsed, drained	400 g (1 lb)	1 kg (2½ lb)
fresh oregano, chopped	1 tbsp	2½ tbsp
fresh rosemary, chopped	1 tbsp	2½ tbsp
clear honey	1 tbsp	2½ tbsp
seasoning		

1 Season the lamb shanks. Heat the oil in a suitable braising pan, fry the shanks on all sides until golden brown. Remove from pan, set aside.

2 Add the chopped onion and garlic, sweat until soft.

3 Add the diced aubergine and courgettes, cook for 5 mins.

4 Stir in the chopped plum tomatoes and stock.

5 Place the lamb shank back with the vegetables. Bring to boil, reduce heat, cover and braise in the oven for 1 hour.

6 Remove the lamb. Stir in the flageolet beans, add the herbs and honey. Simmer, check all the vegetables are soft.

7 Replace the lamb, allow the shanks to seep in the vegetables.

8 Correct the seasoning and consistency.

9 Serve with mashed potatoes or couscous.

19 Irish stew

1 portion provides:
1339 kJ/319 kcal
11.2 g fat
(of which 5.2 g saturated)
26.1 g carbohydrate
(of which 5.7 g sugars)
30.2 g protein
5.0 g fibre

	4 portions	10 portions
stewing lamb	500 g (1¼ lb)	1½ kg (3 lb)
bouquet garni		
potatoes	400 g (1 lb)	1 kg (1½ lb)
onions	100 g (4 oz)	250 g (10 oz)
celery	100 g (4 oz)	250 g (10 oz)
Savoy cabbage	100 g (4 oz)	250 g (10 oz)
leeks	100 g (4 oz)	250 g (10 oz)
button onions	100 g (4 oz)	250 g (10 oz)
chopped parsley		

HEALTHY EATING TIP

Trim as much fat as possible from the stewing lamb and skim all fat from the finished dish.
Use a minimum amount of salt.
Serve with colourful seasonal vegetables to create a 'healthy' dish.

Fig 9.10 Irish stew

Fig 9.11 Preparation for an Irish stew

1   Trim the meat and cut into even pieces. Blanch and refresh.

2   Place in a shallow saucepan, cover with water, bring to the boil, season with salt and skim. If tough meat is being used, allow ½–1 hour stewing before adding any vegetables.

3   Add the bouquet garni. Turn the potatoes into barrel shapes.

4   Cut the potato trimmings, onions, celery, cabbage and leeks into small neat pieces and add to the meat; simmer for 30 minutes.

5   Add the button onions and simmer for a further 30 minutes.

6   Add the potatoes and simmer gently, with a lid on the pan until cooked.

7   Correct the seasoning and skim off all fat.

8   Serve sprinkled with chopped parsley.

Note: Optional accompaniments include Worcester sauce and/or pickled red cabbage.

20   White lamb stew

Blanquette d'agneau

Using butter, 2.5 tbsp. low fat yoghurt, 1 portion provides:
1181 kJ/283 kcal energy
15.5 g fat
(of which 7.8 g saturated)
9.2 g carbohydrate
(of which 3.9 g sugars)
27.3 g protein
0.7 g fibre

continued over ▶

▶ *White lamb stew continued*

	4 portions	10 portions
stewing lamb	500 g (1¼ lb)	1½ kg (3 lb)
white stock	750 ml (1½ pt)	1½ litre (3 pt)
studded onion	50 g (2 oz)	125 g (5 oz)
carrot	50 g (2 oz)	125 g (5 oz)
bouquet garni		
butter, margarine or oil	25 g (1 oz)	60 g (2½ oz)
flour	25 g (1 oz)	60 g (2½ oz)
cream, yoghurt or quark	2–3 tbsp	5 tbsp
chopped parsley		

HEALTHY EATING TIP

Trim as much fat as possible from the lamb before cooking. Use a minimum amount of salt. Reduce the fat content by using low fat yoghurt in place of the cream when reheating. Serve with mashed potato with spring onion and colourful vegetables.

1 Trim the meat and cut into even pieces. Blanch and refresh.

2 Place in a saucepan and cover with cold water.

3 Bring to the boil then place under running cold water until all the scum has been washed away.

4 Drain and place in a clean saucepan and cover with stock, bring to the boil and skim.

5 Add whole onion and carrot, bouquet garni, season lightly with salt and simmer until tender, approximately 1–1½ hours.

6 Meanwhile prepare a blond roux with the butter and flour and make into a velouté with the cooking liquor. Cook out for approximately 20 minutes.

7 Correct the seasoning and consistency and pass through a fine strainer on to the meat, which has been placed in a clean pan.

8 Reheat, mix in the cream and serve, finished with chopped parsley.

9 To enrich this dish a liaison of yolks and cream is sometimes added at the last moment to the boiling sauce, which must not be allowed to reboil, otherwise the eggs will scramble.

21 Cornish pasties

1 portion provides:
1217 kJ/290 kcal
16.2 g fat
(of which 6.0 g saturated)
29.3 g carbohydrate
(of which 1.2 g sugars)
8.7 g protein
1.8 g fibre

	4 portions	10 portions
short paste	200 g (½ lb)	500 g (1¼ lb)
finely diced potato (raw)	100 g (4 oz)	250 g (10 oz)
raw lamb or beef, chuck or skirt (cut in thin pieces)	100 g (4 oz)	250 g (10 oz)
chopped onion or leeks	50 g (2 oz)	125 g (5 oz)
finely diced swede (raw) (optional)	50 g (2 oz)	125 g (5 oz)

HEALTHY EATING TIP

Using less meat and more vegetables will proportionally reduce the amount of fat in the pasty.

1 Roll out the short paste 3 mm (⅛ inch) thick and cut into rounds 12 cm (5 inches) diameter.

2 Mix the remaining ingredients together, moisten

with a little water and place in the rounds in piles. Eggwash the edges.

3   Fold in half and seal, flute the edge and brush with eggwash.

4   Cook in a moderate oven at 150–200°C (Reg. 2–6; 300–400°F) for ¾–1 hour.

5   Serve with a suitable sauce, see pages 60–62, or hot or cold as a snack.

Note: Cooked meat can be used in place of raw.

Variation

- Potato, onion or leek and turnip or swede, fresh herbs.

- Bacon, hard boiled eggs and leeks

- Lamb, carrot and potato

- Apples, cinnamon, cloves, brown sugar, cider.

22 Hot pot of lamb or mutton

Using sunflower oil, 1 portion provides:
1505 kJ/360 kcal
17.0 g fat
(of which 6.4 g saturated)
22.0 g carbohydrate
(of which 1.8 g sugars)
29.0 g protein
2.5 g fibre

	4 portions	10 portions
stewing lamb	500 g (1¼ lb)	1¼ kg (3 lb)
salt and pepper		
onions	100 g (4 oz)	250 g (10 oz)
potatoes	400 g (1 lb)	1¼ kg (1½ lb)
brown stock	1 litre (2 pt)	2½ litre (5 pt)
oil	25 g (1 oz)	60 g (2½ oz)
chopped parsley		

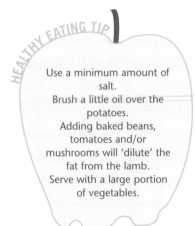

HEALTHY EATING TIP

Use a minimum amount of salt.
Brush a little oil over the potatoes.
Adding baked beans, tomatoes and/or mushrooms will 'dilute' the fat from the lamb.
Serve with a large portion of vegetables.

1   Trim the meat and cut into even pieces.

2   Place in a deep earthenware dish. Season with salt and pepper.

3   Mix the shredded onion and thinly sliced potatoes together.

4   Season and place on top of the meat; three parts cover with stock.

5   Neatly arrange an overlapping layer of 2 mm thick (1⁄12 inch) sliced potatoes on top.

6   Thoroughly clean the edges of the dish and place to cook in a hot oven at 230–250°C (Reg. 8–9; 450–500°F) until lightly coloured.

7   Reduce the heat and simmer gently until cooked, approximately 1½–2 hours.

8   Press the potatoes down occasionally during cooking.

9   Serve with the potatoes brushed with butter or margarine and sprinkle with chopped parsley.

Note: Variations include:

- Use leek in place of onion.

- Add 200 g (½ lb) lambs' kidneys.

- Quickly fry off the meat and sweat onions before putting in the pot.

- Add 100–200 g (4–8 oz) sliced mushrooms.

- Add a small tin of baked beans, or a layer of thickly sliced tomatoes before adding the potatoes.

- Use sausages in place of lamb.

Using sunflower oil with hard margarine in topping, 1 portion provides:
1744 kJ/415 kcal
25.3 g fat
(of which 9.1 g saturated)
22.1 g carbohydrate
(of which 2.5 g sugars)
26.3 g protein
1.6 g fibre

HEALTHY EATING TIP

Use an oil rich in unsaturates (olive or sunflower) to lightly oil the pan. Drain off any excess fat after the lamb has been fried.
Try replacing some of the meat with baked beans or lentils and add tomatoes and/or mushrooms to the dish. When served with a large portion of green vegetables, a 'healthy balance' is created.

23 Shepherd's pie (cottage pie)

	4 portions	10 portions
chopped onion	100 g (4 oz)	250 g (10 oz)
oil	35 g (1½ oz)	100 g (4 oz)
cooked lamb or mutton (minced)	400 g (1 lb)	1¼ kg (1½ lb)
salt and pepper		
Worcester sauce	2–3 drops	5 drops
jus-lié or demi-glace	125–250 ml (¼–½ pt)	300–600 ml (¾–1½ pt)
cooked potato	400 g (1 lb)	1¼ kg (1½ lb)
butter or margarine	25 g (1 oz)	60 g (2½ oz)
milk		

1 Cook the onion in the fat or oil without colouring.

2 Add the cooked meat from which all fat and gristle has been removed.

3 Season, add Worcester sauce and add sufficient sauce to bind.

4 Bring to the boil; simmer for 10–15 minutes.

5 Place in a pie or earthenware dish.

6 Prepare the mashed potatoes and pipe or arrange neatly on top.

7 Brush with milk or eggwash.

8 Colour lightly under salamander or in a hot oven.

9 Serve accompanied with a sauceboat of jus-lié.

Note: This dish prepared with cooked beef is known as cottage pie. When using reheated meats, care must be taken to heat thoroughly and quickly.

Variations include:

- Add 100–200 g (4–8 oz) sliced mushrooms.

- Add a layer of thickly sliced tomatoes (sprinkle with rosemary).

- Mix a tin of baked beans in with the meat.

- Sprinkle with grated cheese and brown.

- Vary the flavour of the mince by adding herbs or spices.

- The potato topping can also be varied by mixing in grated cheese, chopped spring onions or herbs, or by using duchess potato mixture.

- A meatless recipe (using TVP) will be found on page 407.
- Serve lightly sprinkled with garam masala with grilled pitta bread.

24 Minced lamb or mutton

Hachis d'agneau ou de mouton

Prepare the meat for shepherd's pie (recipe 23). Then place on a dish that has been previously piped with a border of duchess potatoes dried for a few minutes in the oven, eggwashed and lightly browned.

Variations include the addition of sliced mushrooms, sweetcorn, or cooked small pasta and also as above.

25 Moussaka

This is a dish of Greek origin.

	4 portions	10 portions
onions	50 g (2 oz)	125 g (5 oz)
small clove garlic	1	2
butter, margarine or oil	25 g (1 oz)	60 g (2½ oz)
tomato purée	25 g (1 oz)	60 g (2½ oz)
cooked mutton, diced or minced	400–600 g (1–1½ lb)	1½ kg (3 lb)
demi-glace or jus-lié	125 ml (¼ pt)	300 ml (⅝ pt)
aubergine	200 g (½ lb)	500 g (1¼ lb)
tomatoes	200 g (½ lb)	500 g (1¼ lb)
flour, white or wholemeal		
oil	60 ml (⅛ pt)	150 ml (⅓ pt)
breadcrumbs	25 g (1 oz)	60 g (2½ oz)
grated Parmesan cheese	25 g (1 oz)	60 g (2½ oz)
melted butter, margarine or oil, as necessary		

Using hard margarine and sunflower oil, 1 portion provides:
1909 kJ/455 kcal
33.3 g fat
(of which 11.1 g saturated)
10.5 g carbohydrate
(of which 5.1 g sugars)
28.9 g protein
2.8 g fibre

HEALTHY EATING TIP

Use an oil rich in unsaturates (olive or sunflower) to lightly oil the pan. Use a minimum amount of salt. Ovenbake the aubergines to reduce the fat content and omit the butter from the topping of breadcrumbs and cheese. Serve with a large mixed salad.

1 Finely chop the onions and garlic.

2 Cook in the butter, margarine or oil without colour.

3 Mix in the tomato purée and the cooked mutton.

4 Add the demi-glace and bring to the boil.

5 Correct the seasoning and allow to simmer for 10–15 minutes. The mixture should be fairly dry.

6 Peel the aubergines and cut into ½ cm (¼ inch) slices.

continued over ▶

▶ *Moussaka continued*

7 Pass the slices of aubergine through the flour.

8 Fry the slices of aubergine in shallow hot oil on both sides and drain.

9 Peel the tomatoes and cut into ½ cm (¼ inch) slices.

10 Place the mixture of mutton into an earthenware dish.

11 Cover the mixture with the slices of tomato, and then neatly with the slices of aubergine.

12 Season with salt and pepper.

13 Sprinkle with breadcrumbs, cheese and melted butter.

14 Gratinate in a hot oven at 230–250°C (Reg. 8–9; 450–500°F).

15 Sprinkle with chopped parsley and serve.

Note: Variations include:

- Minced beef may be used in place of mutton.

- It may be seasoned with a little cinnamon and oregano.

- It may be finished by masking the dish, when all the ingredients have been added, with 250 ml (½ pint) (600 ml (½ pint) for 10 portions) of thin béchamel sauce to which 2 beaten eggs have been added. If this method is being adopted, then the breadcrumbs, cheese and melted butter should be added after the béchamel.

- A vegetarian recipe for Moussaka is on page 414.

1 portion provides:
614 kJ/147 kcal energy
10.3 g fat
(of which 5.9 g saturated)
0.1 g carbohydrate
(of which 0.1 g sugars)
13.7 g protein
0.0 g fibre

26 Grilled lambs' kidneys

Rognons grillés

1 Season the prepared skewered kidneys. See page 223.

2 Brush with melted butter, margarine or oil.

3 Place on preheated greased grill bars or on a greased baking tray.

4 Grill fairly quickly on both sides, approximately 5–10 minutes depending on size.

5 Serve with parsley butter, pickled watercress and straw potatoes.

Note: Devilled kidneys are brushed with a flavoured mustard mixture during cooking.

HEALTHY EATING TIP

Use a minimum amount of salt. Serve with plenty of starchy carbohydrate and vegetables.

27 Kidney sauté

Rognons sautés

Using sunflower oil, 1 portion provides:
1680 kJ/400 kcal
28.3 g fat
(of which 4.3 g saturated)
15.5 g carbohydrate
(of which 3.7 g sugars)
21.8 g protein
1.8 g fibre

	4 portions	10 portions
sheep's kidneys	8	20
butter, margarine or oil	50 g (2 oz)	125 g (5 oz)
demi-glace or jus-lié	250 ml (½ pt)	625 ml (1¼ pt)

HEALTHY EATING TIP

Lightly oil the pan using an unsaturated oil (olive or sunflower). Drain off any excess fat.
Add a minimum amount of salt to the demi-glace and serve with plenty of starchy carbohydrates and vegetables.

1 Skin and halve the kidneys. Remove the sinews.

2 Cut each half into 3 or 5 pieces and season.

3 Fry quickly in a frying-pan using the butter or oil for approximately 4–5 minutes.

4 Place in a colander to drain and discard the drained liquid.

5 Deglaze pan with demi-glace, correct the seasoning and add the kidneys.

6 Do not reboil before serving as kidneys will toughen.

7 After draining the kidneys, the pan may be deglazed with white wine, sherry or port.

8 As an alternative, a sauce suprême (page 56) may be used in place of demi-glace.

Note: A variation includes Kidney sauté Turbigo. Cook as for kidney sauté then add 100 g (4 oz) small button mushrooms cooked in a little butter, margarine or oil, and 8 small 2 cm (1 inch) long grilled or fried chipolatas. Serve with the kidneys in an entrée dish, garnished with heart-shaped croûtons (double these amounts for 10 portions).

28 Braised lambs' hearts

Coeurs d'agneau braisés

Using sunflower oil, 1 portion provides:
1489 kJ/354 kcal
19.0 g fat
(of which 5.6 g saturated)
5.0 g carbohydrate
(of which 4.3 g sugars)
41.2 g protein
1.7 g fibre

	4 portions	10 portions
lambs' hearts	4	10
salt and pepper		
fat or oil	25 g (1 oz)	60 g (2½ oz)
onions	100 g (4 oz)	250 g (10 oz)
carrots	100 g (4 oz)	250 g (10 oz)
brown stock	500 ml (1 pt)	1¼ litre (2½ pt)
bouquet garni		
tomato purée	10 g (½ oz)	25 g (1 oz)
demi-glace or jus-lié	250 ml (½ pt)	625 ml (1¼ pt)

continued over ▶

▶ *Braised lambs' hearts continued*

HEALTHY EATING TIP
Lightly oil the pan using an unsaturated oil (olive or sunflower). Drain off any excess fat and skim all fat from the finished dish. Keep added salt to a minimum.

1 Remove tubes and excess fat from the hearts.

2 Season and colour quickly on all sides in hot fat to seal the pores.

3 Place into a small braising pan (any pan with a tight-fitting lid that may be placed in the oven) or in a casserole.

4 Place the hearts on the lightly fried, sliced vegetables.

5 Add the stock, which should be two-thirds of the way up the meat; season lightly.

6 Add the bouquet garni and tomato purée and if available add a few mushroom trimmings.

7 Bring to the boil, skim and cover with a lid and cook in a moderate oven at 150–200°C (Reg. 2–6; 300–400°F).

8 After 1½ hours add the demi-glace or jus-lie, reboil, skim and strain.

9 Continue cooking until tender.

10 Remove the hearts and correct the seasoning, colour and consistency of the sauce.

11 Pass the sauce on to the sliced hearts and serve.

Variation: the hearts can be prepared and cooked as above and prior to cooking the tube cavities can be filled with a firm stuffing, see page 221.

29 Fried lambs' liver and bacon

Foie d'agneau au lard

Using oil, jus-lié, reduced stock, 1 portion provides:
1039 kJ/250 kcal energy
20.1 g fat
(of which 3.8 g saturated)
0.1 g carbohydrate
(of which 0.1 g sugars)
17.2 g protein
0.0 g fibre

	4 portions	**10 portions**
liver	300 g (12 oz)	1 kg (2 lb)
butter, margarine or oil for frying	50 g (2 oz)	125 g (5 oz)
streaky bacon (4 rashers)	50 g (2 oz)	125 g (5 oz)
jus-lié	125 ml (¼ pt)	300 ml (⅝ pt)

HEALTHY EATING TIP
Keep the added salt to a minimum. Use a small amount of an unsaturated oil to fry the liver. Serve with plenty of potatoes and vegetables.

1 Skin the liver and remove the gristle. Cut in thin slices on the slant.

2 Pass the slices of liver through seasoned flour. Shake off the excess flour.

3 Quickly fry on both sides in hot fat.

4 Remove the rind and bone from the bacon and grill on both sides.

5 Serve the liver and bacon with a cordon of jus-lié and a sauceboat of jus-lié.

Lamb sweetbreads

See recipes for veal sweetbreads, pages 278–9.

Beef

Butchery

Side of beef (approximate weight 180 kg/ 360 lb)

A whole side is divided between the wing ribs and the fore ribs.

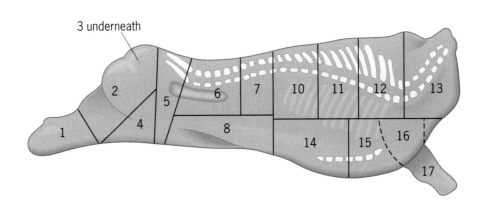

3 underneath

Fig 9.12 Side of beef

Hindquarter of beef

Dissection of the hindquarter

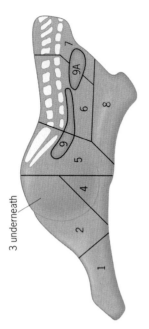

- Remove the rump suet and kidney.
- Remove the thin flank.
- Divide the loin and rump from the leg (topside, silverside, thick flank and shin).
- Remove the fillet.
- Divide rump from the sirloin.
- Remove the wing ribs.
- Remove the shin.
- Bone-out the aitchbone.
- Divide the leg into the three remaining joints (silverside, topside and thick flank).

Fig 9.13 Hindquarter of beef

Joints, uses and weights of hindquarter

Joint	Uses	Approximate weight (kg)	(lb)
(1) shin	consommé, beef tea, stewing	7	14
(2) topside	braising, stewing, second-class roasting	10	20
(3) silverside	pickled in brine then boiled	14	28
(4) thick flank	braising and stewing	12	24
(5) rump	grilling and frying as steaks, braised in the piece	10	20
(6) sirloin	roasting, grilling and frying in steaks	9	18
(7) wing ribs	roasting, grilling and frying in steaks	5	10
(8) thin flank	stewing, boiling, sausages	10	20
(9) fillet	roasting, grilling and frying in steaks	3	6
fat and kidney		10	20
	total weight	90	180

Preparation of joints and cuts of hindquarter

- *Shin* Bone-out, remove excess sinew. Cut or chop as required.
- *Topside*

  roasting: remove excess fat, cut into joints and tie with string;

braising: as for roasting;

stewing: cut into dice or steaks as required.

- *Silverside* Remove the thigh bone. This joint is usually kept whole and pickled in brine prior to boning.
- *Thick flank* As for topside.
- *Rump* Bone-out. Cut off the first outside slice for pies and puddings. Cut into approximately 1½ cm (¾ inch) slices for steaks. The point steak, considered the tenderest, is cut from the pointed end of the slice.

Forequarter of beef
Dissection of the forequarter

- Remove the shank.
- Divide in half down the centre.
- Take off the fore ribs.
- Divide into joints.

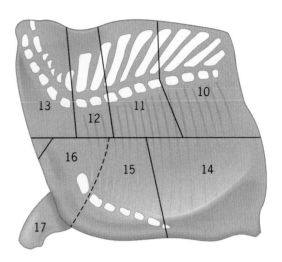

Fig 9.14 Forequarter of beef

Joints, uses and weights of forequarter

Joint	Uses	Approximate weight	
		(kg)	(lb)
(10) fore rib	roasting and braising	8	16
(11) middle rib	roasting and braising	10	20
(12) chuck rib	stewing and braising	15	30
(13) sticking piece	stewing and sausages	9	18
(14) plate	stewing and sausages	10	20
(15) brisket	pickled in brine and boiled, pressed beef	19	38
(16) leg of mutton cut	braising and stewing	11	22
(17) shank	consommé, beef tea	6	12
	total weight	88	176

Beef offal

Offal	Uses
tongue	pickled in brine, boiling, braising
heart	braising
liver	braising, frying
kidney	stewing, soup
sweetbread	braising, frying
tripe	boiling, braising
tail	braising, soup
suet	suet paste and stuffing or rendered down for first-class dripping
bones	beef stocks
marrow	savouries and sauces

Fig 9.15 ✐ Left to right: minute steak; sirloin steak; double sirloin steak

Fig 9.16 ✐ T-bone steak; rump cut into steaks

Quality of beef

- The lean meat should be bright red, with small flecks of white fat (marbled).

- The fat should be firm, brittle in texture, creamy white in colour and odourless. Older animals and dairy breeds have fat that is usually a deeper yellow colour.

30 Brine

Saumure

cold water	2½ litres (8 pt)
saltpetre	15 g (¾ oz)
salt	½–1 kg (1–2 lb)
bay leaf	1
juniper berries	6
brown sugar	50 g (2 oz)
peppercorns	6

1 Boil the ingredients together for 10 minutes, skimming frequently.
2 Strain into a china, wooden or earthenware container.
3 When the brine is cold, add the meat.
4 Immerse the meat for up to 10 days under refrigeration.

Preparation of joints and cuts
Sirloin

- *Roasting* Carefully cut back the covering fat in one piece for approximately 10 cm (4 inch). Trim off the sinew, replace the covering fat and tie with string if necessary.

Method I: whole on the bone Aloyau de boeuf
Saw through the chine bone, lift back the covering fat in one piece for approx. 10 cm (4 inch). Trim off the sinew and replace the covering fat. String if necessary. Ensure that the fillet has been removed.

Fig 9.17 Left to right: slice of rump; whole fillet; piece of sirloin

Method II: boned-out
The fillet is removed and the sirloin boned-out and the sinew is removed as before. Remove the excess fat and sinew from the boned side. This joint may be roasted open, or rolled and tied with string.

- *Grilling and frying* Prepare as above and cut into steaks as required.

  Minute steaks Cut into 1 cm (½ inch) slices, flatten with a cutlet bat dipped in water, making as thin as possible, then trim.

  Sirloin steaks (Entrecôte) Cut into 1 cm (½ inch) slices and trim (approximate weight 150 g, 6 oz).

Fig 9.18 Top: fillet chain, joint; left to right: chateaubriand, fillet steak, tournedos, tail, tail cut for Stroganoff

  Double sirloin steaks Cut into 2 cm (1 inch) thick slices and trim (approximate weight 250–300 g, 10–12 oz).

  Porterhouse and T-bone steak Porterhouse steaks are cut including the bone from the rib end of the sirloin; T-bone steaks are cut from the rump end of the sirloin, including the bone and fillet.

Fillet

As a fillet of beef can vary from 2½–4½ kg (5–9 lb) it follows that there must be considerable variation in the number of steaks obtained from it. A typical breakdown of a 3 kg (6 lb) fillet would be as follows.

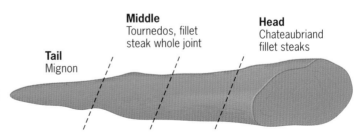

Middle
Tournedos, fillet steak whole joint

Head
Chateaubriand fillet steaks

Tail
Mignon

Fig 9.19 Cuts of fillet of beef

- *Chateaubriand* Double fillet steak 3–10 cm (1½–5 inches) thick, 2–4 portions. Average weight 300 g–1 kg (¾–2 lb). Cut from the head of the fillet, trim off all the nerve and leave a little fat on the steak.

- *Fillet steaks* Approximately 4 steaks of 100–150 g (4–6 oz) each 1½–2 cm (¾–1 inch) thick. These are cut as shown in Fig 9.19 and trimmed as for chateaubriand.

- *Tournedos* Approximately 6–8 at 100 g (4 oz) each, 2–4 cm (1–1½ inches) thick. Continue cutting down the fillet. Remove all the nerve and all the fat and tie each tournedos with string.

- *Tail of fillet* Approximately ½ kg (1 lb). Remove all fat and sinew and slice or mince as required.

- *Whole fillet* Preparation for roasting and pot roasting (poêlé): remove the head and tail of the fillet leaving an even centre piece from which all the nerve and fat is removed. This may be larded by inserting pieces of fat bacon cut into long strips, with a larding needle.

Wing rib

Côte de boeuf

This joint usually consists of the last three rib bones, which, because of their curved shape, act as a natural trivet and because of its prime quality make it a first-class roasting joint, for hot or cold, particularly when it is to be carved in front of the customer.

To prepare, cut seven-eighths of the way through the spine or chine bone, remove the nerve, saw through the rib bones on the underside 5–10 cm (2–4 inch) from the end. Tie firmly with string. When the joint is cooked the chine bone is removed to facilitate carving.

- *Thin flank* Trim off excessive fat and cut or roll as required.

Forequarter

Fore ribs and middle ribs – prepare as for wing ribs.

Chuck ribs	
Sticking piece	bone-out, remove excess
Brisket	fat and sinew, use as
Plate	required.
Leg of mutton cut	
Shank	

Beef offal

Tongue	Remove bone and gristle from the throat end.
Hearts	Remove arterial tubes and excess fat.
Liver	Skin, remove the gristle and cut in thin slices on the slant.
Kidney	Skin, remove the gristle and cut as required.
Sweetbreads	Soak in salted water for 2–3 hours to remove any traces of blood. Wash well, trim, blanch and refresh.
Tripe	Wash well and soak in cold water, then cut into even pieces.
Tail	Cut between the natural joints, trim off excess fat. The large pieces may be split in two.

Beef recipes

31 **Horseradish sauce**

Sauce raifort

	4 portions	10 portions
grated horseradish	25–30 g (1–1½ oz)	60–85 g (2½–4 oz)
lightly whipped cream	120 ml (¼ pt)	300 ml (⅝ pt)
vinegar or lemon juice	1 tbsp	2½ tbsp
pepper, salt		

HEALTHY EATING TIP

Add a minimum amount of salt.

1   Wash, peel and rewash the horseradish.

2   Grate finely and mix all the ingredients together.

32 Yorkshire pudding

Using semi-skimmed milk and oil, 1 portion provides:
809 kJ/193 kcal energy
9.3 g fat
(of which 1.9 g sugars)
22.4 g carbohydrate
(of which 3.3 g sugars)
6.4 g protein
0.8 g fibre

	4 portions	**10 portions**
flour	100 g (4 oz)	250 g (10 oz)
salt		
egg	1	2–3
milk or milk and water	250 ml (½ pt)	600 ml (1¼ pt)
dripping or oil	25 g (1 oz)	60 g (2½ oz)

HEALTHY EATING TIP

Use semi-skimmed milk to make the batter and a minimum amount of salt.
Use an unsaturated oil to cook the batter.

1   Sieve the flour and salt into a basin and make a well in the centre.

2   Break in the egg, add half the liquid and whisk to a smooth mixture, gradually adding the rest of the liquid and allow to rest.

3   Select a shallow pan 15 cm (6 inches) in diameter (preferably a sauté pan).

4   Add dripping from the joint and heat in the oven.

5   Pour in the mixture and cook in a hot oven at 230–250°C (Reg. 8–9; 450–500°F) for approximately 15 minutes.

33 Roasting of beef

Boeuf rôti

1 portion provides:
911 kJ/217 kcal
10.3 g fat
(of which 4.7 g saturated)
0.0 g carbohydrate
(of which 0.0 g sugars)
31.2 g protein
0.0 g fibre

HEALTHY EATING TIP

Use an unsaturated vegetable oil (e.g. sunflower)
Make sure the fat is hot so that less will be absorbed during the roasting. The beef will produce additional fat as it roasts.

Where applicable, name the origin and breed of the beef e.g. Aberdeen Angus, Hereford. For further information contact British Meat.

Suitable joints

First class – sirloin, wing ribs, fore ribs, fillet. Second class – topside, middle ribs.

1   Season joints with salt, place on a trivet, or bones, in a roasting tray.

2   Place a little dripping or oil on top and cook in a hot oven at 230–250°C (Reg. 8–9; 450–500°F).

3   Baste frequently and reduce the heat gradually when necessary, as for example in the case of large joints.

continued over ▶

▶ *Roasting of beef continued*

4   Roasting time is approximately 15 minutes per ½ kg (1 lb) and 15 minutes over.

5   To test if cooked, place on a tray and press firmly in order to see if the juices released contain any blood.

6   Beef is normally cooked underdone and a little blood should show in the juice.

7   On removing the joint from the oven, rest for 15 minutes to allow the meat to set and facilitate carving, then carve against the grain.

Note: Serve the slices moistened with a little gravy. Serve with Yorkshire pudding (recipe 32) (allowing 25 g (1 oz) flour per portion) and garnish with watercress. Serve sauceboats of gravy and horseradish sauce separately.

Some roughly chopped onion, carrot and celery can be added to the roasting tray approximately 30 minutes before the joint is cooked to give additional flavour to the gravy.

Roast gravy

This can be made when the joint is cooked and removed from the roasting tray (see page 220).

Testing for cooking of meat joints
Using a temperature probe

When using a temperature probe, insert it into the thickest part of the joint before placing the food in the oven. The internal temperature reached should be:

Rare meat   55–60°C (130–140°F)
Medium done   66–71°C (150–160°F)
Just done   78–80°C (172–176°F)

Without using a temperature probe:

• Remove the joint from the oven and place onto a plate or dish.

• Firmly press the surface of the meat so that some juice issues.

• Check the colour of the juice:

  red indicates the meat is underdone;

  pink indicates the meat is medium done;

  clear indicates the meat is cooked through.

34 Boiled silverside, carrots and dumplings

1 portion provides:
1068 kJ/254 kcal
10.1 g fat
(of which 4.6 g saturated)
15.5 g carbohydrate
(of which 5.5 g sugars)
26.3 g protein
2.6 g fibre

	4 portions	10 portions
silverside pre-soaked in brine, (page 242)	400 g (1 lb)	1¼ kg (1½ lb)
onions	200 g (8 oz)	500 g (1¼ lb)
carrots	200 g (8 oz)	500 g (1¼ lb)
suet paste (page 566)	100 g (4 oz)	250 g (10 oz)

HEALTHY EATING TIP

Adding carrots, onions, boiled potatoes and a green vegetable will produce a 'healthy balance'.

1   Soak the meat in cold water to remove excess brine for 1–2 hours.

2   Place in a saucepan and cover with cold water, bring to the boil, skim and simmer for 45 minutes.

3   Add the whole prepared onions and carrots and simmer until cooked.

4   Divide the suet paste into even pieces, lightly mould into balls.

5   Add the dumplings and simmer for a further 15–20 minutes.

6   Serve by carving the meat across the grain, garnish with carrots, onions and dumplings and moisten with a little of the cooking liquor.

Note: It is usual to cook a large joint of silverside (approximately 6 kg (12 lb)), in which case soak it overnight and allow 25 minutes per ½ kg (1 lb) plus 25 minutes.

Variations

●   herbs can be added to the dumplings.

●   boiled brisket and tongue can be served with the silverside.

Note: French style boiled beef is prepared using unsalted thin flank or brisket with onions, carrots, leeks, celery, cabbage and a bouquet garni all cooked and served together accompanied with pickled gherkins and coarse salt.

35   Brown beef stew

Ragoût de boeuf

> Using sunflower oil 1 portion provides:
> 907 kJ/216 kcal
> 11.0 g fat
> (of which 2.9 g saturated)
> 7.7 g carbohydrate
> (of which 2.5 g sugars)
> 21.9 g protein
> 1.0 g fibre

Fig 9.20 Right: (background) boiled beef French-style; (foreground) boiled silverside with carrots, onions and dumplings Left: (top) ingredients for boiled beef French-style; (bottom) boiled silverside ingredients

247

continued over ▶

▶ *Brown beef stew continued*

	4 portions	**10 portions**
prepared stewing beef	400 g (1 lb)	1¼ kg (1½ lb)
dripping or oil	25 g (1 oz)	60 g (2½ oz)
onions	75 g (3 oz)	180g (7½ oz)
carrots	75 g (3 oz)	180g (7½ oz)
flour, white or wholemeal	25 g (1 oz)	60 g (2½ oz)
tomato purée	1 tbsp	2½ tbsp
brown stock	750 ml (1½ pt)	2¼ litre (4½ pt)
bouquet garni		
clove of garlic (if desired)	1	2
seasoning		

Fig 9.21 ✎ Beef bourguignonne (see below)

HEALTHY EATING TIP

Trim as much fat as possible from the raw beef and fry in a small amount of an unsaturated oil. Keep added salt to a minimum. Add a cooked pulse bean, a jacket potato and green vegetables to proportionally reduce the overall fat content.

1 Remove excess sinew and fat from the beef.

2 Cut into 2 cm (1 inch) pieces.

3 Fry quickly in hot fat until lightly browned.

4 Add roughly cut onion and carrot and continue frying to a golden colour.

5 Add the flour and mix in; singe in the oven or brown on top of the stove for a few minutes, or use previously browned flour.

6 Add the tomato purée and stir in with a wooden spoon.

7 Mix in the stock, bring to the boil and skim.

8 Add the bouquet garni and garlic, season and cover with a lid; simmer gently until cooked, preferably in the oven, approximately 1½–2 hours.

9 When cooked place the meat into a clean pan.

10 Correct the sauce and pass on to the meat.

11 Serve with chopped parsley sprinkled on top of the meat.

Note: Variations include:

- Add a cooked pulse bean (butter, haricot, flageolet).

- Add lightly sautéed mushrooms, wild or cultivated, once sauce is strained.

- Glazed vegetables can be added as a garnish.

Beef bourguignonne is a brown beef stew using red wine in place of stock and garnishing with glazed button onions, sautéed button mushrooms and lardons of bacon and heart-shaped croûtons.

36 Glazed vegetables

Glazed carrots, turnips, button onions, peas, diamonds of French beans and mushrooms may be used. The vegetables are cooked separately and they may be mixed in, arranged in groups or sprinkled on top of the stew.

HEALTHY EATING TIP

Keep the amount of butter used to a minimum so that only a few grams per portion remain. Use little or no salt.

1   To cook glazed carrots and turnips, turn or cut into even shapes.

2   Barely cover with water in separate thick-bottomed pans and add 25–50 g (1–2 oz) butter or margarine per ½ kg (1 lb) of vegetables.

3   Season very lightly and allow to cook fairly quickly so as to evaporate the water.

4   Check that the vegetables are cooked, if not add a little more water; then toss over a quick fire to give a glossy appearance and a little colour.

5   Care should be taken with turnips as they may break up easily.

6   Button mushrooms, if of good quality, need not be peeled, but a slice should be removed from the base of the stalk. Wash well, then use whole, halved, quartered or turned, depending on their size. They may be coloured first in the oil, butter or margarine, then cooked in a little stock and butter and seasoned lightly; cover with a lid and cook for a few minutes only.

37 Grilled beef

1 portion (100 g cooked weight) provides:
706 kJ/168 kcal
6.0 g fat
(of which 2.7 g saturated)
0.0 g carbohydrate
(of which 0.0 g sugars)
28.6 g protein
0.0 g fibre

Approximate weight per portion 100–150 g (4–6 oz); in many establishments these weights will be exceeded.

Rump steak
Point steak
Double fillet steak (chateaubriand)
Fillet steak
Tournedos
Porterhouse or T-bone steak (see page 243)
Sirloin steak (entrecôte)
Double sirloin steak
Minute steak

All steaks may be lightly seasoned with salt and pepper and brushed on both sides with oil. Place on hot preheated greased grill bars. Turn half-way through the cooking and brush occasionally with oil. Cook to the degree ordered by the customer.

Serve garnished with watercress and deep-fried potato, and offer a suitable sauce, such as compound butter or sauce béarnaise.

Fig 9.22 Stages involved in grilling steak, and a safety grill scraper

Degrees of cooking grilled meats

- Very rare (or blue) – cooked over a fierce heat for a few seconds on each side.
- Rare – the cooked meat has a reddish tinge
- Medium – the cooked meat is slightly pinkish
- Well done – thoroughly cooked with no sign of pinkness

Using a temperature probe

Rare   45–50°C (115–125°F)
Medium   55–60°C (130–140°F)
Well done   75–77°C (167–172°F)

Without a temperature probe

Test with finger pressure, and the springiness or resilience of the meat together with the amount of blood issuing from the meat indicates the degree to which the steak is cooked. This calls for experience, but if the meat is placed on a plate and tested, then the more underdone the steak the greater the springiness and the more blood will be shown on the plate.

To barbecue

1. Choice of meat – some fat is required for flavour, but not too much. Ensure size and thickness are uniform to allow even cooking. Suitable cuts include: T-bone steaks, rib steaks, double lamb chops and noisettes, well trimmed pork cutlets and steaks.

2. Seasoning – add salt and pepper, brush lightly with oil before placing on BBQ. Take care when using marinades, some may contain glucose, which burns easily. Try marinating with wine and herbs, avoid marinating oils, which may ignite and spoil the BBQ.

3. Choice and preparation of barbecue – gas is the preferred choice for temperature control. Allow time to pre-heat BBQ, 30 minutes for gas, 1½

hours for charcoal. If cooking on charcoal always wait for the flames to go out and the embers to start glowing before cooking.

A) Secure a layer of tinfoil over the barbecue.

B) Wait until grill bars are hot or charcoal embers glow.

C) Remove tin foil and brush grill bars with a firm, long-handled wire brush to remove any unwanted debris.

4. Cooking – place the seasoned and lightly oiled meat at a 45° angle on the BBQ and seal one side. Rotate through another 45° angle, allow to cook and then turn the meat and repeat the process. Ensure the temperature is controlled and that the meat does not burn or blacken unnecessarily. Only cook as much meat as required at one time; if left for too long it will dry out and become tough. Use a meat probe to ensure the correct internal temperature is reached, 72°C for 2 minutes.

5. Serve – with fresh crisp vegetables or salads and traditional barbecue dips and sauces.

Note: Burgers and sausages should be cut open and checked and cooked for longer if necessary. Barbecued food may look well cooked when it isn't. Further advice is available from British Meat Food Service.

38 Sirloin steak with mushroom, tomato, tarragon and white wine sauce

Entrecôte chasseur

Using 175 kg steak, 1 portion provides:
1878 kJ/449 kcal energy
24.5 g fat
(of which 13.7 g saturated)
1.5 g carbohydrate
(of which 1.3 g sugars)
55.7 g protein
0.5 g fibre

	4 portions	10 portions
butter or oil	50 g (2 oz)	125 g (5 oz)
sirloin steaks 150–200 g (6–8 oz)	4	10
dry white wine	60 ml (⅛ pt)	150 ml (⅓ pt)
chasseur sauce (page 58)	¼ litre (½ pt)	625 ml (1¼ pt)
chopped parsley		

Use little or no salt to season the steaks.
Fry in a small amount of an unsaturated oil and drain off all excess fat after frying.
Serve with plenty of boiled new potatoes or a jacket potato and a selection of vegetables.

1 Heat the butter in a sauté pan.

2 Lightly season the steaks on both sides with salt and pepper.

3 Fry the steaks quickly on both sides, keep them underdone.

4 Dress the steaks on a serving dish.

5 Pour off the fat from the pan.

6 Deglaze with the white wine. Reduce by half and strain.

7 Add the chasseur sauce, reboil, correct the seasoning.

8 Coat the steaks with the sauce.

9 Sprinkle with chopped parsley and serve.

39 Sirloin steak with red wine sauce

Entrecôte bordelaise

Using sunflower oil, 1 portion (150 g/6 oz raw steak) provides:
3013 kJ/717 kcal
62.2 g fat
(of which 21.6 g saturated)
6.0 g carbohydrate
(of which 3.0 g sugars)
26.1 g protein
1.4 g fibre

Using sunflower oil, 1 portion (200 g/8 oz raw steak) provides:
3584 kJ/853 kcal
73.6 g fat
(of which 26.2 g saturated)
6.0 g carbohydrate
(of which 3.0 g sugars)
34.4 g protein
1.4 g fibre

	4 portions	10 portions
butter or oil	50 g (2 oz)	125 g (5 oz)
sirloin steaks 150–200 g (6–8 oz)	4	10
red wine	60 ml (⅛ pt)	150 ml (⅓ pt)
red wine sauce (page 57)	¼ litre (½ pt)	½ litre (1 pt)
chopped parsley	100 g (4 oz)	250 g (10 oz)

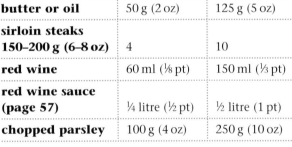

Use little or no salt to season the steaks.
Fry in a small amount of an unsaturated oil and drain off all excess fat after frying.
Serve with plenty of boiled new potatoes or a jacket potato and a selection of vegetables.

continued over ▶

▶ *Sirloin steak with red wine sauce continued*

1   Heat the butter in a sauté pan.

2   Lightly season the steaks on both sides with salt and pepper.

3   Fry the steaks quickly on both sides, keep them underdone.

4   Dress the steaks on a serving dish.

5   Pour off the fat from the pan.

6   Deglaze with the red wine. Reduce by half and strain.

7   Add the bordelaise sauce, reboil and correct seasoning.

8   Coat the steaks with the sauce.

9   Sprinkle with chopped parsley and serve.

Note: Traditionally, two slices of beef bone marrow, poached in stock for 2–3 minutes, would be placed on each steak.

40   Tournedos

Lightly season and shallow fry on both sides in a sauté pan and serve with the appropriate garnish or sauce. Traditionally tournedos is cooked underdone and served on a round croûte of bread fried in butter.

Tournedos can be served with a variety of sauces such as chasseur, red wine, mushroom, etc. and numerous garnishes (diced cubed potatoes, wild or cultivated mushroom, etc.).

HEALTHY EATING TIP

Use little or no salt to season the steaks. Fry in a small amount of an unsaturated oil and drain off all excess fat after frying. Serve on toasted bread with plenty of vegetables.

41   Curried beef (see page 228)

Kari de boeuf

Proceed as for Curried lamb on page 228 using 500 g (1¼ lb) stewing beef. Adjust cooking times until meat is tender.

HEALTHY EATING TIP

Trim as much fat as possible before frying and drain all surplus fat after frying. Use a minimum amount of salt to season the meat. Skim all fat from the finished dish and add low fat yoghurt. Serve with plenty of rice, chapatis and dhal.

42   Steak pudding

1 portion provides:
1369 kJ/326 kcal
17.3 g fat
(of which 7.8 g saturated)
20.6 g carbohydrate
(of which 1.0 g sugars)
23.0 g protein
1.1 g fibre

	4 portions	10 portions
suet paste (page 566)	200 g (8 oz)	500 g (1¼ lb)
prepared stewing beef (chuck steak)	400 g (1 lb)	1¼ kg (1½ lb)
Worcester sauce		
chopped parsley	1 tsp	2½ tsp
salt, pepper		
onion, chopped (optional)	50–100 g (2–4 oz)	200 g (8 oz)
water (approximately)	125 ml (¼ pt)	300 ml (⅝ pt)

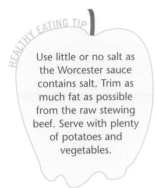

1   Line a greased ¾ litre (1½ pint) basin with three-quarters of the used paste and retain one-quarter for the top.

2   Mix all the other ingredients together.

3   Place in the basin with the water to within 1 cm (½ inch) of the top.

4   Moisten the edge of the suet paste, cover with the top and seal firmly.

5   Cover with greased greaseproof paper and also, if possible, foil or a pudding cloth securely tied with string.

6   Cook in a steamer for at least 3½ hours.

7   Serve with the paper and cloth removed, clean the basin, place on a round flat dish and fasten a serviette round the basin.

Note: Extra gravy should be served separately. If the gravy in the pudding is to be thickened, the meat can be lightly floured.

Variations include:

- Add 50–100 g (2–4 oz) ox or sheep's kidneys cut in pieces with skin and gristle removed.

- Add 50–100 g (2–4 oz) sliced or quartered mushrooms.

Steak pudding can also be made with a cooked filling, in which case simmer the meat until cooked in brown stock with onions, parsley, Worcester sauce and seasoning. Cool quickly and proceed as before, steaming for 1–1½ hours.

43 Sauté of beef

Sauté de boeuf

This term is often applied to a brown beef stew, and it will be found that the word 'sauté' in this case is used instead of the word 'ragoût'. Alternatively, a sauté may be made using first-quality meat, e.g. fillet. The meat is then sautéed quickly and served in a finished sauce; this would be a typical à la carte dish.

44 Beef Stroganoff

Sauté de boeuf Stroganoff

Using sunflower oil, 1 portion provides:
1364 kJ/325 kcal
23.7 g fat
(of which 7.9 g saturated)
1.7 g carbohydrate
(of which 1.7 g sugars)
21.2 g protein
0.3 g fibre

	4 portions	**10 portions**
fillet of beef (tail end)	400 g (1 lb)	1¼ kg (2½ lb)
butter, margarine or oil	50 g (2 oz)	125 g (5 oz)
finely chopped shallots	25 g (1 oz)	60 g (2½ oz)
dry white wine	125 ml (¼ pt)	300 ml (⅝ pt)
cream	125 ml (¼ pt)	300 ml (⅝ pt)
lemon, juice of	¼	½
chopped parsley		

continued over ▶

▶ *Beef Stroganoff continued*

	4 portions	10 portions
prepared stewing beef	400 g (1 lb)	1¼ kg (1½ lb)
lard or oil	35 g (1½ oz)	100 g (4 oz)
onions, chopped	100 g (4 oz)	250 g (10 oz)
flour	25 g (1 oz)	60 g (2½ oz)
paprika	10–25 g (½–1 oz)	25–60 g (1¼–2½ oz)
tomato purée	25 g (1 oz)	60 g (2½ oz)
stock or water (approximately)	750 ml (1½ pt)	2 litre (4 pt)
turned potatoes or small new potatoes	8	20
choux paste	125 ml (¼ pt)	300 ml (1 pt)

1 Cut the meat into strips approximately 1 × 5 cm (½ × 2 inches).

2 Place the butter in a sauteuse over a fierce heat.

3 Add the beef strips, lightly season with salt and pepper and allow to cook rapidly for a few seconds. The beef should be brown but underdone.

4 Drain the beef into a colander. Pour the butter back into the pan.

5 Add the shallots, cover with a lid and allow to cook gently until tender.

6 Drain off the fat, add the wine and reduce to one-third.

7 Add the cream and reduce by a quarter.

8 Add the lemon juice and the beef strips; do not reboil. Correct the seasoning.

9 Serve lightly sprinkled with chopped parsley. Accompany with rice pilaff (see page 161).

45 Goulash (Hungarian)

Goulash de boeuf

1 portion provides:
1625 kJ/389 kcal energy
20.4 g fat
(of which 6.0 g saturated)
26.1 g carbohydrate
(of which 3.9 g sugars)
26.9 g protein
1.7 g fibre

1 Remove excess fat from the beef. Cut into 2 cm (1 inch) square pieces.

2 Season and fry in the hot fat until slightly coloured. Add the chopped onion.

3 Cover with a lid and sweat gently for 3 or 4 minutes.

4 Add the flour and paprika and mix in with a wooden spoon.

5 Cook out in the oven or on top of the stove. Add the tomato purée, mix in.

6 Gradually add the stock, stir to the boil, skim, season and cover.

7 Allow to simmer, preferably in the oven, for approximately 1½–2 hours until the meat is tender.

8 Add the potatoes and check that they are covered with the sauce. (Add more stock if required.)

9 Re-cover with the lid and cook gently until the potatoes are cooked.

10 Skim and correct the seasoning and consistency. A little cream or yoghurt may be added at the last moment.

11 Serve sprinkled with a few gnocchis, reheated in hot salted water or lightly tossed in butter or margarine.

46 Choux paste for gnocchi

(as a garnish, sufficient for 8 portions)

1 Prepare the choux paste following the recipe on page 567, omitting the sugar.

2 Place the mixture into a piping bag with a ½ cm (¼ inch) or 1 cm (½ inch) plain tube.

3 Pipe into a shallow pan of gently simmering salted water, cutting the mixture into 2 cm (1 inch) lengths with a small knife, dipping the knife into the water frequently to prevent sticking.

4 Poach very gently for approximately 10 minutes. If not required at once lift out carefully into cold water and when required reheat in hot salted water.

47 Steak pie

Using puff pastry, using McCance data, 1 portion provides:
1442 kJ/346 kcal energy
22.2 g fat
(of which 2.9 g saturated)
13.6 g carbohydrate
(of which 1.8 g sugars)
24.3 g protein
0.4 g fibre

	4 portions	10 portions
prepared stewing beef (chuck steak)	400 g (1 lb)	1½ kg (2½ lb)
oil or fat	50 ml (2 fl oz)	125 ml (5 fl oz)
onion, chopped (optional)	100 g (4 oz)	250 g (10 oz)
water, stock, red wine or dark beer	125 ml (¼ pt)	300 ml (⅝ pt)
salt, pepper		
few drops Worcester sauce		
chopped parsley	1 tsp	3 tsp
cornflour	10 g (½ oz)	25 g (1 oz)
short, puff or rough puff pastry (pages 562–5)	100 g (4 oz)	250 g (10 oz)

HEALTHY EATING TIP

Use little or no salt as the Worcester sauce contains salt. Fry in a small amount of an unsaturated oil and drain off all excess fat after frying. There will be less fat in the dish if short paste is used. Serve with boiled potatoes and plenty of vegetables.

1 Cut the meat into 2 cm (1 inch) strips then cut into squares.

2 Heat the oil in a frying pan until smoking, add the meat and quickly brown on all sides.

3 Drain the meat off in a colander.

4 Lightly fry the onion.

5 Place the meat, onion, Worcester sauce, parsley and the liquid in a pan, season lightly with salt and pepper.

6 Bring to the boil, skim, then allow to simmer gently until the meat is tender.

continued over ▶

▶ *Steak pie continued*

7   Dilute the cornflour with a little water, stir into the simmering mixture, reboil and correct seasoning.

8   Place the mixture into a pie dish and allow to cool.

9   Cover with pastry, eggwash and bake at 200°C (Reg. 6; 400°F) for approximately 30–45 minutes.

Note: 25–50% wholemeal flour may be used in place of plain flour.

Variations include:

- Adding 50–100 g (2–4 oz) ox or sheep's kidneys with skin and gristle removed and cut into neat pieces.
- Adding 50–100 g (2–4 oz) sliced or quartered mushrooms.
- Adding 1 heaped teaspoon tomato purée and some mixed herbs.
- In place of cornflour the meat can be tossed in flour before frying-off.

48   Carbonnade of beef (Belgian)

Carbonnade de boeuf

> 1 portion provides:
> 1037 kJ/247 kcal energy
> 9.1 g fat
> (of which 1.8 g saturated)
> 14.0 g carbohydrate
> (of which 8.1 g sugars)
> 24.7 g protein
> 1.1 g fibre

	4 portions	**10 portions**
lean beef (topside)	400 g (1 lb)	1¼ kg (2½ lb)
flour, white or wholemeal	25 g (1 oz)	60 g (2½ oz)
dripping or oil	25 g (1 oz)	60 g (2½ oz)
sliced onions	200 g (8 oz)	500 g (1¼ lb)
beer	250 ml (½ pt)	625 ml (1¼ pt)
caster sugar	10 g (½ oz)	25 g (1 oz)
tomato purée	25 g (1 oz)	60 g (2½ oz)
brown stock	500 ml (1 pt)	1¼ litres (2½ pt)

HEALTHY EATING TIP

Trim as much fat as possible before frying and drain off all surplus fat after frying. Use a minimum amount of salt to season the meat. Skim all fat from the finished sauce. Serve with plenty of potatoes and vegetables.

1   Cut the meat into thin slices.

2   Season with salt and pepper and pass through the flour.

3   Quickly colour on both sides in hot fat and place in a casserole.

4   Fry the onions to a light brown colour. Add to the meat.

5   Add the beer, sugar and tomato purée and sufficient brown stock to cover the meat.

6   Cover with a tight-fitting lid and simmer gently in a moderate oven at 150–200°C (Reg. 2–6; 300–400°F) until the meat is tender, for approximately 2 hours.

7   Skim, correct the seasoning and serve.

49   Braised steaks

> Using oil and white flour, 1 portion provides:
> 990 kJ/237 kcal energy
> 12.1 g fat
> (of which 3.2 g saturated)
> 9.3 g carbohydrate
> (of which 3.8 g sugars)
> 23.1 g protein
> 1.1 g fibre

	4 portions	10 portions
stewing beef	400 g (1 lb)	1¼ kg (2½ lb)
dripping or oil	25 g (1 oz)	60 g (2½ oz)
onions	75 g (3 oz)	180 g (7½ oz)
carrots	75 g (3 oz)	180 g (7½ oz)
flour, browned in the oven	25 g (1 oz)	60 g (2½ oz)
tomato purée	25 g (1 oz)	60 g (2½ oz)
brown stock	750 ml (1½ pt)	2 litre (4 pt)
bouquet garni		
clove of garlic (if desired)	1	2–3
seasoning		

HEALTHY EATING TIP

Trim as much fat as possible before frying and drain off all surplus fat after frying. Use a minimum amount of salt. Skim all fat from the finished sauce. Serve with plenty of potatoes and vegetables.

1 Remove excess sinew and fat from the beef.

2 Cut into ½–1 cm (¼–½ inch) thick steaks.

3 Fry quickly in hot fat until lightly browned.

4 Add the roughly cut onion and carrot and continue frying to a golden colour. Mix in the flour.

5 Add the tomato purée and stir in with a wooden spoon.

6 Mix in the stock, bring to the boil and skim.

7 Add the bouquet garni and garlic, season and cover with a lid and simmer gently until cooked, preferably in the oven, approximately 1½–2 hours.

8 When cooked place the meat into a clean pan.

9 Correct the sauce and pass on to the meat.

10 Serve lightly sprinkled with chopped parsley.

Note: Braised steaks may be garnished with vegetables (turned or cut in neat, even pieces), or a pasta, e.g., noodles.

---

50 Braised beef

Boeuf braisé

Using sunflower oil, 1 portion provides:
1380 kJ/329 kcal
14.3 g fat
(of which 3.3 g saturated)
26.8 g carbohydrate
(of which 4.7 g sugars)
24.7 g protein
2.4 g fibre

	4 portions	10 portions
lean beef (topside or thick flank)	400 g (1 lb)	1¼ kg (2½ lb)
dripping or oil	25 g (1 oz)	60 g (2½ oz)
onions	100 g (4 oz)	250 g (10 oz)
carrots	100 g (4 oz)	250 g (10 oz)
brown stock	500 ml (1 pt)	1¼ litre (2½ pt)
bouquet garni		
tomato purée	25 g (1 oz)	60 g (2½ oz)
demi-glace or jus-lié	250 ml (½ pt)	625 ml (1¼ pt)

HEALTHY EATING TIP

Trim as much fat as possible before frying and drain off all surplus fat after frying. Use a minimum amount of salt. Skim all fat from the finished sauce. Serve with plenty of potatoes or noodles and spring vegetables.

Method I

1 Trim and tie the joint securely.

2 Season and colour quickly on all sides in hot fat to seal the pores.

continued over ▶

▶ *Braised beef continued*

3 Place into a small braising pan (any pan with a tight-fitting lid which may be placed in the oven) or in a casserole.

4 Place the joint on the lightly fried, sliced vegetables.

5 Add the stock, which should be two-thirds of the way up the meat, season lightly.

6 Add the bouquet garni and tomato purée and if available add a few mushroom trimmings.

7 Bring to the boil, skim and cover with a lid and cook in a moderate oven at 150–200°C (Reg. 2–6; 300–400°F).

8 After approximately 1½ hours' cooking, remove the meat.

9 Add the demi-glace or jus-lié, reboil, skim and strain.

10 Replace the meat, do not cover, but baste frequently and continue cooking for approximately 2–2½ hours in all. Braised beef should be well cooked (approximately 35 minutes per ½ kg (1 lb) plus 35 minutes). To test if cooked, pierce with a trussing needle, which should penetrate the meat easily and there should be no sign of blood.

11 Remove the joint and correct the colour, seasoning and consistency of the sauce.

12 To serve: remove the string and carve slices across the grain. Pour some of the sauce over the slices and serve the remainder of the sauce in a sauceboat.

Note: Suitable garnishes include spring vegetables (see page 249), or pasta, e.g., noodles (page 148).

Red wine may be used in place of stock.

Method II

As for Method I, but use for cooking liquor either:

• jus-lié;

• half brown stock or red wine and half demi-glace.

Method III

As for Method I, but when the joint and vegetables are browned, sprinkle with 25 g (1 oz) (60 g, 2½ oz for 10 portions) flour and singe in the oven, add the tomato purée, stock and bouquet garni; season and complete the recipe.

51 Braised steak and dumplings

Using margarine reduced to half, 1 portion provides:
1224 kJ/292 kcal energy
14.7 g fat
(of which 5.0 g saturated)
16.1 g carbohydrate
(of which 4.8 g sugars)
25.0 g protein
1.5 g fibre

HEALTHY EATING TIP
Use little or no salt to season the steaks. Fry in a small amount of an unsaturated oil and drain off all excess fat after frying. Skim all fat from the finished dish and serve with plenty of vegetables.

1 Cut the beef into ½–1 cm (¼–½ inch) thick steaks and proceed as for brown beef stew (recipe 35).

2 Prepare 100 g (4 oz) suet paste (page 566) and make 8 dumplings (increase the amount for 10 portions).

3 After the meat has cooked for 1½ hours, pick out the meat and place into a clean pan.

4 Strain the sauce on to the meat.

5 Reboil and correct the seasoning and consistency, which should be fairly thin. Add sufficient to cover the dumplings.

6 Cover with a lid.

7 Complete cooking, preferably in the oven for ¾–1 hour at 150–200°C (Reg. 2–6; 300–400°F). Alternatively, the dumplings can be cooked gently in simmering salted water for approximately 20 minutes, drained and served with the braised steak.

8 Skim off all the fat and serve.

52 Beef olives

Paupiettes de boeuf

> Using 625 ml stock, 1 portion provides:
> 1134 kJ/271 kcal energy
> 13.1 g fat
> (of which 2.6 g saturated)
> 13.6 g carbohydrate
> (of which 5.0 g sugars)
> 25.4 g protein
> 1.5 g fibre

	4 portions	10 portions
stuffing	50 g (2 oz)	125 g (5 oz)
lean beef (topside)	400 g (1 lb)	1¼ kg (2½ lb)
dripping or oil	35 g (1½ oz)	100 g (4 oz)
carrot	100 g (4 oz)	250 g (10 oz)
onion	100 g (4 oz)	250 g (10 oz)
flour (browned in the oven)	25 g (1 oz)	60 g (2½ oz)
tomato purée	25 g (1 oz)	60 g (2½ oz)
brown stock	500–750 ml (1–1½ pt)	1¼–1½ litre (2½–3 pt)
bouquet garni		

HEALTHY EATING TIP: Use little or no salt to season the steaks. Fry in a small amount of an unsaturated oil and drain off all excess fat after frying. Serve with a large portion of potatoes and vegetables

1 Prepare the stuffing.
2 Cut the meat into thin slices across the grain and bat out.
3 Trim to approximately 10 × 8 cm (4 × 3 inches), chop the trimmings finely and add to the stuffing.
4 Season the slices of meat lightly with salt and pepper and spread a quarter of the stuffing down the centre of each slice.
5 Roll up neatly and secure with string.
6 Fry off the meat to a light brown colour, add the vegetables and continue cooking to a golden colour.
7 Drain off the fat into a clean pan and make up to 25 g (1 oz) fat if there is not enough (increase the amount for 10 portions). Mix in the flour.
8 Mix in the tomato purée, cool, and mix in the boiling stock.
9 Bring to the boil, skim, season and pour on to the meat.
10 Add the bouquet garni.
11 Cover and simmer gently, preferably in the oven, for approximately 1½–2 hours.
12 Remove the string from the meat.
13 Skim and correct the sauce and pass on to the meat.

53 Stuffing

	4 portions	10 portions
white or wholemeal breadcrumbs	50 g (2 oz)	125 g (5 oz)
chopped parsley	1 tsp	3 tsp
pinch of thyme		
egg to bind	approx ½	1
prepared chopped suet	5 g (¼ oz)	25 g (1 oz)
sweated onion, finely chopped chopped	25 g (1 oz)	60 g (2½ oz)
salt, pepper		

HEALTHY EATING TIP: Use a minimum amount of salt.

Mix all the ingredients together with the chopped meat trimmings. Other stuffings may be used, for example sausage meat, various herbs, duxelle, etc.

Veal, pork or chicken olives can be prepared and cooked by this method.

1 portion provides:
681 kJ/162 kcal
6.7 g fat
(of which 1.9 g saturated)
12.7 g carbohydrate
(of which 1.0 g sugars)
13.8 g protein
1.0 g fibre

HEALTHY EATING TIP

Use a small amount of an unsaturated oil to cook the onion and to shallow fry the meat. The minced beef will produce more fat, which should be drained off.
Serve with plenty of starchy carbohydrate and vegetables.

54 Hamburg or Vienna steak

Bitok

	4 portions	10 portions
finely chopped onion	25 g (1 oz)	60 g (2½ oz)
butter, margarine or oil	10 g (½ oz)	25 g (1 oz)
leaned minced beef	200 g (½ lb)	500 g (1¼ lb)
small egg	1	2–3
breadcrumbs	100 g (4 oz)	250 g (10 oz)
cold water or milk (approximately)	2 tbsp	60 ml (⅛ pt)
salt and pepper		

1 Cook the onion in the fat without colour, then allow to cool.

2 Add to the rest of the ingredients and mix in well.

3 Divide into even pieces and, using a little flour, make into balls, flatten and shape round.

4 Shallow fry in hot fat on both sides, reducing the heat after the first few minutes, making certain they are cooked right through.

5 Serve with a light sauce, such as sauce piquante (page 61).

Note: The steaks may be garnished with French fried onions (page 451) and sometimes with a fried egg.

55 Hamburger, American style

Hamburgers, now more commonly known as burgers, were originally made using 200 g (8 oz) of minced beef per portion. The meat should be pure beef with 20–25% beef fat by weight. Less fat than this will cause a tough, dry hamburger. If more fat is used the hamburgers will be unpalatable, nutritionally undesirable and will shrink considerably during cooking.

The meat should be passed twice through a mincer, which helps to make for a more tender product. The minced meat should be lightly mixed and moulded into patties. Overmixing the beef can cause toughness.

Hamburgers should not be pricked whilst cooking as the juices will seep out leaving a dry product.

Variations in seasonings and ingredients can be added to the minced beef, but traditionally the sauces and garnishes offered are sufficient. These can include: ketchup, mustard, mayonnaise, chilli sauce, horseradish, cheese, raw onion rings, lettuce, avocado slices, bacon and various pickles and relishes; freshly fried chips and/or cut pieces of raw vegetables (carrot, celery, spring onions, etc.) can be added. The bun may be plain or seeded (sesame seeds).

Alternative fillings can include:

- *cheese*: either on its own, or added to the beef;
- *egg*: a freshly fried egg, or added to the beef;
- *chicken*: a freshly grilled portion of chicken either minced, or in the piece;
- *fish*: a freshly grilled portion of a whole fish (cod or haddock);
- *vegetables*: a selection of freshly grilled, or fried vegetables (onions, peppers, aubergines, mushrooms, etc.).

Note: Mini burgers (one mouthful) can be served as hot snacks at receptions.

56 Tripe and onions

> Using semi-skimmed milk and water 50/50, 1 portion provides:
> 430 kJ/102 kcal energy
> 1.7 g fat
> (of which 0.9 g saturated)
> 12.6 g carbohydrate
> (of which 5.7 g sugars)
> 9.9 g protein
> 0.7 g fibre

	4 portions	**10 portions**
tripe	400 g (1 lb)	1¼ kg (2½ lb)
milk and water	500 ml (1 pt)	1¼ litre (2½ pt)
onions	200 g (8 oz)	500 g (1¼ lb)
salt, pepper		
flour or cornflour	25 g (1 oz)	60 g (2½ oz)

HEALTHY EATING TIP

Keep the added salt to a minimum. Thicken with cornflour and semi-skimmed milk for a lower fat dish.

1   Wash the tripe well. Cut into neat 5 cm (2 inches) squares.

2   Blanch and refresh.

3   Cook the tripe in the milk and water with the sliced onions.

4   Season and simmer for 1½–2 hours.

5   Gradually add the diluted flour or cornflour, stir with a wooden spoon to the boil.

6   Simmer for 5–10 minutes, correct the seasoning and serve.

Note: An alternative thickening is 125 ml (¼ pt) (310 ml, ⅝ pt for 10 portions) of béchamel in place of the cornflour and milk.

57 Ox tongue

Langue de boeuf

Ox tongues are usually pickled in brine. Wash and place in cold water, bring to the boil, skim and simmer for 3–4 hours. Cool slightly and peel off the skin and trim off the root. Secure into a neat shape on a board, in a wooden frame, or in a mould if required for cold buffet display. Unsalted ox tongues may also be braised whole.

58 Braised ox tongue with Madeira sauce

Langue de boeuf braisé au Madère

Cut the cooked tongue in 3 mm (⅛ inch) thick slices and arrange neatly in an entrée dish. Sauce over with Madeira sauce (page 60) and heat through slowly and thoroughly without being allowed to boil.

HEALTHY EATING TIP

Use little or no salt to season the liver.
Fry in a small amount of an unsaturated oil and drain off all excess fat after frying.
Serve with boiled new potatoes and plenty of vegetables.

59 Braised ox liver and onions

Foie de boeuf lyonnaise

	4 portions	10 portions
liver	300 g (12 oz)	1 kg (2 lb)
flour, white or wholemeal	25 g (1 oz)	60 g (2½ oz)
dripping or oil	50 g (2 oz)	125 g (5 oz)
onions, sliced	200 g (½ lb)	500 g (1¼ lb)
brown stock	500 ml (1 pt)	1¼ litre (2½ pt)
tomato purée	25 g (1 oz)	60 g (2½ oz)
bouquet garni		
clove garlic	1	2

1 Prepare the liver by removing the skin and tubes then cut into slices.

2 Pass the sliced liver through seasoned flour.

3 Fry on both sides in hot fat. Place in a braising pan or casserole.

4 Fry the onion to a golden brown, drain and add to the liver.

5 Just cover with the stock and add the tomato purée, bouquet garni and garlic.

6 Lightly season and cover with a lid.

7 Simmer gently in the oven until tender for approximately 1½–2 hours.

8 Correct the sauce and serve.

60 Stewed oxtail

Ragoût de queue de boeuf

HEALTHY EATING TIP

Keep added salt to a minimum.
Fry in a small amount of an unsaturated oil and drain off all excess fat after frying.
Serve with mashed potato and additional green vegetables.

	4 portions	10 portions
oxtail	1 kg (2 lb)	2½ kg (5 lb)
dripping or oil	50 g (2 oz)	125 g (5 oz)
onion	100 g (4 oz)	250 g (10 oz)
carrot	100 g (4 oz)	250 g (10 oz)
flour, browned in the oven	35 g (1½ oz)	100 g (4 oz)
tomato purée	25 g (1 oz)	60 g (2½ oz)
brown stock	1 litre (2 pt)	2½ litre (5 pt)
bouquet garni		
clove garlic	1	2
salt and pepper		

1 Cut the oxtail into sections. Remove the excess fat.
2 Fry on all sides in hot fat.
3 Place in a braising pan or casserole.
4 Add the fried roughly cut onion and carrot.
5 Mix in the flour.
6 Add tomato purée, brown stock, bouquet garni, garlic and season lightly.
7 Bring to the boil, skim.
8 Cover with a lid and simmer in the oven until tender, approximately 3 hours.
9 Remove the meat from the sauce, place in a clean pan.
10 Correct the sauce and pass on to the meat and reboil.
11 Serve sprinkled with chopped parsley.

Note: This dish, also known as braised oxtail, is usually garnished with glazed turned or neatly cut carrots and turnips, button onions, peas and diamonds of beans. Oxtail must be very well cooked so that the meat comes away easily from the bone.

Haricot oxtail can be made as for the previous recipe with the addition of 100 g (4 oz) (250 g, 10 oz for 10 portions) cooked haricot beans, added approximately ½ hour before the oxtail has completed cooking.

Veal

Veal is obtained from good quality carcasses weighing around 100 kg (200 lb). This quality of veal is required for first-class cookery and is produced from calves slaughtered at between 12–24 weeks.

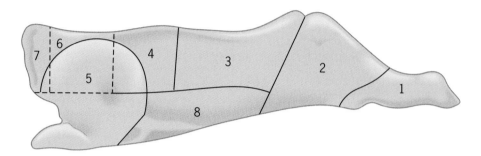

Fig 9.23 Side of veal

Butchery

1 Knuckle   4 Best-end   7 Scrag

2 Leg   5 Shoulder   8 Breast

3 Loin   6 Neck-end

Joints, uses and weights

Joint	Uses	Approximate weight (kg)	(lb)
(1) knuckle	osso buco, sauté, stock	2	4
(2) leg	roasting, braising, escalopes, sauté	5	10
(3) loin	roasting, frying, grilling	3½	7
(4) best-end	roasting, frying, grilling	3	6
(5) shoulder	braising, stewing	5	10
(6) neck-end	stewing, sauté	2½	5
(7) scrag	stewing stock	1½	3
(8) breast	stewing, roasting	2½	5
kidneys	stewing (pies and puddings), sauté	—	—
liver	frying	—	—
sweetbreads	braising, frying	—	—
head	boiling, soup	4	8
brains	boiling, frying	—	—
bones	used for stock	—	—

Joints of the leg

Average weight of English or Dutch milk-fed veal calves is 18 kg (36 lb).

Cuts (English)	Weight	Proportion of leg	Uses
cushion or nut	2.75 kg (5½ lb)	15%	escalopes, roasting, braising, sauté
undercushion or under nut	3 kg (6 lb)	17%	escalopes, roasting, braising, sauté
thick flank	2.5 kg (5 lb)	14%	escalopes, roasting, braising, sauté
knuckle (whole)	2.5 kg (5 lb)	14%	osso buco, sauté
bones (thigh and aitch)	2.5 kg (5 lb)	14%	stock, jus-lié, sauces
usable trimmings	2 kg (4 lb)	11%	pies, stewing
skin and fat	2.75 kg (5½ lb)	15%	

Corresponding joints in beef

- Cushion = topside
- Undercushion = silverside
- Thick flank = thick flank

Dissection of a leg of veal

1 Remove the knuckle by dividing the knee joint (A) and cut through the meat away from the cushion-line A–B.

2 Remove aitch bone (C) at thick end of the leg separating it at the ball and socket joint.

3 Remove all the outside skin and fat thus exposing the natural seams. It will now be seen that the thigh bone divides the meat into two-thirds and one-third (thick flank).

4 Stand the leg on the thick flank with point D uppermost. Divide the cushion from the undercushion, following the natural seam, using the hand and the point of a knife. Having reached the thigh bone, remove it completely.

5 When the boned leg falls open, the three joints can easily be seen joined only by membrane. Separate and trim the cushion removing the loose flap of meat.

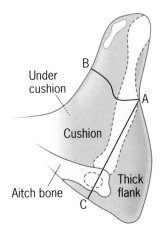
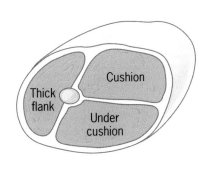

Fig 9.24 Dissection of leg of veal

6 Trim the undercushion removing the layer of thick gristle. Separate into three small joints through the natural seams. It will be seen that one of these will correspond with the round in silverside of beef.

7 Trim the thick flank by laying it on its round side and making a cut along the length about 2.5 cm (1 inch) deep. A seam is reached and the two trimmings can be removed.

The anticipated yield of escalopes from this size leg would be 62.5 kg (13¾ lb), that is 55 kg × 100 g (4 oz) or 73 kg × 80 g (3 oz).

Order of dissection

- Remove the shoulders.
- Remove the breast.
- Take off the leg.
- Divide the loin and best-end from the scrag and neck-end.
- Divide the loin from the best-end.

Preparation of the joints and cuts of veal

Shin

- *Stewing (on the bone) (osso buco)* Cut and saw into 2–4 cm (1–1½ inches) thick slices through the knuckle.
- *Sauté* Bone-out and trim and cut into even 25 g (1 oz) pieces.

Leg

- *Braising or roasting whole* Remove the aitch bone, clean and trim 4 cm (1½ inch) off the knuckle bone. Trim off the excess sinew.
- *Braising or roasting the nut* Remove all the sinew and if there is insufficient fat on the joint then bard thinly and secure with string.
- *Escalopes* Remove all the sinew and cut into

large 50–75 g (2–3 oz) slices against the grain and bat out thinly.

- *Sauté* Remove all the sinew and cut into 25 g (1 oz) pieces.

Loin and Best-end

- *Roasting* Bone-out and trim the flap, roll out and secure with string. This joint may be stuffed before rolling.
- *Frying* Trim and cut into cutlets.

Shoulder

- *Braising* Boned-out as for lamb and usually stuffed.
- *Stewing* Bone-out, remove all the sinew and cut into 25 g (1 oz) pieces.

Neck-end and Scrag

- *Stewing and sauté* Bone-out and remove all the sinew and cut into approximately 25 g (1 oz) pieces.

Breast

- *Stewing* As for neck-end.
- *Roasting* Bone-out, season, stuff and roll up then tie with string.

Kidneys

Remove the fat and skin and cut down the middle lengthwise. Remove the sinew and cut into thin slices or neat dice.

Liver

Skin if possible, remove the gristle and cut into thin slices on the slant.

Sweetbreads

Soak in several changes of cold salted water to remove blood, which would darken the sweetbreads during cooking. Blanch and refresh and peel off membranes and connective tissues. The sweetbreads can then be pressed between two trays with a weight on top and refrigerated.

Head

- Bone-out by making a deep incision down the middle of the head to the nostrils.
- Follow the bone carefully and remove all the flesh in one piece.
- Lastly remove the tongue.
- Wash the flesh well and keep covered in acidulated water.
- Wash off, blanch and refresh.
- Cut into 2–5 cm (1–2 inch) squares.
- Cut off the ears and trim the inside of the cheek.

Brains

Using a chopper or saw, remove the top of the skull, making certain that the opening is large enough to remove the brain undamaged. Soak the brains in running cold water, then remove the membrane, or skin and wash well to remove all blood. Keep in cold salted water until required.

Quality of veal

- Veal is available all the year round.
- The flesh should be pale pink in colour.
- The flesh should be firm in structure, not soft or flabby.
- Cut surfaces should be slightly moist, not dry.
- Bones, in young animals, should be pinkish white, porous and with a degree of blood in their structure.
- The fat should be firm and pinkish white.
- The kidney should be firm and well covered with fat.

Veal recipes

Where applicable give the origin and breed of the veal. For further information contact British Meat.

61 Brown veal stew

Ragoût de veau

Proceed as for Brown beef stew recipe (page 247) using veal in place of beef and allowing 1–1½ hours cooking time.

62 White stew or blanquette of veal

Blanquette de veau

Proceed as for White lamb stew recipe (page 231) using 400 g (1 lb) of prepared stewing veal.

HEALTHY EATING TIP

Use a minimum amount of salt.
Reduce the fat content by using low fat yoghurt in place of the cream when reheating.
Serve with mashed potato with spring onion and colourful vegetables.

Using butter, 1 portion provides:
992 kJ/236 kcal
13.6 g fat
(of which 7.5 g saturated)
5.3 g carbohydrate
(of which 0.4 g sugars)
23.3 g protein
0.2 g fibre

HEALTHY EATING TIP

Add a minimum amount of salt.
Serve with oven-baked croûtons brushed with olive oil or sippets.
A large serving of starchy carbohydrates and vegetables will help to proportionally reduce the fat content.

63 Fricassée of veal

Fricassée de veau

	4 portions	10 portions
boned stewing veal (shoulder or breast)	400 g (1 lb)	1¼ kg (2½ lb)
margarine, butter or oil	35 g (1½ oz)	100 g (4 oz)
flour	25 g (1 oz)	60 g (2½ oz)
white veal stock	500 ml (1 pt)	1¼ litre (2½ pt)
salt, pepper		
egg yolk	1	2–3
cream (dairy or vegetable)	2–3 tbsp	5–7 tbsp
few drops of lemon juice		

1 Trim the meat. Cut into even 25 g (1 oz) pieces.
2 Sweat the meat gently in the butter without colour in a sauté pan.
3 Mix in the flour with a wooden spoon and cook out without colour.
4 Allow to cool.
5 Gradually add boiling stock just to cover the meat, stir until smooth.
6 Season, bring to the boil, skim.
7 Cover and simmer gently on the stove until tender, 1½–2 hours.
8 Pick out the meat into a clean pan. Correct the sauce.
9 Pass on to the meat and reboil. Mix the yolk and cream in a basin.
10 Add a little of the boiling sauce, mix in and pour back on to the meat, shaking the pan until thoroughly mixed; do not reboil. Add the lemon juice.
11 Serve, finished with chopped parsley and heart-shaped croûtons fried in butter or oil.

Note: A variation is to add mushrooms and button onions. Proceed as in recipe 63; after 1 hour's cooking pick out the meat, strain the sauce back on to the meat and add 8 small button onions. Simmer for 15 minutes, add 8 small white button mushrooms, washed and peeled if necessary, then complete the cooking. Finish and serve as in recipe 63.

This is known as fricasée de veau à l'ancienne.

64 Braised veal

Noix de veau braisée

1 portion provides:
792 kJ/190 kcal energy
90.0 g fat
(of which 1.7 g saturated)
5.3 g carbohydrate
(of which 4.5 g sugars)
21.9 g protein
1.1 g fibre

	4 portions	10 portions
carrots	100 g (4 oz)	250 g (10 oz)
onions	100 g (4 oz)	250 g (10 oz)
butter, margarine or oil	25 g (1 oz)	60 g (2½ oz)
cushion or nut of veal	400 g (1 lb)	1¼ kg (2½ lb)
tomato purée	25 g (1 oz)	60 g (2½ oz)
bouquet garni		
brown veal stock	250 ml (½ pt)	625 ml (1¼ pt)
jus-lié	250 ml (½ pt)	625 ml (1¼ pt)

HEALTHY EATING TIP

Lightly oil the pan with an unsaturated oil to fry the carrots and onions. Skim any fat from the finished sauce.
Use a minimum amount of salt.
Serve with plenty of noodles and green vegetables.

1 Slice the carrots and onions thickly. Fry lightly and place in a braising pan.
2 Trim and tie the joint with string and fry quickly on all sides.
3 Place on the bed of roots.
4 Add the tomato purée, bouquet garni, stock, jus-lié, and some mushroom trimmings if available. Season lightly.
5 Bring to the boil, skim, cover with a lid and cook gently in a moderate oven at 150–200°C (Reg. 2–6; 300–400°F) for 1 hour.
6 Remove the lid and continue cooking with the lid off for a further 30 minutes, basting frequently.
7 Remove the joint from the sauce, take off the strings.
8 Correct the colour, consistency and seasoning of the sauce.
9 Pass through a fine conical strainer. Carve in slices against the grain.
10 Pour some of the sauce over the slices and serve a sauceboat of sauce separately.

Note: For larger joints allow 30–35 minutes per ½ kg (1 lb) plus 35 minutes (approximately) cooking time; 125 ml (¼ pt) red wine may replace the same amount of jus-lié. Noodles are often served with this dish.

HEALTHY EATING TIP

Little or no salt is
needed – plenty in the
bacon.
Serve with plenty of
starchy carbohydrate
and vegetables to
proportionally reduce
the fat.

65 Hot veal and ham pie

	4 portions	10 portions
bacon rashers	100 g (4 oz)	250 g (10 oz)
stewing veal without bone	400 g (1 lb)	1¼ kg (2½ lb)
chopped or quartered hardboiled egg	1	2
chopped parsley	1 tsp	2 tsp
chopped onion	50 g (2 oz)	125 g (5 oz)
salt, pepper		
stock (white)	250 ml (½ pt)	625 ml (1¼ pt)
rough puff or puff paste (page 565/564)	100 g (4 oz)	250 g (10 oz)

1 Bat out the bacon thinly and line the bottom and sides of a ½ litre (1 pint) pie dish, leaving two or three pieces for the top.

2 Trim the veal, cut into small pieces and mix with the egg, parsley and onion. Season and place in the pie dish.

3 Just cover with stock. Add the rest of the bacon.

4 Roll out the pastry, eggwash the rim of the pie dish and line with a strip of pastry 1 cm (½ inch) wide. Press this down firmly and eggwash.

5 Without stretching the pastry, cover the pie and seal firmly.

6 Trim off excess pastry with a sharp knife, notch the edge neatly, eggwash and decorate.

7 Allow to rest in the refrigerator or a cool place.

8 Place on a baking sheet in a hot oven at 200°C (Reg. 7; 425°F) for 10–15 minutes until the paste has set and is lightly coloured.

9 Remove the pie from oven, cover with foil and return to the oven reducing the heat to 190°C (Reg. 5; 375°F) for 15 minutes, then to 160°C (Reg. 3; 325°F) for a further 15 minutes, then to 140°C (Reg. 1; 275°F).

10 Complete the cooking at this temperature ensuring that the liquid is gently simmering.

Note: Variations include rabbit, pork, chicken or guinea fowl in place of veal.

66 Grilled veal cutlet

Côte de veau grillée

1 Lightly season the prepared chop with salt and mill pepper.
2 Brush with oil. Place on previously heated grill bars.
3 Cook on both sides for 8–10 minutes in all.
4 Brush occasionally to prevent the meat from drying.
5 Serve with watercress, a deep-fried potato and a suitable sauce or butter, such as béarnaise or compound butter, or on a bed of plain or flavoured mashed potato, see page 468.

Note: Sprigs of rosemary may be added to the chop before or half way through cooking.

67 Fried veal cutlet

Côte de veau sautée

Season and cook in a sauté pan, in clarified butter or oil and butter, on both sides for 8–10 minutes in all. Chops must be started in hot fat, the heat reduced to allow the meat to cook through.

Serve with a suitable garnish (jardinière of vegetables or braised celery) or noodles and finish with a cordon of jus-lié.

Note: Crumbed veal cutlet can be made as an alternative: cook as for the previous recipe and finish with nut brown butter, a cordon of jus-lié and a suitable garnish.

Using sunflower oil, 1 portion provides:
990 kJ/236 kcal
9.7 g fat
(of which 2.6 g saturated)
0.0 g carbohydrate
(of which 0.0 g sugars)
36.9 g protein
0.0 g fibre

HEALTHY EATING TIP

Use a minimum amount of salt to season the meat. Serve with a small amount of sauce or butter and a large portion of mixed vegetables.

Fig 9.25 Veal escalope Holstein
Anton Edelmann

Fig 9.25a Veal escalope Holstein
John Campbell

68 Escalope of veal

Fried in sunflower oil, butter to finish, 1 portion provides:
2079 kJ/495 kcal
39.8 g fat
(of which 11.4 g saturated)
10.3 g carbohydrate
(of which 0.5 g sugars)
24.7 g protein
1.0 g fibre

	4 portions	10 portions
nut or cushion of veal	400 g (1 lb)	1¼ kg (2½ lb)
seasoned flour	25 g (1 oz)	60 g (2½ oz)
egg	1	2
breadcrumbs	50 g (2 oz)	125 g (5 oz)
oil | **for**	50 g (2 oz)	125 g (5 oz)
butter | **frying**	50 g (2 oz)	125 g (5 oz)
beurre noisette	50 g (2 oz)	125 g (5 oz)
butter for finishing (optional)		

HEALTHY EATING TIP

Use an unsaturated oil to fry the veal. Make sure the fat is hot so that less will be absorbed into the crumb. Drain the cooked escalope on kitchen paper. Use a minimum amount of salt. Serve with plenty of starchy carbohydrate and vegetables.

1 Trim and remove all sinew from the veal.

2 Cut into four even slices and bat out thinly using a little water.

3 Flour, egg and crumb. Shake off surplus crumbs. Mark with a palette knife.

Fig 9.26 Escalope of Veal Viennoise garnished with purée of three vegetables *Anton Edelmann*

4 Place the escalopes into shallow hot fat and cook quickly for a few minutes on each side.

5 Dress on a serving dish or plate.

6 An optional finish is to pour over 50 g (2 oz) beurre noisette (nut brown butter), and finish with a cordon of jus-lié (page 63).

Note: Variations include:

- *Escalope of veal Viennoise* As recipe 68, but garnish the dish with chopped yolk, white of egg and chopped parsley. On top of each escalope place a slice of peeled lemon decorated with chopped egg yolk, egg white and parsley, an anchovy fillet and a stoned olive. Finish with a little lemon juice and nut brown butter.

- *Veal escalope Holstein* Prepare and cook the escalopes as for recipe 68. Add an egg fried in butter or oil, and place two neat fillets of anchovy criss-crossed on each egg. Serve.

- *Escalope of veal with spaghetti and tomato sauce* Prepare escalopes as for recipe 68, and garnish with spaghetti with tomato sauce (page 64) allowing 10 g (½ oz) spaghetti per portion.

69 **Breadcrumbed veal escalope with ham and cheese**

Escalope de veau cordon bleu

	4 portions	**10 portions**
nut or cushion of veal	400 g (1 lb)	1¼ kg (2½ lb)
slices of cooked ham	4	10
slices of Gruyère cheese	4	10
seasoned flour	25 g (1 oz)	60 g (2½ oz)
egg	1	2
breadcrumbs	50 g (2 oz)	125 g (5 oz)
oil	50 g (2 oz)	125 g (5 oz)
butter	100 g (4 oz)	250 g (10 oz)
jus-lié (page 63)	60 ml (⅛ pt)	150 ml (⅓ pt)

Fried in sunflower oil, butter to finish, 1 portion provides:
2632 kJ/627 kcal
48.1 g fat
(of which 16.3 g saturated)
12.0 g carbohydrate
(of which 1.3 g sugars)
37.1 g protein
0.7 g fibre

HEALTHY EATING TIP

No added salt is needed as there is plenty in the ham and cheese.
This is a high fat dish, so serve with plenty of starchy carbohydrate and vegetables to 'dilute' the fat.

1   Trim and remove all sinew from the veal.

2   Cut into 8 (20 for 10 portions) even slices and bat out thinly using a little water.

3   Place a slice of ham and a slice of cheese on to 4 (10 for 10 portions) of the veal slices, cover with the remaining slices and press firmly together.

4   Flour, egg and crumb. Shake off all surplus crumbs. Mark on one side with a palette knife.

5   Place the escalopes marked side down into the hot fat and cook quickly for a few minutes on each side, until golden brown.

6   An optional finish is to serve coated with 50 g (2 oz) (125 g, 5 oz for 10 portions) nut brown butter (beurre noisette) and a cordon of jus-lié.

Note: Veal escalopes may be cooked plain (not crumbed) in which case they are only slightly batted out.

Fig 9.27 Veal cordon bleu   *John Campbell*

70 Veal escalope with Madeira

Escalope de veau au Madère

	4 portions	10 portions
butter or margarine	50 g (2 oz)	125 g (5 oz)
seasoned flour	25 g (1 oz)	60 g (2½ oz)
veal escalopes (slightly batted)	4	10
Madeira	30 ml (¹⁄₁₆ pt)	75 ml (⅛ pt)
demi-glace or jus-lié	125 ml (¼ pt)	300 ml (⅝ pt)

1 Heat the butter in a sauté pan.

2 Lightly flour the escalopes. Fry to a light brown colour on both sides.

3 Drain off the fat from the pan. Deglaze with the Madeira.

4 Add the demi-glace and bring to the boil.

5 Correct the seasoning and consistency.

6 Pass through a fine strainer onto the escalopes and serve.

Note: In place of Madeira, sherry or Marsala may be used.

71 Veal escalope with cream and mushrooms

Escalope de veau à la crème et champignons

	4 portions	10 portions
butter, margarine or oil	50 g (2 oz)	125 g (5 oz)
seasoned flour	25 g (1 oz)	60 g (2½ oz)
veal escalopes (slightly batted)	4	10
button mushrooms	100 g (4 oz)	250 g (10 oz)
sherry or white wine	30 ml (¹⁄₁₆ pt)	125 ml (¼ pt)
double cream	125 ml (¼ pt)	300 ml (⅝ pt)
salt, cayenne		

1 Heat the butter in a sauté pan. Lightly flour the escalopes.

2 Cook the escalopes on both sides with the minimum of colour. They should be a delicate light brown.

3 Place the escalopes in a serving dish, cover and keep warm.

4 Peel, wash and slice the mushrooms.

5 Gently sauté the mushrooms in the same butter and pan as the escalopes and add them to the escalopes.

6 Drain off all the fat from the pan. Deglaze the pan with the sherry.

7   Add the cream, bring to the boil and season.

8   Reduce to a lightly thickened consistency. Correct the seasoning.

9   Pass through a fine strainer over the escalopes and mushrooms.

Note: An alternative method of preparing the sauce is to use half the amount of cream and an equal amount of chicken velouté (page 55).

Fig 9.28 Veal escalope with cream and mushrooms
John Campbell

72 Veal escalopes with Parma ham and Mozzarella cheese

Involtini di vitello

	4 portions	**10 portions**
	(8 in total)	(20 in total)
small, thin veal escalopes	400 g (1 lb)	1¼ kg (2¼ lb)
Parma ham thinly sliced	100 g (4 oz)	250 g (10 oz)
Mozzarella cheese, thinly sliced	200 g (8 oz)	500 g (1¼ lb)
fresh leaves of sage *or*	8	20
dried sage	1 tsp	2½ tsp
seasoning		
butter, margarine or oil	50 g (2 oz)	125 g (5 oz)
grated Parmesan cheese		

1 portion provides:
1642 kJ/394 kcal energy
26.1 g fat
(of which 15.5 g saturated)
0.1 g carbohydrate
(of which 0.1 g sugars)
39.8 g protein
0.0 g fibre

HEALTHY EATING TIP

Use a small amount of oil to fry the escalopes and drain the cooked escalopes on kitchen paper. No added salt is necessary as there is plenty of salt in the cheese.
Serve with plenty of vegetables.

1   Sprinkle each slice of veal lightly with flour and flatten.

2   Place a slice of Parma ham on each escalope.

3   Add several slices of Mozzarella cheese to each.

4   Add a sage leaf or a light sprinkling of dried sage.

5   Season, roll up each escalope and secure with a toothpick or cocktail stick.

6   Melt the butter in a sauté pan, add the escalopes and brown on all sides.

7   Transfer the escalopes and butter to a suitably sized ovenproof dish.

8   Sprinkle generously with grated Parmesan cheese and bake in a moderately hot oven at 190°C (Reg. 5; 375°F) for 10 minutes.

9   Clean the edges of the dish and serve.

Using sunflower oil, 1 portion provides:
824 kJ/196 kcal
9.0 g fat
(of which 1.9 g saturated)
5.0 g carbohydrate
(of which 4.1 g sugars)
24.0 g protein
1.1 g fibre

73 Braised stuffed shoulder of veal

	4 portions	10 portions
onion	100 g (4 oz)	250 g (10 oz)
carrot	100 g (4 oz)	250 g (10 oz)
dripping or oil	25 g (1 oz)	60 g (2½ oz)
shoulder of veal (boned)	400 g (1 lb)	1¼ kg (2½ lb)
tomato purée	50 g (2 oz)	125 g (5 oz)
brown veal stock	250 ml (½ pt)	625 ml (1¼ pt)
bouquet garni		
jus-lié or demi-glace	250 ml (½ pt)	625 ml (1¼ pt)
clove garlic, crushed	1	2

1. Bone-out the shoulder, season, stuff (recipe 74) and secure with string. Cook and serve as for braised veal (recipe 64).

2. For larger joints allow 30–35 minutes per ½ kg (1 lb) plus 35 minutes (approximately) cooking time.

74 Roast stuffed breast of veal

Poitrine de veau farcie

Bone, trim, season and stuff. Tie with string and cook and serve as for roast leg of veal.

Veal stuffing

HEALTHY EATING TIP
Use a minimum amount of salt; rely on the herbs and lemon for flavour. Use a little unsaturated oil to cook the onion.

Using 100 g meat, 1 portion provides:
1154 kJ/276 kcal energy
14.0 g fat
(of which 7.2 g saturated)
14.8 g carbohydrate
(of which 1.4 g sugars)
23.4 g protein
0.6 g fibre

	4 portions	10 portions
white or wholemeal breadcrumbs	100 g (4 oz)	250 g (10 oz)
onion cooked in oil, butter or margarine without colour	50 g (2 oz)	125 g (5 oz)
pinch of chopped parsley		
chopped suet	50 g (2 oz)	125 g (5 oz)
good pinch of powdered thyme or rosemary		
grated zest and juice of lemon	½	1
salt, pepper		

1. Combine all the ingredients.

2. This may be used for stuffing joints or may be cooked separately in buttered paper or in a basin in the steamer for approximately 1 hour.

Note: The stuffing for veal joints may be varied by using:

- orange in place of lemon;
- addition of duxelle;
- leeks in place of onion;
- various herbs;
- adding a little spice (ginger, nutmeg, allspice).

75 Braised shin of veal

Osso buco

Using hard margarine and sunflower oil, 1 portion provides:
1748 kJ/416 kcal
28.6 g fat
(of which 7.8 g saturated)
9.3 g carbohydrate
(of which 4.1 g sugars)
28.5 g protein
1.9 g fibre

	4 portions	10 portions
meaty knuckle of veal	1½ kg (3 lb)	3¾ kg (7½ lb)
flour	25 g (1 oz)	60 g (2½ oz)
butter or margarine	50 g (2 oz)	125 g (5 oz)
oil	60 ml (⅛ pt)	150 ml (⅓ pt)
onion	50 g (2 oz)	125 g (5 oz)
small clove garlic	1	2–3
carrot	50 g (2 oz)	125 g (5 oz)
leek	25 g (1 oz)	60 g (2½ oz)
celery	25 g (1 oz)	60 g (2½ oz)
dry white wine	60 ml (⅛ pt)	150 ml (⅓ pt)
white stock	60 ml (⅛ pt)	150 ml (⅓ pt)
tomato purée	25 g (1 oz)	60 g (2½ oz)
bouquet garni		
tomatoes	200 g (½ lb)	500 g (1¼ lb)
grated zest and juice of lemon or orange	½	1
chopped parsley and basil		

HEALTHY EATING TIP

Use a minimum amount of salt to season the meat and in the finished sauce. Lightly oil the pan with an unsaturated oil and drain off any excess after the frying is complete. Serve with a large portion of risotto.

1 Prepare the veal knuckle by cutting and sawing through the bone in 5 cm (2 inch) thick pieces.

2 Season the veal pieces with salt and pepper and pass through flour on both sides.

3 Melt the butter and oil in a sauté pan.

4 Add the veal slices and cook on both sides, colouring slightly.

5 Add the finely chopped onion and garlic, cover with a lid and allow to sweat gently for 2–3 minutes.

6 Add the carrot, leek and celery cut in brunoise, cover with a lid and allow to sweat for 3–4 minutes. Pour off the fat.

7 Deglaze with the white wine and stock. Add the tomato purée.

8 Add the bouquet garni, replace the lid and allow the dish to simmer gently, preferably in an oven, for 1 hour.

9 Add the concasséd tomatoes, correct the seasoning.

10 Replace the lid, return to the oven and allow to continue simmering until the meat is so tender that it can be pulled away from the bone easily with a fork.

11 Remove the bouquet garni, add the lemon juice, correct seasoning and serve sprinkled with a mixture of chopped fresh basil, parsley and grated orange and lemon zest known as gremolata.

Note: A risotto with saffron may be served separately. *Osso buco* is an Italian regional dish that has many variations.

76 Calf's liver and bacon

Foie de veau au lard

> 1 portion provides:
> 998 kJ/238 kcal
> 13.4 g fat
> (of which 5.0 g saturated)
> 2.8 g carbohydrate
> (of which 2.7 g sugars)
> 26.9 g protein
> 1.1 g fibre

	4 portions	10 portions
calf's liver	300 g (12 oz)	1 kg (2 lb)
oil for frying	50 g (2 oz)	125 g (5 oz)
streaky bacon	50 g (2 oz)	125 g (5 oz)
jus-lié	125 ml (¼ pt)	300 ml (⅝ pt)

HEALTHY EATING TIP

Bacon is salty, so no added salt is needed. Use a little unsaturated oil to fry the liver and drain off any excess fat. Serve with boiled new potatoes and a variety of vegetables.

1 Skin the liver and remove the gristle.

2 Cut in slices on the slant.

3 Pass the slices of liver through flour. Shake off the excess flour.

4 Quickly fry on both sides in hot fat.

5 Remove the rind and bone from the bacon and grill on both sides.

6 Serve the liver and bacon with a cordon of jus-lié and a sauceboat of jus-lié separately.

Note: Variations include:

- Fry in butter and sprinkle with powdered sage.

- Fry in butter, remove the liver, deglaze the pan with raspberry vinegar and powdered thyme.

- When cooked, sprinkle with chopped parsley and a few drops of lemon juice.

- Flour, egg and breadcrumb the liver before cooking.

- Liver may be lightly brushed with oil and grilled.

77 Braised veal sweetbreads (white)

Ris de veau braisé (à blanc)

Sweetbreads are glands, and two types are used for cooking. The thymus glands (throat) are usually long in shape and are of inferior quality. The pancreatic glands (stomach) are heart-shaped and of superior quality.

> Using hard margarine and sunflower oil, 1 portion provides:
> 1103 kJ/263 kcal
> 20.7 g fat
> (of which 4.4 g saturated)
> 1.7 g carbohydrate
> (of which 0.0 g sugars)
> 17.6 g protein
> 0.0 g fibre

	4 portions	10 portions
heart-shaped sweetbreads	8	20
salt, pepper		
onion	100 g (4 oz)	250 g (10 oz)
carrot	100 g (4 oz)	250 g (10 oz)
oil, margarine or butter	50 g (2 oz)	125 g (5 oz)
bouquet garni		
veal stock	250 ml (½ pt)	625 ml (1¼ pt)

1 Wash, blanch, refresh and trim the sweetbreads (see page 266).

2 Season and place in a casserole or sauté pan on a bed of roots smeared with the oil, margarine or butter.

3 Add the bouquet garni and stock.

4 Cover with buttered greaseproof paper and a lid.

5 Cook in a moderate oven at 150–200°C (Reg. 2–6; 300–400°F) for approximately 45 minutes.

6 Remove the lid, baste occasionally with cooking liquor to glaze.

7 Serve with some of the cooking liquor, thickened with diluted arrowroot if necessary, and passed on to the sweetbreads.

Note: Variations include:

- *Braised veal sweetbreads (brown).* Prepare as in the recipe above and place on a lightly browned bed of roots. Barely cover with brown veal stock, or half-brown veal stock and half jus-lié. Cook in a moderate oven at 150–200°C (Reg. 2–6; 300–400°F) without a lid, basting frequently (approximately 1 hour). Cover with the corrected, strained sauce to serve. (If veal stock is used, thicken with arrowroot.)

- *Braised veal sweetbreads with vegetables.* Braise white with a julienne of vegetables in place of the bed of roots, the julienne served in the sauce.

78 Sweetbread escalope

Escalope de ris de veau

Braise the sweetbreads white, press slightly between two trays and allow to cool. Cut into thick slices, ½–1 cm (¼–½ inch) thick and shallow fry.

Serve with the garnish and sauce, e.g. on a bed of leaf spinach; coat with Mornay sauce and glaze.

79 Sweetbread escalope (crumbed)

Escalope de ris de veau

Braise the sweetbreads white, press slightly and allow to cool. Cut into thick slices. Then flour, egg and crumb and shallow fry. Serve with a suitable garnish (e.g. asparagus tips) and a cordon of jus-lié. Finish with nut brown butter (optional).

80 Grilled veal sweetbreads

Blanch, braise, cool and press the sweetbreads. Cut in halves crosswise, pass through melted butter and grill gently on both sides. Serve with a sauce and garnish as indicated.

In some recipes they may be passed through butter and crumbs before being grilled, garnished with noisette potatoes, buttered carrots, purée of peas and béarnaise sauce.

Pork and bacon

The keeping quality of pork is less than that of other meat; therefore it must be handled, prepared and cooked with great care. Pork should always be well cooked.

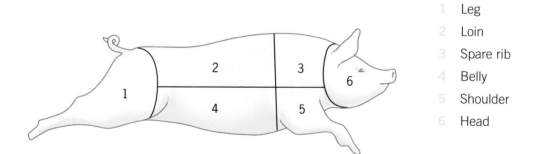

1 Leg
2 Loin
3 Spare rib
4 Belly
5 Shoulder
6 Head

Fig 9.29 Pig carcass dissection

Butchery
Cuts, uses and weights

Joint	Uses	Approximate weight (kg)	(lb)
(1) leg	roasting and boiling	5	10
(2) loin	roasting, frying, grilling	6	12
(3) spare rib	roasting, pies	1½	3
(4) belly	pickling, boiling, stuffed, rolled and roasted	2	4
(5) shoulder	roasting, sausages, pies	3	6
(6) head (whole)	brawn	4	8
(7) trotters	grilling, boiling		
kidneys	sauté, grilling		
liver	frying, pâté		

When 5–6 weeks old a piglet is known as a sucking or suckling pig. The weight is then between 5–10 kg (10–20 lb).

Order of dissection

- Remove the head.
- Remove the trotters.
- Remove the leg.
- Remove the shoulder.
- Remove the spare ribs.
- Divide the loin from the belly.

Preparation of joints and cuts
Leg

- *Roasting* Remove the pelvic or aitch bone, trim and score the rind neatly; that is, with a sharp-pointed knife, make a series of 3 mm (⅛ inch) deep incisions approximately 2 cm (1 inch) apart all over the skin of the joint. Trim and clean the knuckle bone.
- *Boiling* It is usual to pickle the joint either by rubbing dry salt and saltpetre into the meat or by soaking in a brine solution (page 242). Then remove the pelvic bone, trim and secure with string if necessary.

Loin

- *Roasting (on the bone)* Saw down the chine bone in order to facilitate carving; trim the excess fat and sinew and score the rind in the direction that the joint will be carved. Season and secure with string.
- *Roasting (boned-out)* Remove the fillets and bone-out carefully. Trim off the excess fat and sinew, score the rind and neaten the flap, season, replace the filet mignon, roll up and secure the string. This joint is sometimes stuffed (page 283).
- *Grilling or frying chops* Remove the skin, excess fat and sinew, then cut and saw or chop through the loin in approximately 1 cm (½ inch) slices; remove the excess bone and trim neatly.

Spare rib

- *Roasting* Remove the excess fat, bone and sinew and trim neatly.
- *Pies* Remove the excess fat and sinew, bone-out and cut as required.

Belly

Remove all the small rib bones, season with salt, pepper and chopped sage, roll and secure with string. This joint may be stuffed.

Shoulder

- *Roasting* The shoulder is usually boned-out, the excess fat and sinew removed, seasoned, scored and rolled with string. It may be stuffed and can also be divided into two smaller joints.
- *Sausages and pies* Skin, bone-out and remove the excess fat and sinew and cut into even pieces or mince.

Head

These are usually boned and pressed by specialist pork butchers to make a cold meat called brawn.

Trotters

Boil in water for a few minutes, scrape with the back of a knife to remove the hairs, wash off in cold water and split in half.

Kidneys

Remove the fat and skin, cut down the middle lengthwise. Remove the sinew and cut into slices or neat dice.

Liver

Skin if possible, remove the gristle and cut into thin slices on the slant.

Signs of quality

- Lean flesh should be pale pink, firm and of a fine texture.

- The fat should be white, firm, smooth and not excessive.
- Bones should be small, fine and pinkish.
- The skin or rind should be smooth.

Pork recipes

Where applicable name the origin and breed of the pork e.g. Gloucester Spot, Tamworth. For further information contact British Meat.

81 Roast leg of pork

4 oz (113 g) portion, 1 portion provides:
1357 kJ/323 kcal
22.4 g fat
(of which 8.9 g saturated)
0.0 g carbohydrate
(of which 0.0 g sugars)
30.4 g protein
0.0 g fibre

1 Prepare leg for roasting as on page 281.
2 Moisten with water, oil, cider, wine or butter and lard then sprinkle with salt, rubbing it well into the cracks of the skin. This will make the crackling crisp.
3 Place on a trivet in a roasting tin with a little oil or dripping on top.
4 Start to cook in a hot oven at 230–250°C (Reg. 7–9; 450–500°F) basting frequently.
5 Gradually reduce the heat, allowing approximately 25 minutes per ½ kg (1 lb) and 25 minutes over. Pork must always be well cooked. If using a probe, the minimum temperature should be 72°C (161°F) for two minutes.
6 When cooked remove from the pan and prepare a roast gravy from the sediment (see page 63).
7 Remove the crackling and cut into even pieces for serving.
8 Serve the joint garnished with picked watercress and accompanied by roast gravy, apple sauce and sage and onion dressing. If to be carved, proceed as for roast lamb (page 220).

Note: Other joints can also be used for roasting (loin, shoulder and spare rib).

82 Sage and onion dressing for pork

	4 portions	10 portions
white breadcrumbs	100 g (4 oz)	250 g (10 oz)
pork dripping	50 g (2 oz)	125 g (5 oz)
pinch chopped parsley		
chopped onion	50 g (2 oz)	125 g (5 oz)
good pinch powdered sage		
salt, pepper		

Use a small amount of unsaturated oil to cook the onion. Add a minimum amount of salt.

1 Cook the onion in the dripping without colour.

2 Combine all the ingredients. Dressing is usually served separately.

83 Apple sauce

cooking apples	400 g (1 lb)
sugar	50 g (2 oz)
margarine or butter	25 g (1 oz)

1 Peel, core and wash the apples.

2 Place with other ingredients in a covered pan and cook to a purée.

3 Pass through a sieve or liquidise.

84 Grilled pork chop

Côte de porc grillé

Using lean meat only, 1 portion provides:
816 kJ/194 kcal energy
7.4 g fat
(of which 2.7 g saturated)
7.3 g carbohydrate
(of which 6.8 g sugars)
24.4 g protein
0.2 g fibre

Pork is a fatty meat. Grilling will reduce the overall fat content.

1 Season the chop on both sides with salt and mill pepper.

2 Brush with melted fat and either grill on both sides with moderate heat for approximately 10 minutes or cook in a little fat in a plat à sauté.

3 Serve accompanied by a sharp sauce, e.g., of charcutière (page 62).

85 Baked pork chop with apple

Côte de porc à la flamande

Using lean meat only, 1 portion provides:
730 kJ/173 kcal energy
4.9 g fat
(of which 1.7 g saturated)
8.9 g carbohydrate
(of which 8.9 g sugars)
24.0 g protein
1.4 g fibre

	4 portions	10 portions
pork chops	4	10
dessert apples	300 g (12 oz)	750 g (2 lb 14 oz)

continued over ▶

▶ *Baked pork chop with apple continued*

1 Season the chops with salt and mill pepper.

2 Half cook on both sides in a little oil in a sauté pan.

3 Peel, core and slice the apples and place in an earthenware dish.

4 Put the chops on the apples. Sprinkle with a little fat.

5 Complete the cooking in a moderate oven at 180–200°C (Reg. 4–6; 350–400°F) for approximately 10–15 minutes. Clean the dish and serve.

Variations:

- pineapple rings may be used in place of apple

- the chops may be grilled and garnished with slices of peeled cooked apples sprinkled with caster or demerara sugar.

- brushed with honey and grilled

- grilled and served with braised red cabbage and a slice of onion and sage tart (made with short pastry, covered with lightly fried onions, sprinkled with sage and baked).

86 Barbecued spare ribs of pork

Using sunflower oil, 1 portion provides:
6151 kJ/1465 kcal
126 g fat
(of which 37.3 g saturated)
20.3 g carbohydrate
(of which 17.1 g sugars)
63.5 g protein
0.3 g fibre

	4 portions	**10 portions**
finely chopped onion	100 g (4 oz)	250 g (10 oz)
clove of garlic (chopped)	1	2
oil	60 ml (⅛ pt)	150 ml (⅓ pt)
vinegar	60 ml (⅛ pt)	150 ml (⅓ pt)
tomato purée	150 g (6 oz)	375 g (15 oz)
honey	60 ml (⅛ pt)	150 ml (⅓ pt)
brown stock	250 ml (½ pt)	625 ml (1¼ pt)
Worcester sauce	4 tbsp	10 tbsp
dry mustard	1 tsp	2 tsp
pinch thyme		
salt		
spare ribs of pork	2 kg (4 lb)	5 kg (10 lb)

1 Sweat the onion and garlic in the oil without colour.

2 Mix in the vinegar, tomato purée, honey, stock, Worcester sauce, mustard, thyme and season with salt.

3 Allow the barbecue sauce to simmer for 10–15 minutes.

4 Place the prepared spare ribs fat side up on a trivet in a roasting tin.

5 Brush the spare ribs liberally with the barbecue sauce.

6 Place in a moderately hot oven at 180–200°C (Reg. 4–6; 350–400°F).

7 Cook for ¾–1 hour.

8 Baste generously with the barbecue sauce every 10–15 minutes.

9 The cooked spare ribs should be brown and crisp.

10 Cut the spare ribs into individual portions and serve.

87 Pork escalopes

Pork escalopes are usually cut from the prime cuts of meat in the leg or loin and can be dealt with in the same way as a leg of veal. They may be cut into 75–100 g (3–4 oz) slices, flattened with a meat bat and used plain or crumbed and served with vegetables or a pasta (noodles) with a suitable sauce e.g. Madeira or as for pork medallions, or as with veal escalope recipes (page 272).

88 Pork medallions

Pork fillet can be cut into 2 cm pieces, sautéed on both sides and finished with a variety of sauces and garnishes e.g. a coarse grain mustard and red onion sauce, or a sauce made from 4 parts apple pureé and 1 part cream or natural yoghurt with a smooth consistency.

Fig 9.30 Breadcrumbed pork escalope with noodles in tomato sauce *John Campbell*

89 Pork escalopes with Calvados sauce

Using lean meat only, and double cream, 1 portion provides:
1856 kJ/447 kcal energy
34.2 g fat
(of which 20.3 g saturated)
12.7 g carbohydrate
(of which 12.5 g sugars)
22.8 g protein
1.1 g fibre

HEALTHY EATING TIP

Use a little unsaturated oil to sauté the chops. Add a minimum amount of salt. Try using yoghurt stabilised with a little cornflour, or half cream and half yoghurt

	4 portions	10 portions
4 pork escalopes (recipe 87)	4 × 100 g (4 oz)	10 × 100 g (4 oz)
shallot or onion finely chopped	50 g (2 oz)	125 g (5 oz)
butter, margarine or oil	50 g (2 oz)	125 g (5 oz)
Calvados	30 ml (1/16 pt)	75 ml (1/8 pt)
double cream or natural yoghurt	125 ml (1/4 pt)	300 ml (5/8 pt)
chopped basil, sage or rosemary		
salt, cayenne pepper		
crisp eating apples (e.g. russet)	2	5
cinnamon		
lemon juice		
brown sugar		
butter, melted		

1 Core and peel the apples.

2 Cut into ½ cm (¼ inch) thick rings and sprinkle with a little cinnamon and a few drops of lemon juice.

3 Place onto a baking sheet, sprinkle with brown sugar, a little melted butter and caramelise under the salamander or in the top of a hot oven.

4 Lightly sauté the escalopes on both sides in the butter.

5 Remove from the pan and keep warm.

6 Add the chopped shallots to the same pan, cover with a lid and cook gently without colouring (use a little more butter if necessary).

7 Strain off the fat leaving the shallots in the pan and deglaze with the Calvados.

8 Reduce by a half, add the cream or yoghurt, seasoning and herbs.

9 Reboil, correct the seasoning and consistency and pass through a fine strainer onto the meat.

10 Garnish with slices of caramelised apples.

Note: Calvados can be replaced with twice the amount of cider and reduced by three quarters as an alternative. Add a crushed clove of garlic and 1 tablespoon of continental mustard (2–3 cloves and 2½ tablespoons for 10 portions).

Special care must be taken if using yoghurt not to overheat, otherwise the sauce will curdle.

90 Sausage toad in the hole

	4 portions	**10 portions**
sausages	8	20
Yorkshire pudding (page 245)		

1 Place the sausages in a roasting tray or ovenproof dish with a little oil or dripping.

2 Place in a hot oven at 230–250°C (Reg. 8–9; 450–500°F) for 5–10 minutes.

3 Remove, add the Yorkshire pudding and return to the hot oven until the sausages and Yorkshire pudding are cooked, approximately 15–20 minutes.

4 Cut into portions and serve with a lightly thickened gravy or sauce.

Note: Other meats may be cooked and served this way: chops, steak, corned beef, vegetarian sausages etc.

91 Forcemeat

This is a term given to numerous mixtures of meats (usually veal and pork); meat and poultry; poultry; game; fish; vegetables and bread.

Forcemeats range from a simple sausagemeat to the finer mixtures used in the making of hot mousses (ham, chicken, fish) and soufflés. Also included are mixtures of bread, vegetables and herbs, which alternatively are referred to as stuffings.

Forcemeats are used for galantines, raised pies, terrines, meat balls and a wide variety of other dishes.

92 Crepinettes

These are small sausages usually made from a forcemeat of veal, lamb, pork or chicken encased either in caul or paper thin slices of salt pork. Other ingredients are sometimes added e.g. chopped mushrooms or truffle. Crepinettes are usually covered with melted butter or good quality oil, coated with fresh white breadcrumbs and grilled, sautéed or cooked in the oven. Traditionally they are served with potato purée and a well flavoured demi-glace type sauce.

HEALTHY EATING TIP

Drain off some of the fat after cooking the sausages. Use semi-skimmed milk to make the batter. Serve with boiled, mashed or jacket potatoes and plenty of seasonal vegetables.

Using sunflower oil, 1 portion provides:
3067 kJ/730 kcal
43.9 g fat
(of which 9.2 g saturated)
69.7 g carbohydrate
(of which 54.7 g sugars)
13.4 g protein
1.6 g fibre

HEALTHY EATING TIP

Use hot sunflower oil to fry the pork and a small amount of an unsaturated oil to fry the vegetables. No added salt is needed, as the soy sauce is high in sodium. Serve with plenty of rice or noodles, and additional vegetables.

93 Sweet and sour pork

	4 portions	10 portions
loin of pork (boned)	250 g (10 oz)	600 g (1½ lb)
sugar	12 g (½ oz)	30 g (1¼ oz)
dry sherry	70 ml (⅛ pt)	180 ml (⅓ pt)
soy sauce	70 ml (⅛ pt)	180 ml (⅓ pt)
vegetable oil	70 ml (⅛ pt)	180 ml (⅓ pt)
cornflour	50 g (2 oz)	125 g (5 oz)
oil	2 tbsp	5 tbsp
clove garlic	1	2
fresh root ginger	50 g (2 oz)	125 g (5 oz)
onion, chopped	75 g (3 oz)	180 g (7½ oz)
green pepper in 1 cm (½ inch) dice	1	2½
chillies, chopped	2	5
sweet and sour sauce	210 ml (⅜ pt)	500 ml (1 pt)
pineapple rings (fresh or canned)	2	5
spring onions	2	5

1 Cut the boned loin of pork into 2 cm (¼ inch) pieces.

2 Marinate the pork for 30 minutes in the sugar, sherry and soy sauce.

3 Pass the pork through cornflour, pressing the cornflour in well.

4 Deep fry the pork pieces in oil at 190°C (375°F) until golden brown, drain. Add the tablespoons of oil to a sauté pan.

5 Add the garlic and ginger, fry until fragrant.

6 Add the onion, pepper and chillies, sauté for a few minutes.

7 Stir in sweet and sour sauce, bring to boil.

8 Add the pineapple cut into small chunks, thicken slightly with diluted cornflour. Simmer for 2 minutes.

9 Deep fry the pork again until crisp. Drain, mix into vegetables and sauce or serve separately.

10 Serve garnished with rings of spring onions or button onions.

94 Sweet and sour sauce

	4 portions	**10 portions**
white vinegar	375 ml (¾ pt)	1 litre (2 pt)
brown sugar	150 g (6 oz)	375 g (15 oz)
tomato ketchup	125 ml (¼ pt)	300 ml (⅝ pt)
Worcester sauce	1 tbsp	2½ tbsp
seasoning		

1 portion provides:
877 kJ/207 kcal energy
0.0 g fat
(of which 0.0 g saturated)
49.3 g carbohydrate
(of which 48.9 g sugars)
1.1 g protein
0.3 g fibre

1 Boil the vinegar and sugar in a suitable pan.

2 Add the tomato ketchup, Worcester sauce and seasoning.

3 Simmer for a few minutes then use as required. This sauce may also
be lightly thickened with cornflour.

95 Stir-fried pork fillet

pork fillet	400 g (1 lb)	2 kg (1½ lb)
olive oil		
shallots, finely chopped	2	6
garlic (optional) chopped	1 clove	2 cloves
button mushrooms	200 g (8 oz)	400 g (1 lb)
Chinese five spice	1 pinch	2 pinches
soy sauce	1 tbsp	2 tbsp
dry white wine	2 tbsp	5 tbsp
clear honey	2 tsp	3 tsp
salt and pepper		

1 portion provides:
831 kJ/199 kcal energy
9.8 g fat
(of which 2.2 g saturated)
5.1 g carbohydrate
(of which 4.2 g sugars)
22.9 g protein
0.8 g fibre

1 Gently fry the shallots, garlic and sliced mushrooms in a little oil in
a frying pan or wok.

2 Add the pork cut in strips, stir well, increase the heat, season and
add the Chinese five spice powder, cook for 3–4 minutes then cover
the heat.

3 Add the soy sauce, honey, wine and reduce for 2–3 minutes.

4 Correct seasoning and serve.

HEALTHY EATING TIP

Use a small amount of an
unsaturated oil to fry the
vegetables and the pork.
No extra salt, as soy sauce
is added.
Adding more vegetables
and a large portion of rice
or noodles can reduce
the overall fat
content.

Based on edible portion of meat –
135 g, 1 portion provides:
2317 kJ/554 kcal energy
31.3 g fat
(of which 7.7 g saturated)
23.2 g carbohydrate
(of which 20.7 g sugars)
46.0 g protein
0.9 g fibre

HEALTHY EATING TIP

Use a minimum
amount of salt
in the pesto and
risotto.

96 Braised honey glaze blade of pork with sage and onion pesto, served in a garlic flavoured risotto

	4 portions	**10 portions**
pork blade cut from the forequarter of pork	4 × 250 g (10 oz)	10 × 250 g (10 oz)
Marinade **honey**	250 mls (½ pt)	625 mls (1¼ pt)
soft brown sugar	75 g (3 oz)	180 g (7½ oz)
star anise	4	10
cider vinegar	2 tbsp	5 tbsp
well reduced stock brown	125 ml (¼ pt)	375 ml (⅜ pt)
Pesto **sage leaves**	50 g (2 oz)	125 g (5 oz)
flat parsley	25 g (1 oz)	62 g (1½ oz)
Parmesan	25 g (1 oz)	62 g (1½ oz)
toasted pinenuts	25 g (1 oz)	62 g (1½ oz)
chopped shallots	12 g (½ oz)	30 g (1¼ oz)
clove garlic crushed and chopped	3 tbsp	8 tbsp
olive oil		
seasoning		

1 For the pesto, chop all the ingredients together finely in a processor to form a sauce-like consistency.

2 Marinate the pork for 24 hours in the honey marinade.

3 Pack into single portions and steam. Cook at 89°C for 5 hours.

4 Reheat the well reduced stock mix with a little of the marinade, place the pork on a suitable dish, mask with the stock and marinade, then glaze in the oven.

5 Serve on a bed of garlic flavoured risotto, page 162. Mask with the glaze, place a little pesto around the plate.

Note: It is advisable to vacuum pack the blades for steaming at 89°C for 5 hours. Once cooked these can be rapidly chilled in a water bath and kept in the refrigerator at 3°C. They can then be reheated and glazed for service. For service, the blade may be boned before glazing.

Blade is a modern cut of pork that is popular in gastropubs and bistros.

Bacon

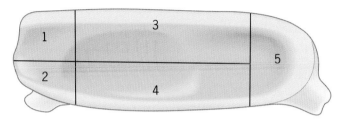

1. Collar
2. Hock
3. Back
4. Streaky
5. Gammon

Grilling cuts

Gammon

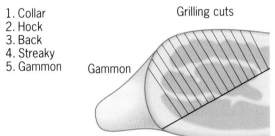

Fig 9.31 Cuts of bacon

Bacon is the cured flesh of a bacon weight pig that is specifically reared for bacon, because its shape and size yields economic bacon joints. Bacon is cured either by dry salting and then smoking or by soaking in brine followed by smoking. Green bacon is brine-cured but not smoked; it has a milder flavour but does not keep as long as smoked bacon.

Depending on the degree of salting during the curing process bacon joints may or may not require soaking in cold water for a few hours before being cooked.

Butchery
Cuts, uses and weights

Joint	Uses	Approximate weight	
		(kg)	(lb)
(1) collar	boiling, grilling	4½	9
(2) hock	boiling, grilling	4½	9
(3) back	grilling, frying	9	18
(4) streaky	grilling, frying	4½	9
(5) gammon	boiling, grilling, frying	7½	15

Preparation of joints and cuts
Collar

- *Boiling* Remove bone (if any) and tie with string.
- *Grilling* Remove the rind and trim off the outside surface and cut into thin slices (rashers), across the joint.

Hock

- *Boiling* Leave whole or bone-out and secure with string.

Back and streaky

- *Grilling* Remove all bones and rind and cut into thin rashers.
- *Frying* Remove the rind, trim off the outside surface and cut into rashers or chops of the required thickness.

Gammon

- *Grilling* Fairly thick slices are cut from the middle of the gammon. They are then trimmed and the rind removed.
- *Frying* As for grilling.

Quality

- There should be no sign of stickiness.
- There should be a pleasant smell.
- The rind should be thin, smooth and free from wrinkles.
- The fat should be white, smooth and not excessive in proportion to the lean.
- The lean should be a deep pink colour and firm.

Note: Do not confuse ham with gammon.

Bacon recipes

97 Boiled bacon (hock, collar or gammon)

Using 4 oz (113 g) per portion, 1 portion provides:
1543 kJ/367 kcal
30.5 g fat
(of which 12.2 g saturated)
0.0 g carbohydrate
(of which 0.0 g sugars)
23.1 g protein
0.0 g fibre

1 Soak the bacon in cold water for 24 hours before cooking. Change the water (see note page 291).
2 Bring to the boil, skim and simmer gently, approximately 25 minutes per ½ kg (1 lb) and 25 minutes over. Allow to cool in the liquid.
3 Remove the rind and brown skin and carve.
4 Serve with a little of the cooking liquor.

Note: Boiled bacon may be served with pease pudding (page 459) and a suitable sauce such as parsley sauce (page 55).

98 Grilled back or streaky rashers

Arrange on a baking tray and grill on both sides under the salamander.

99 Roasted joint of bacon

1 portion provides:
1021 kJ/245 kcal energy
14.8 g fat
(of which 4.9 g saturated)
0.0 g carbohydrate
(of which 0.0 g sugars)
28.0 g protein
0.0 g fibre

1 Soak the joint in cold water for 24 hours (see note page 291).
2 Remove from the water. Dry well.
3 Place on a roasting tray and roast for approximately 25 minutes per ½ kilo (1 lb) and 25 minutes over.

4   Remove from oven and allow to stand for 5 minutes before carving.

5   Use the sediment for roast gravy having checked for saltiness.

The joint may be cooked in foil and for the last 25–30 minutes cooked out of the foil.

100 Baked bacon and pineapple

> Using 1 ring of pineapple, 1 portion provides:
> 1101 kJ/264 kcal energy
> 14.8 g fat
> (of which 4.9 g saturated)
> 4.9 g carbohydrate
> (of which 4.9 g sugars)
> 28.1 g protein
> 0.2 g fibre

Remove some of the outer fat after boiling. Serve with plenty of potatoes and vegetables.

1   Hock, collar or gammon may be used.

2   Soak the bacon joint in cold water for approximately 24 hours (if necessary – see note page 291).

3   Change the water.

4   Cover with water, bring to the boil and skim; simmer gently for half the required cooking time (30 minutes per ½ kg (per pound) and 30 minutes over).

5   Allow to cool. Remove rind and brown skin.

6   Cover the fat surface of the joint with demerara sugar and press well into surface. Stud with 12–24 cloves.

7   Arrange a layer of tinned pineapple rings down the centre of the joint (secure with cocktail sticks if necessary).

8   Place joint in a baking tin for second half of the cooking time.

9   Bake in a moderate oven at 200°C (Reg. 6; 400°F),

basting frequently with pineapple juice until well cooked.

10 Remove the cloves and pineapple.

11 Carve in thickish slices and serve garnished with the pineapple.

Variations include:

- Replace pineapple with tinned peaches or apricots.

- Use clear honey in place of demerara sugar and according to requirements delete or use the fruit.

101 Bacon chops with honey and orange sauce

> 1 portion provides:
> 1233 kJ/296 kcal energy
> 17.9 g fat
> (of which 9.0 g saturated)
> 15.1 g carbohydrate
> (of which 13.9 g sugars)
> 19.4 g protein
> 2.7 g fibre

	4 portions	10 portions
4 bacon chops (trimmed weight)	4 × 100 g (4 oz)	10 × 100 g (4 oz)
butter, margarine or oil	50 g (2 oz)	125 g (5 oz)
oranges	2	5
honey	1 dsp	2½ dsp
lemon, juice of	½	1½
arrowroot	½ tsp	1 tsp

Grill or dry fry the chops. Serve with plenty of potatoes and vegetables.

continued over ▶

▶ *Bacon chops with honey and orange sauce continued*

1 Ensure that the chops are well trimmed of fat.

2 Lightly fry the chops on both sides in the butter, margarine or oil without colouring.

3 Remove from the pan and keep warm.

4 Thinly remove the zest from one orange so that no white pith remains; cut into very fine julienne; blanch and refresh.

5 Peel and segment both oranges ensuring that all the white pith and pips are removed. Retain all the juice.

6 Boil the orange and lemon juice and honey and lightly thicken with diluted arrowroot.

7 Strain the sauce, add the julienne of orange and pour over the chops.

8 Garnish with the segments of orange.

Note: Variations include:

• using 1 orange and 1 pink grapefruit instead of 2 oranges;

• using a small tin of peaches or apricots or pineapple in place of the oranges.

102 Griddled gammon with apricot salsa

	4 portions	10 portions
gammon steaks	4 × 150 g (6 oz)	10 × 150 g (6 oz)
Apricot salsa **fresh apricots or dried reconstituted stoned and chopped**	200 g (8 oz)	500 g (1 lb 4 oz)
lime, grated rind and juice	1	3
grated fresh root ginger	2 tsp	5 tsp
clear honey	2 tsp	5 tsp
olive oil	1 tbsp	2½ tsp
chopped sage fresh	1 tbsp	2½ tbsp
spring onions chopped	4	10
seasoning		

1 portion provides:
1112 kJ/266 kcal energy
14.2 g fat
(of which 4.2 g saturated)
8.1 g carbohydrate
(of which 7.4 g sugars)
26.9 g protein
1.0 g fibre

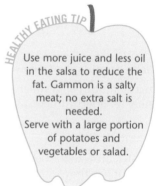

HEALTHY EATING TIP

Use more juice and less oil in the salsa to reduce the fat. Gammon is a salty meat; no extra salt is needed. Serve with a large portion of potatoes and vegetables or salad.

1 Heat the griddle pan, lightly oil, cook the gammon steaks.

2 Make the salsa, mix together in a processor the apricots, lime rind and juice, ginger, honey, olive oil and sage.

3 Add the finely chopped spring onions, then mix well.

Note: The texture should be the consistency of thick cream but coarse. A little extra olive oil may be required or some apricot juice.

103 Sauerkraut with frankfurters and garlic sausage

Choucroûte garni

	4 portions	10 portions
lard or margarine	50 g (2 oz)	125 g (5 oz)
sauerkraut	400 g (1 lb)	1¼ kg (2½ lb)
streaky bacon	300 g (12 oz)	1 kg (2 lb)
whole peeled carrots	2	5
onion studded	1	3
bouquet garni		
juniper berries	10	25
peppercorns	5	12
seasoning		
white wine	125 ml (¼ pt)	300 ml (⅝ pt)
bacon rind	100 g (4 oz)	250 g (10 oz)
garlic sausage	200 g (8 oz)	500 g (1¼ lb)
frankfurter sausages	8	20
boiled potatoes	8	20

Using margarine, 1 portion provides:
2832 kJ/682 kcal energy
50.2 g fat
(of which 19.1 g saturated)
28.8 g carbohydrate
(of which 7.4 g sugars)
30.4 g protein
5.3 g fibre

HEALTHY EATING TIP

Lightly oil the braising pan and drain off as much fat as possible after the bacon and sausage are cooked. Serve with plenty of boiled potatoes and colourful vegetables.

1 Well grease a braising pan with the lard or margarine.

2 Place a layer of sauerkraut in the bottom of the pan.

3 Place the piece of streaky bacon on top with the carrots, onion and bouquet garni; add juniper berries and peppercorns tied in a muslin bag.

4 Cover with the remainder of the sauerkraut, season and add white wine.

5 Cover with bacon rind and a tight-fitting lid.

6 Place in a moderate oven at 180°C (Reg. 4; 350°F) and braise gently for 1 hour.

7 Remove the streaky bacon and replace with the garlic sausage. Continue braising for another hour until the sauerkraut is tender.

8 Reheat the frankfurters if canned or poach in water or stock if fresh.

9 Remove the sauerkraut from the oven and discard the bacon rind.

10 Slice the streaky bacon, garlic sausage, carrots and frankfurters.

11 Dress the sauerkraut in an earthenware dish with the sliced items.

12 Serve plain boiled potatoes separately.

Note: Sauerkraut is pickled white cabbage and is a traditional German dish.

Using 100 g per portion, 1 portion provides:
958 kJ/228 kcal
12.2 g fat
(of which 4.8 g saturated)
0.0 g carbohydrate
(of which 0.0 g sugars)
29.5 g protein
0.0 g fibre

104 Grilled gammon rashers

Brush the rashers with fat on both sides and cook on greased, preheated grill bars on both sides for approximately 5–10 minutes in all. Serve with watercress and any other food as indicated, such as tomatoes, mushrooms, eggs. If a sauce is required, serve any sharp demi-glace sauce.

Using sunflower oil, 1 portion (50 g) provides:
977 kJ/233 kcal
20.3 g fat
(of which 7.2 g saturated)
0.0 g carbohydrate
(of which 0.0 g sugars)
12.5 g protein
0.0 g fibre

105 Fried bacon

Fry on both sides in a frying-pan in very little fat.

Poultry

The term in its general sense is applied to all domestic fowl bred for food and means turkeys, geese, ducks, fowls and pigeons.

Originally fowl were classified according to size and feeding by specific names as follows:

		Weight (kg)	(lb)	Number of portions
single baby chicken	} poussin	³⁄₁₀–½	¾–1	1
double baby chicken		½–¾	1–1½	2
small roasting chicken		¾–1	1½–2	3–4
medium roasting chicken		1–2	2–4	4–6
large roasting or boiling chicken		2–3	4–6	6–8
capon		3–4½	6–9	8–12
old boiling fowl		2½–4	5–8	

There is approximately 15–20% bone in poultry.

Types

- *Spring chickens* Poussin 4–6 weeks old used for roasting and grilling.
- *Broiler chickens* 3–4 months old used for roasting, grilling, casserole.
- *Medium roasting chickens* Fully grown, tender prime birds are used for roasting, grilling, sauté, casserole, suprêmes and pies.
- *Large roasting or boiling chickens* used for roasting, boiling, casserole, galantine.
- *Capons* Specially bred, fattened cock birds used for roasting.
- *Old hens* Used for stocks and soups.

Food value

The flesh of poultry is more easily digested than that of butchers' meat. It contains protein and is therefore useful for building and repairing body tissues and providing heat and energy. The fat content is low and contains a high percentage of unsaturated acids.

Storage

Chilled birds should be stored between 3°C and 5°C. Oven-ready birds are eviscerated and should be stored in a refrigerator. Frozen birds must be kept in deep freeze until required but must be completely thawed, preferably in a refrigerator, before being cooked. This procedure is essential to reduce the risk of food poisoning: chickens are potential carriers of salmonella and if birds are cooked from the frozen state there is the risk of the required degree of heat to kill off salmonella not reaching the centre of the birds.

Frozen poultry should be checked that:

- the packaging is undamaged;
- there are no signs of freezer burns, which are indicated by white patches on the skin.

Frozen birds should be defrosted by removing them from the freezer to a refrigerator.

Signs of quality

- Plump breast, pliable breast bone and firm flesh.
- Skin white and unbroken. Broiler chickens have a faint bluish tint.

- Corn-fed are yellow. Free range have more colour, firmer texture and more flavour.
- Bresse chickens are specially bred in France and are highly esteemed.

Old birds have coarse scales and large spurs on the legs and long hairs on the skin.

Trussing

Roasting

- Clean the legs by dipping in boiling water for a few seconds then remove the scales with a cloth.
- Cut off the outside claws leaving the centre ones, trim these to half their length.
- To facilitate carving remove the wish-bone.
- Place the bird on its back.
- Hold the legs back firmly.
- Insert the trussing needle through the bird, midway between the leg joints.
- Turn on to its side.
- Pierce the winglet, the skin of the neck, the skin of the carcass and the other winglet.
- Tie the ends of string securely.
- Secure the legs by inserting the needle through the carcass and over the legs, take care not to pierce the breast.

Boiling and pot roasting

- Proceed as for roasting.
- Cut the leg sinew just below the joint.
- Bend back the legs so that they lie parallel to the breast and secure when trussing, *or*
- Insert the legs through incisions made in the skin at the rear end of the bird and secure when trussing.

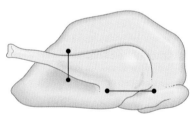

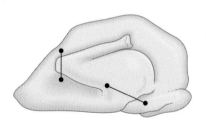

Fig 9.32 Trussing chicken for roasting and boiling

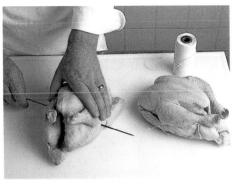
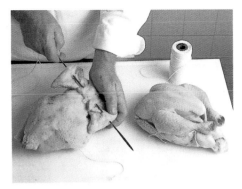

Fig 9.33 ✎ Trussing of chicken for roasting

Cutting for sauté, fricassée, pies, etc.

- Remove the feet at the first joint.
- Remove the legs from the carcass.
- Cut each leg in two at the joint.
- Remove the wish-bone. Remove the winglets and trim.
- Remove the wings carefully, leaving two equal portions on the breast.
- Remove the breast and cut in two.
- Trim the carcass and cut into three pieces.

Cuts of chicken

The pieces of cut chicken are named as follows:

Leg ⎰ (4)   drumstick
    ⎱ (3)   thigh
      (1)   wing
      (2)   breast
      (5)   winglet
      (6)   carcass

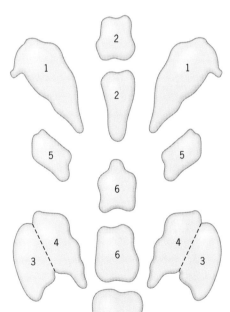

Fig 9.34 ✎ Cuts of chicken

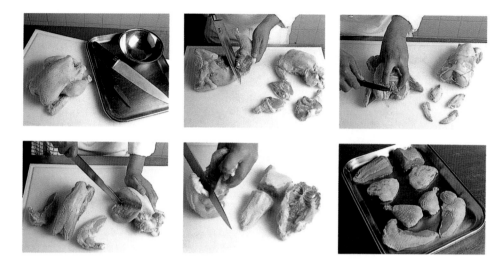

Fig 9.35 🔪 Preparing chicken for sauté

Preparation for grilling

- Remove the wish-bone.
- Cut off the claws at the first joint.
- Place the bird on its back.
- Insert a large knife through the neck-end and out of the vent.
- Cut through the backbone and open out.
- Remove back and rib bones.

Preparation for suprêmes

Fig 9.36 🔪 Preparation of chicken for spatchcock and grilling

(Illustrated opposite)

A suprême is the wing and half the breast of a chicken with the trimmed wing bone attached; the white meat of one chicken yields two suprêmes.

- Use a chicken weighing 1¼–1½ kg (2½–3 lb).
- Cut off both the legs from the chicken.
- Remove the skin from the breasts.
- Remove the wish-bone.
- Scrape the wing bone bare adjoining the breasts.
- Cut off the winglets near the joints leaving 1½–2 cm (½–¾ inch) of bare bone attached to the breasts.
- Cut the breasts close to the breastbone and follow the bone down to the wing joint.
- Cut through the joint.

- Lay the chicken on its side and pull the suprêmes off, assisting with the knife.
- Lift the fillets from the suprêmes and remove the sinew from each.
- Make an incision lengthways, along the thick side of the suprêmes, open and place the fillets inside.
- Close, lightly flatten with a bat moistened with water and trim if necessary.

Fig 9.37 Preparation of chicken for suprêmes

Preparation for ballottines

A ballottine is a boned stuffed leg of bird.

- Using a small sharp knife remove the thigh bone.
- Scrape the flesh off the bone of the drumstick towards the claw joint.
- Sever the drumstick bone leaving approximately 2–3 cm (¾–1 inch) at the claw joint end.
- Fill the cavities in both the drumstick and thigh with a savoury stuffing.
- Neaten the shape and secure with string using a trussing needle.

Ballottines of chicken may be cooked and served using any of the recipes for chicken sauté. See Fig 9.40

Cutting of cooked chicken (roasted or boiled)

- Remove the legs and cut in two (drumstick and thigh). (See pages 300, 306.)
- Remove the wings.

- Separate the breast from the carcass and divide in two.
- Serve a drumstick with a wing and the thigh with the breast.

Poultry – Turkey

Turkeys can vary in weight from 3½–20 kg (7–40 lb). They are trussed in the same way as chicken. The wish-bone should always be removed before trussing to facilitate carving. The sinews should be drawn out of the legs. Allow 200 g (½ lb) per portion raw weight.

When cooking a large turkey the legs may be removed, boned, rolled, tied and roasted separately from the remainder of the bird. This will reduce the cooking time and enable the legs and breast to cook more evenly (see page 304).

Stuffings may be rolled in foil, steamed or baked and thickly sliced. If a firmer stuffing is required, mix in one or two raw eggs before cooking.

Signs of quality

- Large full breast with undamaged skin and no signs of stickiness.
- Legs smooth with supple feet and a short spur.

As birds age the legs turn scaly and the feet harden.

Poultry – Duck, Duckling, Goose, Gosling

Sizes (approximate)

- *Duck* 3–4 kg (4–6 lb)
- *Duckling* 1½–2 kg (3–4 lb)
- *Goose* 6 kg (12 lb)
- *Gosling* 3 kg (6 lb)

Signs of quality

- Plump breasts.
- Lower back bends easily.
- Webbed feet tear easily.
- Feet and bill should be yellow.

Preparation for roasting

This is the same as for chicken (page 298). The gizzard is not split but trimmed off with a knife. Roast goose is cooked and served as for roast duck.

Game

For information and recipes for game, please refer to *Advanced Practical Cookery* by Ceserani and Foskett.

Chicken and turkey recipes

106 Roast turkey

Dinde rôti

	4 portions	10 portions
Chestnut stuffing		
chestnuts	200 g (½ lb)	500 g (1¼ lb)
sausage meat	600 g (1½ lb)	1½ kg (3¾ lb)
chopped onion	50 g (2 oz)	125 g (5 oz)
Parsley and thyme stuffing		
chopped onion	50 g (2 oz)	125 g (5 oz)
oil, butter or margarine	100 g (4 oz)	250 g (10 oz)
salt, pepper		
white or wholemeal breadcrumbs	100 g (4 oz)	250 g (10 oz)
pinch powdered thyme		
pinch chopped parsley		
chopped turkey liver (raw)		
turkey	5 kg (10 lb)	12 kg (25 lb)
fat bacon	100 g (4 oz)	250 g (10 oz)
brown stock	375 ml (¾ pt)	1 litre (2 pt)
bread sauce (page 64)		

No accompaniments, 1 portion (200 g raw with skin, bone) provides:
836 kJ/200 kcal
11.75 g fat
(of which 4.0 g saturated)
0.0 g carbohydrate
(of which 0.0 g sugars)
29.0 g protein
0.0 g fibre

With stuffing, roast gravy, bread sauce, 1 portion (200 g raw, with skin, bone) provides:
1589 kJ/380 kcal
24.0 g fat
(of which 8.4 g saturated)
8.6 g carbohydrate
(of which 1.6 g sugars)
34.0 g protein
0.9 g fibre

1 Slit the chestnuts on both sides using a small knife.

2 Boil the chestnuts in water for 5–10 minutes.

3 Drain and remove the outer and inner skins whilst warm.

4 Cook the chestnuts in a little stock for 5 minutes.

5 When cold, dice and mix into the sausage meat and cooked onion.

6 For the parsley and thyme stuffing, cook the onion in oil, butter or margarine without colour.

7 Remove from the heat, add the seasoning, crumbs and herbs.

8 Mix in the raw chopped liver (optional) from the bird.

9 Truss the bird firmly (removing the wish-bone first).

10 Season with salt and pepper.

11 Cover the breast with fat bacon.

12 Place the bird in a roasting tray on its side and coat with 200 g (4 oz) dripping or oil.

13 Roast in a moderate oven at 200–230°C (Reg. 6–8; 400–450°F).

continued over ▶

▶ *Roast turkey continued*

14 Allow to cook on both legs and complete the cooking with the breast upright for the last 30 minutes.

15 Baste frequently and allow 15–20 minutes per lb. If using a temperature probe, insert in the thickest part of the leg for a reading of 77°C (170°F).

16 Bake the two stuffings separately in greased trays until well cooked.

17 Prepare the gravy from the sediment and the brown stock. Correct the seasoning and remove the fat.

18 Remove the string and serve with stuffings, roast gravy, bread sauce and/or hot cranberry sauce.

19 The turkey may be garnished with chipolata sausages and bacon rolls.

Note: When the turkey is cooked, to facilitate carving, remove and debone the legs.

For ease of carving, before cooking turkeys may be completely boned and each leg must have the tough sinew removed.

The breasts and the legs can both be stuffed, rolled and tied prior to roasting.

107 Turkey escalopes

100 g (4 oz) slices cut from boned out turkey breast can be:

A) lightly floured and gently cooked on both sides in butter, oil or margarine with a minimum of colour.

B) floured, egged and crumbed and shallow fried.

Served with a suitable sauce and/or garnish e.g. pan fried turkey escalope cooked with oyster mushrooms and finished with white wine and cream.

108 Cranberry sauce

cranberries	400 g (1 lb)
water	100 ml (¼ pt)
sugar	50 g (2 oz)

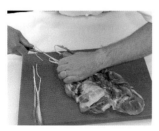

Fig 9.38 Boning, stuffing, rolling and tying turkey

Simmer all ingredients together in a covered pan (not iron or aluminium) until soft. The sauce may be sieved or liquidised if required. For a variation half orange juice and half water plus some grated orange zest may be used.

109 Roast chicken

Poulet rôti

	4 portions	10 portions
chicken 1¼–1½ kg (2½–3 lb)	1	2½
oil, butter or margarine	50 g (2 oz)	125 g (5 oz)
brown stock	125 ml (¼ pt)	300 ml (⅜ pt)
game chips	25 g (1 oz)	60 g (2½ oz)
bread sauce (page 64)	125 ml (¼ pt)	300 ml (⅜ pt)

1 Lightly season the chicken inside and out with salt.

2 Place on its side in a roasting tin.

3 Cover with the oil, butter or margarine.

4 Place in hot oven for approximately 20–25 minutes. Turn on to the other leg.

5 Cook for a further 20–25 minutes approximately. Baste frequently.

6 To test if cooked, pierce with a fork between the drumstick and thigh and hold over a plate. The juice issuing from the chicken should not show any sign of blood. If using a temperature probe, proceed as for turkey (recipe 106).

7 Make roast gravy with the stock and sediment in the roasting tray.

8 Serve with game chips.

Note: Roast gravy and bread sauce are served separately. Always remove the trussing string from the bird before serving.

- *Roast chicken and bacon* – serve with four grilled rashers of streaky bacon, which may be rolled (after cooking).

- Spring chickens can also be cooked and served as above with a reduced cooking time according to the weight of the birds. They can also be served with a savoury sauce e.g. chasseur, Italienne, pepper, piquante or Madeira.

Without accompaniments, 1 portion (200 g raw with skin, bone) provides:
1134 kJ/270 kcal
16.0 g fat
(of which 5.3 g saturated)
0.0 g carbohydrate
(of which 0.0 g sugars)
28.3 g protein
0.0 g fibre

With game chips, bread sauce, 1 portion (200 g raw with skin, bone) provides:
2513 kJ/598 kcal
46.8 g fat
(of which 17.3 g saturated)
6.9 g carbohydrate
(of which 2.4 g sugars)
37.8 g protein
1.1 g fibre

HEALTHY EATING TIP

Use only a little salt to season the chicken and an unsaturated oil to cover the chicken. Drain all fat from the roasting tray before making the roast gravy. Serve with plenty of potatoes and vegetables.

110 Roast chicken with dressing

Poulet rôti à l'anglaise

As for roast chicken, but served with dressing.

chopped onion	25 g (1 oz)
oil, butter or margarine	50 g (2 oz)
salt, pepper	
pinch chopped parsley	
pinch powdered thyme	
white or wholemeal breadcrumbs	50 g (2 oz)
the chopped chicken liver (raw) (optional)	

1 Gently cook the onion in the oil, butter or margarine without colour.

2 Add the seasoning, herbs and crumbs.

3 Mix in the liver.

4 Correct seasoning and bake or steam separately, approximately 20 min.

Fig 9.39 Portioning of roast chicken

111 Sauté of chicken

Poulet sauté

	4 portions	10 portions
chicken 1¼–1½ kg (2½–3 lb)	1	2½
butter, margarine or oil	50 g (2 oz)	125 g (5 oz)
salt, pepper		
jus-lié or demi-glace	250 ml (½ pt)	625 ml (1¼ pt)
chopped parsley		

1 Prepare the chicken for sauté (see page 300).

2 Place the butter, margarine or oil in a sauté pan on a fairly hot stove.

3 Season the pieces of chicken and place in the pan in the following order: drumsticks, thighs, carcass, wings, winglets and breast (tougher pieces first as they take longer to cook).

4 Cook to a golden brown on both sides.

5 Cover with a lid and cook on the stove or in the oven until tender.

6 Dress the chicken pieces neatly in an entrée dish.

7 Drain off all fat from the sauté pan.

8 Return to the heat and add the jus-lié or demi-glace, and simmer for 3–4 minutes.

9 Correct the seasoning and skim.

10 Pass through a fine strainer on to the chicken.

11 Sprinkle with chopped parsley and serve.

Note: The cleaned chicken giblets may be used in the making of the sauce.

Based on average edible portion of roasted meat – 100 g, 1 portion provides:
1329 kJ/320 kcal energy
22.3 g fat
(of which 8.1 g saturated)
0.3 g carbohydrate
(of which 0.3 g sugars)
29.3 g protein
0.0 g fibre

HEALTHY EATING TIP

Use a minimum amount of salt to season the chicken. The fat content can be reduced if the skin is removed from the chicken. Use a little unsaturated oil to cook the chicken and drain off all excess fat from the cooked chicken.
Serve with a large portion of new potatoes and seasonal vegetables.

112 Chicken sauté with mushrooms

Poulet sauté aux champignons

	4 portions	10 portions
butter, margarine or oil	50 g (2 oz)	125 g (5 oz)
chicken 1¼–1½ kg (2½–3 lb)	1	2½
chopped shallot	10 g (½ oz)	25 g (1 oz)
button mushrooms	100 g (4 oz)	250 g (10 oz)
dry white wine	60 ml (⅛ pt)	150 ml (⅓ pt)
demi-glace or jus-lié	250 ml (½ pt)	625 ml (1¼ pt)
salt, pepper		
chopped parsley		

Based on average edible portion of roasted meat – 100 g, 1 portion provides:
947 kJ/227 kcal energy
12.6 g fat
(of which 5.4 g saturated)
0.8 g carbohydrate
(of which 0.7 g sugars)
27.4 g protein
0.0 g fibre

continued over ▶

▶ *Chicken sauté with mushrooms continued*

1 Prepare chicken for sauté (page 300).

2 Pour off the fat, add the white wine and reduce by half.

3 Add the demi-glace or jus-lie, simmer for 5 minutes and correct the seasoning.

4 Pour over the pieces of chicken, sprinkle with chopped parsley.

Using butter, 1 portion provides:
2430 kJ/579 kcal
45.8 g fat
(of which 20.7 g saturated)
2.1 g carbohydrate
(of which 1.6 g sugars)
37.6 g protein
1.5 g fibre

HEALTHY EATING TIP

Use a minimum amount of salt to season the chicken. The fat content can be reduced if the skin is removed from the chicken. Use a little unsaturated oil to cook the chicken and drain off all excess fat from the cooked chicken. Serve with a large portion of new potatoes and seasonal vegetables.

113 Chicken sauté chasseur

Poulet sauté chasseur

	4 portions	10 portions
butter, margarine or oil	50 g (2 oz)	125 g (5 oz)
chicken cut for sauté 1¼–1½ kg (2½–3 lb)	1	2½
chopped shallots	10 g (½ oz)	25 g (1 oz)
button mushrooms	100 g (4 oz)	250 g (10 oz)
dry white wine	3 tbsp	8 tbsp
jus-lié or demi-glace	250 ml (½ pt)	625 ml (1¼ pt)
tomatoes	200 g (8 oz)	500 g (1¼ lb)
chopped parsley and tarragon		

1 Place the butter, margarine or oil in a sauté pan on a fairly hot stove.

2 Season the pieces of chicken and place in the pan in the following order: drumsticks, thighs, carcass, wings, winglets and breast.

3 Cook to a golden brown on both sides.

4 Cover with a lid and cook on the stove or in the oven until tender. Dress neatly in a suitable dish.

5 Add the shallot to the sauté pan, cover with a lid, cook on a gentle heat for 1–2 minutes without colour.

6 Add the washed sliced mushrooms and cover with a lid; cook gently for 3–4 minutes without colour. Drain off the fat.

7 Add the white wine and reduce by half. Add the sauce.

8 Add the tomate concassé; simmer for 5 minutes.

9 Correct the seasoning and pour over the chicken.

10 Sprinkle with chopped parsley and tarragon and serve.

Note: Ballottines of chicken chasseur can be prepared as above or lightly braised (as Fig 9.40).

114 Chicken spatchcock

Poulet grillé à la crapaudine

	4 portions	**10 portions**
chicken 1¼–1½ kg (2½–3 lb)	1	2½

1 Truss the chicken as for boiling (page 298), but do not tie with string.

2 Cut horizontally from below the point of the breast over the top of the legs down to the wing joints without removing the breasts. Fold back the breasts.

3 Snap and reverse the backbone into the opposite direction so that the point of the breast now extends forward to resemble the nose and face of a toad.

4 Flatten slightly. Remove any small bones.

5 Skewer the wings and legs in position.

6 Season with salt and mill pepper.

7 Brush with oil or melted butter.

8 Place on preheated grill bars or on a flat tray under a salamander.

9 Brush frequently with melted fat or oil during cooking and allow approximately 15–20 minutes on each side.

10 Test if cooked by piercing the drumstick with a needle or skewer – there should be no sign of blood.

11 When serving, two eyes for the 'toad' may be made from slices of hard boiled white of egg with a pupil of truffle or gherkin.

12 Serve garnished with picked watercress and offer a suitable sauce separately (e.g. devilled sauce or a compound butter).

1 portion provides:
1560 kJ/372 kcal
24.1 g fat
(of which 8.0 g saturated)
0.0 g carbohydrate
(of which 0.0 g sugars)
38.9 g protein
0.0 g fibre

HEALTHY EATING TIP

Use a minimum amount of salt to season the chicken. The fat content can be reduced if the skin is removed from the chicken. Use a small amount of an unsaturated oil to brush the chicken. Serve with a large portion of potatoes and vegetables.

115 Grilled chicken

Poulet grillé

1 Season the chicken prepared for grilling (see page 300) with salt and mill pepper.

2 Brush with oil or melted butter or margarine and place on preheated greased grill bars or on a barbecue or on a flat baking tray under a salamander.

3 Brush frequently with melted fat during cooking and allow approximately 15–20 minutes each side.

4 Test if cooked by piercing the drumstick with a skewer or trussing needle; there should be no sign of blood issuing from the leg.

5 Serve garnished with picked watercress and offer a suitable sauce separately.

Note: Grilled chicken is frequently served garnished with streaky bacon, tomatoes and mushrooms.

Based on chicken with bone, wing and leg quarters,
1 portion provides:
975 kJ/234 kcal energy
15.7 g fat
(of which 4.3 g saturated)
0.0 g carbohydrate
(of which 0.0 g sugars)
23.3 g protein
0.0 g fibre

HEALTHY EATING TIP

Use a minimum amount of salt and an unsaturated oil. Garnish with grilled tomatoes and mushrooms. Serve with Delmonico potatoes and green vegetables.

Fig 9.40 🖋 Ballottines of chicken chasseur

The chicken may be marinated for 2–3 hours before grilling, in a mixture of oil, lemon juice, spices, herbs, freshly grated ginger, finely chopped garlic, salt and pepper. Chicken or turkey portions can also be grilled and previously marinated if wished (breasts or boned-out lightly battered thighs of chicken).

Fig 9.41 🖋 Chicken suprêmes with asparagus and truffle

Fig 9.42 🖋 Presentation of spatchcock chicken

1 portion provides:
1672 kJ/402 kcal energy
28.2 g fat
(of which 17.3 g saturated)
5.5 g carbohydrate
(of which 0.7 g sugars)
31.2 g protein
0.2 g fibre

HEALTHY EATING TIP

The fat content can be reduced if the skin is removed from the chicken. Use a small amount of an unsaturated oil to cook the chicken and drain off all the fat from the pan. The fat content will be less if half cream and half velouté is used.
Serve with boiled potatoes and vegetables.

116 Suprême of chicken in cream sauce

Suprême de volailles à la crème

	4 portions	**10 portions**
butter, margarine or oil	50 g (2 oz)	125 g (5 oz)
flour	25 g (1 oz)	60 g (2½ oz)
suprêmes of chicken (page 301)	4	10
sherry or white wine	30 ml (1/16 pt)	125 ml (¼ pt)
double cream or non-dairy cream	125 ml (¼ pt)	300 ml (⅝ pt)
salt, cayenne		

1 Heat the butter or margarine in a sauté pan. Lightly flour the suprêmes.

2 Cook the suprêmes gently on both sides (7–9 minutes) with the minimum of colour.

3 Place the suprêmes in an earthenware serving dish, cover to keep warm.

4 Drain off the fat from the pan.

5 Deglaze the pan with the sherry or white wine.

6 Add the cream, bring to the boil and season.

7 Allow to reduce to a lightly thickened consistency. Correct the seasoning.

8   Pass through a fine strainer on to the suprêmes and serve.

Note: An alternative method of preparing the sauce is to use half the amount of cream (fresh or non-dairy) and an equal amount of chicken velouté (page 55).

117 Fried chicken (deep fried)

Cut the chicken as for sauté and 1) coat with either flour, egg and crumbs (pané) or 2) pass through a light batter (page 177) to which herbs can be added. For suprêmes, make an incision, stuff with a compound butter (page 68), flour, egg and crumb and deep-fry such as in Chicken Kiev.

> 1 portion provides:
> 1754 kJ/421 kcal energy
> 28.6 g fat
> (of which 6.1 g saturated)
> 14.5 g carbohydrate
> (of which 0.4 g sugars)
> 27.2 g protein
> 0.5 g fibre

HEALTHY EATING TIP

The fat content can be reduced if the skin is removed from the chicken.

Fig 9.43 Preparation and presentation of grilled chicken

118 Crumbed breast of chicken with asparagus
(Illustration page 310)
Suprême de volaille aux pointes d'asperges

> 1 portion provides:
> 1831 kJ/439 kcal energy
> 26.4 g fat
> (of which 8.9 g saturated)
> 15.7 g carbohydrate
> (of which 1.5 g sugars)
> 35.5 g protein
> 1.3 g fibre

	4 portions	**10 portions**
suprêmes of chicken (page 301)	4 × 125 g (5 oz)	10 × 125 g (5 oz)
egg	1	2
breadcrumbs, white or wholemeal	50 g (2 oz)	125 g (5 oz)
oil	50 g (2 oz)	125 g (5 oz)
butter or margarine	50 g (2 oz)	125 g (5 oz)
butter	50 g (2 oz)	125 g (5 oz)
jus-lié	60 ml (⅛ pt)	150 ml (⅓ pt)
asparagus	200 g (½ lb)	500 g (1¼ lb)

311

continued over ▶

▶ *Crumbed breast of chicken with asparagus continued*

1 Pané the chicken suprêmes. Shake off all surplus crumbs.

2 Neaten and mark on one side with a palette knife.

3 Heat the oil and fat in a sauté pan.

4 Gently fry the suprêmes to a golden brown on both sides (6–8 minutes).

5 Dress the suprêmes on a flat dish and keep warm.

6 Mask the suprêmes with the remaining butter cooked to the nut brown stage.

7 Surround the suprêmes with a cordon of jus-lié.

8 Garnish each suprême with a neat bundle of asparagus points (previously cooked, refreshed and reheated with a little butter).

9 Place a cutlet frill on to each wing bone and serve (optional).

Based on 125 g serving, 1 portion provides:
1435 kJ/346 kcal energy
27.7 g fat
(of which 4.8 g saturated)
2.0 g carbohydrate
(of which 1.7 g sugars)
22.3 g protein
0.2 g fibre

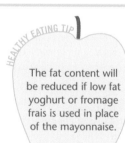

119 Coronation chicken

This is a popular dish usually served on buffets and as a sandwich filler. It consists of pieces of cooked chicken bound with curry flavoured mayonnaise. There are a number of variations: a dice of fresh pineapple and sultanas may be added to the chicken. The curried mayonnaise may be finished with lightly whipped cream or fromage frais, or a Greek yoghurt.

A typical recipe:

boiled chicken cut into slices or 2 cm (1 inch) dice	800 g (2 lb)
fresh pineapple 1 cm (½ inch) dice	100 g (4 oz)
mayonnaise	250 mls (½ pt)
curry paste or curry powder	1 tbsp
olive oil	2 tbsp
onion finely chopped	50 g (2 oz)

1 Either mix the curry paste in the mayonnaise or sweat onion in olive oil. Add the curry powder, sweat for further 2–3 mins. Allow to cool, add to the mayonnaise.

2 Add the pineapple to the chicken, bind with the curried mayonnaise. Serve on fresh lettuce leaves. Garnish with strips of fresh red pimento.

Alternatively, decorate with flakes of fresh coconut.

Low fat Greek yoghurt may be used as an alternative to mayonnaise, again lightly flavoured with curry.

120 Boiled or poached chicken with rice and suprême sauce

Poulet poché au riz, sauce suprême

	4 portions	10 portions
boiling fowl 2–2½ kg (4–5 lb)	1	2–3
studded onion	50 g (2 oz)	125 g (5 oz)
bouquet garni		
carrot	50 g (2 oz)	125 g (5 oz)
celery	50 g (2 oz)	125 g (5 oz)
peppercorns	6	12
Pilaff **chopped onion**	50 g (2 oz)	125 g (5 oz)
butter, margarine or oil	50 g (2 oz)	125 g (5 oz)
rice (long-grain)	200 g (8 oz)	500 g (1¼ lb)
chicken stock	500 ml (1 pt)	1¼ litre (2½ pt)
Sauce **butter, margarine or oil**	75 g (3 oz)	180 g (7½ oz)
flour	75 g (3 oz)	180 g (7½ oz)
chicken stock	1 litre (2 pt)	2½ litre (5 pt)
cream (non-dairy cream)	4 tbsp	10 tbsp
few drops of lemon juice		

Using hard margarine, 1 portion provides:
5259 kJ/1252 kcal
86.0 g fat
(of which 35.7 g saturated)
59.6 g carbohydrate
(of which 1.5 g sugars)
63.3 g protein
1.9 g fibre

HEALTHY EATING TIP

Use a minimum amount of salt.
Remove the skin from the cooked chicken.
Try reducing or omitting the cream used to finish the sauce.
Serve with plenty of rice and vegetables or salad.

1   Place the chicken in cold water. Bring to the boil and skim.

2   Add peeled, whole vegetables, bouquet garni, peppercorns and salt.

3   Simmer until cooked. To test, remove the chicken from the stock and hold over a plate to catch the juices from the inside of the bird. There should be no sign of blood. Also test the drumstick with a trussing needle, which should penetrate easily to the bone.

4   Prepare ½ litre (1 pint) (1½ litre (2½ pint) for 10 portions) of velouté from the cooking liquor, cook out, correct the seasoning and pass through a fine strainer.

5   Finish with cream. Prepare a pilaff of rice (see page 161).

6   To serve, cut into portions. Dress the rice neatly in an entrée dish, arrange the portions of chicken on top and coat with sauce.

Using butter, hard margarine, 1 portion provides:
1226 kJ/292 kcal
16.7 g fat
(of which 7.8 g saturated)
3.2 g carbohydrate
(of which 0.8 g sugars)
30.4 g protein
0.9 g fibre

HEALTHY EATING TIP

Use a minimum amount of salt.
Remove the skin from the cooked chicken.
Try reducing or omitting the cream used to finish the sauce.
Serve with plenty of rice and vegetables or salad.

121 Chicken à la king

Emincé de volaille à la king

	4 portions	**10 portions**
button mushrooms	100 g (4 oz)	250 g (10 oz)
butter, margarine or oil	25 g (1 oz)	60 g (2½ oz)
red pimento (skinned)	50 g (2 oz)	125 g (5 oz)
cooked boiled chicken	400 g (1 lb)	1¼ kg (2½ lb)
sherry	30 ml (⅛ pt)	75 ml (¼ pt)
chicken velouté	125 ml (¼ pt)	150 ml (⅓ pt)
cream or non-dairy cream	30 ml (¹⁄₁₆ pt)	75 ml (¼ pt)

1 Wash, peel and slice the mushrooms.

2 Cook them without colour in the butter or margarine.

3 If using raw pimento, discard the seeds, cut the pimento in dice and cook with the mushrooms.

4 Cut the chicken in small, neat slices.

5 Add the chicken to the mushrooms and pimento.

Fig 9.44 Chicken à la king

John Campbell

6   Drain off the fat. Add the sherry.

7   Add the velouté, bring to the boil.

8   Finish with the cream and correct the seasoning.

9   Place into a serving dish and decorate with small strips of cooked pimento.

Note: 1 or 2 egg yolks may be used to form a liaison with the cream mixed into the boiling mixture at the last possible moment and immediately removed from the heat. Chicken à la king may be served in a border of golden brown duchesse potato or a pilaff of rice may be offered as an accompaniment. It is suitable for a hot buffet dish.

122 Chicken vol-au-vent

Vol-au-vent de volaille

	8 portions
puff pastry (page 564)	400 g (1 lb)
boiling chicken 2 kg (4 lb)	1
chicken velouté	½ litre (1 pt)
cream	4 tbsp

Using hard margarine, 1 portion provides:
2754 kJ/656 kcal
50.7 g fat
(of which 21.2 g saturated)
20.0 g carbohydrate
(of which 0.6 g sugars)
31.0 g protein
0.9 g fibre

1   Prepare the puff pastry using ½ kg (1 lb) flour and ½ kg (1 lb) margarine and ¼ litre (½ pint) water.

2   Roll out sufficient to cut eight rounds 8 cm (3 inch) diameter.

3   Turn upside down on a lightly greased, damped baking sheet.

4   Using a smaller plain cutter dipped in hot oil, make incisions half-way through each, leaving approximately ½ cm (¼ inch) border.

5   Eggwash, rest for 20 minutes and bake in a hot oven at 230–250°C (Reg. 8–9; 450–500°F) for approximately 15–20 minutes.

6   When cool remove the lids carefully with a small knife.

7   Empty out the raw pastry from the centre.

8   Cook the chicken as for boiled chicken (page 313).

9   Make a velouté and cook out, correct the seasoning and pass through a fine strainer; finish with cream.

10   Remove all skin and bone from the chicken.

11   Cut into neat pieces, mix with the sauce.

12   Fill the warm vol-au-vent to overflowing.

13   Add the lids, garnish with picked parsley and serve.

HEALTHY EATING TIP

Use a minimum amount of salt. Try leaving out the added cream from the velouté. The addition of mushrooms will slightly 'dilute' the overall fat.

Note: Chicken and mushroom vol-au-vent can be made with the addition of 100 g (4 oz) of washed button mushrooms cut into quarters and cooked in a little stock with a few drops of lemon juice and 5 g (¼ oz) butter.

123 Chicken pancakes

Crêpes de volaille

HEALTHY EATING TIP

Use semi-skimmed milk
and a minimum amount
of salt to make the
pancakes.
Lightly oil a well-
seasoned pan with an
unsaturated oil to fry the
pancakes.
Season the chicken with
a minimum amount of
salt.

	4 portions	10 portions
Pancake **flour**	100 g (4 oz)	250 g (10 oz)
egg	1	2–3
salt, pepper		
chopped parsley		
milk, whole or skimmed	¼ litre (½ pt)	600 ml (1¼ pt)
melted butter or margarine	10 g (½ oz)	25 g (1 oz)
Filling **thick béchamel or chicken velouté**	125 ml (¼ pt)	300 ml (⅝ pt)
cooked chicken free from bone and skin	200 g (½ lb)	500 g (1¼ lb)
salt, pepper		

1 Sieve the flour into a bowl and make a well in the centre.

2 Add the egg, salt, pepper, parsley and milk.

3 Gradually incorporate the flour from the sides of the bowl and whisk to a smooth batter.

4 Mix in the melted butter.

5 Heat the pancake pan, clean thoroughly.

6 Add 5 g (¼ oz) lard or oil and heat until smoking.

7 Add sufficient mixture to thinly cover the bottom of the pan.

8 Cook for a few seconds until lightly brown.

9 Turn and cook on the other side. Turn onto a plate.

10 Wipe the pan clean and make a total of 8 small or 4 large pancakes (20 or 10 pancakes for 10 portions).

11 Meanwhile prepare the filling by boiling the sauce.

12 Cut the chicken in neat small pieces and add to the sauce.

13 Mix in and correct the seasoning.

14 Divide the mixture between the pancakes, roll up each one and place in an earthenware dish.

15 Reheat in a hot oven and serve.

Note: Additions to the pancake filling can include mushrooms, ham, sweetcorn, etc., and the pancakes can be finished with a sauce such as Mornay, chasseur, etc.

124 Fricassée of chicken

Fricassée de volaille

	4 portions	10 portions
chicken 1¼–1½ kg (2½–3 lb)	1	2–3
butter, margarine or oil	50 g (2 oz)	125 g (5 oz)
flour	35 g (1½ oz)	100 g (4 oz)
chicken stock	½ litre (1 pt)	1¼ litre (2½ pt)
yolks of eggs	1–2	5
cream or non-dairy cream	4 tbsp	10 tbsp
chopped parsley		

Using butter, 1 portion provides:
2699 kJ/643 kcal
51.3 g fat
(of which 23.3 g saturated)
7.4 g carbohydrate
(of which 0.6 g sugars)
38.2 g protein
0.4 g fibre

HEALTHY EATING TIP

Keep added salt to a minimum throughout the cooking. Use a little unsaturated oil to cook the chicken and drain off all excess fat after cooking. Try oven-baking the croûtons brushed with olive oil. The sauce is high in fat, so serve with plenty of starchy carbohydrate and vegetables.

1 Cut the chicken as for sauté and season with salt and pepper.

2 Place the butter in a sauté pan. Heat gently.

3 Add pieces of chicken. Cover with a lid.

4 Cook gently on both sides without colouring. Mix in the flour.

5 Cook out carefully without colouring. Gradually mix in the stock.

6 Bring to the boil and skim. Allow to simmer gently until cooked.

7 Mix the yolks and cream in a basin (liaison).

8 Pick out the chicken into a clean pan.

9 Pour a little boiling sauce on to the yolks and cream and mix well.

10 Pour all back into the sauce, combine thoroughly but do not reboil.

11 Correct the seasoning and pass through a fine strainer.

12 Pour over the chicken, reheat without boiling.

13 Serve sprinkled with chopped parsley.

14 May be garnished with heart-shaped croûtons, fried in butter.

Note: A fricassée of chicken with button onions and mushrooms can be made similarly with the addition of 50–100 g (2–4 oz) button onions and 50–100 g (2–4 oz) button mushrooms. They are peeled and the mushrooms left whole, turned or quartered depending on size and quality. The onions are added to the chicken as soon as it comes to the boil and the mushrooms 15 minutes later. Heart-shaped croûtons may be used to garnish. This is a classic dish known as Fricassée de Volaille à l'Ancienne.

Fig 9.45 Fricassée of chicken   *John Campbell*

Using hard margarine in pastry, 1 portion provides:
3357 kJ/799 kcal
62.6 g fat
(of which 25.1 g saturated)
16.4 g carbohydrate
(of which 1.9 g sugars)
43.3 g protein
1.8 g fibre

HEALTHY EATING TIP

Add little or no salt –
the bacon is salty.
Remove the skin from
the chicken.
Serve with plenty of
starchy carbohydrate
and a large mixed
salad.

125 Chicken pie

	4 portions	**10 portions**
chicken 1¼–1½ kg (2½–3 lb)	1	2–3
salt, pepper		
streaky bacon	100 g (4 oz)	250 g (10 oz)
button mushrooms	100 g (4 oz)	250 g (10 oz)
chopped onion	1	2½
chicken stock	¼ litre (½ pt)	625 ml (1¼ pt)
pinch of chopped parsley		
hard-boiled egg (chopped)	1	2
puff pastry (page 564)	200 g (8 oz)	500 g (1¼ lb)

1   Cut the chicken as for sauté or bone-out completely and cut into pieces 4 × 1 cm (1½ × ½ inch).

2   Season lightly with salt and pepper.

3   Wrap each piece in very thin streaky bacon. Place in a pie dish.

4   Add the washed sliced mushrooms and remainder of the ingredients.

5   Add sufficient cold stock to barely cover the chicken.

6   Cover with puff pastry and allow to rest in a refrigerator.

7   Eggwash and bake at 200°C (Reg. 6; 400°F) for approximately 30 minutes until the paste has set and the juice is simmering.

8   Reduce heat to 160–180°C (Reg. 3–4; 325–350°F) and continue cooking for 1 hour.

Note: If the pie is to be served cold, a soaked leaf of gelatine can be laid on the chicken before covering with pastry.

126 Curried chicken
Kari de poulet

	4 portions	**10 portions**
chicken (1¼–1½ kg) (2½–3 lb)	1	2–3
oil	50 g (2 oz)	125 g (5 oz)
onion	200 g (8 oz)	500 g (1¼ lb)
clove garlic	1	2
flour	10 g (½ oz)	25 g (1 oz)
curry powder	10 g (½ oz)	25 g (1 oz)
tomato purée	25 g (1 oz)	60 g (2½ oz)
chicken stock	½ litre (1 pt)	1¼ litre (2½ pt)
sultanas	25 g (1 oz)	60 g (2½ oz)
chopped chutney	25 g (1 oz)	60 g (2½ oz)
desiccated coconut	10 g (½ oz)	25 g (1 oz)
chopped apple	50 g (2 oz)	125 g (5 oz)
grated root ginger *or*	10 g (½ oz)	25 g (1 oz)
ground ginger	5 g (¼ oz)	12 g (⅝ oz)

Using sunflower oil, 1 portion provides:
2755 kJ/656 kcal
49.9 g fat
(of which 17.1 g saturated)
15.1 g carbohydrate
(of which 11.8 g sugars)
37.4 g protein
2.3 g fibre

HEALTHY EATING TIP

Use a minimum amount of salt.
Remove the skin from the chicken. Use a small amount of an unsaturated vegetable oil to brown the chicken.
Skim all the fat from the finished dish.
Use low-fat yoghurt to finish the sauce.
Serve with plenty of rice and a vegetable dish.

1 Cut the chicken as for sauté, season lightly with salt.

2 Heat the oil in a sauté pan, add the chicken.

3 Lightly brown on both sides.

4 Add the chopped onion and garlic.

5 Cover with lid; cook gently for 3–4 minutes.

6 Mix in the flour and curry powder.

7 Mix in the tomato purée. Moisten with stock.

8 Bring to the boil, skim.

9 Add the remainder of the ingredients. Simmer until cooked.

10 The sauce may be finished with 2 tablespoons cream or yoghurt.

Note: Accompany with 100 g (4 oz) plain boiled rice and/or grilled poppadum; see also page 229 for extra accompaniments.

This is a European recipe in use today. For a traditional Asian recipe the curry powder would be replaced by either curry paste or a mixture of freshly ground spices (turmeric, cumin, allspice, fresh ginger, chilli and clove). See also chapter 10 on international cooking.

127 Braised rice with chicken livers

Pilaff aux foies de volailles

Using hard margarine, 1 portion provides:
1115 kJ/265 kcal
17.0 g fat
(of which 7.2 g saturated)
22.4 g carbohydrate
(of which 0.3 g sugars)
7.0 g protein
0.6 g fibre

	4 portions	10 portions
chicken livers	100 g (4 oz)	250 g (10 oz)
salt, mill pepper		
butter, margarine or oil	25 g (1 oz)	60 g (2½ oz)
demi-glace or jus-lié	60 ml (⅛ pt)	150 ml (⅓ pt)
braised rice (page 161)	200 g (½ lb)	500 g (1¼ lb)

1 Trim the livers, cut into 1 cm (½ inch) pieces.
2 Season lightly with salt and pepper.
3 Fry quickly in the butter in a frying-pan. Drain well.
4 Mix with the demi-glace or the jus-lié; do not reboil.
5 Correct the seasoning.
6 Make a well with the riz pilaff on the dish.
7 Serve the livers in the centre of the rice.

128 Chicken in red wine

Coq au vin

Using sunflower oil, hard margarine, 1 portion provides:
4794 kJ/1141 kcal
95.7 g fat
(of which 32.9 g saturated)
16.6 g carbohydrate
(of which 2.3 g sugars)
49.0 g protein
1.7 g fibre

	4 portions	10 portions
roasting chicken 1½ kg (3 lb)	1	2–3
lardons	50 g (2 oz)	125 g (5 oz)
small chipolatas	4	10
button mushrooms	50 g (2 oz)	125 g (5 oz)
sunflower oil	3 tbsp	7 tbsp
butter or margarine	50 g (2 oz)	125 g (5 oz)
small button onions	12	30
red wine	125 ml (¼ pt)	300 ml (⅝ pt)
brown stock or red wine	500 ml (1 pt)	900 ml (1½ pt)
butter or margarine	25 g (1 oz)	60 g (2½ oz)
flour	25 g (1 oz)	60 g (2½ oz)
heart-shaped croûtons	4	10
chopped parsley		

HEALTHY EATING TIP

Use a well-seasoned pan to dry fry the lardons and chipolatas, then add the mushrooms. Use a minimum amount of added salt.
Drain all the fat from the cooked chicken and garnish with oven baked croutons. Serve with plenty of starchy carbohydrate and vegetables.

1 Cut the chicken as for sauté. Blanch the lardons.
2 If the chipolatas are large divide into two.
3 Wash and cut the mushrooms in quarters.

4 Sauté the lardons, mushrooms and chipolatas in a mixture of butter/margarine and oil. Remove when cooked.

5 Lightly season the pieces of chicken and place in the pan in the correct order with button onions. Sauté until almost cooked. Drain off fat.

6 Just cover with red wine and brown stock, cover with a lid and finish cooking.

7 Remove chicken and onions, place into a clean pan.

8 Lightly thicken the liquor with a beurre manié from the 25 g (1 oz) butter/margarine and 25 g (1 oz) flour.

9 Pass sauce over the chicken and onions, add mushrooms, chipolatas and lardons. Correct seasoning and reheat.

10 Serve garnished with heart-shaped croûtons with the points dipped in chopped parsley.

Duck recipes

129 Roast duck or duckling

Canard ou caneton rôti

With apple sauce, watercress, 1 portion provides:
3083 kJ/734 kcal
60.5 g fat
(of which 16.9 g saturated)
8.2 g carbohydrate
(of which 7.8 g sugars)
40.0 g protein
1.4 g fibre

	4 portions	**10 portions**
duck	1	2–3
oil		
salt		
brown stock	¼ litre (½ pt)	600 ml (1¼ pt)
bunch watercress	1	2
apple sauce (page 283)	125 ml (¼ pt)	300 ml (⅝ pt)

HEALTHY EATING TIP

Use a minimum amount of salt to season the duck and the roast gravy. Take care to remove all the fat from the roasting tray before making the gravy. This dish is high in fat and should be served with plenty of boiled new potatoes and a variety of vegetables.

1 Lightly season the duck inside and out with salt.

2 Truss and brush lightly with oil.

3 Place on its side in a roasting tin, with a few drops of water.

4 Place in a hot oven for 20–25 minutes.

5 Turn on to the other side.

6 Cook for a further 20–25 minutes. Baste frequently.

7 To test if cooked, pierce with a fork between the drumstick and thigh and hold over a plate. The juice issuing from the duck should not show any signs of blood. If using a probe, the temperature should be +62°C (144°F).

8 Prepare the roast gravy with the stock and the sediment in the roasting tray. Correct the seasoning, remove the surface fat.

9 Serve garnished with picked watercress.

10 Accompany with a sauceboat of hot apple sauce and a sauceboat of gravy and game chips. Also serve a sauceboat of sage and onion dressing as prepared in the following recipe.

Note: If the duck is required pink, the temperature should be 57°C (135°F).

130 Dressing for duck

	4 portions	10 portions
chopped onion	100 g (4 oz)	250 g (10 oz)
duck fat or butter	100 g (4 oz)	250 g (10 oz)
powdered sage	¼ tsp	½ tsp
chopped parsley	¼ tsp	½ tsp
salt, pepper		
white or wholemeal breadcrumbs	100 g (4 oz)	250 g (10 oz)
chopped duck liver (optional)	50 g (2 oz)	125 g (5 oz)

1   Gently cook the onion in the dripping without colour.

2   Add the herbs and seasoning. Mix in the crumbs and liver. Cook the stuffing separately. Cook and serve as for roast duck.

Fig 9.46 🔖 Duck with orange   *Anton Edelmann*

131 Duckling with orange sauce

Caneton bigarade

	4 portions	10 portions
duckling 2 kg (4 lb)	1	2–3
butter	50 g (2 oz)	125 g (5 oz)
carrots	50 g (2 oz)	125 g (5 oz)
onions	50 g (2 oz)	125 g (5 oz)
celery	25 g (1 oz)	60 g (2½ oz)
bayleaf	1	2–3
small sprig thyme	1	2–3
brown stock	250 ml (½ pt)	625 ml (1¼ pt)
arrowroot	10 g (½ oz)	25 g (1 oz)
oranges	2	5
lemon	1	2
vinegar	2 tbsp	5 tbsp
sugar	25 g (1 oz)	60 g (2½ oz)

Using butter, 1 portion provides:
3125 kJ/744 kcal
60.1 g fat
(of which 17.1 g saturated)
11.8 g carbohydrate
(of which 9.3 g sugars)
39.9 g protein
0.1 g fibre

HEALTHY EATING TIP

Use a minimum amount of salt to season the duck and the final sauce.
Take care to remove all the fat from the roasting tray before deglazing with the stock.
Reduce the fat by removing the skin from the duck and 'balance' this fatty dish with a large portion of boiled potatoes and vegetables.

1 Clean and truss the duck. Use a fifth of the butter to grease a deep pan. Add the mirepoix (vegetables and herbs).

2 Season the duck. Place the duck on the mirepoix.

3 Coat the duck with the remaining butter.

4 Cover the pan with a tight fitting lid.

5 Place the pan in oven at 200–230°C (Reg. 6–8; 400–450°F).

6 Baste occasionally; cook for approximately 1 hour.

7 Remove the lid and continue cooking the duck, basting frequently, until tender (about a further 30 minutes).

8 Remove the duck, cut out the string and keep the duck in a warm place. Drain off all the fat from the pan.

9 Deglaze with the stock, bring to the boil and allow to simmer for a few minutes.

10 Thicken by adding the arrowroot diluted in a little cold water.

Fig 9.47 Duck with orange   *Anton Edelmann*

11 Reboil, correct the seasoning, degrease and pass through a fine strainer.

12 Thinly remove the zest from one orange and the lemon and cut into fine julienne.

13 Blanch the julienne of zest for 3–4 minutes and refresh.

14 Place the vinegar and sugar in a small sauteuse and cook to a light caramel stage.

15 Add the juice of the oranges and the lemon.

16 Add the sauce and bring to the boil.

17 Correct the seasoning and pass through a fine strainer.

18 Add the julienne to the sauce, keep warm.

19 Remove the legs from the duck, bone out and cut in thin slices.

20 Carve the duck breasts into thin slices and neatly dress.

21 Coat with the sauce and serve.

Note: An alternative method of service is to cut the duck into eight pieces, which may then be either left on the bone or the bones removed.

132 Duck confit

Confit de canard

Duck and goose confit is part of French regional cooking.

> Based on 100 g raw meat, and 10 g pork fat per person,
> 1 portion provides:
> 845 kJ/203 kcal energy
> 13.5 g fat
> (of which 2.0 g saturated)
> 0.0 g carbohydrate
> (of which 0.0 g sugars)
> 20.4 g protein
> 0.0 g fibre

HEALTHY EATING TIP

Make sure that all excess salt is removed before cooking the duck.
This is a very fatty dish. Adding to a stew of haricot beans will help to 'dilute' the fat.

	4 portions	**10 portions**
rock salt	600 g (1½ lb)	2 kg (4 lb)
dried herbs (thyme, marjoram, crushed bay leaves)	2 tbsp	5 tbsp
crushed peppercorns	½ tbsp	1¼ tbsp
cloves	2 cloves	5 cloves
juniper berries roasted and crushed	¼ tbsp	½ tbsp
saltpetre (optional)	½ tsp	1 tsp
caster sugar	250 g (10 oz)	625 g (1 lb 9 oz)
duck legs	4	10
duck fat	625 ml (1¼ pt)	1 litre (2 pt)
pork fat	625 ml (1¼ pt)	1 litre (2 pt)
lard for sealing the confit		

1 Mix the salt, herbs, peppercorns, cloves, saltpetre and caster sugar.

2 Place a layer of this aromatic salt mixture into a suitable bowl.

3 Place the duck legs on top and cover with rest of spiced salt.

4 Cover with muslin or cling film and leave in refrigerator for at least 24 hours.

5 Remove the duck legs (retain the salt for further batches).

6 Brush off excess salt, and wipe clean.

7 In a suitable pan, heat the duck and pork fat, place the duck legs, so that they are completely covered.

8 Slowly heat so that the fat boils but does not smoke. This is a slow cooking process and will take approximately 2 hours before a needle will easily penetrate the meat.

9 Carefully remove the legs, remove meat from the bones.

10 Prepare earthenware crocks by layering with fat, allow to set. Place a single layer of duck meat on top, making sure that the meat does not touch the sides of the crock. Cover with another layer of fat and so on until all the duck is covered.

11 Allow to set hard in the fridge.

12 The next day cover the surface of the fat with a layer of melted lard to form a totally airtight seal.

13 The longer the confit is left in the fat the better the flavour.

14 Each time you want to use a piece of the confit, first remove the lard and the cooking fat. After removing the duck, replace with duck and pork fat.

Note: A whole duck may be used, cut into 4 pieces, 2 legs and 2 breasts.

Goose and pork may also be preserved in the same way.

Confit is used hot or cold as a combination to other dishes. As a starter it may be served with mixed salad leaves and a cranberry and orange dressing. Confit may be added to a stew of haricot beans.

133 Cranberry and orange dressing

Using margarine reduced to half, 1 portion provides:
398 kJ/93 kcal energy
0.2 g fat
(of which 0.0 g saturated)
22.7 g carbohydrate
(of which 22.7 g sugars)
1.3 g protein
4.2 g fibre

	4 portions	10 portions
cranberries	400 g (1 lb)	1 kg (2 lb 8 oz)
granulated sugar	50 g (2 oz)	125 g (5 oz)
red wine	125 ml (¼ pt)	250 ml (½ pt)
red wine vinegar	2 tbsp	5 tbsp
orange zest and juice	2	4

1 Place the cranberries in a suitable saucepan with the rest of the ingredients.

2 Bring to boil and gently simmer for approximately 1 hour, stirring from time to time.

3 Remove from heat and leave to cool. Use as required.

The dressing may also be liquidised if a smooth texture is required.

134 Haricot bean stew with duck confit

Based on 100 g raw meat, and 10 g pork fat per person, 1 portion provides:
2777 kJ/666 kcal energy
45.3 g fat
(of which 16.0 g saturated)
29.6 g carbohydrate
(of which 5.4 g sugars)
36.9 g protein
9.4 g fibre

	4 portions	10 portions
haricot beans (dried)	200 g (8 oz)	500 g (1 lb 4 oz)
carrot	1	2
onions studded with cloves	1	2
pork rinds cut into 5 mm (¼ inch) dice	200 g (8 oz)	500 g (1 lb 4 oz)
belly of pork	200 g (8 oz)	500 g (1 lb 4 oz)
thyme	1 sprig	2 sprigs
chicken stock	1 litre (2 pt)	2¼ litres (5 pt)
duck fat	2 tbsp	4½ tbsp
onions finely chopped	50 g (2 oz)	125 g (5 oz)
crushed chopped garlic	2	5
tomato purée	2 tbsp	4½ tbsp
plum tomatoes, skinned seeded and diced	300 g (12 oz)	750 g (1 lb 14 oz)
white wine	125 ml (¼ pt)	250 ml (½ pt)
belly of pork (salted)	200 g (8 oz)	500 g (1 lb 4 oz)
duck confit	2 legs	10 legs
ground white pepper to taste		

HEALTHY EATING TIP

No added salt is needed as salt pork is added.
Try using a larger amount of bean stew and less pork and duck to reduce the fat content.

continued over ▶

▶ *Haricot bean stew with duck confit continued*

1 Place the haricot beans in a suitable saucepan, cover with water and bring to boil and simmer for 15 minutes.

2 Drain, place in another saucepan with the carrot, onion, pork rind, belly of pork and thyme.

3 Cover with chicken stock in water. Bring to boil and simmer for 1 hour.

4 Remove the carrot, onion and thyme.

5 Lightly sauté the chopped onion and garlic until golden brown in the duck fat.

6 Add the tomato purée, the tomatoes and the white wine.

7 Cook for 10 minutes, add the beans.

8 Purée the salt pork in a food processor (remove any bones first). Fold this into the beans. Continue to cook for approximately 1 hour.

9 Take special care during the cooking, making sure that the beans do not become too dry. If necessary moisten with white wine, stock or water.

10 During the last ten minutes of cooking add the duck confit.

11 Correct the seasoning.

Serve immediately in a suitable dish garnished with flat parsley sprigs.

Ostrich

Ostrich meat has the taste, colour and texture of red meat, closely resembling beef, but has less fat and cholesterol and fewer calories per gram than chicken. These features, coupled with its unique flavour and delicate texture, have made ostrich meat a premium product in the European marketplace.

Uses

Liver Pâté; risotto
Heart Braised, sliced and served as an entrée
Neck Soups, braised like oxtail

The tenderloin, top loin, inside strip and outside strip are very easy to portion, cut into medallions.

The fan is a large thick fillet, which can be cut into steaks.

Source: American Ostrich Association, 1998.

Recipes using ostrich meat in place of other meats

Stroganoff page 253, recipe 44.
Ostrich Olives (paupiettes), page 259, recipe 52.
Hamburg or Vienna steak, page 260, recipe 54.

135 Ostrich stir-fry

> Turkey analysis used as subsitute for ostrich, 1 portion provides:
> 383 kJ/92 kcal energy
> 3.3 g fat
> (of which 0.6 g saturated)
> 6.6 g carbohydrate
> (of which 4.5 g sugars)
> 8.6 g protein
> 1.7 g fibre

		4 portions	**10 portions**
ostrich strips		100 g (4 oz)	250 g (8 oz)
green pepper	finely shredded	1	3
red pepper		1	3
onion, finely chopped		50 g (2 oz)	125 g (5 oz)
bean sprouts		50 g (2 oz)	125 g (5 oz)
Chinese leaves, finely shredded		50 g (2 oz)	125 g (5 oz)
soy sauce		4 tbsp	10 tbsp
cloves of garlic chopped and crushed		2	5
root ginger, grated		12 g (½ oz)	30 g (1¼ oz)
balsamic vinegar		4 tbsp	10 tbsp
olive oil			

1 Marinate the ostrich strips with garlic and ginger and balsamic vinegar.

2 Heat sufficient olive oil in wok. Drain the ostrich from the balsamic vinegar, quickly fry the ostrich with the garlic and ginger and chopped onion.

3 Add the peppers, stir rapidly for 2 minutes.

4 Add the Chinese leaves and bean sprouts, stir well over the heat.

5 Add the soy sauce and season. Heat through.

6 Serve immediately on a bed of braised rice.

Garnish with fresh coriander leaves.

136 Grilled ostrich steaks with lemon, garlic and rosemary, served with puy lentils

Turkey analysis used as subsitute for ostrich, 1 portion provides:
1766 kJ/420 kcal energy
13.2 g fat
(of which 2.0 g saturated)
37.0 g carbohydrate
(of which 5.2 g sugars)
40.7 g protein
6.7 g fibre

	4 portions	10 portions
ostrich steaks	4 × 100 g (4 oz)	10 × 100 g (4 oz)
red onions finely chopped	1	3
fresh rosemary finely chopped	1 tbsp	3 tbsp
clove of garlic crushed and chopped	2	5
lemon zest and juice	1	3
olive oil	2 tbsp	5 tbsp
seasoning		
puy lentils	250 g (10 oz)	625 g (1 lb 9 oz)
olive oil	2 tbsp	5 tbsp
red wine	500 ml (1 pt)	1¼ litres (2½ pt)
red onion	1 small	3 small

HEALTHY EATING TIP

Reduce the amount of oil used to fry the onions and coat the lentils. Keep the added salt to a minimum; rely on the flavours from the wine, rosemary, lemon and garlic.
Serve with a large portion of rice or potato, and leaf spinach.

1 Marinate the steaks with onion, garlic, rosemary, grated zest and juice of lemons, olive oil and seasoning, for 24 hours.

2 Cook the lentils: first quickly fry the onion in the oil, stir in the lentils, making sure they are well coated in the oil.

3 Add the red wine and rosemary. Allow to simmer very gently for about 30 minutes until the liquid is absorbed and the lentils are cooked.

4 Remove the steaks from the marinade, place in a suitable grill tray and grill each side, keeping the steaks undercooked. Baste with the marinade juices to keep the steaks moist.

5 Season the lentils with salt and mill pepper.

6 Place the lentils on plates with the steaks on top.

7 Garnish with flat-leaf parsley and a sprig of fresh rosemary.

Note: A sauce may be made from the marinade by heating the marinade and allowing to simmer for 2–3 mins. Add 250 ml (½ pt) or 625 ml (1¼ pt) of jus-lié. Strain and serve separately.

Chicken palak, naan bread
John Campbell

Caesar salad
John Campbell

continued...

International cookery

Ethnic means a group of people with common national or cultural traditions. Many ethnic groups move and settle from country to country and as our multi-ethnic society continues to grow it becomes increasingly important to have a basic understanding of the commodities available, the styles of cooking and some of the more popular dishes. Many countries such as China, Japan and India and those in the Middle East have long established cookery traditions with a wide range of foods dating back two or three thousand years.

In many groups religious influences affect what people eat. Muslims are traditionally forbidden alcohol and pork and only meat that has been prepared by a halal butcher is permitted. Most Hindus do not eat meat and none eat beef as the cow is a sacred animal to them (strict Hindus are vegetarians). Many

Sikhs also are vegetarians as are strict Buddhists. The Jewish religion has strict dietary laws. Shellfish, pork and birds of prey are forbidden. Strict Jews eat only meat that has been specially slaughtered, known as Kosher meat. Milk and meat must neither be used together in cooking nor served at the same meal and three hours should elapse between eating food containing milk and food containing meat.

Ethnic cookery also varies within specific countries: Great Britain subdivides into England, Scotland, Wales and Northern Ireland. The once subcontinent of India subsequently became India, Pakistan and Bangladesh. In terms of cookery styles and dishes there are often further divisions within these and most other countries according to area or region.

Asian, Middle Eastern and Far-Eastern cookery makes considerable use of a range of spices and herbs.

Ideally spices are freshly ground (in some dishes there may be up to five or six spices) and then carefully fried at the beginning of recipes to extract the maximum flavour. Inevitably, to save time and labour, a variety of different strengths and blends of ready-prepared mixes of spices is available (curry powder or paste) which may be hot, medium or mild or may be named after the area of the country in which it is traditionally used. Garam masala and five spice powder are two other mixes. Many ready-prepared sauces are also available.

It would be impossible within a chapter and even within a book to give a comprehensive study of international cookery but the recipes that follow are examples from a number of countries.

Caribbean cooking

The history of the West Indies shows the many cultural influences brought to the islands over the centuries, which makes it difficult to generalise or to standardise the various types of cuisine that still exist. The Dutch, English, French and Spanish have left their individual traditions and African, Chinese and Creole immigrants have brought their styles to add to the culture and gastronomy.

In the Caribbean there is an abundance of exotic fruits and vegetables, fresh fish and shellfish, pork as the main source of meat, plenty of poultry and dried pulses and cereals, all cooked in interesting combinations with simplicity but with an emphasis on the intense aroma of spices to make it more significant.

1 Metagee (saltfish with coconut and plantains)

Using salt cod, 1 portion provides:
1675 kJ/399 kcal energy
16.5 g fat
(of which 13.5 g saturation)
46.4 g carbohydrate
(of which 11.3 g sugars)
18.3 g protein
6.5 g fibre

	4 portions	10 portions
saltfish pieces	200 g (8 oz)	500 g (1¼ lb)
green plantains	400 g (1 lb)	1 kg (2½ lb)
yam	100 g (4 oz)	250 g (10 oz)
sweet potato	100 g (4 oz)	250 g (10 oz)
shredded onion	100 g (4 oz)	250 g (10 oz)
tomato, skinned de-seeded, diced	100 g (4 oz)	250 g (10 oz)
sprig of thyme		
desiccated coconut	100 g (4 oz)	250 g (10 oz)
white stock	250 ml (½ pt)	600 ml (1¼ pt)
okra	4	10

HEALTHY EATING TIP

This is a salty dish. Serve with extra okra and a large portion of rice.

1 Soak the saltfish in cold water for 30 minutes.

2 Dice the plantain, yam and sweet potato into 1 cm (½ inch) cubes and place in a pan with the onion and tomato.

3 Sprinkle with thyme. Arrange pieces of saltfish on top. Sprinkle with desiccated coconut. Cover with white stock.

4 Top and tail the okra. Do not cut, otherwise the starchy substance will be released. Place the okra in with the fish and vegetables.

5 Bring to the boil and simmer gently until the vegetables and fish are cooked.

6 Serve hot in a suitable dish, decorated with the okra on top.

Note: When possible it is preferable to use coconut milk in place of white stock and desiccated coconut.

Chinese cooking

The People's Republic of China has twenty-eight provinces, five major religions, eight dialects with Mandarin as the common speech, and more than one thousand million inhabitants. There are, however, only four main styles of cookery, these being the Canton, Peking, Shanghai and Szechwan styles, which correspond to the southern, northern, eastern and western regions respectively.

The gastronomy of China is recognised as one of the world's greatest. A certain depth of knowledge is necessary to understand the fundamentals of Chinese cookery and service, which are, however, based on meagre peasant diets and long traditions that ensured that everything was used, no food thrown away and a few ingredients stretched inventively with accent on taste, flavour and aroma. The repertoire is extensive even though the staple ingredient is rice and almost everything is cooked in a wok or a steamer. The sequence of courses as we know it is not followed in a Chinese meal, as several dishes are laid on the table at once, although there is a progress from light to heavy and back to light. The use of chopsticks means that everything is cut small before it is cooked and the chefs use only a chopper for all work, even for the very realistic carvings in vegetables and fruit for which they are famous.

A résumé of the four regions shows Cantonese as being the best – where rice is most widely used, sweet and sour dishes are favoured, duck and other foods are given a glossy finish and a lot of the dishes are cooked by steaming. Peking cookery features noodles rather than rice and there are other farinaceous items such as steamed dumplings and pancake dishes. The dishes are more substantial and the cookery is more cosmopolitan than elsewhere in the country; more foods are deep-fried and generally there is more crispness of texture. Shanghai cookery is more robust with more use of flour and oil, greater emphasis on garlic, ginger and other spices, and a more peppery result. Here also it is the tradition to serve noodles instead of rice. The cookery of the western region of Szechwan bordering on India and Myanmar is noted for its hot spiciness, including the use of chillies.

2 Almond chicken

Using butter, and canned bamboo shoots, 1 portion provides:
2380 kJ/572 kcal energy
41.0 g fat
(of which 11.1 g saturated)
12.9 g carbohydrate
(of which 7.4 g sugars)
38.8 g protein
3.6 g fibre

	4 portions	10 portions
peanut oil	60 ml (⅛ pt)	150 ml (⅓ pt)
suprêmes of chicken, thinly sliced	4	10
onion, finely chopped	100 g (4 oz)	250 g (10 oz)
chopped chives	25 g (1 oz)	60 g (2½ oz)
cucumber	100 g (4 oz)	250 g (10 oz)
carrot	100 g (4 oz)	250 g (10 oz)
water chestnuts, sliced	200 g (8 oz)	500 g (1¼ lb)
bamboo shoots, sliced	50 g (2 oz)	125 g (5 oz)
mushrooms, finely sliced	100 g (4 oz)	250 g (10 oz)
soy sauce	60 ml (⅛ pt)	150 ml (⅓ pt)
whole blanched almonds	100 g (4 oz)	250 g (10 oz)
butter, margarine or oil	50 g (2 oz)	125 g (5 oz)

The fat content can be significantly reduced by using half the amount of oil, skinning the chicken and dry-frying the almonds. Serve with plenty of rice and a vegetable dish.

2 Add the onion, chives, cucumber, carrot, water chestnuts, bamboo shoots and mushrooms, and season.

3 Continue to stir-fry over a fierce heat for 5 minutes.

4 Add the soy sauce and cook for 1 minute.

5 Meanwhile sauté the almonds in a little butter, margarine or oil until golden brown.

6 Place the chicken and vegetables into a suitable dish for serving and garnish with the almonds.

7 Serve with a braised or pilaff rice.

1 Heat the peanut oil in a sauté pan or wok, season and stir-fry the chicken over a fierce heat for 2–3 minutes.

Fig 10.1 🖋 Oriental cooking equipment

1 portion provides:
1471 kJ/352 kcal energy
20.3 g fat
(of which 3.3 g saturated)
32.8 g carbohydrate
(of which 2.7 g sugars)
11.5 g protein
1.7 g fibre

HEALTHY EATING TIP

Rely on the soy sauce for flavour, no added salt is needed.
Use a little unsaturated oil to fry the bean sprouts and pork. Serve with plenty of noodles and extra vegetables or salad.

3 Fried noodles with shredded pork

	4 portions	10 portions
pork fillet, cut into batons	100 g (4 oz)	250 g (10 oz)
dark soy sauce	1½ tsp	4–5 tsp
granulated sugar	1 tsp	2–3 tsp
cornflour	10 g (½ oz)	25 g (1 oz)
water	60 ml (⅛ pt)	150 ml (⅓ pt)
vegetable oil	60 ml (⅛ pt)	150 ml (⅓ pt)
Chinese egg noodles	150 g (6 oz)	375 g (15 oz)
bean sprouts	150 g (6 oz)	375 g (15 oz)
Chinese dried mushrooms	2	5
dry sherry	1 tsp	2–3 tsp
chicken stock	125 ml (¼ pt)	300 ml (½ pt)
light soy sauce	1 tsp	2–3 tsp
sesame oil	½ tsp	1 tsp
spring onions for garnish	2 tsp	5 tsp

1 Marinate the pork in half the dark soy sauce, and half the sugar and cornflour, seasoning, half the water and half the oil. Allow to stand for 15 minutes.

2 Blanch the noodles in boiling salted water for 1 minute, refresh and drain.

3 In a suitable pan, heat sufficient oil to deep fry the noodles. Drain on kitchen paper or in a cloth.

4 Heat the remainder of the oil in a wok. Add the bean sprouts. Cook quickly and remove.

5 Add the pork and cook until lightly browned.

6 Add the bean sprouts to the pork and add the mushrooms.

7 Blend the remaining cornflour with the rest of the water and add all the remaining ingredients. Stir this into the pork and simmer until thickened.

8 Place the noodles in a suitable serving dish, place the pork in the centre and garnish with chopped spring onions.

4 Sole with mushrooms and bamboo shoots

	4 portions	10 portions
fillet of lemon or Dover sole, cut into goujons	200 g (8 oz)	500 g (1¼ lb)
sherry	2 tbsp	5 tbsp
soy sauce	2 tbsp	5 tbsp
cornflour	10 g (½ oz)	25 g (1 oz)
egg white, lightly beaten	1	2
fresh ginger (grated)	10 g (½ oz)	25 g (1 oz)
finely chopped onion	25 g (1 oz)	60 g (2½ oz)
mushrooms, sliced	50 g (2 oz)	125 g (5 oz)
bamboo shoots, sliced	50 g (2 oz)	125 g (5 oz)
pinch of monosodium glutamate (MSG), optional		
white stock	30 ml (1/16 pt)	75 ml (¼ pt)

HEALTHY EATING TIP

Use an unsaturated oil to fry the goujons and drain on kitchen paper. Omit the MSG – flavour is provided by the soy sauce, sherry and ginger. Serve with a large portion of rice or noodles and extra vegetables.

1 Place the goujons of fish into a small basin, add half the sherry and half the soy sauce.

2 Season, mix in half the cornflour and stir in the egg white.

3 Carefully take out the goujons and deep fry until golden brown. Drain.

4 Heat a little oil in a frying pan or wok, add the grated ginger and chopped onion; fry for 1 minute.

5 Add the mushrooms and bamboo shoots; fry for 1 minute.

6 Blend the remaining sherry and cornflour together, add the monosodium glutamate and stock. Pour into the wok and cook, stirring, for 1–2 minutes.

7 Place the sole into a suitable serving dish, mask with the mushroom and bamboo shoot sauce and serve.

Using canned bamboo shoots, 1 portion provides:
2332 kJ/554 kcal energy
21.6 g fat
(of which 1.8 g saturated)
80.6 g carbohydrate
(of which 5.7 g sugars)
14.3 g protein
1.9 g fibre

HEALTHY EATING TIP

Keep added salt to a minimum.
Use an unsaturated oil (olive or sunflower) and reduce the quantity used.

5 Chinese vegetables and noodles

(Illustrated on page 338 with prawns)

	4 portions	10 portions
Chinese noodles	400 g (1 lb)	1¼ kg (2½ lb)
oil	60 ml (⅛ pt)	150 ml (⅓ pt)
celery	100 g (4 oz)	250 g (10 oz)
carrot cut in paysanne	100 g (4 oz)	250 g (10 oz)
bamboo shoots	50 g (2 oz)	125 g (5 oz)
mushrooms, finely sliced	75 g (3 oz)	180 g (7½ oz)
Chinese cabbage, shredded	75 g (3 oz)	180 g (7½ oz)
bean sprouts	100 g (4 oz)	250 g (10 oz)
soy sauce	30 ml (¹⁄₁₆ pt)	75 ml (¼ pt)
garnish: spring onions, sliced lengthways and quickly stir-fried	4	10

1 Cook the noodles in boiling salted water for about 5–6 minutes until *al dente*. Refresh and drain.

2 Heat the oil in a wok and stir fry all the vegetables except the bean sprouts, for 1 minute. Then add the bean sprouts and cook for a further 1 minute.

3 Add the drained noodles, stirring well; allow to reheat through.

4 Correct the seasoning.

5 Serve in a suitable dish, garnished with the spring onions.

Dim Sum

Dim Sum are tasty little snacks of over 1500 varieties, which are steamed, fried or baked. A selection should be offered, traditionally served with Chinese tea. They are suitable for snack meals and can be offered as cocktail appetisers. Two examples, recipes 6 and 7, follow.

6 Har gau wontons

	Makes 25–30
Dough	
wheat starch	75 g (3 oz)
fécule	40 g (1¾ oz)
boiling water	125 ml (¼ pt)
extra fécule for kneading	
Filling	
minced shoulder of pork or chicken	125 g (5 oz)
raw prawns, chopped	125 g (5 oz)
water chestnuts, diced	30 g (1¼ oz)
bamboo shoots, diced	30 g (1¼ oz)
salt	
sugar	1 tsp
sesame oil	½ tsp
cornflour	1 tbsp
small beaten egg	
oil	

Cornflower analysis used for fecule, minced pork used, 1 portion provides:
140 kJ/33 kcal energy
0.7 g fat
(of which 0.2 g saturated)
4.5 g carbohydrate
(of which 0.3 g sugars)
2.6 g protein
0.1 g fibre

HEALTHY EATING TIP

Season with minimum amount of salt.
If chicken (rather than pork) is used, this provides a healthy balanced dish.

1   Sieve the wheat starch and fécule into a bowl. Gradually add the boiling water and beat to form a softish dough.

2   Sprinkle fécule over the work surface, place dough on work surface and knead well for approximately 10 minutes until a smooth dough is obtained. Cover until needed.

3   Mix the pork, prawns and vegetables together.

4   Add salt, sugar and sesame oil, cornflour and egg.

5   Mix thoroughly.

6   Divide dough into two pieces and roll out to form four thin sausages, roughly 2 cm (1 inch) in diameter.

7   Cut off a piece 2 cm (1 inch) long and roughly flatten. Using a suitable implement, such as a small Chinese cleaver, flatten to form a round. (The cleaver should be lightly oiled.) These should be wafer thin, known as a wrapper.

8   Spoon about 1 teaspoon of filling into the middle of each wrapper. Hold the dumpling in one hand and shape it around the filling. Seal it by making a series of pleats across the top.

9   Place them in a lightly oiled steamer basket and steam for 10 minutes.

Cornflower analysis used for fécule, minced pork used, 1 portion provides:
138 kJ/33 kcal energy
0.8 g fat
(of which 0.2 g saturated)
4.6 g carbohydrate
(of which 0.2 g sugars)
2.1 g protein
0.1 g fibre

HEALTHY EATING TIP

Rely on the soy sauce for flavour, no added salt is needed.
If chicken (rather than pork) is used, this provides a healthy balanced dish.

7 Sui mai

	Makes 25–30
Dough	
Use same as har gau recipe	
minced pork or chicken	175 g (7 oz)
raw prawns, chopped	60 g (2½ oz)
spring onion	40 g (1¾ oz)
water chestnuts (diced)	30 g (¾ oz)
bamboo shoots, chopped	30 g (¾ oz)
salt	1 tsp
sugar	1 tsp
soy sauce, light	1 tsp
sesame oil	1 tsp
cornflour	1 tsp
small egg, beaten	
diced crab coral for garnish	
oil	

1 Prepare the dough as in recipe number 6.
2 Mix the meat, prawns, and vegetables together.
3 Add salt, sugar, soy, sesame oil, cornflour and egg.
4 Mix well to combine all ingredients.
5 Chill mixture well.
6 Place a wonton wrapper in the palm of the hand. Spoon approximately 10–15 g (½ oz) of filling into the middle.
7 Using the fingers to shape and the palm of the hand to press, shape the wrapper around the stuffing. The top stays open but the wonton wrapper fits the filling like a tight coat.
8 Dot the filling with crab coral garnish.
9 Place into a lightly oiled steamer.
10 Steam for 15–20 minutes and serve at once.

Fig 10.2 Chinese vegetables and noodles with prawns

Fig 10.3 ✐ Preparation for stir-fry vegetables

Greek cooking

Greek cooking offers very fresh ingredients, well flavoured with herbs and a hint of spiciness and cooked as simply as possible, that is, stewed, grilled or roasted with an emphasis on the use of olive oil, olives, yoghurt and lemon juice to enhance the products. Fish is used in great variety, including salt cod, baby squid, octopus, sea urchins and fresh sardines. Lamb is very popular, as is veal and poultry.

8 Taramasalata (paste of smoked cod's roe)

Served as an hors-d'oeuvre or appetiser. Tarama is the salted roe of the grey mullet, tuna fish or smoked cod's roe.

> 1 portion provides:
> 2933 kJ/709 kcal energy
> 64.0 g fat
> (of which 9.6 g saturated)
> 21.1 g carbohydrate
> (of which 3.2 g sugars)
> 12.6 g protein
> 0.8 g fibre

continued over ▶

▶ *Taramasalata continued*

	4 portions	10 portions
white bread, without crusts	150 g (6 oz)	375 g (15 oz)
milk	125 ml (¼ pt)	300 ml (⅝ pt)
smoked cod's roe, skinned	150 g (6 oz)	375 g (15 oz)
finely chopped onion, optional	50 g (2 oz)	125 g (5 oz)
clove garlic, optional	1	2–3
olive or vegetable oil	250 ml (½ pt)	625 ml (1¼ pt)
seasoning		
stoned olives, lemon, to serve		

HEALTHY EATING TIP

Season with minimum amount of salt. Serve with crudités and plenty of hot pitta bread.

1   Soak the bread in the milk for 2–3 minutes. Squeeze dry.

2   Place all the ingredients except the oil in a food processor, liquidise and gradually add the oil to make a smooth paste.

3   Place into individual ramekin dishes, decorate with stoned olives, garnish with lemon. Serve with hot toast, or hot pitta bread.

9 Avgolemono soup (egg and lemon soup)

> 1 portion provides:
> 278 kJ/66 kcal energy
> 3.1 g fat
> (of which 0.9 g saturated)
> 8.0 g carbohydrate
> (of which 0.5 g sugars)
> 2.1 g protein
> 0.0 g fibre

	4 portions	10 portions
chicken stock	750 ml (1½ pt)	2 litres (4 pt)
patna rice	35 g (1½ oz)	100 g (4 oz)
seasoning		
yolks plus egg (the egg is optional)	2 plus 1	5 plus 2
lemon, juice of	½	1

1   Bring the stock to the boil, add the rice and stir well.

2   Season and cook for 12–15 minutes, remove from heat.

3   In a basin thoroughly mix the yolks, egg and lemon juice.

4   Add 1 tablespoon of the stock a little at a time to the egg and lemon mixture, beating continuously.

5   Add a further 6 tablespoons, mixing continuously. If added too quickly the mixture will curdle.

6   Return the mixture to the stock and heat gently, mixing all the time to cook the egg and to thicken before serving.

10 Kalamarakia yemista (stuffed squid)

> Using approx 400 g raw squid, 1 portion provides:
> 1984 kJ/474 kcal energy
> 26.2 g fat
> (of which 3.0 g saturated)
> 42.2 g carbohydrate
> (of which 20.5 g sugars)
> 19.9 g protein
> 1.9 g fibre

	4 portions	10 portions
medium-sized squid	4	10
onion, finely chopped	50 g (2 oz)	125 g (5 oz)
clove garlic, crushed and chopped	1	2–3
oil	60 ml (⅛ pt)	150 ml (⅓ pt)
wholegrain rice	100 g (4 oz)	250 g (10 oz)
fish stock	250 ml (½ pt)	725 ml (1¼ pt)
pine kernels	50 g (2 oz)	125 g (5 oz)
raisins	100 g (4 oz)	250 g (10 oz)
chopped parsley		
seasoning		
dry white wine	125 ml (¼ pt)	250 ml (½ pt)
tomatoes, skinned, de-seeded, diced	200 g (8 oz)	500 g (1¼ lb)

4   Add the rice and moisten with half the fish stock. Stir and add the chopped tentacles, nuts, raisins and chopped parsley. Season. Stir well and allow to simmer for 5–8 minutes so that the rice is partly cooked.

5   Stuff the squid loosely with this mixture. Seal the end by covering with aluminium foil.

6   Lay the squid into a sauté pan with the remaining fish stock, white wine and tomatoes.

7   Cover with a lid and cook in a moderate oven at 180°C (Reg. 4; 350°F) for 30–40 minutes turning the squid gently during the cooking. Cook very gently or the squid will burst.

8   When cooked, remove the squid and place into a suitable serving dish.

9   Reboil the cooking liquor and reduce by one-third. Strain the ink into the sauce, boil and reduce for 5 minutes. Check the seasoning.

10 Mask the squid with the sauce and finish with chopped parsley to serve.

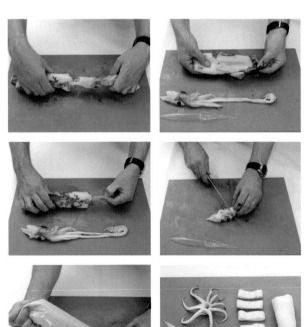

Fig 10.4   Preparation of stuffed squid

HEALTHY EATING TIP

Season with minimum amount of salt. Use an unsaturated oil (olive or sunflower) and reduce the quantity used. Serve with a large mixed salad.

1   Prepare the squid: pull the body and head apart, remove the transparent pen from the bag and any soft remaining part. Rinse under cold water. Pull off the thin purple membrane on the outside.

2   Remove the tentacles and cut into pieces. Remove the ink sac. Reserve the ink to finish the sauce.

3   Sweat the onion and garlic in the oil.

11 Dolmades (stuffed vine leaves)

1 portion provides:
1457 kJ/350 kcal energy
25.6 g fat
(of which 3.4 g saturated)
28.1 g carbohydrate
(of which 7.6 g sugars)
3.7 g protein
1.1 g fibre

HEALTHY EATING TIP

Use less olive oil to sweat the onion and garlic.
Serve with a small amount of avgolemono sauce, or lightly dress with vinaigrette.
Season with minimum amounts of salt.

	4 portions	10 portions
vine leaves	8	20
Filling		
onion, finely chopped	50 g (2 oz)	125 g (5 oz)
clove garlic, crushed and chopped	1	2–3
olive oil	60 ml (⅛ pt)	150 ml (⅓ pt)
brown rice	100 g (4 oz)	250 g (10 oz)
tomato purée	25 g (1 oz)	50 g (2 oz)
white stock (approximately)	60 ml (⅛ pt)	150 ml (⅓ pt)
seasoning		
pine kernels	25 g (1 oz)	50 g (2 oz)
fresh chopped mint		
fresh chopped dillweed		
currants	25 g (1 oz)	50 g (2 oz)
clove garlic, crushed and chopped	1	2–3
lemon, juice of	½	1
pinch of sugar		
olive oil		

The word *dolmades* comes from a Turkish verb meaning 'to stuff'.

1 Blanch the fresh vine leaves in boiling salted water for 1 minute, refresh and drain.

2 To make the filling: sweat the onion and garlic in the oil without colour.

3 Add the brown rice and tomato purée and moisten with the stock. Stir in the nuts, herbs and currants. Simmer on top of the stove, or cover with a lid and place in the oven, until half cooked.

4 Correct the seasoning. Stuff each vine leaf with the rice mixture and roll up, making sure that the ends are closed.

5 In a sauté pan add the other clove of garlic and the lemon juice and sprinkle with sugar and oil.

6 Lay the stuffed vine leaves in the sauté pan and sprinkle with more lemon juice.

7 Add 125 ml (¼ pt) water or white stock and season. Cover with aluminium foil.

8 Bring to the boil, draw to the side of the stove, gently cook until tender. Alternatively, place in a moderate oven at 180°C (Reg. 4; 350°F) covered with a lid for about 30 minutes until tender.

9 When cooked, serve in a suitable earthenware dish in their cooking liquor, which has been thickened with egg yolks and finished with lemon juice. This is avgolemono sauce.

Note: Dolmades may also be eaten cold, served with a lemon vinaigrette dressing, and as part of an assorted hors-d'oeuvre.

12 Avgolemono sauce

1 portion provides:
131 kJ/32 kcal energy
2.7 g fat
(of which 0.8 g saturated)
0.3 g carbohydrate
(of which 0.2 g sugars)
1.5 g protein
0.0 g fibre

	4 portions	10 portions
egg yolks	2	5
lemon, juice of	½	1
stock (cooking liquor)	250 ml (½ pt)	625 ml (1¼ pt)

1 Beat egg yolks and lemon juice over a bain-marie until light.

2 Add the stock gradually and return to the saucepan.

3 Cook over a low heat until the sauce thickens but does not boil.

13 Baklavas (filo pastry with nuts and sugar)

Using ¼ recipe of filo pastry, and ghee, 1 portion provides:
5488 kJ/1314 kcal energy
83.5 g fat
(of which 35.8 g saturated)
132.6 g carbohydrate
(of which 85.2 g sugars)
16.6 g protein
6.1 g fibre

	4 portions	10 portions
filo pastry, sheets of	12 (200 g)	30 (500 g)
clarified butter or ghee	200 g (8 oz)	500 g (1¼ lb)
hazelnuts, flaked	100 g (4 oz)	250 g (10 oz)
almonds, nibbed	100 g (4 oz)	250 g (10 oz)
caster sugar	100 g (4 oz)	250 g (10 oz)
cinnamon	10 g (½ oz)	25 g (1 oz)
grated nutmeg		
Syrup unrefined sugar or caster sugar	200 g (8 oz)	500 g (1¼ lb)
lemons, grated zest and juice of	2	5
water	60 ml (⅛ pt)	150 ml (⅓ pt)
orange, grated zest and juice of	1	2
cinnamon stick	1	2
rose water		

HEALTHY EATING TIP

Use oil to brush the sheets of filo pastry. Less sugar can be used in the filling as it should be sweet enough with the syrup used for masking.

1 Prepare a shallow tray slightly smaller than the sheets of filo pastry by brushing with melted clarified butter or ghee.

2 Place on sheets of filo pastry, brushing each with the fat.

3 Now prepare the filling by mixing the nuts, sugar and spices together, and place into the prepared tray, layered alternately with filo pastry. Brush each layer with the clarified fat so that there are at least 2–3 layers of filling separated by filo pastry.

continued over ▶

▶ *Baklavas continued*

4   Cover completely with filo pastry and brush with the clarified fat.

5   Mark the pastry into diamonds, sprinkle with water and bake in a moderately hot oven at 190°C (Reg. 5; 375°F) for approximately 40 minutes.

6   Meanwhile make the syrup: place all the ingredients in a saucepan and bring to the boil. Simmer for 5 minutes, pass through a fine strainer and finish with 2–3 drops of rose water.

7   When the baklavas are baked, cut into diamonds, place on a suitable serving dish and mask with the syrup.

14 Filo pastry

	4 portions	**10 portions**
strong flour	1 kg (2 lb)	2½ kg (5 lb)
water	250–375 ml (½–¾ pt)	¾ litre (1½ pt)
vinegar	1 tbsp	2–3 tbsp
salt	2 tsp	5 tsp
olive oil	4 tbsp	10 tbsp

1   Sift the flour in a bowl.

2   Add water, vinegar and salt to the bowl and mix ingredients to a thick paste.

3   Add the oil, very slowly, while working the mixture.

4   Mix until the dough becomes smooth and elastic. Cover for 30 minutes.

5   Split the paste into suitable pieces.

6   First roll out with an ordinary rolling pin, then use a very thin rolling pin or pasta machine, to make the paste wafer thin.

7   The pastry is now ready for use. It must be covered with a damp or oiled cloth when not being rolled out or before use.

Note: Always cover filo pastry with a damp cloth or polythene when not using, otherwise it dries quickly and is difficult to handle. Filo pastry is usually purchased ready made.

Indian cooking

There are 25 States in this subcontinent, each with its own capital, and India is the second most populous country in the world with the majority being Hindus. Religion plays an important part in the choice of food and the method of cookery.

The northern part of India and Pakistan use what is called the Mogul style of cooking, the Mogul dynasty of the Shahs having installed itself as long ago as 1526 at the capital Delhi. They were hearty meat-eaters and used wheat more than rice. Tandoori cooking is done here and there is greater emphasis on presentation than elsewhere in the subcontinent. Apart from this there is not very much difference from the other countries of this region.

15 Chemmeen kari

A prawn curry from the South of India.

	4 portions	10 portions
large king size prawns, raw (preferably) or cooked	400 g (1 lb)	1 kg (2½ lb)
malt vinegar	4 tsp	10 tsp
onion, finely chopped	50 g (2 oz)	125 g (5 oz)
vegetable oil	4 tsp	10 tsp
red chillies	4	10
desiccated coconut	100 g (4 oz)	250 g (10 oz)
mustard seeds	1 tsp	2½ tsp
curry leaves	10	25
fresh ginger, finely chopped	25 g (1 oz)	62 g (2½ oz)
cloves garlic, crushed and chopped	2	5
ground turmeric	1 tsp	2½ tsp
ground coriander	12 g (½ oz)	30 g (1¼ oz)
tomato flesh, de-seeded and chopped	100 g (4 oz)	250 g (10 oz)
hot water	125 ml (¼ pt)	312 ml (⅛ pt)

1 portion provides:
1205 kJ/290 kcal energy
22.1 g fat
(of which 14.1 g saturated)
4.8 g carbohydrate
(of which 3.7 g sugars)
20.5 g protein
3.9 g fibre

HEALTHY EATING TIP

No added salt is needed, plenty of other flavours. Use a little unsaturated oil to sweat the onions. Serve with a large portion of rice and a vegetable dish.

1   Shell the prawns and de-vein them by slitting the back.

2   Rub the prawns with salt and half the teaspoons of vinegar and keep aside.

3   Sweat the onions in a little of the oil until very slightly golden brown in colour. Remove from heat, add the chillies, coconut and mustard seeds. Place in the oven stirring occasionally for approximately 8 minutes, or continue to sweat on top of the stove to extract the flavours. Remove from heat, place in a food processor and blend to a fine paste. This is the masala.

4   Heat the oil in a wok or other suitable pan and fry the curry leaves for 1 minute. Add the ginger and garlic and fry for a further 1 minute. Now add the turmeric, ground coriander and chilli powder and the masala. Stir-fry for 1–2 minutes.

5   Add the tomatoes, salt to taste and the hot water. Bring to the boil, simmer for 5 minutes.

6   Drain the prawns. Add them to the pan. Mix well, continue to cook until the prawns are tender (if you are using raw prawns this usually takes 8–10 minutes). They will curl and turn a pinky/orange colour. Add the remaining vinegar. Do not overcook the prawns otherwise they will become hard and dry.

7   Serve immediately, garnished with coriander leaves.

HEALTHY EATING TIP

Use a minimum amount of salt and less butter.
Serve with a large portion of Indian flat bread, salad and cucumber raita.

16 Tandoori prawns (grilled spiced prawns)

	4 portions	10 portions
king size prawns	12	30
unsalted butter	100 g (4 oz)	250 g (10 oz)
fresh ginger, grated	1 tsp	2½ tsp
clove garlic, crushed and chopped	1	2–3
chilli powder	1 tsp	2½ tsp
ground cumin	1 tsp	2½ tsp
ground coriander	1 tsp	2½ tsp
fresh coriander leaves		
seasoning		
Garnish lettuce leaves		
onion rings		
chillies, chopped	2	5
lemon, cut into wedges	1	2

1 Shell and wash the prawns, leaving the head attached. Place in a shallow tray.
2 Melt the butter and add all the spices, including the coriander leaves.
3 Pour this melted butter mixture over the prawns.
4 Gently grill on both sides under the salamander for 5–6 minutes.
5 Serve on a bed of lettuce, garnished with onion, chillies and lemon.

Note: This dish should be prepared using live prawns, but, if unobtainable, cooked prawns may be used, in which case the prawns should be reheated for 2–3 minutes. Tandoori prawns may be served as a first or fish course.

17 Palak lamb

A medium spiced dish from the Punjab.

	4 portions	10 portions
vegetable ghee or oil	62 ml (⅛ pt)	155 ml (⅓ pt)
cumin seeds	1 tsp	2½ tsp
onion, finely chopped	50 g (2 oz)	125 g (5 oz)
fresh ginger, finely chopped	12 g (½ oz)	30 g (1¼ oz)
clove garlic, crushed and chopped	1	3
shoulder loin or leg of lamb	400 g (1 lb)	1 kg (2½ lb)
hot curry paste	2 tsp	5 tsp
natural yoghurt	125 ml (¼ pt)	312 ml (⅝ pt)
tomato purée	25 g (1 oz)	625 g (2½ oz)
spinach, chopped	200 g (8 oz)	500 g (1¼ lb)
salt to taste		
coriander and lemon for garnish		

Using lean meat, vegetable oil,
1 portion provides:
1669 kJ/403 kcal energy
32.0 g fat
(of which 8.8 g saturated)
5.9 g carbohydrate
(of which 5.0 g sugars)
23.5 g protein
1.4 g fibre

HEALTHY EATING TIP

Use a smaller amount of unsaturated oil. Drain off the excess fat after cooking the lamb and before adding the curry paste and yoghurt. Add a minimum amount of salt; there is plenty of flavour from the spices.
Serve with a large portion of rice and a vegetable dish.

1   Heat the ghee or oil in a frying pan.

2   Add the cumin seeds; fry for 1 minute.

3   Add the onion; fry until golden brown.

4   Add the ginger and garlic; stir-fry until all is brown.

5   Add the lamb cut in 2 cm (1 inch) dice; simmer for 15–20 minutes.

6   Add the curry paste, yoghurt and salt.

7   Cook for 5 minutes; add water if necessary to prevent sticking.

8   Stir in the tomato purée and spinach. Cover and simmer for 10–15 minutes until lamb is tender.

9   Serve garnished with lemon quarters and coriander leaves.

Using lean meat, unsalted butter,
1 portion provides:
1686 kJ/405 kcal energy
31.5 g fat
(of which 15.4 g saturated)
7.4 g carbohydrate
(of which 5.6 g sugars)
24.6 g protein
1.0 g fibre

HEALTHY EATING TIP

Use a smaller amount of
unsaturated oil. Drain off
the excess fat before
adding the water. Add a
minimum amount of salt
and try adding natural
yoghurt in place of the
cream. Serve with a large
portion of rice and a
vegetable dish.

18 Lamb pasanda

	4 portions	10 portions
ghee or unsalted butter	32 g (1½ oz)	80 g (3¾ oz)
onion, finely chopped	150 g (6 oz)	375 g (15 oz)
shoulder, leg or loin of lamb, diced	400 g (1 lb)	1 kg (2½ lb)
clove garlic, crushed and chopped	2	4
fresh ginger, finely chopped	12 g (½ oz)	30 g (1¼ oz)
natural yoghurt	125 ml (¼ pt)	312 ml (⅝ pt)
ground turmeric	2½ g (½ tsp)	5½ g (1¼ tsp)
ground coriander	10 g (2 tsp)	25 g (5 tsp)
ground cumin	5 g (1 tsp)	12½ g (2½ tsp)
ground nutmeg	2½ g (½ tsp)	5½ g (1¼ tsp)
pinch of cayenne pepper		
single cream	125 ml (¼ pt)	312 ml (⅝ pt)
ground almonds	25 g (1 oz)	62½ g (2½ oz)
salt	2¼ g (½ tsp)	5½ g (1½ tsp)
garam masala	5 g (1 tsp)	12½ g (2½ tsp)

1   Melt the butter in a frying pan. Sweat the onions until just lightly brown.

2   Add the lamb and cook until sealed.

3   Add the garlic, ginger, yoghurt, turmeric, coriander, cumin, nutmeg and cayenne pepper. Just cover with water and bring to the boil.

4   Cover with a suitable lid; simmer for 30–45 minutes or until the meat is tender.

5   Stir in the cream, ground almonds, salt and garam masala.

6   Bring back to the boil. Simmer for a further 5 minutes.

7   Serve garnished with toasted almonds.

19 Kashmira lamb

A medium spiced dish from North India.

	4 portions	10 portions
tikka paste	100 g (4 oz)	250 g (10 oz)
natural yoghurt	125 ml (¼ pt)	312 ml (⅝ pt)
shoulder loin or leg of lamb	400 g (1 lb)	1 kg (2½ lb)
ghee or oil	62 ml (⅛ pt)	155 ml (⅓ pt)
cumin seeds	1 tsp	2½ tsp
cardamom pods	4	10
cloves	4	10
cinnamon sticks	4	10
onions, finely chopped	100 g (4 oz)	250 g (10 oz)
clove garlic, crushed and chopped	1	1½
fresh ginger, finely chopped	12 g (½ oz)	30 g (1¼ oz)
ground chilli	½ tsp	1¼ tsp
salt to taste		
fresh coriander and roasted almonds		

Using lean meat, vegetable oil, 1 portion provides:
1812 kJ/437 kcal energy
36.0 g fat
(of which 8.8 g saturated)
6.5 g carbohydrate
(of which 4.5 g sugars)
23.0 g protein
0.4 g fibre

HEALTHY EATING TIP

Use a smaller amount of unsaturated oil. Drain off the excess fat after frying the lamb. Add a minimum amount of salt.
Serve with rice, dhal and a vegetable dish.

1 Mix together tikka paste and yoghurt in a suitable bowl.

2 Dice the lamb into 2 cm (1 inch) cubes and marinate in the yoghurt mixture for a minimum of 1 hour.

3 Heat the ghee or oil in a suitable frying pan.

4 Add the cumin seeds, cardamom, cloves and cinnamon; fry for 1 minute.

5 Add the onion, garlic and ginger. Fry for 5 minutes or until golden brown.

6 Add the lamb; fry together for 10–15 minutes. Add a little water if necessary to prevent sticking.

7 Add salt and chilli. Cover and simmer for a further 15 minutes or until the lamb is tender.

8 Serve garnished with coriander leaves and roasted almonds.

Using lean meat, vegetable oil,
1 portion provides:
1329 kJ/320 kcal energy
22.8 g fat
(of which 5.1 g saturated)
5.4 g carbohydrate
(of which 4.0 g sugars)
23.6 g protein
0.8 g fibre

HEALTHY EATING TIP

Use a smaller amount of unsaturated oil to fry the beef and the onion rings. Drain off the excess fat after frying the meat and onions. Drain the onion rings on kitchen paper. Use a minimum amount of salt. Serve with rice or flat bread and a vegetable dish.

20 Beef do-piazza

A medium spiced dish from the Punjab.

	4 portions	10 portions
topside or chuck steak, cubed	400 g (1 lb)	1 kg (2½ lb)
vegetable ghee or oil	62 ml (⅛ pt)	155 ml (⁵⁄₁₆ pt)
onion, finely chopped	100 g (4 oz)	250 g (10 oz)
fresh ginger, finely chopped	12 g (½ oz)	30 g (1¼ oz)
clove garlic, crushed and chopped	1	3
medium curry powder	3 tsp	7½ tsp
natural yoghurt	125 ml (¼ pt)	312 ml (⅝ pt)
lemon, juice of	½	1¼
salt to taste		
julienne of lemon rind		
large onion, cut into rings	1	2

1 Fry the beef in the oil until brown.

2 Add the onions and continue to fry until brown. Drain off the excess oil.

3 Add the ginger, garlic and curry powder; fry for a further 5 minutes.

4 Remove from heat; add the yoghurt and lemon juice.

5 Simmer for 1–1½ hours, adding small amounts of water or stock during the cooking to prevent sticking.

6 Fry the onion rings in oil until golden brown. Keep some for the garnish, add the remainder to the beef. Season with the salt.

7 Serve garnished with the onion rings and the julienne of lemon rind.

21 Beef Madras

A hot curry from the South of India.

	4 portions	10 portions
topside or chuck steak, cubed	400 g (1 lb)	1 kg (2½ lb)
onion, finely chopped	100 g (4 oz)	250 g (10 oz)
clove garlic, crushed and chopped	2	5
vegetable ghee or oil	68 ml (⅛ pt)	155 ml (5/16 pt)
hot Madras curry paste	3 tsp	7½ tsp
brown beef stock	500 ml (1 pt)	1¼ litre (2½ pt)
tomato purée	50 g (2 oz)	125 g (5 oz)
mango chutney, chopped	5 g (2 oz)	125 g (5 oz)
lemon, juice of	½	1½
season to taste		
coriander leaves for garnish		

1 Fry the beef in the oil until sealed and brown, add the onion and garlic, continue to fry for a further 5 minutes.

2 Add the curry paste and mix well; cook for a further 2 minutes.

3 Add the remaining ingredients, cover with brown stock and bring to the boil. Simmer for 1–1½ hours, or until tender.

4 Correct the seasoning and consistency.

5 Garnish with coriander leaves and serve with pilaff rice.

HEALTHY EATING TIP

Use a smaller amount of unsaturated oil to fry the beef and drain off the excess fat before adding the curry paste. Use a minimum amount of salt. Serve with pilaff rice and a vegetable dish.

Fig 10.5 Accompaniments to curry (see page 329)

22 Keema Matar (medium spiced mince and peas)

Using lean meat, vegetable oil, 1 portion provides:
1726 kJ/417 kcal energy
34.1 g fat
(of which 8.8 g saturated)
5.6 g carbohydrate
(of which 2.6 g sugars)
22.0 g protein
1.7 g fibre

	4 portions	10 portions
minced beef	400 g (1 lb)	1 kg (2½ lb)
vegetable ghee or oil	62 ml (⅛ pt)	155 ml (⁵⁄₁₆ pt)
onion, finely chopped	100 g (4 oz)	250 g (10 oz)
clove garlic, crushed and chopped	1	3
fresh ginger, finely chopped	12 g (½ oz)	30 g (1¼ oz)
medium curry paste	4 tsp	10 tsp
brown stock or water	250 ml (½ pt)	625 ml (1¼ pt)
frozen peas	100 g (4 oz)	250 g (10 oz)
chopped fresh coriander	4 tsp	10 tsp
lemon, juice of	½	1¼

1 Fry the beef in the oil until brown.
2 Add the onions and garlic. Fry for a further 5 minutes.
3 Add the ginger, curry paste; cook for a further 8 minutes, adding spoonfuls of water or stock to prevent burning.
4 Add the rest of the water or stock, peas, chopped coriander and lemon juice.
5 Simmer for 20 minutes or until cooked. Serve.

Note: This recipe is suitable for low-cost catering.

23 Tandoori chicken

Estimated edible meat used, vegetable oil used, 1 portion provides:
1436 kJ/342 kcal energy
14.1 g fat
(of which 4.6 g saturated)
10.1 g carbohydrate
(of which 8.6 g sugars)
44.6 g protein
0.3 g fibre

chicken cut as for sauté	1¼–1½ kg (2½–3 lb)
salt	1 tsp
lemon, juice of	1
plain yoghurt	12 fl oz
small onion, chopped	1
clove garlic, peeled	1
ginger, piece of, peeled and quartered	5 cm (2 inch)
fresh hot green chilli, sliced	½
garam masala	2 tsp
ground cumin	1 tsp
few drops each red and yellow colouring	

HEALTHY EATING TIP

Lightly oil the pan to fry the beef and onion and drain off any excess fat. Skim any fat from the surface of the finished dish.
Use a minimum amount of salt.
Serve with pilaff rice and a vegetable dish.

HEALTHY EATING TIP

Skin the chicken and reduce the salt by half.
Serve with rice and vegetables.

Fig 10.6 ✍ Tandoori chicken   *John Campbell*

1   Cut slits bone deep in the chicken pieces.

2   Sprinkle the salt and lemon juice on both sides of the pieces, lightly rubbing into the slits; leave for 20 minutes.

3   Combine the remaining ingredients in a blender or food processor.

4   Brush the chicken pieces on both sides ensuring the marinade goes into the slits. Cover and refrigerate for 6–24 hours.

5   Preheat the oven to the maximum temperature.

6   Shake off as much of the marinade as possible from the chicken pieces, place on skewers and bake for 15–20 minutes or until cooked.

7   Serve with red onion rings and lime or lemon wedges.

24 Chicken palak (chicken fried with spinach and spices)

Estimated edible meat used, butter used, 1 portion provides:
1575 kJ/378 kcal energy
21.9 g fat
(of which 9.5 g saturated)
4.4 g carbohydrate
(of which 3.5 g sugars)
41.3 g protein
1.9 g fibre

	4 portions	10 portions
chicken, cut for sauté	1 × 1½ kg (3 lb)	2 × 1½ kg (6 lb)
ghee or butter, margarine or oil	50 g (2 oz)	125 g (5 oz)
onion, finely chopped	50 g (2 oz)	125 g (5 oz)
clove garlic, crushed and chopped	1	2–3
fresh ginger	25 g (1 oz)	60 g (2½ oz)
green chilli	1	2
ground cumin	1 tsp	2½ tsp
ground coriander	1 tsp	2½ tsp
spinach, washed and finely chopped	250 g (10 oz)	625 g (1½ lb)
tomatoes, skinned, de-seeded, diced	200 g (8 oz)	500 g (1¼ lb)
chicken stock	250 ml (½ pt)	625 ml (1¼ pt)

HEALTHY EATING TIP

Skin the chicken and fry in a small amount of unsaturated oil. Skim excess fat from the finished dish. Serve with plenty of rice, dhal, chapatis and a vegetable dish.

1   Gently fry the chicken in the fat until golden brown.

2   Remove the chicken and fry the onion and garlic until lightly browned. Add the spices and sweat for 3 minutes.

3   Stir in the spinach, add the tomatoes and season. Add the chicken pieces.

4   Add the chicken stock, bring to the boil.

continued over ▶

▶ *Chicken palak continued*

5 Cover with a lid and cook in a moderate oven at 180°C (Reg. 4; 350°F) for 30 minutes or until the chicken is tender. Stir occasionally, adding more stock if necessary.

6 Serve in a suitable dish with rice, chapatis (see page 361) and dhal (see page 355).

25 Chicken tikka

HEALTHY EATING TIP

Skin the chicken and keep the added salt to a minimum. Use half the amount of unsaturated oil. Serve with rice and a vegetable dish.

Estimated edible meat used, 1 portion provides:
1780 kJ/427 kcal energy
27.1 g fat
(of which 5.2 g saturated)
5.5 g carbohydrate
(of which 5.1 g sugars)
41.3 g protein
0.6 g fibre

	4 portions	10 portions
chicken, cut for sauté	1 × 1½ kg (3 lb)	2½ × 1½ kg (6 lb)
natural yoghurt	125 ml (¼ pt)	250 ml (½ pt)
grated ginger	1 tsp	2½ tsp
ground coriander	1 tsp	2½ tsp
ground cumin	1 tsp	2½ tsp
chilli powder	1 tsp	2½ tsp
clove garlic, crushed and chopped	1	2–3
lemon, juice of	½	1
tomato purée	50 g (2 oz)	125 g (5 oz)
onion, finely chopped	50 g (2 oz)	125 g (5 oz)
oil	60 ml (⅛ pt)	150 ml (⅓ pt)
lemon, wedges of	4	10
seasoning		

1 Place the chicken pieces into a suitable dish.

2 Mix together the yoghurt, seasoning, spices, garlic, lemon juice and tomato purée.

3 Pour this over the chicken, mix well and leave to marinate for at least 3 hours.

4 In a suitable shallow tray, add the chopped onion and half the oil.

5 Lay the chicken pieces on top and grill under the salamander, turning the pieces over once or gently cook in a moderate oven at 180°C (Reg. 4; 350°F) for 20–30 minutes.

6 Baste with the remaining oil.

7 Serve on a bed of lettuce garnished with wedges of lemon.

26 Kori cassi (Mangalorean chicken)

Estimated edible meat used, 1 portion provides:
3827 kJ/924 kcal energy
78.3 g fat
(of which 48.3 g saturated)
16.2 g carbohydrate
(of which 13.6 g sugars)
46.3 g protein
10.4 g fibre

	4 portions	10 portions
chicken cut for sauté	1	2½
cloves of garlic	8	20
coconut, freshly grated	500 g (1 lb 4 oz)	1.25 kg (2½ lb)
fenugreek seeds	1 tsp	2¼ tsp
cumin seeds	2½ tsp	6¼ tsp
black malabar peppercorns	2½ tsp	6 tsp
coriander seeds	40 g (1¾ oz)	100 g (4 oz)
red chillies	60 g (1¼ oz)	150 g (6 oz)
salt		
turmeric	2 tsp	5 tsp
oil	50 ml (⅛ pt)	125 ml (¼ pt)
onion, finely chopped	250 g (10 oz)	625 g (1 lb 9 oz)
water		
tamarind pulp	25 g (1 oz)	62 g (2½ oz)
Tarka **ghee**	30 g (1⅛ oz)	75 g (3 oz)
ground fenugreek	½ tsp	1¼ tsp
ground cumin	1 tsp	2½ tsp
finely chopped onion	50 g (2 oz)	125 g (5 oz)

1 In a little oil, roast chillies, coriander, peppercorns, cumin and fenugreek, separately.

2 Grind these spices with the coconut and garlic to a fine paste in a processor, adding a little water.

3 Marinate the chicken with salt and turmeric.

4 Heat the oil in a suitable pan and sauté the chopped onions until light brown. Remove from heat and add the coconut spice mixture.

5 Return to heat and simmer for approximately 20 minutes. Add 250 ml (½ pt) of water, bring to boil, add the chicken. Simmer for approximately 15mins.

6 Add the tamarind pulp and continue to simmer until the chicken is cooked through.

7 Prepare the tarka: heat the ghee, fry the spices, add the onion and sauté until lightly coloured.

8 Pour over the chicken and serve.

27 Dhal

Dhal is made from lentils and is an important part of the basic diet for many Indians. It can also be made using yellow split peas.

> Using butter, 1 portion provides:
> 1083 kJ/258 kcal energy
> 11.1 g fat
> (of which 6.6 g saturated)
> 29.6 g carbohydrate
> (of which 2.0 g sugars)
> 12.4 g protein
> 2.7 g fibre

	4 portions	10 portions
lentils	200 g (8 oz)	500 g (1¼ lb)
turmeric	1 tsp	2½ tsp
ghee, butter or oil	50 g (2 oz)	125 g (5 oz)
onion, finely chopped	50 g (2 oz)	125 g (5 oz)
garlic clove of, crushed and chopped	1	2–3
green chilli, finely chopped, optional	1	2–3
cumin seeds	1 tsp	2½ tsp

HEALTHY EATING TIP

Lightly oil the pan using an unsaturated oil to roast the spices. Reduce the amount of oil used to sauté the onions and skim fat from the cooked chicken. Little or no salt is needed. Serve with plenty of rice and vegetables.

continued over ▶

▶ *Dhal continued*

Lightly oil a pan to sweat the onion. This dish is high in protein and starchy carbohydrate and low in fat. It is a very useful accompaniment for many higher fat dishes and will help to 'dilute' the overall fat content.

1 Place the lentils in a saucepan and cover with water. Add the turmeric, bring to the boil and gently simmer until cooked. Stir occasionally.

2 In a suitable pan, heat the fat and sweat the onion, garlic, chilli (if using) and cumin seeds. Stir into the lentils and season.

3 Serve hot to accompany other dishes. The consistency should be fairly thick but spoonable.

28 Alu-Chole (vegetarian curry)

A dish from North India.

Using lemon juice, vegetable oil, 1 portion provides:
1214 kJ/290 kcal energy
17.5 g fat
(of which 1.6 g saturated)
26.6 g carbohydrate
(of which 5.3 g sugars)
10.6 g protein
5.5 g fibre

	4 portions	10 portions
vegetable ghee or oil	45 ml (3 tsp)	112 ml (7½ tsp)
small cinnamon sticks	4	10
bay leaves	4	10
cumin seeds	5 g (1 tsp)	12½ g (2½ tsp)
onion, finely chopped	100 g (4 oz)	250 g (10 oz)
cloves garlic, finely chopped and crushed	2	5
plum tomatoes, canned, chopped	400 g (1 lb)	1 kg (2½ lb)
hot curry paste	45 ml (3 tsp)	112 g (7½ tsp)
salt to taste		
chick peas, canned, drained	400 g (1 lb)	1 kg (2½ lb)
potato in 1 cm (½ inch) dice	100 g (4 oz)	250 g (10 oz)
water	125 ml (¼ pt)	312 ml (⅝ pt)
tamarind sauce or lemon juice	30 g (2 tsp)	75 g (5 tsp)
chopped coriander leaves	50 g (2 oz)	125 g (5 oz)

Use a small amount of unsaturated oil to fry the spices and onion. Skim the fat from the finished dish. No added salt is necessary. This can be served as a vegetarian dish with rice or to accompany meat and chicken dishes.

1 Heat the ghee in a suitable pan.

2 Add the cinnamon, bay leaves and cumin seeds; fry for 1 minute.

3 Add the onion and garlic. Fry until golden brown.

4   Add the chopped tomatoes, curry paste and salt and fry for a further 2–3 minutes.

5   Stir in the potatoes and water. Bring to the boil. Cover and simmer until the potatoes are cooked.

6   Add the chick peas; allow to heat through.

7   Stir in the coriander and lemon juice, and serve.

29 Pepper bhajee

Reduced to half using margarine, 1 portion provides:
852 kJ/204 kcal energy
13.1 g fat
(of which 1.5 g saturated)
20.0 g carbohydrate
(of which 8.8 g sugars)
4.0 g protein
5.3 g fibre

	4 portions	10 portions
oil	45 ml (3 tsp)	112 ml (7½ tsp)
onion, finely chopped	100 g (4 oz)	250 g (10 oz)
black mustard seeds	5 g (1 tsp)	12½ g (2½ tsp)
hot curry powder	30 ml (2 tsp)	75 ml (5 tsp)
plum tomatoes, canned, chopped	100 g (4 oz)	250 g (10 oz)
potatoes cut in 1 cm (½ inch) cubes	200 g (8 oz)	500 g (1¼ lb)
mixed red and green peppers, cut in half, de-seeded and finely shredded	600 g (½ lb)	1½ kg (3¼ lb)
salt to taste		

Use a small amount of unsaturated oil to fry the spices and onion. Skim the fat from the finished dish.
No added salt is necessary.
Use to accompany meat dishes.

1   Heat oil in a suitable pan. Fry the mustard seeds for 1 minute.

2   Add the onions and fry until golden brown in colour.

3   Stir in the curry powder. Cook for 1 minute. Add the tomatoes.

4   Add the potatoes, red and green peppers. Mix well.

5   Add a little water to prevent sticking occurring. Cover the pan and cook for 15 minutes. Season and serve.

30 Onion bhajias

Reduced to half, using margarine, 1 portion provides:
630 kJ/152 kcal energy
12.1 g fat
(of which 1.3 g saturated)
8.5 g carbohydrate
(of which 1.7 g sugars)
2.9 g protein
2.4 g fibre

	4 portions	10 portions
bessan or gram flour	45 g (3 tsp)	112 g (7½ tsp)
hot curry powder	5 g (1 tsp)	12½ g (2½ tsp)
salt		
water	75 ml (5 tsp)	187 ml (12½ tsp)
onion, finely shredded	100 g (4 oz)	250 g (10 oz)

Use a minimum amount of salt. Make sure the oil is hot so that less is absorbed into the surface. Drain on kitchen paper.

1   Mix together the flour, curry powder and salt.

2   Blend in the water carefully to form a smooth, thick batter.

continued over ▶

▶ *Onion bhajias continued*

3   Stir in the onion, stir well.

4   Drop the mixture off a tablespoon into deep oil at 200°C (400°F). Fry for 5–10 minutes until golden brown.

5   Drain well and serve as a snack with mango chutney as a dip.

31 Pakora (batter-fried vegetables and shrimps)

A reception or bar snack or as a main course.

> Using vegetable oil, mix of veg & shrimps used, 1 portion provides:
> 1040 kJ/249 kcal energy
> 13.9 g fat
> (of which 1.7 g saturated)
> 18.4 g carbohydrate
> (of which 3.3 g sugars)
> 14.0 g protein
> 5.0 g fibre

	4 portions	10 portions
bessan (chick-pea flour)	125 g (5 oz)	250 g (10 oz)
water	375 ml (¾ pt)	750 ml (1½ pt)
turmeric	¼ tsp	½ tsp
ground coriander	1 tsp	2 tsp
cayenne	¼ tsp	½ tsp
salt		

HEALTHY EATING TIP
Use a minimum amount of salt. Make sure the oil is hot so that less is absorbed into the surface. Drain on kitchen paper.

Vegetables such as batons of carrot, florets of cauliflower, florets of broccoli, sliced aubergines, batons of celery, slices of par-boiled peeled or unpeeled potato, batons of parsnip, and large cooked shrimps or prawns (peeled and seasoned with salt and curry powder) can be used.

1   Sieve the flour and slowly add the water, whisking continuously.

2   Pass through a strainer.

3   Add the turmeric, coriander and cayenne pepper, season with salt. Allow to stand for 15 minutes.

4   Dip the vegetables and shrimps or prawns into the batter, coating well.

5   Deep fry in hot oil at 190°C (375°F) until a light saffron colour.

6   Drain well and serve with chutney.

Note: Unlike plain wheat flour, batter made with bessan produces a non-porous surface and no fat will penetrate to the food inside.

32 Samosas

	40–60 pasties	100–150 pasties
short pastry made from ghee fat and fairly strong flour as the dough should be fairly elastic	400 g (1 lb)	1 kg (2½ lb)

HEALTHY EATING TIP
Use a minimum amount of salt. Use a small amount of unsaturated oil to fry the mustard seeds and onion. Skim any fat from the finished dish.

Brush the pastry with ghee or vegetable oil after rolling into a smooth ball.

33 Potato filling

peeled potatoes	200 g (8 oz)	500 g (1¼ lb)
vegetable oil	1½ tsp	3¾ tsp
black mustard seeds	½ tsp	1¼sp
onions, finely chopped	50 g (2 oz)	125 g (5 oz)
fresh ginger, finely chopped	12 g (½ oz)	30 g (1¼ oz)
fennel seeds	1 tsp	2½ tsp
cumin seeds	¼ tsp	1 tsp
turmeric	¼ tsp	1 tsp
frozen peas	75 g (3 oz)	187 g (7½ oz)
salt to taste		
water	2½ tsp	6¼ tsp
fresh coriander, finely chopped	1 tsp	2½ tsp
garam masala	½ tsp	2½ tsp
pinch of cayenne pepper		

> 1 portion provides:
> 257 kJ/86 kcal energy
> 7.4 g fat
> (of which 1.3 g saturated)
> 4.6 g carbohydrate
> (of which 0.1 g sugars)
> 0.7 g protein
> 0.3 g fibre

1 Cut the potatoes into ½ cm (¼ inch) dice; cook in water until only just cooked.

2 Heat the oil in a suitable pan, add the mustard seeds and cook until they pop.

3 Add the onions and ginger. Fry for 7–8 minutes, stirring continuously until golden brown.

4 Stir in the fennel, cumin and turmeric, add the potatoes, peas, salt and water.

5 Reduce to a low heat, cover the pan and cook for 5 minutes.

6 Stir in the coriander; cook for a further 5 minutes.

7 Remove from the heat, stir in the garam masala and the cayenne seasoning.

8 Remove from the pan, place into a suitable bowl to cool before using.

Fig 10.7 Preparation of samosas

1 portion provides:
516 kJ/125 kcal energy
11.6 g fat
(of which 3.4 g saturated)
3.9 g carbohydrate
(of which 0.1 g sugars)
1.6 g protein
0.2 g fibre

HEALTHY EATING TIP

No added salt is
necessary.
Use a small amount of
unsaturated oil to fry
the onions and lamb.
Drain off the excess fat
before adding the
water.

34 Lamb filling

saffron	½ tsp	1¼ tsp
boiling water	2½ tsp	6¼ tsp
vegetable oil	3 tsp	7½ tsp
fresh ginger, finely chopped	12 g (½ oz)	30 g (1¼ oz)
cloves garlic, crushed and chopped	2	5
onions, finely chopped	50 g (2 oz)	125 g (5 oz)
salt to taste		
lean minced lamb	400 g (1 lb)	1 kg (2½ lb)
pinch of cayenne pepper		
garam masala	1 tsp	2½ tsp

1 Infuse the saffron in the boiling water; allow to stand for 10 minutes.

2 Heat the vegetable oil in a suitable pan. Add the ginger, garlic, onions and salt, stirring continuously. Fry for 7–8 minutes, until the onions are soft and golden brown.

3 Stir in the lamb, add the saffron with the water. Cook, stirring the lamb until it is cooked.

4 Add the cayenne, garam masala, reduce the heat, and allow to cook gently for a further 10 minutes.

5 The mixture should be fairly tight with very little moisture.

6 Transfer to a bowl and allow to cool before using.

35 To fill the samosas

1 Take a small piece of dough, roll into a ball 2 cm (1 inch) in diameter. Keep the rest of the dough covered with either a wet cloth, cling film or plastic, otherwise a skin will form on the dough.

2 Roll the ball into a circle about 9 cm (3½ inches) round on a lightly floured surface. Cut the circle in half.

3 Moisten the straight edge with eggwash or water.

4 Shape the semicircle into a cone. Fill the cone with approximately 1½ teaspoons of filling, moisten the top edges and press them well together.

5 The samosas may be made in advance, covered with cling film or plastic and refrigerated before being deep fried.

6 Deep fry at 180°C (375°F) until golden brown; remove from fryer and drain well.

7 Serve on a suitable dish garnished with coriander leaves. Serve a suitable chutney separately.

36 Chapatis

Chapatis are cooked on a *tawa* or frying pan. They are made fresh for each meal, and are dipped into sauces and used to scoop up food.

	4 portions	10 portions
wholewheat flour	200 g (8 oz)	500 g (1¼ lb)
pinch of salt		
water	125 ml (¼ pt)	213 ml (1⁵⁄₁₆ pt)
vegetable oil		

HEALTHY EATING TIP

Use a minimum amount of salt. Lightly oil a well-seasoned pan to cook the chapati or dry-fry. They are a useful accompaniment for fattier meat dishes.

> 1 portion provides:
> 1066 kJ/254 kcal energy
> 12.1 g fat
> (of which 1.4 g saturated)
> 32.0 g carbohydrate
> (of which 1.1 g sugars)
> 6.4 g protein
> 4.5 g fibre

1 Sieve the flour and salt, add the water and knead to a firm dough.

2 Knead on a floured table until smooth and elastic.

3 Cover with a damp cloth or polythene and allow to relax for 30–40 minutes.

4 Divide into 8 pieces (20 pieces for 10 portions), flatten each and roll into a circle 12–15 cm (5–6 inches) in diameter.

5 Lightly grease a frying pan with oil, add the chapati and cook as for a pancake. Traditionally chapatis are allowed to puff by placing them over an open flame.

6 Just before serving reheat the chapatis under the salamander.

37 Naan bread

This recipe comes from Punjab and goes well with tandoori meat dishes as well as vindaloos.

Traditionally, naans are baked in clay ovens. They must be eaten fresh and hot, and served immediately.

> Clarified butter – using ghee, 1 portion provides:
> 1619 kJ/386 kcal energy
> 20.5 g fat
> (of which 12.0 g saturated)
> 48.3 g carbohydrate
> (of which 5.0 g sugars)
> 10.1 g protein
> 1.8 g fibre

	6 portions
strong flour	350 g (14 oz)
caster sugar	1½ tsp
baking powder	½ tsp
salt	1 tsp
fresh yeast	15 g (½ oz)
warm milk 38˚C	150 ml (approx ¼ pt)
unsweetened plain yoghurt	150 ml (approx ¼ pt)
butter	100 g (4 oz)
poppy seeds	2 tbsp

1. Sift the flour into a suitable bowl and add the sugar, salt and baking powder.
2. Dissolve the yeast in the milk and stir in the yoghurt. Mix thoroughly with the flour to form a dough.
3. Knead the dough until it is smooth. Cover with a clean cloth and leave it to rise in a warm place for about 4 hours.
4. Divide the risen dough into 12 equal portions and roll into balls, on a lightly floured surface.
5. Flatten the balls into oblong shapes, using both hands and slapping the naan from one hand to the other.
6. Cook the naan bread on the sides of the tandoori oven or on a lightly greased griddle or heavy bottomed frying pan.

Cook the naan on one side only. Brush the raw side with clarified butter and poppy seeds, turn over, cook other side or brown under a salamander.

Indonesian cooking

Indonesia includes Bali, Borneo, Java and Sumatra and was previously known as the East Indies; it is an agricultural economy that produces rice as its staple food and many kinds of spice, mainly for export. The first two cultural and religious influences were the arrival of Buddhists and Hindus from India who were followed by Portuguese settlers, then a hundred years later by the Dutch. Immigrants came in large numbers from China and had a great deal of influence on the islands' cookery.

HEALTHY EATING TIP

Cook the bread without added fat. Naan bread is a useful accompaniment for fattier meat dishes.

38 Gado-gado (vegetable salad with peanut dressing)

This dish is popular throughout Indonesia. It may be served as a starter or with a main meal and rice.

	4 portions	10 portions
white cabbage, finely shredded and washed	200 g (8 oz)	500 g (1¼ lb)
bean sprouts, washed	100 g (4 oz)	250 g (10 oz)
cooked potato, cut in 1 cm (½ inch) dice	200 g (8 oz)	500 g (1¼ lb)
tomato, skinned, de-seeded, diced	50 g (2 oz)	125 g (5 oz)
eggs, hard-boiled	2	5
vegetable oil	60 ml (⅛ pt)	150 ml (⅓ pt)
Dressing **onion, finely chopped**	50 g (2 oz)	125 g (5 oz)
clove garlic, crushed and chopped	1	2–3
green chilli, finely chopped	1	2–3
crunchy peanut butter	50 g (2 oz)	125 g (5 oz)
malt vinegar	2 tsp	5 tsp
coconut milk	125 ml (¼ pt)	250 ml (½ pt)

1 portion provides:
1329 kJ/320 kcal energy
24.8 g fat
(of which 3.8 g saturated)
16.0 g carbohydrate
(of which 6.6 g sugars)
9.0 g protein
3.1 g fibre

HEALTHY EATING TIP

Lightly oil a pan using an unsaturated oil to fry the onion. The peanut butter and coconut milk are high in fat, so use less sauce and more vegetables.

1   Drain the cabbage and bean sprouts and mix together.

2   Add the potato and the tomato, lightly season.

3   Arrange neatly into individual dishes just prior to service and decorate with quarters of hard-boiled egg.

4   Prepare the dressing: heat the oil in a sauteuse and stir fry the onion, garlic and chilli for 2 minutes.

5   Stir in the peanut butter, vinegar and coconut milk, simmer for a further 2–3 minutes.

6   Pour the hot sauce over the salad or serve separately.

1 portion provides:
2090 kJ/504 kcal energy
40.8 g fat
(of which 24.1 g saturated)
7.5 g carbohydrate
(of which 4.6 g sugars)
27.1 g protein
5.6 g fibre

HEALTHY EATING TIP

Lightly oil a pan using an unsaturated oil to fry the onion. Skim any fat from the finished dish. Little or no salt is required. Serve with rice or noodles and additional vegetables.

39 Rendang (Indonesian beef curry)

	4 portions	10 portions
cooking oil	45 ml (3 tsp)	112 ml (7½ tsp)
onion, finely chopped	100 g (4 oz)	250 g (10 oz)
cloves garlic, crushed and chopped	2	5
fresh ginger, finely chopped	12 g (½ oz)	30 g (1¼ oz)
hot Thai curry blend	30 g (2 tsp)	75 g (5 tsp)
ground lemon grass	5 g (1 tsp)	12½ g (2½ tsp)
desiccated coconut	100 g (4 oz)	250 g (10 oz)
rump or sirloin cut into thin strips	400 g (1 lb)	1 kg (2½ lb)
creamed coconut	100 g (4 oz)	250 g (10 oz)
hot water	250 ml (½ pt)	625 ml (1¼ pt)
salt to taste		

1 Heat the oil in a suitable pan. Fry the onions, garlic and ginger until lightly coloured.

2 Add the curry blend and lemongrass; continue to fry for a further 2 minutes.

3 Add the desiccated coconut; fry for a further 1 minute.

4 In a separate pan, quickly fry the beef, to seal. Drain off the excess oil and place the beef in a clean saucepan. Season.

5 Blend the coconut and hot water to make coconut milk and add to beef.

6 Add the other ingredients that have been prepared.

7 Bring to boil, simmer until the beef is tender and the liquid has evaporated; stir occasionally. The curry should be quite dry.

8 Serve with prawn crackers.

40 Nasi goreng (rice with bacon, chicken and soy sauce)

1 portion provides:
2334 kJ/562 kcal energy
42.6 g fat
(of which 13.9 g saturated)
25.2 g carbohydrate
(of which 2.2 g sugars)
21.0 g protein
0.6 g fibre

	4 portions	**10 portions**
vegetable oil	60 ml (⅛ pt)	150 ml (⅓ pt)
onion, finely chopped	100 g (4 oz)	250 g (10 oz)
clove garlic, crushed and chopped	1	2–3
red chilli, finely chopped	1	2–3
small lardons of bacon	200 g (8 oz)	500 g (1¼ lb)
cooked chicken, cut into 2 cm (1 inch) slices	100 g (4 oz)	250 g (10 oz)
soy sauce	2 tbsp	5 tbsp
rice cooked as pilaff, dry and fluffy	250 g (10 oz)	625 g (1½ lb)
Garnish **eggs, beaten and seasoned**	2	5
finely sliced cucumber	50 g (2 oz)	125 g (5 oz)

HEALTHY EATING TIP

Use a small amount of an unsaturated vegetable oil to fry the onion and bacon. Drain off any excess fat before adding the cooked chicken. This dish will be high in salt from the bacon and soy sauce.

1   Heat a little oil in a wok, add the onion, garlic and chilli and stir-fry. Add the lardons of bacon and cook quickly.

2   Add the cooked chicken and cook for a further 2–3 minutes.

3   Add the soy sauce and cooked rice. Reheat the rice thoroughly. Stir occasionally.

4   For the garnish, heat a little oil in a small frying pan. Beat the egg well with seasoning. Pour this into the frying pan, cook one side, turn over and cook the other. Turn out onto a board. Cut into thin strips.

5   Serve in a suitable dish, garnished with strips of the cooked egg and slices of cucumber.

Note: Prawns are sometimes added to this dish.

Japanese cooking

Japanese cuisine is a reflection of the traditional Japanese art and culture that draws inspiration from the beauty of seasonal changes, and attempts to achieve harmony with the natural surroundings.

The underlying philosophy of the cuisine is to capture the essence of the seasonal changes by using vegetables, fruits and fish associated with the particular time of year and by retaining the natural flavour of the ingredients. Aesthetic and artistic presentation of the food is paramount. Ingredients are often used raw or with minimum cooking, with the preparation focused on the enhancement of the natural flavour and texture of the ingredients. As a result, the freshness and quality of the ingredients becomes essential. It is these Japanese presentation skills and cooking approaches that gave inspiration to nouvelle cuisine.

Key components of a traditional Japanese diet are rice, noodles, vegetables, seaweeds, fish, shellfish, soybean products (tofu, miso, and age) and fruits. The Japanese did not eat meat until late 1800 because of the Buddhist principles that forbade eating four-legged animal meat. However, today meat – mainly beef, pork and chicken – is very much a part of the general Japanese diet, though the amount consumed is small by European standards.

Japanese cookery is widely recognised as being beneficial to health because no saturated fat or dairy products – other than eggs – are generally used.

Traditional Japanese cooking methods are boiling, simmering, steaming, grilling, and frying (deep, shallow and stir). No oven is required.

The main Japanese seasoning ingredients are:

- **Dashi stock** – stock made with dried bonito flakes (Hana-gatsuo) and dried kelp seaweed (Konbu) or dried *Shiitake* mushrooms.

- **Japanese soy sauces (dark and light)** are made from fermented soybeans, wheat and salt. Japanese soy sauces have different flavour from the Chinese varieties. They are less salty and lighter in colour. It is important to use the correct kind.

- **Sake** – rice wine. It is the same kind as the one served as a drink.

- **Mirin** – light golden syrupy wine, which has approximately 14% alcohol content, and is used only in cooking either to add sweetness or to glaze grilled food.

- **Miso** – fermented soybean paste. It comes in a wide variety, each having a distinct aroma, degree of saltiness, fermentation and colour. They are used primarily for soups and dressings in a wide variety of dishes.

- **Sesame oil** – it is generally used in small amounts for flavouring.

One type of Japanese cooking that has become global is sushi. **Sushi** refers to dishes that use vinegared rice. Sushi can be made with numerous kinds of cooked or raw ingredients. There is sushi unique to each region of Japan, using cooked or raw fish, shellfish, braised or raw vegetables or thin, miniature omelettes, or a combination of these. A Japanese set meal (tei-shoku) usually has five components – two bowl dishes and three plate dishes. The two bowls are hot steamed rice and hot soup. The three plates comprise a meat or fish dish and a vegetable or a soybean, or a plate combining the two. All dishes are served together at the same time.

The following are some of the authentic Japanese recipes that go well with European dishes.

41 Sushi rice

Sushi rice is called 'Shari' in Japanese. Shari makes sushi. It is very important to get proper Japanese rice. In order to make the correct texture of sushi rice the ratio 1 (rice): 1 (liquid) is critical. The total liquid quantity includes the amount of rice vinegar in sushi vinegar mixture that will be added to the hot cooked rice later. Sushi rice can be made in advance, stored in a container then covered with a damp tea towel. A 200 ml cup is used for this recipe.

Preparation time: 15 minutes
Cooking time: 15 minutes plus cooling time

	4 portions
Japanese short-grain rice	2 cups (400 ml)
water	340 ml
Sushi Vinegar **Japanese rice vinegar**	60 ml (4 tbsp)
caster sugar	1½ tbsp
salt	½ tsp

1   Put the rice into a bowl and rinse with water until the water runs clear.

2   Drain the washed rice in a sieve and leave it for 5 minutes or until the water drains off completely.

3   Prepare the sushi vinegar by dissolving the sugar and salt in vinegar.

4   Place the rice in a heavy bottomed medium-sized pan or rice cooker and add 340 ml of water.

5   Cover tightly and bring the pan slowly over the medium heat to the boiling point. Continue to boil for 2 minutes, and then reduce the heat to simmer and cook for further 5–8 minutes or until

all the water has been absorbed and you can hear a crackling noise. It is crucial not to take off the lid during this cooking process to make the right firm texture.

6 Turn the heat off and allow the pan to sit on the stove undisturbed for 1–2 minutes.

7 Take the cover off the pan and turn the rice into a large bowl. Sprinkle the vinegar mixture over the hot rice and mix it carefully with a wooden spatula without crushing the grains. To keep the grains separate, toss the rice with horizontal cutting movements. Remember, unless the rice is just cooked, the vinegar will not be absorbed.

8 Spread the rice onto a large chopping board or sushi wooden tub. Cool the rice down to room temperature by fanning. This prevents the rice going soggy and produces a sheen.

9 Once the rice is cooled down to room temperature, it is ready for use.

10 To keep sushi rice from drying out, place in a container and cover with a damp tea cloth. Sushi rice should be eaten the same day it is prepared. It does not keep more than 1 day. It should not be refrigerated as the rice will harden and become unpleasant to the palate.

42 Steamed rice

To cook Japanese rice, the water to rice ratio is 1 (rice): 1 (water). Steamed rice can be made in advance, wrapped in cling film and freezes very well. Re-heat in a microwave oven for approximately 1 or 2 minutes. 1 cup is 200 ml.

Ingredients: To serve 4

2 cups Japanese short grain rice
400 ml water

1 Put the rice into a bowl and rinse with water until the water runs clear.

2 Place the rice in a heavy bottomed medium-sized pan or rice cooker and add 400 ml of water.

3 Cover tightly and bring the pan slowly over the medium heat to the boiling point, continue to boil over high heat for 2 minutes. Cook, and then turn the heat down to simmer and cook further for 5–8 minutes or until all water has been absorbed and you can hear a crackling noise. To make the right texture, it is crucial not to take off the lid during the cooking process.

4 Turn off the heat and let it steam for 5 minutes, then the rice is ready to serve.

43 Tempura

To make a success of Tempura, it is essential that all ingredients are ice-cold, the batter should not be lumpy and you should fry a few pieces at one time. Any vegetable with firm texture can be used.

1 portion provides:
3397 kJ/815 kcal energy
55.9 g fat
(of which 7.4 g saturated)
67.4 g carbohydrate
(of which 5.3 g sugars)
14.8 g protein
5 g fibre

	4 portions
courgettes, sliced	2
sweet potato, scrubbed and sliced	1
green pepper, remove the seeds, cut into strips	1
Shiitake mushroom, remove the stalk, halve them if they are large	4
onion, sliced as half-moon	1
parsley sprigs	4
vegetable oil	500 ml
Batter: all ingredients must be stored in fridge until just before mixing **plain flour, sifted**	100 g
ice cold water	200 ml
egg yolk	
Tentsuyu dipping sauce (optional)	
dashi stock	200 ml
mirin	3 tbsp
soy sauce	3 tbsp
grated ginger	½ tsp

continued over ▶

▶ *Tempura continued*

Use sunflower or groundnut oil for frying. Drain excess oil on kitchen paper.

Accompaniment: Grated white radish

1   To prevent splattering during the frying, make sure to dry all deep-fry ingredients thoroughly first with a kitchen towel.

2   Beat the egg yolk lightly and mix with ice cold water.

3   Add ½ quantity of flour to the egg and water mixture. Give the mixture a few strokes. Add the rest of the flour all at once. Stroke the mixture a few times with chopsticks or fork, until ingredients are loosely combined. The batter should be very lumpy. If you over-mix it, Tempura will be oily and heavy.

4   Heat the oil to 160°C.

5   Dip the vegetables and seafood into the batter a few pieces at a time. Fry until just crisp and golden, about 1½ minutes.

6   Drain cooked vegetables and seafood on a kitchen towel.

7   Serve immediately with a pinch of salt and lemon wedges, dry-roasted salt or with Tentsuyu dipping sauce in a small bowl with grated ginger.

If you prefer to have the Tempura with the Tentsuyu sauce, combine the dipping sauce ingredients in a small saucepan before sifting the flour and heat it through and leave aside.

44   Teri-yaki chicken (Pan-fried chicken coated with soya mirin Sauce)

1 portion provides:
596 kJ/143 kcal energy
9.8 g fat
(of which 2.6 g saturated)
0.5 g carbohydrate
(of which 0 g sugars)
13.4 g protein
0 g fibre

	4 portions
large boned chicken thighs with skin	4
Sauce **mirin (syrupy Japanese rice wine)**	4 tsp
sake (Japanese rice wine)	1 tsp
Japanese soy sauce	1½ tsp
Garnish **spring onion, thinly sliced**	1 tbsp
toasted black sesame seeds	1 tsp

No added salt is needed. Serve with a large portion of rice and additional vegetables.

1   Heat a non-stick frying pan over a moderate heat until hot.

2   Add the chicken pieces skin-side down. In order to squeeze the fat and excess moisture out of the skin, cook skin-side until the skin becomes crispy and golden brown. If the skin is browning too quickly, take the pan off the heat occasionally to slow down the process and prevent burning.

3   When the skins are all crisp and golden brown, take the pieces out of the frying pan then place onto a piece of kitchen towel and drain the fat.

4   Wipe the remaining chicken fat clean from the frying pan using the kitchen towel.

5   Return the chicken pieces to the cleansed frying pan, then cook the flesh-side for 1 minute.

6   Reverse the chicken pieces yet again to skin-side and add mirin, sake and soy sauce to the pan.

7   Increase the heat slightly to bring the sauces to the boil. When the sauce is syrupy and starts to bubble, turn the chicken pieces frequently to coat with the sauce without burning. A pair of tongs is ideal for this operation.

8   When all the chicken pieces are cooked through, add grated ginger to the sauce. The chicken should look glossy and well coated with the sauce. Serve immediately with the remaining thickened sauce. Sprinkle with spring onion slices and sesame seeds for garnish.

45 Tofu steak

This is an excellent alternative to steak for non-meat eaters.

> 1 portion provides:
> 602 kJ/144 kcal energy
> 7.6 g fat
> (of which 0.9 g saturated)
> 9.2 g carbohydrate
> (of which 1.4 g sugars)
> 10.2 g protein
> 0.1 g fibre

HEALTHY EATING TIP

Use a little sunflower or olive oil to fry the bean curd, or dry-fry. The soy sauce is high in sodium; no added salt is needed.

	4 portions
Japanese bean curd	2 blocks
or	*or*
Chinese bean curd	1 block 5 cm (2 inch) square
Shiitake mushroom, sliced	4
cornflour seasoned with salt and pepper	1 tbsp
Sauce **finely sliced spring onion**	2 tbsp
grated fresh ginger	1 tbsp
vegetable oil	1 tbsp
Japanese soy sauce	2 tbsp
sake (Japanese rice wine)	2 tbsp
mirin (Japanese sweet wine)	1 tbsp
sugar	½ tsp
water	2 tbsp
cornflour (diluted with water)	1 tsp (1 tbsp)
Garnish **finely sliced spring onion**	2 tbsp
lettuce leaves	4
tomato, thinly sliced	1

1 Drain off any liquid from the package of bean curd.

2 To refresh the bean curd, rinse the blocks with cold water, then steep them in warm or hot water for 10 minutes. Pat the blocks dry with paper towels. Wrap the blocks with tea towels and weigh them down with the chopping board for 10 minutes to drain excess water.

3 Cut the blocks in half (quarter if it is 5 cm square) and dust with seasoned cornflower.

4 Add a half quantity of vegetable oil in a frying pan or skillet. When sizzling, sear the block of bean curd in one row over high heat. Turn the blocks over to sear them golden brown on both sides. Set aside these blocks and keep them warm.

5 Add the remaining vegetable oil in a small saucepan over medium heat and sauté ginger and spring onion for ½ minute. Add sliced mushroom and continue to sauté further ½ minute. Then add soy sauce, sake and rice vinegar, sugar, reserved mushroom liquid or water (if fresh mushrooms are used) and then stir, bring to the boil. Then add the diluted cornflour to thicken and keep stirring, bring quickly to the boil and adjust the seasoning with salt and pepper if required.

6 Place the bean curd blocks on a warm individual plate arranged with lettuce and tomato and pour the sauce over each block. Garnish the centre of each bean curd block with spring onion. Serve hot.

Fig 10.8 Sashimi and (below) tempura

Mexican cooking

The food of this Spanish-speaking nation has become very popular in many countries. Mexico has an old established cuisine that stems from the native Indians to the Aztecs and then from the Spanish who arrived there in 1519, along with some French influence, which came with the installation of Emperor Maximilian. It is based on an abundance of native ingredients made extremely hot by the use of chillies, cooked simply without roasting or baking, supported by accompaniments made of maize, which plays a much larger part in the diet than wheat.

46 Tortillas

> 1 portion provides:
> 1064 kJ/254 kcal energy
> 10.3 g fat
> (of which 1.1 g saturated)
> 35.4 g carbohydrate
> (of which 0.4 g sugars)
> 5.5 g protein
> 2.2 g fibre

Tortillas are served with all Mexican meals. Although in Mexico a special flour is used, tortillas may be produced using cornmeal and wholemeal flour.

	4 portions	10 portions
wholemeal flour	100 g (4 oz)	250 g (10 oz)
cornmeal flour	100 g (4 oz)	250 g (10 oz)
water	250 ml (½ pt)	625 ml (1¼ pt)

HEALTHY EATING TIP

Use a very little unsaturated vegetable oil to cook the tortillas. A filling of kidney beans with a little grated cheese and chilli sauce can be used to make enchiladas. Serve with a mixed salad.

1   Sieve the flours together into a bowl, add a pinch of salt and enough water to make a smooth dough.

2   Knead well until elastic. Divide into 12 or 16 pieces (30 or 40 for 10 portions), depending on the size of the tortilla required.

3   Place a ball of dough between two pieces of well oiled greaseproof paper (or use silicone paper). Roll the dough into a circle, diameter 10–15 cm (4–6 inches).

4   Lightly oil a frying pan. Peel off the top layer of paper and place the tortilla in the pan. Cook for 2 minutes. Remove the top paper, turn over and cook the other side for 2 minutes. Both sides should be quite pale and dry.

5   Keep the tortillas warm for service, stacking between pieces of dry greaseproof paper.

Note: The tortilla can be served in different ways. When crisp and golden it is called a **tostada**. These are served with red kidney beans, cheese and a chilli sauce.

Tacos are tortillas curled into a shell shape and fried, usually filled with picadillo (see following recipe) and served with salad and chilli sauce.

Tortillas that are rolled and filled, then served with a sauce, are called **enchiladas**.

Chilli sauce is usually purchased as a commercial product, but it can be made by mixing together tomato ketchup and tabasco sauce, or by making a fresh tomato coulis (page 64), strengthened with tomato purée and finished with tabasco.

Tortillas may be made lighter by adding 1 teaspoon (2½ teaspoons for 10 portions) baking powder.

Using gherkins to replace capers,
1 portion provides:
1945 kJ/467 kcal energy
32.6 g fat
(of which 6.6 g saturated)
18.6 g carbohydrate
(of which 13.4 g sugars)
26.2 g protein
2.4 g fibre

HEALTHY EATING TIP

Dry-fry the minced
beef in a well-seasoned
pan and drain off all
excess fat. Use a
minimum amount of
salt.
Use to fill the tortillas
and serve with a
green salad.

47 Picadillo

Used as a filling for tacos.

	4 portions	10 portions
oil	60 ml (⅛ pt)	150 ml (⅓ pt)
minced lean beef	400 g (1 lb)	1 kg (2½ lb)
onion, finely chopped	100 g (4 oz)	250 g (10 oz)
clove garlic, crushed and chopped	1	2–3
chilli, finely chopped	1	2–3
tomatoes, skinned, de-seeded, diced	100 g (4 oz)	250 g (10 oz)
tomato purée	50 g (2 oz)	125 g (5 oz)
cumin seed	¼ tsp	½ tsp
raisins	50 g (2 oz)	125 g (5 oz)
brown stock or water	250 ml (½ pt)	625 ml (1¼ pt)
cornflour	18 g (¾ oz)	36 g (1½ oz)
green olives, chopped	25 g (1 oz)	60 g (2½ oz)
capers, chopped	25 g (1 oz)	60 g (2½ oz)
flaked almonds, roasted	50 g (2 oz)	125 g (5 oz)

1   Heat the oil in a frying pan, add the minced beef and brown quickly.

2   Add the onion, garlic, and the chopped chilli pepper. Season and cook for a further 3 minutes.

3   Pour off the excess oil and place the meat into a suitable saucepan.

4   Add to the saucepan the tomatoes, tomato purée, cumin seed and raisins.

5   Barely cover with brown stock or water and gently simmer for 30 minutes.

6   Lightly thicken with a little diluted cornflour and stir in the olives and capers.

7   Correct the seasoning and consistency. Finish by adding the roasted flaked almonds.

48 Burritos (Mexican pancakes)

The pancakes are filled with meat and served with a cheese sauce.

	4 portions	10 portions
pancake batter (see below)	250 ml (½ pt)	625 ml (1¼ pt)
portions chilli con carne (page 394)	4	10
Mornay sauce flavoured with Dijon-type mustard	500 ml (1 pt)	1¼ litre (2½ pt)
grated cheese, Parmesan or Cheddar		

1 Make the pancakes in the normal way (see below).

2 Fill the pancakes with chilli con carne. Place in a suitable earthenware dish.

3 Mask with Mornay sauce and sprinkle with grated cheese.

4 Glaze under the salamander or in a hot oven and serve.

> 1 portion provides:
> 3481 kJ/832 kcal energy
> 47.6 g fat
> (of which 13.0 g saturated)
> 60.2 g carbohydrate
> (of which 9.8 g sugars)
> 45.2 g protein
> 10.3 g fibre

> HEALTHY EATING TIP
> No added salt is needed; there is plenty of salt in the cheese. Serve with a large mixed salad.

49 Pancake batter

	4 portions	10 portions
flour, white or wholemeal	100 g (4 oz)	250 g (10 oz)
pinch of salt		
egg	1	2
milk, whole or skimmed	250 ml (½ pt)	625 ml (1¼ pt)
melted butter, margarine or oil	10 g (½ oz)	25 g (1 oz)
oil for frying		

1 Sieve the flour and salt into a bowl, make a well in the centre.

2 Add the egg and milk, gradually incorporating the flour from the sides; whisk to a smooth batter.

3 Mix in the melted butter. Heat the pancake pan, clean thoroughly.

4 Add a little oil, heat until smoking.

5 Add enough mixture to just cover the bottom of the pan thinly.

6 Cook for a few seconds until brown.

7 Turn and cook on the other side. Turn on to a plate.

8 Repeat until all the batter is used up.

> Using whole milk and vegetable oil, 1 portion provides:
> 1034 kJ/248 kcal energy
> 15.4 g fat
> (of which 3.4 g saturated)
> 22.2 g carbohydrate
> (of which 3.2 g sugars)
> 6.3 g protein
> 0.8 g fibre

Middle Eastern cooking

The countries of the middle east have shared their past and this has been given unity in the kitchen. The spread of Islam has played a significant role in the development of the traditional cuisine. The death of the prophet Muhammad in the year AD 632 was followed by victorious wars waged by the followers of his faith. The establishment of an Islamic empire, stretching across Asia, North Africa, Spain and Sicily, brought together cooking styles and refinements in eating habits. Great value is attached to food as a means of offering hospitality. Regional differences do not have much to do with national boundaries but depend more on geography, history and local produce.

HEALTHY EATING TIP

Use a minimum amount of salt. Serve with plenty of hot pitta bread and crudités to make a healthy starter.

1 Cook the chick peas in simmering water for 2 hours. Drain well.

2 Purée the peas in a food processor, add seasoning, sesame seed paste, garlic and onion. Finish with lemon juice.

3 Place into a suitable serving dish decorated with a line of paprika.

50 Hummus (chick pea and sesame seed paste)

Served with pitta bread as a starter or as an accompaniment to main dishes.

> 1 portion provides:
> 1546 kJ/367 kcal energy
> 15.3 g fat
> (of which 2.0 g saturated)
> 39.2 g carbohydrate
> (of which 3.0 g sugars)
> 20.9 g protein
> 1.7 g fibre

	4 portions	10 portions
soaked chick peas	300 g (12 oz)	750 g (1 lb 14 oz)
seasoning		
sesame seed paste (tahini)	75 g (3 oz)	187 g (7½ oz)
clove garlic, crushed and chopped	1	2–3
onion, finely chopped	50 g (2 oz)	125 g (5 oz)
lemon, juice of	1	2
paprika	5 g (¼ oz)	10 g (½ oz)

51 Tabbouleh (cracked wheat salad)

Serve with hummus or kebabs.

> 1 portion provides:
> 582 kJ/140 kcal energy
> 7.9 g fat
> (of which 0.9 g saturated)
> 15.5 g carbohydrate
> (of which 1.0 g sugars)
> 2.1 g protein
> 0.3 g fibre

	4 portions	10 portions
cracked wheat (burghul)	75 g (3 oz)	187 g (7½ oz)
onion, finely chopped	25 g (1 oz)	60 g (2½ oz)
diced cucumber	50 g (2 oz)	125 g (5 oz)
tomato, peeled, de-seeded, diced	50 g (2 oz)	125 g (5 oz)
salt, pepper		
vegetable oil	30 ml (¹⁄₁₆ pt)	75 ml (¼ pt)
lemon, juice of	½	1
chopped fresh parsley and mint		

HEALTHY EATING TIP

Use a minimum amount of salt. Use half the amount of an unsaturated oil.

	4 portions	10 portions
burghul (cracked wheat)	200 g (8 oz)	500 g (1¼ lb)
leg or shoulder of lamb, boned and diced	400 g (1 lb)	1 kg (2½ lb)
onion, finely chopped	50 g (2 oz)	125 g (5 oz)
cinnamon	1 tsp	2½ tsp
seasoning		
cold water	2 tbsp	5 tbsp
Filling onion, finely chopped	50 g (2 oz)	125 g (5 oz)
clove garlic, crushed and chopped	1	2
oil	60 ml (⅛ pt)	150 ml (⅓ pt)
minced lamb	200 g (8 oz)	500 g (1¼ lb)
allspice	½ tsp	1 tsp
pine kernels	50 g (2 oz)	125 g (5 oz)
chopped raisins	50 g (2 oz)	125 g (5 oz)
melted butter or margarine	50 g (2 oz)	125 g (5 oz)

1   Cover the cracked wheat with cold water and leave to soak for 10 minutes. Drain well, place into a suitable basin.

2   Add the onion, cucumber and tomato, season with salt and pepper.

3   Mix in the oil and lemon juice, stir in the chopped parsley and chopped mint.

4   Serve on individual side plates, dressed in lettuce leaves.

52   Kibbeh bil sanieh (spiced lamb with cracked wheat)

Eaten with salad, pitta bread, hummus and yoghurt. Served hot or cold.

Using butter, 1 portion provides:
3338 kJ/803 kcal energy
51.6 g fat
(of which 16.7 g saturated)
49.5 g carbohydrate
(of which 10.6 g sugars)
36.7 g protein
0.9 g fibre

HEALTHY EATING TIP

Use a small amount of an unsaturated oil to sweat the onion and brown the lamb. Drain off any excess fat from the filling. Serve with plenty of pitta bread, salad, yoghurt and hummus.

1   Cover the cracked wheat with cold water and allow to stand for 5 minutes. Drain well.

2   Place the lamb in a food processor with the finely chopped onion, cinnamon and seasoning, and blend to a smooth paste. Add the cold water, mix well.

3   Add the well drained cracked wheat. Blend in a processor until a smooth paste is formed.

Fig 10.9 Couscous

continued over ▶

▶ *Kibbeh bil sanieh continued*

4   For the filling: first, sweat the onion and garlic together in the oil. Add the minced lamb, allow to brown quickly.

5   Mix in the allspice, pine kernels and raisins.

6   In a suitable dish, spread half of the lamb and wheat mixture on the bottom (the kibbeh). Cover with the filling. Finish by topping with the rest of the kibbeh.

7   Cut diagonal lines over the top to make diamond shapes and brush the melted fat over the top.

8   Bake in a moderately hot oven, 190°C (Reg. 5; 375°F) for approximately 45 minutes. The surface should be brown and crisp. Baste occasionally with a few tablespoons of stock, so that the interior is moist.

53 Couscous

(Illustrated on page 375)

This is the national dish of the Maghreb, the North African countries of Morocco, Tunisia and Algeria of Berber origin. A couscous has been adopted by other Arab countries, who call it Maghebia, which is different from the North African dish. Couscous itself is a type of fine semolina.

The basic process for the preparation of couscous is the steaming of the grain over a stew or broth. This is generally made with lamb or chicken and a variety of vegetables. Chick peas are usually added and sometimes raisins. The broth is often coloured red with tomato purée or yellow with saffron.

The actual process of cooking the couscous is very simple, but calls for careful handling of the grain. The aim is to make it swell and become extremely light, each grain soft, delicate and separate. The grain must never cook in the broth or sauce, but only in the steam. The couscousier, the pot traditionally used, is in two parts: the bottom part is the round pan in which the stew is cooked; the top consists of a sieve, which holds the couscous.

The treatment of the grain is always the same, whatever the sauce. This recipe is for a basic Moroccan couscous.

Using lamb and butter, 1 portion provides:
2146 kJ/515 kcal energy
28.5 g fat
(of which 12.6 g saturated)
42.2 g carbohydrate
(of which 14.7 g sugars)
25.3 g protein
2.8 g fibre

	4 portions	10 portions
couscous	200 g (8 oz)	500 g (1¼ lb)
lean stewing lamb *or* **stewing lamb and**	400 g (1 lb) 200 g (8 oz)	1 kg (2½ lb) 500 g (1¼ lb)
stewing beef *or* **chicken, cut for sauté**	200 g (8 oz) 1 × 1½ kg (3 lb)	500 g (1¼ lb) 2 × 1½ kg (7 lb)
olive oil	2 tbsp	5 tbsp
onion, finely chopped	50 g (2 oz)	125 g (5 oz)
clove garlic, crushed and chopped	1	2–3
celery	100 g (4 oz)	250 g (10 oz)
leek	100 g (4 oz)	250 g (10 oz)
carrot	100 g (4 oz)	250 g (10 oz)
chick peas	25 g (1 oz)	60 g (2½ oz)
ground ginger (optional)	¼ tsp	½ tsp
saffron (optional)	¼ tsp	½ tsp
raisins	50 g (2 oz)	125 g (5 oz)
courgettes	100 g (4 oz)	250 g (10 oz)
tomatoes, skinned, de-seeded, diced	50 g (2 oz)	125 g (5 oz)
chopped parsley		
tomato purée	50 g (2 oz)	125 g (5 oz)
cayenne pepper		
paprika	½ tsp	1 tsp
butter or margarine	50 g (2 oz)	125 g (5 oz)

HEALTHY EATING TIP

No additional salt is needed.
Add only a small amount of fat to the couscous before adding the meat and vegetables. The fat content will be reduced if skinned chicken is used or less lamb/beef and more vegetables.

54 Couscous with chorizo sausage and chicken

1 portion provides:
1590 kJ/380 kcal energy
13.1 g fat
(of which 4.3 g saturated)
34.1 g carbohydrate
(of which 1.7 g sugars)
33.1 g protein
0.3 g fibre

	4 portions	10 portions
couscous	250 g (10 oz)	625 g (1½ lb)
chorizo sausage	150 g (6 oz)	400 g (1 lb)
suprêmes of chicken (skinned)	3	7
sunblush tomatoes	75 g (3 oz)	200 g (8 oz)
olive oil	1 tbsp	1½ tbsp
garlic cloves (finely chopped)	2	3
fresh parsley	¼ tsp	½ tsp

1 Soak the couscous in warm water for 10 minutes.

2 Fry the meat in the oil until browned and sealed. Remove quickly, fry the onions and garlic.

3 Drain, place the meat, onions and garlic into a saucepan.

4 Add the celery, leeks, carrots cut into 1 cm (½ inch) dice. Add the chick peas, cover with water, season.

5 Add the ginger and saffron. Bring to the boil and simmer for about 1 hour.

6 Drain the couscous, place in the top part of the couscousier and steam for 30 minutes. Alternatively, place the couscous in a metal colander lined with muslin. Fit into the top of the saucepan, making sure that the liquid from the stew does not touch the steamer as the couscous will become lumpy. Stir occasionally.

7 Add to the stew the raisins and courgettes, the tomato, chopped parsley and tomato purée. Cook for a further 30 minutes.

8 Remove approximately 250 ml (½ pint) sauce from the stew and stir in the cayenne pepper, enough to make it strong and fiery. Finish with paprika.

9 To serve, pile the couscous into a suitable serving dish, preferably earthenware, add knobs of butter or margarine and work into the grains with a fork.

10 Carefully arrange the meat and vegetables over the couscous and pour the broth over. Serve the hot peppery sauce separately.

11 Alternatively, the couscous, meat and vegetables, the broth and the peppery sauce can be served in separate bowls.

Note: A pre-cooked couscous is also available.

HEALTHY EATING TIP

Using an unsaturated oil (sunflower or olive), lightly oil the pan to sauté the garlic. Drain off any excess fat after cooking the sausage and chicken. Serve with mixed leaves.

1 Prepare the couscous in a suitable bowl and gently pour over 300 ml of boiling water.

2 Stir well, cover and leave to stand for 5 minutes.

3 Heat the olive oil in a suitable frying pan, add the chopped garlic, then sauté for 1 minute.

4 Add the chorizo sausage, (sliced 1 cm, ½ inch thick) and the chicken cut into fine strips. Cook for 5–6 minutes.

5 Add the couscous, sunblush tomatoes (skinned or diced) and parsley, mix thoroughly and heat for a further 2–3 minutes.

6 Drizzle with olive oil, serve as a warm salad.

Garnish with mixed leaves and flat parsley.

1 portion provides:
1554 kJ/370 kcal energy
16.3 g fat
(of which 1.1 g saturated)
51.3 g carbohydrate
(of which 50.9 g sugars)
7.6 g protein
6.9 g fibre

55 Khoshaf (dried fruit with nuts, perfumed with rose and orange water)

During Ramadan, Muslims fast all day and only eat after sunset. This is one of the dishes enjoyed during Ramadan. It is served hot or cold.

	4 portions	10 portions
dried apricots	100 g (4 oz)	250 g (10 oz)
prunes	100 g (4 oz)	250 g (10 oz)
dried figs	100 g (4 oz)	250 g (10 oz)
raisins	100 g (4 oz)	250 g (10 oz)
rose water	1 tbsp	2½ tbsp
orange blossom water	1 tbsp	2½ tbsp
blanched almonds (halved)	50 g (2 oz)	125 g (5 oz)
pine kernels	50 g (2 oz)	125 g (5 oz)

1 Wash the fruit if necessary, soak overnight.
2 Drain, place fruit in a large saucepan, cover with water and bring to boil. Simmer for 10 minutes.
3 Add the rose water and the orange blossom water.
4 Place into a serving dish sprinkled with nuts.

Fig 10.10 Khoshaf

Israeli kosher cooking

Israel, although a Middle Eastern country, is like a European state set down in Asia. It is populated by a total of some 4 million Jewish and Arab people. The Jewish people in Israel are mainly immigrants from Europe who have come from Germany, Poland and Russia; there are also immigrants from Spain and Portugal and more recently the Jewish minorities from North African countries including Ethiopia, Syria and Iran have made their homes in Israel. No matter where they originated from, Jewish people still carry out the cooking traditions of the time when Israel was their God-given homeland and in accordance with the food laws as written in the Torah, which is comprised of the first five books of the Old Testament. *Kosher* is a Jewish word meaning 'pure' or 'clean'. This lists the fish, birds and animals that orthodox Jews are allowed to eat, how they must be slaughtered, and how the meat must be koshered; milk and meat may not be cooked together nor eaten at the same meal and separate cooking and serving utensils must be kept specifically for each. After eating any form of meat it is not permitted to consume any milk foods, including cheese, for 3 hours. Products bearing the seal of the Beth Din – the authority appointed and approved by the Chief Rabbi – should be used. Shellfish, game birds and pork products are forbidden.

The laws also govern the way certain foods are stored, the kitchen and its equipment and the cook's personal knives. Knives in use for general catering may not be used for kosher catering.

Many interesting dishes are made for the many Jewish festivals in the calendar and only unleavened bread called *matzos* may be eaten during the Feast of the Passover, which commemorates the night when a destroying angel smote the first-born of the Egyptians but spared those in the houses where the doorposts and lintels had been daubed with blood.

56   Potato latkes

1 portion provides:
909 kJ/218 kcal energy
12.9 g fat
(of which 1.8 g saturated)
22.1 g carbohydrate
(of which 1.4 g sugars)
4.7 g protein
1.6 g fibre

	4 portions	10 portions
potatoes, washed, peeled and grated	400 g (1 lb)	1 kg (2½ lb)
onion, finely chopped	50 g (2 oz)	125 g (5 oz)
salt and pepper		
egg	1	2
plain flour or breadcrumbs	1 tbsp	2½ tbsp

HEALTHY EATING TIP

Use a minimum amount of salt. Use a little unsaturated oil to fry the potato mixture, then drain on kitchen paper.

1. Wash the grated potatoes, drain well and mix in a basin with the finely chopped onion.
2. Season with salt and pepper and add the beaten egg, flour or breadcrumbs and season.
3. Heat a little oil in a shallow pan and place potato mixture in 50 g (2 oz) pieces in the pan.
4. Cook on both sides for 3–4 minutes until golden brown; serve immediately.

Note: A little grated carrot or courgette may be added to the potato.

Using white flour, gherkin analysis used for capers, 1 portion provides:
849 kJ/201 kcal energy
6.0 g fat
(of which 2.4 g saturated)
14.3 g carbohydrate
(of which 2.8 g sugars)
23.3 g protein
0.7 g fibre

HEALTHY EATING TIP

Add little or no salt, rely on the Worcester sauce for flavour. Skim any fat from the stock after cooking the meat balls.
Serve with pasta or noodles and a green salad.

57 Koenigsberger klops (meat balls)

A reception snack *or* main course.

	4 portions	**10 portions**
bread, white or wholemeal	75 g (3 oz)	187 g (7½ oz)
egg	1	2
minced beef	200 g (8 oz)	500 g (1¼ lb)
minced veal	200 g (8 oz)	500 g (1¼ lb)
onion, chopped	50 g (2 oz)	125 g (5 oz)
salt and pepper		
chopped parsley		
paprika	¼ tsp	½ tsp
grated lemon rind	½ tsp	1 tsp
lemon, juice of	½	1
Worcester sauce	1 tsp	2½ tsp
brown vegetable stock	1 litre (2 pt)	2½ litre (5 pt)
cornflour or arrowroot		
tomato purée		
capers	25 g (1 oz)	60 g (2½ oz)
gherkins	25 g (1 oz)	60 g (2½ oz)

1   Remove the crusts from the bread and soak the bread in water.

2   Mix together the beaten egg and meat.

3   Sweat the chopped onion in a little oil until soft, then allow to cool and add to the meat.

4   Season with salt and pepper and add the chopped parsley.

5   Squeeze out excess water from the bread, add to the meat.

6   Add the paprika, lemon rind and juice, and Worcester sauce, and mix well.

7   Form into 18 g (¾ oz) balls for a reception snack or 75 g (3 oz) balls for a main course (2 per portion).

8   Cook in boiling vegetable stock, cover and simmer until cooked. Remove when cooked and keep warm.

9   Boil the remaining stock, lightly thicken with arrowroot or cornflour and colour slightly by adding a little tomato purée.

10 Season with salt and pepper and add the chopped capers and gherkins.

11 Reheat the meat balls in the gravy. Serve the small balls with cocktail sticks.

58 Cholla bread

	2 loaves
butter or margarine	56 g (2¼ oz)
strong flour	500 g (1¼ lb)
caster sugar	18 g (¾ oz)
salt	1 tsp
egg	63 g (2½ oz)
yeast	25 g (1 oz)
tepid water (26°C; 80°F)	185 ml (8 fl oz)

Fig 10.11 Cholla

1 Rub the butter or margarine into the sieved flour in a suitable basin.

2 Mix the sugar, salt and egg together.

3 Disperse the yeast in the water.

4 Add all these ingredients to the sieved flour and mix well to develop the dough. Cover with a damp cloth or plastic and allow it to ferment for about 45 minutes.

5 Divide into 125–150 g (5–6 oz) strands and begin to plait.

For 4-strand plait	*5-strand plait*
2 over 3	2 over 3
4 over 2	5 over 2
1 over 3	1 over 3

6 After moulding place on a lightly greased baking sheet and eggwash lightly.

7 Prove in a little steam until double in size. Eggwash again lightly and decorate with maw seeds.

8 Bake in a hot oven, at 220°C (Reg. 7; 425°F) for 25–30 minutes.

59 Matzo fritters

	4 portions	10 portions
matzos (wafers of unleavened bread)	3	7
milk	250 ml (½ pt)	625 ml (1¼ pt)
eggs, separated	2	5
matzo meal	150 g (6 oz)	375 g (15 oz)
brown sugar	100 g (4 oz)	250 g (10 oz)
salt		
cinnamon		
vegetable oil	60 ml (⅛ pt)	150 ml (⅓ pt)

Using semi-skimmed milk, matzo biscuits used as matzo flour, 1 portion provides:
2079 kJ/494 kcal energy
21.2 g fat
(of which 3.7 g saturated)
68.2 g carbohydrate
(of which 31.1 g sugars)
12.0 g protein
1.4 g fibre

HEALTHY EATING TIP
Use a minimum amount of salt. Fry in a small amount of an unsaturated oil and drain on kitchen paper.

continued over ▶

▶ *Matzo fritters continued*

1 Sprinkle warm water over the matzos. Place on a baking sheet and dry in a hot oven for 1 minute.

2 In a suitable basin beat the milk and egg yolks together, add the matzo meal, sugar, salt and cinnamon.

3 Fold in the stiffly beaten egg whites.

4 Spread this mixture on one side of each matzo. Fry in hot oil on the batter side until brown.

5 Spread batter on other side and fry again until brown.

6 Serve hot, sprinkled with sugar.

Using semi-skimmed milk, plain flour used, 1 portion provides:
2971 kJ/710 kcal energy
41.5 g fat
(of which 17.3 g saturated)
68.9 g carbohydrate
(of which 28.9 g sugars)
19.7 g protein
3.1 g fibre

60 Blitz kuchen (baked fluffy batter with nuts and cinnamon)

	4 portions	10 portions
cake flour	200 g (8 oz)	500 g (1¼ lb)
baking powder	10 g (½ oz)	25 g (1 oz)
butter or margarine	100 g (4 oz)	250 g (10 oz)
caster sugar	100 g (4 oz)	250 g (10 oz)
eggs, separated	4	10
lemon, grated rind of		
milk	60 ml (⅛ pt)	150 ml (⅓ pt)
egg white	1	2–3
water	1 tbsp	2–3 tbsp
chopped mixed nuts	100 g (4 oz)	250 g (10 oz)
cinnamon		

1 Sieve the flour and baking powder into a suitable bowl.

2 Cream the butter and sugar together until light and white.

3 Gradually add the egg yolks to the butter and sugar, beating continuously. Add the lemon rind.

4 Gradually add the flour, beating well, then add the milk. Cream well. (Add a little more milk if necessary.)

5 Beat 4 egg whites until full peak.

6 Gently fold the egg whites into the batter.

7 Heat a lightly oiled 20 cm (8 inch) frying pan, suitable for placing in the oven. Pour in sufficient batter to cover the surface and spread with diluted egg white.

8 Sprinkle liberally with caster sugar, cinnamon and chopped mixed nuts.

9 Bake in a moderate oven at 190°C (Reg. 5; 375°F) for about 20 minutes. Serve hot or cold.

Fig 10.12 Blitz kuchen
John Campbell

Spanish cooking

The flavours of Spain like much else of its culture are strangely influenced by the Moors who, for seven centuries, ruled a large part of the country. Its closeness to North Africa and the almost tropical culture of its southern and eastern coastal strip, have done much to preserve a culinary tradition reliant on almonds, saffron, chick peas, egg yolk, honey and quince, as well as onion, garlic, olive oil, tomato and lamb common to Mediterranean countries. The cooking can be rich and distinctive. Many of its popular dishes are mixtures of fish, shellfish, meat, poultry, and game with an assortment of vegetables and cereals.

61 Paella (savoury rice with chicken, fish, vegetables and spices)

	4 portions	10 portions
cooked lobster	1 × 400 g (1 lb)	2½ × 400 g (2½ lb)
squid	200 g (8 oz)	500 g (1¼ lb)
gambas (Mediterranean prawns), cooked	400 g (1 lb)	1 kg (2½ lb)
mussels	400 g (1 lb)	1 kg (2½ lb)
white stock	1 litre (2 pt)	2½ litre (5 pt)
pinch of saffron		
onion, finely chopped	50 g (2 oz)	125 g (5 oz)
clove garlic, finely chopped	1	2–3
red pepper, diced	50 g (2 oz)	125 g (5 oz)
green pepper, diced	50 g (2 oz)	125 g (5 oz)
roasting chicken, cut for sauté	1½ kg (3 lb)	2 × 1½ kg (6 lb)
olive oil	60 ml (⅛ pt)	150 ml (⅓ pt)
short grain rice	200 g (8 oz)	500 g (1¼ lb)
thyme, bay leaf and seasoning		
tomatoes, skinned, de-seeded, diced	200 g (8 oz)	500 g (1¼ lb)

Using edible chicken meat,
1 portion provides:
3383 kJ/804 kcal energy
31.0 g fat
(of which 6.2 g saturated)
48.8 g carbohydrate
(of which 3.8 g sugars)
85.7 g protein
1.3 g fibre

HEALTHY EATING TIP

To reduce the fat, skin the chicken and use a little unsaturated oil to sweat the onions and fry the chicken. No added salt is necessary. Serve with a large green salad.

1 Prepare the lobster: cut it in half, remove the claws and legs, discard the sac and trail. Remove meat from the claws and cut the tail into 3–4 pieces, leaving the meat in the shell.

continued over ▶

▶ *Paella continued*

2 Clean the squid, pull the body and head apart. Extract the transparent 'pen' from the body. Rinse well, pulling off the thin purple membrane on the outside. Remove the ink sac. Cut the body into rings and tentacles into 1 cm (½ inch) lengths.

3 Prepare the gambas by shelling the body.

4 Shell the mussels and retain the cooking liquid.

5 Boil the white stock and mussel liquor together, infused with saffron. Simmer for 5–10 minutes.

6 Sweat the finely chopped onion in a suitable pan, without colour. Add the garlic and the peppers.

7 Sauté the chicken in olive oil until cooked and golden brown, then drain.

8 Add the rice to the onions and garlic and sweat for 2 minutes.

9 Add about 200 ml (⅓ pint) white stock and mussel liquor.

10 Add the thyme, bay leaf and seasoning. Bring to the boil, then cover with a lightly oiled greaseproof paper and lid. Cook for 5–8 minutes, in a moderately hot oven at 180°C (Reg. 4; 350°F).

11 Add the squid and cook for another 5 minutes.

12 Add the tomatoes, chicken and lobster pieces, mussels and gambas. Stir gently, cover with a lid and reheat the rice in the oven.

13 Correct the consistency of the rice if necessary by adding more stock, so that it looks sufficiently moist without being too wet. Correct the seasoning.

14 When all is reheated and cooked, place in a suitable serving dish, decorate with 4 gambas and 4 mussels halved and shelled. Finish with wedges of lemon.

Note: For a traditional paella a raw lobster may be used, which should be prepared as follows. Remove the legs and claws and crack the claws. Cut the lobster in half crosswise, between the tail and the carapace. Cut the carapace in two lengthwise. Discard the sac. Cut across the tail in thick slices through the shell. Remove the trail, wash the lobster pieces and cook with the rice.

Fig 10.13 ✎ Paella

62 Cocido madrileno (pork with chick peas)

	4 portions	10 portions
garlic sausage or Spanish chorizo	100 g (4 oz)	250 g (10 oz)
loin of pork, boned	400 g (1 lb)	1 kg (2½ lb)
smoked bacon	50 g (2 oz)	125 g (5 oz)
chick peas (dried)	100 g (4 oz)	250 g (10 oz)
potato	100 g (4 oz)	250 g (10 oz)
carrot	100 g (4 oz)	250 g (10 oz)
onion, finely chopped	100 g (4 oz)	250 g (10 oz)
seasoning		

Using chorizo, 1 portion provides:
1424 kJ/339 kcal energy
13.3 g fat
(of which 4.7 g saturated)
21.5 g carbohydrate
(of which 4.8 g sugars)
34.6 g protein
1.3 g fibre

HEALTHY EATING TIP

Skim all the fat from the surface of the liquid after cooking the meat. No added salt is needed.

1 Cut the sausage and the pork into 1 cm (½ inch) dice, the bacon into lardons.

2 Place the sausage, bacon and pork into a large saucepan, cover with water or white stock, and add the chick peas. Bring to the boil and skim.

3 Simmer gently for 30 minutes, then add the vegetables. Add more water or white stock if necessary, season well and simmer for another hour until the meat is very tender.

4 Traditionally the broth is served first, then the vegetables and meat.

Thai cooking

Among the South-East Asian cuisines Thai owes the least to any European influences and could be described as a cross between Chinese and Indian, sharing similarities with Malaysian and Indonesian. Rice is the staple food, as in other Asian countries, and is eaten at all meals. Presentation of carved fruit and vegetables is important. The four predominant elements are hot, salty, sweet and sour. These are supplied by chillies, garlic, ginger, galangal (a relation of ginger), soya sauce, coconut, basil and lemongrass. Hampla (a sauce of fermented figs) and coriander also play a major part in the flavouring components.

1 portion provides:
395 kJ/95 kcal energy
5.8 g fat
(of which 0.9 g saturated)
0.7 g carbohydrate
(of which 0.2 g sugars)
10.0 g protein
0.1 g fibre

HEALTHY EATING TIP

No added salt is needed.
Use a little unsaturated oil to fry the fish cakes and drain on kitchen paper. Serve with plenty of fragrant Thai rice and extra vegetables.

63 Thai fish cakes

	4 portions	**10 portions**
salmon filleted and skinned	100 g (4 oz)	250 g (10 oz)
cod filleted and skinned	100 g (4 oz)	250 g (10 oz)
sesame oil	½ tsp	1¼ tsp
garlic cloves	2	5
root ginger, grated	1 tbsp	2¼ tbsp
red chillies (small)	½	1
soy sauce	1 tsp	1½ tsp
lemon grass	12 g (½ oz)	30 g (1¼ oz)
salt	2 g	5 g
pepper	2 g	5 g
lime juice	10 ml (2 tsp)	25 ml (5 tsp)
sunflower oil for cooking	10 ml (2 tsp)	25 ml (5 tsp)

1 Pass all ingredients except the oil for cooking in a food processor, blend until bound together and smooth.

2 Turn out and divide into 12 small cakes for 4 portions, 30 for 10 portions. The cakes should be at least 1 inch, 2 cm thick.

3 Heat the oil in a suitable pan, place the fish cakes in, allow approximately 3 minutes each side.

4 Serve immediately garnished with flat leaf parsley and Thai cucumber salad.

Fig 10.14 Thai fish cakes with cucumber salad

64 Thai cucumber salad

	4 portions	**10 portions**
rice or white wine vinegar	125 ml (¼ pt)	300 ml (⅝ pt)
brown sugar	40 g (2 tbsp)	100 g (5 tbsp)
cucumbers	200 g (8 oz)	500 g (1¼ lb)
shallots	4	10
chilli pepper flakes	¼ tsp	¾ tsp
cilantro or parsley chopped	1 tsp	2½ tsp

> 1 portion provides:
> 234 kJ/56 kcal energy
> 0.1 g fat
> (of which 0.0 g saturated)
> 12.7 g carbohydrate
> (of which 12.2 g sugars)
> 0.8 g protein
> 0.6 g fibre

1 In a suitable bowl, whisk together the vinegar, sugar, salt and pepper.

2 Cut the cucumber into fine slices and finely shred the shallots. Place these in a bowl with the pepper flakes, cilantro or parsley.

3 Pour over the vinegar sugar mixture, toss together, marinate for 30 minutes before serving.

Cilantro – another name for fresh coriander.

65 Barbequed tofu

	4 portions	**10 portions**
solid tofu, cubes	400 g (1 lb)	1 kg (2½ lb)
toasted ground sesame seeds	1 tbsp	2½ tbsp
spring onions chopped	3	7
garlic cloves crushed and chopped	4	10
sesame oil	30 ml (2 tbsp)	75 ml (5 tbsp)
rice wine or sake	30 ml (2 tbsp)	75 ml (5 tbsp)
maple syrup or honey	30 ml (2 tbsp)	75 ml (5 tbsp)
black pepper	2 g	5 g
soy sauce	60 ml (4 tbsp)	90 ml (10 tbsp)
broccoli florets	10	25

> Using maple syrup, 1 portion provides:
> 821 kJ/198 kcal energy
> 13.5 g fat
> (of which 1.9 g saturated)
> 7.8 g carbohydrate
> (of which 5.2 g sugars)
> 10.5 g protein
> 0.5 g fibre

HEALTHY EATING TIP

Grill the marinated tofu and serve with fragrant Thai rice and vegetables to make an interesting vegetarian dish.

1 Mix together the chopped onions, garlic, maple syrup, pepper, soy sauce, rice wine or sake and the sesame seeds until thoroughly mixed.

2 Marinate the tofu in this mixture for several hours.

3 Remove from the marinade, grill or fry the tofu.

4 Boil the marinade and serve with the tofu in individual bowls with cooked broccoli florets.

5 Serve separately on a bed of plain boiled or steamed fragrant Thai rice.

66 Chicken dumplings (approx. 50 dumplings)

Kha nom jeeb sai gai

Using stock for nam pla, vegetable oil for garlic oil, this recipe provides:
3243 kJ/775 kcal energy
27.8 g fat
(of which 3.6 g saturated)
100.6 g carbohydrate
(of which 16.5 g sugars)
30.6 g protein
1.9 g fibre

Reduce the fat by skinning the chicken and using a little unsaturated oil to fry the garlic mixture and chicken. Brush the cooked dumplings lightly with garlic oil before serving.

glutinous rice flour	3 tbsp
rice flour	250 g (10 oz) + 2 tbsp
arrowroot	3 tbsp
water	350 ml (¾ pt)
vegetable oil	2½ tbsp
banana leaves for steaming	
Filling **vegetable oil**	4 tbsp
garlic mixture	2 tbsp
minced chicken	450 g (1 lb 2 oz)
onion finely chopped	50 g (2 oz)
nam pla (fish sauce)	3 tbsp
sugar	3 tbsp
To serve **garlic oil**	1–2 tbsp
lettuce leaves	
cucumber slices	
spring onion	
vinaigrette	

1 Prepare the dough. Place the glutinous rice flour in a suitable pan with 250 g (10 oz) of rice flour and 1 tablespoon of the arrowroot. Stir in the water and oil.

2 Place over a gentle heat and cook, stirring constantly, until the mixture forms a ball, leaving the sides of the pan clean.

3 Transfer the mixture to a bowl and allow to cool slightly. When the dough is just warm, add a further 2 tablespoons of rice flour and rest of the arrowroot, knead until smooth and shiny. Cover with a damp cloth.

4 Heat 2 tablespoons of oil in a frying pan, add the garlic mixture and stir-fry for one minute.

5 Add the chicken and stir-fry for 3–5 minutes until cooked.

6 Add the onion, nam pla and sugar, cook, stirring until all the liquid has been absorbed. Place the mixture into a bowl, set aside until cold.

7 Roll the dough into small balls, about 1 cm (½ inch) in diameter, flatten each ball into a round.

8 Place approximately 1 teaspoon of filling into the centre of each round.

9 Draw up the sides to enclose the filling in an onion shape. Alternatively, place the filling on one half of each dough round, and fold the remaining halves over to form semi-circles. Crimp the edges.

10 Place a layer of torn banana leaves in the top of a bamboo steamer. Brush the leaves with oil and prick them all over with a fork.

11 Arrange the dumplings on top of the leaves. Steam for 10–15 minutes until cooked.

12 To serve, brush the dumplings generously with garlic oil. Serve with lettuce, cucumber and onion salad.

67 Garlic mixture

Kru tium prig tai

This is an essential ingredient in many Thai dishes.

crushed garlic	2 tbsp
chopped coriander root or stem	2 tbsp
ground black pepper	½ tbsp

Pound all ingredients together to form a smooth paste.

This mixture may be made in advance and stored in the refrigerator.

68 Fish sauce

Nam pla

This is a commercially prepared bottle sauce made from anchovies, similar to anchovy essence. It is widely used in Thai cooking to accentuate the flavours of other ingredients, rather than impart its own 'fishy' flavour.

69 Thai pork spare ribs

Seeh krong mhoo

	4 portions	10 portions
pork spare ribs	400 g (1 lb)	1 kg (2½ lb)
garlic mixture	2 tbsp	5 tbsp
salt		
dark soy sauce	2 tbsp	5 tbsp
ground ginger	1 tsp	2½ tsp
brown sugar	1 tbsp	2½ tbsp
honey	2 tbsp	5 tbsp

Using stock sauce for nam pla, canned bamboo shoots used, 1 portion provides:
913 kJ/218 kcal energy
9.8 g fat
(of which 3.5 g saturated)
18.1 g carbohydrate
(of which 16.7 g sugars)
15.7 g protein
0.2 g fibre

1 Mix all the ingredients together.

2 Place the spare ribs in a suitable dish, pour over the ingredients, mix well so that they are well coated. Allow to marinate for at least 2 hours.

3 Bake the spare ribs with the marinade in a moderate oven 180°C (350°F) until well cooked for approximately 1 hour.

4 Serve immediately.

HEALTHY EATING TIP

No added salt is needed. Drain off the fat from the cooked spare ribs and serve with plenty of rice and vegetables.

Using stock for nam pla, 1 portion
provides:
1697 kJ/401 kcal energy
9.3 g fat
(of which 1.7 g saturated)
69.8 g carbohydrate
(of which 6.8 g sugars)
13.9 g protein
2.8 g fibre

HEALTHY EATING TIP

No added salt is
needed.
Use a small amount of
unsaturated oil to fry
the beef and drain off
any excess fat.

70 Thai spicy fried rice

Khow bhud khie mau

	4 portions	10 portions
minced beef	100 g (4 oz)	250 g (10 oz)
red kidney beans (cooked)	100 g (4 oz)	250 g (10 oz)
nam pla	1½ tbsp	3 tbsp
dark soy sauce	1 tbsp	2½ tbsp
red chillies, seeded and finely chopped	4	10
cloves of garlic crushed and chopped	3	7
vegetable oil	2 tbsp	5 tbsp
green beans cut into 1 cm (½ inch) lengths	10	25
cooked Thai rice	750 g (1 lb 8 oz)	1.875 kg (3 lb 12 oz)
sugar	1 tbsp	2½ tbsp
salt	½ tsp	1¼ tsp
fresh basil or mint leaves		

1 Combine the minced beef and kidney beans in a shallow dish. Stir in the nam pla and soy sauce. Cover and set aside for 30 minutes to allow flavours to blend.

2 In a small basin, mix the chillies, garlic and salt together.

3 Heat the oil in a wok, add the chilli mixture and stir-fry for 1 minute.

4 Add the beef mixture, cook, stirring continuously for 3 minutes. Add the green beans and stir-fry for 3 minutes more.

5 Stir in the rice and sugar, stir until the rice is well heated through. *Check core temperature 72°C.* Make sure all the ingredients are thoroughly mixed. Correct seasoning.

6 Serve in a suitable dish, garnish with basil or mint leaves.

71 Thai pork with chilli and basil

Bhud prig noh mai

Using stock for nam pla, 1 portion provides:
493 kJ/119 kcal energy
8.1 g fat
(of which 1.5 g saturated)
2.7 g carbohydrate
(of which 2.1 g sugars)
8.9 g protein
0.7 g fibre

	4 portions	**10 portions**
vegetable oil	2 tbsp	5 tbsp
clove garlic crushed and chopped	1	3
chillies finely chopped	2	5
pork fillet thinly sliced	150 g (6 oz)	375 g (15 oz)
ground black pepper		
nam pla	1 tbsp	2½ tbsp
sugar	½ tsp	1¼ tsp
bamboo shoots – shredded	50 g (2 oz)	125 g (5 oz)
onion finely chopped	50 g (2 oz)	125 g (5 oz)
green pepper de-seeded and finely shredded	½	1
chicken stock or water	4 tbsp	10 tbsp
fresh basil leaves chopped	4 tbsp	10 tbsp

HEALTHY EATING TIP

Use less unsaturated vegetable oil to fry the pork.
Serve with plenty of steamed Thai rice and vegetables.

1 Heat the oil in a wok. Add the garlic and chilli and stir-fry until the garlic is golden.

2 Add the pork, pepper, nam pla and sugar, stirring constantly.

3 Stir in the bamboo shoots with the onion, green pepper and stock.

4 Cook for approximately 5 minutes. Stir in the basil leaves and cook for a further minute. Season with black pepper.

5 Serve immediately with steamed Thai rice.

Variations

In place of pork, use fillet or rump steak, chicken breast, ostrich or shelled prawns. If bamboo shoots are omitted, the dish is called Bhud kra prau.

72 Thai mussaman curry

Using oyster sauce for shrimp paste, glaze = stock
reduced, tamarind pulp diluted for liquid, 1 portion
provides:
1977 kJ/475 kcal energy
33.2 g fat
(of which 18.1 g saturated)
19.4 g carbohydrate
(of which 9.7 g sugars)
26.9 g protein
1.8 g fibre

	4 portions	10 portions
Curry paste		
cayenne pepper	¾ tsp	2 tsp
ground coriander	1 tbsp	2½ tbsp
ground cumin	½ tsp	1½ tsp
ground cinnamon	½ tsp	1½ tsp
whole green cardamoms	2	4½
lemon, grated rind	½	1½
vegetable oil	1 tbsp	2½ tbsp
onion, finely chopped	75 g (3 oz)	187 g (7½ oz)
cloves garlic, crushed and chopped	3	7
dried shrimp paste	¼ tsp	¾ tsp

1 Place all spices and lemon rind together in a suitable bowl.
2 Lightly fry the onion and garlic in the oil until cooked but not coloured.
3 Add the shrimp paste and stir well.
4 Place in a liquidiser with the spices and 3 tablespoons cold water. Blend until smooth.

	4 portions	10 portions
shoulder or loin of lamb, diced	400 g (1 lb)	1 kg (2½ lb)
diced potatoes	200 g (8 oz)	500 g (1¼ lb)
creamed coconut	175 g (7 oz)	400 g (1 lb)
hot water	500 ml (1 pt)	1½ litre (2½ pt)
fish glaze	1 tbsp	2 tbsp
whole green cardamoms	8	20
cinnamon stick	½	1¼
tamarind liquid	5 tsp	12 tsp
lemon, juice of	½	1
caster sugar	12 g (½ oz)	30 g (1¼ oz)
roasted peanuts	50 g (2 oz)	125 g (5 oz)

1 Fry the lamb quickly in vegetable oil to a golden brown colour.
2 Place the lamb in a saucepan with the potatoes, coconut milk, fish glaze, cardamoms and cinnamon and bring slowly to the boil, stirring continuously.
3 Allow to simmer for one hour.
4 Stir in the curry paste, tamarind liquid, lemon juice and sugar. Simmer for a further 5 minutes.
5 Serve garnished with roasted peanuts.

USA cooking

It is not easy to encompass all that can be classed as American cookery, as it is an amalgam of the waves of immigrants who went there seeking a better way of life than that of their mother country. These people had to adopt their styles of cooking to the conditions that prevailed where they settled but kept to the basis that it

HEALTHY EATING TIP
Use very little unsaturated oil to fry the onion for the curry paste.
Drain any fat from the fried lamb and skim all fat from the cooked sauce. Serve with plenty of rice and vegetables to 'dilute' the fat.

Fig 10.15 Preparation of Caesar salad

Indigenous cooking has grown up in which dishes developed from forgotten cultures, simply inspired by local ingredients, have developed. The style of cooking sometimes referred to as Tex Mex, using beans, chilli pepper and corn pancakes, and corn chips with avocado pear as basic ingredients, is typical of this development.

73 Caesar salad

Using toast for croûtons, 1 portion provides:
1494 kJ/361 kcal energy
32.2 g fat
(of which 7.9 g saturated)
5.1 g carbohydrate
(of which 2.0 g sugars)
12.9 g protein
1.2 g fibre

	4 portions	10 portions
cos lettuce (medium size)	2	4
croûtons 2 cm (1 inch) square	16	40
eggs, fresh	2	4
garlic, finely chopped	1 tsp	2 tsp
anchovy fillets, mashed	4	8
lemon juice	1	2
virgin olive oil	6 tbsp	15 tbsp
white wine vinegar	1 tbsp	2 tbsp
salt, black mill pepper		
Parmesan, freshly grated	75 g (3 oz)	150 g (6 oz)

(garlic, finely chopped through salt, black mill pepper bracketed as *dressing*)

is still possible to find communities with what are now regional specialities but which were originally alien.

The major influences may have been Dutch, French, English and native Indian but almost every other nationality in the world is now represented in the USA, and in addition to Creole and Cajun in the deep south there are Spanish, Mexican, Jewish, German, Swiss, Scandinavian, Chinese, Japanese and many other forms of cookery included in the basic American mode of living, but very much more noticeable in the places where these people live.

America is the world's greatest producer of foods thus allowing a very interesting and widely varied menu and many good dishes are accepted as international favourites.

continued over ▶

▶ *Caesar salad continued*

HEALTHY EATING TIP

No added salt is needed; anchovies and cheese are high in salt. Oven bake the croûtons and serve with fresh bread or rolls.

1 Separate the lettuce leaves, wash, dry thoroughly and refrigerate.

2 Lightly grill or fry (in good fresh oil) the croûtons on all sides.

3 Plunge the eggs into boiling water for one minute, remove and set aside.

4 Break the lettuce into serving pieces and place into a salad bowl.

5 Mix the dressing, break the eggs, spoon out the contents, mix with a fork, add to the dressing and mix into the salad.

6 Mix in the cheese, scatter the croûtons on top and serve.

Note: Because of the lightly cooked eggs they must be perfectly fresh and the salad must be prepared and served immediately.

In the interests of food safety, the eggs are sometimes hard boiled.

Alternatively the salad may be garnished with hard boiled gull's eggs.

74 Chilli con carne (beef with beans in chilli sauce)

Originally from Texas and Mexico, chilli con carne is now eaten throughout the United States.

---

1 portion provides:
1741 kJ/414 kcal energy
18.9 g fat
(of which 3.1 g saturated)
28.0 g carbohydrate
(of which 6.2 g sugars)
35.7 g protein
9.1 g fibre

---

	4 portions	10 portions
dried kidney beans or pinto beans	200 g (8 oz)	500 g (1¼ lb)
lean topside of beef	400 g (1 lb)	1 kg (2½ lb)
sunflower oil	60 ml (⅛ pt)	150 ml (⅓ pt)
onions, finely chopped	100 g (4 oz)	250 g (10 oz)
cloves garlic, crushed and chopped	2	5
chilli powder	2 tsp	5 tsp
oregano	1 tsp	2–3 tsp
ground cumin	½ tsp	1 tsp
tomato purée	50 g (2 oz)	125 g (5 oz)
tomatoes, skinned, de-seeded, diced	200 g (8 oz)	500 g (1¼ lb)
white or brown stock	500 ml (1 pt)	1¼ litre (2½ pt)

HEALTHY EATING TIP

Lightly oil the pan using an unsaturated oil. Drain all fat from the cooked beef. Adding more beans and serving with rice and extra vegetables will 'dilute' the fat.

1 Soak the beans in cold water for 24 hours. Drain, cover with cold water and bring to the boil. Boil for 10 minutes then gently simmer until tender.

2 Prepare the beef by removing all the excess fat and cutting into batons 5 cm (2 inches) long × ½ cm (¼ inch) wide or mincing.

3 Heat a little of the oil in a frying pan and quickly fry the beef until golden brown.

4 Drain the beef, place in a suitable saucepan.

5 Add a little more oil to the frying pan, add the onions and garlic and quickly fry until a light golden colour.

6 Stir in the chilli powder, oregano and cumin and cook for a further 3 minutes. Add to the beef.

7 Stir in the tomato purée, tomatoes and seasoning, and cover with white or brown stock.

8 Gently cook by simmering on the stove or cover and cook in a moderate oven at 180°C (Reg. 4; 350°F) for 1½–2 hours.

9 Check constantly to make sure that the meat does not become too dry. Add a little more stock or water if necessary.

10 Drain the cooked beans and add to the cooked beef.

11 Serve in an earthenware dish sprinkled with chopped parsley.

Note: This dish must be quite moist, the consistency of a stew. Chilli powders and chilli seasonings vary in strength, therefore the amount used may be varied.

75 Hash brown potatoes

1 portion provides:
954 kJ/228 kcal energy
11.3 g fat
(of which 5.3 g saturated)
25.8 g carbohydrate
(of which 0.9 g sugars)
7.1 g protein
2.0 g fibre

	4 portions	10 portions
potatoes	600 g (1½ lb)	2 kg (4 lb)
butter or margarine	25 g (1 oz)	60 g (2½ oz)
lardons of bacon	100 g (4 oz)	250 g (10 oz)
seasoning		

HEALTHY EATING TIP

Dry fry the lardons in a well-seasoned pan. Brush a little oil over the potatoes and cook in a hot oven. Use a minimum amount of salt.

1 Wash, peel and rewash the potatoes.

2 Coarsely grate the potatoes, rewash quickly and then drain well.

3 Melt the butter in a suitable frying pan. Add the lardons of bacon, fry until crisp and brown, remove from the pan and drain.

4 Pour the fat back into the frying pan, add the grated potato and season.

5 Press down well, allow 2 cm (1 inch) thickness, and cook over a heat for 10–15 minutes or in a moderate oven at 190°C (Reg. 5; 190°C) until a brown crust forms on the bottom.

6 Turn out onto a suitable serving dish and sprinkle with the lardons of bacon and chopped parsley.

76 Clam chowder
(See page 87)

A chowder is usually an unpassed shellfish soup. It originated in the USA where there are many regional variations. Clams, oysters, scallops and fresh or frozen crabs may be used.

77 Succotash (butter beans, sweetcorn and bacon in cream sauce)

1 portion provides:
1157 kJ/277 kcal energy
15.3 g fat
(of which 7.9 g saturated)
25.6 g carbohydrate
(of which 2.8 g sugars)
10.7 g protein
5.4 g fibre

	4 portions	10 portions
lardons of bacon	50 g (2 oz)	125 g (5 oz)
butter or margarine	25 g (1 oz)	60 g (2½ oz)
butter beans, cooked	350 g (14 oz)	1 kg (2 lb)
sweetcorn, cooked	150 g (6 oz)	375 g (15 oz)
cream sauce	125 ml (¼ pt)	300 ml (⅝ pt)
seasoning		
single cream (or yoghurt)	60 ml (⅛ pt)	150 ml (⅓ pt)

continued over ▶

▶ *Succotash continued*

Dry fry the lardons in a well-seasoned pan and drain off the excess fat. Add a minimum amount of salt. Serve with starchy carbohydrate to 'dilute' the fat.

1   Quickly fry the lardons of bacon in the fat.

2   Add the drained butter beans and sweetcorn.

3   Bind with cream sauce, correct the seasoning and finish with cream.

4   Serve in a suitable dish sprinkled with chopped parsley.

78   Pecan pie

1 portion provides:
4178 kJ/1001 kcal energy
65.0 g fat
(of which 19.8 g saturated)
97.2 g carbohydrate
(of which 93.3 g sugars)
13.0 g protein
2.9 g fibre

	4 portions	10 portions
sweet pastry	150 g (6 oz)	375 g (15 oz)
eggs	3	7–8
soft brown sugar	200 g (8 oz)	500 g (1¼ lb)
vanilla essence		
pinch of salt		
melted butter or margarine	75 g (3 oz)	180 g (7½ oz)
treacle syrup	6 tbsp	15 tbsp
coarsely chopped pecan nuts	200 g (8 oz)	500 g (1¼ lb)

1   Line an 18–20 cm (7–8 inch) flan ring with the sweet pastry and partly bake blind.

2   Prepare the filling from the remaining ingredients. Lightly heat the eggs and sugar together with the vanilla essence and salt.

3   Stir in the melted butter or margarine and syrup, and add the chopped pecan nuts.

4   Pour this mixture into the flan case and decorate with pecan halves.

5   Bake in a moderately hot oven at 180°C (Reg. 4; 350°F) for 30–35 minutes until the filling is set. Cover with aluminium foil if the pastry starts to get too dark.

6   Serve with cream, ice-cream or yoghurt.

Fig 10.16   Pecan pie   *Yolande Stanley*

Vegetarian dishes

Asparagus wrapped in puff pastry
with Gruyère cheese
John Campbell

Mexican bean pot and salad
John Campbell

Polenta and lentil cakes with
roasted vegetables, cucumber
and yoghurt sauce
John Campbell

Vegetarian

The professional chef today has to cater for a much wider, discerning clientele. This includes being able to produce exciting, well balanced vegetarian dishes for a growing vegetarian market. Vegetarian cookery can, with imagination and creativity, be as interesting in ingredient usage and presentation as many of the other styles of cookery.

Vegetarians and vegans do not eat fish, meat, poultry or game and vegans in addition do not consume milk, dairy products and eggs.

1 Chinese-style stir-fry vegetables

	4 portions	**10 portions**
beansprouts	100 g (4 oz)	250 g (10 oz)
button mushrooms	100 g (4 oz)	250 g (10 oz)
carrots	100 g (4 oz)	250 g (10 oz)
celery	100 g (4 oz)	250 g (10 oz)
cauliflower	100 g (4 oz)	250 g (10 oz)
broccoli	100 g (4 oz)	250 g (10 oz)
baby sweetcorn	50 g (2 oz)	125 g (5 oz)
French beans	50 g (2 oz)	125 g (5 oz)
red peppers	50 g (2 oz)	125 g (5 oz)
green peppers	50 g (2 oz)	125 g (5 oz)
sunflower oil	125 ml (¼ pt)	300 ml (⅝ pt)
grated root ginger	5 g (¼ oz)	12 g (⅝ oz)
soy sauce	60 ml (⅛ pt)	150 ml (⅓ pt)
ground white or mill pepper to season		

1 portion provides:
1429 kJ/340 kcal
31.9 g fat
(of which 4.2 g saturated)
9.1 g carbohydrate
(of which 4.2 g sugars)
4.7 g protein
4.5 g fibre

HEALTHY EATING TIP

No additional salt is needed; flavour from soy sauce, ginger and pepper. Use a smaller amount of sunflower oil. Serve with a large portion of rice or noodles.

1 Wash the beansprouts, wash and slice the mushrooms. Peel the carrots, cut into large batons. Trim the celery, cut into large batons. Wash the cauliflower and broccoli and cut into florets. Top and tail the French beans, cut in halves. Wash and slice the peppers. The green vegetables may be quickly blanched and refreshed to retain colour.

2 Heat the sunflower oil in a wok or frying pan and add all the vegetables. Fry and continuously stir for approximately 3 minutes.

3 Add the grated ginger, cook for 1 minute. Add the soy sauce, stir well.

4 Correct the seasoning, serve immediately.

Fig 11.1 ✐ Preparation of Chinese-style stir-fry vegetables

HEALTHY EATING TIP

Use a little unsaturated oil (sunflower or olive) to sweat the mushrooms and shallots. Try using half cream and half yoghurt for the sauce. Use a minimum amount of salt.

2 Courgette moulds with mushrooms served with a white wine sauce

	4 portions	10 portions
mushrooms	300 g (12 oz)	750 g (1 lb 14 oz)
butter	25 g (1 oz)	62 g (2½ oz)
shallots, finely chopped	25 g (1 oz)	62 g (2½ oz)
chopped fresh thyme	½ tsp	1¼ tsp
large courgettes	2	5
white wine	250 ml (½ pt)	625 ml (1¼ pt)
double cream	250 ml (½ pt)	625 ml (1¼ pt)
lemon juice	½ lemon	1
seasoning salt/pepper		
garnish		
tomatoes skinned, de-seeded and diced	2	5
asparagus tips	8	20

1 Place the butter into a suitable sized pan, add the mushrooms, shallots and thyme. Sweat together until cooked. Make sure all the liquid has evaporated.

2 Cut the courgettes into long thin strips using a potato peeler or a mandoline. Blanch in boiling water for 1 minute. Remove, drain on a cloth.

3 Lightly oil dariole moulds or ramekins and line with the courgettes. Place one strip across the centre of the mould then add another three, working around the mould so that the sides are completely covered.

4 Add the white wine to the mushroom mixture and reduce by half. Add the cream and cook for a further 5 minutes until thickened. Season.

5 Strain the mushroom mixture, retaining the liquid (this forms the basis of the sauce).

6 Place the liquid in a clean saucepan, then add the lemon juice.

7 Divide the mushroom mixture between the courgette moulds. Fold the courgettes over the top. Press down.

8 Turn the moulds onto clean plates, mask with the sauce, garnish with warm tomato concassée and hot steamed asparagus tips.

Courgette moulds may also be filled with cooked risotto, page 162. The risotto may be garnished with cooked, diced mushroom and cooked diced red, yellow, green pimentos. Serve with a fresh tomato sauce.

3 Caribbean fruit curry

Using single cream, 1 portion provides:
1729 kJ/412 kcal
19.6 g fat
(of which 6.1 g saturated)
57.2 g carbohydrate
(of which 51.6 g sugars)
5.4 g protein
8.3 g fibre

	4 portions	10 portions
pineapple	1 small	1 large
small dessert pears	2	5
dessert apples	2	5
mangoes	2	5
bananas	2	5
paw paw	1	2–3
guava	1	2–3
grated rind and juice of lime	1	2–3
onion, chopped	50 g (2 oz)	125 g (5 oz)
sunflower margarine	25 g (1 oz)	60 g (2½ oz)
sunflower oil	60 ml (⅛ pt)	150 ml (⅓ pt)
Madras curry powder	50 g (2 oz)	125 g (5 oz)
wholemeal flour	25 g (1 oz)	60 g (2½ oz)
fresh grated ginger	10 g (½ oz)	25 g (1 oz)
desiccated coconut	50 g (2 oz)	125 g (5 oz)
tomato, skinned, de-seeded and diced	100 g (4 oz)	250 g (10 oz)
tomato purée	25 g (1 oz)	60 g (2½ oz)
sultanas	50 g (2 oz)	125 g (5 oz)
fruit juice	½ litre (1 pt)	1¼ litre (2½ pt)
yeast extract	5 g (¼ oz)	12 g (⅝ oz)
cashew nuts	50 g (2 oz)	125 g (5 oz)
single cream or smetana	60 ml (⅛ pt)	150 ml (⅓ pt)

HEALTHY EATING TIP

Lightly oil a well-seasoned pan with the sunflower oil to fry the onion.
No added salt is needed.
Try finishing the dish with low fat yoghurt in place of the cream.
Serve with plenty of starchy carbohydrate and salad.

1 Skin, cut the pineapple in half, remove the tough centre. Cut in 1 cm (½ inch) chunks. Peel the apples and pears, remove the cores, cut into 1 cm (½ inch) pieces. Peel and slice the mangoes. Skin and cut the bananas into 1 cm (½ inch) pieces. Cut the guavas and paw paws in half, remove the seeds, peel, dice into 1 cm (½ inch) pieces. Marinate the fruit in lime juice.

2 Fry the onion in the sunflower margarine and oil until lightly brown, add the curry powder, sweat together, add the wholemeal flour and cook for 2 minutes.

3 Add the ginger, coconut, tomato concassé, tomato purée and sultanas.

4 Gradually add sufficient boiling fruit juice to make a light sauce.

5 Add yeast extract, stir well. Simmer for 10 minutes.

6 Add the fruit and cashew nuts, stir carefully, allow to heat through.

7 Finish with cream or smetana.

8 Serve in a suitable dish; separately serve poppadums, wholegrain pilaff rice and a green salad.

1 portion provides:
2135 kJ/514 kcal energy
41.8 g fat
(of which 15.5 g saturated)
29.5 g carbohydrate
(of which 2.0 g sugars)
8.4 g protein
0.9 g fibre

HEALTHY EATING TIP

Use a little unsaturated oil (e.g. sunflower) to sweat the onion and garlic. Try using half cream and half fromage frais to finish the sauce. Serve the Hollandaise sauce separately and add a large portion of mixed leaves and herbs.

4 Mushrooms en croûte with Madeira served with Hollandaise sauce

	4 portions	10 portions
puff pastry	400 g (1 lb)	1 kg (2¼ lb)
eggwash		
Parmesan cheese	25 g (1 oz)	62 g (2½ oz)
dried porcini mushrooms	25 g (1 oz)	62 g (2½ oz)
fresh oyster mushrooms **trumpet mushrooms** **chestnut mushrooms**	200 g (8 oz)	500 g (1 lb)
Madeira wine, dry	125 ml (¼ pt)	312 ml (⅝ pt)
finely chopped onion	50 g (2 oz)	125 g (5 oz)
butter	25 g (1 oz)	62 g (2½ oz)
crushed chopped cloves of garlic	3	7
flour	25 g (1 oz)	62 g (2½ oz)
chopped fresh thyme	½ tsp	1¼ tsp
double cream	62 ml (⅛ pt)	155 ml (⅜ pt)
seasoning salt/pepper		
nutmeg		
hollandaise sauce	125 ml (¼ pt)	312 ml (⅝ pt)

1 Re-constitute the dried mushrooms in 275 ml (approximately ½ pt) boiling water for 25 g (1 oz); or 680 ml (2½ oz), for approximately 30 minutes.

2 Roll out the puff pastry to prepare either square or round vol au vents, approximately 8 cm (3 inch) round or squares.

3 Turn upside down on a lightly greased, dampened baking sheet.

4 Using a small cutter dipped in hot oil, make incisions half way through each, leaving approximately ½ cm (¼ inch) border.

5 Eggwash, rest for 20 minutes, sprinkle with Parmesan cheese and bake in a hot oven at 200°C (400°F) for approximately 15–20 minutes.

6 Remove from oven, allow to cool, remove lids carefully using a sharp knife, empty out the pastry from the centre. Keep the lids.

7 To make the mushroom filling, melt the butter in a suitable saucepan, add the chopped onion and garlic, sweat without colour. Add the flour. Stir well.

8 Add the chopped fresh mushrooms and the soaked mushrooms, roughly chopped.

9 Stir in the water the mushrooms have been soaked in. Stir well.

10 Season lightly with salt, pepper and nutmeg. Add the thyme.

11 Add the Madeira. Cover with a tight fitting lid and allow to cook slowly for approximately 1½ hours, simmering very gently. Stir from time to time, making sure the liquid has not evaporated. Finish with the cream.

12 To serve, place on suitable plates. Fill the vol au vents with the mushroom mixture. Replace the lids. Mask with a little hollandaise sauce, garnish with fresh basil. Serve hollandaise sauce separately.

5 Bean goulash

	4 portions	10 portions
red kidney or haricot beans	200 g (8 oz)	500 g (1¼ lb)
sunflower oil	60 ml (⅛ pt)	150 ml (⅓ pt)
onion, finely chopped	50 g (2 oz)	125 g (5 oz)
clove garlic, crushed	1	2–3
paprika	25 g (1 oz)	60 g (2½ oz)
red peppers	2	5
green pepper	1	2–3
yellow pepper	1	2–3
sliced button mushrooms	200 g (8 oz)	500 g (1¼ lb)
tomato purée	50 g (2 oz)	125 g (5 oz)
vegetable stock	750 ml (1½ pt)	2 litre (4 pt)
bouquet garni		
seasoning		
small turned potatoes (cooked)	8	20

1 portion provides:
1728 kJ/411 kcal
17.9 g fat
(of which 2.7 g saturated)
50.0 g carbohydrate
(of which 7.3 g sugars)
17.3 g protein
18.5 g fibre

HEALTHY EATING TIP

Use less sunflower oil to sweat the onions. Add a pinch of salt. Serve with rice or noodles and a green salad or mixed vegetables.

1 Soak the beans for 24 hours in cold water. Drain, place into a saucepan. Cover with cold water, bring to the boil and simmer until tender.

2 Heat the oil in a sauté pan, sweat the onion and garlic without colour for 2–3 minutes and add the paprika; sweat for a further 2–3 minutes.

3 Add the peppers, cut in halves, remove seeds and cut into 1 cm (½ inch) dice. Add the button mushrooms; sweat for a further 2 minutes.

4 Add the tomato purée, vegetable stock and bouquet garni. Bring to the boil and simmer until the pepper and mushrooms are cooked.

5 Remove the bouquet garni. Add the drained cooked beans, correct seasoning and stir.

6 Garnish with potatoes or gnocchi and chopped parsley.

7 Serve wholegrain pilaff or wholemeal noodles separately.

Fig 11.2 Bean goulash

1 portion provides:
344 kJ/83 kcal energy
5.9 g fat
(of which 0.6 g saturated)
2.6 g carbohydrate
(of which 0.8 g sugars)
4.9 g protein
1.8 g fibre

Use a minimum amount of salt.

6 Broccoli sauce

	4 portions	10 portions
cooked broccoli	200 g (8 oz)	500 g (1¼ lb)
sunflower seeds	40 g (1½ oz)	100 g (4 oz)
smetana or silken tofu (page 640)	125 ml (¼ pt)	300 ml (⅝ pt)
lemon, juice of	½	1–1½
seasoning		

1 Place the broccoli, sunflower seeds and approximately 500 ml (½ pint) of water into a liquidiser with the smetana and lemon juice. Liquidise until smooth.

2 Strain through a coarse strainer into a small saucepan. Correct the seasoning and consistency.

3 Heat *very* gently before serving. *Do not boil.*

1 portion provides:
1904 kJ/458 kcal energy
33.6 g fat
(of which 12.1 g saturated)
23.8 g carbohydrate
(of which 0.7 g sugars)
16.5 g protein
1.0 g fibre

No additional salt is needed as cheese is added.

7 Gougère

Choux pastry (page 567)

	4 portions	10 portions
water	250 ml (½ pt)	625 ml (1¼ pt)
sunflower margarine	100 g (4 oz)	250 g (10 oz)
strong flour	125 g (5 oz)	300 g (12½ oz)
eggs (medium)	4	10
Gruyère cheese, diced	75 g (3 oz)	180 g (7½ oz)
seasoning		

1 Make the choux pastry, cool and add the finely diced Gruyère cheese.

2 With a 1 cm (½ inch) plain tube, pipe individual rings approximately 8 cm (3 inches) diameter on to a very lightly greased baking sheet.

3 Brush lightly with eggwash and relax for approximately 15 minutes.

4 Bake in a preheated oven at 190°C (Reg. 5; 375°F) for 20 to 30 minutes.

5 When cooked, place on individual plates. Fill the centre with a suitable filling, such as:

- ratatouille
- stir-fry vegetables
- cauliflower cheese
- button mushrooms in a tomato and garlic sauce
- leaf spinach with chopped onions in a béchamel sauce
- button mushrooms and sweetcorn in a béchamel yoghurt sauce.

8 Courgette and potato cakes with mint and feta cheese

	6 portions
courgettes	3 large
potatoes	350 g (14 oz)
chopped fresh mint	2 tbsp
feta cheese	200 g (8 oz)
spring onions, finely chopped	2
eggs	1
plain flour	25 g (1 oz)
butter	25 g (1 oz)
olive oil	1 tbsp
seasoning salt/pepper	

1 portion provides:
910 kJ/219 kcal energy
13.6 g fat
(of which 7.4 g saturated)
15.4 g carbohydrate
(of which 2.4 g sugars)
9.5 g protein
1.6 g fibre

HEALTHY EATING TIP

Make sure the puréed courgettes are rinsed well to remove the added salt. Use a little sunflower oil to brush the cakes before cooking.

1 Lightly scrape the courgettes to remove the outside skin. Place in a food processor to purée. Remove, sprinkle with salt to remove the excess moisture, leave for 1 hour. Rinse under cold water, squeeze out all excess moisture, dry on a clean cloth.

2 Steam or par-boil the potatoes for 8–10 minutes. Cool and peel.

3 Carefully grate the potatoes, place in a bowl, then season.

4 Add the courgettes, mint, spring onion, chopped feta cheese and the beaten egg. Mix well.

5 Divide the mixture into 6, shape into cakes approximately 1 cm (½ inch) thick.

6 Dust with flour.

7 Brush the cakes with melted butter and oil, place on a baking sheet, cook in an oven 200°C (400°F) for 15 minutes, turn over, continue to cook for a further 15 minutes.

8 Serve on suitable plates garnished with fresh blanched mint leaves and a salsa verde.

1 portion provides:
2017 kJ/485 kcal energy
37.7 g fat
(of which 15.0 g saturated)
23.4 g carbohydrate
(of which 2.5 g sugars)
15.9 g protein
0.8 g fibre

HEALTHY EATING TIP

The puff pastry and cheese make this dish high in fat. Serve with plenty of starchy carbohydrate to 'dilute' the fat.

9 Asparagus wrapped in puff pastry with Gruyère

	4 portions	10 portions
puff pastry (page 564)	350 g (14 oz)	875 g (2 lb 3 oz)
eggwash or milk for brushing		
freshly cooked asparagus	350 g (14 oz)	875 g (2 lb 3 oz)
Gruyère cheese	175 g (7 oz)	400 g (1 lb)
freshly grated Parmesan	3 tbsp	7 tbsp
crème fraîche	250 ml (½ pt)	625 ml (1¼ pt)
seasoning salt/pepper		
watercress for garnish		

1   Cut the Gruyère cheese into 1 cm (½ inch) dice. In a suitable bowl, mix the Parmesan cheese, crème fraîche and season.

2   Roll out the puff pastry to approximately ¼ cm (⅛ inch) thick, cut into squares approximately 18 × 18 cm (7 × 7 inches).

3   Brush the edges with eggwash or milk.

4   Divide the crème fraîche onto the centre of each square. Lay the asparagus on top. Place the diced Gruyère cheese firmly between the asparagus.

5   Fold the opposite corners of each square to meet in the centre like an envelope. Firmly pinch the seams together to seal them. Make a small hole in the centre of each one to allow the steam to escape. Place on a lightly greased baking sheet.

6   Allow to relax for 20 minutes in the refrigerator. Brush with eggwash or milk, sprinkle with Parmesan.

7   Bake in a hot oven 200°C (400°F) for approximately 20–25 minutes until golden brown.

8   Serve garnished with watercress.

Fig 11.3 🖊 Asparagus wrapped in puff pastry with Gruyère
John Campbell

10 Meatless shepherd's pie

	4 portions	10 portions
lentils	100 g (4 oz)	250 g (10 oz)
vegetable stock	500 ml (1 pt)	1¼ litre (2½ pt)
textured vegetable protein (TVP) mince, natural flavour	100 g (4 oz)	250 g (10 oz)
onions, finely chopped	100 g (4 oz)	250 g (10 oz)
dried mixed herbs	3 g (⅛ oz)	8 g (⅛ oz)
sunflower margarine	50 g (2 oz)	125 g (5 oz)
wholemeal flour	25 g (1 oz)	60 g (2½ oz)
tomato purée	50 g (2 oz)	125 g (5 oz)
yeast extract	10 g (½ oz)	25 g (1 oz)
seasoning		
drops Worcester sauce	2–3	5–6
duchess potatoes (page 469)	500 g (1 lb)	1¼ kg (2½ lb)
grated Cheddar cheese	50 g (2 oz)	125 g (5 oz)

1 portion provides:
2198 kJ/523 kcal
22.3 g fat
(of which 6.0 g saturated)
54.3 g carbohydrate
(of which 4.9 g sugars)
29.9 g protein
7.5 g fibre

HEALTHY EATING TIP

Use a small amount of unsaturated oil to sweat the onions. No added salt; plenty in the yeast extract, Worcester sauce and cheese. Serve with a selection of colourful vegetables.

1 Cook the lentils in the vegetable stock.

2 Reconstitute the TVP by soaking in cold water for the recommended time according to the manufacturer's instructions.

3 Sweat the onion and mixed herbs in the margarine without colour.

4 Stir in the wholemeal flour and cook out for 1–2 minutes.

5 Add the TVP and vegetable stock from the lentils, simmer for 10 minutes.

6 Mix in the lentils, tomato purée and yeast extract.

7 Correct the seasoning and consistency, add 2–3 drops of Worcester sauce to taste.

8 Place this mixture into a pie dish; allow to cool.

9 Pipe the duchess potato on top using a star tube.

10 Sprinkle with the grated Cheddar cheese.

11 Bake in a preheated oven at 180°C (Reg. 4; 350°F) for approximately 20 minutes until golden brown.

Note: In place of the TVP a selection of freshly diced blanched vegetables may be used or twice the amount of lentils.

1 portion provides:
672 kJ/161 kcal
1.2 g fat
(of which 0.2 g saturated)
27.0 g carbohydrate
(of which 4.6 g sugars)
12.3 g protein
14.0 g fibre

HEALTHY EATING TIP
No added salt is needed; plenty in the yeast extract. Serve with a selection of colourful vegetables.

11 Mexican bean pot

	4 portions	10 portions
dry red beans or haricot beans	300 g (12 oz)	1 kg (2 lb)
onions, finely chopped	100 g (4 oz)	250 g (10 oz)
carrots, sliced	100 g (4 oz)	250 g (10 oz)
tomato, skinned, de-seeded and diced	200 g (8 oz)	500 g (1¼ lb)
cloves garlic, crushed and chopped	2	5
paprika	10 g (½ oz)	25 g (1 oz)
dried marjoram	3 g (⅛ oz)	9 g (⅓ oz)
small fresh chilli, finely chopped	1	2–3
small red pepper, finely diced	1	2–3
yeast extract	5 g (¼ oz)	12 g (⅝ oz)
chopped chives		
seasoning		

1 Soak the beans in cold water for 24 hours, drain. Place into a saucepan, cover with cold water, bring to the boil and simmer gently.

2 When three-quarters cooked, add all the other ingredients except the chopped chives.

3 Continue to simmer until all is completely cooked.

4 Serve sprinkled with chopped chives.

Fig 11.4 ✐ Mexican bean pot　　　*John Campbell*

12 Ratatouille pancakes with a cheese sauce

	4 portions	10 portions
Pancake batter (see page 509)		
flour	100 g (4 oz)	250 g (10 oz)
skimmed milk	250 ml (½ pt)	625 ml (1¼ pt)
egg	1	2–3
pinch of salt		
melted sunflower margarine	10 g (½ oz)	25 g (1 oz)
Ratatouille (see page 434)		
courgettes	200 g (8 oz)	500 g (1¼ lb)
aubergines	200 g (8 oz)	500 g (1¼ lb)
red pepper	1	2–3
green pepper	1	2–3
tomatoes	100 g (4 oz)	250 g (10 oz)
yellow pepper	1	2–3
onion, chopped	50 g (2 oz)	125 g (5 oz)
clove garlic, chopped	1	2
sunflower oil	4 tbsp	10 tbsp
tin plum tomatoes	1 × 400 g (1 lb)	1¼ kg (2½ lb)
tomato purée	50 g (2 oz)	125 g (5 oz)
Cheese sauce (page 55)		
skimmed milk	500 ml (1 pt)	1¼ litre (2½ pt)
sunflower oil	50 g (1 tbsp)	125 g (2½ tbsp)
flour	50 g (2 oz)	125 g (5 oz)
onion studded with clove	1	2–3
grated Parmesan	25 g (1 oz)	60 g (2½ oz)
egg yolk	1	2–3
seasoning		

HEALTHY EATING TIP

Less oil is needed to prepare the ratatouille. No added salt is needed; cheese is salty. Serve with a large mixed salad.

1   Prepare and make the pancakes.

2   Prepare the ratatouille and cheese sauce.

3   Season with salt and cayenne pepper.

4   Fill the pancakes with the ratatouille, roll up and serve on individual plates or on a service dish, coated with cheese sauce, sprinkled with grated Parmesan cheese and finished by gratinating under the salamander.

1 portion provides:
1814 kJ/432 kcal
35.5 g fat
(of which 7.4 g saturated)
23.5 g carbohydrate
(of which 16.3 g sugars)
6.4 g protein
6.7 g fibre

HEALTHY EATING TIP

Use a small amount of an unsaturated oil to sweat the onions. No added salt if the stock contains yeast extract.

13 Vegetable curry with rice pilaff

	4 portions	10 portions
mixed vegetables (cauliflower, broccoli, peppers, carrots, courgettes, mushrooms, aubergines)	600 g (1½ lb)	1½ kg (3¾ lb)
sunflower margarine	100 g (4 oz)	250 g (10 oz)
onions, chopped finely	150 g (6 oz)	375 g (15 oz)
garam masala	25 g (1 oz)	60 g (2½ oz)
creamed coconut or 2 oz (50 g) desiccated coconut	25 g (1 oz)	60 g (2½ oz)
curry sauce made from vegetable stock (pages 62 and 51)	500 ml (1 pt)	1¼ litre (2½ pt)

1 Prepare the vegetables: cut the cauliflower and broccoli into small florets, blanch and refresh; cut the peppers into half, remove the seeds, cut into 1 cm (½ inch) dice; cut the carrots into large dice, blanch and refresh; and the courgettes into 1 cm (½ inch) dice; leave the mushrooms whole; cut the aubergines into 1 cm (½ inch) dice.

2 Heat the margarine and sweat the onion.

3 Add the garam masala; sweat for approximately 2 minutes and add the coconut.

4 Add all the vegetables; sweat together for approximately 5 minutes.

5 Add the curry sauce, bring to the boil and gently simmer until all the vegetables are cooked but crunchy in texture.

6 Serve in a suitable dish with a rice pilaff garnished with flaked almonds, poppadoms and a curry tray with mango chutney.

Note: To the basic recipe of rice pilaff (page 161) using 100 g (4 oz) rice, add 50 g (2 oz) roasted flaked almonds after cooking (increase the quantities by 2½ for 10 portions).

A recipe for Alu-Chole, a vegetarian curry from Northern India, can be found on page 356.

14 Tomato savarin filled with cucumber, apple and walnut dressing

1 portion provides:
1215 kJ/289 kcal
25.8 g fat
(of which 9.2 g saturated)
4.8 g carbohydrate
(of which 4.7 g sugars)
9.8 g protein
1.8 g fibre

	4 portions	**10 portions**
can of plum tomatoes	1×400 g (1 lb)	1¼ kg (2½ lb)
tomato purée	25 g (1 oz)	60 g (2½ oz)
agar-agar (vegetarian gelatine substitute)	25 g (1 oz)	60 g (2½ oz)
mayonnaise	125 ml (¼ pt)	300 ml (⅝ pt)
lemon, juice of	½	1
green pepper	½	1
yellow pepper	½	1
sticks of celery	3	7
egg whites	2	5
whipping cream or natural yoghurt	125 ml (¼ pt)	300 ml (⅝ pt)
seasoning		

HEALTHY EATING TIP
Use a minimum amount of salt. The fat content will be lower if yoghurt is used in place of cream.

1 Purée the tomatoes with their juice to measure 500 ml (1 pint).

2 Bring to the boil, and whisk in tomato purée.

3 Dissolve the agar-agar in hot water, add to the tomatoes and vegetables, cut in large dice.

4 Place the mixture in a basin on a bowl of ice, stir until cool.

5 Season, whisk in the mayonnaise and lemon juice.

6 Continue to cool until setting point is reached, carefully fold in stiffly beaten egg whites and whipping cream.

7 Pour into an 18–19 cm (7–8 inch) savarin mould and set in refrigerator.

8 Unmould onto a suitable serving dish, fill the centre with cucumber, apple and walnut dressing. Decorate with tomato and mint leaves.

Note: Soaked leaf gelatine may be used to replace the agar-agar, although gelatine is not a vegetarian but an animal product.

It is advisable to use pasteurised egg whites.

15 Cucumber, apple and walnut dressing

1 portion provides:
923 kJ/222 kcal energy
14.9 g fat
(of which 2.1 g saturated)
15.6 g carbohydrate
(of which 15.4 g sugars)
7.2 g protein
2.5 g fibre

	4 portions	**10 portions**
small cucumber	1	2–3
dessert apples	3	8
lime, juice of	1	2–3
crushed walnuts	75 g (3 oz)	180 g (7½ oz)
natural yoghurt	250 ml (½ pt)	625 ml (1¼ pt)

1 Peel the cucumber and cut into ½ cm (¼ inch) dice.

2 Peel and cut the dessert apples into 2 cm (¾ inch) dice, sprinkle with the lime juice.

3 Place the cucumber and apple into a basin, add the walnuts and bind with the natural yoghurt.

4 Use this mixture to fill the centre of the tomato savarin and serve with a green salad of mixed lettuce.

16 Vegetarian kedgeree

1 portion provides:
2367 kJ/563 kcal
39.6 g fat
(of which 6.3 g saturated)
46.4 g carbohydrate
(of which 11.7 g sugars)
8.7 g protein
8.9 g fibre

HEALTHY EATING TIP

Use a little unsaturated oil to sweat the onion. No added salt is necessary. Reheat the vegetables in a hot oven, or fry in a little oil and drain on kitchen paper.

	4 portions	10 portions
cauliflower	100 g (4 oz)	250 g (10 oz)
French beans	100 g (4 oz)	250 g (10 oz)
courgettes	100 g (4 oz)	250 g (10 oz)
mange-tout	100 g (4 oz)	250 g (10 oz)
sunflower oil	125 ml (¼ pt)	300 ml (⅝ pt)
onion, finely chopped	50 g (2 oz)	125 g (5 oz)
clove garlic, crushed and chopped	1	2–3
curry powder	25 g (1 oz)	60 g (2½ oz)
grated root ginger	10 g (½ oz)	30 g (1¼ oz)
ground cardamom	3 g (⅛ oz)	9 g (⅓ oz)
turmeric	3 g (⅛ oz)	9 g (⅓ oz)
Basmati rice	100 g (4 oz)	250 g (10 oz)
vegetable stock	180 ml (⅛ pt)	500 ml (1 pt)
cooked green lentils	75 g (3 oz)	180 g (7½ oz)
curry sauce (page 62) using vegetable stock	500 ml (1 pt)	1¼ litre (2½ pt)

1 Prepare the vegetables in the following way: cut the cauliflower into small florets, cook in boiling salted water; top and tail French beans, cut in half and cook in boiling salted water; remove the ends from the courgettes, peel carefully, cut into 1 cm (½ inch) lengths, blanch in boiling salted water; top and tail the mange-tout, leave whole, blanch in boiling salted water for 30 seconds. Refresh and drain all the vegetables.

2 Heat half the oil in a sauté pan, add the chopped onion and garlic, sweat without colour.

3 Add the curry powder, ginger, cardamom and turmeric; sweat for 1 minute.

4 Add the Basmati rice, stir well. Add the boiling vegetable stock, cover with a greased greaseproof paper and lid. Cook in a moderately hot oven, 200–230°C (Reg. 6–8; 400–450°F) until the rice is tender but retains a bite.

5 When cooked, remove from the oven and stir in the cooked lentils.

6 Reheat the vegetables by lightly frying them in the remaining oil, keeping all the vegetables crisp.

7 Drain the vegetables, stir into the rice and serve, with the curry sauce.

17 Vegetarian lasagne

	4 portions	**10 portions**
sheets of lasagne	10	30
sunflower oil	125 ml (¼ pt)	300 ml (⅝ pt)
finely chopped onion	100 g (4 oz)	250 g (10 oz)
garlic cloves, chopped	2	5
mushrooms, sliced	200 g (8 oz)	500 g (1¼ lb)
seasoning		
medium-sized courgettes	2	5
oregano	3 g (⅛ oz)	9 g (⅓ oz)
tomato skinned, de-seeded and diced	200 g (8 oz)	500 g (1¼ lb)
tomato purée	50 g (2 oz)	125 g (5 oz)
broccoli (small florets)	300 g (12 oz)	750 g (2 lb)
carrots	100 g (4 oz)	250 g (10 oz)
pine kernels	25 g (1 oz)	60 g (2½ oz)
béchamel	250 ml (½ pt)	625 ml (1¼ pt)
grated Parmesan cheese	50 g (2 oz)	125 g (5 oz)
natural yoghurt	250 ml (½ pt)	625 ml (1¼ pt)

1 portion provides:
2993 kJ/713 kcal
46.2 g fat
(of which 8.5 g saturated)
54.6 g carbohydrate
(of which 16.5 g sugars)
22.9 g protein
11.8 g fibre

HEALTHY EATING TIP

Try using a mixture of white and green lasagne. Use a little unsaturated oil to sweat the onion. Make the béchamel with semi-skimmed milk. No added salt is needed.

1 Cook the lasagne sheets in boiling salted water until *al dente*, refresh and drain.

2 Heat half the oil and sweat the onion and garlic.

3 Add the mushrooms and continue to cook without colour. Season.

4 Heat the remaining oil in a sauteuse, add the courgettes, cut in 1 cm (½ inch) dice, and lightly fry; sprinkle with the oregano. Cook until crisp, add the tomato concassé and tomato purée.

5 Add the broccoli florets and carrots (cut in ½ cm (¼ inch) dice), previously blanched and refreshed. Mix together with the pine kernels.

6 Make a cheese sauce using the béchamel and half the grated cheese, finish with the natural yoghurt.

7 Well grease a suitable ovenproof dish with the sunflower oil and place a layer of lasagne in the bottom.

8 Cover with a layer of mushrooms, then a layer of lasagne, then the broccoli and tomato mixture, then lasagne, then cheese sauce. Continue to do this, finishing with a layer of cheese sauce on the top.

9 Sprinkle with remaining grated Parmesan cheese.

10 Bake in a preheated oven at 180°C (Reg. 4; 350°F) for 20–25 minutes.

18 Vegetarian moussaka

1 portion provides:
2249 kJ/536 kcal
29.1 g fat
(of which 7.0 g saturated)
46.2 g carbohydrate
(of which 11.4 g sugars)
25.5 g protein
6.4 g fibre

HEALTHY EATING TIP

Use a little unsaturated oil to cook the onion and garlic.
No added salt is needed.
Try oven-baking the aubergines brushed with a little oil.

	4 portions	10 portions
finely chopped onion	50 g (2 oz)	125 g (5 oz)
clove garlic, chopped	1	2–3
sunflower oil	4 tbsp	10 tbsp
TVP mince (natural flavour)	100 g (4 oz)	250 g (10 oz)
tomato skinned, de-seeded and diced	200 g (8 oz)	500 g (1¼ lb)
tomato purée	50 g (2 oz)	125 g (5 oz)
pinch oregano		
seasoning		
vegetable stock	500 ml (1 pt)	1¼ litre (2½ pt)
yeast extract	5 g (¼ oz)	12 g (⅜ oz)
arrowroot	10 g (½ oz)	25 g (1 oz)
potatoes	400 g (1 lb)	1¼ kg (2½ lb)
large aubergines	2	5
Cheese sauce **sunflower margarine**	25 g (1 oz)	60 g (2½ oz)
wholemeal flour	25 g (1 oz)	60 g (2½ oz)
skimmed milk	250 ml (½ pt)	625 ml (1¼ pt)
Parmesan cheese	25 g (1 oz)	60 g (2½ oz)
egg yolk	1	2–3
natural yoghurt	2 tbsp	5 tbsp
grated Parmesan cheese	50 g (2 oz)	125 g (5 oz)

1 Presoak the TVP mince in cold water for 2–3 hours. Cook the onion and garlic in the sunflower oil until lightly coloured.

2 Add the drained TVP.

3 Add the tomato concassé, tomato purée, oregano and seasoning.

4 Add the vegetable stock to cover. Bring to the boil; simmer for 5 minutes.

5 Add the yeast extract, stir well.

6 Dilute the arrowroot with a little water and gradually stir into the TVP.

7 Bring back to the boil. Simmer for 2 minutes.

8 Cook the potatoes with the skins on, by steaming or boiling. Peel and slice into ½ cm (¼ inch) slices.

9 Slice the aubergines into ½ cm (¼ inch) slices, pass through the wholemeal flour, shallow fry in the sunflower oil on both sides, until golden brown. Drain on kitchen paper.

10 In a suitable ovenproof dish arrange layers of TVP mixture and overlapping slices of potato and aubergines.

11 Make the cheese sauce (page 55) and pour on top, sprinkle with the grated Parmesan cheese.

12 Bake in a preheated oven at 190°C (Reg. 5; 375°F) for approximately 30 minutes.

19 Vegetable biryani

	4 portions	10 portions
Basmati rice	400 g (1 lb)	1¼ kg (2½ lb)
oil	2 tbsp	5 tbsp
cinnamon stick	½	1
cardamom pods	4	10
cloves	4	10
sliced onions	100 g (4 oz)	250 g (10 oz)
clove garlic	1	2–3
green chilli, finely chopped	1	2–3
grated root ginger	1 tbsp	2–3 tbsp
mixed vegetables (carrots, celery, broccoli, cauliflower, French beans)	600 g (1½ lb)	1½ kg (3¾ lb)
tomatoes, blanched, de-seeded and chopped or canned plum tomatoes	400 g (1 lb)	1¼ kg (2½ lb)
tomato purée	25 g (1 oz)	60 g (2½ oz)
chopped coriander leaves		

1 Wash, soak and drain the rice.

2 Partly cook the rice in boiling salted water for 3 minutes. Refresh and drain well.

3 Heat the oil in a suitably sized pan. Add the crushed cinnamon, cardamom and cloves and sweat for 2 minutes.

4 Add the sliced onions, garlic, chilli and ginger. Continue to sweat until soft.

5 Prepare the vegetables: cut the carrots and celery into batons, the cauliflower and broccoli into florets and the French beans into 2.5 cm (1 inch) lengths.

6 Add the vegetables and fry for 2–3 minutes.

7 Add the tomatoes and tomato purée. Season.

8 Make sure there is sufficient moisture in the pan to cook the vegetables. Usually a little water needs to be added. Ideally the vegetables should cook in their own juices combined with the tomatoes.

9 When the vegetables are partly cooked, layer them in a casserole or suitable pan with the rice. (Make sure that there is sufficient liquid to cook the rice.)

10 Cover the casserole, finish cooking in a moderate oven at 180°C (Reg. 4; 350°F) for about 20 minutes, or until the rice is tender.

11 Sprinkle with chopped coriander leaves and serve.

1 portion provides:
2014 kJ/482 kcal energy
7.3 g fat
(of which 0.9 g saturated)
91.3 g carbohydrate
(of which 9.9 g sugars)
12.2 g protein
4.6 g fibre

HEALTHY EATING TIP
Keep added salt to a minimum. Use a little unsaturated oil to sweat the spices, onions and vegetables

20 Vegetable and nut Stroganoff

	4 portions	10 portions
sunflower oil	4 tbsp	10 tbsp
onions, finely chopped	50 g (2 oz)	125 g (5 oz)
Chinese leaves, shredded	300 g (12 oz)	1 kg (2 lb)
celery, in paysanne	6 sticks	15 sticks
button mushrooms, sliced	300 g (12 oz)	1 kg (2 lb)
mixed nuts (peanuts, cashews, hazelnuts)	200 g (8 oz)	500 g (1¼ lb)
paprika	1 tsp	2–3 tsp
English or continental mustard	1 tsp	2–3 tsp
white wine	125 ml (¼ pt)	300 ml (⅝ pt)
unsweetened vegetable creamer or smetana	125 ml (¼ pt)	300 ml (⅝ pt)
seasoning		

1 Heat the oil and sweat the onions for 2–3 minutes.

2 Add the Chinese leaves, celery and mushrooms. Cook for 5 minutes.

3 Add the nuts whole. Stir in the paprika and diluted mustard.

4 Add the white wine, bring to the boil and simmer for 5 minutes.

5 Season. Cool slightly, add heat-stable unsweetened vegetable creamer or smetana. Serve with a dish of plain-boiled wholewheat noodles tossed in sunflower margarine or wholegrain pilaff rice.

Fig 11.5 Almonds: whole, flaked, nibbed, ground

21 Oriental stir-fry Quorn

1 portion provides:
836 kJ/200 kcal energy
11.8 g fat
(of which 1.3 g saturated)
11.6 g carbohydrate
(of which 7.3 g sugars)
12.7 g protein
5.6 g fibre

		4 portions	10 portions
Quorn pieces, defrosted		200 g (8 oz)	500 g (1 lb 4 oz)
soy sauce		62 ml (⅛ pt)	156 ml (⁵⁄₁₆ pt)
freshly grated ginger		12 g (½ oz)	30 g (1¼ oz)
spring onions		8	20
vegetable oil		1 tbsp	3 tbsp
red pepper	halved,	1	3
yellow pepper	de-seeded and	1	3
green pepper	finely sliced	1	3
blanched almonds or cashews		50 g (2 oz)	100 g (4 oz)
dry sherry		1 tbsp	3 tbsp
vegetable stock		62 ml (⅛)pt	156 ml (⁵⁄₁₆ pt)
sugar		¼ tsp	1 tsp
cornflour		6 g (¼ oz)	15 g (⅝ oz)

HEALTHY EATING TIP

Use a little unsaturated oil to fry the quorn, onions and peppers. No added salt is needed; plenty of flavour from the soy sauce, ginger and stock.

1 Prepare a marinade by mixing the soy sauce with the ginger and season with black pepper.

2 Add the Quorn pieces, mix well and chill for 1 hour.

3 Strain the Quorn from the marinade. In a wok, add half the vegetable oil, stir-fry the Quorn quickly for approximately 4 minutes. Remove from the wok.

4 Add the remaining oil and fry the spring onion and the peppers for another 1–2 minutes.

5 Return the Quorn to the wok.

6 Add the strained marinade, sherry, stock and sugar. Bring to boil.

7 Thicken lightly with the cornflour. Stir gently to enable the ingredients to be covered with the sauce.

8 Serve with noodles or rice.

Quorn may be used in stews, pies and casseroles in place of meat.

See page 213 for information on Quorn.

22 Vegetarian strudel

1 portion provides:
2117 kJ/504 kcal
27.6 g fat
(of which 4.0 g saturated)
54.1 g carbohydrate
(of which 10.5 g sugars)
14.3 g protein
9.7 g fibre

HEALTHY EATING TIP

Use a minimum amount of salt. Use a little unsaturated oil to cook the onion and garlic.

Strudel dough	4 portions	10 portions
strong flour	200 g (8 oz)	500 g (1¼ lb)
pinch of salt		
sunflower oil	25 g (1 oz)	60 g (2½ oz)
egg	1	2–3
water at 37°C (100°F)	83 ml (⅙ pt)	125 ml (¼ pt)
large cabbage leaves	200 g (8 oz)	500 g (1¼ lb)
sunflower oil	4 tbsp	10 tbsp
finely chopped onion	50 g (2 oz)	125 g (5 oz)
cloves garlic, chopped	2	5
courgettes	400 g (1 lb)	1 kg (2½ lb)
carrots	200 g (8 oz)	500 g (1¼ lb)
turnips	100 g (4 oz)	250 g (10 oz)
tomato skinned, de-seeded and diced	300 g (12 oz)	750 g (30 oz)
tomato purée	25 g (1 oz)	60 g (2½ oz)
toasted sesame seeds	25 g (1 oz)	60 g (2½ oz)
wholemeal breadcrumbs	50 g (2 oz)	125 g (5 oz)
fresh chopped basil	3 g (⅛ oz)	9 g (⅓ oz)
seasoning		

1 Make strudel paste by sieving the flour with the salt, make a well.

2 Add the oil, egg and water, gradually incorporate the flour to make a smooth dough and knead well.

3 Place in a basin, cover with a damp cloth; relax for 3 minutes.

4 Meanwhile prepare the filling: take the large cabbage leaves, wash and discard the tough centre stalks, blanch in boiling salted water for 2 minutes, until limp. Refresh and drain well in a clean cloth.

5 Heat the oil in a sauté pan, gently fry the onion and garlic until soft.

6 Peel and chop the courgettes into ½ cm (¼ inch) dice, blanch and refresh. Peel and dice the carrots and turnips, blanch and refresh.

7 Place the well drained courgettes, carrots and turnips into a basin, add the tomato concassé, tomato purée, sesame seeds, breadcrumbs, chopped basil. Mix well, season.

8 Roll out strudel dough to a thin rectangle, place on a clean cloth and stretch until extremely thin.

9 Lay the drained cabbage leaves on the stretched strudel dough, leaving approximately 1 cm (½ inch) gap from the edge.

10 Place the filling in the centre. Eggwash the edges.

11 Fold in the longer side edges to meet in the middle. Roll up.

12 Transfer to a lightly oiled baking sheet. Brush with the sunflower oil.

13 Bake for 40 minutes in a preheated oven at 180–200°C (Reg. 4–6; 350–400°F).

14 When cooked serve hot, sliced on individual plates with a cordon of tomato sauce made with vegetable stock and without bacon.

23 Vegetarian pizza

1 portion provides:
2272 kJ/541 kcal
26.6 g fat
(of which 4.8 g saturated)
64.0 g carbohydrate
(of which 13.7 g sugars)
17.0 g protein
10.4 g fibre

HEALTHY EATING TIP

Use a little unsaturated oil to cook the onion and garlic. Serve with a large mixed salad.

Pizza dough	4 portions	10 portions
flour	300 g (12 oz)	750 g (1½ lb)
soya flour	10 g (½ oz)	25 g (1¼ oz)
pinch of salt		
warm water at 32°C/90°F	180 ml (⅛ pt)	500 ml (1 pt)
fresh yeast	10 g (½ oz)	25 g (1 oz)
ascorbic acid	5 g (¼ oz)	12 g (⅝ oz)
onions, finely chopped	200 g (8 oz)	500 g (1¼ lb)
cloves of garlic, crushed	2	5
sunflower oil	4 tbsp	10 tbsp
tomatoes, skinned, de-seeded and diced	400 g (1 lb)	1 kg (2½ lb)
tomato purée	50 g (2 oz)	125 g (5 oz)
fresh parsley	10 g (½ oz)	25 g (1 oz)
fresh chopped basil	10 g (½ oz)	25 g (1 oz)
cooked artichoke bottoms	2	5
pine kernels	25 g (1 oz)	60 g (2½ oz)
sesame seeds	10 g (½ oz)	25 g (1 oz)
capers	10 g (½ oz)	25 g (1 oz)
green olives	8	20
black olives	8	20
sultanas	25 g (1 oz)	60 g (2½ oz)
Mozzarella cheese	50 g (2 oz)	125 g (5 oz)

1 Sieve the flour, soya flour and a pinch of salt into a basin.

2 Warm the water, place in a separate basin with the yeast, disperse the yeast in the warm water, allow sufficient flour to make a light batter, sprinkle a little flour over the ferment, cover with a damp cloth and allow the ferment to break through the flour.

3 When the ferment is ready, pour into the rest of the flour.

4 Add the ascorbic acid, incorporate the flour until a smooth elastic dough is obtained.

5 Turn out onto a floured surface and continue to knead the dough until smooth.

6 Return to the basin, cover with a damp cloth and allow to prove in a warm place until double in size.

7 Knock back the dough to bring the yeast back into contact with the dough and to equalise the dough.

8 Roll out the dough into 15 cm (6 inch) rounds or in a rectangle, and cover a lightly greased swiss roll tin.

9 Allow to prove for 10 minutes in a warm atmosphere.

10 Bake for 4–5 minutes in a preheated oven at 200°C (Reg. 5–6; 400°F).

11 Sweat the onions and garlic in the oil.

12 Add the tomato concassé and purée. Stir well.

13 Add the chopped parsley and basil. Cook out the tomatoes for about 15 minutes. Season.

14 Spread this tomato mixture on the pizza base.

15 Arrange neatly on top the artichoke bottoms into small pieces, sprinkle on the pine kernels, sesame seeds, capers, stoned olives and sultanas.

continued over ▶

▶ *Vegeterian pizza continued*

16 Finally, sprinkle with grated Mozzarella cheese.

17 Bake in oven for about 15 minutes at 200°C (Reg. 6; 400°F). Serve very hot.

Note: Alternatively a ratatouille mixture, or a variation of it, may be used as a pizza topping with grated cheese.

24 Polenta and vegetable terrine

Using cream cheese, 1 portion provides:
2106 kJ/508 kcal energy
32.7 g fat
(of which 15.6 g saturated)
45.1 g carbohydrate
(of which 5.0 g sugars)
8.2 g protein
3.8 g fibre

	6 portions
butter	150 g (6 oz)
water	1.5 litres (2½ pt)
polenta	325 g (13 oz)
extra virgin olive oil	45 ml (3 tbsp)
white mill pepper	
salt	
grated nutmeg	
cream cheese or	25 g (1 oz)
freshly grated Parmesan	

Use little or no salt; plenty in the cheese.
Try to add less butter to the polenta.

Vegetables for the terrine

A variety of vegetables may be used. For example, cooked broccoli, button onions, courgettes, carrots, green beans, baby sweetcorn, red, green or yellow peppers (blanched).

For a 6 oz portion terrine allow approximately 2 courgettes, 2 peppers (one of each colour), 6 florets of broccoli, 2 baby sweetcorn, and 50 g (2 oz) green beans.

1 Preparing the polenta, bring the water to the boil, with butter, nutmeg and seasoning.

2 Rain in the polenta and mix thoroughly for about 5–10 minutes.

3 Mix in the cream cheese or Parmesan (some fresh chopped herbs may also be added at this stage).

4 Lightly oil a suitable terrine or loaf tin, line with cling film – this makes the turning out of the terrine more easy.

5 Pour a thin layer of warm polenta into the bottom of the tin. Arrange a layer of vegetables on the polenta, cover this layer with more polenta; repeat the process until the terrine is full.

6 Cover with cling film and chill for several hours until firm to the touch.

7 Turn out, slice and serve on a suitable plate on a mirror of fresh tomato sauce or another suitable vegetable sauce, garnish with coriander.

This terrine makes a very suitable vegetarian starter.

Note: The terrine may be made using roasted vegetables (page 455).

25 Polenta and lentil cakes with roasted vegetables served with cucumber and yoghurt sauce

1 portion provides:
1898 kJ/452 kcal energy
15.2 g fat
(of which 4.1 g saturated)
55.6 g carbohydrate
(of which 7.9 g sugars)
25.2 g protein
4.3 g fibre

	4 portions	10 portions
fine polenta	75 g (3 oz)	187 g (7½ oz)
puy lentils	250 g (10 oz)	625 g (1 lb 9 oz)
vegetable stock	250 ml (½ pt)	625 ml (1¼ pt)
grated Parmesan cheese	25 g (1 oz)	62 g (2½ oz)
beaten egg	1	3
leek finely chopped and blanched	75 g (3 oz)	187 g (7½ oz)
crushed garlic chopped finely	1	3
olive oil	3 tbsp	8 tbsp
Sauce cucumber	250 g (10 oz)	625 g (1 lb 9 oz)
natural yoghurt	250 ml (¼ pt)	625 ml (1¼ pt)
chopped chives	1 tsp	2½ tsp
chopped mint	¼ tsp	1¼ tsp

HEALTHY EATING TIP

No additional salt is needed.
Use less olive oil to fry the cakes, and drain on kitchen paper. Brush the vegetables with a little unsaturated oil when roasting.

1. Wash the lentils and cook in salted water for about 25 minutes until tender but still firm. Drain well, refresh and drain again. Dry on a suitable cloth.

2. Bring the vegetable stock to the boil, rain in the polenta, cook gently stirring until thickened.

3. Add the Parmesan cheese, beaten egg and season.

4. Mix the lentils, polenta, leek and garlic.

5. Correct seasoning, cool, shape into 4 round cakes.

6. Place in the fridge and chill well for at least 1 hour.

7. Heat the olive oil in a suitable pan, gently fry the cakes for about 3–4 minutes on each side until heated through and well browned.

8. To make the sauce, liquidise the peeled cucumber with the yoghurt, finish with chopped mint and chives.

9. To serve, place a small amount of sauce into a plate, the cakes on top. Garnish the plate with freshly roasted vegetables.

Fig 11.6 Polenta and lentil cakes with roasted vegetables, served with cucumber and yoghurt sauce
John Campbell

26 Warm tofu and asparagus salad

Using increased quantity of fresh tomatoes, 1 portion provides:
723 kJ/173 kcal energy
11.7 g fat
(of which 2.0 g saturated)
8.5 g carbohydrate
(of which 6.2 g sugars)
9.1 g protein
2.6 g fibre

	4 portions	10 portions
asparagus, cooked	200 g (8 oz)	500 g (1¼ lb)
firm tofu	200 g (8 oz)	500 g (1¼ lb)
olive oil	1 tbsp	2½ tbsp
red onion, finely chopped	1 small	2
clove garlic	1	2
sundried tomatoes cut in julienne	100 g (4 oz)	250 g (9 oz)
lemon	½	1½
toasted cashews	50 g (2 oz)	125 g (5 oz)
vegetable stock	2 tbsp	5 tbsp
seasoning		
ground black pepper		
mixed leaves for garnish – raddichio, lamb's lettuce, frisée, endive etc.		

HEALTHY EATING TIP

Use a little olive oil in a well-seasoned pan to fry the onions and garlic. Add a minimum amount of salt. Serve with warm bread rolls to increase the starchy carbohydrate.

1 Heat the olive oil in a suitable pan. Add the crushed and chopped clove/s of garlic and the onion and quickly fry until lightly coloured.

2 Add the sundried tomatoes and sauté for a further minute.

3 Add lemon juice and grated lemon zest.

4 Season and add the tofu and the vegetable stock.

5 Cover and simmer gently for approximately 10 minutes.

6 Place the tofu mixture on suitable plates, garnish with mixed leaves.

7 Finish by placing the warmed asparagus on top. Sprinkle with toasted cashew nuts.

Fig 11.7 Warm tofu and asparagus salad   *John Campbell*

27 Tofu dressings and dips

soft or silken tofu	800 g (2 lb)
lemon juice or vinegar	3 tbsp
seasoning	

HEALTHY EATING TIP

Add a minimum amount of salt.

Blend in a food processor until smooth. Add the following, as required.

Garlic and dill
2 cloves crushed and chopped garlic
2 tsps of chopped dill

Curry
1 finely chopped onion sweated in 1 tablespoon of olive oil. Add 2 teaspoons of curry powder. Sweat for a further two minutes. Add to the tofu and mix well.

Cheese and garlic
Add 50 g (2 oz) freshly grated Parmesan and 2 cloves of crushed and chopped garlic.

Ginger
Add 2 teaspoons of freshly grated ginger, dash of tabasco and 1 teaspoon freshly chopped parsley.

Avocado
Add the purée of two avocado pears, 50 g (2 oz) of finely chopped onion and dash of tabasco.

Herb
Add 3 teaspoons of freshly chopped herbs – basil, oregano, tarragon, chives, parsley.

28 Crispy deep fried tofu

50 g provides:
543 kJ/131 kcal energy
8.9 g fat
(of which 0.0 g saturated)
1.0 g carbohydrate
(of which 0.5 g sugars)
11.8 g protein
0.0 g fibre

HEALTHY EATING TIP

Use an unsaturated oil to fry the tofu. Make sure the oil is hot so that less is absorbed. Alternatively, try dry frying the tofu.

Firm tofu cut into cubes.

Coat with any of the following:

- flour, egg and breadcrumbs;
- milk and flour;
- cornstarch;
- arrowroot.

Deep fry tofu at 180°C/350°F until golden brown. Drain. Serve garnished with freshly grated ginger and julienne of herbs.

Serve with a tomato sauce flavoured with coriander.

HEALTHY EATING TIP

Use a little unsaturated oil to cook the onion and garlic. Add a minimum amount of salt.
Serve with a warm bread roll.

29 Fresh tomato and tofu soup

This is a summer soup – serve cold.

	4 portions	10 portions
tomatoes, skinned, de-seeded, cut concassé	100 g (4 oz)	250 g (10 oz)
onion, finely chopped	1 large	2
tomato juice	500 ml (2 pt)	1.25litre (5 pt)
cloves of garlic, crushed and chopped	2	5
soft tofu	300 g (12 oz)	750 g (1 lb 14 oz)
tabasco		
chopped parsley		
chopped basil		

1 Sweat the chopped onion in the oil without colour. Add the garlic. Mix well.
2 Allow to cool.
3 Add tofu, season well.
4 Add a dash of tabasco to taste.
5 Liquidise, pass through a fine strainer.
6 Correct seasoning and consistency.
7 Serve well chilled, garnished with tomato concassé. Sprinkle with chopped basil and parsley.

continued...

Prepare and cook vegetable dishes

Fresh vegetables are important foods both from an economic and nutritional point of view. Vegetables are an important part of our diet therefore the recognition of quality, purchasing, storage and efficient preparation and cooking is essential if the nutritional content of vegetables is to be conserved. Potatoes are discussed separately in Chapter 13.

Purchasing

The purchasing of vegetables is affected by:

- the perishable nature of the products;
- varying availability owing to seasonal fluctuations and supply and demand;
- the effects of preservation, e.g. freezing, drying, canning vegetables.

The high perishability of vegetables causes problems not encountered in other markets. Fresh vegetables are living organisms and will lose quality quickly if not properly stored and handled. Automation in harvesting and packaging speeds the handling process and helps retain quality.

The EEC vegetable quality grading system is:

- *Extra class* Produce of the highest quality.
- *Class 1* Produce of good quality.
- *Class 2* Produce of reasonably good quality.
- *Class 3* Produce of low market quality.

Food value

Root vegetables contain starch or sugar for energy, a small but valuable amount of protein, some mineral salts and vitamins. They are also useful sources of cellulose and water. Green vegetables are rich in mineral salts and vitamins, particularly vitamin C and carotene. The greener the leaf the larger the quantity of vitamins present. The chief mineral salts are calcium and iron.

Quality and purchasing points

Root vegetables must be:

- clean, free from soil;
- firm, not soft or spongy;
- sound;
- free from blemishes;
- of an even size;
- of an even shape.

Green vegetables must be absolutely fresh and have leaves bright in colour, crisp and not wilted. In addition:

- Cabbage and Brussels sprouts should be compact and firm.
- Cauliflowers should have closely grown flowers, a firm white head and not too much stalk, or too many outer leaves.
- Peas and beans should be crisp and of medium size. Pea pods should be full and beans not stringy.
- Blanched stems must be firm, white, crisp and free from soil.

Storage

- Store all vegetables in a cool, dry, well ventilated room at an even temperature of 4–8°C (39–46°F), which will help to minimise spoilage. Check vegetables daily and discard any that are unsound.
- Remove root vegetables from their sacks and store in bins, or racks.
- Store green vegetables on well ventilated racks.
- Store salad vegetables in a cool place and leave in their containers.

- Store frozen vegetables at −18°C (0°F) or below. Keep a check on use-by dates, damaged packages and any signs of freezer burn.
- The fresher the vegetables the better the flavour so ideally they should not be stored at all. However, as in many cases storage is necessary, then it should be for the shortest time possible.
- Green vegetables lose vitamin C quickly if they are bruised, damaged, stored for too long, or overcooked.

Health, safety and hygiene

Chapter 1 contains information on these aspects. In addition:

- If vegetables are stored at the incorrect temperature micro-organisms may develop.
- If vegetables are stored in damp conditions moulds may develop.
- To prevent bacteria from raw vegetables passing on to cooked vegetables, store them in separate areas.
- Thaw out frozen vegetables correctly and *never* refreeze them once they have thawed out.

Cooking

Approximate times are given for the cooking of vegetables as quality, age, freshness and size all affect the length of cooking time required. Young, freshly picked vegetables will cook for a shorter time than vegetables allowed to grow older and which may have been stored after picking.

As a general rule all root vegetables are started to cook in cold salted water, with the exception of new potatoes: those vegetables that grow above the ground are started in boiling salted water. This is so that they may be cooked as quickly as possible for the *minimum* period of time so that *maximum* flavour, food value and colour are retained.

Fig 12.1 Cuts of vegetables (from left to right): macédoine, paysanne, jardinière, julienne, brunoise

All vegetables cooked by boiling may also be cooked by steaming. The vegetables are prepared in exactly the same way as for boiling, placed into steamer trays, lightly seasoned with salt and steamed under pressure for the minimum period of time in order to conserve maximum food value and retain colour. High speed steam cookers are ideal for this purpose and also because of the speed of cooking; batch cooking (cooking in small quantities throughout the service) can be practised instead of cooking large quantities prior to service, refreshing and reheating.

Many vegetables are cooked from raw by the stir-fry method, a quick and nutritious method of cooking.

Cuts of vegetables

The size to which the vegetables are cut may vary according to their use; however, the shape does not change.

- **Julienne** (strips)
  - Cut the vegetables into 2 cm (1 inch) lengths. (Short julienne)
  - Cut the lengths into thin slices.
  - Cut the slices into thin strips.
  - Double the length gives a long julienne, used for garnishing e.g. salads, meats, fish, poultry dishes.

- **Brunoise** (small dice)
  - Cut the vegetables into convenient-sized lengths.
  - Cut the lengths into 2 mm ($\frac{1}{12}$ inch) slices.
  - Cut the slices into 2 mm ($\frac{1}{12}$ inch) strips.
  - Cut the strips into 2 mm ($\frac{1}{12}$ inch) squares.

- **Macédoine** ($\frac{1}{2}$ cm ($\frac{1}{4}$ inch) dice)
  - Cut the vegetables into convenient lengths.
  - Cut the lengths into $\frac{1}{2}$ cm ($\frac{1}{4}$ inch) slices.
  - Cut the slices into $\frac{1}{2}$ cm ($\frac{1}{4}$ inch) strips.
  - Cut the strips into $\frac{1}{2}$ cm ($\frac{1}{4}$ inch) squares.

- **Jardinière** (batons)
  - Cut the vegetables into 1$\frac{1}{2}$ cm ($\frac{3}{4}$ inch) lengths.
  - Cut the lengths into 3 mm ($\frac{1}{4}$ inch) slices.
  - Cut the slices into batons (3 × 3 × 18 mm ($\frac{1}{8}$ × $\frac{1}{8}$ × $\frac{3}{4}$ inch)).

- **Paysanne**
  There are at least four accepted methods of cutting paysanne. In order to cut economically, the shape of the vegetables should decide which method to choose. All are cut thinly.
  - 1 cm sided ($\frac{1}{2}$ inch) triangles.
  - 1 cm sided ($\frac{1}{2}$ inch) squares.
  - 1 cm diameter ($\frac{1}{2}$ inch) rounds.
  - 1 cm diameter ($\frac{1}{2}$ inch) rough-sided rounds.

Concassé
Roughly chopped, e.g. skinned and de-seeded tomatoes are roughly chopped for many food preparations. See page 457.

Vegetable recipes

Not including sauce, 1 portion
provides:
32 kJ/8 kcal
0.0 g fat
(of which 0.0 g saturated)
1.4 g carbohydrate
(of which 1.4 g sugars)
0.6 g protein
0.0 g fibre

1 Globe artichokes

Artichauts en branche

1 Allow 1 artichoke per portion.

2 Cut off the stems close to the leaves.

3 Cut off about 2 cm (1 inch) across the tops of the leaves.

4 Trim the remainder of the leaves with scissors or a small knife.

5 Place a slice of lemon at the bottom of each artichoke.

6 Secure with string.

7 Simmer in gently boiling lightly salted water (to which a little ascorbic acid – one vitamin C tablet – may be added) until the bottom is tender (20–30 minutes).

8 Refresh under running water until cold.

9 Remove the centre of the artichoke carefully.

10 Scrape away all the furry inside and leave clean.

11 Replace the centre, upside down.

12 Reheat by placing in a pan of boiling salted water for 3–4 minutes.

13 Drain and serve accompanied by a suitable sauce.

Note: Artichokes may also be served cold with vinaigrette sauce.

Do not cook artichokes in an iron or aluminium pan because these metals cause a chemical reaction that will discolour the artichokes.

2 Artichoke bottoms

Fonds d'artichauts

1 Cut off the stalk and pull out all the underneath leaves.

2 With a large knife cut through the artichoke leaving only 1½ cm (¾ inch) at the bottom of the vegetable.

3 With a small sharp knife, whilst holding the artichoke upside down, peel carefully, removing all the leaf and any green part, keeping the bottom as smooth as possible. If necessary smooth with a peeler.

4 Rub immediately with lemon and keep in lemon water or ascorbic acid solution.

5 Using a spoon or the thumb, remove the centre furry part, which is called the choke. The choke is sometimes removed after cooking.

6 Artichoke bottoms should always be cooked in a blanc (see over).

Note: Artichoke bases may be served as a vegetable; they are sometimes filled with another vegetable (peas, spinach, etc.). When they are served ungarnished they are usually cut into quarters.

3 Blanc

	4 portions	10 portions
cold water	½ litre (1 pt)	1 litre (2 pt)
flour	10 g (¼ oz)	20 g (⅜ oz)
lemon, juice of	½	1
salt		

1 Mix the flour and water together.
2 Add the salt and lemon juice. Pass through a strainer.
3 Place in a pan, bring to the boil, stirring continuously.

Note: Alternatively, artichokes may be cooked in ½ litre (1 pint) water, 2 vitamin C tablets (ascorbic acid) and 30 ml (1⁄16 pt) oil and salt (increase the quantities 2½ times for 10 portions).

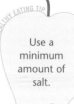

Use a minimum amount of salt.

4 Purée of Jerusalem artichokes

Topinambours en purée

	4 portions	10 portions
Jerusalem artichokes	600 g (1½ lb)	1½ kg (3¾ lb)
butter	25 g (1 oz)	60 g (2½ oz)
salt, pepper		

1 portion provides:
291 kJ/69 kcal
5.1 g fat
(of which 3.3 g saturated)
4.1 g carbohydrate
(of which 0.0 g sugars)
2.1 g protein
0.0 g fibre

1 Wash, peel and rewash the artichokes.
2 Cut in pieces if necessary. Barely cover with water; add a little salt.
3 Simmer gently until tender. Drain well.
4 Pass through a sieve, mouli or liquidise.
5 Return to the pan, reheat and mix in the butter and correct the seasoning and serve.

Note: 125 ml (¼ pint) (300 ml, ⅝ pint for 10 portions) cream or natural yoghurt may be mixed in before serving.

Use a minimum amount of salt.

5 Jerusalem artichokes in cream sauce

Topinambours à la crème

1 Wash and peel the artichokes and rewash. Cut to an even size.
2 Barely cover with water, add a little salt and simmer until tender; do not overcook.
3 Drain well and add 250 ml (½ pint) (600 ml, 1¼ pint for 10 portions) cream sauce (page 55).

Note: Cream sauce may be made using skimmed milk and natural yoghurt.

Use a minimum amount of salt. Try using half the amount of cream sauce and half natural yoghurt.

1 portion provides:
580 kJ/138 kcal
12.3 g fat
(of which 7.8 g saturated)
1.7 g carbohydrate
(of which 1.7 g sugars)
5.2 g protein
2.3 g fibre

6 Asparagus

Asperges

Allow 6–8 good-sized pieces per portion. An average bundle will yield 3–4 portions.

1 Using the back of a small knife, carefully remove the tips of the leaves.

2 Scrape the stem, either with the blade of a small knife or a peeler.

3 Wash well. Tie into bundles of about 12 heads.

4 Cut off the excess stem.

5 Cook in lightly salted boiling water for approximately 15 minutes.

6 Test if cooked by gently pressing the green part of the stem, which should be tender; do not overcook.

7 Lift carefully out of the water. Remove the string, drain well and serve.

Note: Serve a suitable sauce separately (hollandaise or melted butter). Asparagus are usually served as a separate course. They may also be served cold, in which case they should be immediately refreshed when cooked in order to retain the green colour. Serve with vinaigrette or mayonnaise.

7 Asparagus points or tips

Pointes d'asperges

Young thin asparagus, 50 pieces to the bundle, is known as sprew or sprue.

They are prepared in the same way as asparagus except that, when they are very thin, removing of the leaf tips is dispensed with. They may be served as a vegetable.

They are also used in numerous garnishes for soups, egg dishes, fish, meat and poultry dishes, cold dishes, salad, etc.

1 portion provides:
994 kJ/225 kcal
20.0 g fat
(of which 3.8 g saturated)
10.1 g carbohydrate
(of which 5.9 g sugars)
1.9 g protein
5.2 g fibre

8 Fried aubergine

Aubergine frite

1 Allow ½ aubergine per portion.

2 Remove alternate strips with a peeler.

3 Cut into ½ cm (¼ inch) slices on the slant.

4 Pass through seasoned flour or milk and flour.

5 Shake off all surplus flour.

6 Deep fry in hot fat at 185°C (365°F). Drain well and serve.

Note: Aubergines may also be shallow fried, grilled or griddled.

9 Griddled aubergines with lemon pesto

1 portion provides:
1297 kJ/313 kcal energy
27.5 g fat
(of which 5.9 g saturated)
5.7 g carbohydrate
(of which 5.1 g sugars)
11.3 g protein
4.4 g fibre

	4 portions	10 portions
aubergines, sliced into rounds	4	10
baby aubergine sliced lengthways	4	10
lemon pesto basil chopped	1 tbsp	3 tbsp
roasted pine nuts	75 g (3 oz)	175 g (7 oz)
crushed chopped garlic cloves	1	3
Parmesan cheese, grated	75 g (3 oz)	175 g (7 oz)
lemon's grated rind	2	5
lemon juice	3 tbsp	7 tbsp
olive oil	3 tbsp	7 tbsp
seasoning		

HEALTHY EATING TIP

No added salt is needed – plenty in the cheese.

1 Heat the griddle pan, place the aubergines on the pan and cook for 3 minutes on each side. Remove and arrange on serving dish.

2 Make the pesto, place the basil, pine nuts, garlic, Parmesan, lemon rind and juice, olive oil and seasoning in a food processor, then blend until smooth.

3 Drizzle the lemon pesto over the aubergines and serve.

Other vegetables may also be used, for example courgettes.

1 portion provides:
579 kJ/138 kcal
12.6 g fat
(of which 1.7 g saturated)
5.2 g carbohydrate
(of which 4.6 g sugars)
1.3 g protein
2.4 g fibre

Use a little unsaturated oil to cook the onions. Use a minimum amount of salt.

10 Ratatouille

Ratatouille

	4 portions	10 portions
baby marrow	200 g (8 oz)	500 g (1¼ lb)
aubergines	200 g (8 oz)	500 g (1¼ lb)
tomatoes	200 g (8 oz)	500 g (1¼ lb)
oil	50 ml (⅛ pt)	125 ml (¼ pt)
onion, finely sliced	50 g (2 oz)	125 g (5 oz)
clove garlic, peeled and chopped	1	2
red peppers, diced	50 g (2 oz)	125 g (5 oz)
green peppers, diced	50 g (2 oz)	125 g (5 oz)
salt, pepper		
chopped parsley	1 tsp	2–3 tsp

1 Trim off both ends of the marrow and aubergines.
2 Remove the skin using a peeler.
3 Cut into 3 mm (⅛ inch) slices.
4 Concassé the tomatoes (peel, remove seeds, roughly chop).
5 Place the oil in a thick-bottomed pan and add the onions.
6 Cover with a lid and allow to cook gently 5–7 minutes without colouring.
7 Add the garlic, the marrow and aubergine slices and the peppers.
8 Season lightly with salt and mill pepper.
9 Allow to cook gently for 4–5 minutes, toss occasionally and keep covered.
10 Add the tomato and continue cooking for 20–30 minutes or until tender.
11 Mix in the parsley, correct the seasoning and serve.

Fig 12.2 Ingredients of ratatouille

11 Stuffed aubergine

Aubergine farcie

	4 portions	10 portions
aubergines	2	5
shallots, chopped	10 g (½ oz)	25 g (1 oz)
mushrooms	100 g (4 oz)	250 g (10 oz)
chopped parsley		
tomato concassé	100 g (4 oz)	250 g (10 oz)
salt, pepper		
demi-glace or jus-lié	125 ml (¼ pt)	300 ml (⅝ pt)

1 Cut the aubergines in two lengthwise.

2 With the point of a small knife make a cut round the halves approximately ½ cm (¼ inch) from the edge, then make several cuts ½ cm (¼ inch) deep in the centre.

3 Deep fry in hot fat at 185°C (365°F) for 2–3 minutes; drain well.

4 Scoop out the centre pulp and finely chop it.

5 Cook the shallots in a little oil or fat without colouring.

6 Add the well-washed mushrooms. Cook gently for a few minutes.

7 Mix in the pulp, parsley and tomato; season. Replace in the aubergine skins.

8 Sprinkle with breadcrumbs and melted butter. Brown under the salamander.

9 Serve with a cordon of demi-glace or jus-lié. Illustrated on page 444.

12 Broccoli

Cook and serve as for any of the cauliflower recipes (page 442). Green and purple broccoli, because of their size, need less cooking time than cauliflower.

Broccoli is usually broken down into florets and as such require very little cooking. Once brought to the boil, 1–2 minutes should be sufficient. This leaves the broccoli slightly crisp.

1 portion provides:
76 kJ/18 kcal
0.0 g fat
(of which 0.0 g saturated)
1.6 g carbohydrate
(of which 1.5 g sugars)
3.1 g protein
4.1 g fibre

1 portion provides:
297 kJ/71 kcal
5.1 g fat
(of which 3.3 g saturated)
5.8 g carbohydrate
(of which 5.8 g sugars)
0.7 g protein
2.8 g fibre

Use a minimum amount of salt.

13 Buttered carrots

Carottes au beurre

	4 portions	10 portions
carrots	400 g (1 lb)	1 kg (2½ lb)
salt, pepper		
butter	25 g (1 oz)	60 g (2½ oz)
chopped parsley		

1   Peel and wash the carrots.

2   Cut into neat even pieces or turn barrel shape.

3   Place in a pan with a little salt, a pinch of sugar and butter. Barely cover with water.

4   Cover with a buttered paper and allow to boil steadily in order to evaporate all the water.

5   When the water has completely evaporated check that the carrots are cooked; if not, add a little more water and continue cooking. Do not overcook.

6   Toss the carrots over a fierce heat for 1–2 minutes in order to give them a glaze.

7   Serve sprinkled with chopped parsley.

1 portion provides:
410 kJ/99 kcal energy
5.6 g fat
(of which 3.4 g saturated)
11.9 g carbohydrate
(of which 11.1 g sugars)
0.9 g protein
3.6 g fibre

14 Purée of carrots

Purée de carottes

	4 portions	10 portions
carrots	600 g (1½ lb)	1½ kg (3¾ lb)
butter or margarine	25 g (1 oz)	60 g (2½ oz)
salt, pepper		

1   Wash, peel and rewash the carrots. Cut in pieces.

2   Barely cover with water, add a little salt. Simmer gently or steam until tender.

3   Drain well. Pass through a sieve or mouli.

4   Return to the pan, reheat and mix in the butter, correct the seasoning, and serve.

Use a minimum amount of salt.

Using water only, 1 portion provides:
338 kJ/82 kcal energy
5.4 g fat
(of which 3.4 g saturated)
8.0 g carbohydrate
(of which 7.5 g sugars)
0.7 g protein
2.4 g fibre

15 Vichy carrots

Carottes Vichy

1   Allow the same ingredients as for buttered carrots, substitute Vichy water for the liquid.

2   Peel and wash the carrots (which should not be larger than 2 cm (1 inch) in diameter).

3   Cut into 2 mm (¹⁄₁₂ inch) thin slices on the mandolin.

4   Cook and serve as for buttered carrots.

Use a
minimum
amount of
salt.

16 Carrots in cream sauce

Carottes à la crème

	4 portions	10 portions
carrots	400 g (1 lb)	1 kg (2½ lb)
cream sauce (page 55)	¼ litre (½ pt)	600 ml (1¼ pt)
butter or margarine	10 g (½ oz)	25 g (1 oz)
salt, pepper		

Using a cream sauce based on béchamel with single cream added 40:10, 1 portion provides:
511 kJ/123 kcal energy
8.2 g fat
(of which 4.6 g saturated)
11.5 g carbohydrate
(of which 7.8 g sugars)
1.4 g protein
2.5 g fibre

Prepare and cook carrots as for buttered carrots. Mix with the sauce, correct the seasoning and serve.

Note: The cream sauce may be made with wholemeal flour, skimmed milk and natural yoghurt.

Use a minimum amount of salt. Try using half the amount of cream sauce and half natural yoghurt.

17 Stuffed mushrooms

Champignons farcis

	4 portions	10 portions
grilling mushrooms	300 g (12 oz)	1 kg (2 lb)
shallots, chopped	10 g (½ oz)	25 g (1 oz)
butter, margarine or oil	50 g (2 oz)	125 g (5 oz)
breadcrumbs	25 g (1 oz)	60 g (2½ oz)

Using sunflower oil, 1 portion provides:
577 kJ/137 kcal
13.1 g fat
(of which 1.8 g saturated)
3.2 g carbohydrate
(of which 0.3 g sugars)
1.9 g protein
2.1 g fibre

1   Peel, remove the stalk and wash well.

2   Retain 8 or 12 of the best mushrooms. Finely chop the remainder with the well washed peelings and stalks.

3   Cook the shallots, without colour, in a little fat.

4   Add the chopped mushrooms and cook for 3–4 minutes (duxelle).

5   Grill the mushrooms as in the recipe 18.

6   Place the duxelle in the centre of each mushroom.

7   Sprinkle with a few breadcrumbs and melted butter.

8   Reheat in the oven or under the salamander and serve.

Use a little unsaturated oil to cook the shallots.

18 Grilled mushrooms

Champignons grillés

Using sunflower oil, 1 portion provides:
499 kJ/119 kcal
12.8 g fat
(of which 1.7 g saturated)
0.0 g carbohydrate
(of which 0.0 g sugars)
0.9 g protein
1.3 g fibre

	4 portions	10 portions
grilling mushrooms	200 g (8 oz)	500 g (1¼ lb)
salt, pepper		
butter, margarine or oil	50 g (2 oz)	125 g (5 oz)

Use a minimum amount of salt.

1 Peel the mushrooms, remove the stalks and wash and drain well.

2 Place on a tray and season lightly with salt and pepper.

3 Brush with melted fat or oil and grill on both sides for 3–4 minutes. Serve with picked parsley.

19 Cabbage

Chou vert

1 portion provides:
38 kJ/9 kcal
0.0 g fat
(of which 0.0 g saturated)
1.1 g carbohydrate
(of which 1.1 g sugars)
1.3 g protein
2.5 g fibre

½ kg (1 lb) will serve 3–4 portions (1¼ kg, 2½ lb will serve 8–10 portions).

1 Cut cabbage in quarters.

2 Remove the centre stalk and outside leaves.

3 Shred and wash well.

4 Place into boiling lightly salted water.

5 Boil steadily or steam until cooked, 5–10 minutes, according to the age and type. Do not overcook.

6 Drain immediately in a colander and serve.

Note: Overcooking will lessen the vitamin content and also spoil the colour. This is also true when cooking any green vegetable.

20 Spring greens

Choux de printemps

Prepare and cook as for cabbage for 10–15 minutes according to the age and type. Do not overcook. ½ kg (1 lb) will serve 3–4 portions.
(1¼ kg, 2½ lb will serve 8–10 portions).

21 Stir-fry cabbage with mushrooms and beansprouts

1 portion provides:
393 kJ/94 kcal energy
6.3 g fat
(of which 0.8 g saturated)
5.9 g carbohydrate
(of which 4.7 g sugars)
4.0 g protein
3.3 g fibre

	4 portions	10 portions
sunflower oil	2 tbsp	5 tbsp
spring cabbage, shredded	400 g (1 lb)	1 kg (2½ lb)
soy sauce	2 tbsp	5 tbsp
mushrooms	200 g (8 oz)	500 g (1¼ lb)
beansprouts	100 g (4 oz)	250 g (10 oz)
freshly ground pepper		

Reduce the oil by half when cooking the cabbage. No added salt is needed as soy sauce is added.

Use a minimum amount of salt; rely on the stock for flavour.

1 Heat the oil in a suitable pan (wok).

2 Add the cabbage and stir for 2 minutes.

3 Add the soy sauce, stir well. Cook for a further 1 minute.

4 Add the mushrooms cut into slices and cook for a further 2 minutes.

5 Stir in the beansprouts and cook for 1–2 minutes.

6 Stir well. Season with freshly ground pepper and serve.

Note: This recipe can be prepared without the mushrooms and/or beansprouts if desired. Pak Choi, a small Chinese cabbage, is ideal for this dish.

22 Braised cabbage

Choux braisés

1 portion provides:
215 kJ/52 kcal energy
0.6 g fat
(of which 0.2 g saturated)
9.4 g carbohydrate
(of which 8.5 g sugars)
2.6 g protein
4.0 g fibre

	4 portions	10 portions
cabbage	½ kg (1 lb)	1¼ kg (2½ lb)
carrot	100 g (4 oz)	250 g (10 oz)
onion	100 g (4 oz)	250 g (10 oz)
white stock	250 ml (½ pt)	625 ml (1¼ pt)
salt, pepper		
bouquet garni		
jus-lié	125 ml (¼ pt)	300 ml (⅝ pt)

1 Quarter the cabbage, remove the centre stalk and wash.

2 Retain four (or ten) light green leaves, shred the remainder.

3 Blanch the leaves and shredded cabbage for 2–3 minutes; refresh.

4 Lay the blanched leaves flat on the table.

5 Place the remainder of the cabbage on the centre of each and season.

6 Wrap each portion of cabbage in a tea-cloth and shape into a fairly firm ball.

7 Remove from the tea-cloth. Place on a bed of roots.

8 Add the stock half way up cabbage, season and add bouquet garni.

9 Bring to the boil, cover with a lid and cook in the oven for 1 hour.

10 Dress the cabbage in a serving dish.

11 Add the cooking liquor to the jus-lié, correct the seasoning and consistency and strain.

12 Pour over the cabbage and serve.

Note: Braised stuffed cabbage can be made with the addition of 25–50 g (1–2 oz) (60–125 g, 2½–5 oz for 10 portions) sausage meat placed in the centre before shaping into a ball. This recipe can also be prepared using Chinese leaves.

23 Sauerkraut (pickled white cabbage)

Choucroûte

1 portion provides:
75.5 kJ/19 kcal energy
0.1 g fat
(of which 0.0 g saturated)
3.2 g carbohydrate
(of which 2.8 g sugars)
1.3 g protein
2.7 g fibre

	4 portions	10 portions
sauerkraut	400 g (1 lb)	1¼ kg (2½ lb)
studded onion	50 g (2 oz)	125 g (5 oz)
carrot	50 g (2 oz)	125 g (5 oz)
bouquet garni		
peppercorns	6	15
juniper berries	6	15
white stock	250 ml (½ pt)	625 ml (1¼ pt)

1 Season the sauerkraut and place in a casserole or pan, suitable for placing in the oven.

2 Add the whole onion and carrot, the bouquet garni and the peppercorns and berries.

3 Barely cover with good white stock. Cook with a buttered paper and lid.

4 Cook slowly in a moderate oven for 3–4 hours.

5 Remove the bouquet garni and onion. Cut the onion in slices.

6 Serve the sauerkraut garnished with slices of carrot.

Note: Garnished sauerkraut can be served as a main course (see page 295).

24 Braised red cabbage

Choux à la flamande

1 portion provides:
754 kJ/180 kcal
15.2 g fat
(of which 8.4 g saturated)
7.8 g carbohydrate
(of which 7.7 g sugars)
3.4 g protein
3.2 g fibre

	4 portions	10 portions
red cabbage	300 g (12 oz)	1 kg (2 lb)
salt, pepper		
butter	50 g (2 oz)	125 g (5 oz)
vinegar or red wine	125 ml (¼ pt)	300 ml (⅝ pt)
bacon trimmings (optional)	50 g (2 oz)	125 g (5 oz)
cooking apples	100 g (4 oz)	250 g (10 oz)
caster sugar	10 g (½ oz)	25 g (1 oz)

HEALTHY EATING TIP

The fat and salt content will be reduced by omitting the bacon.

1 Quarter, trim and shred the cabbage. Wash well and drain.

2 Season lightly with salt and pepper.

3 Place in a well-buttered casserole or pan suitable for placing in the oven (not aluminium or iron because these metals will cause a chemical reaction that will discolour the cabbage).

4 Add the peeled and cored apples. Cut into 1 cm (½ inch) dice and sugar.

5 Add the vinegar and bacon (if using), cover with a buttered paper and lid.

6 Cook in a moderate oven at 150–200°C (Reg. 2–6; 300–400°F) for 1½ hours.

7 Remove the bacon (if used) and serve.

Note: Other optional flavourings include 50 g (2 oz) sultanas, grated zest of one orange, pinch of ground cinnamon.

Use a minimum amount of salt. Use little or no bacon or suet.

Fig 12.3 Braised red cabbage

25 Braised celery

Céleri braisé

1 portion provides:
505 kJ/120 kcal
10.2 g fat
(of which 4.1 g saturated)
4.8 g carbohydrate
(of which 4.5 g sugars)
2.8 g protein
3.8 g fibre

	4 portions	10 portions
heads of celery	2	5
carrots, sliced	100 g (4 oz)	250 g (10 oz)
onion, sliced	100 g (4 oz)	250 g (10 oz)
bouquet garni		
white stock	¼ litre (½ pt)	625 ml (1¼ pt)
salt, pepper		
fat bacon or suet	50 g (2 oz)	125 g (5 oz)
crusts of bread	2	5

1 Trim the celery heads and the root, cut off the outside discoloured stalks and cut the heads to approximately 15 cm (6 inch) lengths.

2 Wash well under running cold water.

3 Place in a pan of boiling water. Simmer for about 20 minutes until limp. Refresh and rewash.

4 Place the sliced vegetables in a sauté pan, sauteuse or casserole.

5 Add celery heads whole or cut them in half lengthwise, fold over and place on the bed of roots.

6 Add the bouquet garni, barely cover with stock and season lightly.

7 Add the fat bacon or suet, the crusts of bread, cover with a buttered greaseproof paper and a tight lid and cook gently in a moderate oven at 150–200°C (Reg. 2–6; 300–400°F) for 2 hours or until tender.

8 Remove the celery from the pan, drain well and dress neatly.

9 Add the cooking liquor to an equal amount of jus-lié or demi-glace, reduce and correct the seasoning and consistency.

10 Mask the celery, finish with chopped parsley, and serve.

26 Brussels sprouts

Choux de bruxelles

1 portion provides:
82 kJ/20 kcal
0.0 g fat
(of which 0.0 g saturated)
1.9 g carbohydrate
(of which 1.8 g sugars)
3.1 g protein
3.2 g fibre

continued over ▶

▶ *Brussels sprouts continued*

½ kg (1 lb) will yield 3–4 portions (1¼ kg, 2½ lb will serve 8–10 portions).

1 Using a small knife trim the stems and cut a cross 2 mm (¹⁄₁₂ inch) deep and remove any discoloured leaves. Wash well.

2 Cook in boiling lightly salted water or steam for 5–10 minutes according to size. Do not overcook.

3 Drain well in a colander and serve.

Note: Brussels sprouts with butter are cooked and served as in previous recipe, but brushed with 25–50 g (1–2 oz) melted butter (60–125 g, 2½–5 oz for 10 portions).

Brussels sprouts with chestnuts. To every 400 g (1 lb) sprouts add 100 g (4 oz) cooked peeled chestnuts.

27 Cauliflower

Chou-fleur nature

> Using no additions, 1 portion provides:
> 142 kJ/34 kcal energy
> 0.9 g fat
> (of which 0.2 g saturated)
> 3.0 g carbohydrate
> (of which 2.5 g sugars)
> 3.6 g protein
> 1.8 g fibre

Allow 1 medium-sized cauliflower for 4 portions.

1 Trim the stem and remove the outer leaves.

2 Hollow out the stem with a peeler or cut into florets. Wash.

3 Cook in lightly salted boiling water or steam for approximately 10–15 minutes. Do not overcook (florets 3–5 mins).

4 Drain well and serve cut into 4 even portions.

Note: Buttered cauliflower is brushed with 25–50 g (1–2 oz) melted butter before serving and can be sprinkled with chopped parsley.

Other variations include:

- *Cauliflower fried in butter*
  1 Cut the cooked cauliflower in 4 portions.

2 Lightly colour on all sides in 25–50 g (1–2 oz) butter.

- *Cauliflower, cream sauce*
  1 Cook and serve as for cauliflower.
  2 Accompany with ¼ litre (½ pint) cream sauce in a sauceboat.

- *Cauliflower, melted butter*
  As for cauliflower, with a sauceboat of 100 g (4 oz) melted butter (see page 175).

- *Cauliflower, hollandaise sauce*
  As for cauliflower, accompanied by a sauceboat of ⅛ litre (¼ pint) hollandaise sauce (see page 67).

Note: Increase the above quantities 2½ times for 10 portions.

28 Cauliflower and garlic mash

Blend one cooked cauliflower with four roasted and peeled garlic cloves, 1 tablespoon of virgin olive oil, season and finish with chopped parsley. Suitable for serving with roast or baked cod.

29 Cauliflower au gratin or Cauliflower Mornay

Chou-fleur Mornay

> 1 portion (au gratin) provides:
> 632 kJ/150 kcal
> 10.4 g fat
> (of which 3.9 g saturated)
> 8.6 g carbohydrate
> (of which 3.8 g sugars)
> 6.3 g protein
> 2.0 g fibre

HEALTHY EATING TIP

No additional salt is needed as cheese is added.

1   Cut the cooked cauliflower into four.

2   Reheat in a pan of hot salted water (chauffant), or reheat in butter in a suitable pan.

3   Place in vegetable dish or on greased tray.

4   Coat with ¼ litre (½ pint) Mornay sauce (see page 55).

5   Sprinkle with grated cheese.

6   Brown under the salamander and serve.

30 Cauliflower polonaise

Chou-fleur polonaise

1 portion provides:
575 kJ/139 kcal energy
11.9 g fat
(of which 6.9 g saturated)
4.1 g carbohydrate
(of which 1.9 g sugars)
4.0 g protein
1.7 g fibre

1   Cut the cooked cauliflower into four, reheat in a chauffant or in butter in a suitable pan.

2   Heat 50 g (2 oz) butter, add 10 g (½ oz) fresh breadcrumbs in a frying-pan and lightly brown. Pour over the cauliflower, sprinkle with sieved hard-boiled egg and chopped parsley.

31 Sea-kale

Chou de mer

1 portion provides:
33 kJ/8 kcal energy
0.0 g fat
(of which 0.0 g saturated)
0.6 g carbohydrate
(of which 0.6 g sugars)
1.4 g protein
0.0 g fibre

½ kg (1 lb) will yield about 3 portions.

1   Trim the roots, remove any discoloured leaves.

2   Wash well and tie into a neat bundle.

3   Cook in boiling lightly salted water for 15–20 minutes. Do not overcook.

4   Drain well, serve accompanied with a suitable sauce (melted butter, hollandaise, etc.).

32 Sea-kale Mornay or Sea-kale au gratin

Chou de mer Mornay

1 portion provides:
628 kJ/157 kcal
10.4 g fat
(of which 3.9 g saturated)
8.4 g carbohydrate
(of which 3.6 g sugars)
6.1 g protein
1.4 g fibre

1   Trim the roots. Remove any discoloured leaves. Wash well and tie into a neat bundle. Cook in boiling salted water for 15–20 minutes. Do not overcook.

2   Reheat and cut into 5 cm (2 inch) lengths; place in a vegetable dish.

3   Coat with ¼ litre (½ pint) Mornay sauce (page 55) and sprinkle with grated cheese.

4   Brown under the salamander and serve.

33 Marrow

Courge

1 portion provides:
44 kJ/11 kcal
0.0 g fat
(of which 0.0 g saturated)
2.1 g carbohydrate
(of which 2.0 g sugars)
0.6 g protein
0.9 g fibre

1   Peel the marrow with a peeler or small knife.

2   Cut in half lengthwise.

3   Remove the seeds with a spoon.

4   Cut into even pieces approximately 5 cm (2 inches) square.

5   Cook in lightly salted boiling water or steam for 10–15 minutes. Do not overcook.

6   *Drain well* and serve.

Note: All the variations for cauliflower may be used with marrow.

1 portion with sausage stuffing
provides:
805 kJ/194 kcal energy
17.4 g fat
(of which 7.9 g saturated)
6.0 g carbohydrate
(of which 2.9 g sugars)
3.6 g protein
0.8 g fibre

HEALTHY EATING TIP

Use a minimum
amount of salt.
Use little or no bacon
or suet to cook the
marrow.
Use less fatty meat and
more rice in the
stuffing.

34 Stuffed marrow

Courge farcie

1 Peel the marrow and cut in half lengthwise.

2 Remove the seeds with a spoon.

3 Season and add the stuffing. Replace the two halves.

4 Cook as for braised celery (page 441) allowing about 1 hour.

5 To serve, cut into thick slices and dress neatly in a vegetable dish. Baby marrows are ideal for this.

Note: Various stuffings may be used: 100 g (4 oz) sausage meat or 100 g (4 oz) rice for 4 portions: cooked rice with chopped cooked meat, seasoned with salt, pepper and herbs; well-seasoned cooked rice with sliced mushroom, tomatoes, etc.

Fig 12.4 Stuffed aubergine, courgette, tomato

Squash are a vegetable of many varieties which may be used as for any of the recipes for marrow and courgettes. Squash can also be used for ratatouille. See figure 12.5.

35 Courgettes and peppers griddled with penne and Brie

		4 portions	10 portions
courgettes, finely sliced		4	10
red peppers	cored,	1	3
green peppers	deseeded,	1	3
yellow peppers	sliced	1	3
penne		400 g (1 lb)	1 kg (2½ lb)
Brie		175 g (7 oz)	400 g (1 lb)
olive oil	.	2 tbsp	3 tbsp
dill chopped		1 tbsp	2½ tbsp.
seasoning			

1 portion provides:
2498 kJ/593 kcal energy
21.0 g fat
(of which 8.9 g saturated)
82.3 g carbohydrate
(of which 10.4 g sugars)
23.8 g protein
6.0 g fibre

HEALTHY EATING TIP

No added salt is needed – plenty in the cheese.

1 Heat a griddle pan, lightly oil, place courgettes and peppers on the pan, cook for 5 minutes, turning occasionally.

2 Cook the penne *al dente*, refresh, drain, reheat in olive oil.

3 Add the griddled vegetables, diced Brie and dill. Season and serve.

Note: Gorgonzola, Camembert or other suitable cheeses may be used.

36 Marrow provençale

Courge provençale

	4 portions	10 portions
marrow	400 g (1 lb)	1 kg (2½ lb)
chopped onion	50 g (2 oz)	125 g (5 oz)
clove garlic, chopped	1	2–3
oil or butter	50 g (2 oz)	125 g (5 oz)
salt, pepper		
tomatoes, skinned, de-seeded and diced	400 g (1 lb)	1 kg (2½ lb)
chopped parsley		

1 portion provides:
524 kJ/126 kcal energy
10.6 g fat
(of which 6.5 g saturated)
6.4 g carbohydrate
(of which 5.7 g sugars)
1.8 g protein
1.4 g fibre

HEALTHY EATING TIP

Use a little unsaturated oil to cook the onion. Use a minimum amount of salt.

1 Peel the marrow, remove the seeds and cut into 2 cm (1 inch) dice.

2 Cook the onion and garlic in the oil in a pan for 2–3 minutes without colouring.

3 Add the marrow, season lightly with salt and pepper.

4 Add the tomato concassé.

continued over ▶

▶ *Marrow provençale continued*

5   Cover with a lid, cook gently in the oven or on the side of the stove for 1 hour or until tender.

6   Sprinkle with chopped parsley and serve.

Note: Baby marrows may be served similarly, but reduce the cooking time to 5–10 minutes.

> 1 portion provides:
> 113 kJ/27 kcal
> 0.1 g fat
> (of which 0.0 g saturated)
> 5.9 g carbohydrate
> (of which 0.4 g sugars)
> 1.0 g protein
> 0.8 g fibre

37 Baby marrow (Courgette)

Courgette

¾ kg (1½ lb) yields about 4 portions (2 kg, 4 lb yields about 10 portions). Because they are tender, courgettes are not peeled or de-seeded.

1   Wash. Top and tail and cut into round slices 3–6 cm (⅛–¼ inch) thick.

2   Gently boil in lightly salted water or steam for 2 or 3 minutes. Do not overcook.

3   Drain well and serve either plain or brushed with melted butter or margarine and/or sprinkled with chopped parsley.

> Using butter, 1 portion provides:
> 456 kJ/111 kcal energy
> 10.7 g fat
> (of which 6.6 g saturated)
> 1.9 g carbohydrate
> (of which 1.8 g sugars)
> 1.9 g protein
> 0.9 g fibre

38 Shallow-fried courgettes

Courgettes sautées

1   Prepare as recipe 37.

2   Gently fry in hot oil or butter for 2 or 3 minutes, drain and serve.

> Using vegetable oil, 1 portion provides:
> 481 kJ/117 kcal energy
> 11.4 g fat
> (of which 1.4 g saturated)
> 1.8 g carbohydrate
> (of which 1.7 g sugars)
> 1.8 g protein
> 0.9 g fibre

39 Deep-fried courgettes

Courgettes frites

1   Prepare as recipe 37.

2   Pass through flour, or milk and flour, or batter and deep fry in hot fat at 185°C (365°F). Drain well and serve.

40 Braised chicory

Endive au jus

½ kg (1 lb) will yield 3 portions.

1 Trim the stem, remove any discoloured leaves, wash.

2 Place in a well-buttered casserole or pan suitable to place in the oven.

3 Season lightly with salt and a little sugar if desired (to counteract the bitterness).

4 Add the juice of half a lemon to prevent discoloration.

5 Add 25–50 g (1–2 oz) butter per ½ kg (1 lb) and a few drops of water.

6 Cover with a buttered paper and lid.

7 Cook gently in a moderate oven at 150–200°C (Reg. 2–6; 300–400°F) for 1 hour.

8 Dress and serve.

> Using 25 g butter per ½ kg, 1 portion provides:
> 304 kJ/73 kcal
> 6.8 g fat
> (of which 4.3 g saturated)
> 1.8 g carbohydrate
> (of which 0.0 g sugars)
> 1.0 g protein
> 1.0 g fibre

41 Shallow-fried chicory

Endive meunière

Cook the chicory as in the previous recipe. Drain, shallow fry in a little butter, and colour lightly on both sides. Serve with 10 g (½ oz) per portion nut brown butter, lemon juice and chopped parsley.

> Using 37.5 g of butter, 1 portion provides:
> 484 kJ/118 kcal energy
> 12.0 g fat
> (of which 7.3 g saturated)
> 4.8 g carbohydrate
> (of which 1.3 g sugars)
> 0.9 g protein
> 1.5 g fibre

42 Leaf spinach

Epinards en branches

½ kg (1 lb) will yield 2 portions.

1 Remove the stems and discard them.

2 Wash the leaves very carefully in plenty of water, several times if necessary.

3 Cook in lightly salted boiling water for 3–5 minutes; do not overcook.

4 Refresh under cold water, squeeze dry into a ball.

5 When required for service, either reheat and serve plain or place into a pan containing 25–50 g (1–2 oz) butter, loosen with a fork and reheat quickly without colouring.

> Using 25 g butter per ½ kg, 1 portion provides:
> 515 kJ/123 kcal
> 10.8 g fat
> (of which 6.6 g saturated)
> 1.4 g carbohydrate
> (of which 1.2 g sugars)
> 5.2 g protein
> 6.3 g fibre

Using 25 g of butter, 1 portion provides:
588 kJ/143 kcal energy
11.9 g fat
(of which 6.7 g saturated)
3.3 g carbohydrate
(of which 3.1 g sugars)
5.7 g protein
4.2 g fibre

43 Spinach purée

Epinards en purée

1 Cook, refresh and drain the spinach as above.

2 Pass through a sieve or mouli, or use a food processor.

3 Reheat in 25–50 g (1–2 oz) butter, mix with a wooden spoon, correct the seasoning and serve.

Note: Creamed spinach purée can be made by mixing in 30 ml (⅛ pint) cream, 60 ml (¼ pint) béchamel or natural yoghurt before serving. Serve with a border of cream. An addition would be 1 cm (½ inch) triangle-shaped croûtons fried in butter. Spinach may also be served with toasted pine kernels or finely chopped garlic.

1 portion of 100 g provides:
344 kJ/81 kcals
0.6 g fat
(of which 0.1 g saturated)
5.0 g carbohydrate
(of which 0.4 g sugars)
7.9 g protein
6.5 g fibre

44 Broad beans

Fèves

½ kg (1 lb) will yield about 2 portions.

1 Shell the beans and cook in boiling salted water for 10–15 minutes until tender. Do not overcook.

2 If the inner shells are tough remove before serving.

Note: Variations include:

- Brushing with butter.
- Brushing with butter, then sprinkling with chopped parsley.
- Binding with ¼ litre (½ pint) cream sauce or fresh cream.

Fig 12.5 Various vegetables (from top left): beef tomato, green pepper, red pepper, squash, aubergine, courgette flowers, yellow courgette, green courgette, baby cauliflower, yellow pepper, mooli, baby corn, squash

45 French beans

Haricots verts

½ kg (1 lb) will yield 3–4 portions.

1   Top and tail the beans, carefully and economically.

2   Using a large sharp knife cut the beans into strips 5 cm × 3 mm (2 × ⅛ inch).

3   Wash.

4   Cook in lightly salted boiling water or steam for 5–10 minutes, until tender.

5   Do not overcook. Drain well and serve.

Note: Variations include:

- Brushing the beans with butter.

- Gently tossing the cooked beans in butter over heat without colouring.

- Adding to 400 g (1 lb) cooked French beans, 50 g (2 oz) shallow-fried onions.

- Combining 400 g (1 lb) cooked French beans with 100 g (4 oz) cooked flageolet beans.

> 1 portion provides:
> 646 kJ/154 kcal
> 2.9 g fat
> (of which 0.5 g saturated)
> 28.5 g carbohydrate
> (of which 2.1 g sugars)
> 5.1 g protein
> 5.9 g fibre

46 Runner beans

Wash and string the beans with a small knife, then cut them into thin strips approximately 4–6 cm (2–3 inches) long. Cook in boiling lightly salted water or steam for approximately 10 minutes. Drain well and serve. Do not overcook.

> 1 portion provides:
> 80 kJ/19 kcal
> 0.2 g fat
> (of which 0.0 g saturated)
> 2.7 g carbohydrate
> (of which 1.3 g sugars)
> 1.9 g protein
> 3.4 g fibre

47 Corn on the cob

Maïs

Allow 1 cob per portion.

1   Trim the stem.

2   Cook in lightly salted boiling water for 10–20 minutes or until the corn is tender. Do not overcook.

3   Remove the outer leaves and fibres.

4   Serve with a sauceboat of melted butter.

Note: Creamed sweetcorn can be made by removing the corn from the cooked cobs, draining well, and lightly binding with cream (fresh or non-dairy), béchamel or yoghurt.

> 1 portion provides:
> 646 kJ/154 kcal
> 2.9 g fat
> (of which 0.5 g saturated)
> 28.5 g carbohydrate
> (of which 2.1 g sugars)
> 5.1 g protein
> 5.9 g fibre

48 Celeriac

Using butter, 1 portion provides:
264 kJ/65 kcal energy
5.5 g fat
(of which 3.3 g saturated)
2.3 g carbohydrate
(of which 1.8 g sugars)
1.2 g protein
3.7 g fibre

Celeriac or celery root is a versatile vegetable that can be prepared and served raw as an hors d'oeuvre, makes an excellent soup or as a hot vegetable using any of the carrot recipes, pages 436–7.

49 Buttered turnips, swedes or celeriac

1 portion provides:
253 kJ/60 kcal
5.4 g fat
(of which 3.3 g saturated)
2.5 g carbohydrate
(of which 2.5 g sugars)
0.7 g protein
1.9 g fibre

	4 portions	10 portions
turnips, swedes or celeriac	400 g (1 lb)	1 kg (2½ lb)
salt, sugar		
butter	25 g (1 oz)	60 g (2½ oz)
chopped parsley		

1 Peel and wash the vegetables.
2 Cut into neat pieces or turn barrel shape.
3 Place in a pan with a little salt, a pinch of sugar and butter. Barely cover with water.
4 Cover with a buttered paper and allow to boil steadily in order to evaporate all the water.
5 When the water has completely evaporated check that the vegetables are cooked; if not, add a little more water and continue cooking. Do not overcook.
6 Toss the vegetables over a fierce heat for 1–2 minutes to glaze.
7 Drain well, and serve.

50 Purée of turnips, swedes, celeriac or parsnips

Using mix veg, 25 g butter used, 1 portion provides:
395 kJ/95 kcal energy
5.9 g fat
(of which 3.3 g saturated)
9.2 g carbohydrate
(of which 6.4 g sugars)
1.8 g protein
4.7 g fibre

	4 portions	10 portions
turnips, swedes, celeriac or parsnips	600 g (1½ lb)	1½ kg (3¾ lb)
salt, pepper		
butter	25 g (1 oz)	60 g (2½ oz)

1 Wash, peel and rewash the vegetables. Cut in pieces if necessary.
2 Barely cover with water; add a little salt.
3 Simmer gently until tender or steam. Drain well.
4 Pass through a sieve or mouli, or use a food processor.
5 Return to the pan, reheat and mix in the butter, correct the seasoning and serve.

Combination vegetable purée can include, for example: swede and carrot, parsnip and potato.

51 Fried onions

Oignons sautées ou oignons lyonnaise

½ kg (1 lb) will yield approximately 2 portions.

Using peanut oil, 1 portion provides:
681 kJ/162 kcal
12.9 g fat
(of which 2.4 g saturated)
10.4 g carbohydrate
(of which 10.4 g sugars)
1.8 g protein
2.6 g fibre

1 Peel and wash the onions, cut in halves, slice finely.

2 Cook slowly in 25–50 g (1–2 oz) oil in a frying-pan, turning frequently until tender and nicely browned; season lightly with salt.

52 French-fried onions

Oignons frites à la française

> Using 50 g onions, to give 83.5 g finished wt., 1 portion provides:
> 661 kJ/159 kcal energy
> 11.7 g fat
> (of which 1.6 g saturated)
> 12.3 g carbohydrate
> (of which 3.5 g sugars)
> 2.0 g protein
> 1.0 g fibre

Fig 12.6 Preparation and cooking of French-fried onions

53 Braised onions

Oignons braisés

> 1 portion provides:
> 245 kJ/58 kcal
> 0.4 g fat
> (of which 0.1 g saturated)
> 10.9 g carbohydrate
> (of which 10.4 g sugars)
> 3.4 g protein
> 2.8 g fibre

1 Peel and wash the onions.

2 Cut in 2 mm (½₂ inch) slices, against the grain. Separate into rings.

3 Pass through milk and seasoned flour.

4 Shake off the surplus. Deep fry in hot fat at 185°C (365°F).

5 Drain well on kitchen paper, season lightly with salt and serve.

1 Select medium even-sized onions, allow 2–3 portions per ½ kg (1 lb).

2 Peel, wash and cook in lightly salted boiling water for 30 minutes or steam.

3 Drain and place in a pan or casserole suitable for use in the oven.

4 Add a bouquet garni, half-cover with stock and a lid and braise gently at 180–200°C (Reg. 4–6; 350–400°F) in the oven until tender.

5 Drain well and dress neatly in a vegetable dish.

6 Reduce the cooking liquor with an equal amount of jus-lié or demi-glace. Correct the seasoning and consistency and pass. Mask the onions and sprinkle with chopped parsley.

1 portion provides:
62 kJ/260 kcal
0.4 g fat
(of which 0.1 g saturated)
9.8 g carbohydrate
(of which 3.7 g sugars)
5.4 g protein
4.8 g fibre

54 Peas

Fresh peas 1 kg (2 lb) will yield about 4 portions.

1   Shell and wash the peas.

2   Cook in lightly salted boiling water or steam with a sprig of mint until tender. Do not overcook. Drain in a colander.

3   Add 25 g (1 oz) butter and ½ teaspoon caster sugar, toss gently.

4   Serve with blanched, refreshed mint leaves.

Frozen peas ¼ kg (½ lb) will yield about 4 portions.

1   Cook in lightly salted boiling water for approximately 1 minute or until tender. Drain in a colander.

2   Add 25 g (1 oz) butter and ½ teaspoon caster sugar; toss gently (optional).

3   Serve with blanched refreshed mint leaves.

Mange-tout ½ kg (1 lb) will yield 4–6 portions

1   Top and tail, wash and drain.

2   Cook in boiling salted water for 2–3 minutes, until slightly crisp.

3   Serve whole, brushed with butter.

Sugar snap peas

Proceed as for mange-tout.

1 portion provides:
515 kJ/123 kcal
5.6 g fat
(of which 3.4 g saturated)
12.9 g carbohydrate
(of which 5.8 g sugars)
5.9 g protein
5.7 g fibre

55 Peas French-style

Petit pois à la française

	4 portions	**10 portions**
peas (in the pod)	1 kg (2 lb)	2½ kg (5 lb)
spring or button onions	12	40
small lettuce	1	2–3
butter	25 g (1 oz)	60 g (2½ oz)
salt		
caster sugar	½ tsp	1 tsp
flour	5 g (¼ oz)	12 g (⅜ oz)

1   Shell and wash the peas and place in a sauteuse.

2   Peel and wash the onions, shred the lettuce and add to the peas with half the butter, a little salt and the sugar.

3   Barely cover with water. Cover with a lid and cook steadily, preferably in the oven, until tender.

4   Correct the seasoning.

5   Mix the remaining butter with the flour and shake into the boiling peas until thoroughly mixed, and serve.

Note: When using frozen peas, allow the onions to almost cook before adding the peas.

56 Stuffed pimento

Piment farci

	4 portions	**10 portions**
medium-sized red pimentos	4	10
Pilaff		
rice (long-grain)	200 g (8 oz)	500 g (1¼ lb)
onion, chopped	50 g (2 oz)	125 g (5 oz)
butter	50 g (2 oz)	125 g (5 oz)
salt, pepper		
carrots, sliced	50 g (2 oz)	125 g (5 oz)
onions, sliced	50 g (2 oz)	125 g (5 oz)
bouquet garni		
white stock	½ litre (1 pt)	1¼ litre (2½ pt)

1 portion provides:
1291 kJ/308 kcal
11.4 g fat
(of which 6.7 g saturated)
48.8 g carbohydrate
(of which 5.3 g sugars)
5.4 g protein
3.1 g fibre

HEALTHY EATING TIP

This dish is low in fat if the pimentos are placed in the oven or under the salamander and the butter/oil kept to a minimum. Add little or no salt.
If extra vegetables are added to the rice, and a vegetable stock used, this dish can be a useful vegetarian starter.

1   Place the pimentos on a tray in the oven or under the salamander for a few minutes, or deep fry in hot oil at 180°C (365°F), until the skin blisters.

2   Remove the skin and stalk carefully and empty out all the seeds.

3   Stuff with a well-seasoned pilaff of rice, which may be varied by the addition of mushrooms, tomatoes, ham, etc.

4   Replace the stem.

5   Place the pimentos on the sliced carrot and onion in a pan suitable for the oven; add the bouquet garni, stock and seasoning. Cover with a buttered paper and lid.

6   Cook in a moderate oven at 180–200°C (Reg. 4–6; 350–400°F) for 1 hour or until tender.

7   Serve garnished with picked parsley.

57 Salsify

Salsifi

½ kg (1 lb) will yield 2–3 portions.

1   Wash, peel and rewash the salsify.

2   Cut into 5 cm (2 inch) lengths.

3   Cook in a blanc as for artichokes (recipe 431). Do not overcook.

1 portion provides:
76 kJ/18 kcal
0.0 g fat
(of which 0.0 g saturated)
2.8 g carbohydrate
(of which 2.8 g sugars)
1.9 g protein
0.0 g fibre

continued over ▶

► *Salsify continued*

4   They may then be served as for any of the cauliflower recipes, pages 442–3.

5   Salsify may also be passed through batter and deep fried.

1 portion provides:
1386 kJ/336 kcal energy
32.1 g fat
(of which 4.7 g saturated)
9.0 g carbohydrate
(of which 8.2 g sugars)
2.9 g protein
3.8 g fibre

HEALTHY EATING TIP

Use less oil in the marinade and lightly brush the vegetables with the marinade before grilling. Add little or no salt to the marinade.

58 Grilled vegetables

(also known as griddled vegetables)

	4 portions	10 portions
courgettes	2	5
aubergine	1	3
red pepper	1	3
yellow pepper	1	3
tomatoes	2	5
balsamic vinegar	2 tbsp	5 tbsp
seasoning		
Marinade **olive oil extra virgin**	2 tbsp	5 tbsp
crushed and chopped cloves of garlic	2	5
fresh thyme chopped	1 tsp	2½ tsp
fresh basil leaves chopped	1 tsp	2½ tsp
fresh rosemary chopped	1 tsp	2½ tsp

1   Cut the courgettes lengthways into 3 mm (⅛ inch slices) and aubergines into 5 mm (¼ inch rounds). Cut each pepper in half, de-seed and cut each half into two. Skin the tomatoes, halve and de-seed. Marinate the vegetables with the prepared marinade, making sure that all the vegetables are coated. Cover and leave for 8–12 hours.

2   Brush suitable grill tray with oil and place on the vegetables from the marinade.

3   Courgettes and tomatoes grill for approximately 2 minutes. Aubergines and peppers grill for approximately 4 minutes.

4   Season lightly. Place on suitable serving dishes, sprinkle with balsamic vinegar.

Other vegetables that may be included are celery, fennel and chicory.

It is advisable to blanch celery, fennel and chicory in boiling water for 30–60 seconds, refresh and drain before marinating and grilling.

Fig 12.7 Grilled vegetables
John Campbell

59 Roasted vegetables

	4 portions	10 portions
red onions, small	1	3
red peppers	1	3
yellow peppers	1	3
courgettes	2	5
aubergines	1	3
garlic, coarsely chopped	1–2 cloves	2–4 cloves
olive oil	1 tbsp	2½ tbsp
balsamic vinegar	1 tbsp	2½ tbsp
fresh rosemary roughly		
fresh basil chopped		
black mill pepper		
sea salt		

1 portion provides:
343 kJ/82 kcal energy
3.6 g fat
(of which 0.6 g saturated)
10.0 g carbohydrate
(of which 8.6 g sugars)
3.0 g protein
3.8 g fibre

HEALTHY EATING TIP

Lightly brush the vegetables with the olive oil and add a minimum amount of salt.

1   Peel the vegetables, cut the onion into 8 pieces, the peppers into half, de-seed and cut each into approximately 4–6 even pieces. Cut the courgettes into 2 cm × 1 cm (1 inch × ½ inch) batons. Cut the aubergine into 2 cm × 1 cm (1 inch × ½ inch) batons.

2   Place all vegetables into a suitable roasting dish, sprinkle with the olive oil and balsamic vinegar.

3   Season lightly with sea salt and pepper.

4   Sprinkle with rosemary and basil.

5   Place in a pre-heated oven at 180°C (350°F) for approximately 15 minutes.

6   Serve immediately.

These vegetables may also be chilled and served with a salad as a starter.

60 Grilled tomatoes

Tomates grillées

Allow 1 or 2 per portion according to size; ½ kg (1 lb) will yield 3–4 portions.

1   Wash the tomatoes, and remove the eyes with a small knife.

2   Place on a greased, seasoned baking tray.

3   Make an incision 2 mm (¹⁄₁₂ inch) cross-shape on the opposite side to the eye and peel back the four corners.

Using sunflower oil, 1 portion provides:
121 kJ/29 kcal
1.3 g fat
(of which 0.3 g saturated)
3.5 g carbohydrate
(of which 3.5 g sugars)
1.1 g protein
1.9 g fibre

continued over ▶

► *Grilled tomatoes continued*

HEALTHY EATING TIP

Use a little
unsaturated oil to
brush over the
tomatoes.
Add a minimum
amount of salt.

4   Brush with oil and season lightly with salt and
    pepper.

5   Grill under a moderately hot salamander. Serve garnished with
    picked parsley or fresh basil leaves.

Fig 12.8 Roasted vegetables   *John Campbell*

1 portion provides:
430 kJ/102 kcal energy
5.9 g fat
(of which 3.5 g saturated)
10.6 g carbohydrate
(of which 5.7 g sugars)
2.5 g protein
2.2 g fibre

HEALTHY EATING TIP

Use a small amount of an
unsaturated oil to cook
the shallots and brush
over the stuffed tomatoes.
Add a minimum amount
of salt.
Adding cooked rice to the
stuffing will increase the
amount of starchy
carbohydrate.

61 Stuffed tomatoes

Tomates farcies

	4 portions	10 portions
medium-sized tomatoes	8	20
Duxelle **shallots, chopped**	10 g (½ oz)	25 g (1¼ oz)
butter or oil	25 g (1 oz)	60 g (2½ oz)
mushrooms	150 g (6 oz)	375 g (15 oz)
salt, pepper		
clove garlic, crushed (optional)	1	2–3
white or wholemeal **breadcrumbs**	25 g (1 oz)	60 g (2½ oz)
chopped parsley		

1   Wash the tomatoes, remove the eyes.

2   Remove ¼ of the tomato with a sharp knife.

3   Carefully empty out the seeds without damaging the flesh.

4   Place on a greased baking tray.

5 Cook the shallots in a little oil or butter or margarine without colouring.

6 Add the washed chopped mushrooms, season with salt and pepper; add the garlic if using and cook for 2–3 minutes.

7 Add a little of the strained tomato juice, the breadcrumbs and the parsley; mix to a piping consistency. Correct the seasoning. At this stage several additions may be made: chopped ham, cooked rice, etc.

8 Place the mixture in a piping bag with a large star tube and pipe into the tomato shells. Replace the tops.

9 Brush with oil, season lightly with salt and pepper.

10 Cook in a moderate oven at 180–200°C (Reg. 4–6; 350–400°F) for 4–5 minutes.

11 Serve garnished with picked parsley or fresh basil or rosemary. Illustrated on page 444.

62 Beetroot

Betterave

Select medium-sized or small beetroots, carefully twist off the green leaves (do not cut). Wash well in cold water, cover with water and simmer gently until the skin is easily removed by rubbing between the fingers. Do *not* cut or prick with knife as the beetroots will 'bleed' and turn pale. Beetroots may also be cooked in a steamer.

> 1 portion provides:
> 92 kJ/22 kcal
> 0.0 g fat
> (of which 0.0 g saturated)
> 5.0 g carbohydrate
> (of which 5.0 g sugars)
> 0.9 g protein
> 1.3 g fibre

Beetroot can also be served hot:

- in cream sauce;

- coated in herb flavoured oil, see page 69;

- coated in butter and marmalade.

63 Basic tomato preparation

Tomate concassée

This is a cooked preparation that is usually included in the normal *mise en place* of a kitchen as it is used in a great number of dishes.

	4 portions	10 portions
tomatoes	400 g (1 lb)	1¼ kg (2½ lb)
shallots or onions, chopped	25 g (1 oz)	60 g (2½ oz)
butter, margarine or oil	25 g (1 oz)	60 g (2½ oz)
salt, pepper		

1 Plunge the tomatoes into *boiling* water for 5–10 seconds, the riper the tomatoes the less time required. Refresh *immediately*.

continued over ▶

▶ *Basic tomato preparation continued*

2 Remove the skins, cut in halves across the tomato and remove all the seeds.

3 Roughly chop the flesh of the tomatoes.

4 Meanwhile cook the chopped onion or shallot without colouring in the butter or margarine.

5 Add the tomatoes and season lightly.

6 Simmer gently on the side of the stove until the moisture is evaporated.

1 portion provides:
130 kJ/31 kcal
0.0 g fat
(of which 0.0 g saturated)
5.6 g carbohydrate
(of which 5.4 g sugars)
2.3 g protein
2.8 g fibre

64 Braised leeks

Poireaux braisés

½ kg (1 lb) of leeks will yield 2 portions.

1 Cut the roots from the leek, remove any discoloured outside leaves and trim the green.

2 Cut through lengthwise and wash well under running water.

3 Tie into a neat bundle.

4 Place in boiling lightly salted water for 5 minutes or steam.

5 Place on a bed of root vegetables.

6 Barely cover with stock, add the bouquet garni and season lightly.

7 Cover with a lid and cook for ½–1 hour or until tender.

8 Remove the leeks from the pan and fold neatly; arrange in a vegetable dish.

9 Meanwhile add jus-lié to the cooking liquor and correct the seasoning and consistency.

10 Pour the sauce over the leeks.

Note: Boiled leeks are prepared as above, cooking for 10–15 minutes. Drain well, cut the string and serve plain, or brushed with melted butter. Leeks may also be served coated with cream or parsley sauce.

1 portion provides:
235 kJ/56 kcal
0.0 g fat
(of which 0.0 g saturated)
13.5 g carbohydrate
(of which 2.7 g sugars)
1.3 g protein
2.5 g fibre

65 Parsnips

Panais

Wash well. Peel the parsnips and again wash well. Cut into quarters lengthwise, remove the centre root if tough. Cut into neat pieces and cook in lightly salted water until tender or steam. Drain and serve with melted butter or in a cream sauce. Parsnips may be roasted in the oven in a little fat or in with a joint and can be cooked and prepared as a purée.

66 Kohlrabi

Information about this vegetable can be found in *Advanced Practical Cookery*.

67 Pease pudding

	4 portions	10 portions
yellow split peas, soaked	200 g (8 oz)	500 g (1¼ lb)
water	½ litre (1 pt)	1¼ litre (2½ pt)
studded onion	50 g (2 oz)	125 g (5 oz)
carrot	50 g (2 oz)	125 g (5 oz)
bacon trimmings	50 g (2 oz)	125 g (5 oz)
butter or margarine	50 g (2 oz)	125 g (5 oz)
salt, pepper		

Using hard margarine, 1 portion provides:
1277 kJ/304 kcal
15.6 g fat
(of which 6.5 g saturated)
29.6 g carbohydrate
(of which 2.3 g sugars)
13.1 g protein
6.5 g fibre

HEALTHY EATING TIP

No added salt is needed. Reduce the amount of butter or margarine added to the puréed peas.

1 Place all the ingredients, except the butter and margarine, in a saucepan with a tight-fitting lid.

2 Bring to the boil, cook in a moderate oven at 180–200°C (Reg. 4–6; 350–400°F) for 2 hours.

3 Remove the onion, carrot and bacon and pass the peas through a sieve or use a food processor.

4 Return to a clean pan, mix in the butter or margarine, correct the seasoning and consistency (this should be firm).

68 Mixed vegetables

Macédoine de légumes, Jardinière de légumes

	4 portions	10 portions
carrots	100 g (4 oz)	250 g (10 oz)
turnips	50 g (2 oz)	125 g (5 oz)
salt		
French beans	50 g (2 oz)	125 g (5 oz)
peas	50 g (2 oz)	125 g (5 oz)

1 portion provides:
58 kJ/14 kcal
0.1 g fat
(of which 0.0 g saturated)
2.5 g carbohydrate
(of which 1.7 g sugars)
1.0 g protein
2.1 g fibre

1 Peel and wash the carrots and turnips; cut into ½ cm (¼ inch) dice (macédoine) or batons (jardinière); cook separately in lightly salted water, do not overcook. Refresh.

2 Top and tail the beans; cut into ½ cm (¼ inch) dice, cook and refresh, do not overcook.

3 Cook the peas and refresh.

4 Mix the vegetables and when required reheat in hot salted water.

5 Drain well, serve brushed with melted butter.

1 portion provides:
21 kJ/5 kcal
0.0 g fat
(of which 0.0 g saturated)
0.7 g carbohydrate
(of which 0.7 g sugars)
0.6 g protein
2.2 g fibre

69 Fennel

Fenouil

The foliage of this plant is a herb of distinctive flavour used in fish cookery and salads. One good-sized bulb will serve 2–4 portions.

1 Trim the bulb, remove the stalks and leaves and wash well.

2 Cook in lightly salted boiling water for 15–20 minutes. Do not overcook.

3 Drain well, cut into portions and serve as for any of the cauliflower recipes on pages 442–3.

Note: Fennel may also be braised as for celery, page 441.

70 Mixed fried vegetables in batter

Légumes en fritot

The vegetables are prepared in small pieces and may also be served individually.

Fried in peanut oil, 1 portion provides:
1062 kJ/253 kcal
16.5 g fat
(of which 3.6 g saturated)
22.7 g carbohydrate
(of which 2.7 g sugars)
4.9 g protein
3.1 g fibre

HEALTHY EATING TIP

Use semi-skimmed milk and a pinch of salt to make the batter. Make sure the fat is hot so that less will be absorbed into the batter. Drain on kitchen paper.

cauliflower

fennel

broccoli

parsnips

celery

salsify

French beans

courgettes

1 Boil or steam the vegetables (except the courgettes) keeping them slightly firm.

2 Marinate in oil, lemon juice and chopped parsley.

3 Dip in batter (see page 181).

4 Deep fry in hot fat 180°C (356°F) until golden brown.

5 Drain on kitchen paper and serve.

71 Straw vegetables

	4 portions	10 portions
carrots	50 g (2 oz)	125 g (5 oz)
leeks	50 g (2 oz)	125 g (5 oz)
celery	50 g (2 oz)	125 g (5 oz)
potatoes	100 g (4 oz)	250 g (10 oz)
fennel	50 g (2 oz)	125 g (5 oz)
parsnip	100 g (4 oz)	250 g (10 oz)

1 Wash and prepare all the vegetables.
2 Cut each vegetable into fine julienne.
3 Wash well, drain on a cloth and dry well.
4 Fry the vegetables in hot oil (185°C/365°F) until golden brown and crisp. Drain.

Use as garnish.

72 Vegetable crisps

Vegetable crisps may be made from the following vegetables:

parsnips

beetroot

carrots

mouli

root ginger

potato

courgette

aubergine

sweet potato

Peel and slice the vegetables very thinly (wash and dry the potatoes) using a mandoline.

Deep fry in deep hot oil at 185°C (365°F) until crisp. Drain well on kitchen paper, use as a garnish.

HEALTHY EATING TIP

Make sure the fat is hot so that less fat will be absorbed. Drain on kitchen paper. Limit the amount of these fatty vegetables when used as a garnish.

73 Ladies' fingers (okra) in cream sauce

Okra à la crème

> Using hard margarine, 1 portion provides:
> 928 kJ/221 kcal
> 20.2 g fat
> (of which 9.8 g saturated)
> 5.7 g carbohydrate
> (of which 5.7 g sugars)
> 4.4 g protein
> 3.2 g fibre

	4 portions	10 portions
ladies' fingers	400 g (1 lb)	1¼ kg (2½ lb)
butter or margarine	50 g (2 oz)	125 g (5 oz)
cream sauce	¼ litre (½ pt)	625 ml (1¼ pt)

HEALTHY EATING TIP

Use a little unsaturated oil to sweat the okra. Try using half cream sauce and half yoghurt, adding very little salt.

1 Top and tail the ladies' fingers.
2 Blanch in lightly salted boiling water, or steam; drain.
3 Sweat in the margarine or butter for 5–10 minutes, or until tender.
4 Carefully add the cream sauce.
5 Bring to the boil, correct seasoning and serve in a suitable dish.

Note: Okra may also be served brushed with butter or sprinkled with chopped parsley.

74 Vegetable moulds (mousse)

> Using carrots, 1 portion provides:
> 839 kJ/203 kcal energy
> 17.4 g fat
> (of which 9.0 g saturated)
> 5.3 g carbohydrate
> (of which 5.0 g sugars)
> 6.8 g protein
> 2.5 g fibre

Many vegetables are suitable for making into moulds (usually dariole or small timbale moulds): asparagus, broccoli, carrot, cauliflower, aubergine, fennel, spinach, etc.

	4 portions	10 portions
seasoned vegetable purée	400 g (1 lb)	1 kg (2½ lb)
eggs	3–4	7–10
double cream	2 tbsp	5 tbsp

1 Thoroughly mix the eggs without overbeating.
2 Pass them through a fine strainer on to the cold vegetable purée; add the cream and combine thoroughly.
3 Three quarter fill the buttered moulds (this allows for expansion during cooking).
4 Place the moulds in a bain-marie of hot water and bake at 190°C (Reg. 5; 375°F) until set.
5 Remove from oven and allow to stand for 10 minutes before turning out.

Note: Variations include:

- Béchamel sauce can be used in place of cream.
- Extra ingredients, spices or herbs, may be added to the various moulds (chopped garlic with aubergine; toasted pine nuts in spinach; chopped coriander in carrot; grated Parmesan cheese with broccoli, etc.).

Vegetable moulds can be served as vegetables, as a garnish or as a light course, in which case they would be served with a suitable sauce (asparagus mousse, mushroom sauce, page 56).

Fig 12.9 🥄 Carrot, broccoli and cauliflower mousse *John Campbell* **Fig 12.10** 🥄 Vegetable soufflés

Vegetable soufflé uses the same basic recipe; keep the purée stiff. Separate the eggs, mix the yolks into the purée then fold in the stiffly beaten whites. Place the mixture into buttered and floured soufflé moulds; bake in a hot oven 220°C (Reg. 7; 425°F) until set.

Pulse dishes

Pulses are the dried seeds of plants that form pods and they fall into three types: peas, beans and lentils.

There are numerous varieties of pulse and as the majority are grown in warm temperate climates most of those used in the UK are imported. Pulses are available in three forms: fresh, dried and tinned. Fresh pulses can be cooked for any of the recipes in the vegetable section pages.

Food value

Pulses are a good source of protein and carbohydrate and therefore help to provide the body with energy. They also contain iron and vitamin B, are high in fibre and, with the exception of the soy bean, contain no fat.

Storage

Chapter 1 contains details of stock rotation procedures. In addition:

- Store fresh pulses in a refrigerator at a temperature below 5°C (41°F).

- Store frozen pulses in a freezer at a temperature below −18°C (0°F).

- Store dried pulses in clean airtight containers off the floor in the dry store.

- Unpack tinned pulses and check that the tins are sound and undamaged.

Health and hygiene

Chapter 1 contains details of health and food safety. In addition:

- Always check pulses for food pests (flour moths) and any foreign matter (stones, etc.).

- When storing cooked pulses, keep them covered and in a refrigerator at a temperature below 5°C (41°F).

- To prevent risk of cross-contamination, store cooked pulses away from any raw foods.

Types of pulses

Beans

- *Aduki* Small, round, deep red, shiny, nutty and sweet (the flavour used in oriental confectionery).

- *Black* Glistening black skins, creamy flesh.

- *Black-eyed* White beans with a black blotch, savoury flavour.

- *Broad* Also known as java beans, strongly flavoured.

463

- *Borlotti* Pink blotched, mottled, kidney-shaped with pleasant flavour.
- *Butter* Also known as Lima beans, available large or small.
- *Cannellini* Italian haricot, slightly larger than the English.
- *Dutch brown* Light brown in colour.
- *Flageolet* Pale green, kidney-shaped with delicate flavour.
- *Ful medames* Also known as Egyptian brown beans, small, brown and knobbly, known as the field bean in England.
- *Haricot* White, smooth, oval, used for baked beans.
- *Pinto* Pink, blotched, mottled colour.
- *Red kidney* Used in chilli con carne. They contain an enzyme that must be destroyed by presoaking, washing off, then boiling and ensuring that the beans are well cooked. Failure to do this may cause chemical food poisoning.
- *Soissons* Finest haricot beans.
- *Soy* Soy beans are very high in nutrients, especially protein, and they contain all the essential amino acids. They are processed into many forms: soy flour, TVP (meat substitute), tofu (curd), oils, margarines, soy milk and soy sauce.
- *Mung beans* Small, olive green in colour, good flavour, available split, whole and skinless. Widely used by being sprouted for their shoots.

Peas

- *Blue* Also known as marrowfat peas, pleasant flavour, floury texture, retain shape when cooked.
- *Chick* Available whole and split skinless. Whole chick peas look like the kernel of a hazelnut. They have a nutty taste.
- *Split green* A sweeter variety than the blue pea; cook to a purée easily.

- *Split yellow* Cook to a purée easily.

Both yellow and green split peas are used for vegetable purées and soups.

Lentils

- *Orange* Several types, which vary in size and shade and may be sold whole or split.
- *Green or continental* Retain shape after cooking, available in small or large varieties.
- *Yellow* Of Asian origin, often used as a dhal accompaniment to curry dishes.
- *Red* Purée easily, used for soups and stews etc.
- *Indian brown* Red lentils from which the seed coat has not been removed; they purée easily.
- *Puy* Dark French lentils, varied in size, retain their shape when cooked and are considered the best of their type.
- *Dhal* The Hindi word for dried peas and beans.

Use of pulses

Pulses are one of the most versatile commodities. They can be used extensively in a wide range of dishes. Imaginative and experimental use of different herbs, spices, flavourings and vegetables can give individual variation to the pulse recipes.

There are several recipes given in this book:

- Haricot bean and Three bean salads (page 120).
- Pulse soups (page 73).
- Pease pudding (page 459).
- Bean goulash (page 403).
- Meatless shepherd's pie (lentils) (page 407).
- Mexican bean pot (page 408).
- Moussaka (TVP) (page 414).
- Vegetable recipes (page 426).

Cooking

Some pulses require presoaking in cold water before cooking; the soaking time will vary according to the type and quality and the length of time they have been stored.

For soaking, pulses should be amply covered with cold water (they will expand gradually) and kept in a cold place. In some cases this may be for a few hours; in others it may be overnight, in which case they should be stored in the refrigerator at a temperature below 5°C (41°F). After soaking, salt should NOT be added before or during the cooking as this causes the pulses to toughen. Salt, however, may be added if required towards the end of the cookery process.

75 Dried beans (Pulse)

½ kg (1 lb) will yield 8 portions. Black-eyed, borlotti, butter, haricot, kidney, flageolet beans only require soaking if they have been stored for a long time.

1 If necessary soak in cold water overnight in a cool place.

2 Change the water, refresh.

3 Cover with cold water. Do not add salt (as salt toughens the skin and lengthens the cooking time). Bring to the boil.

4 Skim when necessary.

5 Add 50 g (2 oz) carrot, 50 g (2 oz) studded onion, 50 g (2 oz) bacon bone or trimmings (optional) and bouquet garni.

6 Simmer until tender. Season lightly with salt.

7 Drain and serve.

> 1 portion provides:
> 29 kJ/7 kcals
> 0.0 g fat
> (of which 0.0 g saturated)
> 1.1 g carbohydrate
> (of which 0.8 g sugars)
> 0.8 g protein
> 3.2 g fibre

Note: Pulse beans can be served sprinkled with chopped parsley, mixed fresh herbs or chives. They can also be lightly dressed with a good quality oil (natural or flavoured) and/or a suitably flavoured warm vinaigrette.

Puy lentils are a popular, green-coloured lentil that do not require soaking and hold their shape when cooked. They require only about 30 minutes cooking and they can be braised in a little stock, vegetables, herbs, wine, etc. Usually cooked *al dente*, they are a suitable accompaniment for many meat, game and poultry dishes and can be used as a garnish for roast and baked fish.

13 Potatoes

Variations in shape
for fondant potatoes
John Campbell

Delmonico potatoes

Mashed potatoes with spring onions
John Campbell

Potatoes

Several named varieties of potato are grown in Britain and these will be available according to the season. The different varieties have differing characteristics and some are more suitable for certain methods of cooking than others; e.g.:

- *Maris Piper* Suitable for boiling, mashing, baking, roasting, frying.
- *Desirée, Wilja, Cara* Excellent for chips.
- *King Edwards* Excellent for most purposes.

Potatoes are also imported from Cyprus, Egypt, Spain, France, Greece, Italy, the Canary Islands, The Netherlands and Belgium.

Purchasing

Potatoes should be of even shape and free from dirt, blemishes (possible disease), green patches, mechanical damage and any growth shoots.

Storage

Store in paper sacks or on vegetable racks in a cool, dry, dark, airy store. If kept near warmth they will start to turn green and sprout; if kept in damp conditions they will quickly deteriorate. These are signs that the potatoes are producing poisonous alkaloids, which can be a potential health hazard, and must not be used for human consumption.

Food value

Potatoes are a source of vitamin C and they also contain iron, calcium, thiamin, nicotine acid, protein and fibre.

Yield

½ kg (1 lb) old potatoes will yield approximately 3 portions. ½ kg (1 lb) new potatoes will yield approximately 4 portions. 1½ kg (3 lb) old potatoes will yield approximately 10 portions. 1¼ kg (2½ lb) new potatoes will yield approximately 10 portions.

Ready prepared

Potatoes are obtainable in many convenience forms: peeled, turned, cut into various shapes for frying, or scooped into balls (Parisienne) or olive shape.

Chips are available fresh, frozen, chilled or vacuum packed.

Frozen potatoes are available as croquettes, hash browns, sauté and roast. Mashed potato powder is also available.

1 Plain boiled potatoes

Pommes nature

> Using old potatoes, 1 portion provides:
> 487 kJ/116 kcal
> 0.1 g fat
> (of which 0.0 g saturated)
> 28.6 g carbohydrate
> (of which 0.6 g sugars)
> 2.0 g protein
> 1.5 g fibre

1   Wash, peel and rewash the potatoes.
2   Cut or turn into even-sized pieces allowing 2–3 pieces per portion.
3   Cook carefully in lightly salted water for approximately 20 minutes.
4   Drain well and serve.

2 Parsley potatoes

Pommes persillées

> Using 10 g butter per portion, old potatoes, 1 portion provides:
> 798 kJ/190 kcal
> 8.3 g fat
> (of which 5.2 g saturated)
> 28.6 g carbohydrate
> (of which 0.6 g sugars)
> 2.1 g protein
> 1.5 g fibre

1   Prepare and cook the potatoes as for plain boiled.
2   Brush with melted butter and sprinkle with chopped parsley.

3 Mashed potatoes

Pommes purée

> Using old potatoes, butter and whole milk, 1 portion provides:
> 763 kJ/182 kcal
> 7.1 g fat
> (of which 4.4 g saturated)
> 29.0 g carbohydrate
> (of which 1.1 g sugars)
> 2.4 g protein
> 1.5 g fibre

HEALTHY EATING TIP

Add a minimum amount of salt. Add a little olive oil in place of butter and semi-skimmed milk.

1   Wash, peel and rewash the potatoes. Cut to an even size.
2   Cook in lightly salted water or steam.
3   Drain off the water, cover and return to a low heat to dry out the potatoes.
4   Pass through a medium sieve or a special potato masher.

5 Return the potatoes to a clean pan.

6 Add 25 g (1 oz) butter per ½ kg (1 lb) and mix in with a wooden spoon.

7 Gradually add warm milk 30 ml (⅛ pint) stirring continuously until a smooth creamy consistency is reached.

8 Correct the seasoning and serve.

Note: Variations of mashed potatoes can be achieved by:

- dressing in a serving dish and surrounding with a cordon of fresh cream;
- placing in a serving dish, sprinkling with grated cheese, melted butter and browning under a salamander;
- adding 50 g (2 oz) diced cooked lean ham, 25 g (1 oz) diced red pepper and chopped parsley;
- adding lightly sweated chopped spring onions;
- adding a good quality olive oil in place of butter;
- addition of a little garlic juice (use a garlic press);
- addition of a little fresh chopped rosemary or chives;
- mixing with equal quantities of parsnip;
- addition of a little freshly grated horseradish or horseradish cream.

4 Duchess potatoes (basic recipe)

Pommes duchesse

Using old potatoes, whole milk, hard margarine, 1 portion provides:
819 kJ/195 kcal
8.2 g fat
(of which 3.3 g saturated)
28.6 g carbohydrate
(of which 0.6 g sugars)
3.5 g protein
1.5 g fibre

1 Wash, peel and rewash the potatoes. Cut to an even size.

2 Cook in lightly salted water.

3 Drain off the water, cover and return to a low heat to dry out the potatoes.

4 Pass through a medium sieve or a special potato masher or mouli.

5 Place the potatoes in a clean pan.

6 Add 1 egg yolk per ½ kg (1 lb) and stir in vigorously with a wooden spoon.

7 Mix in 25 g (1 oz) butter or margarine per ½ kg (1 lb). Correct the seasoning.

8 Place in a piping bag with a large star tube and pipe out into neat spirals about 2 cm (1 inch) diameter and 5 cm (2 inches) high on to a lightly greased baking sheet.

9 Place in a hot oven at 230°C (Reg. 8; 450°F) for 2–3 minutes in order to firm the edges slightly.

10 Remove from the oven and brush with eggwash.

11 Brown lightly in a hot oven or under the salamander.

5 Croquette potatoes

Pommes croquettes

Using hard margarine and frying in peanut oil, 1 portion provides:
1699 kJ/405 kcal
25.4 g fat
(of which 6.6 g saturated)
40.8 g carbohydrate
(of which 1.1 g sugars)
6.0 g protein
2.2 g fibre

HEALTHY EATING TIP

Add a minimum amount of salt. Use peanut or sunflower oil to fry the croquettes and drain on kitchen paper.

1 Use a duchess mixture moulded cylinder shape 5 × 2 cm (2 × 1 inches).

2 Pass through flour, eggwash and breadcrumbs.

continued over ▶

▶ *Croquette potatoes continued*

3   Reshape with a palette knife and deep fry in hot deep oil (185°C) (365°F) in a frying-basket (see illustration below).

4   When the potatoes are a golden colour, drain well and serve.

Fig 13.1 ✎ Deep frying croquette potatoes

6 Potato cakes

1 portion provides:
1058 kJ/254 kcal energy
17.7 g fat
(of which 4.9 g saturated)
21.5 g carbohydrate
(of which 0.8 g sugars)
3.4 g protein
1.6 g fibre

Use a duchess mixture moulded into flat cakes, 3 cm (1½ inches) diameter, 1 cm (½ inch) thick. Shallow fry as for Macaire potatoes (recipe 21).

7 Almond potatoes

Pommes amandines

1 portion provides:
1613 kJ/387 kcal energy
26.5 g fat
(of which 6.0 g saturated)
30.2 g carbohydrate
(of which 1.5 g sugars)
8.9 g protein
2.9 g fibre

Prepare, cook and serve as for croquette potatoes (recipe 5), using nibbed almonds in place of breadcrumbs.

8 Marquis potatoes

Pommes marquise

Using 200 g potato per portion, 1 portion provides:
643 kJ/153 kcal
0.2 g fat
(of which 0.0 g saturated)
36.5 g carbohydrate
(of which 0.8 g sugars)
3.8 g protein
3.6 g fibre

1   Pipe duchess mixture in the shape of an oval nest, 5 × 2 cm (2 × 1 inches).

2   Cook and glaze as for duchess potatoes (recipe 4).

3   Place a spoonful of cooked tomato concassé (page 457) in the centre, sprinkle with a little chopped parsley and serve.

9 Baked jacket potatoes

Pommes au four

Using medium potato, 180 g analysis given per potato, 1 portion provides:
401 kJ/94 kcal energy
0.2 g fat
(of which 0.0 g saturated)
21.8 g carbohydrate
(of which 0.9 g sugars)
2.7 g protein
1.6 g fibre

HEALTHY EATING TIP
Oven bake without sea salt. Fillings based on vegetables with little or no cheese or meat will make a 'healthy' snack meal.

1   Select good-sized potatoes and allow one potato per portion.

2   Scrub well, make a 2 mm (½ inch) deep incision round the potato.

3   Place on a tray in a hot oven at 230–250°C (Reg. 8–9; 450–500°F) for about 1 hour. Turn the potatoes over after 30 minutes.

4   Test by holding the potato in a cloth and squeezing gently; if cooked it should feel soft.

Note: If the potatoes are being cooked by microwave, prick the skins first.

Variations include:

Split and filled with any of the following: grated cheese, minced beef or chicken, baked beans, chilli con carne, creamed cheese and chives, mushrooms, bacon, ratatouille, prawns in mayonnaise, coleslaw, etc.

The cooked potatoes can also be cut in halves lengthwise, the potato spooned out from the skins, seasoned, mashed with butter, returned to the skins, sprinkled with grated cheese and reheated in an oven or under the grill.

10 Steamed potatoes

Pommes vapeur

> Using old potatoes, 1 portion provides:
> 487 kJ/116 kcal
> 0.1 g fat
> (of which 0.0 g saturated)
> 28.6 g carbohydrate
> (of which 0.6 g sugars)
> 2.0 g protein
> 2.9 g fibre

1   Prepare the potatoes as for plain boiled (recipe 1); season lightly with salt.

2   Cook in a steamer and serve.

11 Steamed jacket potatoes

Pommes en robe de chambre

> Using old potatoes, 1 portion provides:
> 487 kJ/116 kcal
> 0.1 g fat
> (of which 0.0 g saturated)
> 28.6 g carbohydrate
> (of which 0.6 g sugars)
> 2.0 g protein
> 1.5 g fibre

1   Select small even-sized potatoes and scrub well.

2   Cook in a steamer or boil in lightly salted water and serve unpeeled.

Note: This method is frequently used with small new potatoes.

12 Sauté potatoes

Pommes sautées

> Using old potatoes and sunflower oil, 1 portion provides:
> 1249 kJ/297 kcal
> 11.4 g fat
> (of which 1.3 g saturated)
> 46.8 g carbohydrate
> (of which 0.4 g sugars)
> 4.9 g protein
> 1.7 g fibre

HEALTHY EATING TIP

Use a little hot sunflower oil to fry the potatoes. Add little or no salt; the customer can add more if required.

1   Select medium even-sized potatoes. Scrub well.

2   Plain boil or cook in the steamer. Cool slightly and peel.

3   Cut into 3 mm (⅛ inch) slices.

4   Toss in hot shallow oil in a frying-pan until lightly coloured; season lightly with salt.

5   Serve sprinkled with chopped parsley.

(See page 472 for an example of service of this dish.)

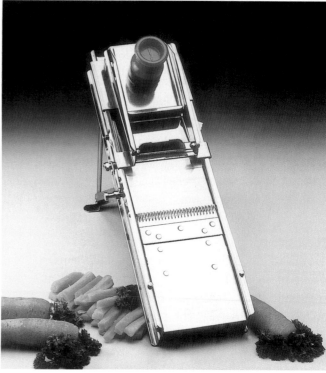

Fig 13.2 🍴 Deep fried potatoes: background, clockwise from left: fried, matchstick, croquette, bataille; foreground, left to right: straw, game chips, wafer

Fig 13.3 🍴 Mandolin

Fig 13.4 🍴 Ingredients for and service of sauté potatoes with onions

13 Sauté potatoes with onions

Pommes lyonnaise

1   Allow ¼ kg (8 oz) onion to ½ kg (1 lb) potatoes.

2   Cook the onions as for fried onions (page 450).

3   Prepare sauté potatoes as for the previous recipe.

4   Combine the two and toss together.

5   Serve as for sauté potatoes.

14 Crisps (game chips)

Pommes chips

1 Wash, peel and rewash the potatoes.
2 Cut in thin slices on the mandolin.
3 Wash well and dry in a cloth.
4 Cook in hot deep fat (185°C/365°F) until golden brown and crisp.
5 Drain well and season lightly with salt.

Note: Crisps are not usually served as a potato by themselves, but are used as a garnish and are also served with drinks and for snacks.

Crisps can also be made from other root vegetables e.g. parsnips, carrots, beetroot, turnips, swedes.

Vegetable straw can be made by the same method using any root vegetable or combination of vegetables.

Vegetable crisps and straw can be used to garnish meat and poultry dishes and with salads, sandwiches and snacks.

15 Wafer potatoes

Pommes gaufrettes

1 Wash, peel and rewash the potatoes.
2 Using a corrugated mandolin blade, cut in slices, giving a half turn in between each cut in order to obtain a wafer or trellis pattern.
3 Cook and serve as for crisps.

16 Matchstick potatoes

Pommes allumettes

1 Select medium even-sized potatoes.
2 Wash, peel and rewash.
3 Trim on all sides to give straight edges.
4 Cut into slices 5 cm × 3 mm (2 × ⅛ inch).
5 Cut the slices into 5 cm × 3 mm × 3 mm (2 × ⅛ × ⅛ inch) strips.
6 Wash well and dry in a cloth.
7 Fry in hot deep fat (185°C/365°F) until golden brown and crisp. Drain.
8 Season lightly with salt and serve.

Note: These may also be blanched as for fried potatoes (recipe 18).

Using old potatoes and peanut oil, 1 portion (25 g) provides:
424 kJ/101 kcal
9.0 g fat
(of which 1.7 g saturated)
4.9 g carbohydrate
(of which 0.1 g sugars)
0.4 g protein
0.3 g fibre

HEALTHY EATING TIP

Use hot sunflower oil to fry the potatoes and drain on kitchen paper. Add a minimum amount of salt; the customer can add more if required.

17 Straw potatoes

Pommes pailles

Using old potatoes and peanut oil, 1 portion (25 g) provides:
424 kJ/101 kcal
9.0 g fat
(of which 1.7 g saturated)
4.9 g carbohydrate
(of which 0.1 g sugars)
0.4 g protein
0.3 g fibre

1 Wash, peel and rewash the potatoes.
2 Cut into fine julienne.
3 Wash well and drain in a cloth.
4 Cook in hot deep fat (185°C/365°F) until golden brown and crisp.
5 Drain well and season lightly with salt.

Note: This potato is generally used as a garnish, usually for grills of meat.

18 Fried or chipped potatoes

Pommes frites

Using old potatoes and peanut oil, 1 portion provides:
1541 kJ/367 kcal
15.8 g fat
(of which 2.8 g saturated)
54.1 g carbohydrate
(of which 0.0 g sugars)
5.5 g protein
1.5 g fibre

1 Prepare and wash the potatoes.
2 Cut into slices 1 cm (½ inch) thick and 5 cm (2 inches) long.
3 Cut the slices into strips 5 × 1 × 1 cm (2 × ½ × ½ inch).
4 Wash well and dry in a cloth.
5 Cook in a frying-basket without colour in moderately hot fat (165°C/330°F).
6 Drain and place on kitchen paper on trays until required.

7 When required, place in a frying-pan and cook in hot fat (185°C/365°F) until crisp and golden.
8 Drain well, season lightly with salt and serve.

Note: Because chips are so popular, the following advice from the Potato Marketing Board is useful:

- Cook chips in small quantities, which will allow the oil to regain its temperature more quickly; the chips cook faster and absorb less fat.
- Do not let the temperature of the oil exceed 199°C (390°F) as this will accelerate the fat breakdown.
- Use oils high in polyunsaturates for a healthier chip.
- Ideally use a separate fryer for chips and ensure that it has the capacity to raise the fat temperature rapidly to the correct degree when frying chilled or frozen chips.
- Although the majority of chipped potatoes are purchased frozen, the Board recommends the following potatoes for those who prefer to make their own chips: Maris Piper, Cara, Désirée.

19 Deep fried potato wedges in batter

Using yeast batter, 1 portion provides:
1651 kJ/392 kcal energy
13.0 g fat
(of which 2.1 g saturated)
63.3 g carbohydrate
(of which 4.4 g sugars)
9.5 g protein
3.2 g fibre

	4 portions	10 portions
medium sized potatoes, unpeeled, but well scrubbed	4	10
flour (self-raising) made into a batter (page 177)	200 g (8 oz)	500 g (20 oz)
grated peeled potato, washed and pressed dry	150 g (6 oz)	375 g (15 oz)

	4 portions	10 portions
potatoes	400 g (1 lb)	1¼ kg (2½ lb)
onions	100 g (4 oz)	250 g (10 oz)
salt, pepper		
white stock	¼ litre (½ pt)	600 ml (1¼ pt)
butter, margarine *or* oil	25–50 g (1–2 oz)	60–100 g (4–5 oz)
chopped parsley		

1 Cut each potato into 8 even-sized wedges.

2 Steam the wedges until cooked, but still firm.

3 Add the grated potato to the batter.

4 Dip the wedge into the batter and deep fry in hot fat or oil (185°C/365°F).

Note: Potato wedges can be used as snacks, used with dips and served with main courses.

20 Savoury potatoes

Pommes Boulangère

Using 25 g hard margarine, 1 portion provides:
595 kJ/142 kcal
5.3 g fat
(of which 2.2 g saturated)
22.3 g carbohydrate
(of which 1.8 g sugars)
2.8 g protein
2.4 g fibre

Using 50 g hard margarine, 1 portion provides:
787 kJ/187 kcal
10.3 g fat
(of which 4.4 g saturated)
22.3 g carbohydrate
(of which 1.8 g sugars)
2.8 g protein
2.4 g fibre

1 Cut the potatoes into 2 mm (½ inch) slices on a mandolin. Keep the best slices for the top.

2 Peel, halve and finely slice the onions.

3 Mix the onions and potatoes together and season lightly with pepper and salt.

4 Place in a well-buttered shallow earthenware dish or roasting tin.

5 Barely cover with stock.

6 Neatly arrange overlapping slices of potato on top.

7 Brush lightly with oil.

8 Place in a hot oven at 230–250°C (Reg. 8–9; 450–500°F) for 20 minutes until lightly coloured.

9 Reduce the heat and allow to cook steadily, pressing down firmly from time to time with a flat-bottomed pan.

10 When ready all the stock should be cooked into the potato. Allow 1½ hours cooking time in all.

continued over ▶

▶ *Savoury potatoes continued*

11 Serve sprinkled with chopped parsley. If cooked in an earthenware dish, clean the edges of the dish with a cloth dipped in salt, and serve in the dish.

Note: Leeks can be used in place of onions for variety.

21 Macaire potatoes (potato cakes)

Pommes Macaire

> Using hard margarine and sunflower oil, this recipe provides:
> 4392 kJ/1047 kcal
> 65.7 g fat
> (of which 14.7 g saturated)
> 109.8 g carbohydrate
> (of which 2.7 g sugars)
> 11.4 g protein
> 10.8 g fibre

1 ½ kg (1 lb) will yield 2–3 portions.

2 Prepare and cook as for baked jacket potatoes (recipe 9).

3 Cut in halves, remove the centre with a spoon, and place in a basin.

4 Add 25 g (1 oz) butter per ½ kg (1 lb), a little salt and milled pepper.

5 Mash and mix as lightly as possible with a fork.

6 Using a little flour, mould into a roll, then divide into pieces, allowing one or two per portion.

7 Mould into 2 cm (1 inch) round cakes, flour lightly.

8 Shallow fry on both sides in very hot oil and serve.

Note: Additions to potato cakes can include:

- chopped parsley or fresh herbs or chives or duxelle;
- cooked chopped onion;
- grated cheese.

22 Byron potatoes

Pommes Byron

> Using 1 tbs each of cheese and double cream per person, analysis given per potato, 1 portion provides:
> 2099 kJ/505 kcal energy
> 39.0 g fat
> (of which 18.7 g saturated)
> 33.4 g carbohydrate
> (of which 1.8 g sugars)
> 7.1 g protein
> 2.4 g fibre

1 Prepare and cook as for Macaire potatoes.

2 Using the back of a dessertspoon make a shallow impression on each potato.

3 Carefully sprinkle the centres with grated cheese. Make sure no cheese is on the edge of the potato.

4 Cover the cheese with cream.

5 Brown lightly under the salamander and serve.

23 Fondant potatoes

Pommes fondantes

1   Select small or even-sized medium potatoes.

2   Wash, peel and rewash.

3   Turn into eight-sided barrel shapes, allowing 2–3 per portion, about 5 cm (2 inches) long, end diameter 1½ cm (¾ inch), centre diameter 2½ cm (1¼ inches).

4   Brush with melted butter, margarine or oil.

5   Place in a pan suitable for the oven.

6   Half cover with white stock, season lightly with salt and pepper.

7   Cook in a hot oven at 230–250°C (Reg. 8–9; 450–500°F), brushing the potatoes frequently with melted butter, margarine or oil.

8   When cooked the stock should be completely absorbed by the potatoes.

9   Brush with melted butter, margarine or oil and serve.

Note: Fondant potatoes can be lightly sprinkled with:

- thyme, rosemary or oregano (or this can be added to the stock)
- grated cheese (Gruyère and Parmesan or Cheddar)
- Chicken stock in place of white stock.

Using old potatoes and hard margarine, 1 portion (125 g raw potato) provides:
956 kJ/228 kcal
7.0 g fat
(of which 2.1 g saturated)
39.6 g carbohydrate
(of which 0.9 g sugars)
4.1 g protein
1.5 g fibre

HEALTHY EATING TIP

Use a little unsaturated oil to brush over the potatoes before and after cooking. No added salt, rely on the stock for flavour.

Fig 13.5 Variations in shape for fondant potatoes
John Campbell

Using old potatoes and peanut oil,
1 portion (125 g raw potato)
provides:
956 kJ/228 kcal
7.0 g fat
(of which 1.1 g saturated)
39.6 g carbohydrate
(of which 0.9 g sugars)
4.1 g protein
1.5 g fibre

HEALTHY EATING TIP

Brush the potatoes
with peanut or
sunflower oil, with
only a little in the
roasting tray. Drain
off all fat when
cooked.

24 Roast potatoes

Pommes rôties

1 Wash, peel and rewash the potatoes.
2 Cut into even-sized pieces, allow 3–4 pieces per portion.
3 Heat a good measure of oil or dripping in a roasting tray.
4 Add the well-dried potatoes and lightly brown on all sides.
5 Season lightly with salt and cook for about 1 hour in a hot oven at 230–250°C (Reg. 8–9; 450–500°F).
6 Turn the potatoes over after 30 minutes.
7 Cook to a golden brown. Drain and serve.

Note: Roast potatoes can be part-boiled for 10 minutes, refreshed and well dried before roasting. This will cut down on the cooking time and can also give a crisper potato.

25 Château potatoes

Pommes château

1 Select small even-sized potatoes and wash.
2 If they are of fairly even size, they need not be peeled, but can be turned into barrel-shaped pieces approximately the size of fondant potatoes.
3 Place in a saucepan of boiling water for 2–3 minutes, refresh immediately. Drain in a colander.
4 Finish as for roast potatoes (recipe 24).

26 Cocotte potatoes

Pommes cocotte

Proceed as for château potatoes, but with the potatoes a quarter the size, cooking them in a sauté pan or frying-pan.

27 Noisette potatoes

Pommes noisette

½ kg (1 lb) will yield 2 portions.

1 Wash, peel and rewash the potatoes.
2 Scoop out balls with a noisette spoon.
3 Cook in a little oil in a sauté pan or frying-pan. Colour on top of the stove and finish cooking in the oven at 230–250°C (Reg. 8–9; 450–500°F).

28 Potatoes with bacon and onions

Pommes au lard

	4 portions	10 portions
peeled potatoes	400 g (1 lb)	1¼ kg (2½ lb)
streaky bacon (lardons)	100 g (4 oz)	250 g (10 oz)
button onions	100 g (4 oz)	250 g (10 oz)
white stock	¼ litre (½ pt)	600 ml (1¼ pt)
salt and pepper		
chopped parsley		

1 Cut the potatoes in 1 cm (½ inch) dice.

2 Cut the bacon into ½ cm (¼ inch) lardons, lightly fry in a little fat together with the onions and brown lightly.

3 Add the potatoes, half cover with stock, season lightly with salt and pepper. Cover with a lid and cook steadily in the oven at 230–250°C (Reg. 8–9; 450–500°F) for approximately 30 minutes.

4 Correct the seasoning, serve in a vegetable dish and sprinkle with chopped parsley.

HEALTHY EATING TIP

Dry fry the bacon in a well-seasoned pan and drain off any excess fat. Add little or no salt.

29 Potatoes cooked in milk with cheese

Gratin dauphinoise

	4 portions	10 portions
potatoes	500 g (1¼ lb)	1¼ kg (2½ lb)
milk	250 ml (½ pt)	600 ml (1¼ pt)
salt and pepper		
grated cheese, preferably Gruyère	50 g (2 oz)	125 g (5 oz)

1 Slice the peeled potatoes ½ cm (¼ inch) thick.

2 Place in an ovenproof dish and cover with milk.

3 Season, sprinkle with grated cheese and cook in a moderate oven 190°C (375°F, Reg. 5) until the potatoes are cooked and golden brown.

30 Delmonico potatoes

Pommes Delmonico

1 Wash, peel and rewash the potatoes.

2 Cut into 6 mm (¼ inch) dice.

3 Barely cover with milk, season lightly with salt and pepper and allow to cook for 30–40 minutes.

continued over ▶

▶ *Delmonico potatoes continued*

4   Place in an earthenware dish, sprinkle with crumbs and melted butter, brown in the oven or under the salamander and serve.

31 New potatoes

Pommes nouvelles

1 portion provides:
383 kJ/91 kcal
0.1 g fat
(of which 0.0 g saturated)
22.0 g carbohydrate
(of which 0.8 g sugars)
1.9 g protein
2.4 g fibre

Method I

1   Wash the potatoes and boil or steam in their jackets until cooked.

2   Cool slightly, peel while warm and place in a pan of cold water.

3   When required for service add a little salt and a bunch of mint to the potatoes and heat through slowly.

4   Drain well, serve brushed with melted butter and sprinkle with chopped mint or decorate with blanched refreshed mint leaves.

Method II

1   Scrape the potatoes and wash well.

2   Place in a pan of lightly salted boiling water with a bunch of mint and boil gently until cooked for about 20 minutes. Serve as above.

Note: The starch cells of new potatoes are immature; to help break down these cells new potatoes are started to cook in boiling water.

Fig 13.6 🖉 A variety of new potatoes   *John Campbell*

32 New rissolée potatoes

Pommes nouvelles rissolées

Using peanut oil, 1 portion provides:
610 kJ/145 kcal
6.1 g fat
(of which 1.1 g saturated)
22.0 g carbohydrate
(of which 0.8 g sugars)
1.9 g protein
2.4 g fibre

New potatoes are cooked, drained and fried to a golden brown in oil or butter, or a combination of both.

33 Parmentier potatoes

Pommes parmentier

½ kg (1 lb) will yield 2–3 portions.

1 Select medium to large size potatoes.
2 Wash, peel and rewash.
3 Trim on three sides and cut into 1 cm (½ inch) slices.
4 Cut the slices into 1 cm (½ inch) strips.
5 Cut the strips into 1 cm (½ inch) dice.
6 Wash well and dry in a cloth.
7 Cook in hot shallow oil in a frying-pan until golden brown.
8 Drain, season lightly and serve sprinkled with chopped parsley.

Using peanut oil, 1 portion provides:
1819 kJ/433 kcal
33.5 g fat
(of which 6.3 g saturated)
32.8 g carbohydrate
(of which 0.7 g sugars)
2.3 g protein
1.7 g fibre

34 Swiss potato cakes (rösti)

1 Allow 100 g (4 oz) unpeeled potato per portion.
2 Parboil in salted water (or steam) for approximately 5 minutes.
3 Cool, then shred in large flakes on a grater.
4 For 4 portions heat 50 g (2 oz) oil, butter or margarine in a frying pan.
5 Add potatoes, season lightly with salt and pepper.
6 Press the potato together and cook on both sides until brown and crisp.

The potato can be made in a 4 portion cake or in individual rounds.

Using butter, 1 portion provides:
700 kJ/168 kcal energy
10.5 g fat
(of which 6.5 g saturated)
17.3 g carbohydrate
(of which 0.7 g sugars)
2.2 g protein
1.3 g fibre

Variations:

- add sweated chopped onion
- add sweated lardons of bacon
- use 2 parts of grated potato to 1 part grated apple.

HEALTHY EATING TIP

Lightly oil a well-seasoned pan with sunflower oil to fry the rösti.
Use a minimum amount of salt.

Fig 13.7 Rösti

John Campbell

14 Pastry

Cream caramel, fruit crumble, strawberry mousse

Chocolate éclair, bread and butter pudding, rum and raisin ice cream on a crisped (baked) slice of apple

Chocolate mousse, lemon sorbet on a chocolate cup, chocolate clafoutis
John Campbell

continued...

continued...

Baking, patisserie, confectionery and healthy eating

Today bakery goods, pastry and confectionery remain popular with the consumer, however there is a demand for products that have a reduced fat and sugar content as many people pursue a healthy lifestyle. Therefore chefs will continue to respond to this demand by modifying recipes to reduce the fat and sugar content. They may also use alternative ingredients, such as low calorie sweeteners where possible and unsaturated fats.

Egg custard-based dessert

Egg custard mixture provides the chef with a versatile basic set of ingredients that cover a wide range of sweets. Often the mixture is referred to as crème renversée. Some examples of sweets produced from this mixture are:

- Cream caramel
- Bread and butter pudding
- Diplomat pudding
- Cabinet pudding
- Queen of puddings
- Crème beau rivage
- Baked egg custard

Savoury egg custard is used to make:

- Quiches
- Tartlets
- Flans

When a starch such as flour is added to the ingredients for an egg custard mix, this changes the characteristic of the end product.

Pastry cream (also known as confectioner's custard) is a filling used for many sweets, gâteaux, flans, tartlets and as a basis for soufflé mixes. *Sauce anglaise* is used as a base for some ice-creams. It is also used in its own right as a sauce to accompany a range of sweets.

Basic egg custard sets by coagulation of the egg protein. Egg white coagulates at approximately 60°C (140°F), egg yolks at 70°C (158°F). Whites and yolks mixed will give a coagulation at 66°C (151°F). If the egg protein is overheated or overcooked, it will shrink and water will be lost from the mixture causing undesirable bubbles in the custard. This loss of water is called syneresis.

Ingredients for egg custards

Eggs

Egg yolk is high in saturated fat. The yolk is a good source of protein and also contains vitamins and iron. The egg white is made up of protein (albumen) and water. The egg yolk also contains lecithin, which acts as an emulsifier in dishes such as mayonnaise.

Milk

Full cream, skimmed or semi-skimmed can be used for these desserts.

Cream

Cream is often added to egg custard desserts to enrich and to improve the feel in the mouth of the final product. Fat contents of various types are listed in the table on page 559.

Whipping and double cream may be whipped to make them lighter and to increase volume.

All cream products must be kept in the refrigerator for health and safety reasons. Cream will whip more easily if it is kept at refrigeration temperature. All dairy products must be kept in the refrigerator as these present the perfect medium for the growth of micro-organisms. Handle these products with care and remember that they will also absorb odour. Never store near onions or other strong-smelling foods.

Traditional custard made from custard powder

Custard powder is used to make custard sauce. Custard powder is made from vanilla-flavoured cornflour with yellow colouring and is a substitute for eggs. The fat content is reduced when using semi-skimmed milk.

Ice-cream

Traditional ice-cream is made from a basic egg custard sauce. The sauce is cooled and mixed with fresh cream. It is then frozen by a rotating machine where the water content forms ice crystals.

Ice-cream should be served at −5°C to −6°C (21°F–23°F). This is the correct eating temperature, otherwise it is too hard.

Long-term storage should be at −18°C to −20°C (−0.4°F to −4°F).

The manufacture of ice-cream is governed by the Food and Drugs Act 1962 and the Food Standard Regulations 1970.

Points to remember
Egg custard-based desserts

- Always work in a clean and tidy way, complying with food hygiene regulations.
- Prevent cross-contamination occurring by not allowing any foreign substances to come into contact with the mixture.
- Always heat the egg yolks or egg to 70°C, otherwise use pasteurised egg yolks or eggs.
- Follow the recipe carefully.
- Ensure that all heating and cooling temperatures are followed.
- Always store the end-product carefully at the right temperature.
- Check all weighing scales.
- Check all raw materials for correct use-by dates.
- Always wash your hands when handling fresh eggs or dairy products and other pastry ingredients.
- Never use cream to decorate a product that is still warm.
- Always remember to follow the Food Hygiene (Amendments) Regulations 1993/95.
- *Check at all times the temperature of the refrigerators and freezers* that they comply with the current regulations.

Fresh cream

- Piping is a skill; like all other skills it takes practice to become proficient. The finished item should look attractive, the piping being neat, simple, clean and tidy.
- All piping bags should be sterilised after each use as these may well be a source of contamination.
- Make sure that all the equipment you need for this operation is hygienically cleaned before and after use to avoid cross-contamination.

Egg whites

- To avert danger of salmonella, if the egg white is not going to be cooked or will not reach a temperature of 70°C (158°F), use pasteurised egg whites. Egg white is available chilled, frozen or dried.
- Equipment must be scrupulously clean, free from any traces of fat, as these prevent the whites from whipping. Fat or grease prevents the albumen strands from bonding and trapping the air bubbles.
- Take care that there are no traces of yolk in the white, as yolk contains fat.
- A little acid (cream of tartar or lemon juice) strengthens the egg white, extends the foam and produces more meringue. The acid also has the effect of stabilising the meringue.
- If the foam is overwhipped, the albumen strands, which hold the water molecules with the sugar suspended on the outside of the bubble, are overstretched. The water and sugar make contact and the sugar dissolves making the meringue heavy and wet. This sometimes can be rescued by further whisking until it foams up but very often you will find that you may have to discard the mixture and start again.

Meringues

Egg white forms a foam that is used for aerating sweets and many other desserts.

Note: See page 511.

Quality requirements and purchasing points

Fresh fruit should be:

- whole and of fresh appearance (for maximum flavour the fruit must be ripe but not overripe);
- firm according to the type and variety;
- clean, free from traces of pesticides and fungicides;
- free from external moisture;
- free from any unpleasant foreign smell or taste;
- free from pests or disease;
- sufficiently mature; it must be capable of being handled and travelling without damage;
- free from any defects characteristic of the variety in shape, size and colour;
- free of bruising and any other damage due to weather conditions.

Soft fruits deteriorate quickly, especially if not sound. Care must be taken to see that they are not damaged or over-ripe when purchased. Soft fruits should look fresh; there should be no signs of wilting, shrinking or mould. The colour of certain soft fruits is an indication of ripeness (e.g. strawberries or dessert gooseberries).

Food value

Fruit is rich in antioxidant minerals and vitamins. Antioxidants protect cells from damage by oxygen, which may lead to heart disease and cancer. The current recommendation is to eat five portions of fruit and vegetables each day.

Storage

Hard fruits, such as apples, are left in boxes and kept in a cool store.

Soft fruits, such as raspberries and strawberries, should be left in their punnets or baskets in a cold room.

Stone fruits are best placed in trays so that any damaged fruit can be seen and discarded.

Peaches and citrus fruits are left in their delivery trays or boxes.

Bananas should not be stored in too cold a place because the skins turn black.

Egg custard-based dessert recipes

1 Baked egg custard

Using whole milk, 1 portion provides:
780 kJ/186 kcal
8.4 g fat
(of which 4.3 g saturated)
19.0 g carbohydrate
(of which 19.0 g sugars)
8.7 g protein
0.0 g fibre

	4 portions	10 portions
medium eggs	3	7
sugar, caster or unrefined	50 g (2 oz)	125 g (5 oz)
vanilla essence	2–3 drops	5 drops
milk, whole or skimmed	½ litre (1 pt)	1¼ litre (2½ pt)
grated nutmeg		

1 Whisk the eggs, sugar and essence.

2 Pour on the warmed milk, whisking continuously.

3 Pass through a fine strainer into a pie dish or individual dishes.

4 Add a little grated nutmeg. Wipe the edge of the pie dish or individual dishes clean.

5 Stand in a roasting tray half full of water and cook slowly in a moderate oven at 160°C (Reg. 3; 325°F) for 45 minutes to 1 hour.

6 Clean the edges of the pie dish and serve.

Note: May be served with stewed fruit e.g. rhubarb, apple.

2 Queen of puddings

1 portion provides:
1522 kJ/362 kcal
14.7 g fat
(of which 6.8 g saturated)
50.0 g carbohydrate
(of which 41.2 g sugars)
10.9 g protein
0.9 g fibre

	4 portions	10 portions
milk, whole or skimmed	½ litre (1 pt)	1¼ litre (2½ pt)
eggs	3	7
caster or unrefined sugar	50 g (2 oz)	125 g (5 oz)
vanilla essence		
cake or breadcrumbs	75 g (3 oz)	180 g (7½ oz)
butter or margarine	25 g (1 oz)	60 g (2½ oz)
caster sugar for meringue	50 g (2 oz)	125 g (5 oz)
jam	50 g (2 oz)	125 g (5 oz)

1 Boil the milk.

2 Pour on to 2 yolks, 1 egg (5 yolks, 2 eggs for 10 portions), sugar and vanilla essence, whisk well.

3 Place the crumbs in a buttered pie dish or individual dishes.

4 Strain the custard on to the crumbs.

5 Bake in a moderate oven in a bain-marie for 30 minutes or until set.

6 Allow to cool.

7 Stiffly beat the egg whites; fold in the caster sugar.

8 Spread the warmed jam over the baked mixture.

9 Using a large star tube, pipe the meringue to cover the jam.

10 Brown in a hot oven at 220°C (Reg. 7; 425°F) and serve.

Using whole milk and whipping cream, 1 portion provides:
2280 kJ/543 kcal
29.1 g fat
(of which 17.1 g saturated)
66.2 g carbohydrate
(of which 51.3 g sugars)
8.2 g protein
1.9 g fibre

3 Trifle

	6–8 portions
sponge (3 eggs medium)	1
jam	25 g (1 oz)
tinned fruit (pears, peaches, pineapple)	1
Custard	
custard powder	35 g (1½ oz)
milk, whole or skimmed	375 ml (¾ pt)
caster sugar	50 g (2 oz)
cream (¾ whipped) or non-dairy cream	125 ml (¼ pt)
whipped sweetened cream or non-dairy cream	¼ litre (½ pt)
angelica	25 g (1 oz)
glacé cherries	25 g (1 oz)

1   Cut the sponge in half, sideways, and spread with jam.

2   Place in a glass bowl or individual dishes and soak with fruit syrup; a few drops of sherry may be added.

3   Cut the fruit into small pieces and add to the sponge.

4   Dilute the custard powder in a basin with some of the milk, add the sugar.

5   Boil the remainder of the milk, pour a little on the custard powder, mix well, return to the saucepan and over a low heat stir to the boil. Allow to cool, stirring occasionally to prevent a skin forming; fold in the three-quarters whipped 125 ml (¼ pint) cream.

6   Pour on to the sponge. Leave to cool.

7   Decorate with whipped cream, angelica and cherries.

Note: Other flavourings or liqueurs may be used in place of sherry: whisky, rum, brandy, Tia Maria.

For raspberry or strawberry trifle use fully ripe fresh fruit in place of tinned and decorate with fresh fruit in place of angelica and glacé cherries.

A fresh egg custard may be used with fresh egg yolks (see recipe 18, page 500) and a complete trifle recipe using fresh egg custard will be found in *Advanced Practical Cookery*.

4 Bread and butter pudding

	4 portions	10 portions
sultanas	50 g (2 oz)	100 g (4 oz)
slices of white or wholemeal bread, spread with butter or margarine	2	5
eggs (medium)	3	7
sugar, caster or unrefined	50 g (2 oz)	125 g (5 oz)
vanilla essence or a vanilla pod	2–3 drops	5 drops
milk, whole or skimmed	½ litre (1 pt)	1¼ (2½ pt)

Using white bread and butter,
1 portion provides:
1093 kJ/260 kcal
11.6 g fat
(of which 5.9 g saturated)
30.4 g carbohydrate
(of which 23.4 g sugars)
10.6 g protein
1.0 g fibre

1 Wash the sultanas and place in a pie dish or individual dishes.

2 Remove the crusts from the bread and cut each slice into four triangles, neatly arrange overlapping in the pie dish.

3 Prepare an egg custard as in recipe 1.

4 Strain on to the bread, dust lightly with sugar.

5 Cook and serve as for baked egg custard.

Variations

- Before cooking, add either freshly grated nutmeg or orange zest or a combination of both;

- fruit loaf brioche or panettone in place of bread;

- chocolate bread and butter pudding – add 25 g (1 oz) chocolate powder to the egg custard mix;

- add soft, well-drained poached fruit (or tinned) e.g. peaches, pears.

Note: For a crisp crust finish, sprinkle with icing sugar and brown well under the salamander.

HEALTHY EATING TIP

Try using half wholemeal and half white bread. The fat content will be reduced by using semi-skimmed milk in the custard. Adding more dried fruit would reduce the need for so much sugar.

Fig 14.1 Bread and butter pudding

Using whole milk and 3 eggs,
1 portion provides:
1427 kJ/340 kcal
15.8 g fat
(of which 7.2 g saturated)
40.9 g carbohydrate
(of which 35.5 g sugars)
11.0 g protein
0.7 g fibre

Using whole milk and 4 eggs,
1 portion provides:
1512 kJ/360 kcal
17.3 g fat
(of which 7.7 g saturated)
40.9 g carbohydrate
(of which 35.5 g sugars)
12.7 g protein
0.7 g fibre

5 Cabinet pudding

Pouding cabinet

	4 portions	10 portions
plain sponge cake	100 g (4 oz)	250 g (10 oz)
glacé cherries	25 g (1 oz)	60 g (2½ oz)
currants and sultanas	25 g (1 oz)	60 g (2½ oz)
angelica	10 g (½ oz)	25 g (1 oz)
milk, whole or skimmed	½ litre (1 pt)	1¼ litres (2½ pt)
eggs (medium)	3–4	8–10
caster or unrefined sugar	50 g (2 oz)	125 g (5 oz)
vanilla essence or a vanilla pod	2–3 drops	7 drops

1 Cut the cake into ½ cm (¼ inch) dice.
2 Mix with the chopped cherries and fruits (which can be soaked in rum).
3 Place in a greased, sugared charlotte mould or four dariole moulds. Do not fill more than half-way.
4 Warm the milk and whisk on to the eggs, sugar and essence (or vanilla pod).
5 Strain on to the mould.
6 Place in a roasting tin, half full of water; allow to stand for 5–10 minutes.
7 Cook in a moderate oven at 150–160°C (Reg. 2–3; 300–325°F) for 30–45 minutes.
8 Leave to set for a few minutes before turning out.
9 Serve a fresh egg custard or hot apricot sauce separately.

Note: Diplomat pudding is made as for cabinet pudding, but served cold with either redcurrant, raspberry, apricot or vanilla sauce.

Fig 14.2 Blowlamp. Extreme care must be taken when using a blow lamp. Manufacturer's instructions *must* be followed explicitly because there is the danger of a gas explosion from the canister if used incorrectly.

6 Cream caramel

Crème caramel
(Illustrated on page 494)

> Using whole milk, 1 portion provides:
> 868 kJ/207 kcal
> 7.2 g fat
> (of which 3.3 g saturated)
> 30.2 g carbohydrate
> (of which 30.2 g sugars)
> 7.3 g protein
> 0.0 g fibre

		4 portions	10 portions
sugar, granulated or cube	caramel	100 g (4 oz)	200 g (8 oz)
water		125 ml (¼ pt)	250 ml (½ pt)
milk, whole or skimmed		½ litre (1 pt)	1 litre (2 pt)
eggs (medium)		4	8
sugar, caster or unrefined	custard	50 g (2 oz)	100 g (4 oz)
vanilla essence or a vanilla pod		3–4 drops	6–8 drops

1 Prepare the caramel by placing three-quarters of the water in a thick-based pan, adding the sugar and allowing to boil gently, without shaking or stirring the pan.

2 When the sugar has cooked to a golden brown caramel colour, add the remaining quarter of the water, reboil until the sugar and water mix, then pour into the bottom of dariole moulds.

3 Prepare the cream by warming the milk and whisking on to the beaten eggs, sugar and essence (or vanilla pod).

4 Strain and pour into the prepared moulds.

5 Place in a roasting tin half full of water.

6 Cook in a moderate oven at 150–160°C (Reg. 2–3; 300–325°F) for 30–40 minutes.

7 When thoroughly cold, loosen the edges of the cream caramel with the fingers, shake firmly to loosen and turn out on to a flat dish or plates.

8 Pour any caramel remaining in the mould around the creams.

Note: Cream caramels may be served with whipped cream or a fruit sauce such as passionfruit, and accompanied by a sweet biscuit, e.g. shortbread, palmiers.

7 Burned, caramelised or browned cream

Crème brulée

> 1 portion provides:
> 1154 kJ/278 kcal energy
> 21.9 g fat
> (of which 12.1 g saturated)
> 14.8 g carbohydrate
> (of which 14.8 g sugars)
> 6.2 g protein
> 0.0 g fibre

	4 portions	10 portions
milk	125 ml (¼ pt)	300 ml (⅝ pt)
double cream	125 ml (¼ pt)	300 ml (⅝ pt)
natural vanilla essence or pod		
eggs (medium)	2	5
yolk	1	2–3
caster sugar	25 g (1 oz)	60 g (2½ oz)
demerara sugar		

1 Warm the milk, cream and vanilla essence in a pan.

2 Mix the eggs, egg yolk and sugar in a basin and add the warm milk. Stir well and pass through a fine strainer.

3 Pour the cream into individual dishes and place them into a tray half-filled with warm water.

4 Place in the oven at approximately 160°C (325°F) for about 30–40 minutes, until set.

5 Sprinkle the tops with demerara sugar and glaze

493

continued over ▶

Fig 14.3 Cream caramels (with copper sugar boiler and dariole moulds)

▶ *Burned, caramelised or browned cream continued*

under the salamander or by blowtorch to a golden brown.

6 Clean the dishes and serve.

Variations: Sliced strawberries, raspberries or other fruits, e.g. peaches, apricots, may be placed in the bottom of the dish before adding the cream mixture or placed on top after the creams are caramelised.

Illustrated on page 492.

---

1 portion, using blackcurrants for blueberries, provides:
1565 kJ/378 kcal energy
34.0 g fat
(of which 21.1 g saturated)
16.1 g carbohydrate
(of which 16.1 g sugars)
2.9 g protein
1.5 g fibre

HEALTHY EATING TIP

This dish will contribute to the recommended '5 portions of fruit and vegetables per day'

8 **Vanilla panna cotta served on a fruit compote (Andrew Bennett)**

	6 portions
double cream	375 ml (¾ pt)
milk	125 ml (¼ pt)
vanilla pod	½
aniseeds	2
leaf gelatine (soaked)	2 leaves
caster sugar	50 g (2 oz)
Fruit compote **strawberries**	75 g (3 oz)
kiwi fruit	1
peaches	1
blueberries	75 g (3 oz)
raspberries	50 g (2 oz)
apricot purée	75 g (3 oz)

1 Prepare the fruit compote by boiling the apricot purée and infusing with vanilla pod. Remove pod, allow purée to cool.

2 Finely dice the peach and the kiwi and quarter the strawberries. Mix, add blueberries and raspberries.

3 Bind the fruit with the apricot purée. A little stock syrup may be required to keep the fruit free flowing.

4 For the panna cotta, boil the milk and cream, add aniseeds, infuse with the vanilla pod, remove after infusion.

5 Heat again and add the soaked gelatine and caster sugar. Strain through a fine strainer.

6 Fill individual dariole moulds. Allow to cool.

7 Place the fruit compote with individual fruit plates, turn out the panna cotta, place on top of the compote, finish with a tuile biscuit.

9 Chocolate panna cotta

	4–6 portions	10–12 portions
double cream	500 ml (1 pt)	1.25 litres (2½ pt)
milk	125 ml (¼ pt)	300 ml (⅜ pt)
vanilla essence to taste		
caster sugar	100 g (4 oz)	250 g (10 oz)
Cointreau or brandy	1 tbsp	1½ tbsp
bitter chocolate	50 g (2 oz)	125 g (5 oz)
gelatine leaf (soaked in cold water)	2 leaves	5 leaves

1 portion provides:
2228 kJ/538 kcal energy
47.4 g fat
(of which 29.4 g saturated)
25.2 g carbohydrate
(of which 25.1 g sugars)
2.9 g protein
0.2 g fibre

1 Place the double cream in a suitable saucepan, add the sugar and vanilla essence. Add the Cointreau or brandy.

2 Heat to just below boiling point.

3 Remove from heat, add the chopped chocolate, stir well.

4 Add the soaked and squeezed gelatine.

5 Strain through a fine strainer.

6 Allow to cool, stirring occasionally.

7 When cold, stir and pour into suitable individual moulds.

8 Cover and refrigerate for at least 8 hours.

9 To serve, loosen the sides of the moulds and turn out into suitable plates.

Serve with a quenelle of mascarpone (soft Italian cheese with clotted cream) and segments of orange. Decorate with chocolate run outs.

Using whole milk and whipping cream, 1 portion provides:
970 kJ/231 kcal
18.2 g fat
(of which 10.9 g saturated)
11.8 g carbohydrate
(of which 11.8 g sugars)
5.8 g protein
0.0 g fibre

Use semi-skimmed milk and whipping cream to reduce the overall fat content.

10 Bavarois (basic recipe), often referred to as a mousse

	6–8 portions
gelatine	10 g (½ oz)
medium eggs, separated	2
caster sugar	50 g (2 oz)
milk, whole or skimmed	¼ litre (½ pt)
whipping or double cream or non-dairy cream	125 ml (¼ pt)

1 If using leaf gelatine, soak in cold water.
2 Cream the yolks and sugar in a bowl until almost white.
3 Whisk in the milk, which has been brought to the boil; mix well.
4 Clean the milk saucepan, which should be a thick-based one, and return the mixture to it.
5 Return to a low heat and stir continuously with a wooden spoon until the mixture coats the back of the spoon. The mixture must not boil.
6 Remove from the heat; add the gelatine and stir until dissolved.
7 Pass through a fine strainer into a clean bowl, leave in a cool place, stirring occasionally until almost setting point.
8 Fold in the lightly beaten cream.
9 Fold in the stiffly beaten whites.
10 Pour the mixture into a mould or individual moulds (which may be very lightly greased with almond oil).
11 Allow to set in the refrigerator.
12 Shake and turn out on to a flat dish or plates.

Note: Bavarois may be decorated with sweetened, flavoured whipped cream (crème Chantilly). It is advisable to use pasteurised egg yolks and whites.

Variations include:

- *Chocolate bavarois* Dissolve 50 g (2 oz) chocolate couverture in the milk. Decorate with whipped cream and grated chocolate.

- *Coffee bavarois* Proceed as for bavarois with the addition of coffee essence to taste.

- *Lemon bavarois* As orange bavarois using lemons in place of oranges.

- *Lime bavarois* As orange bavarois using limes in place of oranges.

- *Orange bavarois* Add grated zest and juice of 2 oranges and 1 or 2 drops orange colour to the mixture, and increase the gelatine by 2 leaves. Decorate with blanched, fine julienne of orange zest, orange segments and whipped cream.

- *Vanilla bavarois* Add a vanilla pod or a few drops of vanilla essence to the milk. Decorate with vanilla-flavoured sweetened cream (crème Chantilly).

11 Strawberry or raspberry bavarois (mousse)

	4 portions	10 portions
fruit (picked, washed and sieved)	200 g (½ lb)	500 g (1¼ lb)
medium eggs	2	5
gelatine	10 g (½ oz)	25 g (1 oz)
milk, whole or skimmed	180 ml (⅜ pt)	500 ml (1 pt)
sugar, caster or unrefined	50 g (2 oz)	125 g (5 oz)
whipping or double cream or non-dairy cream	125 ml (¼ pt)	300 ml (⅝ pt)

Using whole milk, whipping cream, 1 portion provides:
1102 kJ/265 kcal energy
17.7 g fat
(of which 10.0 g saturated)
19.0 g carbohydrate
(of which 19.0 g sugars)
8.5 g protein
0.6 g fibre

HEALTHY EATING TIP

Use semi-skimmed milk and whipping cream to reduce the overall fat content.

Prepare as for the basic recipe (recipe 10). When the custard is almost cool add the fruit purée. Decorate with whole fruit and whipped cream.

Ice-creams and sorbets

The Ice-Cream Regulations 1959 and 1963 require ice-cream to be pasteurised by heating to:

- 65°C (150°F) for 30 minutes or
- 71°C (160°F) for 10 minutes or
- 80°C (175°F) for 15 seconds or
- 149°C (300°F) for 2 seconds (sterilised).

After heat treatment the mixture is reduced to 7.1°C (45°F) within 1½ hours and kept at this temperature until the freezing process begins. Ice-cream needs this treatment so as to kill harmful bacteria. Freezing without correct heat treatment does not kill bacteria, it allows them to remain dormant. The storage temperature for ice-cream should not exceed −2°C. All establishments making ice-cream for sale must be licensed by the local authority Environmental Health Officer.

12 Vanilla ice-cream

Glace vanille

Using whole milk and single cream, 1 portion provides:
616 kJ/147 kcal
8.1 g fat
(of which 4.2 g saturated)
15.8 g carbohydrate
(of which 15.8 g sugars)
3.5 g protein
0.0 g fibre

	8–10 portions
egg yolks	4
caster or unrefined sugar	100 g (4 oz)
vanilla pod or essence	
milk, whole or skimmed	375 ml (¾ pt)
cream or non-dairy cream	125 ml (¼ pt)

1   Whisk the yolks and sugar in a bowl until almost white.

2   Boil the milk with the vanilla pod or essence in a thick-based pan.

3   Whisk on to the eggs and sugar; mix well.

4   Return to the cleaned saucepan, place on a low heat.

5   Stir continuously with a wooden spoon until the mixture coats the back of the spoon.

6   Pass through a fine strainer into a bowl.

7   Freeze in an ice-cream machine, gradually adding the cream.

Note Variations include:

- *Coffee ice-cream* Add coffee essence to taste to the custard after it is cooked.

- *Chocolate ice-cream* Add 50–100 g (2–4 oz) of chopped couverture to the milk before boiling.

- *Strawberry ice-cream* Add 125 ml (¼ pint) of strawberry pulp in place of 125 ml (¼ pint) of milk. The pulp is added after the custard is cooked.

- *Rum and raisin* – soak 50 g (2 oz) raisins in 2 tbsp rum for 3–4 hours. Add to mixture before freezing.

13 Lemon sorbet

Sorbet au citron

1 portion provides:
421 kJ/100 kcal
0.0 g fat
(of which 0.0 g saturated)
26.3 g carbohydrate
(of which 26.3 g sugars)
0.4 g protein
0.0 g fibre

	8–10 portions
sugar	200 g (8 oz)
water	½ litre (1 pt)
lemons	2
egg white, pasteurised	1

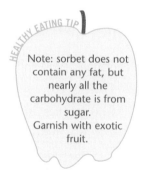

HEALTHY EATING TIP

Note: sorbet does not contain any fat, but nearly all the carbohydrate is from sugar.
Garnish with exotic fruit.

1   Bring the sugar, water and peeled zest of lemons to the boil.

2   Remove from the heat and cool. The saccarometer reading for the syrup should be 18–20° baumé.

3   Add the juice of the lemon.

4   Add the white and mix well.

5   Pass through a fine strainer and freeze.

14 Orange sorbet

Sorbet à l'orange

sugar	200 g (8 oz)
water	½ litre (1 pt)
large oranges	2
lemon	1
egg white, pasteurised	1

Prepare and freeze as for lemon ice, 18–20° baumé.

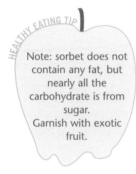

Note: sorbet does not contain any fat, but nearly all the carbohydrate is from sugar.
Garnish with exotic fruit.

15 Raspberry sorbet

Sorbet à la framboise

sugar	200 g (8 oz)
water	375 ml (¾ pt)
lemon	1
raspberry purée	125 ml (¼ pt)
egg white, pasteurised	1

Prepare and freeze as for lemon ice, 18–20° baumé.

Note: Passionfruit or mango sorbet can be made by substituting the relevant purée for raspberry.

Egg-based sauces and creams

16 Sabayon sauce

Sauce sabayon

Using 5 egg yolks, 1 portion provides:
454 kJ/108 kcal energy
3.4 g fat
(of which 1.0 g saturated)
13.3 g carbohydrate
(of which 13.3 g sugars)
1.8 g protein
0.0 g fibre

	8 portions
egg yolks	4–6
caster or unrefined sugar	100 g (4 oz)
dry white wine	¼ litre (½ pt)

1   Whisk the egg yolks and sugar in a 1 litre (2 pint) pan or basin until white.

2   Dilute with the wine.

3   Place the pan or basin in a bain-marie of warm water.

4   Whisk the mixture continuously until it increases to four times its bulk and is firm and frothy.

Note: Sauce sabayon may be offered as an accompaniment to any suitable hot sweet e.g. pudding soufflé or soufflés.

A sauce sabayon may also be made using milk in place of wine, which can be flavoured according to taste: vanilla, or nutmeg, or cinnamon.

17 Sabayon with Marsala

Zabaglione

	4 portions	10 portions
egg yolks	8	20
caster or unrefined sugar	200 g (8 oz)	500 g (1¼ lb)
Marsala	150 ml (⅓ pt)	375 ml (¾ pt)

1 Whisk the egg yolks and sugar in a bowl until almost white.
2 Mix in the Marsala.
3 Place the bowl and contents in a bain-marie of warm water.
4 Whisk mixture continuously until it increases to four times its bulk and is firm and frothy.
5 Pour the mixture into glass goblets.
6 Accompany with a suitable biscuit, e.g. sponge fingers.

Variations: Use sherry, whisky or brandy in place of Marsala.

This is a traditional Italian dessert, which was sometimes prepared in the restaurant in a special Zabaglione pan with a handle.

18 Fresh egg custard sauce

Sauce à l'anglaise

	4 portions	10 portions
egg yolks (4 if using skimmed milk)	2	5
caster or unrefined sugar	25 g (1 oz)	60 g (2½ oz)
vanilla essence or vanilla pod	2–3 drops	5–7 drops
milk, whole or skimmed	250 ml (½ pt)	625 ml (1¼ pt)

1 Mix the yolks, sugar and essence in a basin.
2 Whisk on the boiled milk and return to a thick-bottomed pan.
3 Place on a low heat and stir with a wooden spoon until it coats the back of the spoon. Do not allow to boil or the eggs will scramble.

Note: Other flavours may be used in place of vanilla:

- coffee
- chocolate
- rum
- brandy
- Caloredos
- kirsch
- Curaçao
- Cointreau
- Tia Maria
- whisky
- ground cinnamon
- orange flower water.

19 Pastry cream

Crème pâtissière

			Using white flour and whole milk, this recipe provides:
medium eggs	2		4564 kJ/1087 kcal
caster or unrefined sugar	100 g (4 oz)		31.7 g fat
flour, white or wholemeal	50 g (2 oz)		(of which 16.0 g saturated)
custard powder	10 g (½ oz)		176.6 g carbohydrate
milk, whole or skimmed	½ litre (1 pt)		(of which 129.3 g sugars)
vanilla pod or essence			34.8 g protein
			2.1 g fibre

1 Whisk the eggs and sugar in a bowl until almost white.

2 Mix in the flour and custard powder.

3 Boil the milk in a thick-based pan.

4 Whisk on to the eggs, sugar and flour and mix well.

5 Return to the cleaned pan, stir to the boil.

6 Add a few drops of vanilla essence or a vanilla pod.

7 Remove from the heat and pour into a basin.

8 Sprinkle the top with a little caster or icing sugar to prevent a skin forming.

Note: Pastry cream may be varied with other flavours:

- rum
- brandy
- Tia Maria
- lime
- whisky
- orange
- lemon
- praline
- strawberry
- passion fruit
- almond
- Calvados.

Other variations include:

- Chocolate pastry cream. Dissolve 100 g (4 oz) of couverture or 50 g (2 oz) cocoa powder in the milk and proceed as above.

- Coffee pastry cream. Add coffee essence to taste and proceed as above.

- Pastry cream is a basic preparation used in many pastry dishes, e.g. as a base for soufflés and for some fruit flans or tartlets, as well as in many other pastries. Traditionally chocolate eclairs are filled with chocolate pastry cream and coffee eclairs with coffee pastry cream.

Soufflé puddings

Using white flour and hard margarine, 1 portion provides:
510 kJ/122 kcal
7.6 g fat
(of which 3.2 g saturated)
9.1 g carbohydrate
(of which 5.9 g sugars)
4.8 g protein
0.2 g fibre

20 Soufflé pudding (basic recipe)

Pouding soufflé

	6 portions	10 portions
milk, whole or skimmed	185 ml (⅜ pt)	375 ml (¾ pt)
flour, white or wholemeal	25 g (1 oz)	50 g (2 oz)
butter or margarine	25 g (1 oz)	50 g (2 oz)
caster or unrefined sugar	25 g (1 oz)	50 g (2 oz)
medium eggs, separated	3	6

1 Boil the milk in a sauteuse.

2 Combine the flour, butter and sugar.

3 Whisk into the milk and reboil.

4 Remove from heat, add the yolks one at a time, whisking continuously.

5 Stiffly beat the whites.

6 Carefully fold into the mixture.

7 Three-quarters fill buttered and sugared dariole moulds.

8 Place in a roasting tin, half full of water.

9 Bring to the boil and place in a hot oven at 230–250°C (Reg. 8–9; 450–500°F) for 12–15 minutes.

10 Turn out on to a flat dish and serve with a suitable hot sauce, such as custard or sabayon sauce (recipe 16).

Note: Orange or lemon soufflé pudding is made by flavouring the basic mixture with the grated zest of an orange or lemon and a little appropriate sauce. Use the juice in the accompanying sauce.

21 Vanilla soufflé

Soufflé à la vanille

	4 portions	10 portions
milk	125 ml (¼ pt)	300 ml (⅝ pt)
natural vanilla or pod		
medium eggs, separated	4	10
flour	10 g (½ oz)	25 g (1¼ oz)
caster sugar	50 g (2 oz)	125 g (5 oz)
butter	10 g (½ oz)	25 g (1¼ oz)

1 Lightly coat the inside of a soufflé case/dish with fresh butter.

2 Coat the butter in the soufflé case with caster sugar, tap out surplus.

3 Boil the milk and vanilla in a thick-bottomed pan.

4 Mix half the egg yolks, the flour and sugar to a smooth consistency in a basin.

5 Add the boiling milk to the mixture, stir vigorously until completely mixed.

6 Return this mixture to a clean thick-bottomed pan and stir continuously with a wooden spoon over gentle heat until the mixture thickens, then remove from heat.

7 Allow to cool slightly.

8 Add the remaining egg yolks and mix thoroughly.

9 Stiffly whip the egg whites and *carefully* fold into the mixture, which should be just warm. (An extra egg white can be added for extra lightness.)

10 Place the mixture into the prepared case/s and level it off with a palette knife – do not allow it to come above the level of the soufflé case.

11 Place on a baking sheet and cook in a moderately hot oven, approximately 200–230°C (Reg. 6–8; 400–450°F), until the soufflé is well risen and is firm to touch, approximately 15–20 minutes. (For individual soufflés, reduce time by 5 minutes.)

12 Remove carefully from oven, dredge with icing sugar and serve at once. A hot soufflé *cannot* be allowed to stand or it may sink.

Note: A pinch of egg white powder (merri-white) added when whisking the whites will strengthen them and assist in the aeration process.

1 portion provides:
1179 kJ/280 kcal energy
13.3 g fat
(of which 5.7 g saturated)
31.7 g carbohydrate
(of which 30.4 g sugars)
10.1 g protein
0.1 g fibre

22 Soufflé without flour – Hot lemon curd soufflé

	4 portions	10 portions
eggs, medium	4	9
lemon, zest and juice	2	5
caster sugar	75 g (3 oz)	187 g (7½ oz)
cream of tartar	pinch	large pinch
egg white powder	pinch	large pinch
Lemon curd		
lemons	2	5
medium eggs	1	2
caster sugar	37 g (1½ oz)	100 g (4 oz)
butter, unsalted	25 g (1 oz)	60 g (2½ oz)
cornflour	6 g (¼ oz)	15 g (⅜ oz)

1 Lightly grease the individual soufflé dishes with butter or margarine and lightly dust with caster sugar.

2 Prepare lemon curd by whisking the eggs with the caster sugar over a bain-marie of hot water, add the butter cut into small pieces and the cornflour. Whisk well until the mixture thickens.

3 Divide the lemon curd into the soufflé dishes.

4 Separate the egg whites and egg yolks. Mix the yolks with the caster sugar, the lemon zest and juice. Whisk well to thoroughly incorporate.

5 Carefully whisk the egg whites to soft peaks with a pinch of cream of tartar and egg white powder to strengthen.

6 Carefully fold the whites into the yolk and lemon mixture. Do not overmix.

7 Divide the mixture into soufflé dishes.

8 Place on a baking sheet and cook in a pre-heated oven 170°C (325°F) for approximately 12–16 minutes. Remove, dust with icing sugar and serve immediately.

23 Cold lemon soufflé

Soufflé milanaise

1 portion provides:
1385 kJ/330 kcal
18.6 g fat
(of which 10.6 g saturated)
36.2 g carbohydrate
(of which 36.2 g sugars)
6.7 g protein
0.0 g fibre

	6 portions
leaf gelatine	10 g (½ oz)
lemons	2
pasteurised yolks	4
pasteurised whites	4
caster sugar	200 g (8 oz)
whipping or double cream or non-dairy cream	¼ litre (½ pt)

1 Prepare a soufflé dish or individual dishes by tying a 8 cm (3 inch) wide strip of greaseproof paper around the outside top edge with string, so that it extends 2–4 cm (1–1½ inches) above the top of the dish.

2 Soak the gelatine in cold water.

3 *Lightly* grate the zest of the lemons.

4 Squeeze the juice of the lemons into a bowl.

5 Add the lemon zest, yolks, sugar and whisk over a pan of hot water until the mixture thickens and turns a very light colour.

6 Dissolve the gelatine in a few drops of water over heat, mix in, remove from heat.

7 Lightly whisk the cream until three-quarters stiff.

Fig 14.4 Lemon curd soufflé (without flour)   *Yolande Stanley*

continued over ▶

▶ *Cold lemon soufflé continued*

8 Stiffly beat the egg whites.

9 Stir the basic mixture frequently until almost on setting point.

10 Gently fold in the cream. Gently fold in the egg whites.

11 Pour into the prepared dishes.

12 Place in a refrigerator to set.

13 To serve, remove the paper collar and decorate sides with green chopped almonds or pistachio nuts. The top may be similarly decorated or by using rosettes of sweetened vanilla-flavoured whipped cream.

Steamed puddings

24 Steamed currant roll

Using water, 1 portion provides:
1997 kJ/476 kcal energy
22.7 g fat
(of which 11.4 g saturated)
66.4 g carbohydrate
(of which 25.2 g sugars)
5.5 g protein
1.9 g fibre

	6 portions	12 portions
flour	300 g (12 oz)	600 g (1½ lb)
with baking powder	10 g (½ oz)	20 g (1½ lb)
or **self-raising flour**	300 g (12 oz)	600 g (1½ lb)
pinch salt		
chopped suet	150 g (6 oz)	300 g (12 oz)
sugar, caster or unrefined	75 g (3 oz)	150 g (6 oz)
currants	100 g (4 oz)	200 g (8 oz)
water or milk	185 ml (⅜ pt)	375 ml (¾ pt)

1 Sieve the flour, salt and baking-powder into a bowl.

2 Mix in the suet. Mix in the sugar and currants.

3 Add sufficient water or milk to make a fairly firm dough.

4 Roll in greased greaseproof paper and a pudding cloth or foil. Tie with string at both ends. Steam for 1½ –2 hours.

5 Remove the cloth and paper and serve with a sauceboat of custard.

Note: Sultanas, raisins or dates may be used instead of currants.

Fig 14.5 ✐ Left: preparation of steamed puddings. Right: steamed puddings (clockwise from left): sultana, chocolate and lemon with chocolate sauce (p. 524), lemon sauce (p. 522) and custard sauce (p. 500)

Vegetarian suet is available. Using raisins, sultanas, and a pinch of mixed spice gives an old English pudding known as Spotted Dick, which can also be prepared in individual moulds and steamed for one hour.

25 Steamed dried fruit pudding

	6 portions	12 portions
flour	100 g (4 oz)	200 g (8 oz)
with baking powder	10 g (½ oz)	25 g (1 oz)
or **self-raising flour**	100 g (4 oz)	200 g (8 oz)
pinch salt		
breadcrumbs	100 g (4 oz)	200 g (8 oz)
suet	100 g (4 oz)	200 g (8 oz)
sugar, caster or unrefined	100 g (4 oz)	200 g (8 oz)
fruit (currants, raisins, dates or sultanas)	100 g (4 oz)	200 g (8 oz)
egg (medium) beaten	1	2
milk, whole or skimmed	125 ml (¼ pt)	250 ml (½ pt)

> 1 portion provides:
> 1586 kJ/378 kcal energy
> 17.1 g fat
> (of which 8.4 g saturated)
> 53.4 g carbohydrate
> (of which 30.6 g sugars)
> 5.7 g protein
> 1.2 g fibre

1 Mix all the dry ingredients together. Add the liquid and mix.

2 Place in a greased pudding basin or individual moulds (one hour cooking time), cover and steam 1½ –2 hours.

3 Serve with custard sauce or vanilla sauce.

26 Golden syrup or treacle pudding

	6 portions	12 portions
flour	150 g (6 oz)	300 g (12 oz)
with baking powder	10 g (½ oz)	20 g (1 oz)
or **self-raising flour**	150 g (6 oz)	300 g (12 oz)
pinch salt		
chopped suet	75 g (3 oz)	150 g (6 oz)
caster or unrefined sugar	50 g (2 oz)	100 g (4 oz)
lemon, zest of	1	2
egg	1	2
milk, whole or skimmed	125 ml (¼ pt)	250 ml (½ pt)
golden syrup or light treacle	125 ml (¼ pt)	250 ml (½ pt)

> 1 portion provides:
> 1315 kJ/313 kcal
> 13.0 g fat
> (of which 5.9 g saturated)
> 47.8 g carbohydrate
> (of which 26.6 g sugars)
> 4.3 g protein
> 0.9 g fibre

1 Sieve the flour, salt and baking powder into a bowl.

2 Mix the suet, sugar and zest.

3 Mix to a medium dough, with the beaten egg and milk.

4 Pour the syrup in a well-greased basin or individual moulds (one hour cooking time). Place the mixture on top.

continued over ▶

▶ *Golden syrup or treacle pudding continued*

5 Cover securely; steam for 1½ –2 hours.

6 Serve with a sauceboat of warm syrup containing the lemon juice.

Vegetarian suet is available for recipes 24, 25 and 26.

27 Steamed sponge pudding (basic recipe)

	6 portions	12 portions
butter or margarine	100 g (4 oz)	200 g (8 oz)
caster or soft brown sugar	100 g (4 oz)	200 g (8 oz)
medium eggs	2	4
flour, white or wholemeal	150 g (6 oz)	300 g (12 oz)
baking powder	10 g (½ oz)	20 g (1 oz)
few drops of milk		

1 Cream the butter or margarine and sugar in a bowl until fluffy and almost white.

2 Gradually add the beaten eggs, mixing vigorously.

3 Sieve the flour and baking powder.

4 Gradually incorporate into the mixture as lightly as possible keeping to a dropping consistency by the addition of the milk.

5 Place in a greased pudding basin or individual moulds (45 minutes cooking time).

6 Cover securely with greased greaseproof paper. Steam for 1–1½ hours.

Note: Variations include (double the quantities for 12 portions):

- *Vanilla sponge pudding* Add a few drops of vanilla essence to the basic mixture, and serve with a vanilla-flavoured sauce (page 522).

- *Chocolate sponge pudding* Add 25 g (1 oz) chocolate or cocoa powder in place of 25 g (1 oz) flour, that is 125 g (5 oz) flour, 25 g (1 oz) chocolate to basic recipe. Serve with a chocolate sauce (page 524).

- *Lemon sponge pudding* Add the grated zest of one or two lemons, and a few drops of lemon essence to basic recipe. Serve with a lemon (page 522) or vanilla sauce.

- *Orange sponge pudding* Proceed as for lemon pudding, but using oranges in place of lemons. Serve with an orange sauce (page 522) or vanilla sauce.

- *Cherry sponge pudding* Add 100 g (4 oz) chopped or quartered glacé cherries to basic recipe. Serve with a custard sauce (page 522) or almond sauce (page 523).

- *Sultana/currant/raisin sponge pudding* Add 100 g (4 oz) of washed well dried fruit to basic recipe. Serve with custard sauce (page 522).

Using butter, 1 portion provides:
1295 kJ/309 kcal energy
16.3 g fat
(of which 9.4 g saturated)
37.8 g carbohydrate
(of which 18.1 g sugars)
5.2 g protein
0.8 g fibre

28 Christmas pudding

8–10 portions	1 litre (2 pt) basin
shredded suet	100 g (4 oz)
self-raising flour	50 g (2 oz)
white or brown breadcrumbs	100 g (4 oz)
mixed spice	1 tsp
ground nutmeg	¼ tsp
cinnamon	1 tsp
soft dark brown sugar	200 g (8 oz)
sultanas	100 g (4 oz)
raisins	100 g (4 oz)
currants	100 g (4 oz)
mixed chopped candied peel	25 g (1 oz)
ground almonds	25 g (1 oz)
cooking apples peeled and chopped	75 g (3 oz)
grated zest of ½ orange	
grated zest of ½ lemon	
eggs	2
barley wine	70 ml (⅛ pt)
Guinness stout	70 ml (⅛ pt)
rum	2 tbsp

1 Place all the dried fruit, with added candied peel in a mixing bowl, and soak overnight with the barley wine, Guinness and rum.

2 Sift the flour with the mixed spice, nutmeg and cinnamon.

3 Add breadcrumbs, suet and sugar to the flour.

4 Drain the fruit from the alcohol. Add to the flour along with the nuts, apple and grated zest.

5 In a separate basin, beat the eggs with the alcohol.

6 Add the dried fruit to the flour, mix thoroughly.

7 Pack into a lightly greased basin, 1 litre (2 pt).

8 Cover with a sheet of silicone and aluminium foil. Secure well.

9 Steam for 8 hours at normal atmospheric pressure.

10 Remove from steamer and allow to cool, remove foil and silicone, replace with fresh. Secure well.

11 Allow to mature for at least 2 months. Reheat by steaming for a further 2 hours.

12 Serve with rum and brandy sauce.

Pancakes

29 Pancakes with lemon or orange

Crêpes au citron ou à l'orange

> Using white flour, whole milk, hard margarine and peanut oil, 1 portion provides:
> 1275 kJ/304 kcal
> 16.2 g fat
> (of which 4.8 g saturated)
> 35.5 g carbohydrate
> (of which 16.4 g sugars)
> 6.1 g protein
> 0.9 g fibre

	4 portions	10 portions
flour, white or wholemeal	100 g (4 oz)	250 g (10 oz)
pinch of salt		
egg	1	2–3
milk, whole or skimmed	¼ litre (½ pt)	625 ml (1¼ pt)
melted butter, margarine or oil	10 g (½ oz)	25 g (1 oz)
oil for frying		
sugar, caster or unrefined	50 g (2 oz)	125 g (5 oz)

HEALTHY EATING TIP

Use semi-skimmed milk to make the batter.

continued over ▶

▶ *Pancakes with lemon or orange continued*

1 Sieve the flour and salt into a bowl, make a well in the centre.

2 Add the egg and milk, gradually incorporating the flour from the sides, whisk to a smooth batter.

3 Mix in the melted butter.

4 Heat the pancake pan, clean thoroughly.

5 Add a little oil; heat until smoking.

6 Add enough mixture to just cover the bottom of the pan thinly.

7 Cook for a few seconds until brown.

8 Turn and cook on the other side. Turn on to a plate.

9 Sprinkle with sugar. Fold in half then half again.

Note: When making a batch of pancakes it is best to keep them all flat one on top of the other on a plate. Sprinkle sugar between each. Fold them all when ready for service, sprinkle again with sugar and dress neatly overlapping on a serving dish or hot plates. Garnish with quarters of lemon or orange free from pips. Serve very hot, two per portion.

30 Pancakes with jam

Crêpes à la confiture

	4 portions	**10 portions**
warm jam	50 g (2 oz)	125 g (5 oz)
sugar	25 g (1 oz)	60 g (2½ oz)
pancakes (recipe 29)		

off

HEALTHY EATING TIP
Use semi-skimmed milk to make the batter.

1 Prepare the pancakes as above. Spread each with warm jam.

2 Roll like a swiss roll, trim the ends. Dredge with caster sugar and serve.

31 Pancakes with apple

Crêpes normande

HEALTHY EATING TIP
Use semi-skimmed milk to make the batter.

Method I

Cook as for the basic recipe and spread with a hot purée of apple (page 573); roll up and sprinkle with caster sugar.

Method II

Place a little cooked apple in the pan, add the pancake mixture and cook on both sides. Turn out, sprinkle with caster sugar and roll up.

Meringues

32 Meringue

Meringue

(Illustrated on page 512)

	4 portions	10 portions
egg whites, pasteurised	4	10
caster sugar	200 g (8 oz)	500 g (1¼ lb)

This recipe provides:
3491 kJ/831 kcal
0.0 g fat
(of which 0.0 g saturated)
210.0 g carbohydrates
(of which 210.0 g sugars)
10.8 g protein
0.0 g fibre

1 Whip the egg whites stiffly.

2 Sprinkle on the sugar and carefully mix in.

3 Place in a piping bag with a large plain tube and pipe on to silicone paper on a baking sheet.

4 Bake in the slowest oven possible or in a hot plate (110°C/Reg. ¼; 225°F). The aim is to dry out the meringues without any colour whatsoever.

Note: To gain maximum efficiency when whipping egg whites, the following points should be observed:

- Because of possible weakness in the egg white protein it is advisable to strengthen the protein by adding a pinch of cream of tartar and a pinch of dried egg white powder. If all dried egg white powder is used no additions are necessary.

- Eggs should be fresh.

- When separating yolks from whites *no* speck of egg yolk must be allowed to remain in the white; egg yolk contains fat, the presence of which can prevent the white being correctly whipped.

- The bowl and whisk must be scrupulously clean, dry and free from any grease.

- When egg whites are whipped the addition of a little sugar (15 g to 4 egg whites) will assist the efficient beating and lessen the chance of overbeating.

The reason egg whites increase in volume when whipped is because they contain so much protein (11%). The protein forms tiny filaments, which stretch on beating, incorporate air in minute bubbles then set to form a fairly stable puffed-up structure expanding to seven times its bulk.

Fig 14.6 Preparation and piping of meringues   *Yolande Stanley*

Fig 14.7 Vacherin and a selection of meringue pastries

33 Meringue with whipped cream

Meringue Chantilly

1 Allow two meringues per portion.
2 Join together with a little sweetened, vanilla-flavoured whipped cream, or non-dairy cream (known as crème Chantilly).
3 Decorate with whipped cream, glacé cherries and angelica, or crystallised violets or roses.

34 Meringue and ice-cream

Meringue glacée Chantilly

1 Allow 2 meringues per portion.
2 Join together with a small ball of vanilla ice-cream.
3 Serve in a coupe or ice-cream dish.
4 Decorate with whipped cream.

35 Vacherin with strawberries and cream

Vacherin aux fraises

Using 280 g strawberries, whipped cream,
1 portion provides:
1436 kJ/341 kcal energy
12.6 g fat
(of which 7.9 g saturated)
56.3 g carbohydrate
(of which 56.3 g sugars)
3.9 g protein
0.6 g fibre

A vacherin is a round meringue shell piped into a suitable shape so that the centre may be filled with sufficient fruit such as strawberries, stoned cherries, peaches, apricots, and whipped cream to form a rich sweet.

The vacherin may be prepared in one, two, four or larger portion sizes.

	4 portions	10 portions
egg whites	4	10
caster sugar	200 g (8 oz)	500 g (1¼ lb)
strawberries (picked and washed)	100–300 g (¼ –¾ lb)	250–750 g (10 oz–1¾ lb)
cream (whipped and sweetened) or non-dairy cream	125 ml (¼ pt)	300 ml (⅝ pt)

Try 'diluting' the fat in the cream with some low fat fromage frais.

1 Stiffly whip the egg whites.
2 Carefully fold in the sugar.

3 Place the mixture into a piping bag with a 1 cm (½ inch) plain tube.
4 Pipe on to silicone paper on a baking sheet.
5 Start from the centre and pipe round in a circular fashion to form a base 16 cm (6 inch) then pipe around the edge 2–3 cm (1–1½ inches) high.
6 Bake in a cool oven at 110°C (Reg. ¼; 225°F) until the meringue case is completely dry. Do not allow to colour.
7 Allow meringue case to cool then remove from the paper.
8 Spread a thin layer of cream on the base. Add the strawberries.
9 Decorate with the remainder of the cream.

Note: Melba sauce (page 523) may be used to coat the strawberries before decorating with cream. Refer to recipe 32 notes before whipping the egg whites.

Raspberries can be used instead of strawberries.

36 Baked Alaska

Omelette soufflée surprise

1 portion provides:
2190 kJ/521 kcal
16.4 g fat
(of which 7.3 g saturated)
91.3 g carbohydrate
(of which 81.2 g sugars)
7.7 g protein
0.6 g fibre

	4 portions	10 portions
sponge cake	4 pieces	10 pieces
fruit syrup	60 ml (⅛ pt)	150 ml (⅓ pt)
vanilla ice-cream	4 scoops	10 scoops
egg whites	4	10
caster sugar	200 g (8 oz)	500 g (1¼ lb)

1 Neatly arrange the pieces of sponge cake in the centre of a flat ovenproof dish or individual dishes.
2 Sprinkle the sponge cake with a little fruit syrup.

continued over ▶

▶ *Baked Alaska continued*

3   Place a flattened scoop of vanilla ice-cream on each piece of sponge.

4   Meanwhile stiffly whip the egg whites and fold in the sugar.

5   Use half the meringue and completely cover the ice-cream and sponge. Neaten with a palette knife.

6   Place the remainder of the meringue into a piping bag with a large tube (plain or star) and decorate over.

7   Place into a hot oven at 230–250°C (Reg. 8–9; 450–500°F) and colour a golden brown or brown with a blow torch. Serve immediately.

Note: The fruit syrup for soaking the sponge may be flavoured with rum, sherry, brandy, whisky, Tia Maria, Curaçao or any other suitable liqueur.

Variations include:

•   *Baked Alaska with peaches* Proceed as for the basic recipe, adding a little maraschino to the fruit syrup and using raspberry ice-cream instead of vanilla ice-cream. Cover the ice-cream with four halves of peaches.

•   *Baked Alaska with pears* Proceed as for the basic recipe, adding a little kirsch to the fruit syrup and adding halves of poached pears to the ice-cream.

Milk puddings

37   **Baked rice pudding**

   Pouding de riz

Using whole milk, hard margarine, 1 portion provides:
1006 kJ/239 kcal
7.0 g fat
(of which 3.9 g saturated)
40.7 g carbohydrate
(of which 19.0 g sugars)
5.8 g protein
0.6 g fibre

	4 portions	10 portions
rice (short- or whole-grain)	50 g (2 oz)	125 g (5 oz)
sugar, caster or unrefined	50 g (2 oz)	125 g (5 oz)
milk, whole or skimmed	½ litre (1 pt)	1¼ litre (2½ pt)
butter or margarine	10 g (½ oz)	25 g (1 oz)
vanilla essence	2–3 drops	6–8
grated nutmeg		

Use semi-skimmed milk.

1   Wash the rice, place in a pie dish or individual dishes.

2   Add the sugar and milk, mix well.

3   Add the butter, essence and nutmeg.

4   Place on a baking sheet; clean the rim of the pie dish.

5   Bake at 180–200°C (Reg. 4–6; 350–400°F), until the milk starts simmering.

6   Reduce the heat and allow the pudding to cook slowly, allowing 1½ –2 hours in all (less time for individual dishes).

38 Rice pudding

Ingredients as for baked rice pudding.

1   Boil the milk in a thick-based pan.
2   Add the washed rice, stir to the boil.
3   Simmer gently, stirring frequently until the rice is cooked.
4   Mix in the sugar, flavouring and butter (at this stage an egg yolk may also be added). A vanilla pod can be used in place of essence.
5   Pour into a pie dish or individual dishes, place on a baking tray and brown lightly under the salamander.

Note: Candied fruit and chopped nuts may be added for variety.

HEALTHY EATING TIP

Use semi-skimmed milk.

39 Semolina pudding

	4 portions	**10 portions**
milk, whole or skimmed	½ litre (1 pt)	1¼ litre (2½ pt)
semolina	35 g (1½ oz)	85 g (4¼ oz)
sugar, caster or unrefined	50 g (2 oz)	125 g (5 oz)
butter or margarine	10 g (½ oz)	25 g (1 oz)
lemon juice or lemon essence	2–3 drops	6–8

Using whole milk and hard margarine, 1 portion provides:
753 kJ/179 kcal
6.9 g fat
(of which 3.9 g saturated)
25.8 g carbohydrate
(of which 19.0 g sugars)
5.1 g protein
0.3 g fibre

1   Boil the milk in a thick-based pan.
2   Sprinkle in the semolina and stir to the boil.
3   Simmer for 15–20 minutes.
4   Add the sugar, butter, flavouring (and an egg yolk if desired).
5   Pour into a pie dish or individual dishes. Brown under the salamander.

Note: Sago, tapioca and ground rice pudding are made in the same way, using sago, tapioca or ground rice in place of semolina and vanilla essence for lemon essence.

Miscellaneous

40 Bread pudding

	4 portions	**10 portions**
stale bread	½ kg (1 lb)	1¼ kg (2½ lb)
sugar, caster or unrefined	125 g (5 oz)	300 g (12½ oz)
currants or sultanas	125 g (5 oz)	300 g (12½ oz)
mixed spice	½ tsp	1¼ tsp
margarine	75 g (3 oz)	180 g (7½ oz)
egg	1	3

Using white bread, 1 portion provides:
2797 kJ/661 kcal energy
19.4 g fat
(of which 1.0 g saturated)
115.8 g carbohydrate
(of which 57.4 g sugars)
13.2 g protein
2.5 g fibre

continued over ▶

▶ *Bread pudding continued*

1   Soak the bread in cold water or milk until soft.

2   Squeeze the bread dry and place in a bowl.

3   Mix in four-fifths sugar and the rest of the ingredients.

4   Place in a greased baking tray. Sprinkle with the remaining sugar.

5   Bake at 180°C (Reg. 4; 350°F) for about 1 hour.

Note: Cut into suitable sized pieces, it may be served cold or hot with a custard-type sauce.

1 portion provides:
4103.6 kJ/980 kcal energy
60.4 g fat
(of which 36.7 g saturated)
106.7 g carbohydrate
(of which 78.9 g sugars)
9.1 g protein
1.8 g fibre

41 Sticky toffee pudding with butterscotch sauce

	4 portions	10 portions
Medjool dates stoned and chopped	150 g (6 oz)	375 g (15 oz)
water	250 ml (½ pt)	625 ml (1¼ pt)
bicarbonate of soda	1 tsp	2½ tsp
unsalted butter	50 g (2 oz)	125 g (5 oz)
caster sugar	150 g (6 oz)	375 g (15 oz)
medium eggs	2	5
self-raising flour	150 g (6 oz)	375 g (15 oz)
vanilla essence	1 tsp	2½ tsp
Sauce **double cream**	250 ml (½ pt)	625 ml (1¼ pt)
butter	62 g (2½ oz)	155 g (6¼ oz)
demerara sugar	100 g (4 oz)	250 g (10 oz)

1   For four portions, grease a baking tin approximately 28 × 18 cm (11 × 7 inch) in size.

2   Boil the dates in water for approximately five minutes until soft, then add the bicarbonate of soda.

3   Cream the butter and sugar together until light and white, gradually beat in the eggs.

4   Mix in the dates, flour and vanilla essence, stir well.

5   Form into the greased baking tin and bake in a pre-heated oven 180°C (250°F) for approximately 30–40 minutes, until firm to the touch.

6   Carefully portion the sponge.

7   Make the sauce by boiling the cream, whisk in the butter and sugar, simmer for 3 minutes. Carefully pour over the pudding.

Note: May also be prepared in individual moulds.

42 Chocolate fondant

	4 portions	10 portions
couverture chocolate	150 g (6 oz)	375 g (15 oz)
unsalted butter	125 g (5 oz)	312 g (12½ oz)
eggs	3	7
yolks	2	5
caster sugar	75 g (3 oz)	182 g (7½ oz)
flour	75 g (3 oz)	182 g (7½ oz)

1 portion provides:
2830 kJ/675 kcal energy
46.8 g fat
(of which 29.6 g saturated)
55.9 g carbohydrate
(of which 40.9 g sugars)
11 g protein
0.6 g fibre

1 Lightly grease and flour individual dariole moulds.

2 Carefully melt the chocolate and butter in a suitable bowl, either in a microwave oven or over a pan of hot water (bain-marie).

3 In a separate bowl whisk the eggs, egg yolks and caster sugar until aerated to ribbon stage. Pour into the chocolate and butter mix, then whisk together.

4 Add the flour, then mix until smooth.

5 Pour into the moulds, bake in the oven at 200°C (400°F) for 15 minutes.

6 Remove from oven, leave for 5 minutes before turning out onto suitable plates.

Serve with a suitable ice-cream: vanilla, pistachio, almond or Bailey's.

43 Bailey's ice-cream

	6 portions
milk	500 ml (1 pt)
double cream	250 ml (½ pt)
Bailey's Irish cream liqueur	250 ml (½ pt)
vanilla pod	1
egg yolks	6
caster sugar	125 g (5 oz)

1 portion provides:
2179 kJ/524 kcal energy
36 g fat
(of which 16.4 g saturated)
36 g carbohydrate
(of which 36 g sugars)
6.4 g protein
0 g fibre

1 Bring the milk, cream and Bailey's with the vanilla pod to the boil. Remove from the heat.

2 Whisk the egg yolks and sugar, then cream well.

3 Pour a third of the milk mixture onto the egg yolks and sugar. Whisk well, add to the remainder of the milk, stir the custard over a low heat. **Do not boil**. When it coats the back of a spoon, strain.

4 Allow to cool, churn in an ice-cream machine.

44 Chocolate and griottine* clafoutis
John Campbell

Cherry batter	
eggs	2
sugar	2½ tbsp
milk	180 ml (6 fl oz)
kirsch	2 tsp, from the griottines
plain flour	2½ tbsp
Chocolate batter	
plain chocolate	200 g (7 oz)
butter	100 g (4 oz)
eggs	2
sugar	2 tbsp
plain flour	2 tbsp
cornflour	1 tbsp
Chocolate sauce (optional)	
sugar	165 g (5½ oz)
cocoa	55 g (2 oz)
water	125 ml (4 fl oz)
To finish	
drained griottines	220 g (8 oz)
icing sugar, for dusting	

For the cherry batter

In a large bowl, beat the eggs and sugar together until smooth. Add the milk and kirsch, then sieve in the flour. Mix well, then strain the batter through a sieve and set aside.

*Griottines are a type of cherry.

For the chocolate batter

1 Melt the chocolate and butter in a bowl placed over a pan of simmering water on a low heat.

2 Meanwhile, place the eggs and sugar in a mixing bowl or a mixer with a whisk attachment and whisk to a thick white foam.

3 Switch the machine to the slowest speed, add both flours and mix for 30–60 seconds.

4 Stir the chocolate and butter together then use a hand whisk to fold this mixture into the whisked egg mixture, ensuring total incorporation.

5 Carefully mix the two batters together to make one thick batter. This mixture can be stored in the refrigerator for up to 4 days.

For the chocolate sauce

Place all the ingredients in a saucepan and bring to the boil, stirring to dissolve.

Remove from the heat, cool and store covered in the refrigerator until ready to serve, or for up to 1 month.

To complete: Preheat the oven to 180°C (Reg. 4; 350°F). Lightly, but thoroughly, butter some individual dishes. Alternatively use another ovenproof dish such as a gratin dish. Place 10–12 griottine cherries in the base of each dish and divide the batter between them. Place the dishes on a baking shelf and bake for 8–10 minutes until just cooked.

Remove the clafoutis from the oven and allow it to cool slightly. Dust with icing sugar and serve, with the chocolate sauce served separately if desired.

45 Lemon tart
Tarte au citron

1 portion provides:
1878 kJ/450 kcal energy
28.0 g fat
(of which 15.2 g saturated)
42.7 g carbohydrate
(of which 36.1 g sugars)
9.4 g protein
0.3 g fibre

	8 portions
medium eggs	8
caster sugar	300 g (12 oz)
double cream	250 ml (½ pt)
lemons	juice of 3 zest from 4
sweet pastry	150 g (6 oz)

1   Prepare 150 g (6 oz) of sweet pastry adding the zest of 1 lemon to the mix.

2   Line a 16 cm (8 inch) flan ring.

3   Bake blind for approximately 15 minutes.

4   Prepare the filling, mix the eggs and sugar together until smooth, add the cream, lemon juice and zest. Whisk well.

5   Pour into the flan case, bake for 30–40 minutes at 150°C (300°F) until set.

6   Remove from oven and allow to cool.

7   Dust with icing sugar and glaze under the grill or use a blow torch. Portion and serve.

Note: Take care when almost cooked as overcooking will cause the filling to rise.

Alternatively, limes may be used in place of lemons. If so, use the zest and juice of 5 limes or use a mixture of lemons and limes.

Note: The mixture will fill one 16 cm (8 inch) × 4 cm (2 inch) or two 16 cm (8 inch) × 2 cm (1 inch) flan rings.

If using two flan rings, double the amount of pastry and reduce the baking time when the filling is added.

Fig 14.8 Lemon tart

Yolande Stanley

Fig 14.9 White chocolate mousse

Yolande Stanley

Using whole milk, whipped cream,
1 portion provides:
2208 kJ/532 kcal energy
41.3 g fat
(of which 24.4 g saturated)
31.5 g carbohydrate
(of which 31.5 g sugars)
10.4 g protein
0.0 g fibre

Using whole milk, yoghurt,
1 portion provides:
1436 kJ/343 kcal energy
17.9 g fat
(of which 9.7 g saturated)
34.7 g carbohydrate
(of which 34.7 g sugars)
12.7 g protein
0.0 g fibre

46 White chocolate mousse

	4 portions	10 portions
milk, whole or skimmed	125 ml (¼ pt)	300 ml (⅝ pt)
orange, grated zest	1	2–3
white chocolate	150 g (6 oz)	375 g (15 oz)
medium eggs	2	5
caster sugar	25 g (1 oz)	60 g (2½ oz)
leaf gelatine	6 g (¼ oz)	12 g (⅝ oz)
whipping cream, fromage frais or natural yoghurt	250 ml (½ pt)	625 ml (1¼ pt)

1   Heat the milk to boiling point with the grated zest of the orange.

2   Add the white chocolate and melt. Stir well, away from the heat.

3   Whisk the eggs and sugar together, add the hot milk and return to the saucepan.

4   Stir on the side of the stove until the mixture coats the back of a spoon but do not boil. Remove from the heat.

5   Add the soaked and squeezed gelatine and bring down to setting point.

6   Fold in the whipped cream or alternative. Carefully and immediately pour into the mould.

7   Turn out and use as required.

Note: The mousse can be prepared in individual moulds, turned out onto plates, topped with poached fruit (pears, peaches, apricots) or fresh berries (loganberries, raspberries, strawberries). It can be coated with a suitable sauce (lemon, orange, lime, strawberry, Grand Marnier, grenadine).

Sweet sauces and flavourings

¼ litre (½ pt) = 4–8 portions.

47 Jam sauce

jam	200 g (8 oz)
water	100 ml (³⁄₁₆ pt)
lemon juice	2–3 drops
cornflour	10 g (½ oz)

> 1 portion provides:
> 595 kJ/139 kcal energy
> 0.0 g fat
> (of which 0.0 g saturated)
> 37.0 g carbohydrate
> (of which 34.7 g sugars)
> 0.2 g protein
> 0.0 g fibre

1   Boil the jam, water and lemon juice together.

2   Adjust the consistency with a little cornflour or arrowroot diluted with water.

3   Reboil until clear and pass through a conical strainer.

48 Apricot sauce

Sauce abricot

apricot jam	200 g (8 oz)
water	100 ml (³⁄₁₆ pt)
lemon juice	2–3 drops
cornflour	10 g (½ oz)

> 1 portion provides:
> 595 kJ/139 kcal energy
> 0.0 g fat
> (of which 0.0 g saturated)
> 37.0 g carbohydrate
> (of which 34.7 g sugars)
> 0.2 g protein
> 0.0 g fibre

Proceed as for recipe 47.

49 Orange, lemon or lime sauce

sugar, caster or unrefined	50 g (2 oz)
water	250 ml (½ pt)
cornflour or arrowroot	10 g (½ oz)
oranges, lemons or limes	1–2

Using oranges, cornflour, 1 portion provides:
306 kJ/72 kcal energy
0.1 g fat
(of which 0.0 g saturated)
18.5 g carbohydrate
(of which 16.2 g sugars)
0.4 g protein
0.6 g fibre

1 Boil the sugar and water.
2 Add the cornflour diluted with water, stirring continuously.
3 Reboil until clear, strain.
4 Add blanched julienne of orange zest and the strained orange juice.

Note: A little Curaçao or Cointreau may be added for additional flavour.

50 Syrup sauce

syrup	200 g (8 oz)
water	125 ml (¼ pt)
lemon, juice of	1
cornflour or arrowroot	10 g (½ oz)

Using cornflour, 1 portion provides:
677 kJ/159 kcal energy
0.0 g fat
(of which 0.0 g saturated)
42.0 g carbohydrate
(of which 39.7 g sugars)
0.2 g protein
0.0 g fibre

Bring the syrup, water and lemon juice to the boil and thicken with diluted cornflour. Boil for a few minutes and strain.

51 Custard sauce

custard powder	10 g (½ oz)
milk, whole or semi-skimmed	250 ml (½ pt)
caster or unrefined sugar	25 g (1 oz)

Using whole milk, this recipe provides:
1245 kJ/296 kcal
9.6 g fat
(of which 6.0 g saturated)
47.2 g carbohydrate
(of which 38.0 g sugars)
8.3 g protein
0.3 g fibre

1 Dilute the custard powder with a little of the milk.
2 Boil the remainder of the milk.
3 Pour a little of the boiled milk on to the diluted custard powder.
4 Return to the saucepan.
5 Stir to the boil and mix in the sugar.

Note: See also recipe 18, fresh egg custard sauce.

52 Almond sauce

cornflour	10 g (½ oz)
milk, whole or skimmed	250 ml (½ pt)
caster or unrefined sugar	25 g (1 oz)
few drops almond essence	

Using whole milk, cornflour,
1 portion provides:
314 kJ/75 kcal energy
2.5 g fat
(of which 1.6 g sugars)
11.7 g carbohydrate
(of which 9.4 g sugars)
2.1 g protein
0.0 g fibre

1 Dilute the cornflour with a little of the milk.

2 Boil the remainder of the milk. Whisk on to the cornflour.

3 Return to the pan, stir to the boil. Simmer for 3–4 minutes.

4 Mix in the sugar and essence. Pass through a strainer.

53 Rum or brandy cream

Whipped, sweetened cream flavoured with rum or brandy.

54 Rum or brandy butter

Cream equal quantities of butter and sieved icing sugar together and add rum or brandy to taste.

55 Melba sauce

Sauce Melba

Method I

raspberry jam	400 g (1 lb)
water	125 ml (¼ pt)

Boil together and pass through a conical strainer.

1 portion provides:
558 kJ/131 kcal energy
0.0 g fat
(of which 0.0 g saturated)
34.7 g carbohydrate
(of which 34.7 g sugars)
0.2 g protein
0.0 g fibre

Method II

raspberries	400 g (1 lb)
water	125 ml (¼ pt)
sugar, caster or unrefined	100 g (4 oz)

Boil ingredients together, cool, liquidise and strain.

1 portion provides:
265 kJ/62 kcal energy
0.2 g fat
(of which 0.1 g saturated)
15.4 g carbohydrate
(of which 15.4 g sugars)
0.7 g protein
0.0 g fibre

1 portion provides:
474 kJ/111 kcal energy
0.2 g fat
(of which 0.1 g saturated)
28.5 g carbohydrate
(of which 28.3 g sugars)
0.7 g protein
0.0 g fibre

Using cocoa, portion size
57 g/2 oz, 1 portion provides:
336 kJ/79 kcal energy
1.8 g fat
(of which 1.1 g saturated)
15.1 g carbohydrate
(of which 13.3 g sugars)
1.7 g protein
0.2 g fibre

Method III

raspberries	400 g (1 lb)
icing sugar	200 g (8 oz)

Liquidise, pass through a fine sieve and add a little lemon juice.

Note: Methods II and III are also known as raspberry cullis or coulis, which can also be prepared using other fruits, e.g. peach, strawberry or mango.

56 Chocolate sauce

Sauce chocolat

cornflour	10 g (½ oz)
milk	250 ml (½ pt)
cocoa powder	10 g (½ oz)
or chocolate (block)	25 g (1 oz)
sugar	65 g (1½ oz)
butter	5 g (¼ oz)

With cocoa

1   Dilute the cornflour with a little of the milk, mix in the cocoa.
2   Boil the remainder of the milk.
3   Pour a little of the milk on to the cornflour.
4   Return to the saucepan.
5   Stir to the boil. Mix in the sugar and butter.

With chocolate

Shred the chocolate, add to the milk and proceed as above, omitting the cocoa.

Note: Chocolate sauce may be flavoured if desired with rum or Crème de Menthe.

57 Boiled butter cream

medium eggs	2
icing sugar	50 g (2 oz)
granulated sugar or cube sugar	300 g (12 oz)
water	100 g (4 oz)
glucose	50 g (2 oz)
unsalted butter	400 g (1 lb)

1   Beat the eggs and icing sugar until the ribbon stage (sponge).
2   Boil the granulated or cube sugar with water and glucose to 118°C (245°F).

3　Gradually add the sugar at 118°C (245°F) to the eggs and icing sugar at ribbon stage, whisk continuously and allow to cool to 26°C (80°F).

4　Gradually add the unsalted butter while continuing to whisk until a smooth cream is obtained.

Note: Butter cream may be flavoured with numerous flavours and combinations of flavours:

- chocolate and rum
- strawberry and vanilla
- apricot and passionfruit
- coffee and hazelnut
- whisky and orange
- lemon and lime
- brandy and praline

58　Butter cream

icing sugar	150 g (6 oz)
butter	200 g (8 oz)

1　Sieve the icing sugar.

2　Cream the butter and icing sugar until light and creamy.

3　Flavour and colour as required.

Note: Variations include:

- *Rum butter cream* Add rum to flavour and blend in.
- *Chocolate butter cream* Add melted chocolate, sweetened or unsweetened according to taste.

59　Praline

Praline is a basic preparation used for flavouring items such as gâteaux, soufflés, ice-creams and many other sweets.

almonds, shelled	100 g (4 oz)
hazelnuts, shelled	100 g (4 oz)
water	60 ml (⅛ pt)
sugar	200 g (8 oz)

1　Lightly brown the almonds and hazelnuts in an oven.

2　Cook the water and sugar in a copper or thick-based pan until the caramel stage is reached.

3　Remove the pan from the heat. Mix in the nuts.

4　Turn out the mixture on to a lightly oiled marble slab.

5　Allow to become quite cold.

6　Crush to a coarse texture using a rolling pin. Store in an airtight container.

60 Apple Charlotte

Charlotte aux pommes

Using hard margarine, 1 portion provides:
2163 kJ/515 kcal
22.3 g fat
(of which 9.3 g saturated)
74.5 g carbohydrate
(of which 23.4 g sugars)
9.4 g protein
6.1 g fibre

	4 portions	10 portions
stale bread	400 g (1 lb)	1¼ kg (2½ lb)
margarine or butter	100 g (4 oz)	250 g (10 oz)
cooking apples	400 g (1 lb)	1¼ kg (2½ lb)
sugar, caster or unrefined	50–75 g (2–3 oz)	125–150 g (5–6 oz)
breadcrumbs or cake crumbs	35 g (1½ oz)	85 g (4½ oz)

1 Use either one Charlotte mould or four dariole moulds.

2 Cut the bread into 3 mm (⅛ inch) slices and remove the crusts.

3 Cut a round the size of the mould bottom, dip into melted butter or margarine on one side and place in the mould fat side down.

4 Cut fingers of bread 2–4 cm (1–1½ inch) wide, and fit, overlapping well, to the sides of the mould after dipping each one in melted fat. Take care not to leave any gaps.

5 Peel, core and wash the apples, cut into thick slices and three parts cook in a little butter and sugar (a little cinnamon or a clove may be added), and add the breadcrumbs.

6 Fill the centre of the mould with the apple.

7 Cut round pieces of bread to seal the apple in.

8 Bake at 220°C (Reg. 7; 425°F) for 30–40 minutes. Remove from the mould.

9 Serve with apricot (page 521) or custard (page 522) sauce.

61 Apple fritters

Beignets aux pommes

Fried in peanut oil, 1 portion provides:
1034 kJ/246 kcal
10.2 g fat
(of which 1.9 g saturated)
38.9 g carbohydrate
(of which 25.0 g sugars)
2.1 g protein
3.0 g fibre

	4 portions	10 portions
cooking apples	400 g (1 lb)	1 kg (2½ lb)
frying batter (page 177)	150 g (6 oz)	375 g (15 oz)
apricot sauce (page 521)	125 ml (¼ pt)	300 ml (⅝ pt)

1 Peel and core the apples and cut into ½ cm (¼ inch) rings.

2 Pass through flour, shake off the surplus.

3 Dip into frying batter.

4 Lift out with the fingers, into fairly hot deep fat 185°C (365°F).

5 Cook for about 5 minutes on each side.

6 Drain well on kitchen paper, dust with icing sugar and glaze under the salamander.

7 Serve with hot apricot sauce.

62 Banana fritters

Beignets aux bananes

1 portion provides:
1405 kJ/333 kcal energy
11.5 g fat
(of which 1.4 g saturated)
57.9 g carbohydrate
(of which 41.7 g sugars)
3.0 g protein
1.6 g fibre

	4 portions	10 portions
bananas	4	10
frying batter (page 177)	150 g (6 oz)	375 g (15 oz)
apricot sauce (page 521)	125 ml (¼ pt)	300 ml (⅝ pt)

1   Peel and cut the bananas in half lengthwise then in half across.

2   Cook and serve as for apple fritters above.

Note: Bananas may be dipped in hot pastry cream flavoured with rum, allowed to cool on an oiled tray, before passing through flour and dipping in frying batter.

63   Pineapple fritters

Beignets aux ananas

1 portion provides:
1082 kJ/257 kcal energy
11.2 g fat
(of which 1.3 g saturated)
39.6 g carbohydrate
(of which 25.7 g sugars)
1.9 g protein
0.7 g fibre

	4 portions
pineapple, rings of	4
frying batter (page 177)	150 g (6 oz)
apricot sauce (page 521)	125 ml (¼ pt)

Cut the rings in half, cook and serve as for apple fritters (recipe 61).

Note: Pineapple fritters may also be dipped in hot pastry cream flavoured with liqueur, allowed to cool on an oiled tray before passing through flour and dipping in frying batter.

64   Baked apple

Pommes bonne femme

Using hard margarine, 1 portion provides:
663 kJ/156 kcal
5.1 g fat
(of which 2.2 g saturated)
29.7 g carbohydrate
(of which 29.5 g sugars)
0.4 g protein
2.7 g fibre

	4 portions	10 portions
medium-size cooking apples	4	10
sugar, white or unrefined	50 g (2 oz)	125 g (5 oz)
cloves	4	10
butter or margarine	25 g (1 oz)	60 g (2½ oz)
water	60 ml (⅛ pt)	150 ml (⅓ pt)

1   Core the apples and make an incision 2 mm (1/12 inch) deep round the centre of each. Wash well.

2   Place in a roasting tray or ovenproof dish.

3   Fill the centre with sugar and add a clove.

4   Place 5 g (¼ oz) butter on each. Add the water.

5   Bake in a moderate oven at 200–220°C (Reg. 6–7; 400–425°F) for 15–20 minutes.

6   Turn the apples over carefully.

7   Return to the oven until cooked, about 40 minutes in all.

8   Serve with a little cooking liquor and custard, cream or ice-cream.

Note: For stuffed baked apple, proceed as for baked apples, but fill the centre with washed sultanas, raisins or chopped dates, or a combination of these.

65 Apple crumble

	4 portions	**10 portions**
Bramley apples	600 g (1½ lb)	2 kg (4 lb)
sugar	100 g (4 oz)	250 g (10 oz)
cloves	1	2
topping **plain flour**	150 g (6 oz)	400 g (1 lb)
soft brown sugar	100 g (4 oz)	250 g (10 oz)
butter or margarine	50 g (2 oz)	125 g (5 oz)

1 Peel, core and slice the apples.

2 Cook gently with a few drops of water, sugar and clove.

3 Place in a pie dish, then remove the clove.

4 Lightly rub the fat into the flour and combine with the sugar.

5 When the fruit is cool, add the topping and bake in a hot oven 220°C (reg. 7, 425°F) for about 30 minutes until lightly browned.

6 Serve with custard, cream or vanilla ice cream.

Variations: apple and blackberry, apple and gooseberry, rhubarb, rhubarb and ginger (all using cooked fruit); raspberry, blackcurrant, damson (using raw fruit).

The topping can be varied by using wholemeal flour, self-raising flour – adding a little spice e.g. cinnamon, nutmeg, mixed spice.

Replacing a quarter of the flour with ground almonds or chopped almonds, walnuts or pecans.

Use half the flour and half porridge oats.

66 Fresh fruit salad

Salade de fruits

(Illustrated on page 530)

All the following fruits may be used: dessert apples, pears, pineapple, oranges, grapes, melon, strawberries, peaches, raspberries, apricots, bananas, cherries. Kiwi fruit, plums, mangoes, paw-paws and lychees may also be used. Kirsch, Cointreau or Grand Marnier may be added to the syrup. All fruit must be ripe. Allow about 150 g (6 oz) unprepared fruit per portion.

		4 portions	10 portions
caster sugar	stock syrup	50 g (2 oz)	125 g (5 oz)
water		125 ml (¼ pt)	⅜ litre (⅝ pt)
lemon, juice of		½	1
orange		1	2–3
dessert apple		1	2–3
dessert pear		1	2–3
cherries		50 g (2 oz)	125 g (5 oz)
grapes		50 g (2 oz)	125 g (5 oz)
banana		1	2–3

1 Boil the sugar with ⅛ litre (¼ pint) (⅜ litre, ⅝ pint) water to make a syrup, place in a bowl.

2 Allow to cool, add the lemon juice.

3 Peel and cut the orange into segments as for cocktail.

4 Quarter the apple and pear, remove the core, peel and cut each quarter into two or three slices, place in the bowl and mix with the orange.

5 Stone the cherries, leave whole.

6 Cut the grapes in half, peel if required, and remove the pips.

7 Mix carefully and place in a glass bowl in the refrigerator to chill.

8 Just before serving, peel and slice the banana and mix in.

As an alternative to water and sugar a fruit juice e.g. apple, orange, grape or passion fruit, can be used.

67 Tropical fruit plate

An assortment of fully ripe fruits e.g. pineapple, papaya, mango (see page 530) peeled, de-seeded, cut into pieces and neatly dressed on a plate. An optional accompaniment could be: yoghurt, vanilla ice-cream, crème fraîche, fresh or clotted cream.

HEALTHY EATING TIP

This colourful dessert helps to meet the target of 'five portions of fruit and vegetables per day'.

Fig 14.10 🖋 Peeling a mango

Fig 14.11 🖋 Fresh fruit salad

Fig 14.12 🖋 Preparation of apple
fritters

Fig 14.13 🖋 Tropical fruit plate

68 Fruit fool

Method I Apple, gooseberry, rhubarb, etc.

> Using whole milk, apples, 1 portion provides:
> 942 kJ/222 kcal energy
> 2.6 g fat
> (of which 1.6 g saturated)
> 50.3 g carbohydrate
> (of which 44.5 g sugars)
> 2.4 g protein
> 1.6 g fibre

	4 portions	10 portions
fruit	400 g (1 lb)	1 kg (2½ lb)
water	60 ml (⅛ pt)	150 ml (⅓ pt)
granulated or unrefined sugar	100 g (4 oz)	250 g (10 oz)
cornflour	25 g (1 oz)	60 g (2½ oz)
milk, whole or skimmed	¼ litre (½ pt)	625 ml (1¼ pt)
caster or unrefined sugar	25 g (1 oz)	60 g (2½ oz)

1 Cook the fruit in water and sugar, to a purée. Pass through a sieve.
2 Dilute the cornflour in a little of the milk, add the sugar.
3 Boil remainder of the milk.
4 Pour on the diluted cornflour, stir well.
5 Return to the pan on a low heat and stir to the boil.
6 Mix with the fruit purée. The quantity of mixture should not be less than ½ litre (1 pint).
7 Pour into four glass coupes or suitable dishes and allow to set.
8 Decorate with whipped sweetened cream or non-dairy cream. The colour may need to be adjusted slightly with food colour.

Method II Raspberries, strawberries, etc.

> Using strawberries, 1 portion provides:
> 1540 kJ/370 kcal energy
> 25.3 g fat
> (of which 15.8 g saturated)
> 35.7 g carbohydrate
> (of which 35.7 g sugars)
> 2.0 g protein
> 1.2 g fibre

fruit in purée	400 g (1 lb)	1 kg (2½ lb)
caster sugar	100 g (4 oz)	250 g (10 oz)
fresh whipped cream	¼ litre (½ pt)	625 ml (1¼ pt)

Mix together and serve in coupes.

Method III Fruit as per Method II

> Using raspberries, double cream used, 1 portion provides:
> 1606 kJ/385 kcal energy
> 25.2 g fat
> (of which 15.6 g saturated)
> 40.0 g carbohydrate
> (of which 31.9 g sugars)
> 2.0 g protein
> 2.7 g fibre

cornflour	35 g (1½ oz)	85 g (4¼ oz)
water	375 ml (¾ pt)	900 ml (1⅞ pt)
sugar	100 g (4 oz)	250 g (10 oz)
fruit	400 g (1 lb)	1¼ kg (2½ lb)
cream	185 ml (⅜ pt)	500 ml (1 pt)

1 Dilute the cornflour in a little of the water.
2 Boil the remainder of the water with the sugar and prepared fruit until soft.
3 Pass through a fine sieve.
4 Return to a clean pan and reboil.
5 Stir in the diluted cornflour and reboil. Allow to cool.
6 Lightly whisk the cream and fold into the mixture.
7 Serve as for Method I.

Note: In methods 2 and 3 the cream content may be reduced by using equal quantities of cream and natural Greek-style yoghurt.

Using pears, 1 portion provides:
531 kJ/126 kcal
0.0 g fat
(of which 0.0 g saturated)
33.5 g carbohydrate
(of which 33.5 g sugars)
0.2 g protein
2.2 g fibre

HEALTHY EATING TIP

Use fruit juice to poach the fruit. If dried fruits are used, no added sugar is needed.

69 Poached fruits or fruit compote

Compote de fruits

	4 portions	**10 portions**
fruit	400 g (1 lb)	1 kg (2½ lb)
sugar or stock syrup water	¼ litre (½ pt)	625 ml (1¼ pt)
sugar	100 g (4 oz)	250 g (10 oz)
lemon	½	1

Apples, pears

1 Boil the water and sugar.
2 Quarter the fruit, remove the core and peel.
3 Place in a shallow pan in sugar syrup.
4 Add a few drops of lemon juice.
5 Cover with greaseproof paper.
6 Allow to simmer slowly, preferably in the oven, cool and serve.

Soft fruits – raspberries, strawberries

1 Pick and wash the fruit. Place in a glass bowl.
2 Pour on the hot syrup. Allow to cool and serve.

Stone fruits – plums, damsons, greengages, cherries

Wash the fruit, barely cover with sugar syrup and cover with greaseproof paper or a lid. Cook gently in a moderate oven until tender.

Rhubarb

Trim off the stalk and leaf and wash. Cut into 5 cm (2 inch) lengths and cook as above, adding extra sugar if necessary. A little ground ginger may also be added.

Gooseberries, blackcurrants, redcurrants

Top and tail the gooseberries, wash and cook as for stone fruit, adding extra sugar if necessary. The currants should be carefully removed from the stalks, washed and cooked as for stone fruits.

Dried fruits – prunes, apricots, apples, pears

Dried fruits should be washed and soaked in cold water overnight. Gently cook in the liquor with sufficient sugar to taste.

Note: A piece of cinnamon stick and a few slices of lemon may be added to the prunes or pears, one or two cloves to the dried or fresh apples.

Any compote may be flavoured with lavender and/or mint.

70 Pear Condé

Poire Condé

	4 portions	10 portions
rice (short- or whole-grain)	75 g (3 oz)	180 g (7½ oz)
milk, whole or skimmed	½ litre (1 pt)	1¼ litre (2½ pt)
sugar, caster or unrefined	50 g (2 oz)	125 g (5 oz)
vanilla essence or pod	3–4 drops	6–7 drops
ripe dessert pears	2	5
apricot glaze	125 ml (¼ pt)	300 ml (⅝ pt)
angelica	10 g (½ oz)	25 g (1¼ oz)
glacé cherries	2	5

> Using whole milk, 1 portion provides:
> 1299 kJ/309 kcal
> 4.9 g fat
> (of which 3.1 g saturated)
> 64.5 g carbohydrate
> (of which 48.3 g sugars)
> 5.7 g protein
> 2.4 g fibre

1 Cook the rice in the milk, sweeten and flavour. Allow to cool.

2 Peel, core, halve the pears; poach them carefully, leave to cool.

3 Dress the rice either in a glass bowl, on individual plates or a flat dish.

4 Drain the pears and neatly arrange them on top.

5 Coat with apricot glaze. Decorate with angelica and cherries.

Note: Many other fruits may be prepared as a condé: banana, pineapple, peach. The rice can be enriched with 10 g (½ oz) butter or margarine and an egg yolk (increase the quantities 2½ times for 10 portions).

71 Pears in red wine

	4 portions	10 portions
whole ripe medium pears	4	10
cooking liquid **water**	250 ml (½ pt)	625 ml (1¼ pt)
sugar	100 g (4 oz)	250 g (10 oz)
red wine	125 ml (¼ pt)	300 ml (⅝ pt)
cinnamon stick	1	2–3
lemon, zest of	1	2–3
few drops of cochineal		

> 1 portion provides:
> 690 kJ/163 kcal energy
> 0.2 g fat
> (of which 0.0 g saturated)
> 42.3 g carbohydrate
> (of which 42.3 g sugars)
> 0.5 g protein
> 3.5 g fibre

1 Boil all the ingredients for the cooking liquid.

2 Peel the pears. Use either whole, in which case the cores should be tunnelled out and half of the stalks left intact; or in halves or quarters with the cores and stalks removed.

continued over ▶

▶ *Pears in red wine continued*

3 Gently poach the pears covered with greaseproof paper in the cooking liquid.

4 The pears may be served hot or cold. An accompaniment might be cream (plain or whipped), ice-cream e.g. vanilla or pistachio, yoghurt or fromage frais.

Note: If the pears are cut up the amount of cooking liquid may be lessened. The amount of red wine can be varied according to taste. Pears in red wine may also be used as a garnish for other dishes e.g. vanilla mousse or bavarois.

72 Avocado mousse with poached pear and strawberry sauce

	4 portions	10 portions
avocado purée	250 ml (½ pt)	625 ml (1¼ pt)
lemon, juice of	½	1
icing sugar	50 g (2 oz)	125 g (5 oz)
leaf gelatine	12 g (½ oz)	25 g (1 oz)
whipped cream, fromage frais or natural yoghurt	125 ml (¼ pt)	300 ml (⅝ pt)
poached pear	4 halves	10 halves

1 Add the lemon juice to the avocado purée.

2 Mix in the icing sugar.

3 Place the soaked and lightly squeezed gelatine into a small pan. Heat gently until it starts to boil.

4 Carefully add the gelatine to the purée, stirring well.

5 When setting point is reached, carefully fold in the whipped cream or alternative.

6 Pour into individual moulds and place in the refrigerator to set.

7 When set, turn out onto plates and garnish each with half a poached pear carefully fanned.

8 Mask with strawberry sauce.

73 Strawberry sauce

strawberry purée	125 ml (¼ pt)	300 ml (⅝ pt)
white wine	125 ml (¼ pt)	300 ml (⅝ pt)
caster sugar	50 g (2 oz)	125 g (5 oz)

Mix all the ingredients together and strain.

Note: Alternative fruit purées that can be used in the mousse are peach, apricot, mango, pawpaw, strawberry and raspberry.

Using whipping cream, 1 portion provides:
1449 kJ/347 kcal energy
24.8 g fat
(of which 10.4 g saturated)
28.4 g carbohydrate
(of which 27.4 g sugars)
4.5 g protein
2.9 g fibre

HEALTHY EATING TIP
Although avocado is rich in fat, this fat is unsaturated and a 'healthier' type of fat. Try using yoghurt or fromage frais in place of the cream.

1 portion provides:
350 kJ/83 kcal energy
0.0 g fat
(of which 0.0 g saturated)
16.5 g carbohydrate
(of which 16.5 g sugars)
0.3 g protein
0.4 g fibre

Alternative sauces include raspberry, peach, apricot, lemon, orange and lime.

For peach sauce proceed as for strawberry sauce, substituting peach purée for strawberry purée.

74 Fruit Melba (peach, pear, banana Melba)

Pêche Melba

> 1 portion provides:
> 607 kJ/145 kcal
> 2.6 g fat
> (of which 1.3 g saturated)
> 30.5 g carbohydrate
> (of which 30.2 g sugars)
> 1.6 g protein
> 1.3 g fibre

	4 portions	10 portions
peaches	2	5
vanilla ice-cream	125 ml (¼ pt)	300 ml (½ pt)
Melba sauce (page 523)	125 ml (¼ pt)	300 ml (½ pt)

1   Dress the fruit on a ball of ice-cream in an ice-cream coupe and coat with Melba sauce. May be decorated with whipped cream.

Note: If using fresh peaches they should be dipped in boiling water for a few seconds, cooled by placing into cold water, peeled and halved.

Fresh pears should be peeled, halved and poached. Bananas should be peeled at the last moment.

75 Pear belle Hélène

Poire belle Hélène

Serve a cooked pear on a ball of vanilla ice-cream in a coupe. Decorate with whipped cream. Serve with a sauceboat of hot chocolate sauce (recipe 56).

76 Peach cardinal

Pêche cardinal

Place half a prepared peach on a ball of strawberry ice-cream in a coupe. Coat with Melba sauce; decorate with whipped cream and sprinkle with toasted almonds cut in slices, if required.

77 Coupe Jacques

Place some fruit salad in a coupe; arrange one scoop each of lemon and strawberry ice-cream on top. Decorate with whipped cream if required.

There are numerous other recipes that include fruit:

- Baked Alaska (page 513).
- Bavarois (page 496).
- Cold lemon soufflé (page 505).
- Dutch apple tart (page 575).
- Flans (page 569).
- Ice-cream (strawberry, raspberry) (page 498).
- Kiwi slice (page 587).
- Lemon meringue pie (page 573).
- Meringue (page 511).
- Pancakes (page 510).
- Pies (page 568).
- Savarin (page 555).
- Sorbets (page 497).
- Soufflé puddings (page 502).
- Steamed sponge puddings (page 508).
- Tartlets and barquettes (page 577).
- Turnovers (page 582).

Many recipes also make use of dried fruit:

- Bread and butter pudding (page 491).
- Bread pudding (page 515).
- Christmas pudding (page 509).
- Mince pies (page 586).

Prepare and cook dough products

Bread and dough products basically contain wheat flour and yeast. Bread and bread products form the basis of our diet; it is not surprising, therefore, that bread is seen as a fundamental staple product in our society. 'Give us our daily bread.' We eat bread at breakfast, lunch and dinner in sandwiches, as bread rolls, as croissants, as French sticks, etc. Bread is also used as an ingredient for many other dishes, either as slices or as breadcrumbs. The basic bread dough of wheat flour, yeast and water may be enriched with fat, sugar, eggs, milk and numerous other added ingredients.

Dough consists of strong flour, water, salt and yeast, which are kneaded together to the required consistency at a suitable temperature. When proving takes place the yeast produces carbon dioxide and water, which aerates the dough. When baked it produces a light digestible product with flavour and colour.

Enriched doughs or enriched breads are:

- buns
- savarins
- brioche
- croissants
- Danish pastries.

Croissants and Danish pastries are enriched doughs where the fat is added by layering or lamination; a softer eating quality is obtained because the fat in the dough insulates the water molecules, keeping the moisture level higher during baking.

Flour-based products provide us with variety, energy, vitamins and minerals. Wholemeal bread products also provide roughage, an essential part of a healthy diet.

Understanding fermentation

For dough to become leavened bread it must go through a fermentation process. This is brought about by the action of yeast, with enzymes in the yeast and dough; these convert sugar into alcohol, thus producing the characteristic flavour of bread. The action also produces carbon dioxide, which makes the bread rise.

Yeast requires ideal conditions for growth; these are:

- *Warmth* A good temperature for dough production is 22–30°C (72–86°F).
- *Moisture* Yeast requires moisture; the liquid should be added at approximately 38°C (100°F).
- *Food* Yeast requires food; this is obtained from the starch in the flour.
- *Time* Time is needed to allow the yeast to grow.

Yeast is a living single-cell micro-organism and in the right conditions, with food, warmth and moisture, it ferments, producing carbon dioxide and alcohol while at the same time reproducing itself. It is rich in protein and vitamin B.

Yeast will not survive in a high concentration of sugar or salt and will slow down in a very rich dough with a high fat and egg content.

When mixing yeast in water or milk, make sure that the liquid is at the right temperature, 38°C (100°F), and disperse the yeast in the liquid. As a living organism cannot be dissolved, we use the word disperse.

Dried yeast has been dehydrated and requires creaming with a little water before use. It will keep for several months in its dry state.

Points to remember

- Yeast should be removed from the refrigerator and used at room temperature.
- Check all ingredients are weighed carefully.
- Work in a clean and tidy manner to avoid cross-contamination.
- Check all temperatures carefully.
- All wholemeal doughs absorb more water than

white doughs. The volume of water absorbed by flour also varies according to the strength (protein and bran content).

- When using machines, check that they are in working order.
- Always remember the health and safety rules when using machinery.
- Divide the dough with a dough divider, hard scraper or hydraulic cutting machine.
- Check the divided dough pieces for weight. When scaling, remember that doughs lose up to 12.5% of water during baking; therefore this needs to be taken into account when scaling.
- Keep the flour, bowl and liquid warm.
- Remember to knock the dough back carefully once proved, as this will expel the gas and allow the greater dispersion of the yeast. It will once again be in direct contact with the dough.
- Proving allows the dough to ferment; the second prove is essential for giving dough products the necessary volume and a good flavour.
- Time and temperature are crucial when cooking dough products.
- When using frozen dough products always follow the manufacturer's instructions. Contamination can occur if the doughs are defrosted incorrectly.

Types
Enriched doughs

- *Savarin* A rich yeast dough used for savarins, babas, marignans.
- *Brioche* A rich yeast dough with a high fat and butter content.

Laminated doughs

- *Croissants* Made from a dough in which the fat content has been layered (laminated) as in puff pastry.

- *Danish* Also a laminated dough; Danish pastries may be filled with fruit, frangipane, apple, custard, cherries and many other ingredients.

Speciality doughs

- *Blinis* A type of pancake.
- *Naan bread* Unleavened bread traditionally cooked in a tandoori oven.
- *Pitta bread* Middle Eastern and Greek bread, also unleavened.
- *Chapatti* Indian unleavened bread made from a fine ground wholemeal flour.

Storage of cooked dough products

Crusty rolls and bread are affected by changes in storage conditions; they are softened by a damp environment and humid conditions. Always store in suitable containers at room temperature and in a freezer for longer storage. Do not store in a refrigerator unless you want the bread to stale quickly for use as breadcrumbs. Staling will also occur quickly in products that contain a high ratio of fat and milk. Many commercial dough products contain anti-staling agents.

Convenience dough products

There are many new different types of product on the market.

- Fresh and frozen preproved dough products:
  - rolls
  - Danish pastries
  - croissants
  - French breads.
- Bake-off products. These are products ready for baking, either frozen or fresh or in modified atmosphere-packaged forms. This method replaces most of the oxygen around the product to slow down spoilage. These products have to be kept refrigerated:

- garlic bread
- rolls
- Danish pastries.

Possible reasons for faults using yeast doughs

- *Close texture:*
  - insufficiently proved
  - insufficiently kneaded
  - insufficient yeast
  - oven too hot
  - too much water
  - too little water.
- *Uneven texture:*
  - insufficient kneading
  - oven too cool
  - over-proving.
- *Coarse texture:*
  - over-proofed, uncovered
  - insufficient kneading
  - too much water
  - too much salt.
- *Wrinkled:*
  - over-proved.
- *Sour:*
  - stale yeast
  - too much yeast.
- *Broken crust:*
  - under-proved at the second stage.
- *White spots on crust:*
  - not covered before second proving.

Breads

It is customary today in a restaurant to be offered a range of different flavoured breads. Internationally there is a wide variety; different nations and regions have their own speciality breads. Bread plays an important part in many religious festivals especially Christian and Jewish.

The traditional breadmaking process is known as the Bulk Fermentation Process. This was used by many bakers before the introduction of high speed mixing and dough conditioners, which both eliminate the need for bulk fermentation time. However this traditional method produces a fine flavour due to the fermentation and is evident in the final product.

Bulk fermentation time (BFT)

This term is used to describe the length of time that the dough is allowed to ferment in bulk. BFT is measured from the end of the mixing method to the beginning of the scaling process. The length of BFT can be from 1–6 hours and is related to the level of salt and yeast in the recipe, as well as the dough temperature.

It is important that during the bulk fermentation process ideal conditions are adhered to:

A) The dough must be kept covered to prevent the dough surface skinning.

B) The appropriate temperature is maintained to control the rate of fermentation.

78 Wholemeal bread

stoneground wholemeal flour	625 g (1 lb 9 oz)
unbleached strong white flour	125 g (5 oz)
salt	1 tbsp
fresh yeast *or* **dried yeast**	25 g (1 oz) 18 g (¾ oz)
water, lukewarm	500m (1 pt)
honey	3 tbsp
unsalted butter or oil	60 g (2½ oz)

1 Melt the butter in a saucepan.

2 Mix together 1 tablespoon of honey and 4 tablespoons of the water in a bowl.

3 Disperse the yeast into the honey mixture.

4 In a basin, place the melted butter, remaining honey and water, the yeast mixture and salt.

5 Add the white flour and half the wholemeal flour. Mix well.

6 Add the remaining wholemeal flour gradually, mixing well between each addition.

7 The dough should pull away from the side of the bowl and form a ball. The resulting dough should be soft and slightly sticky.

8 Turn out onto a floured work surface. Sprinkle with white flour, knead well.

9 Brush a clean bowl with melted butter or oil. Place in the dough, cover with a damp cloth and allow to prove in a warm place. This will take approximately 1–1½ hours.

10 Knock back and further knead the dough. Cover again and rest for 10–15 minutes.

11 Divide the dough into two equal pieces.

12 Form each piece of dough into a cottage loaf or place in a suitable loaf tin.

13 Allow to prove in a warm place for approximately 45 minutes.

14 Place in a pre-heated oven, 190°C (375°F) and bake until well browned, approximately 40–45 minutes.

15 When baked, the bread should sound hollow and the sides should feel crisp when pressed.

16 Cool on a wire rack.

Alternatively, the bread may be divided into 50 g (2 oz) rolls, brushed with eggwash and baked at 200°C for approximately 10 minutes.

Fig 14.14 🖉 Assortment of bread rolls   *John Campbell*

`79` Walnut and sultana rolls

	Makes 16 rolls
wholemeal flour	400 g (1 lb)
fresh yeast	25 g (1 oz)
milk and water	250 ml (½ pt)
caster sugar	½ tsp
sultanas	100 g (4 oz)
butter	25 g (1 oz)

HEALTHY EATING TIP

Only a little salt is necessary to 'control' the yeast. Many customers will prefer less salty bread.

1 Sieve the flour into a suitable bowl and warm in the oven or above the stove.

2 Cream the yeast and sugar together in a bowl, add a ¼ of the liquid.

3 Make a well in the centre of the flour, add the dispersed yeast.

4 Sprinkle over a little flour, cover with a cloth and leave in a warm place until the yeast ferments.

5 Add the remainder of the liquid at 37°C, butter and salt.

6 Knead well until smooth and free from stickiness.

7 Return to the bowl, cover with a cloth and leave in a warm place until double in size.

8 Knock back gently, fold in the sultanas and walnuts.

9 Divide into 16 even pieces.

10 Mould into desired shapes and place onto a lightly greased floured baking sheet.

11 Cover with a cloth, allow to prove in a warm place until double in size.

12 Brush very carefully with eggwash and bake in a hot oven 190°C (375°F) for approximately 12 minutes.

80 Onion and walnut bread

	Makes 1 crown loaf
bread flour	500 g (1 lb)
onion finely chopped	1 large
walnut pieces (lightly toasted)	50 g (2 oz)
fresh yeast	12 g (½ oz)
milk	425 ml (⅞ pt)
vegetable oil	30 ml (¹⁄₁₆ pt)
salt	10 g (2 tsp)
pepper	
melted butter	

HEALTHY EATING TIP

Only a little salt is necessary to 'control' the yeast. Many customers will prefer less salty bread.

1 Warm 60 ml (4 tbsp) of milk to 37°C.

2 Disperse the yeast into the milk.

3 Place the dispersed yeast, remaining milk, half the oil and salt into a large bowl.

4 Stir in half of the flour and mix well with your hand.

5 Gradually add the remaining flour, mixing well after each addition. Mix well until a smooth elastic dough is obtained. Adjust the consistency by adding more flour if necessary. The dough should be soft and slightly sticky.

6 Turn the dough out onto a floured work surface, knead well. Keep kneading until very smooth and elastic. This will take approximately 5–7 minutes.

7 Brush a large bowl with melted butter. Place the dough into the bowl, turn over so that it is covered with butter.

8 Cover with a damp cloth and allow to prove until double in size, approximately 1–1½ hours.

9 Heat the remaining oil in a frying pan. Sauté the finely chopped onion, season with salt and pepper. Sauté until lightly coloured. Allow to cool.

10 When proved, turn the dough out on to a lightly floured table and knock back for approximately 20 seconds, cover and allow to rest for approximately 5 minutes.

11 Knead the onion and walnuts into the dough. Cover and allow to rest for a further 5 minutes.

12 Mould the dough into a ball and form a ring approximately 25–30 cm (10–12 inches) in diameter.

13 Place ring on to a lightly greased baking sheet. Cover and allow to prove to double in size for approximately 45 minutes, preferably in a prover.

14 Brush with eggwash lightly. Using kitchen scissors, snip the top of the ring zig zag fashion.

15 Bake in a pre-heated oven 200°C (400°F) for 45–50 minutes.

16 When baked and golden brown place bread on a wire rack and allow to cool. If tapped, it should sound hollow and the sides should be crisp.

81 Sun-dried tomato bread

	Makes 2 × 450 g (1 lb) loaves
bread flour	500 g (1 lb 4 oz)
suet	10 g (⅜ oz approx)
skimmed milk powder	12½ g (½ oz)
shortening	12½ g (½ oz)
yeast (fresh)	20 g (¾ oz approx)
water	300 ml (½ pt approx)
sugar	12½ g (½ oz)
chopped sundried tomatoes	100 g (4 oz)

1 Soak the sundried tomatoes in boiling water for 30 minutes.

2 Sieve the flour, salt and skimmed milk powder.

3 Add the shortening and rub through the dry ingredients.

4 Disperse the yeast into warm water approximately 37°C. Add and dissolve the sugar. Add to the above ingredients.

5 Mix until a smooth dough is formed.

Note: Check for any extremes in consistency and adjust as necessary until a smooth elastic dough is formed.

6 Cover the dough, keep warm and allow to prove.

7 After approximately 30–40 minutes knock back the dough and mix in the chopped sundried tomatoes (well drained).

8 Mould and prove again for another 30 minutes. (Covered.)

9 Divide the dough into two and mould round.

10 Rest for 10 minutes. Keep covered.

11 Re-mould into ball shape.

12 Place the dough pieces into 15 cm (6 inch) diameter hoops laid out on a baking tray. The hoops must be warm and lightly greased.

14 With the back of the hand flatten the dough pieces.

15 Prove at 38–40°C (100–104°F) in humid conditions, preferably in a prover.

16 Bake at 225°C (437°F) for 25–30 minutes.

17 After baking, remove the bread from the tins immediately and place on a cooling wire.

Rye

This is a prominent cereal in parts of Europe and Russia, mainly because it will grow better than wheat in poor soil and harsh weather conditions. The grains are longer and thinner than wheat grains and yield a flour that is darker than wheat flour, having a low protein content. Its main use is for rye bread.

82 Rye bread with caraway seeds

	1 medium sized loaf
rye flour	250 g (10 oz)
unbleached bread flour	175 g (7 oz)
fresh yeast (or dried yeast may be used)	15 g (½ oz approx)
water	60 ml (4 tbsp)
black treacle	15 ml (1 tbsp)
vegetable oil	15 ml (1 tbsp)
caraway seeds	15 g (½ oz approx)
salt	15 g (½ oz approx)
lager	250 ml (½ pt)
polenta	
eggwash	

HEALTHY EATING TIP

Only a little salt is necessary to 'control' the yeast. Many customers will prefer less salty bread.

1 Disperse the yeast in the warm water (at approximately 37°C)

2 In a basin mix the black treacle, oil, ⅔ of the caraway seeds and the salt. Add the lager. Add the yeast and mix in the sieved rye flour. Mix well.

3 Gradually add the bread flour. Continue to add the flour until the dough is formed and it is soft and slightly sticky.

4 Turn the dough onto a lightly floured surface and knead well.

5 Knead the dough until it is smooth and elastic.

6 Place the kneaded dough into a suitable bowl that has been brushed with oil.

7 Cover with a damp cloth and allow the dough to prove in a warm place until it is double in size. This will take about 1½–2 hours.

8 Turn the dough onto a lightly floured work surface, knock back the dough to original size. Cover and allow to rest for approximately 5–10 minutes.

9 Shape the dough into an oval approximately 25 cm (10 in) long.

10 Place onto a baking sheet lightly sprinkled with polenta.

11 Allow the dough to prove in a warm place, preferably in a prover, until double in size (approximately 45 minutes to 1 hour).

12 Lightly brush the loaf with eggwash, sprinkle with remaining caraway seeds.

13 Using a small sharp knife, make 3 diagonal slashes, approximately 5 mm (¼ inch) deep into the top of the loaf.

14 Place in a pre-heated oven 190°C (375°F) and bake for approximately 50–55 minutes.

15 When cooked, turn out. The bread should sound hollow when tapped and the sides should feel crisp.

16 Allow to cool.

83 Olive bread with sage and oregano

bread flour	300 g (12 oz)
bread flour	525 g (1 lb 5 oz)
black olives de-stoned	150 g (6 oz)
fresh yeast	12½ g (½ oz)
sugar	5 g (1 tsp)
milk	310 ml (⅝ pt)
water	250 ml (½ pt)
olive oil	80 ml (³⁄₁₆ pt)
fresh sage chopped	2 tbsp
fresh oregano chopped	2 tbsp
salt	5 g (1 tsp)

Fig 14.15 Stuffed olives

1 Disperse the yeast in the warm milk approximately 37°C.

2 Whisk in the 300 g (12 oz) of sifted flour and the sugar, stand in a warm place for approximately 30 minutes until the mixture is double in size.

3 Add the oil, the 525 g (1 lb 5 oz) of sifted flour and salt. Mix well.

4 Turn out onto a floured surface and knead to form a smooth and elastic dough.

5 Place the dough into a large greased bowl, cover and allow to prove for approximately 1 hour until the dough has doubled in size.

6 Turn the dough onto a floured board, knock back and knead in remaining ingredients.

7 Roll dough into an oval 30 cm × 35 cm (15 inches × 16 inches). Fold in almost half. Place onto a greased baking sheet, cover, stand in a warm place for about 45 minutes until double in size.

8 Dust with sifted flour and bake in a hot oven approximately 200°C (400°F) for 45 minutes.

84 Polenta soda bread with mixed seeds

	One loaf
polenta	150 g (6 oz)
strong flour	175 g (7 oz)
salt	6 g (¼ oz)
bicarbonate of soda	1 tsp
pumpkin seeds	25 g (1 oz)
sunflower seeds	25 g (1 oz)
poppy seeds	12 g (½ oz)
fine oatmeal	25 g (1 oz)
caster sugar	1 tsp
egg	1
buttermilk	250 ml (½ pt)

1 Sift the flour, salt and bicarbonate of soda together in a large bowl.

2 Add the polenta and the seeds, oatmeal and caster sugar. Mix together well.

3 Whisk the egg and buttermilk together, add to the dry ingredients. Mix to form a smooth and slack dough.

4 Place into a lightly oiled loaf tin, sprinkle with poppy seeds.

5 Bake in a pre-heated oven, 190°C (375°F) for approximately 50–60 minutes.

6 Remove from oven, turn out, place on baking sheet and return to oven for 5 minutes.

7 Remove, allow to cool on a wire rack.

Fig 14.16 Polenta soda bread

John Campbell

85 Soda bread with goat's cheese, potato and thyme

	One loaf
self-raising flour	175 g (7 oz)
goat's cheese	110 g (4½ oz)
spring onions, finely chopped	4
potato grated	175 g (7 oz)
chopped thyme	1 tsp
salt	1 tsp
cayenne pepper	pinch
egg	1
milk	2 tbsp
grain mustard	1 tsp

1 Remove the rind from the goat's cheese, cut into ½ cm (¼ inch) cubes

2 Sift the flour, salt and cayenne into a suitable bowl. Fold in the grated potato, chopped spring onions, chopped thyme and ⅔ of the goat's cheese. Mix thoroughly

3 Add the beaten egg, milk and mustard. Mix to a rough dough.

4 Mould into a round loaf tin, 15 cm (6inch).

5 Place on a lightly greased baking sheet. Press the rest of the cheese evenly on top.

6 Lightly dust with flour and chopped thyme.

7 Place in a pre-heated oven 190°C (375°F) for approximately 45–50 minutes until golden brown. Remove from oven and serve immediately.

Note: Rosemary, basil, oregano or tarragon may be used in place of thyme.

86 Kugelhopf bread with almonds, bacon and herbs

The bread is baked in a Kugelhopf mould traditionally from the Alsace region in France.

bread flour	500 g (1 lb 4 oz)
fresh yeast	25 g (1 oz)
or dried yeast	15 g (¾ oz)
milk	250 ml (½ pt)
unsalted butter, melted	150 g (6 oz)
salt	5 g (1 tsp)
eggs	3
sugar	15 ml (3 tsp)
fresh chopped sage	1 tsp
fresh chopped thyme	1 tsp
flaked almonds	50 g (2 oz)
streaky bacon chopped	125 g (5 oz)

1 Take 60 ml (approximately 4 tablespoons) of warm milk (37°C).

2 Disperse the yeast with the milk.

3 Sift the flour and salt into a suitable bowl.

4 Whisk the eggs and add to the flour with the dispersed yeast. Add the melted butter, sugar and remainder of the warm milk. Take special care that the butter does not exceed 37°C. It should be just melted.

5 Work well and mix thoroughly to a smooth dough.

6 Beat the dough well until it is very elastic. The dough should be very sticky, and reasonably wet.

7 Cover the bowl with a damp cloth and allow to prove in a warm place for 1–1½ hours.

8 Quickly fry the chopped streaky bacon in a pan for 3–4 minutes. Drain off all excess fat. Allow to cool.

9 Knock back the dough, mix in the bacon, almonds and chopped herbs. Mix well.

10 Fill the kugelhopf mould evenly with the dough. Cover with a damp cloth and allow to prove for 30–40 minutes, until double in size.

11 Bake in a pre-heated oven 190°C (375°F) for approximately 45–50 minutes. Unmould onto a wire rack and allow to cool.

Alternatively other nuts and different herbs may be used.

87 Bagels

Bagels are now very popular and are usually filled with a variety of fillings e.g. smoked salmon and cream cheese, and served as a snack.

	makes 12
bread flour	450 g (10 oz)
fresh yeast *or*	12 g (½ oz)
dried yeast	10 g
caster sugar	2 tbsp
milk	250 ml (½ pt)
water	125 ml (¼ pt)
salt	15 g (3 tsp)
eggwash	
poppy seeds	1 tbsp
sea salt	10 g (2 tsp)

1 Warm the water to 37°C, disperse the yeast in the water, add one tablespoon of sugar, cover and stand in a warm place for approximately 10 minutes.

2 Add the sifted flour gradually, mixing into a firm dough.

3 Turn dough onto a floured surface. Knead well until dough is smooth and elastic. Place dough into well greased bowl, cover and stand in a warm place in a prover for 1 hour or until dough has doubled in size.

4 Turn dough out onto a floured surface, knead until smooth. Divide into 12, knead each into a ball. Make a hole in the centre of each.

5 Rotate each ball of dough with the finger until the hole is one third of the size of the bagel.

6 Place bagel on a greased baking sheet approximately 3 cm (1½ inch) apart. Cover and stand in a warm place or prover until double in size.

7 Drop bagels individually into a pan of boiling water. Do not allow them to touch. Turn bagels after 1 minute, simmer for a further 1 minute. Remove, drain well and place on greased baking sheet.

8 Brush each with eggwash, sprinkle with poppy seeds and sea salt. Bake in an oven 200°C (400°F) for about 20 minutes. Remove, cool on a wire rack.

88 Bread rolls

	8 rolls	20 rolls
flour (strong)	200 g (8 oz)	500 g (1½ lb)
yeast	5 g (¼ oz)	12 g (⅝ oz)
liquid (half water, half milk)	125 ml (¼ pt)	300 ml (⅝ pt)
butter or margarine	10 g (½ oz)	25 g (1¼ oz)
caster sugar	¼ tsp	½ tsp
salt		

Using white flour and hard margarine, 1 portion (2 rolls) provides:
426 kJ/102 kcal
1.7 g fat
(of which 0.7 g saturated)
19.5 g carbohydrate
(of which 1.0 g sugars)
3.4 g protein
1.1 g fibre

Using wholemeal flour, 1 portion provides:
379 kJ/90 kcal
1.6 g fat
(of which 0.5 g saturated)
17.1 g carbohydrate
(of which 1.2 g sugars)
3.4 g protein
2.3 g fibre

1 Sieve the flour into a bowl; warm in oven or above the stove.
2 Cream the yeast in a small basin with a quarter of the liquid.
3 Make a well in the centre of the flour; add the dissolved yeast.
4 Sprinkle over a little of the flour, cover with a cloth, leave in a warm place until the yeast ferments (bubbles).
5 Add the remainder of the liquid (warm), the fat, sugar and the salt.
6 Knead firmly until smooth and free from stickiness.
7 Return to the basin, cover with a cloth and leave in a warm place until double its size. (This is called *proving* the dough.)
8 Knock back. Divide into even pieces.
9 Mould into the desired shape.
10 Place on a floured baking sheet. Cover with a cloth.
11 Leave in a warm place to prove (double in size).
12 Brush carefully with eggwash.
13 Bake in a hot oven at 220°C (Reg. 7; 425°F) for about 10 minutes.

Note: At all times during preparation of the dough, extreme heat must be avoided as the yeast will be killed and the dough spoiled.

For variety (increase the quantities 2½ times for 10 portions):

- Use all wholemeal flour, 1 teaspoon raw cane sugar in place of caster sugar and all water and no milk.
- Add 50 g (2 oz) each of chopped walnuts and sultanas.

Fig 14.17 Dough divider

Using hard margarine, 1 portion
(2 buns) provides:
656 kJ/157 kcal
6.4 g fat
(of which 2.7 g saturated)
22.6 g carbohydrate
(of which 4.0 g sugars)
3.6 g protein
1.2 g fibre

89 Bun dough (basic recipe)

	8 buns	20 buns
flour (strong)	200 g (½ lb)	500 g (1¼ lb)
yeast	5 g (¼ oz)	12 g (⅝ oz)
milk and water, approximately	60 ml (⅛ pt)	300 ml (⅝ pt)
medium egg	1	2–3
butter or margarine	50 g (2 oz)	125 g (5 oz)
caster sugar	25 g (1 oz)	60 g (2½ oz)

1 Sieve the flour into a bowl and warm.

2 Cream the yeast in a basin with a little of the liquid.

3 Make a well in the centre of the flour.

4 Add the dispersed yeast, sprinkle with a little flour, cover with a cloth, leave in a warm place until the yeast ferments (bubbles).

5 Add the beaten egg, butter or margarine, sugar and remainder of the liquid. Knead well to form a soft, slack dough, knead until smooth and free from stickiness.

6 Keep covered and allow to prove in a warm place. Use as required.

90 Bun wash

sugar	100 g (¼ lb)
water or milk	125 ml (¼ pt)

Boil together until the consistency of a thick syrup.

91 Fruit buns

Using hard margarine, 1 portion provides:
728 kJ/173 kcal
6.5 g fat
(of which 2.7 g saturated)
26.9 g carbohydrate
(of which 8.0 g sugars)
3.7 g protein
1.7 g fibre

1 Add 50 g (2 oz) washed, dried fruit (currants, sultanas) and a little mixed spice to the basic bun mixture.

2 Mould into 8 round balls.

3 Place on a lightly greased baking sheet.

4 Cover with a cloth, allow to prove.

5 Bake in hot oven at 220°C (Reg. 7; 425°F) for 15–20 minutes.

6 Brush liberally with bun wash as soon as cooked.

92 Hot cross buns

1 Proceed as for fruit buns using a little more spice.
2 When moulded make a cross with the back of a knife, or make a slack mixture of flour and water and pipe on crosses using a greaseproof paper cornet.
3 Allow to prove and finish as for fruit buns.

93 Bath buns

1 Add to basic bun dough 50 g (2 oz) washed and dried fruit (currants and sultanas), and 25 g (1 oz) chopped mixed peel and 25 g (1 oz) sugar nibs.
2 Proceed as for fruit buns. Pull off into 8 rough-shaped pieces.
3 Sprinkle with a little broken loaf sugar or nibs.
4 Cook as for fruit buns.

94 Chelsea buns

1 Take the basic bun dough and roll out into a large square.
2 Brush with melted margarine or butter.
3 Sprinkle liberally with caster sugar.
4 Sprinkle with 25 g (1 oz) currants, 25 g (1 oz) sultanas and 25 g (1 oz) chopped peel.
5 Roll up like a Swiss roll, brush with melted margarine or butter.
6 Cut into slices across the roll 3 cm (1½ inches) wide.
7 Place on a greased baking tray with deep sides.
8 Cover and allow to prove. Complete as for fruit buns.

95 Swiss buns

1 Divide basic bun dough into 8 pieces.
2 Mould into balls, then into 10 cm (4 inch) lengths.
3 Place on a greased baking sheet, cover with a cloth.
4 Allow to prove.
5 Bake at 220°C (Reg. 7; 425°F), for 15–20 minutes.
6 When cool, glaze with fondant or water icing.

96 Water icing, glacé icing

Water icing is used to finish a number of cakes and pastries. For the basic icing simply take 400 g (1 lb) of icing sugar and add 60 ml (4 tablespoons) of warm water; the icing should be thick enough to coat the back of a spoon. If necessary, add more water or icing sugar to adjust the consistency.

Water may be replaced with other liquids to add flavour to the icing.

For example: Orange juice   Mango juice
Lemon juice   Apple juice
Lime juice   Grape juice
Passionfruit juice

or use a combination of juices with Cointreau, kirsch, Grand Marnier, rum, Calvados etc.

97 Doughnuts

Using hard margarine and peanut oil, 1 portion provides:
918 kJ/218 kcal
13.3 g fat
(of which 4.0 g saturated)
22.6 g carbohydrate
(of which 4.0 g sugars)
3.6 g protein
1.2 g fibre

1 Take the basic bun dough (recipe 89) and divide into 8 pieces.
2 Mould into balls. Press a floured thumb into each.
3 Add a little jam in each hole. Mould carefully to seal the hole.
4 Cover and allow to prove on a well-floured tray.
5 Deep fry in moderately hot fat 175°C (347°F) for 12–15 minutes.
6 Lift out of the fat, drain and roll in a tray containing caster sugar mixed with a little cinnamon.

98 Rum baba

Baba au rhum

Using butter, 1 portion provides:
797 kJ/190 kcal
7.6 g fat
(of which 4.2 g saturated)
25.4 g carbohydrate
(of which 6.4 g sugars)
4.9 g protein
1.4 g fibre

	8 portions	20 portions
flour (strong)	200 g (8 oz)	500 g (1¼ lb)
yeast	5 g (¼ oz)	12 g (⅝ oz)
milk	125 ml (¼ pt)	300 ml (⅝ pt)
currants	50 g (2 oz)	125 g (5 oz)
medium eggs	2	5
butter	50 g (2 oz)	125 g (5 oz)
sugar	10 g (½ oz)	25 g (1 oz)
pinch salt		
small glass of rum	1	2–3

1 Sieve the flour in a bowl and warm.

2 Cream the yeast with a little of the warm milk in a basin.

3 Make a well in the centre of the flour and add the dispersed yeast.

4 Sprinkle with a little of the flour from the sides, cover with a cloth and leave in a warm place until it ferments.

5 Add the remainder of the warm milk and the washed, dried currants and the beaten eggs, knead well to a smooth elastic dough.

6 Replace in the bowl, add the butter in small pieces, cover with a cloth and allow to prove in a warm place.

7 Add the sugar and salt, mix well until absorbed.

8 Half fill greased dariole moulds, and allow to prove.

9 Bake in a hot oven at 220°C (Reg. 7; 425°F) for about 20 minutes.

10 Turn out when cooked, cool slightly.

11 Soak carefully in hot syrup.

12 Sprinkle liberally with rum.

13 Brush all over with apricot glaze.

Note: Babas may also be decorated with whipped cream or crème Chantilly (whipped cream sweetened with caster sugar and flavoured with a little vanilla essence) and finished with a glacé cherry and angelica or half walnuts or any glacéed fruit. Babas may also be flavoured with whisky or brandy in place of rum. Points about use of cream (see also pages 558, 559):

- Fresh cream must be cold when required for whipping.

- For preference it should be whipped in china or stainless steel bowls. If any other metal is used, the cream should be transferred to china bowls as soon as possible.

- If fresh cream is whipped too much, it turns to butter. This is more likely to happen in hot conditions. To prevent this, stand the bowl of cream in a bowl of ice while whisking.

- When adding cream to hot liquids dilute the cream with some of the liquid before adding to the main bulk. This helps to prevent the cream from separating.

99 Syrup for baba, savarin and marignans

	4 babas	10 babas
sugar	100 g (4 oz)	250 g (10 oz)
bay leaf	1	2–3
rind and juice of lemon	1	2–3
water	¼ litre (½ pt)	600 ml (1¼ pt)
coriander seeds	2–3	6–7
small cinnamon stick	½	1–1½

Serves 4, 1 portion provides:
422 kJ/99 kcal energy
0.0 g fat
(of which 0.0 g saturated)
26.4 g carbohydrate
(of which 26.4 g sugars)
0.0 g protein
0.0 g fibre

Boil all the ingredients together and strain.

100 Savarin paste (basic recipe)

	8 portions	20 portions
flour (strong)	200 g (8 oz)	500 g (1¼ lb)
yeast	5 g (¼ oz)	12 g (⅜ oz)
milk	125 ml (¼ pt)	300 ml (⅝ pt)
medium eggs	2	5
butter (softened)	50 g (2 oz)	125 g (5 oz)
sugar	10 g (½ oz)	25 g (1 oz)
pinch salt		

1 portion of paste provides:
700 kJ/167 kcal energy
7.4 g fat
(of which 3.9 g saturated)
21.5 g carbohydrate
(of which 2.5 g sugars)
4.9 g protein
0.8 g fibre

Using syrup, 1 portion of
complete Savarin provides:
967 kJ/229 kcal energy
7.4 g fat
(of which 3.9 g saturated)
38.2 g carbohydrate
(of which 19.1 g sugars)
5.0 g protein
0.8 g fibre

1 Sieve the flour in a bowl and warm.

2 Cream the yeast with a little of the warm milk in a basin.

3 Make a well in the centre of the flour and add the dissolved yeast.

4 Sprinkle with a little of the flour from the sides, cover with a cloth and leave in a warm place until it ferments.

5 Add the remainder of the warm milk and the beaten eggs, knead well to a smooth elastic dough.

6 Replace in the bowl, add the butter in small pieces, cover with a cloth and allow to prove in a warm place.

7 Add the sugar and salt, mix well until absorbed.

8 Half fill a greased savarin mould, and prove.

9 Bake in a hot oven at 220°C (Reg. 7; 425°F) for about 30 minutes.

10 Turn out when cooked, cool slightly.

11 Soak carefully in hot syrup (see above).

12 Brush over with apricot glaze (page 571).

Fig 14.18 🖎 Fruit savarin, individual   *Yolande Stanley*

Fig 14.19 🖎 Fruit savarin   *Yolande Stanley*

Fig 14.20 Marignans Chantilly

Yolande Stanley

101 Savarin with fruit

Savarin aux fruits

1 Prepare the basic savarin mixture.

2 Prove and cook for about 30 minutes in a large greased savarin mould.

3 Complete in exactly the same way as rum baba including the cream. The rum is optional for savarin.

4 Fill the centre with fruit salad.

> 1 portion provides:
> 1224 kJ/292 kcal energy
> 13.5 g fat
> (of which 7.7 g saturated)
> 39.1 g carbohydrate
> (of which 20.6 g sugars)
> 5.9 g protein
> 1.0 g fibre

102 Marignans Chantilly

1 Marignans are prepared from a basic savarin mixture, and cooked in barquette moulds.

2 After the marignans have been soaked, carefully make a deep incision along one side.

3 Decorate generously with whipped sweetened vanilla-flavoured cream.

4 Brush with apricot glaze (page 571).

> 1 portion provides:
> 1202 kJ/286 kcal energy
> 13.4 g fat
> (of which 7.7 g saturated)
> 38.0 g carbohydrate
> (of which 19.5 g sugars)
> 5.8 g protein
> 0.8 g fibre

Prepare and cook pastry dishes – Ingredients

Flour

Flour is probably the most common commodity in daily use. It forms the foundation of bread, pastry and cakes and is also used in soups, sauces, batters and other foods.

Production of flour

The endosperm of the wheat grain contains all the material used by the baker. It consists of numerous large cells of net-like form in which starch grains are tightly packed. In addition, the cells contain an insoluble gluten protein. When flour is mixed with water it is converted into a sticky dough. This characteristic is due to the gluten, which becomes sticky when moistened. The relative proportion of starch and gluten varies in different wheats, and those with a low percentage of gluten (soft flour) are not suitable for bread-making. For this reason, wheat is blended.

In milling, the whole grain is broken up, the parts separated, sifted, blended and ground into flour. Some of the outer coating of bran is removed as is also the wheatgerm, which contains oil and is therefore likely to become rancid and so spoil the flour. For this reason wholemeal flour should not be stored for more than 14 days.

Types

White flour contains 72–85% of the whole grain (the endosperm only). Wholemeal flour contains 100% of the whole grain. Wheatmeal flour contains 85–95% of the whole grain. Hovis flour contains 85% of the whole grain. High ratio or patent flour contains 40% of the whole grain. Self-raising flour is white flour with the addition of baking powder. Semolina is granulated hard flour prepared from the central part of the wheat grain. White or wholemeal semolina is available.

Fats

Pastry goods may be made from various types of fat, either a single named fat or a combination. Examples of fats are:

- butter
- margarine
- cake margarine
- pastry margarine
- shortening
- lard.

Butter

Butter is excellent for flavour but does not possess the same qualities of water retention or creaminess as other special manufactured fats.

Margarine

Margarine is often made from a blend of oils that have been hardened or hydrogenated (hydrogen gas is added). Margarine may contain up to 10% butterfat.

Cake margarine

This is again a blend of oils, hydrogenated, to which is added an agent that helps combine water and fat together, an emulsifying agent. Cake margarine may contain up to 10% butterfat.

Pastry margarine

This is used for puff pastry. It is a hard plastic or waxy fat that is suitable for layering.

Shortening (another name for fat used in pastry making)

This is made from oils and is 100% fat, such as hydrogenated lard; another type of shortening is rendered pork fat.

Sugar

Sugar is extracted from sugar beet or sugar cane. The juice is crystallised by a complicated manufacturing process. It is then refined and sieved into several grades, such as granulated, caster or icing sugars.

Loaf or cube sugar is obtained by pressing the crystals whilst slightly wet, drying them in blocks, and then cutting the blocks into squares.

Syrup and treacle are produced during the production of sugar.

Fondant is a cooked mixture of sugar and glucose, which, when heated, is coloured and flavoured and used for decorating cakes, buns, gâteaux and petits fours. Fondant is generally bought ready made.

Raising agents

A raising agent is added to a cake or bread mixture to give lightness to the product. This lightness is based upon the principle that gases expand when heated. The gases used are air, carbon dioxide or water vapour. These gases are introduced before baking or are produced by substances added to the mixture before baking. When the product is cooked, the gases expand. These gases are trapped in the gluten content of the wheat flour. On further heating and cooking, the product, because of the pressure of the gluten, rises and sets.

Baking powder

Chemical raising agents cause reaction between certain acidic and alkaline compounds, which produce carbon dioxide. The alkaline component is almost universally sodium bicarbonate or sodium acid carbonate, commonly known as baking soda. It is ideal because it is cheap to produce, easily purified, non-toxic and naturally tasteless. Potassium bicarbonate is available for those on low sodium diets, but this compound tends to absorb moisture and react prematurely and gives off a bitter flavour.

Baking powder may be used without the addition of acid if the dough or batter is already acidic enough to react with it to produce carbon dioxide. Yoghurt and sour milk contain lactic acid and often are used in place of water or milk in such products; sour milk can also be added along with the baking soda as a separate 'natural' component of the leavening.

Baking powder contains baking soda and an acid in the form of salt crystals that dissolve in water. Ground dry starch is also added to prevent premature reactions in humid air by absorbing moisture and to dilute the powder.

Most baking powders are 'double acting', that is, they produce an initial set of gas bubbles upon mixing the powder into the batter and then a second set during the baking process. The first and smaller reaction is necessary to form many small gas cells in the batter or dough; the second, to expand these cells to a size appropriate to form the final light texture, but late enough in the baking so that the surrounding materials have set, preventing the escape of bubbles or the collapse of the product.

Different commercial baking powders differ mainly in the proportions of the acid salts. Cream of tartar is not normally used due to its high cost.

Carbon dioxide using baking powder

Alkali (bicarbonate of soda) + acid (cream of tartar (potassium hydrogen tartrate).

Calcium phosphate and glucono-delta-lactose are now commonly used in place of cream of tartar.

Sodium aluminium sulphate is an acid that is only active at higher oven temperatures and has an advantage over other powders, which tend to produce gas too early.

Use of water vapour

This is produced during the baking process, from the liquid content used in the mixing. Water vapour has approximately 1600 times the original volume of the water. The raising power is slower than that of a gas. This principle is used in the production of choux pastry, puff pastry, rough puff, flaky and batter products.

Points to remember

- Always buy a reliable brand of baking powder.
- Store in a dry place in an airtight tin.
- Do not store for long periods of time, as the baking powder over time loses some of its residual carbon dioxide and therefore will not be as effective.
- Check the recipe carefully, making sure that the correct preparation for the type of mixture is used; otherwise, under- or over-rising may result.
- Sieve the raising agent with the flour and/or dry ingredients to give an even mix and thus an even reaction.
- Distribute moisture evenly into the mixture to ensure even action of the raising agent.
- If a large proportion of raising agent has been added to a mixture, and is not to be cooked immediately, keep in a cool place to avoid too much reaction before baking.

What happens if too much raising agent is used

Too much raising agent causes:

- Over-risen product that may collapse giving a sunken effect;
- a coarse texture; poor colour and flavour;
- fruit sinking to the bottom of the cake; a bitter taste.

What happens if insufficient proportion of raising agent is used

Insufficient raising agent causes:

- lack of volume;
- insufficient lift;
- close texture;
- shrinkage.

Eggs

Eggs are an important and versatile ingredient in pastry work. They act as enriching and emulsifying agents. Hen's eggs are graded in four sizes – small, medium, large, and very large. For the recipes in this book, use medium (weight 50 g (2 oz)).

Eggs are used in pastry work because of their binding, emulsifying and coating properties. Eggs add both protein and fat, thus improving the nutritional value and flavour.

Cream

Cream is the concentrated milk fat that is skimmed off the top of the milk and should contain at least 18% butterfat. Cream for whipping must contain more than 30% butterfat. Commercially frozen cream is available in 2 and 10 kg (4 and 20 lb) slabs. Types, packaging, storage and uses of cream are listed opposite.

Type of cream	Legal minimum fat (%)	Processing and packaging	Storage	Characteristics and uses
half cream	12	homogenised and may be pasteurised or ultra-heat treated	2–3 days	does not whip; used for pouring; suitable for low-fat diets
cream or single cream	18	homogenised and pasteurised by heating to about 79.5°C (175°F) for 15 seconds then cooled to 4.5°C (40°F). Automatically filled into bottles and cartons after processing. Sealed with foil caps. Bulk quantities according to local suppliers	2–3 days in summer; 3–4 days in winter under refrigeration	a pouring cream suitable for coffee, cereals, soup or fruit. A valuable addition to cooked dishes. Makes delicious sauces. Does not whip
whipping cream	35	not homogenised, but pasteurised and packaged as above	2–3 days in summer; 3–4 days in winter under refrigeration	the ideal whipping cream. Suitable for piping, cake and dessert decoration, ice-cream, cake and pastry fillings
double cream	48	slightly homogenised, and pasteurised and packaged as above	2–3 days in summer; 3–4 days in winter under refrigeration	a rich pouring cream which will also whip. The cream will float on coffee or soup
double cream 'thick'	48	heavily homogenised, then pasteurised and packaged. Usually only available in domestic quantities	2–3 days in summer; 3–4 days in winter under refrigeration	a rich spoonable cream that will not whip
clotted cream	55	heated to 82°C (180°F) and cooled for about 4½ hours. The cream crust is then skimmed off. Usually packed in cartons by hand. Bulk quantities according to local suppliers	2–3 days in summer; 3–4 days in winter under refrigeration	a very thick cream with its own special flavour and colour. Delicious with scones, fruit and fruit pies
ultra-heat treated (UHT) cream	12 18 35	half (12%), single (18%) or whipping cream (35%) is homogenised and heated to 132°C (270°F) for one second and cooled immediately. Aseptically packed in polythene and foil-lined containers. Available in bigger packs for catering purposes	6 weeks if unopened. Needs no refrigeration. Usually date stamped	a pouring cream

Techniques
Adding fat to flour

Fats act as a shortening agent. The fat coats the sub-proteins within the flour, which has the effect of shortening the gluten strands. These gluten strands are easily broken when eaten. The development of gluten in strong flour to the production of puff pastry is very important as we need long strands to trap the expanding gases, which makes the paste rise.

- Rubbing in by hand: short pastry.
- Rubbing in by machine: short pastry.
- Creaming method by machine or by hand: sweet pastry.
- Flour batter method: slab cakes.
- Lamination: puff pastry.
- Boiling: choux pastry.

Terms
Folding

As in folding puff pastry.

Kneading

Used as a term when making doughs or in the first stage of making puff pastry.

Blending

Mixing all the ingredients carefully by weight.

Relaxing

Keeping pastry covered with a damp cloth, cling film or plastic to prevent skinning. Relaxing allows the pastry to lose some of its resistance to rolling.

Cutting

- Always cut with a sharp, damp knife.
- When using cutters, always flour the cutters by dipping in flour. This will give a sharp, neat cut.
- When using a lattice cutter, use only on firm pastry; if the pastry is too soft, you will have difficulty lifting the lattice.

Rolling

- Roll the pastry on a lightly floured surface, turn the pastry to prevent it sticking. Keep the rolling pin lightly floured and free from the pastry.
- Always roll with care, treat lightly, never apply too much pressure.
- Always apply even pressure when using a rolling pin.

Shaping

Shaping refers to producing flans, tartlets, barquettes and other such goods with the pastry. Shaping also refers to crimping with the back of a small knife using the thumb technique.

Docking

Piercing raw pastry with small holes to prevent rising during baking as when cooking blind tartlets.

Glazing

Examples of glazing pastry dishes are as follows:

- Using a hot clear gel produced from a pectin source obtainable commercially for finishing flans and tartlets; always use while still hot. A cold gel is exactly the same except that it is used cold. The gel keeps a sheen on the goods and excludes all oxygen, which might otherwise cause discoloration.
- Using apricot glaze, produced from apricot jam, acts in the same way as gels.
- Using eggwash, prior to baking, to produce a rich glaze on removing from the oven.
- Dusting with icing sugar, then caramelising in the oven or under the grill.

- Using fondant to give a rich sugar glaze, which may be flavoured and/or coloured.
- Using water icing to give a transparent glaze, which also may be flavoured and/or coloured.

Finishing and presentation

It is essential that all products are finished according to the recipe requirements. The finishing and presentation is often a key stage in the process as failure at this point can affect the sales. The way we present goods is an important part of the sales technique. Each product of the same type must be of the same shape, size, colour and finish. The decoration should be attractive, delicate and in keeping with the product range. All piping should be neat, clean and tidy.

- *Dusting*
  This is the sprinkling of icing sugar on to a product using a fine sugar dredger or sieve, or muslin cloth.
- *Piping*
  Using fresh cream, chocolate, or fondant.
- *Filling*
  Products may be finished by filling with fruit, cream, pastry cream, etc. Never overfill as this will often given the product a clumsy appearance.

Storage, health and safety

- Store all goods according to the Food Hygiene (Amendments) Regulations 1993/Food Safety Temperature Control Regulation 1995.
- Handle all equipment carefully to avoid cross-contamination.
- Take special care when using cream and ensure that products containing cream are stored under refrigerated conditions.
- All piping bags must be sterilised after each use.

- Always make sure that storage containers are kept clean and returned ready for re-use. On their return they are hygienically washed and stored.

Points to remember

- Check all weighing scales for accuracy.
- Follow the recipe carefully.
- Check all storage temperatures are correct.
- Fat is better to work with if it is plastic (at room temperature). This will make it easier to cream.
- Always cream the fat and sugar well, before adding the liquid.
- Always work in a clean, tidy and organised way; clean all equipment after use.
- Always store ingredients correctly: eggs should be stored in a refrigerator, flour in a bin with a tight-fitting lid, sugar and other dry ingredients in closed storage containers.
- Ensure all cooked products are cooled before finishing.
- Understand how to use fresh cream; remember that it is easily overwhipped.
- Always plan your time carefully.
- Understand why pastry products must be rested or relaxed and docked. This will prevent excessive shrinkage in the oven and docking will allow the air to escape through the product thus preventing an unevenness.
- Use silicone paper for baking in preference to greaseproof.
- Keep all small moulds clean and dry to prevent rusting.

Convenience pastry

Convenience mixes such as short pastry, sponge mixes and choux pastry mixes are now becoming increasingly used in a variety of establishments.

These products have improved enormously over the last few years. Using such products gives the chef the opportunity to save on time and labour; and with skilful imagination and creativity, the finished products are not impaired.

The large food manufacturer dominates the frozen puff pastry market. Not surprisingly even more caterers, including some luxury establishments, have turned to using frozen puff pastry. Frozen puff pastry is now available in 12-inch squares, ready rolled, thus avoiding the possibility of uneven thickness and waste that can occur when rolling out yourself.

Manufactured puff pastry is available in three types, defined often by the fat content. The cheapest is made with the white hydrogenated fat that gives the product a pale colour and a waxy taste. Puff pastry made with bakery margarine has a better colour and often a better flavour. The best quality puff pastry is that which is made with all butter, giving a richer texture, colour and flavour.

Pastry bought in blocks is cheaper than pre-rolled separate sheets, but has to be rolled evenly to give an even bake. The sizes of sheets do vary with manufacturers; all are interleaved with greaseproof paper.

Filo pastry is another example of a convenient pastry product; this is available in frozen sheets of various size. No rolling out is required, once thawed; it can be used as required and moulded if necessary.

Other convenience pastry products

Apart from convenience pastry mixes, there also exists on the market a whole range of frozen products suitable to serve as sweets and afternoon tea pastries. These include fruit pies, flans, gâteaux and charlottes. The vast majority are ready to serve once defrosted, but very often they do require a little more decorative finish. The availability of such products gives the caterer the advantage of further labour cost reductions, while asking the chef to concentrate on other areas of the menu.

103 Short pastry

Pâte à foncer

Using ½ lard, ½ hard margarine, this recipe (5–8 portions) provides:
6269 kJ/1493 kcal
92.6 g fat
(of which 38.0 g saturated)
155.5 g carbohydrate
(of which 3.1 g sugars)
18.9 g protein
7.2 g fibre

	5–8 portions	10–16 portions
flour (soft)	200 g (8 oz)	500 g (1¼ lb)
pinch salt		
lard or vegetable fat	50 g (2 oz)	125 g (5 oz)
butter or margarine	50 g (2 oz)	125 g (5 oz)
water	2–3 tbsp	5–8 tbsp

1 Sieve the flour and salt.
2 Rub in the fat to a sandy mixture.
3 Make a well in the centre.
4 Add sufficient water to make a fairly firm paste.
5 Handle as little and as lightly as possible.

Note: The amount of water used varies according to:
- the type of flour (a very fine soft flour is more absorbent);
- the degree of heat (prolonged contact with hot hands and weather conditions).

For wholemeal short pastry use ½ to ¾ wholemeal flour in place of white flour.

Short pastry is used in fruit pies, Cornish pasties, etc.

Possible reasons for faults in short pastry

- *Hard*
  - too much water
  - too little fat
  - fat rubbed in insufficiently
  - too much handling and rolling
  - over baking.
- *Soft-crumbly*
  - too little water
  - too much fat.

- *Blistered*
  - too little water
  - water added unevenly
  - fat not rubbed in evenly.
- *Soggy*
  - too much water
  - too cool an oven
  - baked for insufficient time.
- *Shrunken*
  - too much handling and rolling
  - pastry stretched whilst handling.

Fig 14.21 Preparation of puff pastry, recipe 104

104 Puff pastry

Feuilletage

Using hard margarine, 5–8 portions provides:
8997 kJ/2142 kcal
164.8 g fat
(of which 70.9 g saturated)
150.8 g carbohydrate
(of which 3.0 g sugars)
23.2 g protein
7.4 g fibre

	5–8 portions	10–16 portions
flour (strong)	200 g (8 oz)	500 g (1¼ lb)
salt		
margarine or butter	200 g (8 oz)	500 g (1¼ lb)
ice-cold water	125 ml (¼ pt)	300 ml (⅝ pt)
few drops of lemon juice or ascorbic or tartaric acid		

HEALTHY EATING TIP

Add a minimum amount of salt. Puff pastry is very high in fat and should be rolled out thinly.

1 Sieve the flour and salt; 50% wholemeal flour may be used.
2 Rub in one-quarter of the butter or margarine.
3 Make a well in the centre.
4 Add the water and lemon juice (to make the gluten more elastic), and knead well into a smooth dough in the shape of a ball.
5 Relax the dough in a cool place for 30 minutes.
6 Cut a cross half-way through the dough and pull out the corners to form a star shape.

7 Roll out the points of the star square, leaving the centre thick.
8 Knead the remaining butter or margarine to the same texture as the dough. This is most important; if the fat is too soft it will melt and ooze out, if too hard it will break through the paste when being rolled.
9 Place the butter or margarine on the centre square, which is four times thicker than the flaps.
10 Fold over the flaps.
11 Roll out 30 × 15 cm (12 × 18 inches), cover with a cloth or plastic and rest for 5–10 minutes in a cool place.
12 Roll out 60 × 20 cm (24 × 9 inches), fold both the ends to the centre, fold in half again to form a square. This is one double turn.
13 Allow to rest in a cool place for 20 minutes.
14 Half-turn the paste to the right or the left.
15 Give one more double turn; allow to rest for 20 minutes.
16 Give two more double turns, allowing to rest between each.
17 Allow to rest before using.

Care must be taken when rolling out the paste to keep the ends and sides square.

The lightness of the puff pastry is mainly due to the air that is trapped when giving the pastry folds during preparation. The addition of lemon juice (acid) is to strengthen the gluten in the flour, thus helping to make a stronger dough so that there is less likelihood of the fat oozing out; 3 g (⅛ oz) (7½ g, ¼ oz for 10 portions) ascorbic or tartaric acid may be used in place of lemon juice. The rise is caused by the fat separating layers of paste and air during rolling. When heat is applied by the oven, steam is produced causing the layers to rise and give the characteristic flaky formation.

Puff pastry is used for meat pies, sausage rolls, jam puffs, etc. (See page 585 for illustrations of uses of puff pastry.)

Possible reasons for faults in puff pastry

- *Not flaky*
  - fat too warm thus preventing the fat and paste remaining in layers during rolling
  - excessively heavy use of rolling pin.
- *Fat oozes out*
  - fat too soft
  - dough too soft
  - edges not sealed
  - uneven folding and rolling
  - oven too cool.
- *Hard*
  - too much water
  - flour not brushed off between rolling
  - over handling.
- *Shrunken*
  - insufficient resting between rolling
  - overstretching.
- *Soggy*
  - under baked
  - oven too hot.
- *Uneven rise*
  - uneven distribution of fat
  - sides and corners not straight
  - uneven folding and rolling.

105 Rough puff pastry

Using hard margarine, this recipe (5–8 portions) provides:
7464 kJ/1777 kcal
124.3 g fat
(of which 53.2 g saturated)
150.8 g carbohydrate
(of which 3.0 g sugars)
23.2 g protein
7.4 g fibre

	5–8 portions	10–16 portions
flour (strong)	200 g (8 oz)	500 g (1¼ lb)
salt		
butter or margarine	150 g (6 oz)	375 g (15 oz)
ice-cold water	125 ml (¼ pt)	300 ml (⅝ pt)
squeeze of lemon juice or ascorbic or tartaric acid		

1 Sieve the flour and salt; 50% wholemeal flour may be used.
2 Cut the fat into 10 g (½ oz) pieces and lightly mix them into the flour without rubbing in.
3 Make a well in the centre.
4 Add the liquid and mix to a fairly stiff dough.
5 Turn on to a floured table and roll into an oblong strip, about 30 × 10 cm (12 × 4 inches), keeping the sides square.
6 Give one double turn as for puff pastry.
7 Allow to rest in a cool place, covered with cloth or plastic for 30 minutes.
8 Give three more double turns, resting between each. Allow to rest before using.

106 Sugar pastry

Pâte à sucre

Using hard margarine, 5–8 portions provides:
7864 kJ/1872 kcal
109.8 g fat
(of which 46.4 g saturated)
208.0 g carbohydrate
(of which 55.6 g sugars)
25.7 g protein
7.2 g fibre

	5–8 portions	10–16 portions
medium egg	1	2–3
sugar	50 g (2 oz)	125 g (5 oz)
margarine or butter	125 g (5 oz)	300 g (12½ oz)
flour (soft)	200 g (8 oz)	500 g (1¼ lb)
pinch salt		

Method I

1 Taking care not to over soften, cream the egg and sugar.

2 Add the margarine and mix for a few seconds.

3 Gradually incorporate the sieved flour and salt. Mix lightly until smooth.

4 Allow to rest in a cool place before using.

Method II

1 Sieve the flour and salt. Lightly rub in the margarine to a sandy texture.

2 Make a well in the centre. Add the sugar and beaten egg.

3 Mix the sugar and egg until dissolved.

4 Gradually incorporate the flour and margarine and lightly mix to a smooth paste. Rest paste before using.

Note: 50%, 70% or 100% wholemeal flour may be used.

Sugar pastry is used for flans, fruit tartlets, etc.

The butter may be reduced from 125 g to 100 g (5 oz to 4 oz).

107 Suet paste

5–8 portions provides:
6402 kJ/1524 kcal
89.3 g fat
(of which 40.6 g saturated)
171.3 g carbohydrate
(of which 3.0 g sugars)
19.3 g protein
7.2 g fibre

		5–8 portions	10 portions
flour (soft)	or self-raising flour	200 g (8 oz)	500 g (1¼ lb)
baking powder		10 g (½ oz)	25 g (1 oz)
pinch salt			
prepared beef suet		100 g (4 oz)	250 g (10 oz)
water		125 ml (¼ pt)	300 ml (⅝ pt)

1 Sieve the flour, baking powder and salt.

2 Mix in the suet. Make a well. Add the water.

3 Mix lightly to a fairly stiff paste.

Note: Suet paste is used for steamed fruit puddings, steamed jam rolls, steamed meat puddings and dumplings. Vegetarian suet is also available.

Possible reasons for faults in suet paste

- *Heavy and soggy*
  - cooking temperature too low.
- *Tough*
  - too much handling, over-cooking.

Fig 14.22 Preparing choux paste

108 Choux paste

Pâte à choux

> Using hard margarine, 5–8 portion provides:
> 6248 kJ/1488 kcal
> 106.6 g fat
> (of which 43.3 g saturated)
> 99.3 g carbohydrate
> (of which 4.1 g sugars)
> 38.9 g protein
> 4.5 g fibre

	5–8 portions	10–16 portions
water	¼ litre (½ pt)	625 ml (1¼ pt)
pinch of sugar and salt		
butter, margarine or oil	100 g (4 oz)	250 g (10 oz)
flour (strong)	125 g (5 oz)	300 g (12½ oz)
eggs	4	10

1 Bring the water, sugar and fat to the boil in a saucepan. Remove from heat.

2 Add the sieved flour and mix in with a wooden spoon; 50%, 70% or 100% wholemeal flour may be used.

3 Return to a moderate heat and stir continuously until the mixture leaves the sides of the pan.

4 Remove from the heat and allow to cool.

5 Gradually add the beaten eggs, mixing well.

6 The paste should be of dropping consistency.

Note: Choux paste is used for éclairs, cream buns, profiteroles (illustrated on page 589).

Possible reasons for faults in choux paste

- *Greasy and heavy*
  - basic mixture over-cooked.
- *Soft, not aerated*
  - flour insufficiently cooked; eggs insufficiently beaten in the mixture; oven too cool; underbaked.

109 Fruit pies

Apple, blackberry, blackberry and apple, cherry, rhubarb, gooseberry, damson, damson and apple, etc.

Using white flour and apple, 4–6 portions provides:
6808 kJ/1621 kcal
65.0 g fat
(of which 26.6 g saturated)
260.0 g carbohydrate
(of which 144.1 g sugars)
15.3 g protein
15.0 g fibre

Using 50% wholemeal flour and apple, 4–6 portions provides:
6709 kJ/1598 kcal
65.6 g fat
(of which 26.7 g saturated)
251.1 g carbohydrate
(of which 144.5 g sugars)
17.8 g protein
18.8 g fibre

	4–6 portions	10–15 portions
fruit	400 g (1 lb)	1½ kg (2½ lb)
water	2 tbsp	5 tbsp
sugar	100 g (4 oz)	250 g (10 oz)
Short pastry flour (soft)	100 g (4 oz)	250 g (10 oz)
butter or margarine	25 g (1 oz)	60 g (2½ oz)
lard or vegetable fat	25 g (1 oz)	60 g (2½ oz)
water to mix		

1 Prepare the fruit, wash and place half in a ½ litre (1 pint) pie dish or individual dishes.
2 Add the sugar and water and the remainder of the fruit.
3 Place a clove in an apple pie.
4 Roll out the pastry ½ cm (¼ inch) thick to the shape of the pie dish, allow to relax. Damp the rim of the pie dish and edge the rim with a strip of the pastry.
5 Damp the edge of the pastry.
6 Carefully lay the pastry on the dish without stretching it and firmly seal the rim of the pie. Cut off any surplus pastry.
7 Brush with milk and sprinkle with caster sugar.
8 Place the pie on a baking sheet and bake in a hot oven at 220°C (Reg. 7; 425°F) for about 10 minutes.
9 Reduce the heat or transfer to a cooler part of the oven and continue cooking for a further 30 minutes. If the pastry colours too quickly cover with a sheet of paper.
10 Clean the pie dish, and serve with a sauceboat of custard ¼ litre (½ pint); cream or ice-cream.

Preparation of fruit for pies

- *Apples* Peeled, quartered, cored, washed, cut in slices.
- *Cherries* Stalks removed, washed.
- *Blackberries* Stalks removed, washed.
- *Gooseberries* Stalks and tails removed, washed.
- *Damsons* Picked and washed.
- *Rhubarb* Leaves and root removed, tough strings removed, cut into 2 cm (1 inch) pieces, washed.

For fruit crumbles see page 528.

110 Treacle tart

1 portion provides:
1100 kJ/262 kcal energy
10.7 g fat
(of which 5.8 g saturated)
41.1 g carbohydrate
(of which 20.3 g sugars)
2.8 g protein
0.8 g fibre

	4 portions	10 portions
Short paste		
flour	100 g (4 oz)	250 g (10 oz)
lard, margarine or vegetable fat	25 g (1 oz)	60 g (2½ oz)
butter or margarine	25 g (1 oz)	60 g (2½ oz)
pinch of salt		
water to mix		
Filling		
treacle	100 g (4 oz)	250 g (10 oz)
lemon juice	3–4 drops	8–10 drops
fresh white bread or cake crumbs	15 g (¾ oz)	50 g (2 oz)
water	1 tbsp	2½ tbsp

1 Make pastry as in recipe 103, page 562, allow to rest in refrigerator.
2 Roll out to a 3 mm (⅛ in) round.
3 Place onto a lightly greased, oven-proof plate.
4 Warm the treacle, water, lemon juice and add the crumbs.

5 Spread on the pastry and bake at 220°C (Reg 7; 425°F) for about 20 mins.

This tart can also be made in a shallow flan ring. Any pastry debris can be rolled and cut into ½ cm (¼ in) strips and used to decorate the top of the tart before baking.

Treacle tarts can also be made in individual moulds.

111 Flans

(Illustrated on pages 579–80)

Allow 25 g (1 oz) flour per portion and prepare sugar pastry (page 566).

1 Grease the flan ring and baking sheet.
2 Roll out the pastry 2 cm (1 inch) larger than the flan ring.
3 Place the flan ring on the baking sheet.
4 Carefully place the pastry on the flan ring, by rolling it loosely over the rolling-pin, picking up, and unrolling it over the flan ring.
5 Press the pastry into shape without stretching it, being careful to exclude any air.
6 Allow a ½ cm (¼ inch) ridge of pastry on top of the flan ring.
7 Cut off the surplus paste by rolling the pin firmly across the top of the flan ring.
8 Mould the edge with thumb and forefinger. Decorate (a) with pastry tweezers or (b) with thumbs and forefingers, squeezing the pastry neatly to form a corrugated pattern.

Note: A flan jelly (commercial pectin glaze) may be used as an alternative to apricot glaze. This is usually a clear glaze to which food colour may be added.

Using 250 g of fruit, 1 portion provides:
918 kJ/218 kcal energy
6.5 g fat
(of which 3.9 g saturated)
40.2 g carbohydrate
(of which 31.4 g sugars)
2.1 g protein
0.9 g fibre

112 Cherry flan – using fresh cherries

Flan aux cerises

	4 portions	**10 portions**
sugar paste (page 566)	100 g (4 oz)	250 g (10 oz)
cherries	200–300 g (8–12 oz)	500 g (1¼ lb)
sugar	50 g (2 oz)	125 g (5 oz)
red glaze (page 576)	2 tbsp	6 tbsp

1 Line the flan ring and pierce the bottom.
2 Stone the cherries. Arrange neatly in the flan case. Sprinkle with sugar.
3 Bake at 200–230°C (Reg. 6–8; 400–450°F) for about 30 minutes.
4 Remove ring and eggwash sides. Complete the cooking.
5 Brush with hot red glaze (page 576).

Note: A ½ cm (¼ inch) layer of pastry cream or thick custard may be placed in the flan case before adding the cherries.

113 Apple flan

Flan aux pommes

	4 portions	**10 portions**
sugar paste (page 566)	100 g (4 oz)	250 g (10 oz)
sugar	50 g (2 oz)	125 g (5 oz)
cooking apples	400 g (1 lb)	1 kg (2½ lb)
apricot glaze (page 571)	2 tbsp	6 tbsp

1 portion provides:
1428 kJ/340 kcal
13.8 g fat
(of which 5.8 g saturated)
53.8 g carbohydrate
(of which 36 g sugars)
3.5 g protein
2.9 g fibre

1 Line a flan ring. Pierce the bottom several times with a fork.
2 Keep the best-shaped apple and make the remainder into a purée.
3 When cool, place in the flan case.
4 Peel, quarter and wash the remaining apple.
5 Cut in neat thin slices and lay carefully on the apple purée, overlapping each slice. Ensure that each slice points to the centre of the flan then no difficulty should be encountered in joining the pattern up neatly.
6 Sprinkle a little sugar on the apple slices and bake the flan at 200–220°C (Reg. 6–7; 400–425°F) for 30–40 minutes.
7 When the flan is almost cooked, remove the flan ring carefully, return to the oven to complete the cooking. Mask with hot apricot glaze or flan jelly.

Fig 14.23 🖊 Apple slice   *Yolande Stanley*

114 Apricot glaze

Prepare by boiling apricot jam with a little water and passing it through
a strainer. Glaze should be used hot.

Fig 14.24 🖊 Apple meringue tartlet   *Yolande Stanley*

Fig 14.25 Making flans and slices (bands)

115 Apple meringue flan

Flan aux pommes meringué

Cook as for apple flan, without arranging sliced apples. Pipe with meringue (page 511) using two egg whites. Return to the oven at 200°C (Reg. 6; 400°F) to cook and colour meringue (about 5 minutes).

Note: This may be finished with ordinary or Italian meringue.

116 Italian meringue

granulated sugar or cube sugar	200 g (8 oz)
water	60 ml (⅛ pt)
pinch of cream of tartar	
egg whites	4

1 Boil the sugar, water and cream of tartar to hard ball stage 121°C (250°F).

2 Beat the egg whites to full peak and while stiff, beating slowly, pour on the boiling sugar. Use as required.

117 Apple purée

Marmalade de pomme

	4 portions	10 portions
cooking apples	400 g (1 lb)	1 kg (2½ lb)
butter or margarine	10 g (½ oz)	25 g (1¼ oz)
sugar	50 g (2 oz)	125 g (5 oz)

1 Peel, core and slice the apples.

2 Place the butter or margarine in a thick-bottomed pan; heat until melted.

3 Add the apples and sugar, cover with a lid and cook gently until soft.

4 Drain off any excess liquid and pass through a sieve or liquidise.

118 Lemon meringue pie (economic recipe)

	8 portions	20 portions
sugar paste (page 566)	200 g (8 oz)	500 g (1¼ lb)
Lemon curd		
water	125 ml (¼ pt)	300 ml (⅝ pt)
sugar	100 g (4 oz)	250 g (10 oz)
cornflour	25 g (1 oz)	60 g (2½ oz)
butter	25 g (1 oz)	60 g (2½ oz)
lemon	1	2½
yolks	1–2	3–5
Meringue		
egg whites	4	10
caster sugar	200 g (8 oz)	500 g (1¼ lb)

1 portion provides:

1824 kJ/434 kcal

17.5 g fat
(of which 7.8 g saturated)
68.3 g carbohydrate
(of which 46.3 g sugars)
5.2 g protein
1.0 g fibre

1 Line a flan ring and cook blind.

2 Prepare the lemon curd by boiling the water, sugar and zest and juice of lemon to a syrup.

3 Thicken with diluted cornflour, remove from the heat, add the butter and whisk in yolks. Place in the flan case.

4 When set, pipe in the meringue (page 511) and colour in a hot oven at 220°C (Reg. 7; 425°F).

Note: This may also be finished with Italian meringue (recipe 116).

119 Lemon curd (alternative recipe)

	8 portions	20 portions
medium eggs, separated, pasteurised	2	5
caster sugar	100 g (4 oz)	250 g (10 oz)
butter	100 g (4 oz)	250 g (10 oz)
lemon	1	2

1   Cream the egg yolks and sugar in a bowl with a whisk.

2   Add the butter, zest and juice of lemon.

3   Place in a bain-marie on a low heat and whisk continuously until it thickens (20–30 minutes).

120 Baked jam roll

Using white flour, 1 portion provides:
1677 kJ/399 kcal
20.9 g fat
(of which 8.9 g saturated)
50.6 g carbohydrate
(of which 12.4 g sugars)
5.3 g protein
2.2 g fibre

	4 portions	10 portions
short paste (flour with baking powder added when sifting flour, or self-raising flour) (page 562)	200 g (8 oz)	500 g (1¼ lb)
jam	2–3 tbsp	5–7 tbsp

1   Roll out the pastry into a rectangle 30 cm × 16 cm (12 × 6 inches).

2   Spread with jam, leaving 1 cm (½ inch) clear on all edges.

3   Fold over two short sides, 1 cm (½ inch). Roll the pastry from the top.

4   Moisten the bottom edge to seal the roll.

5   Place edge down on a greased baking sheet.

6   Brush with eggwash or milk. Sprinkle with sugar.

7   Bake in a moderate oven at 200°C (Reg. 6; 400°F) for about 40 minutes.

8   Serve with a sauceboat of jam or custard sauce separately.

Note: These can be made in individual portions.

121 Baked apple dumplings

Using lard and margarine, 1 portion provides:
1227 kJ/291 kcal energy
11.6 g fat
(of which 5.1 g saturated)
46.4 g carbohydrate
(of which 23.6 g sugars)
3.2 g protein
2.7 g fibre

	4 portions	10 portions
short paste (page 562)	200 g (8 oz)	500 g (1¼ lb)
cloves	4	12
small cooking apples (4 oz each)	4	10
sugar	50 g (2 oz)	125 g (5 oz)

1   Roll out the pastry 3 mm (⅛ inch) thick into a square.

2   Cut into four even squares. Damp the edges.

3   Place a whole peeled, cored and washed apple in the centre of each square. Pierce the apple with a clove.

4   Fill the centre with sugar.

5   Fold over the pastry to completely seal the apple, without breaking the pastry.

6   Roll out any debris of pastry and cut neat 2 cm (1 inch) fancy rounds and place one on top of each apple.

7   Egg or milkwash and place on a lightly greased baking sheet.

8   Bake in a moderately hot oven at 200°C (Reg. 6; 400°F) for about 30 minutes.

9 Serve with a sauceboat of custard, cream or ice-cream.

Note: Centre of apples may also be filled with different mixtures of candied fruits, dried fruits and nuts and spices, e.g. cinnamon, ginger or nutmeg.

122 Dutch apple tart

1 portion provides:
1628 kJ/386 kcal energy
13.0 g fat
(of which 7.7 g saturated)
67.8 g carbohydrate
(of which 50.3 g sugars)
3.8 g protein
2.6 g fibre

	6–8 portions	15–20 portions
sugar paste (page 566)	200 g (8 oz)	500 g (1¼ lb)
cooking apples	400 g (1 lb)	1¼ kg (2½ lb)
sugar	100 g (4 oz)	250 g (10 oz)
pinch of cinnamon		
lemon, zest of		
sultanas	50 g (2 oz)	125 g (5 oz)

1 Roll out half the pastry 3 mm (⅛ inch) thick into a neat round and place on a greased plate or line a flan ring.

2 Prick the bottom several times with a fork.

3 Peel, core and wash and slice the apples.

4 Place them in a saucepan with the sugar and a little water.

5 Partly cook the apples; add the cinnamon and zest of lemon.

6 Add the washed, dried sultanas and allow to cool.

7 Place on the pastry. Moisten the edges.

8 Roll out the other half of the pastry to a neat round and place on top.

9 Seal firmly, trim off excess pastry, mould the edges.

10 Brush with milk and sprinkle with caster sugar.

11 Place on a baking sheet, bake in a moderately hot oven at 200–220°C (Reg. 6–7; 400–425°F) for about 40 minutes.

12 Remove from the plate carefully before serving.

123 Rhubarb flan

Flan au rhubarbe

Using apricot glaze, 1 portion provides:
955 kJ/226 kcal energy
6.5 g fat
(of which 3.9 g saturated)
42.3 g carbohydrate
(of which 33.5 g sugars)
2.3 g protein
1.4 g fibre

	4 portions	10 portions
sugar paste (page 566)	100 g (4 oz)	250 g (10 oz)
sugar	100 g (4 oz)	250 g (10 oz)
rhubarb	300 g (¾ lb)	1 kg (2 lb)
apricot glaze (page 571) or red glaze (see below)	2 tbsp	5 tbsp

1 Trim the roots and leaves from the rhubarb and remove the tough string. Cut into 2 cm (1 inch) pieces, wash and dry thoroughly.
2 Line flan ring and pierce.
3 Sprinkle with sugar.
4 Arrange the fruit neatly in the flan case.
5 Sprinkle with the remainder of the sugar.
6 Bake at 200–220°C (Reg. 6–7; 400–425°F).
7 When the flan is almost cooked, carefully remove the flan ring and return the flan to the oven to complete the cooking.
8 Mask with hot apricot or red glaze.

Note: A ½ cm (¼ inch) layer of pastry cream or thick custard may be placed in the flan case before adding the rhubarb.

Red glaze

- Boil the sugar and water or fruit syrup with a little red colour and thicken with diluted arrowroot or fecule, reboil until clear; strain.

or

- Red jam and a little water boiled and passed through a strainer.

124 Plum or apricot flan

Flan aux prunes ou aux abricots

Using 250 g plums, apricot glaze used, 1 portion provides:
1028 kJ/243 kcal energy
6.5 g fat
(of which 3.9 g sugars)
47.2 g carbohydrate
(of which 38.4 g sugars)
2.0 g protein
1.4 g fibre

	4 portions	10 portions
sugar paste (page 566)	100 g (4 oz)	250 g (10 oz)
sugar	100 g (4 oz)	250 g (10 oz)
plums or apricots	200–300 g (8–12 oz)	500–700 g (1¼ –2 lb)
apricot glaze (page 571)	2 tbsp	5 tbsp

1 Line a flan ring and pierce. Sprinkle with sugar.
2 Quarter or halve the fruit. Arrange neatly in the flan case.
3 Sprinkle with the remainder of the sugar.
4 Bake at 200–220°C (Reg. 6–7; 400–425°F).
5 When the flan is almost cooked carefully remove the flan ring and return the flan to the oven to complete the cooking.
6 Mask with hot apricot glaze.

Note: A ½ cm (¼ inch) layer of pastry cream or thick custard may be placed in the flan case before adding the fruit.

125 Soft fruit and tinned fruit flans

For soft fruit (strawberry, raspberry, banana) and tinned fruits (pear, peach, pineapple, cherry), the flan case is lined in the same way, the bottom pierced and then cooked 'blind': tear a piece of paper 2 cm (1inch) larger in diameter than the flan ring, place it carefully in the flan case, fill the centre with dried peas, beans or small pieces of stale bread and bake at 200–220°C (Reg. 6–7; 400–425°F) for about 30 minutes. Remove the flan ring, paper and beans before the flan is cooked through, eggwash including the inside and return to the oven to complete the cooking. Add pastry cream and sliced or whole drained fruit. Mask with glaze. The glaze may be made with the fruit juice thickened with arrowroot, approximately 10 g (½ oz) to ¼ litre (½ pt).

126 Strawberry or raspberry flan

Flan aux fraises ou aux framboises

	4 portions	10 portions
sugar paste (page 566)	100 g (4 oz)	250 g (10 oz)
fruit	200 g (8 oz)	500 g (1¼ lb)
red glaze (page 576)	2 tbsp	5 tbsp

> 1 portion provides:
> 567 kJ/135 kcal energy
> 6.5 g fat
> (of which 3.9 g saturated)
> 18.4 g carbohydrate
> (of which 9.7 g sugars)
> 2.0 g protein
> 0.9 g fibre

1 Cook the flan blind, allow to cool. Pick and wash the fruit, drain well.

2 Dress neatly in flan case. Coat with the glaze.

Note: A layer of pastry cream or thick custard may be placed in the flan case before adding the fruit.

127 Fruit tartlets

These are made from the same pastry and the same fruits as the fruit flans. The ingredients are the same. The tartlets are made by rolling out the pastry 3 mm (⅛ inch) thick and cutting out rounds with a fluted cutter and neatly placing them in greased tartlet moulds. Depending on the fruit used, they may sometimes be cooked blind (strawberries, raspberries).

128 Fruit barquettes

Certain fruits (strawberries, raspberries) are sometimes served in boat-shaped moulds. The preparation is the same as for tartlets.

Tartlets and barquettes should be glazed and served allowing one large or two small per portion.

Fig 14.26 🖎 Fruit tartelettes and barquettes

Yolande Stanley

> 1 portion provides:
> 1549 kJ/369 kcal
> 16.0 g fat
> (of which 6.9 g saturated)
> 53.7 g carbohydrate
> (of which 30.3 g sugars)
> 6.0 g protein
> 2.9 g fibre

129 Banana flan

Flan aux bananes

	4 portions	10 portions
sugar paste (page 566)	100 g (4 oz)	250 g (10 oz)
pastry cream or thick custard	125 ml (¼ pt)	250 g (10 oz)
bananas	2	5
apricot glaze (page 571)	2 tbsp	5 tbsp

1 Cook flan blind, allow to cool.

2 Make pastry cream (page 501) or custard and pour while hot into the flan case.

3 Allow to set. Peel and slice the bananas neatly.

4 Arrange overlapping layers on the pastry cream. Coat with glaze.

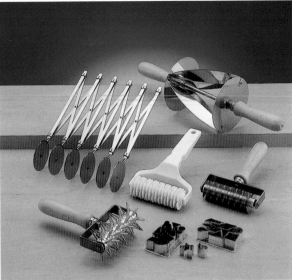

Fig 14.28 🖎 Lattice cutters

Fig 14.27 🖎 Banana flan   *Yolande Stanley*

130 Mincemeat tart

	4 portions	10 portions
sugar paste (page 566)	200 g (8 oz)	500 g (1¼ lb)
mincemeat (page 604)	200 g (8 oz)	500 g (1¼ lb)

1 portion provides:
1492 kJ/355 kcal energy
15.0 g fat
(of which 7.7 g saturated)
55.0 g carbohydrate
(of which 37.5 g sugars)
3.4 g protein
1.4 g fibre

1   Roll out half the pastry 3 mm (⅛ inch) thick into a neat round and place on a greased plate.

2   Prick the bottom several times with a fork.

3   Add the mincemeat. Moisten the edges.

4   Roll out the other half of the pastry to a neat round and place on top.

5   Seal firmly, trim off excess pastry, mould the edges.

6   Brush with milk and sprinkle with caster sugar.

7   Place on a baking sheet and bake at 200–220°C (Reg. 6–7; 400–425°F) for about 40 minutes and serve.

Fig 14.29 🖋 Mincemeat flan with trellis pastry

Yolande Stanley

Using whipping cream, 1 portion provides:
735 kJ/176 kcal
14.9 g fat
(of which 8.6 g saturated)
9.8 g carbohydrate
(of which 6.3 g sugars)
1.2 g protein
0.2 g fibre

131 Cream horns

(Illustrated on page 585)

	Makes 16
puff pastry (page 564)	200 g (8 oz)
cream	½ litre (1 pt)
few drops vanilla essence	
jam	50 g (2 oz)
caster sugar	50 g (2 oz)

1 Roll out the pastry 2 mm (¹⁄₁₂ inch) thick, 30 cm (12 inches) long.

2 Cut into 1½ cm wide (¾ inch) strips. Moisten on one side.

3 Wind carefully round lightly greased cream horn moulds, starting at the point and carefully overlapping each round slightly.

4 Brush with eggwash on one side and place on a greased baking sheet.

5 Bake at 220°C (Reg. 7; 425°F) for about 20 minutes.

6 Sprinkle with icing sugar and return to a hot oven for a few seconds to glaze.

7 Remove carefully from the moulds and allow to cool.

8 Place a little jam in the bottom of each.

9 Add the sugar and essence to the cream and whip stiffly.

10 Place in a piping bag with a star tube and pipe a neat rose into each horn.

Note: These may also be partially filled with pastry cream to which various flavourings or fruit may be added:

- praline
- chocolate
- coffee
- lemon
- raspberries
- strawberries
- mango
- orange segments.

132 Eccles cakes

	Makes 12 cakes
puff or rough puff pastry (pages 564–5)	200 g (8 oz)
Filling	
butter or margarine	50 g (2 oz)
mixed peel	50 g (2 oz)
demerara sugar	50 g (2 oz)
currants	200 g (8 oz)
pinch mixed spice	

1 portion provides:
691 kJ/164 kcal
8.6 g fat
(of which 3.7 g saturated)
22.1 g carbohydrate
(of which 17.3 g sugars)
1.1 g protein
1.4 g fibre

1 Roll out the pastry 2 mm (½ inch) thick.

2 Cut into rounds 10–12 cm (4–5 inch) diameter. Damp the edges.

3 Place a tablespoon of the mixture in the centre of each.

4 Fold the edges over to the centre and completely seal in the mixture.

5 Brush the top with egg white and dip into caster sugar.

6 Place on a greased baking sheet.

7 Cut two or three incisions with a knife so as to show the filling.

8 Bake at 220°C (Reg. 7; 425°F) for 15–20 minutes.

133 Puff pastry slice

Mille-feuilles

> 1 portion provides:
> 1158 kJ/369 kcal energy
> 10.9 g fat
> (of which 1.3 g saturated)
> 67.7 g carbohydrate
> (of which 52.3 g sugars)
> 4.9 g protein
> 0.1 g fibre

	Makes 6–8 slices
puff pastry (page 564)	200 g (8 oz)
apricot jam	100 g (4 oz)
pastry cream	¼ litre (½ pt)
fondant or water icing	200 g (8 oz)

1 Roll out the pastry 2 mm (¹⁄₁₂ inch) thick into an even-sided square.
2 Roll up carefully on a rolling-pin and unroll onto a greased, dampened baking sheet.
3 Using two forks pierce as many holes as possible.
4 Cut in half with a large knife then cut each half in two to form four even-sized rectangles.
5 Bake in a hot oven at 220°C (Reg. 7; 425°F) for 15–20 minutes; turn the strips over after 10 minutes. Allow to cool.
6 Keep the best strip for the top. Spread pastry cream on one strip.
7 Place another strip on top and spread with jam.
8 Place the third strip on top and spread with pastry cream.
9 Place the last strip on top, flat side up.
10 Press down firmly with a flat tray.
11 Decorate by feather-icing as follows:
12 Warm the fondant to blood heat and correct the consistency with sugar syrup if necessary.
13 Separate a little fondant into two colours and place in paper cornets.
14 Pour the fondant over the mille-feuilles in an even coat.
15 Immediately pipe on one of the colours lengthwise in strips 1 cm (½ inch) apart.
16 Quickly pipe on the second colour between each line of the first.
17 With the back of a small knife, wiping after each stroke, mark down the slice at 2 cm (1 inch) intervals.
18 Quickly turn the slice around and repeat in the same direction with strokes in between the previous ones.
19 Allow to set and trim the edges neatly.
20 Cut into even portions with a sharp thin-bladed knife, dip into hot water and wipe clean after each cut.

Note: At stages 15 and 16 baker's chocolate or tempered couverture may be used for marbling.

Whipped fresh cream may be used as an alternative to pastry cream. Also a variety of soft fruits may be incorporated in the layers, such as raspberries; strawberries; canned well-drained pears, peaches or apricots; kiwi fruit; caramelised poached apple slices. The pastry cream or whipped cream may also be flavoured with a liqueur if so desired such as Curaçao, Grand Marnier, Cointreau.

134 Apple turnovers

Chausson aux pommes

	Makes 12
puff pastry (page 564)	200 g (8 oz)
dry, sweetened apple purée	100 g (4 oz)

1 Roll out the pastry 2 mm (½ in) thick.
2 Cut into 8 cm (4 in) diameter rounds.
3 Roll out slightly oval 12 × 10 cm (5 × 4 in).
4 Moisten the edges, place a little apple purée in centre of each.
5 Fold over and seal firmly.
6 Brush with egg white and dip in caster sugar.
7 Place sugar side up on a dampened baking sheet.

Fig 14.30 Puff pastry slice

Yolande Stanley

8   Bake in hot oven, 220°C (Reg 7, 425°F) for 15–20 minutes.

Note: Other types of fruit may be included in the turnovers, such as apple and mango; apple and blackberry; apple and passionfruit; apple, pear and cinnamon.

135 Palmiers

Puff pastry trimmings are suitable for these.

1   Roll out the pastry 2 mm (¹⁄₁₂ inch) thick into a square.

2   Sprinkle liberally with caster sugar on both sides and roll into the pastry.

3   Fold into three from each end so as to meet in the middle, brush with eggwash and fold in two.

4   Cut into strips approximately 2 cm (1 inch) thick; dip one side in caster sugar.

5   Place on a greased baking sheet, sugared side down, leaving a space of at least 2 cm (1 inch) between each.

6   Bake in a very hot oven for about 10 minutes.

7   Turn with a palette knife, cook on the other side until brown and the sugar is caramelised.

Note: Palmiers may be made in all sizes. Two joined together with a little whipped cream may be served as a pastry, small ones for petits fours. They may be sandwiched together with soft fruit, whipped cream and/or ice-cream and served as a sweet.

136 Puff pastry cases

Bouchées and vol-au-vent

Makes 12 bouchées or 6 vol-au-vent cases.

puff pastry (page 564)	200 g (8 oz)

1   Roll out the pastry approximately ½ cm (¼ inch) thick.

2   Cut out with a round, fluted 5 cm (2 inch) cutter.

3   Place on a greased, dampened baking sheet; eggwash.

4   Dip a plain 4 cm (1½ inch) diameter cutter into hot fat or oil and make an incision 3 mm (⅛ inch) deep in the centre of each.

5   Allow to rest in a cool place.

6   Bake at 220°C (Reg. 7; 425°F) for about 20 minutes.

583

continued over ▶

▶ *Puff pastry cases continued*

7 When cool remove the caps or lids carefully and remove all the raw pastry from inside the cases.

Note: Bouchées are filled with a variety of savoury fillings and are served hot or cold. They may also be filled with cream and jam or lemon curd as a pastry.

Large bouchées are known as vol-au-vent. They may be produced in one, two, four or six portion sizes, and a single-sized vol-au-vent would be approximately twice the size of a bouchée. When preparing one and two portion size vol-au-vent the method for bouchées may be followed. When preparing larger sized vol-au-vent it is advisable to have two layers of puff pastry each ½ cm (¼ inch) thick, sealed together with eggwash. One layer should be a plain round, and the other of the same diameter with a circle cut out of the centre.

137 Jalousie

1 portion provides:
1178 kJ/282 kcal energy
17.8 g fat
(of which 5.1 g saturated)
27.2 g carbohydrate
(of which 17.5 g sugars)
3.8 g protein
0.8 g fibre

	8–10 portions
puff pastry (page 564)	200 g (8 oz)
mincemeat (page 604), jam or frangipane (page 611)	200 g (8 oz)

1 Roll out one-third of the pastry 3 mm (⅛ inch) thick into a strip 25 × 10 cm (10 × 4 inches) and place on a greased, dampened baking sheet.

Fig 14.31 🖎 Preparation of vol-au-vent; bouchées; cream horns (page 580); palmiers (page 583)

2 Pierce with a fork. Moisten the edges.

3 Spread on the filling, leaving 2 cm (1 inch) free all the way round.

4 Roll out the remaining two-thirds of the pastry to the same size.

5 Fold in half lengthwise and, with a sharp knife, cut slits across the fold about ½ cm (¼ inch) apart to within 2 cm (1 inch) of the edge.

6 Carefully open out this strip and neatly place on to the first strip.

7 Neaten and decorate the edge. Brush with eggwash.

8 Bake at 220°C (Reg. 7; 425°F) for 25–30 minutes.

9 Sprinkle with icing sugar and return to a very hot oven to glaze.

Fig 14.32 🖎 Puff pastry goods (from top to foreground): bouchées, vol-au-vent, palmiers, cream horns

Fig 14.33 🖎 Gâteau pithiviers *Yolande Stanley*

138 Gâteau pithiviers

1 portion provides:
928 kJ/222 kcal energy
15.6 g fat
(of which 3.8 g saturated)
18.5 g carbohydrate
(of which 8.9 g sugars)
3.8 g protein
0.5 g fibre

	8–10 portions	20 portions
puff pastry (page 564)	200 g (8 oz)	500 g (1¼ lb)
apricot jam	1 tbsp	3 tbsp
frangipane (page 611)	using half the recipe	1½ times

1. Roll out one-third of the pastry into a round 20 cm (8 inches), 2 mm (1/12 inch) thick, moisten the edges and place on a greased, dampened baking sheet; spread the centre with jam.

2. Prepare the frangipane by creaming the margarine and sugar in a bowl, gradually adding the beaten eggs and folding in the flour and almonds.

3. Spread on the frangipane, leaving a 2 cm (1 inch) border round the edge.

4. Roll out the remaining two-thirds of the pastry and cut into a slightly larger round.

5. Place neatly on top, seal and decorate the edge.

6. Using a sharp pointed knife, make curved cuts 2 mm (1/12 inch) deep, radiating from the centre to about 2 cm (1 inch) from the edge. Brush with eggwash.

7. Bake at 220°C (Reg. 7; 425°F) for 25–30 minutes.

8. Glaze with icing sugar as for jalousie.

139 Mince pies

1 portion provides:
718 kJ/171 kcal
10.2 g fat
(of which 4.5 g saturated)
17.7 g carbohydrate
(of which 10.2 g sugars)
1.3 g protein
1.0 g fibre

	Makes 8–12 pies
puff pastry (page 564)	200 g (8 oz)
mincemeat (page 604)	200 g (8 oz)

1. Roll out the pastry 3 mm (⅛ inch) thick.
2. Cut half the pastry into fluted rounds 6 cm (2½ inches) diameter.
3. Place on a greased, dampened baking sheet.
4. Moisten the edges.
5. Place a little mincemeat in the centre of each.
6. Cut the remainder of the pastry into fluted rounds, 8 cm (3 inches) diameter.
7. Cover the mincemeat, seal the edges. Brush with eggwash.
8. Bake at 220°C (Reg. 7; 425°F) for about 20 minutes.
9. Sprinkle with icing sugar and serve warm. Accompany with a suitable sauce (custard, brandy sauce, brandy cream, etc.).

Note: Mince pies may be made with short or sugar pastry.

140 Sausage rolls

1 portion provides:
799 kJ/190 kcal
15.9 g fat
(of which 5.8 g saturated)
7.9 g carbohydrate
(of which 0.2 g sugars)
4.3 g protein
0.4 g fibre

	Makes 12 rolls	10 portions
puff pastry (page 564)	200 g (8 oz)	500 g (1¼ lb)
sausage meat	400 g (1 lb)	1 kg (2½ lb)

1. Roll out the pastry 3 mm (⅛ inch) thick into a strip 10 cm (4 inches) wide.
2. Make sausage meat into a roll 2 cm (1 inch) diameter.
3. Place on the pastry. Moisten the edges of the pastry.
4. Fold over and seal. Cut into 8 cm (3 inch) lengths.
5. Mark the edge with the back of a knife. Brush with eggwash.
6. Place on to a greased, dampened baking sheet.
7. Bake at 220°C (Reg. 7; 425°F) for about 20 minutes.

141 Fruit slice

Bande aux fruits

These may be prepared from any fruit suitable for flans.

> 1 portion provides:
> 767 kJ/183 kcal
> 7.8 g fat
> (of which 3.4 g saturated)
> 28.6 g carbohydrate
> (of which 21.3 g sugars)
> 1.3 g protein
> 1.6 g fibre

	8–10 portions
puff pastry (page 564)	200 g (8 oz)
fruit	400 g (1 lb)
sugar to sweeten	
appropriate glaze	2 tbsp

1. Roll out the pastry 2 mm (½ inch) thick in a strip 12 cm (6 inches) wide.
2. Place on a greased, dampened baking sheet.
3. Moisten two edges with eggwash; lay two 1½ cm (⅜ inch) wide strips along each edge.
4. Seal firmly and mark with the back of a knife. Prick the bottom of the slice.
5. Then depending on the fruit used, either put the fruit (such as apple) on the slice and cook together or cook the slice blind and afterwards place the pastry cream and fruit (such as tinned peaches) on the pastry. Glaze and serve as for flans.

Note: Alternative methods are:

- to use short or sweet pastry for the base and puff pastry for the two side strips;
- to use sweet pastry in a slice mould.

(Apple slice illustrated on page 571).

142 Kiwi slice

Bande aux kiwis

1. Cook the band blind.
2. When cool add the pastry cream.
3. Arrange the slices of kiwi fruit on pastry cream.
4. Coat with the apricot glaze.
5. Decorate with whipped cream.

Note: A whole variety of fruit may be used instead of or in combination with kiwi fruit, such as banana, apricots, raspberries, mango, strawberries, pawpaw, peaches, grapes or pears.

Fig 14.34 Kiwi fruit slice

1 portion provides:
516 kJ/123 kcal
9.5 g fat
(of which 5.7 g saturated)
8.8 g carbohydrate
(of which 7.3 g sugars)
1.1 g protein
0.1 g fibre

143 Chocolate éclairs

Eclairs au chocolat

	Makes 12 éclairs
choux paste (page 567)	125 ml (¼ pt)
fondant	100 g (4 oz)
whipped cream	¼ litre (½ pt)
chocolate couverture	25 g (1 oz)

1   Place the choux paste into a piping bag with a 1 cm (½ inch) plain tube.

2   Pipe into 8 cm (3 inch) lengths onto a lightly greased dampened baking sheet.

3   Bake at 200–220°C (Reg. 6–7; 400–425°F) for about 30 minutes.

4   Allow to cool. Slit down one side, with a sharp knife.

5   Fill with sweetened, vanilla-flavoured whipped cream, using a piping bag and small tube. The continental fashion is to fill with pastry cream.

6   Warm the fondant, add the finely cut chocolate, allow to melt slowly, adjust the consistency with a little sugar and water syrup if necessary. *Do not overheat or the fondant will lose its shine.*

7   Glaze the éclairs by dipping them in the fondant; remove the surplus with the finger. Allow to set.

Note: Traditionally chocolate éclairs were filled with chocolate pastry cream.

Fig 14.35 🍴 Piping éclairs

Fig 14.36 ✎ Glazing chocolate éclairs   *Yolande Stanley*

144 Coffee éclairs

Eclairs au café

Add a few drops of coffee essence instead of chocolate to the fondant.

Coffee éclairs may be filled with coffee-flavoured pastry cream, page 501, or whipped non-dairy cream.

Fig 14.37 ✎ Chocolate éclairs

145 Profiteroles

These are small choux paste buns that can be made in a variety of sizes:

- pea size, for consommé garnish;
- double pea size (stuffed) for garnish;
- half-cream-bun size – filled with cream and served with chocolate sauce.

146 Cream buns

Choux à la crème

(Illustrated on page 592)

	Makes 8 buns
choux paste (page 567)	125 ml (¼ pt)
chopped almonds	25 g (1 oz)
whipped cream	¼ litre (½ pt)

1   Place the choux paste into a piping bag with a 1 cm (½ inch) plain tube.
2   Pipe out on to a lightly greased dampened baking sheet into pieces the size of a walnut.
3   Sprinkle each with chopped almonds. Cook, split and fill as for éclairs.
4   Sprinkle with icing sugar and serve.

147 Profiteroles and chocolate sauce

Profiteroles au chocolat

(Illustrated on page 592)

	8 portions
choux paste (page 567)	125 ml (¼ pt)
chocolate sauce (page 524)	¼ litre (½ pt)
whipped, sweetened, vanilla flavoured cream	¼ litre (½ pt)

1   Proceed as for cream buns (above), pipe out half the size and omit the almonds. Fill with cream and dredge with icing sugar.
2   Serve with a sauceboat of cold chocolate sauce.

Note: Alternatively, coffee sauce may be served and the profiteroles filled with non-dairy cream. Profiteroles may also be filled with chocolate, coffee or rum flavoured pastry cream.

1 portion provides:
919 kJ/219 kcal
16.2 g fat
(of which 9.7 g saturated)
16.4 g carbohydrate
(of which 12.8 g sugars)
2.9 g protein
0.2 g fibre

148 Choux paste fritters

Beignets soufflés, sauce abricot

1 portion provides:
344 kJ/82 kcal
3.9 g fat
(of which 1.3 g saturated)
11.5 g carbohydrate
(of which 8.8 g sugars)
0.9 g protein
0.2 g fibre

	8 portions
choux paste (page 567)	125 ml (¼ pt)
apricot sauce (page 521)	125 ml (¼ pt)

1 Using a tablespoon and the finger, break the paste off into pieces the size of a walnut into a moderately hot deep fat 170°C (347°F).

2 Allow to cook gently for 10–15 minutes.

3 Drain well, sprinkle liberally with icing sugar.

4 Serve with a sauceboat of hot apricot sauce.

149 Steamed fruit puddings

Apple, apple and blackberry, rhubarb, rhubarb and apple, etc.

Using apple, 1 portion provides:
967 kJ/230 kcal
7.4 g fat
(of which 3.4 g saturated)
41.5 g carbohydrate
(of which 27.1 g sugars)
1.9 g protein
3.0 g fibre

	6 portions
suet paste (page 566)	200 g (8 oz)
fruit	¾–1 kg (1½ –2 lb)
sugar	100 g (4 oz)
water	2 tbsp

1 Grease the basin.

2 Line, using three-quarters of the paste.

3 Add prepared and washed fruit and sugar. Add 1–2 cloves in an apple pudding.

4 Add water. Moisten the edge of the paste.

5 Cover with the remaining quarter of the pastry. Seal firmly.

6 Cover with greased greaseproof paper, a pudding cloth or foil.

7 Steam for about 1½ hours and serve with custard.

150 Steamed jam roll

1 portion provides:
673 kJ/160 kcal energy
7.0 g fat
(of which 3.9 g saturated)
24.3 g carbohydrate
(of which 11.7 g sugars)
1.5 g protein
0.5 g fibre

	6 portions	**15 portions**
suet paste (page 566)	200 g (8 oz)	400 g (1 lb)
jam	100 g (4 oz)	200 g (8 oz)

1 Roll out the paste into a rectangle 3 cm × 16 cm (12 × 6 inches).

2 Spread with jam leaving 1 cm (½ inch) clear on all edges.

3 Fold over two short sides, 1 cm (½ inch). Roll the pastry from the top.

4 Moisten the bottom edge to seal the roll.

5 Wrap in buttered greaseproof paper and a pudding cloth or foil, tie both ends. Steam for 1½ –2 hours. Serve with jam or custard sauce.

Note: The jam may be sprinkled with finely chopped nuts (walnuts, hazelnuts, pecan, almonds). May be made in individual portions.

Fig 14.38 (clockwise from top): cream buns, profiteroles and chocolate sauce (page 590)

Prepare and cook cakes and biscuits

Cake mixtures

There are three basic methods of making cake mixtures, also known as cake batters. The working temperature of cake batter should be 21°C (70°F).

Sugar batter method

For this method, the fat (cake margarine, butter or shortening) is blended in a machine with caster sugar. This is the basic or principal stage; the other ingredients are then usually added in the order shown.

Flour batter method

For this method the eggs and sugar are whisked to a half sponge; this is the basic or principal stage, which aims to foam the two ingredients together until half the maximum volume is achieved. Other ingredients are added as shown.

A humectant such as glycerine may be added to assist with moisture retention; if so, add at stage 2.

Blending method

Used for high ratio cake mixtures. This uses high ratio flour specially produced so that it will absorb more liquid. For this method also use a high ratio fat. This is made from oil to which a quantity of emulsifying agent has been added enabling the fat to take up a greater quantity of liquid.

High ratio cakes contain more liquid and sugar, resulting in a fine stable crumb, extended shelf-life, good eating and excellent freezing qualities.

The principal or basic stage is the mixing of the fat and flour to a crumbling texture.

It is essential that each stage of the batter is blended into the next to produce a smooth batter, free from lumps. When using mixing machines, it is important to remember to:

- blend on a slow speed,
- beat on a medium speed, using a paddle attachment.

When blending, always clear the mix from the bottom of the bowl to ensure that any first or second stage butter does not remain in the bowl.

Baking powder

Baking powder may be made from one part sodium bicarbonate to two parts of cream of tartar. In commercial baking the powdered cream of tartar may be replaced by another acid product, such as acidulated calcium phosphate.

When used under the right conditions it produces carbon dioxide gas; to produce gas a liquid and heat are needed. As the acid has a delayed action, only a small amount being given off when the liquid is added, the majority of the gas is released when the mixture is heated. Therefore cakes when mixed do not lose the property of the baking powder if they are not cooked right away.

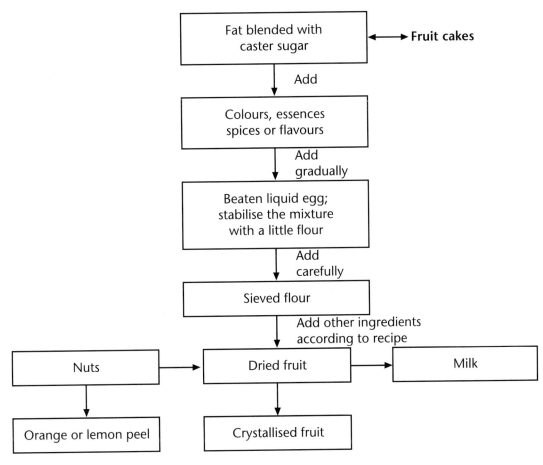

Fig 14.39 Sugar batter method

Possible reasons for faults in cakes

- *Uneven texture*
  - fat insufficiently rubbed in
  - too little liquid
  - too much liquid.
- *Close texture*
  - too much fat
  - hands too hot when rubbing in
  - fat to flour ratio incorrect.
- *Dry*
  - too much liquid

- oven too hot.
- *Bad shape*
  - too much liquid
  - oven too cool
  - too much baking powder.
- *Fruit sunk*
  - fruit wet
  - too much liquid
  - oven too cool.
- *Cracked*
  - too little liquid
  - too much baking powder.

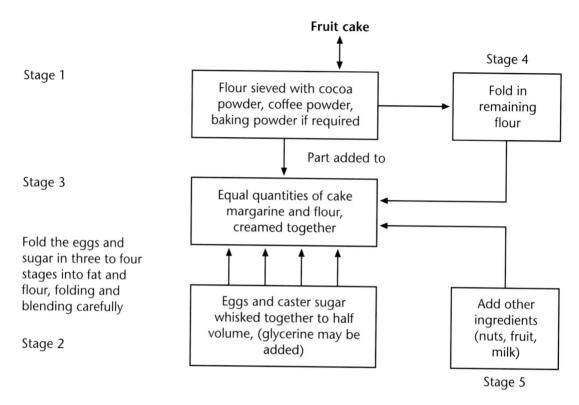

Fig 14.40 🖋 Flour batter method

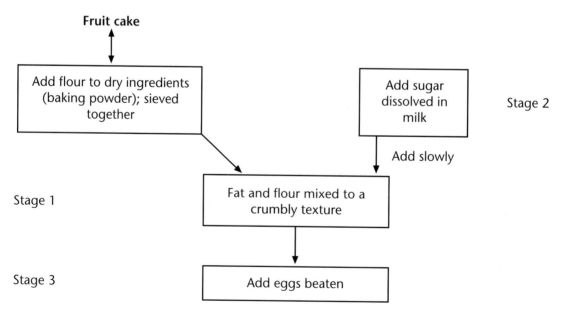

Fig 14.41 🖋 Blending method

Biscuit mixtures

Biscuits may be produced by the following methods:

- rubbing in
- foaming
- sugar batter
- flour batter
- blending.

Rubbing in

This is probably the best known method and is used in producing some of the most famous types of biscuits, such as shortbread. The method is exactly the same as producing short pastry.

- Rub the fat into the flour, by hand or by machine, adding the liquid and the sugar and mixing in the flour to produce a smooth biscuit paste.
- Do not overwork the paste otherwise it will not combine and as a consequence you will not be able to roll it out.

Foaming

This is where a foam is produced from egg whites or egg yolks or both. Sponge fingers are an example of a two foam mixture. Meringue is an example of a single foam mixture using egg whites. Great care must be taken not to overmix the product.

Sugar batter method

Fat and sugar are mixed together to produce a light and fluffy cream. Beaten egg is gradually added. The dry ingredients are then carefully folded in.

Flour batter method

Half the sieved flour is creamed with the fat. The eggs and sugar are beaten together before they are added to the fat and flour mixture. Finally, the remainder of the flour is folded in together with any other dry ingredients.

Blending method

In several biscuit recipes, the method only requires the chef to blend all the ingredients together to produce a smooth paste.

Production methods and examples

- *Rubbing in* Shortbread.
- *Foaming* Sponge fingers.
- *Sugar batter method* Cats' tongues (langues de chat), Sablé biscuits.
- *Flour batter method* Cookies.
- *Blending method* Almond biscuits (using basic almond commercial mixture).

Sponge mixtures

These are produced from a foam of eggs and sugar. The eggs may be whole eggs or separated. Examples of sponge products are: gâteaux, sponge fingers and sponge cakes.

The egg white traps the air bubbles by forming a semi-rigid membrane structure. When eggs and sugar are whisked together, they thicken until maximum volume is reached; then flour is carefully folded in by a method known as cutting in. This is the most difficult operation as the flour must not be allowed to sink to the bottom of the bowl, otherwise it becomes lumpy and difficult to clear. However, the mixture *must not be stirred* as this will disturb the aeration and cause the air to escape, resulting in a much heavier sponge. If butter, margarine or oil is added, it is important that this is added at about 36°C (98°F), otherwise overheating will cause the fat or oil to act on the flour and create lumps, which are difficult, often impossible, to dispense.

Stabilisers are often added to sponges to prevent them from collapsing. The most common are ethylmethyl cellulose and glycerol monostearate; these are added to the eggs and sugar on the commencement of mixing.

Methods of making sponges

Foaming method

Whisking eggs and sugar together to ribbon stage; folding in/cutting flour.

Melting method

As with foaming, adding melted butter, margarine or oil to the mixture. The fat content enriches the sponge, improves the flavour texture and crumb structure and will extend the shelf-life.

Boiling method

Sponges made by this method have a stable crumb texture that is easier to handle than genoese sponge, crumbling less when cut. This method will produce a sponge that is suitable for dipping in fondant. The stages are shown in fig 14.42.

Blending method

High ratio sponges follow the same principles as high ratio cakes. As with cakes, high ratio goods produce a fine stable crumb, even texture, excellent shelf-life and good freezing qualities.

Creaming method

This is the traditional method and is still used today for Victoria sandwich and light fruit cakes. The fat and sugar are creamed together, beaten egg is added and finally the sieved flour with the other dry ingredients as desired.

Separate yolk and white method

This method is used for sponge fingers (page 610).

Possible reasons for faults in sponges

- *Close texture*
  - underbeating
  - too much flour
  - oven too cool or too hot.
- *Holey texture*
  - flour insufficiently folded in
  - tin unevenly filled.
- *Cracked crust*
  - oven too hot.
- *Sunken*
  - oven too hot
  - tin removed during cooking.
- *White spots on surface*
  - insufficient beating.

Possible reasons for faults in genoese sponges

- *Close texture*
  - eggs and sugar overheated
  - eggs and sugar underbeaten
  - too much flour
  - flour insufficiently folded in
  - oven too hot.
- *Sunken*
  - too much sugar
  - oven too hot
  - tin removed during cooking.
- *Heavy*
  - butter too hot
  - butter insufficiently mixed in
  - flour overmixed.

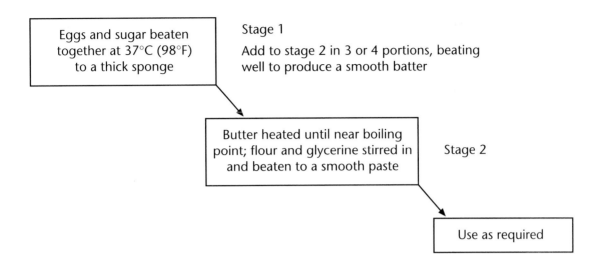

Stage 1

Eggs and sugar beaten together at 37°C (98°F) to a thick sponge

Add to stage 2 in 3 or 4 portions, beating well to produce a smooth batter

Butter heated until near boiling point; flour and glycerine stirred in and beaten to a smooth paste

Stage 2

Use as required

Fig 14.42 Boiling method

Points to remember

- Check all ingredients carefully.
- Make sure scales are accurate; weigh all ingredients carefully.
- Check ovens are at the right temperature, that the shelves are in the correct position.
- Check all work surfaces and equipment are clean.
- Check that all other equipment required, such as cooling wires, are within easy reach.
- Always sieve flour to remove lumps and any foreign material.
- Make sure that eggs and fats are at room temperature.
- Check dried fruits carefully and wash, drain and dry if necessary.
- Always follow the recipe carefully.
- Always scrape down the sides of the mixing bowl when creaming mixtures.
- Always seek help if you are unsure, or lack understanding.
- Try to fill the oven space when baking by planning production carefully; this saves time, labour and money.
- Never guess quantities. Time and temperature are important factors; they too should not be guessed.
- The shape and size of goods will determine the cooking time and temperature, the wider the cake, the longer and more slowly it will need to cook.
- Where cakes contain a high proportion of sugar in the recipe, this will caramelise the surface quickly before the centre is cooked. Therefore cover the cake with sheets of silicone or wetted greaseproof and continue to cook.
- When cake tops are sprinkled with almonds or sugar, the baking temperature needs to be lowered slightly to prevent over colouring of the cake crust.
- When glycerine, glucose and invert sugar, honey or treacle is added to cake mixtures, the oven temperature should be lowered as these colour at a lower temperature than sugar.
- Always work in a clean and hygienic way;

remember the hygiene and safety rules, in particular the Food Safety Act.

- All cakes and sponges benefit from being allowed to cool in their tins as this makes handling easier. If sponges need to be cooled quickly, place a wire rack over the top of the tin and invert, then remove the lining paper and cool on a wire rack.

The introduction of steam or moisture

Because they become too dry whilst baking due to oven temperature producing a dry atmosphere, some cakes require the injection of steam. Combination ovens are ideally suited for this purpose. The steam delays the formation of the crust until the cake batter has become fully aerated and the proteins have set. Alternatively add a tray of water to the oven while baking. If the oven is too hot the cake crust will form early and the cake batter will rise into a peak.

Convenience cake, biscuit and sponge mixes

There is now available on the market a vast range of prepared mixes, as well as frozen goods. Premixes enable the caterer to calculate costs more effectively, reduce labour costs, limit the range of stock items to be held, with less demand for highly skilled labour.

Every year more and more convenience products are introduced on to the market by large and small food manufacturers. The caterer should be encouraged to investigate these products and experiment to assess their quality.

Decorating and finishing for presentation
Filling

Cakes, sponges and biscuits may be filled or sandwiched together with a variety of different types of filling. Examples are:

- *Creams*
- butter cream plain ⎫ flavoured and/or
- pastry cream ⎭ coloured
- whipped cream
- clotted cream.
- *Fruit*
- fresh fruit purée
- jams
- fruit pastries
- fruit mousses
- preserves
- fruit gels.
- *Pastes and spreads*
- chocolate
- praline
- nut
- curds.

Spreading and coating to finish

This is where smaller cakes and gâteaux are covered top and sides with any of the following:

- fresh whipped cream
- fondant
- chocolate
- royal icing
- buttercream
- water icing
- meringue
  - ordinary
  - Italian
  - Swiss
- commercial preparations.

Piping

Piping is a skill that takes practice. There are many different types of piping tube available. The following may be used for piping:

- royal icing
- chocolate
- fondant
- meringue
- boiled sugar
- fresh cream.

Dusting, dredging, sprinkling

These techniques are used to give the product a final design or glaze during cooking using sugar.

- *Dusting* A light even finish.
- *Dredging* Heavier dusting with sugar.
- *Sprinkling* A very light sprinkle of sugar.

The sugar used may be icing, caster, or granulated white; demerara, Barbados or dark brown sugar.

The product may be returned to the oven for glazing or glazed under the salamander.

Remember that decorating is an art form and that there is a range of equipment and materials available to assist you in this work. An example of decorative media is as follows:

- Glacé and crystallised fruits
  - cherries
  - lemons
  - oranges
  - pineapple
  - figs.
- Crystallised flowers
  - rose petals
  - violets
  - mimosa
  - lilac.
- Crystallised stems
  - angelica.
- Nuts
  - almonds (nibbed, flaked)
  - coconut (fresh slices, desiccated)
  - hazelnuts
  - brazil nuts
  - pistachio.
- Chocolate
  - rolls
  - vermicelli
  - flakes
  - chocolate piping
  - chips.

Biscuit pastes

Piped biscuits can be used for decoration:

- piped sablé paste
- cats' tongues (langues de chat)
- almond mixture.

Cakes

151 Scones

Using hard margarine, 1 portion provides:
678 kJ/162 kcal
5.8 g fat
(of which 2.5 g saturated)
26.3 g carbohydrate
(of which 7.5 g sugars)
2.7 g protein
1.0 g fibre

	Makes 8 scones	20 scones
self-raising flour	200 g (8 oz)	500 g (1¼ lb)
baking powder	5 g (¼ oz)	12 g (⅝ oz)
pinch salt		
butter or margarine	50 g (2 oz)	125 g (5 oz)
caster sugar	50 g (2 oz)	125 g (5 oz)
milk or water	95 ml (³⁄₁₆ oz)	250 ml (½ pt)

1   Sieve the flour, baking powder and salt.

2   Rub in the fat to a sandy texture. Make a well in the centre.

3   Add the sugar and the liquid. Dissolve the sugar in the liquid.

4   Gradually incorporate the flour; mix lightly.

5   Roll out two rounds, 1 cm (½ inch) thick. Place on a greased baking sheet.

6   Cut a cross half-way through the rounds with a large knife.

7   Milkwash and bake at 200°C (Reg. 6; 400°F) for 15–20 minutes.

Note: 50% wholemeal flour may be used. The comparatively small amount of fat, rapid mixing to a soft dough, quick and light handling are essentials to produce a light scone.

Add 50 g (2 oz) (125 g, 5 oz for 20 portions) washed and dried sultanas to the scone mixture for fruit scones.

Fig 14.43   Service of scones with strawberry jam and clotted cream

152 Small cakes – basic mixture

Using hard margarine, 1 portion provides:
947 kJ/225 kcal
11.6 g fat
(of which 4.8 g saturated)
28.8 g carbohydrate
(of which 13.4 g sugars)
3.3 g protein
0.7 g fibre

	10 medium or 20 small cakes	25–50 portions
flour (soft) or self-raising	200 g (8 oz)	500 g (1¼ lb)
baking powder (with plain flour)	1 level tsp	
salt		
margarine or butter	125 g (5 oz)	300 g (12½ oz)
caster sugar	125 g (5 oz)	300 g (12½ oz)
medium eggs	2–3	5–7

Method I – rubbing in

1 Sieve the flour, baking powder and salt.
2 Rub in the butter or margarine to a sandy texture. Add the sugar.
3 Gradually add the well-beaten eggs and mix as lightly as possible until combined.

Method II – creaming

1 Cream the margarine and sugar in a bowl until soft and fluffy.
2 Slowly add the well-beaten eggs, mixing continuously and beating really well between each addition.
3 Lightly mix in the sieved flour, baking powder and salt.

Note: In both cases the consistency should be a light dropping one, and if necessary it may be adjusted with the addition of a few drops of milk.

Variations include:

- *Cherry cakes* Add 50 g (2 oz) glacé cherries cut in quarters and 3 to 4 drops vanilla essence to the basic mixture (Method II) and divide into 8–12 lightly greased cake tins or paper cases. Bake in a hot oven at 220°C (Reg. 7; 425°F) for 15–20 minutes.

- *Coconut cakes* In place of 50 g (2 oz) flour, use 50 g (2 oz) desiccated coconut and 3 to 4 drops vanilla essence to the basic mixture (Method II) and cook as for cherry cakes.

- *Raspberry buns* Divide basic mixture (Method I) into 8 pieces. Roll into balls, flatten slightly, dip tops into milk then caster sugar. Place on a greased baking sheet, make a hole in the centre of each, add a little raspberry jam. Bake in a hot oven at 200°C (Reg. 7; 425°F) for 15–20 minutes.

- *Queen cakes* To the basic mixture (Method II) add 100 g (4 oz) washed and dried mixed fruit and cook as for cherry cakes.

153 Rich fruit cake

Ingredients	16 cm (6 inch) dia, 8 cm deep	21 cm (8 inch) dia, 8 cm deep	26 cm (10 inch) dia, 8 cm deep	31 cm (12 inch) dia, 8 cm deep
butter or margarine	150 g (6 oz)	200 g (8 oz)	300 g (12 oz)	550 g (1 lb 6 oz)
caster or soft brown sugar	150 g (6 oz)	200 g (8 oz)	300 g (12 oz)	550 g (1 lb 6 oz)
eggs	4	6	8	10
soft flour	125 g (5 oz)	175 g (7 oz)	275 g (11 oz)	500 g (1 lb 4 oz)
salt pinch	6 g	8 g	10 g	12 g
nutmeg	¾ tsp	1 tsp	1¼ tsp	2 tsp
mixed spice	¾ tsp	1 tsp	1¼ tsp	2 tsp
cinnamon	¾ tsp	1 tsp	1¼ tsp	2 tsp
currants	150 g (6 oz)	200 g (8 oz)	300 g (12 oz)	550 g (1 lb 6 oz)
sultanas	150 g (6 oz)	200 g (8 oz)	300 g (12 oz)	550 g (1 lb 6 oz)
raisins	125 g (5 oz)	150 g (6 oz)	225 g (9 oz)	400 g (1 lb)
glacé cherries	75 g (3 oz)	100 g (4 oz)	125 g (5 oz)	200 g (8 oz)
mixed peel	75 g (3 oz)	100 g (4 oz)	125 g (5 oz)	200 g (8 oz)
ground almonds	75 g (3 oz)	100 g (4 oz)	125 g (5 oz)	200 g (8 oz)
grated lemon rind	½	½	1	2
glycerine	2 tsp	3 tsp	1 tbsp	2 tbsp
oven temperature	150°C (300°F)	150°C (300°F)	130°C (250°F)	110°C (225°F)
time (approx)	3 hours	3½ hours	4½ hours	6–7 hours

1 Cream the butter, margarine and sugar until light and fluffy.

2 Gradually beat in the eggs, creaming continuously.

3 Add the glycerine.

4 Sift the flour, nutmeg, mixed spice and cinnamon. Add the ground almonds and salt, mix well.

5 Carefully fold in the flour, nutmeg, mixed spice, cinnamon, ground almonds and salt into the eggs and sugar.

6 Fold in the dried fruit, mixed peel and glacé cherries and lemon rind.

7 Place the mixture into a prepared cake tin lined with silicone. The outside of the tin should also be well protected with paper. Bake at required temperature for the required time.

8   To test, insert a needle into the centre of the cake; when cooked, it should come out clean and free of uncooked mixture.

9   Remove from the oven, then allow to cool.

10 Wrap in tin foil and allow to mature for 2–3 weeks before coating with marzipan and icing.

Note: The dried fruit may be soaked in brandy for 12 hours. Allow 3 tablespoons of brandy for a 16 cm (6 in) diameter cake; 4 tablespoons for 21 cm (8 in) diameter; 5 tablespoons for 26 cm (10 in) diameter etc.

Alternatively, instead of soaking the fruit before baking, the brandy may be poured over the cake once it leaves the oven after baking.

154 Marzipan or almond paste

Cooked

water	250 ml (½ pt)
caster sugar	1 kg (2 lb)
ground almonds	400 g (1 lb)
yolks	3
almond essence	

Place the water and sugar in a pan and boil. Skim. When the sugar reaches 116°C (241°F) draw aside and mix in the almonds; then add the yolks and essence and mix in quickly to avoid scrambling. Knead well until smooth.

155 Royal icing

icing sugar	400 g (1 lb)
whites of egg, pasteurised	3
lemon, juice of	1
glycerine	2 tsp

Modern practice is to use egg white substitute or dried egg whites. Always follow the manufacturer's instructions for quantities.

Mix well together in a basin the sieved icing sugar and the whites of egg, with a wooden spoon. Add a few drops of lemon juice and glycerine and beat until stiff.

28 g/1 oz provides:
330 kJ/78 kcal energy
2.7 g fat
(of which 1.5 g saturated)
12.1 g carbohydrate
(of which 11.7 g sugars)
0.3 g protein
0.4 g fibre

156 Mincemeat (used for mincepies)

suet (chopped)	100 g (4 oz)
mixed peel (chopped)	100 g (4 oz)
currants	100 g (4 oz)
sultanas	100 g (4 oz)
raisins	100 g (4 oz)
apples (chopped)	100 g (4 oz)
Barbados sugar	100 g (4 oz)
mixed spice	5 g (¼ oz)
lemon grated zest and juice	1
orange grated zest and juice	1
rum	60 ml
brandy	60 ml

Mix the ingredients together, place in jars and use as required.

157 Rock cakes

Using hard margarine, 1 portion provides:
913 kJ/217 kcal
8.7 g fat
(of which 3.6 g saturated)
33.6 g carbohydrate
(of which 14.3 g sugars)
3.4 g protein
1.3 g fibre

	8 cakes	**20 cakes**
flour (soft) or self-raising	200 g (8 oz)	500 g (1¼ lb)
baking powder (with plain flour)	5 g (¼ oz)	12 g (⅝ oz)
pinch salt		
margarine or butter	75 g (3 oz)	180 g (7½ oz)
caster sugar	75 g (3 oz)	180 g (7½ oz)
large egg	1	2–3
dried fruit (currants, sultanas)	50 g (2 oz)	125 g (5 oz)

1 Use Method I, page 601. Keep the mixture slightly firm.

2 Place with a fork into 8–12 rough shapes on a greased baking sheet; milk or eggwash.

3 Bake in a fairly hot oven at 220°C (Reg. 7; 425°F) for about 20 minutes.

Variation: add a small pinch of mixed spice.

Sponges

158 Victoria sandwich

	4 portions	10 portions
butter or margarine	100 g (4 oz)	250 g (10 oz)
caster sugar	100 g (4 oz)	250 g (10 oz)
medium eggs	2	
flour (soft)	100 g (4 oz)	250 g (10 oz)
baking powder	5 g (¼ oz)	12 g (⅝ oz)

1 Cream the fat and sugar until soft and fluffy.
2 Gradually add the beaten eggs.
3 Lightly mix in the sieved flour, and baking powder.
4 Divide into two 18 cm (7 inch) greased sponge tins.
5 Bake at 190–200°C (Reg. 5–6; 375–400°F), for 12–15 minutes.
6 Turn out on to a wire rack to cool.
7 Spread one half with jam, place the other half on top.
8 Dust with icing sugar.

Using hard margarine, this recipe provides:
6866 kJ/1635 kcal
94.3 g fat
(of which 39.3 g saturated)
184.7 g carbohydrate
(of which 106.6 g sugars)
23.3 g protein
3.6 g fibre

159 Genoese sponge

Génoise

	4 portions	10 portions
medium eggs	4	10
caster sugar	100 g (4 oz)	250 g (10 oz)
flour (soft)	100 g (4 oz)	250 g (10 oz)
butter, margarine or oil	50 g (2 oz)	125 g (5 oz)

1 Whisk the eggs and sugar with a balloon whisk in a bowl over a pan of hot water.
2 Continue until the mixture is light, creamy and double in bulk.
3 Remove from the heat and whisk until cold and thick (ribbon stage). Fold in the flour very gently.
4 Fold in the melted butter very gently.
5 Place in a greased, floured Genoese mould.
6 Bake in a moderately hot oven at 200–220°C (Reg. 6–7; 400–425°F) for about 30 minutes.

Using hard margarine, this recipe (4 portions) provides:
5978 kJ/1423 kcal
65.8 g fat
(of which 25.6 g saturated)
182.8 g carbohydrate
(of which 106.6 g sugars)
36.5 g protein
3.6 g fibre

160 Chocolate Genoese

Génoise au chocolat

> 1 portion provides:
> 1518 kJ/362 kcal energy
> 17.6 g fat
> (of which 8.8 g saturated)
> 43.5 g carbohydrate
> (of which 26.6 g sugars)
> 10.1 g protein
> 0.9 g fibre

	4 portions	10 portions
flour (soft)	75 g (3 oz)	180 g (7½ oz)
cocoa powder	10 g (½ oz)	25 g (1 oz)
cornflour	10 g (½ oz)	25 g (1 oz)
medium eggs	4	10
caster sugar	100 g (4 oz)	250 g (10 oz)
butter, margarine or oil	50 g (2 oz)	125 g (5 oz)

Sift the flour and the cocoa together with the cornflour, then proceed as for Genoese sponge.

161 Chocolate gâteau

Gâteau au chocolat

> Using hard margarine and butter, 4 portions provides:
> 20113 kJ/4789 kcal
> 260.9 g fat
> (of which 148.7 g saturated)
> 606.0 g carbohydrate
> (of which 533.2 g sugars)
> 41.6 g protein
> 4.8 g fibre

	4 portions	10 portions
egg chocolate genoese sponge (as previous recipe)	4	10
butter cream **unsalted butter**	200 g (8 oz)	500 g (1¼ lb)
icing sugar	150 g (6 oz)	375 g (15 oz)
block chocolate (melted in a basin in a bain-marie)	50 g (2 oz)	125 g (5 oz)
chocolate vermicelli or flakes	50 g (2 oz)	125 g (5 oz)
stock syrup (page 608)		

1 Cut the genoese into three slices crosswise.

2 Prepare the butter cream as on page 525, and mix in the melted chocolate.

3 Lightly moisten each slice of genoese with stock syrup, which may be flavoured with kirsch, rum, etc.

4 Lightly spread each slice of genoese with butter cream and sandwich together.

5 Lightly coat the sides with butter cream and coat with chocolate vermicelli or flakes.

6 Neatly smooth the top using a little more butter cream if necessary.

Note: Many variations can be used in decorating this gâteau; chocolate fondant may be used on the top and various shapes of chocolate can be used to decorate the top and sides.

Fig 14.44 ✎ Chocolate gâteau

Yolande Stanley

162 Coffee gâteau

Gâteau moka

1 portion provides:
4046 kJ/963 kcal energy
65.5 g fat
(of which 36.0 g saturated)
86.0 g carbohydrate
(of which 66.2 g sugars)
13.1 g protein
1.7 g fibre

	4 portions	10 portions
egg genoese sponge (page 605)	4	10
unsalted butter	200 g (8 oz)	500 g (1¼ lb)
icing sugar	150 g (6 oz)	375 g (15 oz)
coffee essence		
toasted, flaked or nibbed almonds	50 g (2 oz)	125 g (5 oz)
stock syrup		

1 Cut genoese into three slices crosswise.

2 Prepare the butter cream as on page 525, and flavour with coffee essence.

3 Lightly moisten each slice of genoese with stock syrup, which may be flavoured with Tia Maria, brandy etc.

4 Lightly spread each slice with butter cream and sandwich together.

5 Lightly coat the sides with butter cream and coat with almonds.

6 Smooth the top using a little more butter cream if necessary.

7 Decorate by piping the word MOKA in butter cream.

8 Coffee-flavoured fondant may be used in place of butter cream for the top.

163 Stock syrup

	4 portions	10 portions
water	500 ml (1 pt)	1¼ litre (2½ pt)
granulated sugar	150 g (6 oz)	375 g (15 oz)
glucose	50 g (2 oz)	125 g (5 oz)

1 Boil the water, sugar and glucose together, strain and cool.
2 Glucose helps to prevent crystallising.

164 Swiss roll

This recipe (4 portions) provides:
4445 kJ/1058 kcal
25.3 g fat
(of which 8.0 g saturated)
182.7 g carbohydrate
(of which 106.5 g sugars)
36.5 g protein
3.6 g fibre

	4 portions	10 portions
medium eggs	4	10
caster sugar	100 g (4 oz)	250 g (10 oz)
flour (soft)	100 g (4 oz)	250 g (10 oz)
or		
medium eggs	250 ml (½ pt)	625 ml (1¼ pt)
caster sugar	175 g (7 oz)	425 g (17½ oz)
flour (soft)	125 g (5 oz)	300 g (12½ oz)

1 Whisk the eggs and sugar with a balloon whisk in a bowl over a pan of hot water.
2 Continue until the mixture is light, creamy and double in bulk.
3 Remove from the heat and whisk until cold and thick (ribbon stage).
4 Fold in the flour very gently.
5 Grease a Swiss roll tin and line with greased greaseproof or silicone paper.
6 Pour in genoese mixture and bake at 220°C (Reg. 7; 425°F) for about 6 minutes.
7 Turn out on to a sheet of paper sprinkled with caster sugar.
8 Remove the paper from the Swiss roll, spread with warm jam.
9 Roll into a fairly tight roll, leaving the paper on the outside for a few minutes.
10 Remove the paper and allow to cool on a wire rack.

Biscuits and tarts

165 Shortbread biscuits

Method I

	Makes 12 biscuits
flour (soft)	150 g (6 oz)
pinch of salt	
butter or margarine	100 g (4 oz)
caster sugar	50 g (2 oz)

1 Sift the flour and salt.

2 Mix in the butter or margarine and sugar with the flour.

3 Combine all the ingredients to a smooth paste.

4 Roll carefully on a floured table or board to the shape of a rectangle or round, ½ cm (¼ inch) thick. Place on a lightly greased baking sheet.

5 Mark into the desired size and shape. Prick with a fork.

6 Bake in a moderate oven at 180–200°C (Reg. 4–6; 350–400°F) for 15–20 minutes.

Method II

soft flour, white or wholemeal	100 g (4 oz)
rice flour	100 g (4 oz)
butter or margarine	100 g (4 oz)
caster or unrefined sugar	100 g (4 oz)
medium egg (beaten)	1

1 Sieve the flour and rice flour into a basin.

2 Rub in the butter until the texture of fine breadcrumbs. Mix in the sugar.

3 Bind the mixture to a stiff paste using the beaten egg.

4 Roll out to 3 mm (⅛ inch) using caster sugar, prick well with a fork and cut into fancy shapes. Place the biscuits on a lightly greased baking sheet.

5 Bake in a moderate oven at 180–200°C (Reg. 4–6; 350–400°F), for 15 minutes or until golden brown.

6 Remove with a palette knife on to a cooling rack.

continued over ▶

▶ *Shortbread biscuits continued*

Method III

butter or margarine	100 g (4 oz)
icing sugar	100 g (4 oz)
medium egg	1
flour (soft)	150 g (6 oz)

1   Cream the butter or margarine and sugar thoroughly.

2   Add the egg and mix in. Mix in the flour.

3   Pipe on to lightly greased and floured baking sheets using a large star tube.

4   Bake at 200–220°C (Reg. 6–7; 400–425°F), for approximately 15 minutes.

1 portion provides:
145 kJ/34 kcal energy
0.9 g fat
(of which 0.2 g saturated)
5.7 g carbohydrate
(of which 3.3 g sugars)
1.3 g protein
0.1 g fibre

166 Sponge fingers

Biscuits à la cuillère

	Makes 32 fingers
medium eggs	4
caster sugar	100 g (4 oz)
flour (soft)	100 g (4 oz)

1   Cream the egg yolks and sugar in a bowl until creamy and almost white.

2   Whip the egg whites stiffly.

3   Add a little of the whites to the mixture and cut in.

4   Gradually add the sieved flour and remainder of the whites alternately, mixing as lightly as possible.

5   Place in a piping bag with 1 cm (½ inch) plain tube and pipe in 8 cm (3 inch) lengths onto baking sheets lined with greaseproof or silicone paper.

6   Sprinkle liberally with icing sugar. Rest for 5 minutes.

7   Bake in a moderate hot oven at 200–220°C (Reg. 6–7; 400–425°F) for about 10 minutes.

8   Remove from the oven, lift the paper on which the biscuits are piped and place upside down on the table.

9   Sprinkle liberally with water. This will assist the removal of the biscuits from the paper. (No water is needed if using silicone paper.)

167 Bakewell tart

	8 portions
sugar paste (using 8 oz flour) (page 566)	200 g (8 oz)
icing sugar	35 g (1½ oz)
raspberry jam	50 g (2 oz)
apricot glaze	50 g (2 oz)
frangipane **(make as for 168)** **butter or margarine**	100 g (4 oz)
ground almonds	50 g (2 oz)
medium eggs	2
caster sugar	100 g (4 oz)
flour	50 g (2 oz)
almond essence	

Using hard margarine, 1 portion provides:
2105 kJ/501 kcal
28.8 g fat
(of which 11.0 g saturated)
57.5 g carbohydrate
(of which 33.7 g sugars)
6.7 g protein
2.2 g fibre

1 Line a flan ring using three-quarters of the paste 2 mm (1⁄12 inch) thick.

2 Pierce the bottom with a fork.

3 Spread with jam and the frangipane.

4 Roll the remaining paste, cut into neat ½ cm (¼ inch) strips and arrange neatly criss-crossed on the frangipane; trim off surplus paste. Brush with eggwash.

5 Bake in a moderately hot oven at 200–220°C (Reg. 6–7; 400–425°F) for 30–40 minutes. Brush with hot apricot glaze.

6 When cooled brush over with very thin water icing.

168 Frangipane (alternative)

	8 portions
butter	100 g (4 oz)
caster sugar	100 g (4 oz)
medium eggs	2
ground almonds	100 g (4 oz)
flour	10 g (½ oz)

Cream the butter and sugar, gradually beat in the eggs. Mix in the almonds and flour, mix lightly.

Petits fours

These are an assortment of small biscuits, cakes and sweets served with coffee after special meals. There is a wide variety of items that can be prepared and when serving petits fours as large an assortment as possible should be offered.

Basically petits fours fall into two categories – dry and glazed. Dry includes all manner of biscuits, macaroons, meringue (see page 511) and marzipan items.

Glazed includes fruits (recipe 172) dipped in sugar, fondants, chocolates, sweets, and small pieces of neatly cut genoese sponge (see page 605) covered in fondant.

169 Cat's tongues

Langues de chat

icing sugar	125 g (5 oz)
butter	100 g (4 oz)
vanilla essence	
egg whites	3–4
soft flour	100 g (4 oz)

1 Lightly cream the sugar and butter, add 3–4 drops of vanilla essence.
2 Add the egg whites one by one, continually mixing and being careful not to allow the mixture to curdle.
3 Gently fold in the sifted flour and mix lightly.
4 Pipe on to a lightly greased baking sheet using a 3 mm (⅛ inch) plain tube, 2½ cm (1 inch) apart.
5 Bake at 230–250°C (Reg. 8–9; 450–500°F), for a few minutes.
6 The outside edges should be light brown and the centres yellow.
7 When cooked, remove on to a cooling rack using a palette knife.

170 Cornets (see Fig 14.46)

Cornets

1 Ingredients and method to stage 3 as for cat's tongues.
2 Using a 3 mm (⅛ inch) plain tube, pipe out the mixture onto a lightly greased baking sheet into rounds approximately 2½ cm (1¼ inches) in diameter.
3 Bake at 230–250°C (Reg. 8–9; 450–500°F), until the edges turn brown and the centre remains uncoloured.
4 Remove the tray from the oven.
5 Work quickly while the cornets are hot and twist them into a cornet shape using the point of a cream horn mould. (For a tight cornet shape it will be found best to set the pieces tightly inside the cream horn moulds and to leave them until set.)

171 Palmiers

See page 583.

Fig 14.45 Piping langues de chat

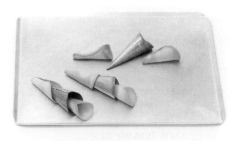

Fig 14.46 Moulding cornets

172 Glazed fruits

1   Dates stoned, stuffed with marzipan (left yellow or lightly coloured pink or green) and rolled in castor sugar.

2   Grapes (in pairs left on the stalk) or tangerine in segments, passed through a syrup and prepared as follows:

Syrup

sugar	400 g (1 lb)
glucose	50 g (2 oz)
water	250 ml (½ pt)
lemon, juice of	1

1   Boil the sugar, glucose and water to 160–165°C (310–315°F).

2   Add the lemon juice, shake in thoroughly, remove from heat.

3   Pass the fruits through this syrup using a fork and place them on to a lightly oiled marble slab to cool and set.

Note: Marzipan (page 603) can be coloured and moulded into a variety of shapes. They can then be either rolled in caster sugar or glazed by dipping in a syrup as in previous recipe.

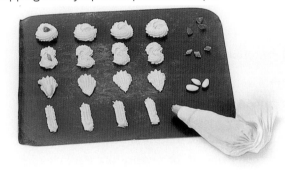

Yolande Stanley

Fig 14.47 ✎ Piping sablé biscuits

173 Piped biscuits

Sablés à la poche

	20–30 biscuits
caster or unrefined sugar	75 g (3 oz)
butter or margarine	150 g (6 oz)
medium egg	1
vanilla or grated lemon zest	
soft flour, white or wholemeal	200 g (8 oz)
ground almonds	35 g (1½ oz)

continued over ▶

► *Piped biscuits continued*

1 Cream the sugar and butter until light in colour and texture.

2 Add the egg gradually, beating continuously, add 3–4 drops vanilla or lemon zest.

3 Gently fold in the sifted flour and almonds, mix well until suitable for piping. If too stiff, add a little beaten egg.

4 Pipe on to a lightly greased and floured baking sheet using a medium-sized star tube (a variety of shapes can be used).

5 Some can be left plain, some decorated with half almonds or neatly cut pieces of angelica and glacé cherries.

6 Bake in a moderate oven at 190°C (Reg. 5; 375°F) for about 10 minutes.

7 When cooked, remove on to a cooling rack using a palette knife.

This recipe provides:
3361 kJ/800 kcal
53.5 g fat
(of which 4.2 g saturated)
62.4 g carbohydrate
(of which 62.4 g sugars)
21.2 g protein
14.4 g fibre

174 Almond biscuits

Biscuits aux amandes

	16–20 biscuits
egg whites	1½
ground almonds	100 g (4 oz)
caster or unrefined sugar	50 g (2 oz)
almond essence	
sheet rice paper	1
glacé cherries and angelica	

1 Whisk the egg whites until stiff.

2 Gently stir in the ground almonds, sugar and 3–4 drops almond essence. Place rice paper on a baking sheet.

3 Pipe mixture, using a medium star tube, into shapes.

4 Decorate with neatly cut diamonds of angelica and glacé cherries.

5 Bake at 180–200°C (Reg. 4–6; 350–400°F), for 10–15 minutes.

6 Trim with small knife to cut through rice paper and place on to a cooling rack using a palette knife.

175 Tuilles

butter	100 g (4 oz)
icing sugar	100 g (4 oz)
flour	100 g (4 oz)
egg whites	2

1   Mix all ingredients, rest for 1 hour.

2   Spread to required shape and size.

3   Bake at 395°C.

4   While hot, mould biscuits to required shape and leave to cool.

Fig 14.48 Moulding tuilles

15 Snacks, light meals, savouries and convenience foods

Selection of cold canapés

John Campbell

Snacks, light meals, savouries

Snacks (to be held in the hand) and light meals are a popular form of catering at any time of day or night and there is a wide variety of foods that can be offered.

Snacks

- Sandwiches made with fresh bread or toasted (page 634) accompanied with potato or vegetable crisps and a little salad.
- Rolls, baps, French bread, croissants, pitta bread, cut through and filled with a variety of fillings.
- Cornish pasties (page 232).
- Fried or grilled chicken pieces (pages 309, 311).
- Hamburgers (page 260).
- Potato chips, crisps and other shapes (page 473).
- Sausage rolls (page 586).
- Fruit fritters (apple, banana, pineapple) (page 526).
- Samosas (page 358).
- Tortillas (page 371).

Light meals

- Soup served with a warm roll or bread.
- Selection of hors-d'oeuvre (page 89).
- Selection of salad greens served with pâté, cheese, shellfish (crab, lobster, prawns, shrimps), smoked fish (mackerel fillet, salmon, trout, eel).
- Cold meat and poultry or quiche or pie with or without salad.
- Any composed salad.
- Plate of assorted smoked fish.
- Plate of assorted preserved meats.
- An egg dish (omelette, boiled, poached, fried or scrambled eggs) (page 132).
- A small dish of pasta (page 143).
- Poached smoked haddock (page 188).
- Kedgeree (page 196).
- A small portion of any fish dish.

- Kebabs (page 223).
- Barbecued spare ribs (page 284).
- Burritos (page 373).
- A small portion of any vegetarian dish (page 398).
- Baked beans on toast.
- Fried egg and chips.
- Pizza.

Savouries

Savouries can be offered usually as the last course for lunch, dinner or supper. Many savouries can also be served as a snack or light meal.

A variety of savouries served on hot buttered toast include:

- *Angels on horseback* – raw oysters wrapped in thinned streaky bacon, skewered and grilled.
- *Devils on horseback* – well-cooked, stoned prunes filled with chopped chutney, rolled in thinned streaky bacon, skewered and grilled.
- *Chicken liver and bacon (Canapé Diane)* – trimmed pieces of chicken liver, wrapped in thinned bacon, skewered and grilled.
- *Mushroom* – peeled open mushrooms, brushed with oil and grilled.
- *Soft herring roes* – floured and fried or grilled on both sides.
- *Soft roes and mushrooms* – cooked roes and grilled mushrooms.
- *Haddock* – lightly grilled pieces of smoked haddock fillet cut to the shape of the pieces of toast.
- *Haddock and bacon* – wrapped pieces of fish in thinned bacon and grilled.
- *Creamed haddock and cheese* – cooked, flaked smoked haddock mixed with béchamel or cream, piled on toast, sprinkled with grated cheese and

lightly browned under the grill. After toasting the bread, remove crusts and leave slices whole or cut into halves.

Convenience foods

What makes a food or product convenient? What constitutes a convenience food? The word 'convenience' encompasses a wide range of prepared and part-prepared food. This means that certain stages or steps in the process have been eliminated, thus less labour is required in their preparation.

Convenience foods can be categorised into: fresh convenience; dried; canned; bottled; frozen; chilled; vacuum packed; and portion controlled food, e.g. butter portions, jam portions.

The range of convenience foods available to the caterer is expanding all the time, as new technology becomes available to the food manufacturer and there continues to be an increased demand for a wide variety of products from the caterer.

Convenience foods require a range of skills for their preparation and service. The caterer must make a full assessment of what products will be suitable to use in specific situations; will the customer accept the product you intend to use? The equipment required for preparation and service will also have to be reviewed. How is this assessment going to be carried out?

Basic level of convenience

This is where the basic stages have been completed such as in peeled potatoes or carrots, but any slicing, chopping or dicing still has to be carried out.

Pre-assembly convenience

There are products where all the basic stages have been completed, together with the dicing, chopping, slicing, etc.

Pre-cooking convenience

This is where the constituents only have to be assembled prior to the cooking.

Pre-service convenience

This is where the products only have to undergo minimal processing prior to service, such as defrosting prior to service (gâteaux), or defrosting followed by cooking and service. The products may simply have to be cooked for a relatively short period in a conventional or microwave oven.

Full service convenience

This is where all the products are ready to be served, when nothing more in certain cases is required than opening a box or can. A guide to convenience foods is shown in the table below.

Type	Packaged items where food is cooked or prepared	Beverages	Packaged items where food is not cooked or fully prepared
full convenience	butter portions jam portions sliced bread potted shrimps gâteaux salad dressings	fruit juices	frozen fruit
pre-service convenience	ice-cream canned fruit canned meats canned soup fruit pies	tea bags liquid coffee	frozen fruit
pre-cooking convenience	canned steak dehydrated soup sausage rolls fish fingers croquettes		uncooked frozen pies, pastries breadcrumbed scampi scallops portioned meat, suprême of chicken
pre-assembly convenience	canned steak frozen pastry fruit pie fillings pastry products	ground coffee	sponge mixes pastry mixes unfrozen scampi fish fillets, portioned meat
basic convenience		coffee beans (to be ground)	peeled vegetables dried fruit jointed meats minced meat, sausages

Using butter, 1 portion provides:
1554 kJ/370 kcal
23.0 g fat
(of which 14.1 g saturated)
22.8 g carbohydrate
(of which 2.7 g sugars)
19.1 g protein
1.7 g fibre

1 Fried ham and cheese savoury

Croque monsieur

	4 portions	10 portions
slices cooked ham	4	10
slices Gruyère cheese	8	20
slices thin toast	8	20
clarified butter, margarine or sunflower oil	50 g (2 oz)	125 g (5 oz)

1   Place each slice of ham between two slices of cheese, then between two slices of lightly toasted bread.

2   Cut out with a round cutter.

3   Gently fry on both sides in clarified butter or oil and serve.

2 Scotch woodcock

Using hard margarine, 1 portion provides:
611 kJ/145 kcal
10.6 g fat
(of which 4.2 g saturated)
8.1 g carbohydrate
(of which 0.5 g sugars)
5.1 g protein
0.8 g fibre

	4 portions	10 portions
medium eggs	2–3	6–8
salt, pepper		
butter or margarine	35 g (1½ oz)	85 g (4¼ oz)
slices toast	2	5
anchovy fillets	5 g (¼ oz)	12 g (⅝ oz)
capers	5 g (¼ oz)	12 g (⅝ oz)

1   Break the eggs into a basin. Season with salt and pepper.

2   Thoroughly mix with a fork or whisk.

3   Place 25 g (1 oz) of butter in a small thick-based pan.

4   Allow to melt over a low heat.

5   Add the eggs and cook slowly, stirring continuously until *lightly* scrambled. Remove from the heat.

6   Spread on four rectangles or round-cut pieces of buttered toast.

7   Decorate each with two thin fillets of anchovy and four capers and serve.

Note: Adding 1 tbsp cream or milk when eggs are almost cooked will help to prevent overcooking.

3 Welsh rarebit

Using hard margarine, 1 portion provides:
1074 kJ/256 kcal
18.6 g fat
(of which 9.7 g saturated)
11.9 g carbohydrate
(of which 2.4 g sugars)
10.1 g protein
0.7 g fibre

	1 portion
butter or margarine	25 g (1 oz)
flour	10 g (½ oz)
milk, whole or skimmed	125 ml (¼ pt)
Cheddar cheese	100 g (4 oz)
egg yolk	1
beer	4 tbsp
salt, cayenne	
Worcester sauce	
English mustard	
butter or margarine	10 g (½ oz)
slices toast	2

HEALTHY EATING TIP

Use sunflower margarine and semi-skimmed milk to make the sauce. No added salt is needed as cheese is added.

1 Melt the butter or margarine in a thick-based pan.

2 Add the flour and mix in with a wooden spoon.

3 Cook on a gentle heat for a few minutes without colouring.

4 Gradually add the cold milk and mix to a smooth sauce.

5 Allow to simmer for a few minutes.

6 Add the grated or finely sliced cheese.

7 Allow to melt slowly over a gentle heat until a smooth mixture is obtained.

8 Add the yolk to the hot mixture, stir in and immediately remove from the heat.

9 Meanwhile, in a separate pan boil the beer and allow it to reduce to half a tablespoon.

10 Add to the mixture with the other seasonings.

11 Allow the mixture to cool.

12 Spread on the four rectangles of buttered toast.

13 Place on a baking sheet and brown gently under the salamander and serve.

Note: Cheese contains a large amount of protein, which will become tough and strong if heated for too long or at too high a temperature. A low-fat Cheddar may be used instead of the traditional full-fat variety.

4 Buck rarebit

Prepare Welsh rarebit and place a well-drained poached egg on each portion.

Note: Variations include:

- lightly cooked slices of tomato and/or mushrooms put on the toast before adding the mixture;

- grilled back rashers or sliced, cooked ham put either under or on top of the mixture;

- the mixture spread on portions of smoked haddock, a little milk added then baked in the oven; thinly sliced cooked tomato or mushroom can also be added.

5 Cheese and ham savoury flan

Quiche lorraine

> This recipe provides:
> 2955 kJ/704 kcal
> 48.4 g fat
> (of which 22.6 g saturated)
> 38.1 g carbohydrate
> (of which 6.5 g sugars)
> 31.6 g protein
> 1.8 g fibre

	4 portions	10 portions
rough puff, puff or short pastry	100 g (4 oz)	250 g (10 oz)
chopped ham	50 g (2 oz)	125 g (5 oz)
grated cheese	25 g (1 oz)	60 g (2½ oz)
medium egg	1	2
milk	125 ml (¼ pt)	300 ml (⅝ pt)
cayenne, salt		

1 Lightly grease four (or 10) good-size barquette or tartlet moulds. Line thinly with pastry.

2 Prick the bottoms of the paste two or three times with a fork.

3 Cook in a hot oven at 230–250°C (Reg. 8–9; 450–500°F) for 3–4 minutes or until the pastry is lightly set.

4 Remove from the oven; press the pastry down if it has tended to rise.

5 Add the chopped ham and grated cheese.

6 Mix the egg, milk, salt and cayenne thoroughly. Strain into the barquettes.

7 Return to the oven at 200–230°C (Reg. 6–8; 400–450°F) and bake gently for 15–20 minutes or until nicely browned and set.

Note: A variation is to line a 12 cm (6 inch) flan ring with short paste and proceed as above. The filling can be varied by using lightly fried lardons of bacon (in place of ham), chopped cooked onions and chopped parsley.

A variety of savoury flans can be made by using imagination and experimenting with different combinations of food: e.g. Stilton and onion; salmon and cucumber; sliced sausage and tomato.

6 Cheese straws

Paillettes au fromage

> This recipe provides:
> 2562 kJ/610 kcal
> 48.1 g fat
> (of which 24.1 g saturated)
> 28.7 g carbohydrate
> (of which 0.6 g sugars)
> 17.4 g protein
> 1.4 g fibre

	4 portions	10 portions
puff or rough puff paste	100 g (4 oz)	250 g (10 oz)
grated cheese	50 g (2 oz)	125 g (5 oz)
cayenne		

1 Roll out the pastry 60 × 15 cm (24 × 6 inches).

2 Sprinkle with cheese and cayenne.

3 Give a single turn, that is, fold the paste one-third the way over so that it covers the first fold.

4 Roll out 3 mm (⅛ inch) thick.

5 Cut out four circles 4 cm (2 inches) diameter.

6 Remove the centre with a smaller cutter leaving a circle ½ cm (¼ inch) wide.

7 Cut the remaining paste into strips 8 × ½ cm (3 × ¼ inches).

8 Twist each once or twice.

9 Place on a lightly greased baking sheet.

10 Bake in a hot oven at 230–250°C (Reg. 8–9; 450–500°F) for 10 minutes or until a golden brown.

11 To serve, place a bundle of straws into each circle.

Note: 50% white and 50% wholemeal flour can be used for the pastry.

7 Cheese soufflé

Soufflé au fromage

Using hard margarine, this recipe provides:
3223 kJ/767 kcal
60.2 g fat
(of which 28.2 g saturated)
17.6 g carbohydrate
(of which 6.1 g sugars)
39.7 g protein
0.5 g fibre

	4 portions	**10 portions**
butter or margarine	25 g (1 oz)	60 g (2½ oz)
flour	15 g (¾ oz)	50 g (2 oz)
milk	125 ml (¼ pt)	300 ml (⅝ pt)
egg yolks	3	8
salt, cayenne		
grated cheese	50 g (2 oz)	125 g (5 oz)
egg whites	4	10

HEALTHY EATING TIP

Use sunflower margarine and semi-skimmed milk to make the sauce. No added salt is needed as cheese is added.

1 Melt the butter in a thick-based pan.

2 Add the flour and mix with a wooden spoon.

3 Cook out for a few seconds without colouring.

4 Gradually add the cold milk and mix to a smooth sauce.

5 Simmer for a few minutes.

6 Add one egg yolk, mix in quickly; immediately remove from the heat.

7 When cool, add the remaining yolks. Season with salt and pepper.

8 Add the cheese.

9 Place the egg whites and a pinch of salt (a pinch of egg white powder will help strengthen the whites) in a scrupulously clean bowl, preferably copper, and whisk until stiff.

10 Add one-eighth of the whites to the mixture and mix well.

11 Gently fold in the remaining seven-eighths of the mixture, mix as lightly as possible. Place into a buttered soufflé case.

12 Cook in a hot oven at 220°C (Reg. 7; 425°F) for 25–30 minutes.

13 Remove from the oven, place on a round flat dish and serve *immediately*.

8 Cheese fritters

Beignets au fromage

1 portion provides:
1409 kJ/340 kcal energy
28.4 g fat
(of which 11.2 g saturated)
11.8 g carbohydrate
(of which 0.4 g sugars)
9.9 g protein
0.5 g fibre

	4 portions	10 portions
water	125 ml (¼ pt)	300 ml (⅝ pt)
butter or margarine	50 g (2 oz)	125 g (5 oz)
flour, white or wholemeal	60 g (2½ oz)	200 g (8 oz)
medium eggs	2	5
grated Parmesan cheese	50 g (2 oz)	125 g (5 oz)
salt, cayenne		

HEALTHY EATING TIP

Use sunflower margarine for the fritters. No extra salt is needed, as cheese is added.
Fry in hot sunflower oil and drain on kitchen paper.

1 Bring the water and butter or margarine to the boil in a thick-based pan. Remove from the heat.

2 Add the flour, mix with a wooden spoon.

3 Return to a gentle heat and mix well until the mixture leaves the sides of the pan. Remove from the heat. Allow to cool slightly.

4 Gradually add the eggs, beating well. Add the cheese and seasoning.

5 Using a spoon, scoop out the mixture in pieces the size of a walnut; place into deep hot fat 185°C (365°F).

6 Allow to cook with the minimum of handling for about 10 minutes.

7 Drain and serve sprinkled with grated Parmesan cheese.

9 Pizza

Using 100% white strong flour, 1 portion provides:
3956 kJ/941 kcal
46.3 g fat
(of which 13 g saturated)
114.4 g carbohydrate
(of which 20.1 g sugars)
23.6 g protein
8.4 g fibre

Pizza is a traditional dish originating from southern Italy. In simple terms it is a flat bread dough that can be topped by a wide variety of ingredients and baked quickly. The only rule is not to add wet ingredients, such as tomatoes, which are too juicy, otherwise the pizza becomes soggy. Traditionally pizzas are baked in a wood-fired brick oven but they can be baked in any type of hot oven for 8–15 minutes depending on the ingredients. A typical recipe is given here.

flour, strong white	200 g (8 oz)
pinch of salt	
margarine	12 g (½ oz)
yeast	5 g (¼ oz)
water or milk at 24°C (75°F)	125 ml (¼ pt)
caster sugar	5 g (¼ oz)
onions	100 g (4 oz)
cloves garlic, crushed	2
sunflower oil	60 ml (⅛ pt)
canned plum tomatoes	200 g (8 oz)
tomato purée	100 g (4 oz)
oregano	3 g (⅛ oz)
basil	3 g (⅛ oz)
sugar	10 g (½ oz)
cornflower	10 g (½ oz)
Mozzarella cheese	100 g (4 oz)

1 Sieve the flour and the salt. Rub in the margarine.

2 Disperse the yeast in the warm milk or water; add the caster sugar. Add this mixture to the flour.

3 Mix well, knead to a smooth dough, place in a basin covered with a damp cloth and allow to prove until doubled in size.

4 Knock back, divide into two and roll out into two 18 cm (7 inches) discs. Place on a lightly greased baking sheet.

5 Sweat the finely chopped onions and garlic in the oil until cooked.

6 Add the roughly chopped tomatoes, tomato purée, oregano, basil and sugar. Bring to the boil and simmer for 5 minutes.

7 Dilute the cornflour in a little water, stir into the tomato mixture and bring back to the boil.

8 Take the discs of pizza dough and spread 125 g (5 oz) of filling on each one.

9 Sprinkle with grated Mozzarella cheese or lay the slices of cheese on top.

10 Bake in a moderately hot oven at 180°C (Reg. 4; 350°F), for about 10 minutes.

Note: The pizza dough may also be made into rectangles so that it can be sliced into fingers for buffet work.

Oregano is sprinkled on most pizzas before baking. This is a basic recipe and many variations exist, some have the addition of olives, artichoke bottoms, prawns, mortadella sausage, garlic sausage, anchovy fillets. A vegetarian pizza recipe is on page 419.

Other combinations include:

- Mozzarella cheese, anchovies, capers and garlic.
- Mozzarella cheese, tomato and oregano.
- Ham, mushrooms, egg and Parmesan cheese.
- Prawns, tuna, capers and garlic.
- Ham, mushrooms and olives.

10 Bruschetta

Bruschetta is a thick slice of toasted or grilled bread rubbed with a fresh clove of garlic and sprinkled with extra virgin olive oil. It can then be embellished with tomato, basil, anchovies, Ricotta cheese or almost any type of topping.

HEALTHY EATING TIP

Use a little olive oil to cook the topping ingredients. Ricotta cheese contains less fat than Mozzarella.

1   Toast or grill the slices of bread and rub them with garlic cloves whilst hot.

2   Cook the raw ingredients for the topping in olive oil and pile on to the bread.

3   Add final ingredients such as cheese, anchovies, herbs.

Note: Toppings include mushrooms, aubergine, onions, spinach, tomatoes, ham, rocket, olives, Parmesan, Mozzarella and anchovies. Traditionally an Italian type bread e.g. ciabatta is used.

One of the most popular ways of serving bruschetta is:

1   Toast or grill thick slices of ciabatta and rub with garlic cloves whilst hot.

2   Add generous topping of diced cheese, e.g. Ricotta or Mozzarella, and diced tomato flesh (skin and de-seed the tomatoes).

3   Sprinkle with a good quality olive oil and finely chopped onion or chives and serve.

Canapés

- Cherry tomatoes, scooped out, filled with crab meat, seasoned and bound with mayonnaise
- Avocado pear purée with lime juice, mixed with a fine dice of yellow peppers
- Slices of rye bread with a slice of lobster, topped with asparagus, garnished with lobster eggs
- Smoked duck on slices of rye bread, garnished with mango
- Small new potatoes, cooked, scooped out, filled with sour cream and chives, garnished with caviar or lumpfish roe
- Small choux pastry éclairs filled with liver pâté
- Brioche croûtes with apricot chutney and gorgonzola
- Marinated and smoked salmon twisted onto the end of silver forms with a mustard dip. The marinade can be a combination of different flavours, e.g. beetroot and soya, lime juice and coriander
- Various types of sushi
- Profiteroles filled with prawns in cocktail sauce.

Examples of *hot* canapés

- Small Yorkshire puddings with a slice of beef topped with horseradish cream
- Oyster beignets, garlic mayonnaise
- Aubergine and goats' cheese tartlet
- Monkfish spring rolls, remoulade sauce
- Chicken and risotto croquettes
- Small pizzas
- Small pieces of chicken on skewers with bacon
- Satay, peanut sauce
- Angels on horseback, page 618
- Vegetable samosas, page 358
- Latkes, page 379

Dips for hot canapés

- Garlic mayonnaise
- Yoghurt, cucumber and mint
- Apricot chutney

Fig 15.1 🖋 Assorted canapés (cold)   *John Campbell*

Fig 15.2 🖋 Assorted canapés with dips (hot)

At some receptions **small** finger pastries are requested. Some examples that can be offered:

- Fruit tartlets, bakewell tarts, lemon meringue tartlets
- Eclairs
- Palmiers with strawberries and cream
- Scones filled with tropical fruit
- Cornets made of brandy snaps filled with cream and stem ginger
- Small scoops of ice-cream dipped in white and dark chocolate
- Lemon meringue tartlets
- Various tuille shapes, caskets filled with lemon mousse

11 Cocktail canapés (traditional)

These are small items of food, hot or cold, served at cocktail parties or buffet receptions, and may be offered as an accompaniment to drinks before any meal (luncheon, dinner or supper). Typical items for cocktail parties and light buffets are:

1 Hot savoury pastry patties or bouchées of lobster, chicken, crab, salmon, mushroom, ham, etc. Small pizzas, quiches, brochettes, hamburgers.

2 Hot sausages (chipolatas), various fillings, such as chicken livers, prunes, mushrooms, tomatoes, gherkins, etc., wrapped in bacon and skewered and cooked under the salamander. Fried goujons of fish.

3 Game chips, gaufrette potatoes, fried fish balls, celery stalks spread with cheese.

12 Lamb satay

	makes 20
lamb fillets or loin of lamb	500 g
clove of garlic, crushed and chopped	3
Thai fish sauce	2 tsp
sweet chilli sauce	2 tbsp
fresh ginger, grated	2 tsp
lime juice	62 ml (⅛ pt)
peanut butter (coarse)	2 tbsp
ground cumin	1 tsp
ground turmeric	1 tsp
Sauce **white vinegar**	62 ml (⅛ pt)
caster sugar	2 tbsp
sweet chilli sauce	1 tbsp
unsalted, roasted peanuts	1 tbsp
fresh coriander leaves, finely chopped	1 tbsp

1 Prepare the lamb, cutting it into thin strips.

2 In a bowl place the garlic, sauces, ginger, lime juice, peanut butter and spices. Mix well.

3 Place the marinade over the lamb, place in refrigerator for 3 hours or overnight.

4 Meanwhile prepare the bamboo skewers in water for about 1 hour to prevent scorching.

5 Thread the lamb onto the skewers. Grill the lamb skewers, turning once until cooked and nicely coloured.

6 Prepare the sauce. Place the vinegar and sugar in a small pan, stir until the sugar has dissolved. Bring to boil, simmer for 2 minutes. Stir in remaining ingredients.

7 Serve the lamb on a suitable platter on banana leaves with the sauce in a bowl in the centre.

13 Crab cakes with chilli lime dipping sauce

	makes 30–40
crab meat	350 g (14 oz)
uncooked prawns, shelled de-veined	650 g (1 lb 10 oz)
red curry paste	1 tbsp
egg	1
spring onions	2
fresh coriander (finely chopped)	2 tbsp
lemongrass, finely chopped	2 tsp
red Thai chilli, deseeded, chopped	1
vegetable oil	2 tbsp
Dipping sauce **lime juice**	2 tbsp
water	2 tbsp
fish sauce	2 tsp
sugar	2 tsp
kaffir lime leaf, chopped	1
red Thai chilli, deseeded, chopped finely	1

1 In a food processor, place crab, prawns, curry paste, egg, onion, coriander, lemongrass and chilli. Combine all ingredients until all mixed together.

2 Shape into small cakes.

3 Heat oil in a shallow pan, stir-fry crab cakes on both sides until golden brown. Drain, place on a suitable dish with dipping sauce.

Dipping sauce

Combine all ingredients together in a suitable bowl, then stir well.

14 Potato wedges with tomato chilli salsa

	makes 40
large potatoes	5
coarse black pepper	1 tsp
sea salt	1 tsp
Tomato chilli salsa **large beef tomatoes, peeled, seeded, finely chopped**	1
red onion	1
chilli, finely chopped	1
lime juice	1 tbsp
chopped fresh basil leaves	1 tbsp

1 Wash the potatoes, cut into wedges.
2 Heat a little oil in a suitable roasting tray, add the wedges skin side down. Sprinkle with salt and pepper.
3 Bake in a hot oven until brown and crisp.
4 Prepare the salsa: place all ingredients into a suitable bowl and mix well.
5 When the potatoes are cooked, place on a suitable serving platter, arranged around a bowl of sour cream and a bowl of the salsa.

15 Pork and corn Thai cakes

	makes 20
minced pork	500 g (1 lb 4 oz)
red curry paste	1 tbsp
egg, lightly beaten	1
spring onions, finely chopped	6
cooked sweetcorn	100 g (4 oz)
breadcrumbs	50 g (2 oz)
coriander leaves, finely chopped	1 tbsp

1 Place the minced pork into a bowl, add the curry paste, egg, onion, sweetcorn and breadcrumbs, mix well. Add coriander leaves, give a further mix.
2 Divide into 20 small balls, flatten into cakes.
3 Place on an oiled tray, bake in a hot oven until cooked and golden brown, turn once.
4 To serve, place on a suitable dish garnished with coriander leaves and in the centre a suitable dipping sauce, e.g. tomato and chilli.

Note: Veal may be used in place of pork.

16 Honey prawns

large uncooked prawns	20
honey	60 ml (⅛ pt)
soy sauce	60 ml (⅛ pt)
hoi sin sauce	1 tbsp
crushed chopped garlic	2 cloves
small chilli, deseeded, chopped	1
toasted sesame seeds	2 tsp

1   Shell and devein the prawns, leaving tails intact.

2   Cut along prawn backs lengthways without separating halves.

3   In a suitable bowl, add the honey, soy sauce, hoi sin sauce, garlic and chilli. Mix well.

4   Pour over prawns, allow to marinate for at least 3 hours or overnight.

5   Flatten the prawns, grill on both sides.

6   Serve on a suitable platter sprinkled with sesame seeds.

17 Lemongrass prawns

uncooked prawns	32
lemons	2
lemongrass, finely chopped	2
sambal ulek (chilli paste)	2 tsp
honey	60 ml (⅛ pt)
lemon juice	2 tbsp
cloves of garlic	2
fresh lemon grass stems	4

1   Shell and devein prawns, leaving tails intact.

2   Peel the two lemons, remove the pith from the rind and cut the rind into a short julienne. Place this in a basin with the chopped lemon grass, sambal ulek, honey, lemon juice and garlic. Mix well.

3   Pour this mixture over the prawns and marinate for at least 3 hours or overnight.

4   Cut off 1 cm (½ inch) base of the lemongrass stems, then discard. Peel away coarse inner layers. Cut each in half crossways, cut one end into a sharp point.

5   Thread 2 prawns into each lemongrass skewer. Grill each skewer gently on both sides.

6   Serve on pieces of coconut shell on a reel of finely sliced cucumber.

18 Bocconcini and tomato bruschetta

Cut small rounds of bruschetta the size of a 50p piece, then lightly toast.

Place a basil leaf on each slice, arrange slices of bocconcini cheese and tomato. Drizzle with garlic flavoured olive oil, season with salt and black pepper. See also recipe 10, page 626.

19 Pumpernickel rounds with smoked salmon, sour cream and dill

Cut small rounds of pumpernickel, pipe a rosette of sour cream flavoured with chopped dill. Arrange smoked salmon on top, then garnish with lemon and dill.

20 Fresh mussels with tomato and cheese

Prepare mussels by removing beards. Place in a pan, surface covered with white wine or fish stock. Add mussels, cook over fierce heat until they open. Drain, discard liquid. Place each mussel in half shell. Place in a tray, cover mussel with cooked tomato concassé, sprinkle with mozzarella cheese. Grill until it is melted.

21 Mini poppadums

May be filled with a variety of fillings e.g. curried eggs, spiced tuna and lime dressing, chicken tikka, curried fish.

22 Deep-fried pork noodles

	makes 36–40
dried egg noodles	50 g (2 oz)
minced pork	250 g (10 oz)
finely chopped onion	100 g (4 oz)
garlic, crushed and chopped	2
grated fresh ginger	2 tsp
coriander, chopped	1 tsp
egg yolk	1
flour	50 g (2 oz)
sambal ulek (chilli paste)	1 tsp
fish sauce	1 tsp
sweet chilli sauce } dip	62 ml (⅛ pt)
lime juice	2 tbsp

1   Crush noodles, place into a suitable bowl, cover with boiling water, stand for 5 minutes, then drain.

2   Add pork, onion, garlic, coriander, egg yolk, flour, sambal and fish sauce.

3   Mix well. Divide into small balls, deep fry until golden brown and cooked through. Drain.

Serve with the dipping sauce of sweet chilli and lime juice.

23 Tuna nori rolls

	makes 36–40 pieces
koshi hikari rice (small round grain white rice)	400 g (1 lb)
rice vinegar	60 ml (⅛ pt)
sugar	2 tbsp
salt	pinch
toasted nori	6 sheets
sashimi tuna	125 g (5 oz)
Lebanese cucumber	125 g (5 oz)
avocado pear	200 g (8 oz)
pickled ginger slices	2 tbsp
wasabi (Japanese white radish)	½ tsp

1   Cook rice in boiling salted water until tender, drain well, stand for 5 minutes, stir in vinegar, sugar and salt. Allow to cool.

2   Place one sheet of nori, rough side up on bamboo sushi mat. Spread ⅙ of the rice mixture over nori, leaving 4 cm (2 inches) on short side. Press rice firmly in place.

3   Make a lengthways hollow across centre of rice. Place ⅙ of each of the tuna, cucumber, avocado, ginger and wasabi in hollow in centre of the rice.

4   Use the bamboo mat to roll the tuna nori, pressing firmly as you roll.

5   Cut into the desired number of pieces (approximately 6), place on serving dish. Repeat with each piece of nori.

6   Serve with soy sauce.

Nori – dried seaweed sold in paper thin sheets.

Sandwiches

For speed of production, sandwiches are made in bands by cutting the bread rectangularly. When filled, the crusts are removed and the sandwiches cut into fingers.

Today bakers will bake the bread to your specification and slice it ready for use. The specification may also include speciality breads like tomato, basil bread, walnut and olive bread.

Sandwiches may also be cut into small cubes and a variety placed on a cocktail stick to represent a mini kebab.

Sandwiches may be made from every kind of bread, fresh or toasted, in a variety of shapes and with an almost endless assortment of fillings. They may be garnished with potato or vegetable crisps and a little salad.

Toasted sandwiches

These are made by inserting a variety of savoury fillings between two slices of hot, freshly buttered toast, e.g. scrambled egg, bacon, fried egg, scrambled egg with chopped ham, or by inserting two slices of buttered bread with the required filling into a sandwich toaster.

Club sandwich

This is made by placing between two slices of hot buttered toast a filling of lettuce, grilled bacon, slices of hard-boiled egg, mayonnaise and slices of chicken.

Bookmaker sandwich

This is an underdone minute steak between two slices of hot buttered toast.

Double-decker and treble-decker sandwiches

Toasted and untoasted bread can be made into double-decker sandwiches, using three slices of bread with two separate fillings. Treble and quadro-decker sandwiches may also be prepared. They may be served hot or cold.

For further information contact British Sandwich Association, 8 Home Farm, Ardington, Wantage, Oxfordshire OX12 8PN.

www.sandwich.org.uk

Open sandwich or Scandinavian smorrëbord

These are prepared from a buttered slice of any bread garnished with any type of meat, fish, eggs, vegetables, salads, etc.

The varieties of open sandwich can include some of the following:

1. Smoked salmon, lettuce, potted shrimps, slice of lemon.
2. Cold sliced beef, sliced tomato, fans of gherkins.
3. Shredded lettuce, sliced hard-boiled egg, mayonnaise, cucumber.
4. Pickled herring, chopped gherkin, capers sieved, hard-boiled egg.

Wraps

These are made enclosing various fillings wrapped in tortillas (plain or flavoured e.g. tomato, herbs) page 371. Any of a wide variety of fillings can be used e.g. chicken and roasted vegetables, beans and red pepper salad with Guacamole (a well flavoured avocado pulp). Flat breads e.g. pitta, ciabatta etc. can be used for various fillings e.g. chicken tikka.

Bagels

Bagels are ring doughnut shaped rolls of leavened bread that are boiled before being baked giving them a hard texture. Traditionally filled with smoked salmon and cream cheese (a Jewish speciality).

Glossary of culinary terms

À la In the style of

À la française In the French style

À la minute Cooked to order

À la carte Dishes prepared to order and priced individually

Abatis de volaille Poultry offal, giblets, etc.

Abats Offal, heads, hearts, liver, kidney etc.

Accompaniments Items offered separately with a dish of food

Agar-agar A vegetable gelling agent obtained from seaweed, used as a substitute for gelatine

Aile Wing of poultry or game birds

Aloyau de boeuf Sirloin of beef

Ambient Room temperature, surrounding atmosphere

Amino acid Organic acids found in proteins

Antibiotic Drug used to destroy disease-producing germs within human or animal bodies

Antiseptic Substance that prevents the growth of bacteria and moulds specifically on or in the human body

Aromates Fragrant herbs and spices

Arroser To baste as in roasting

Ascorbic acid Known as vitamin C, found in citrus fruits and

blackcurrants, necessary for growth and maintenance of health

Aspic A savoury jelly mainly used for decorative larder work

Assorti An assortment

Au bleu When applied to meat it means very underdone

Au beurre With butter

Au four Baked in the oven

Au gratin Sprinkled with cheese or breadcrumbs and browned

Au vin blanc With white wine

Bacterium (singular) Single celled micro-organisms: some are harmful and cause food poisoning; others are useful such as those used in cheese making

Bacteria (plural)

Bactericide Substance that destroys bacteria

Bain-marie
- A container of water to keep foods hot without fear of burning
- A container of water for cooking foods to prevent them burning
- A deep narrow container for storing hot sauces, soups and gravies

Barder To bard, to cover breasts of birds with thin slices of bacon

Barquette A boat-shaped pastry case

Basting Spooning melted fat over the food during cooking to keep the food moist

Bat out To flatten slices of raw meat with a cutlet bat

Bean curd Also known as *tofu*; a curdled, soft, cheese-like preparation made from soybean milk; it is a good source of protein

Bean sprouts Young shoots of dried beans: mung beans, alfalfa and soybean

Beurre manié Equal quantities of flour and butter used for thickening sauces

Blanc A cooking liquor of water, lemon juice, flour and salt; also applied to the white of chicken – the breast and wings

Blanch
- To make white as with bones and meat
- To retain colour as with certain vegetables
- To skin, as for tomatoes
- To make limp as for certain braised vegetables
- To cook without colour as for the first frying of fried (chip) potatoes

Blanquette A white stew cooked in stock from which the sauce is made

Blitz to rapidly purée or foam a light sauce generally using an electric hand blender at the last moment before service

Bombay duck Small, dried, salted fish; fried, it is used as an accompaniment to curry dishes

Bombe An ice-cream speciality of different flavours in bomb shape

Bone out To remove the bones

Botulism Rare form of food poisoning

Bouchée A small puff paste case, literally a mouthful

Bouillon Unclarified stock

Bouquet garni A faggot of herbs: e.g. parsley stalks, thyme and bay leaf, tied in pieces of celery and leek

Brine A preserving solution of water, salt, saltpetre and aromates used for meats (silverside, brisket, tongue)

Brunoise Small dice

Butters
- Black butter (beurre noir)
- Brown butter: nut brown butter (beurre noisette)
- Melted butter (beurre fondu)
- Parsley butter (beurre maître d'hôtel)

Buttermilk Liquid remaining from the churning of butter

Calcium A mineral required for building bones and teeth, obtained from cheese and milk

Calorie A unit of heat or energy, known as a kilocalorie

Canapé A cushion of bread on which are served various foods, hot or cold

Carbohydrate A nutrient that has three groups, sugar, starch and cellulose; the first two provide the body with energy; cellulose provides roughage (dietary fibre)

Carbon dioxide A gas produced by all raising agents

Carrier A person who harbours and may transmit pathogenic organisms without showing signs of illness

Carte du jour Menu for the day

Casserole An earthenware fireproof dish with a lid

Cellulose The coarse structure of fruit, vegetables and cereals that is not digested but used as roughage (dietary fibre)

Châteaubriand The head of the fillet of beef

Chaud-froid A demi-glace or creamed velouté with gelatine or aspic added, used for masking cold dishes

Chiffonade Fine shreds, e.g. spinach, lettuce

Chinois A conical strainer

Chlorophyll The green colour in vegetables

Civet A brown stew of game, usually hare

Clarification To make clear such as stock, jelly, butter

Clostridium perfringens Food poisoning bacterium found in the soil, vegetables and meat

Coagulation The solidification of protein that is irreversible (fried egg, cooking of meat)

Cocotte Porcelain or earthenware fireproof dish

Collagen & elastin Proteins in connective tissue e.g. gristle

Compote Stewed (stewed fruit)

Concassé Coarsely chopped (parsley, tomatoes)

Confit A cooked meat, poultry or game preserved in good fat or oil

Consommé Basic clear soup

Contamination Occurrence of any objectionable matter in food

Contrefilet Boned out sirloin of beef

Cook out The process of cooking the flour in a roux, soup or sauce

Cordon A thread or thin line of sauce

Correcting Adjusting the seasoning, consistency and colour

Côte A rib or chop

Côtelette A cutlet

Coupe An individual serving bowl

Couper To cut

Court-bouillon A well-flavoured cooking liquor for fish

Crème fraîche Whipping cream and buttermilk heated to 24–29°C (75–84°F)

Crêpes Pancakes

Cross-contamination The transfer of micro-organisms from contaminated to uncontaminated hands, utensils or equipment

Credit notes Issued when invoice contains incorrect details; credit is therefore given

Croquettes Cooked foods moulded cylinder shape, coated in flour, egg, crumbed and deep fried

Croûtons Cubes of fried or toasted bread served with soup; also triangular pieces served with spinach, and heart-shaped with certain vegetables and entrées

Crudités Small neat pieces of raw vegetables served with a dip as an appetiser

Cuisse de poulet Chicken leg

Cullis (Coulis) Sauce made of fruit or vegetable purée, e.g. raspberry, tomato

Danger zone of bacterial growth Temperature range within which multiplication of pathogenic bacteria is possible. From 10–63°C (50–145°F)

Dariole A small mould as used for cream caramel

Darne A slice of round fish on the bone e.g. salmon

Dégraisser To skim fat off liquid

Déglacer To swill out a pan in which food has been roasted or fried, with wine, stock or water, in order to use the sediment for the accompanying sauce or gravy

Delivery note Form sent by supplier with delivery of goods

Désosser To bone out meat

Detergent Substance that dissolves grease

Demi-glace Brown stock reduced to a light consistency

Dilute To mix a powder, e.g. cornflour with a liquid

Dish paper A plain dish paper

Disinfectant Substance that reduces the risk of infection

Doily A fancy dish paper

Drain Placing food in a colander, allowing liquid to seep out

Duxelle Finely chopped mushrooms cooked with chopped shallots

Eggwash Beaten egg with a little milk or water

Emulsion A mixture of oil and liquid (such as vinegar), which does not separate on standing (mayonnaise, hollandaise)

Entrecôte A steak cut from a boned sirloin

Enzymes Chemical substances produced from living cells

Escalope A thin slice such as escalope of veal

Farce Stuffing

Fécule Fine potato flour

Feuilletage Puff pastry

Fines herbes Chopped fresh herbs e.g. parsley, tarragon and chervil

First aid materials Suitable and sufficient bandages and dressing including waterproof dressing and antiseptic; all dressings to be individually wrapped

Flake To break into natural segments (fish)

Flan Open fruit tart

Fleurons Small crescent-shaped pieces of puff pastry

Flute A 20 cm (1 inch) diameter French bread used for soup garnishes

Food borne Bacteria carried on food

Food handling Any operation in the storage, preparation, production, processing, packaging, transporting, distribution and sale of food

Frappé Chilled, e.g. melon frappé

Freezer burn Affects frozen items, which are spoiled due to being unprotected for too long

Friandises Sweetmeats, petits fours

Fricassée A white stew in which the meat, poultry or fish is cooked in the sauce

Friture A pan that contains deep fat

Fumé Smoked, e.g. saumon fumé, smoked salmon

Garam masala A combination of spices

Garnish Served as part of the main item, trimmings

Gastroenteritis Inflammation of the stomach and intestinal tract that normally results in diarrhoea

Gâteau A cake of more than one portion

Ghee The Indian name for clarified butter; ghee is pure butterfat

Gibier Game

Glace Ice or ice-cream from which all milk solids have been removed

Glaze To glaze
- To colour a dish under the salamander (fillets of sole bonne femme)
- To finish a flan or tartlet (with apricot jam)
- To finish certain vegetables (glazed carrots)

Gluten This is formed from protein in flour when mixed with water

Gratin A thin coating of grated cheese and/or breadcrumbs on certain dishes then browned under the grill or in an oven

Haché Finely chopped or minced

Hors-d'oeuvre Appetising first course dishes, hot or cold

Humidity Indicates amount of moisture in the air

Incubation period Time between infection and first signs of illness

Infestations Insects breeding on the premises

Insecticide Chemical used to kill insects

Invoices Bill listing items delivered with costs of items

Jardinière Vegetables cut into batons

Julienne Cut into fine strips

Jus-lié Thickened gravy

Larding Inserting strips of fat bacon into meat

Lardons Batons of thick streaky bacon

Liaison A thickening or binding

Macédoine
- A mixture of fruit or vegetables
- Cut into ½ cm (¼ inch) dice

Magnetron The device that generates microwaves in a microwave oven

Marinade A richly spiced pickling liquid used to give flavour and to assist tenderising meats

Marmite Stock pot

Mascarpone An Italian cheese resembling clotted cream

Menu List of dishes available

Micro-organisms Very small living plants or animals (bacteria, yeasts, moulds)

Mignonnette Coarsely ground pepper

Mildew Type of fungus similar to mould

Mineral salts These are mineral elements, small quantities of which are essential for health

Mirepoix Roughly cut onion, carrots, a sprig of thyme and a bay leaf

Mise en place Basic preparation prior to serving

Miso Seasoning made from fermented soybeans

Monosodium glutamate A substance added to food products to increase flavour

Moulds Microscopic plants (fungi) that may appear as woolly patches on food

Mousse A dish of light consistency, hot or cold

Napper To coat or mask with sauce

Natives A menu term for English oysters

Navarin Brown stew of lamb

Niacin Part of vitamin B, found in liver, kidney, meat extract, bacon

Noisette (nut) A cut from a boned-out loin of lamb

Nutrients These are the components of food required for health (protein, fats, carbohydrates, vitamins, mineral salts, water)

Optimum Best, most favourable

Palatable Pleasant to taste

Pané Floured, egg and crumbed

Panettone A very light traditional Italian Christmas cake

Parsley butter Butter containing lemon juice and chopped parsley

Pass To cause to go through a sieve or strainer

Pathogen Disease-producing organism

Paupiette A stuffed and rolled strip of fish or meat

Paysanne Cut in even thin triangular, round or square pieces

Persillé Finished with chopped parsley

Pesticide Chemical used to kill pests

Pests Such as cockroaches, flies, silverfish

Petits fours Very small pastries, biscuits, sweets, sweetmeats

pH value A scale indicating acidity or alkalinity in food

Phosphorus A mineral element found in fish. Required for building bones and teeth

Piquant Sharply flavoured

Piqué Studded clove in an onion

Plat du jour Special dish of the day

Poppadums Dried, thin, large, round wafers made from lentil flour, used as an accompaniment to Indian dishes

Printanier Garnish of spring vegetables

Protein The nutrient needed for growth and repair

Prove To allow a yeast dough to rest in a warm place so that it can expand

Pulses Vegetables grown in pods (peas and beans) and dried; source of protein and roughage

Quark Salt-free soft cheese made from semi-skimmed milk

Ragoût Stew (ragoût de boeuf); brown beef stew

Rare When applied to meat, it means underdone

Réchauffer To reheat

Reduce To concentrate a liquid by boiling

Refresh To make cold under running cold water

Residual insecticide Long lasting insecticide which remains active for a considerable period of time

Riboflavin Part of vitamin B known as B_2. Sources in yeast, liver, eggs, cheese

Rissoler To fry to a golden brown

Rodents Rats and mice

Roux A thickening of cooked flour and fat

Sabayon Yolks of eggs and a little water or wine cooked until creamy

Saccharometer An instrument for measuring the density of sugar

Salamander Type of grill heat from above

Salmonella Food poisoning bacterium found in meat and poultry

Sanitiser Chemical agent used for cleaning and disinfecting surfaces and equipment

Sauté
- Tossed in fat (pommes sautées)
- Cooked quickly in a sauté pan or frying pan
- A brown stew of a specific type, (veal sauté)

Seal To set the surface of meat in a hot oven or pan to colour and retain the juices

Seared Cooked quickly on both sides in a little hot fat or oil

Seasoned flour Flour seasoned with salt and pepper

Set
- To seal the outside surface
- To allow to become firm or firmer (jelly)

Shredded Cut in fine strips (lettuce, onion)

Silicone paper Non-stick paper (siliconised paper)

Singe To brown or colour

Smetana A low fat product; a cross between soured cream and yoghurt

Sodium Mineral element in the form of salt (sodium chloride); found in cheese, bacon, fish, meat

Soufflé A very light dish, sweet or savoury, hot or cold

Soy sauce Made from soybeans and used extensively in Chinese cookery

Spores Resistant resting-phase of bacteria protecting them against adverse conditions such as high temperatures

Staphylococcus Food poisoning bacterium found in the human nose and throat and also in septic cuts

Starch A carbohydrate found in cereals, certain vegetables and farinaceous foods

Steriliser Chemical used to destroy all living organisms

Sterile Free from all living organisms

Sterilisation Process that destroys living organisms

Stock rotation Sequence of issuing goods: first into store, first to be issued

Strain To separate the liquid from the solids by passing through a strainer

Sweat To cook in fat under a lid without colour

Syneresis The squeezing out of liquid from an overcooked protein and liquid mixture (scrambled egg, egg custard)

Table d'hôte A meal at a fixed price; a set menu

Tahini A strong flavoured sesame seed paste

Tally Corresponds to; is the same as

Tartlet A small round pastry case

Terrine An earthenware dish used for cooking and serving pâté; also used as a name for certain products

Thiamine Part of vitamin B known as B_1, it assists the nervous system; sources in yeast, bacon, wholemeal bread

Timbale A double serving dish

Tofu Low fat bean curd made from soybeans (see also bean curd)

Tourné Turned, shaped in barrels or large olives

Tranche A slice

Trichinosis Disease caused by hair-like worms in the muscles of meat, as in pork

Tronçon A slice of flat fish on the bone e.g. turbot

TVP Texturised vegetable protein, derived from soybeans

Vegan A person who does not eat fish, meat, poultry, game, dairy products and eggs

Vegetarian A person who does not eat meat, poultry or game

Velouté
- Basic sauce
- A soup of velvet or smooth consistency

Viruses Microscopic pathogens that multiply in the living cells of their host

Vitamins Chemical substances that assist the regulation of body processes

Vol-au-vent A large puff pastry case

Wok A round-bottomed pan used extensively in Chinese cooking

Yeast extract A mixture of brewer's yeast and salt high in flavour and protein

Yoghurt An easily digested fermented milk product

Index

Page numbers in italics refer to illustrations.